MGF
WORKSHOP MANUAL

Which includes the following publications:

MGF Workshop Manual
RCL 0051ENG (8th Edition)

'K' Series Engine Overhaul Manual
RCL 0057ENG (6th Edition)

PG1 Manual Gearbox Overhaul Manual
RCL 0124 (2nd Edition)

Publication Part No. RCL 0051ENG BB which incorporates
RCL 0051ENG, RCL 0057ENG & RCL 0124
© MG Rover Group 2000

This publication covers all MGF Models from 1995
to the end of production.

Included in this manual are the following publications:

MGF Workshop Manual - RCL 0051ENG (8th Edition) 2000
'K' Series Engine Overhaul Manual - RCL 0057ENG (6th Edition) 2000
PG1 Manual Gearbox Overhaul Manual - RCL 0124 (2nd Edition) 1997

MGF

WORKSHOP
MANUAL

This manual should be used in conjunction with the following overhaul manuals.

RCL 0057   'K' Series Engine
RCL 0124   PG1 Manual Gearbox

Publication Part No. RCL0051ENG - 8th Edition
Published by MG Rover Group Aftersales
© MG Rover Group Limited 2000

INTRODUCTION
GENERAL INFORMATION
INFORMATION

MAINTENANCE

ENGINE

EMISSION CONTROL
ENGINE MANAGEMENT SYSTEM
 - MEMS 1.9 / 2J / 3
FUEL DELIVERY SYSTEM

COOLING SYSTEM

MANIFOLD & EXHAUST SYSTEMS

CLUTCH

MANUAL GEARBOX
AUTOMATIC GEARBOX - EM-CVT

DRIVE SHAFTS

STEERING

SUSPENSION

BRAKES

RESTRAINT SYSTEMS
BODY

HEATING & VENTILATION
AIR CONDITIONING

WIPERS & WASHERS
ELECTRICAL
INSTRUMENTS

MGF Workshop Manual

CONTENTS

Page

INTRODUCTION

INTRODUCTION

How to use this Manual

To assist in the use of this Manual the section title is given at the top and the relevant sub-section is given at the bottom each page.

Each major section starts with a contents page, listing the information contained in the relevant sub-sections. To assist filing of revised information each sub-section is numbered from page 1.

The individual items comprising repair operations are to be followed in the sequence in which they appear. Item numbers in illustrations are referred to in the text.

Adjustment and repair operations include reference to Service tool numbers and the associated illustration depicts the tool. Where usage is not obvious the tool is shown in use. Adjustment and repair operations also include reference to wear limits, relevant data, torque figures, and specialist information and useful assembly details. Each adjustment or repair operation is given a Repair Operation Time number.

WARNINGS, CAUTIONS and NOTES have the following meanings:

 WARNING: Procedures which must be followed precisely to avoid the possibility of injury.

 CAUTION: Calls attention to procedures which must be followed to avoid damage to components.

 NOTE: Gives helpful information.

References

References to the LH or RH side given in this Manual are made when viewing the vehicle from the rear. With the engine and gearbox assembly removed, the crankshaft pulley end of the engine is referred to as the front.

Operations covered in this Manual do not include reference to testing the vehicle after repair. It is essential that work is inspected and tested after completion and if necessary a road test of the vehicle is carried out particularly where safety related items are concerned.

Dimensions

The dimensions quoted are to design engineering specification with Service limits where applicable.

REPAIRS AND REPLACEMENTS

When replacement parts are required it is essential that only Rover recommended parts are used.

Attention is particularly drawn to the following points concerning repairs and the fitting of replacement parts and accessories.

Safety features and corrosion prevention treatments embodied in the car may be impaired if other than Rover recommended parts are fitted. In certain territories, legislation prohibits the fitting of parts not to the manufacturer's specification. Torque wrench setting figures given in this Manual must be used. Locking devices, where specified, must be fitted. If the efficiency of a locking device is impaired during removal it must be renewed.

Owners purchasing accessories while travelling abroad should ensure that the accessory and its fitted location on the car conform to legal requirements.

The Terms of the vehicle Warranty may be invalidated by the fitting of other than Rover recommended parts.

All Rover recommended parts have the full backing of the vehicle Warranty.

Rover Dealers are obliged to supply only Rover recommended parts.

SPECIFICATION

Rover are constantly seeking to improve the specification, design and production of their vehicles and alterations take place accordingly. While every effort has been made to ensure the accuracy of this Manual, it should not be regarded as an infallible guide to current specifications of any particular vehicle.

This Manual does not constitute an offer for sale of any particular vehicle. Rover Dealers are not agents of Rover and have no authority to bind the manufacturer by any expressed or implied undertaking or representation.

ABBREVIATIONS AND SYMBOLS

After Bottom Dead Centre	ABDC		Inches	in
After Top Dead Centre	ATDC		Idle Air Control	IAC
Air Conditioning	A/C		Inertia Fuel Shutoff	IFS
Air Fuel Ratio	AFR		Intake Air Temperature	IAT
Alternating Current	ac		Internal Diameter	i.dia.
Ambient Air Temperature	AAT		International Organisation	
Amperes	A		for Standardization	ISO
Anti-Lock Brake System	ABS		Kilogramme	kg
Before Bottom Dead Centre	BBDC		Kilometre	km
Before Top Dead Centre	BTDC		Kilometres per hour	km/h
Bottom Dead Centre	BDC		KiloOhms	kΩ
British Standards	BS		KiloWatts	kW
Camshaft Position	CMP		Left-Hand	LH
Carbon Dioxide	CO_2		Left-Hand Drive	LHD
Carbon Monoxide	CO		Light Emitting Diode	LED
Celcius (Centigrade)	C		Liquid Crystal Display	LCD
Centimetre	cm		Litre	l
Chlorofluorocarbons	CFC's		Low Compression	lc
Crankshaft Position	CKP		Low tension	lt
Cubic Centimetres	cm^3		Malfunction Indicator Lamp	MIL
Degree (angle)	deg. or °		Manifold Absolute Pressure	MAP
Degree (temperature)	deg. or °		Maximum	max
Diagnostic Control Unit	DCU		MegaWatts	MW
Dial Test Indicator	DTI		Mercury	Hg
Diameter	dia.		Metre	m
Direct Current	dc		Miles Per Hour	mph
Double Overhead Camshaft	DOHC		Milliamp	mA
Engine Coolant Temperature	ECT		Millimetre	mm
Electric Power Assisted Steering	EPAS		Minimum	min
Electrically Eraseable			Minus (of tolerance)	-
Programmable Read Only Memory	EEPROM		Minute (angle)	'
Electronic Control Unit	ECU		Modular Engine Management	
Electronic Air Control valve	EACV		System	MEMS
Electro Mechanical - Continuously			Model Year	MY
Variable Transmission	EM-CVT		Multi-Function Unit	MFU
Electromotive force	e.m.f.		Multi-Point Injection	MPi
Engine Control Module	ECM		Negative (electrical)	-
Exhaust Gas Recirculation	EGR		Negative Temperature Coeficient	NTC
Evaporative Emission	EVAP		Newton Metre	Nm
Field Effect Transistor	FET		Nitrous Oxide	NO_x
			Number	No.
Gramme (mass)	g			
Gearbox Interface Unit	GIU		On Board Diagnostics	OBD
			Ohms	Ω
Heated Oxygen Sensor	HO_2S		Organic Acid Technology	OAT
Hertz	Hz		Outside Diameter	o.dia.
High Compression	hc			
High Tension (electrical)	h.t.			
Hour	h			
Hydraulic Control Unit	HCU			
Hydrocarbons	HC			
Hydrofluorocarbon	HFC			

INTRODUCTION

Percentage	%
Plus or Minus	±
Plus (tolerance)	+
Positive (electrical)	+
Positive Crankcase Ventilation	PCV
Positive Temperature Coefficient	PTC
Pounds Per Square Inch	lbf/in²
Pounds Per Square Inch	psi
Pounds (mass)	lb
Pulse Width Modulation	PWM
Radius	r
Ratio	:
Reference	ref
Revolutions Per Minute	rev/min or rpm
Right-Hand	RH
Right-Hand Drive	RHD
Rover Engineering Standards	RES
Second (angle)	"
Single Overhead Camshaft	SOHC
Specific Gravity	sp.gr
Square Centimetres	cm²
Square inches	in²
Standard	std.
Supplementary Restraint System	SRS
Synchronizer/Synchromesh	synchro
Thousand	k
Throttle Position	TP
Top Dead Centre	TDC
United Kingdom	UK
United States	US
Variable Valve Control	VVC
Vehicle Identification Number	VIN
Volt	V
Water	H₂O
Watt	W

GENERAL INFORMATION

CONTENTS

VEHICLE IDENTIFICATION NUMBER

Location

The Vehicle Identification Number (VIN) is stamped on plates attached to the RH side of the spare wheel compartment, and behind the LH lower corner of the windscreen. The VIN number is also stamped on the RH side front, upper suspension mounting plate. Example given below:

1M0061

Vehicle identification number

S A R R D W B G/T B/M/J/X A D 000001

S= Geographic area

A= Country

R= Manufacturer

RD= Marque/Model

W= Body/Trim Level

B= Body Style (2 door convertible)

G/T= Engine Type
(E- K 1.6 MPi) (G- K 1.8 MPi) (T- K 1.8 VVC)

B/M/J/X= Steering and Transmission
(B- RHD Man) (M- LHD Man)
(J- RHD CVT) (X- LHD CVT)

A= Model Change

D= Assembly Plant

6 figures= Serial number

Paint and Trim colour codes

3-letter codes identifying the original Paint and Trim colours are stamped on the VIN plate

Paint

K M N

K= Basic colour

M= Mark identifier

N= Colour/Shade name

Trim

L Q P

L= Basic colour

Q= Mark identifier

P= Colour/Shade name

IDENTIFICATION NUMBER LOCATIONS

Engine number

'K' Series Engine: Stamped on the front face of the cylinder block adjacent to the gearbox.

Gearbox number

Manual Gearbox: Stamped on a label attached to the front face of the clutch housing.

Body number

The body number is stamped on a plate attached to the centre cross member, under the LH side seat.

Lubricating oils

Avoid excessive skin contact with used lubricating oils and always adhere to the health protection precautions.

⚠ WARNING: Avoid excessive skin contact with used engine oil. Used engine oil contains potentially harmful contaminants which may cause skin cancer or other serious skin disorders.

⚠ WARNING: Avoid excessive skin contact with mineral oil. Mineral oils remove the natural fats from the skin, leading to dryness, irritation and dermatitis.

Health Protection Precautions

- Avoid prolonged and repeated contact with oils, particularly used engine oils.
- Wear protective clothing, including impervious gloves where practicable.
- Do not put oily rags in pockets.
- Avoid contaminating clothes (particularly those next to the skin) with oil.
- Overalls must be cleaned regularly. Discard heavily soiled clothing and oil impregnated footwear.
- First aid treatment should be obtained immediately for open cuts and wounds.
- Apply barrier creams before each work period, to help prevent lubricating oil from contaminating the skin.
- Wash with soap and water to ensure all oil is removed (skin cleansers and nail brushes will help).
- Use moisturisers after cleaning; preparations containing lanolin help replace the skin's natural oils which have been removed.
- Do not use petrol/gasolene, kerosene, diesel fuel, oil, thinners or solvents for cleaning skin.
- If skin disorders develop, obtain medical advice without delay.
- Where practicable, degrease components prior to handling.
- Wear eye protection (e.g. goggles or face shield) if there is a risk of eye contamination. Eye wash facilities should be provided in close vicinity of the work area.

DANGEROUS SUBSTANCES

Modern vehicles contain many materials and liquids which if not handled with care can be hazardous to both personal health and the environment.

⚠ WARNING: Many liquids and other substances used in motor vehicles are poisonous and should not be consumed under any circumstances. As far as possible, ensure such substances are prevented from contact with the skin. These liquids and substances include but are not limited to: acid, anti-freeze, asbestos, brake fluid, fuel, windscreen washer additives, lubricants, refrigerant and various adhesives.

⚠ WARNING: Always read the instructions printed on labels or stamped on components and obey them implicitly. Such instructions are included for reasons of your health and personal safety. Never disregard them.

Synthetic rubber

Many 'O' rings, seals, hoses, flexible pipes and other similar items which appear to be natural rubber, are in fact made of synthetic materials called Fluoroelastomers. Under normal operating conditions this material is safe and does not present a health hazard. However, if the material is damaged by fire or excessive heating, it can break down and produce highly corrosive Hydrofluoric acid.

Contact with Hydrofluoric acid can cause serious burns on contact with skin. If skin contact does occur:

- Remove any contaminated clothing immediately.
- Irrigate affected area of skin with a copious amount of cold water or limewater for 15 to 60 minutes.
- Obtain medical assistance immediately.

Should any material be in a burnt or overheated condition, handle with extreme caution and wear protective clothing (seamless industrial gloves, protective apron etc.).

Decontaminate and dispose of gloves immediately after use.

Local issues

A number of environmental issues will be of particular concern to residents and other neighbours close to the site. The sensitivity of these issues will depend on the proximity of the site and the layout and amount of activity conducted at the site.

Noise is a major concern and therefore consideration should be given to the time spent carrying out noisy activities and the location of those activities that can cause excessive noise.

Car alarm testing, panel beating, hammering and other such noisy activities should, whenever possible, be carried out indoors with doors and windows shut, or as far away as possible from local residents and others who may be affected by the disturbance.

Running vehicle engines may be an outside activity which could cause nuisance to neighbours because of noise and smell.

Be sensitive with regards the time of day when these activities are performed, and minimise the time of the noisy operation, particularly in the early morning and late evening.

Another local concern will be the smell from the various materials used. Using less solvent, paint and petrol could help prevent this annoyance.

Local residents and other business users will also be concerned about traffic congestion, noise and exhaust fumes, be sensitive to these concerns and try to minimise inconvenience caused by deliveries, customers and servicing operations.

Checklist

Always adhere to the following:
• Identify where the neighbours who are likely to be affected are situated.
• Minimise noise, smell and traffic nuisance.
• Prevent litter by putting waste in the correct containers.
• Have waste skips emptied regularly.

Spill kits

Special materials are available to absorb a number of different substances. They can be in granular form, ready to use and bought in convenient containers for storage. Disposal of used spill-absorbing material is dealt with in the 'Waste Management' section.

Land contamination

Oil, fuels and solvents etc. can contaminate any soil that they are allowed to contact. Such materials should never be disposed of by pouring onto soil and every precaution must be taken to prevent spillage reaching soil. Waste materials stored on open ground could also leak, or have polluting substances washed off them that would contaminate the land. Always store these materials in suitable skips or other similarly robust containers.

Checklist

Always adhere to the following:
• Don't pour or spill anything onto the soil or bare ground.
• Don't store waste materials on bare ground, see 'Spillage prevention' list in 'Additional Precautions Checklist'.

Legal compliance

Some sites may have a discharge consent for effluent discharge to the foul drain for a car wash etc. It is important to know what materials are allowed in the drain and to check the results of any monitoring carried out by the local Water authority.

Where paint-spraying operations are carried out, it may be necessary to apply to the Local Authority for an air emissions licence to operate the plant. If such a licence is in operation, additional precautions will be necessary to comply with the requirements, and the results of any air quality monitoring must be checked regularly.

Checklist

Always adhere to the following:
• Know what legal consents and licences apply to the operations.
• Check that the emissions and discharges comply with legal requirements.

GENERAL INFORMATION

ENVIRONMENTAL PRECAUTIONS

General

This section provides general information which if observed, can help reduce environmental damage caused by activities carried out in workshops.

Emissions to air

Many of the activities that are carried out in workshops emit gases and fumes which contribute to global warming, depletion of the ozone layer and/or the formation of photochemical smog at ground level. By considering how the workshop activities are carried out, these gases and fumes can be minimised, thus reducing the impact on the environment.

Exhaust fumes

Running car engines is an essential part of workshop activities and exhaust fumes need to be ventilated to atmosphere. However, the amount of time engines are running and the position of the vehicle should be carefully considered at all times, to reduce the release of poisonous gases and minimise the inconvenience to people living nearby.

Solvents

Some of the cleaning agents used are solvent based and will evaporate to atmosphere if used carelessly, or if cans are left unsealed. All solvent containers should be firmly closed when not being used and solvent should be used sparingly. Suitable alternative methods may be available to replace some of the commonly used solvents. Similarly, many paints are solvent based and the spray should be minimised to reduce solvent emissions.

Refrigerant

It is illegal to release any refrigerants into the atmosphere. Discharge and replacement of these materials from air conditioning units should only be carried out using the correct equipment.

Checklist

Always adhere to the following:

Engines:
• Don't leave engines running unnecessarily.
• Minimise testing times and check where the exhaust fumes are being blown.

Materials:
• Keep lids on containers of solvents.
• Only use the minimum quantity.
• Consider alternative materials.
• Minimise over-spray when painting.

Gases:
• Use the correct equipment for collecting refrigerants.
• Don't burn rubbish on site.

Discharges to water

Most sites will have two systems for discharging water: storm drains and foul drains. Storm drains should only receive clean water, foul drains will take dirty water.

The foul drain will accept many of the normal waste waters such as washing water, detergents and domestic type wastes but oil, petrol, solvent, acids, hydraulic oil, antifreeze and other such substances should never be poured down the drain. If in any doubt, consult the Water Authority responsible for your locality first.

Every precaution must be taken to prevent spillage of oil, fuel, solvents etc. reaching the drains. All handling of such materials must take place well away from the drains and preferably in an area with a kerb or wall around it, to prevent discharge into the drain. If a spillage occurs, it should be soaked up immediately. Having a spill kit available will make this easier.

Additional precautions

Check whether the surface water drains are connected to an oil/water separator, this could reduce the pollution if an incident was to occur. Oil/water separators do need regular maintenance to ensure effectiveness.

Checklist

Always adhere to the following:

Disposal:
• Never pour anything down a drain without first checking that it is environmentally safe to do so, and that it does not contravene any local regulations or bye-laws.
• Have oil traps emptied regularly.

Spillage prevention:
• Store liquids in a walled area.
• Make sure that taps on liquid containers are secure and cannot be accidently turned on.
• Protect bulk storage tanks from vandalism by locking the valves.
• Transfer liquids from one container to another in an area away from open drains.
• Ensure lids are replaced securely on containers.
• Have spill kits available near to points of storage and handling of liquids.

Use of resource

Another environmental concern is the waste of materials and energy that can occur in day to day activities.

Electricity for heating, lighting and compressed air uses resources and releases pollution during its generation.

Fuel used for heating, running cars or vans and mobile plant is another limited resource which consumes large amounts of energy during its extraction and refining processes.

Water has to be cleaned, piped to site and disposed of; all of which creates more potential pollution.

Oil, spares, paint etc., have all produced pollution in the process of manufacture and they become a waste disposal problem if discarded.

Checklist

Always adhere to the following:

Electricity and heating:
- Keep doors and windows closed in the Winter.
- Switch off machinery or lights when not needed.
- Use energy efficient heating systems.
- Switch off computers and photocopiers when not needed.

Fuel:
- Don't run engines unnecessarily
- Think about whether journeys are necessary and drive to conserve fuel.

Water:
- Don't leave taps and hose pipes running.
- Mend leaks quickly.

Compressed air:
- Don't leave valves open.
- Mend leaks quickly.
- Don't leave the compressor running when not needed.

Use of environmentally damaging materials:
- Check whether a less toxic material is available.

Handling and storage of materials:
- Have the correct facilities available for handling liquids to prevent spillage and wastage as listed above.
- Provide suitable locations for storage to prevent frost damage or other deterioration.

Burning used engine oil

Burning of used engine oil in small space heaters or boilers can be recommended only for units of approved design. The heating system must meet the regulatory standards for small burners(s) with a net rated thermal input of less than 3MW. The use of waste oil burners must be licensed by the local authority.

Waste Management

One of the major ways that pollution can be reduced is by the careful handling, storage and disposal of all waste materials that occur on sites. Legislation makes it illegal to dispose of waste materials other than to licensed waste carriers and disposal sites. This means that it is necessary to not only know what the waste materials are, but also to have the necessary documentation and licenses.

Handling and storage of waste

Ensure that waste materials are not poured down the drain or onto soils. They should be stored in such a way as to prevent the escape of the material to land, water or air.

They must also be segregated into different types of waste e.g. oil, metals, batteries, used vehicle components. This will prevent any reaction between different materials and assist in disposal.

Disposal of waste

Disposal of waste materials must only be to waste carriers who are licensed to carry those particular waste materials and all the necessary documentation must be completed. The waste carrier is responsible for ensuring that the waste is taken to the correct disposal sites.

Dispose of waste in accordance with the following guidelines:

- **Fuel, hydraulic fluid, anti-freeze and oil:** keep separate and dispose of to specialist contractor.
- **Refrigerant:** collect in specialist equipment and reuse.
- **Detergents:** safe to pour down the foul drain if diluted.
- **Paint, thinners:** keep separate and dispose of to specialist contractor.
- **Components:** send back to supplier for refurbishment, or disassemble and reuse any suitable parts. Dispose of the remainder in ordinary waste.
- **Small parts:** reuse any suitable parts, dispose of the remainder in ordinary waste.
- **Metals:** can be sold if kept separate from general waste.
- **Tyres:** keep separate and dispose of to specialist contractor.
- **Packaging:** compact as much as possible and dispose of in ordinary waste.
- **Asbestos-containing:** keep separate and dispose of to specialist contractor.
- **Oily and fuel wastes (e.g. rags, used spill kit material):** keep separate and dispose of to specialist contractor.
- **Air filters:** keep separate and dispose of to specialist contractor.
- **Rubber/plastics:** dispose of in ordinary waste.
- **Hoses:** dispose of in ordinary waste.
- **Batteries:** keep separate and dispose of to specialist contractor.
- **Airbags - explosives:** keep separate and dispose of to specialist contractor.
- **Electrical components:** send back to supplier for refurbishment, or disassemble and reuse any suitable parts. Dispose of the remainder in ordinary waste.
- **Electronic components:** send back to supplier for refurbishment, or disassemble and reuse any suitable parts. Dispose of the remainder in ordinary waste.
- **Catalysts:** can be sold if kept separate from general waste.
- **Used spill-absorbing material:** keep separate and dispose of to specialist contractor.
- **Office waste:** recycle paper and toner and ink cartridges, dispose of the remainder in ordinary waste.

PRECAUTIONS AGAINST DAMAGE

Always fit wing and seat covers before commencing work.

Avoid spilling brake fluid or battery acid on paintwork. Wash off with water immediately if this occurs.

Disconnect the battery earth lead before starting work, see **ELECTRICAL PRECAUTIONS**.

Always use the recommended service tool or a satisfactory equivalent where specified.

Protect exposed bearing and sealing surfaces and screw threads from damage.

SAFETY INSTRUCTIONS

Jacking

The recommended jacking points are given in **LIFTING AND TOWING**, always ensure that any lifting apparatus has adequate load and safety capacity for the weight to be lifted. Ensure the vehicle is standing on level ground prior to lifting or jacking. Apply the handbrake and chock the wheels.

Never rely on a jack as the sole means of support when working beneath the vehicle. Use additional safety supports beneath the vehicle.

Do not leave tools, lifting equipment, spilt oil, etc. around or on the work bench area.

Brake shoes and pads

 WARNING: Always fit the correct grade and specification of brake linings and renew brake pads and brake shoes in axle sets only.

Brake hydraulics

Observe the following recommendations when working on the brake system:

- Always use two spanners when loosening or tightening brake pipe or hose connections.
- Ensure that hoses run in a natural curve and are not kinked or twisted.
- Fit brake pipes securely in their retaining clips and ensure that the pipe cannot contact a potential chafing point.
- Containers used for hydraulic fluid must be kept absolutely clean.
- Do not store hydraulic brake fluid in an unsealed container, it will absorb water and in this condition would be dangerous to use due to a lowering of its boiling point.
- Do not allow hydraulic brake fluid to be contaminated with mineral oil, or put new brake fluid in a container which has previously contained mineral oil.
- Do not re-use brake fluid removed from the system.
- Always use clean brake fluid or a recommended alternative to clean hydraulic components.
- After disconnection of brake pipes and hoses, immediately fit suitable blanking caps or plugs to prevent the ingress of dirt.
- Only use the correct brake fittings with compatible threads.
- Absolute cleanliness must be observed when working with hydraulic components.

WARNING: It is imperative that the correct brake fittings are used and that threads of components are compatible.

Engine coolant caps and plugs

Extreme care is necessary when removing engine coolant caps and plugs when the engine is hot and especially if it is overheated. To avoid the possibility of scalding allow the engine to cool before attempting coolant cap or plug removal.

GENERAL FITTING INSTRUCTIONS

Component removal

Whenever possible, clean components and surrounding area before removal.

- Blank off openings exposed by component removal.
- Immediately seal fuel, oil or hydraulic lines when apertures are exposed; use plastic caps or plugs to prevent loss of fluid and ingress of dirt.
- Close the open ends of oilways exposed by component removal with tapered hardwood plugs or conspicuous plastic plugs.
- Immediately a component is removed, place it in a suitable container; use a separate container for each component and its associated parts.
- Clean bench and provide marking materials, labels and containers before dismantling a component.

Dismantling

Observe scrupulous cleanliness when dismantling components, particularly when brake, fuel or hydraulic system parts are being worked on. A particle of dirt or a cloth fragment could cause a serious malfunction in these systems.

- Blow out all tapped holes, crevices, oilways and fluid passages with an air line. Ensure that any 'O' rings used for sealing are correctly replaced or renewed, if disturbed during the process.
- Use marking ink to identify mating parts and ensure correct reassembly. Do not use a centre punch or scriber to mark parts, they could initiate cracks or distortion in marked components.
- Wire together mating parts where necessary to prevent accidental interchange (e.g. roller bearing components).
- Wire labels on to all parts which are to be renewed, and to parts requiring further inspection before being passed for reassembly; place these parts in separate containers from those containing parts for rebuild.
- Do not discard a part due for renewal until after comparing it with a new part, to ensure that its correct replacement has been obtained.

Cleaning components

Always use the recommended cleaning agent or equivalent.

Ensure that adequate ventilation is provided when volatile degreasing agents are being used.

Do not use degreasing equipment for components containing items which could be damaged by the use of this process.

Whenever possible clean components and the area surrounding them before removal. Always observe scrupulous cleanliness when cleaning dismantled components.

General inspection

All components should be inspected for wear or damage before being reassembled.

- Never inspect a component for wear or dimensional check unless it is absolutely clean; a slight smear of grease can conceal an incipient failure.
- When a component is to be checked dimensionally against recommended values, use the appropriate measuring equipment (surface plates, micrometers, dial gauges etc.). Ensure the measuring equipment is calibrated and in good serviceable condition.
- Reject a component if its dimensions are outside the specified tolerances, or if it appears to be damaged.
- A part may be refitted if its critical dimension is exactly to its tolerance limit and it appears to be in satisfactory condition. Use 'Plastigauge' 12 Type PG-1 for checking bearing surface clearances.

GENERAL INFORMATION

Ball and Roller Bearings

When removing and installing bearings, ensure that the following practices are observed to ensure component serviceability.

- Remove all traces of lubricant from bearing under inspection by cleaning with a suitable degreasant; maintain absolute cleanliness throughout operations.

- Conduct a visual inspection for markings on rolling elements, raceways, outer surface of outer rings or inner surface of inner rings. Reject any bearings found to be marked, since marking in these areas indicates onset of wear.

- Hold inner race of bearing between finger and thumb of one hand and spin outer race to check that it rotates absolutely smoothly. Repeat, holding outer race and spinning inner race.

- Rotate outer ring gently with a reciprocating motion, while holding inner ring; feel for any check or obstruction to rotation. Reject bearing if action is not perfectly smooth.

- Lubricate bearing with generous amounts of lubricant appropriate to installation.

- Inspect shaft and bearing housing for discoloration or other markings which indicate movement between bearing and seatings.

- Ensure that shaft and housing are clean and free from burrs before fitting bearing.

- If one bearing of a pair shows an imperfection, it is advisable to replace both with new bearings; an exception could be if the faulty bearing had covered a low mileage, and it can be established that damage is confined to only one bearing.

- Never refit a ball or roller bearing without first ensuring that that it is in a fully serviceable condition.

- When hub bearings are removed or displaced, new bearings must be fitted; do not attempt to refit the old hub bearings.

- When fitting a bearing to a shaft, only apply force to the inner ring of the bearing. When fitting a bearing into a housing, only apply force to the outer ring of the bearing.

- In the case of grease lubricated bearings (e.g. hub bearings) fill the space between bearing and outer seal with the recommended grade of grease before fitting seal.

- Always mark components of separable bearings (e.g. taper roller bearings) when dismantling, to ensure correct reassembly. Never fit new rollers in a used outer ring; always fit a complete new bearing assembly.

Oil seals

Always renew oil seals which have been removed from their working location (whether as an individual component or as part of an assembly). NEVER use a seal which has been improperly stored or handled, such as hung on a hook or nail.

- Carefully examine seal before fitting to ensure that it is clean and undamaged.

- Ensure the surface on which the new seal is to run is free of burrs or scratches. Renew the component if the original sealing surface cannot be completely restored.

- Protect the seal from any surface which it has to pass when being fitted. Use a protective sleeve or tape to cover the relevant surface.

- Lubricate the sealing lips with a recommended lubricant before use to prevent damage during initial use. On dual lipped seals, smear the area between the lips with grease. **Note:** some oil seals are coated with a protective wax and must be fitted dry, unless instructed otherwise.

- If a seal spring is provided, ensure that it is fitted correctly. Place lip of seal towards fluid to be sealed and slide into position on shaft. Use fitting sleeve where possible to protect sealing lip from damage by sharp corners, threads or splines. If a fitting sleeve is not available, use plastic tube or tape to prevent damage to the sealing lip.

- Grease outside diameter of seal, place square to housing recess and press into position using great care, and if possible a 'bell piece' to ensure the seal is not tilted. In some cases it may be preferable to fit seal to housing before fitting to shaft. Never let weight of unsupported shaft rest in seal.

- Use the recommended service tool to fit an oil seal. If the correct service tool is not available, use a suitable tube approximately 0.4 mm (0.015 in) smaller than the outside diameter of the seal. Use a hammer **VERY GENTLY** on drift if a suitable press is not available.

- Press or drift the seal in to the depth of its housing, with the sealing lip facing the lubricant to be retained if the housing is shouldered, or flush with the face of the housing where no shoulder is provided. Ensure that the seal does not enter the housing in a tilted position.

GENERAL INFORMATION

Locking Devices

Always replace locking devices with one of the same design.

Tab washers - always release locking tabs and fit new locking washers. Do not re-use locking tabs.

Locking nuts - always use a backing spanner when loosening or tightening locking nuts, brake and fuel pipe unions.

Roll pins - always fit new roll pins of an interference fit in the hole.

Circlips - always fit new circlips of the correct size for the groove.

Keys and keyways - remove burrs from edges of keyways with a fine file and clean thoroughly before attempting to refit key.

Clean and inspect key closely; keys are suitable for refitting only if indistinguishable from new, as any indentation may indicate the onset of wear.

Split pins -

1M0057

Always fit new split-pins of the correct size for the hole in the bolt or stud. **Do not slacken back nut to enter split-pin.**

Joints and joint faces

Fit joints dry unless specified otherwise.

- When jointing compound is used, apply in a thin uniform film to metal surfaces; take care to prevent jointing compound from entering oilways, pipes or blind tapped holes.

- If gaskets and/or jointing compound is recommended for use; remove all traces of old jointing material prior to reassembly. Do not use a tool which will damage the joint faces and smooth out any scratches or burrs on the joint faces using an oil stone. Do not allow dirt or jointing material to enter any tapped holes or enclosed parts.

- Prior to reassembly, blow through any pipes, channels or crevices with compressed air.

GENERAL INFORMATION

Screw threads

Metric threads to ISO standards are used.

Damaged nuts, bolts and screws must always be discarded.

Cleaning up damaged threads with a die or tap impairs the strength and closeness of fit of the threads and is not recommended.

Castellated nuts must not be slackened back to accept a split-pin, except in those recommended cases when this forms part of an adjustment.

Do not allow oil or grease to enter blind threaded holes. The hydraulic action on screwing in the bolt or stud could split the housing.

Always tighten a nut or bolt to the recommended torque figure. Damaged or corroded threads can affect the torque reading.

To check or re-tighten a bolt or screw to a specified torque figure, first slacken a quarter of a turn, then retighten to the correct torque figure.

Bolt identification

1M0055

An ISO metric bolt or screw made of steel and larger than 6 mm in diameter can be identified by either of the symbols ISO M or M embossed or indented on top of the head.

In addition to marks to identify the manufacturer, the head is also marked with symbols to indicate the strength grade, e.g. 8.8; 10.9; 12.9; 14.9. As an alternative, some bolts and screws have the M and strength grade symbol on the flats of the hexagon.

GENERAL INFORMATION

Nut identification

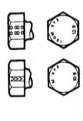

1M0056

A nut with an ISO metric thread is marked on one face or on one of the flats of the hexagon with the strength grade symbol 8, 12, or 14. Some nuts with a strength grade 4, 5 or 6 are also marked and some have the metric symbol M on the flat opposite the strength grade marking.

A clock face system is used as an alternative method of indicating the strength grade. The external chambers or a face of the nut is marked in a position relative to the appropriate hour mark on a clock face to indicate the strength grade.

A dot is used to locate the 12 o'clock position and a dash to indicate the strength grade. If the grade is above 12, two dots identify the 12 o'clock position.

Self-locking nuts

1M0058

Self-locking nuts, i.e. nylon insert or metal stiff nuts can be re-used providing resistance can be felt when the locking portion of the nut passes over the thread of the bolt or stud.

Self-locking bolts and screws

1M0059

Self-locking bolts and screws, i.e. nylon patched or trilobular thread can be re-used providing resistance can be felt when the locking portion enters the female thread.

Nylon patched bolts and screws have a locking agent pre-applied to the threads. They are identified by the presence of a coloured section of thread which extends for up to 180° around the thread.

Trilobular i.e. Powerlok bolts have a special thread form which creates a slight interference in the tapped hole or threads of the nut into which it is screwed.

DO NOT re-use self-locking fasteners in critical locations eg engine bearings. Always use the correct replacement self-locking nut, bolt or screw.

DO NOT fit non self-locking fasteners in applications where a self-locking nut, bolt or screw is specified.

Encapsulated bolts and screws

1M0062

Encapsulated bolts and screws have a micro-encapsulated locking agent pre-applied to the thread. They are identified by the presence of a coloured section of thread which extends completely around the thread - 360°. The locking agent is released and activated by the assembly process and is then chemically cured to provide the locking action.

Unless a specific repair procedure states otherwise, encapsulated bolts may be re-used providing the threads are undamaged and the following procedure is adopted.

Remove loose adhesive from the bolt and housing threads, ensure threads are clean and free of oil and grease. Apply an approved adhesive.

Fit a new encapsulated bolt, or if not available a bolt of equivalent specification treated with an approved adhesive.

GENERAL INFORMATION

SERVICE TOOLS

General

Special service tools have been developed to facilitate removal, dismantling and assembly of mechanical components in a cost effective and time efficient manner. The use of special tools also helps prevent the potential for damage to components.

Some operations described in this Manual cannot be carried out properly without the aid of the relevant service tools.

Special service tools can be obtained from the following suppliers:

Cartool (UK) Limited
Unit 3, Sterling Business Park
Salthouse Road
Brackmills
Northampton
NN4 7EX
England

TEL: +44 (0) 1604 760099
FAX: +44 (0) 1604 760017
e-mail: sales@cartooluk.co.uk

CARTOOL GmbH
Straussenleitenstrasse 15
85053 Ingolstadt
Germany

TEL: +49 (0) 841 9650080
FAX: +49 (0) 841 9650090
e-mail: i.amann@cartool.de

TestBook

TestBook is a computerised workshop tool which provides your dealership with instant access to the very latest Technical Information from ROVER, allowing for accurate and effective fault diagnosis and repair of all Rover Vehicles.

Where specific garage equipment is required for diagnosis and repair, reference should be made to the Service Tools and Equipment Programme where details of the equipment recommended by Rover Service may be found.

Body repairs

Any damage found, that would affect the corrosion resistance of the vehicle during the Warranty period must be rectified by an authorised Rover Dealer to the standards, and by the methods, detailed in the Body Repair Manual.

Replacement body panels

Body panels are supplied coated in cathodic electrocoat primer.

DYNAMOMETER TESTING

General

IMPORTANT: Use a four wheel dynamometer for brake testing if possible.

 WARNING: Do not attempt to test ABS function on a dynamometer.

Four wheel dynamometers

Provided that front and rear rollers are rotating at identical speeds and that normal workshop safety standards are applied, there is no speed restriction during testing except any that may apply to the tyres.

Before testing a vehicle with anti-lock brakes on a four wheel dynamometer, disconnect the ABS modulator. The ABS function will not work, the ABS warning light will illuminate. Normal braking will be available.

Two wheel dynamometers

ABS will not function on a two wheel dynamometer. The ABS light will illuminate during testing. Normal braking will be available.

If brake testing on a two wheel dynamometer is necessary, the following precautions should be taken:

- Traction control must be disabled
- Neutral selected in gearbox

When checking brakes, run engine at idle speed to maintain servo-vacuum.

FUEL HANDLING PRECAUTIONS

General

The following information provides basic precautions which must be observed if petrol (gasoline) is to be handled safely. It also outlines other areas of risk which must not be ignored. This information is issued for basic guidance only, if in doubt consult your local Fire Officer.

Fuel vapour is highly flammable and in confined spaces is also explosive and toxic. The vapour is heavier than air and will always fall to the lowest level. The vapour can be easily distributed throughout a workshop by air currents; consequently, even a small spillage of fuel is potentially very dangerous.

Always have a fire extinguisher containing FOAM, CO_2, GAS or POWDER close at hand when handling or draining fuel or when dismantling fuel systems. Fire extinguishers should also be located in areas where fuel containers are stored.

Always disconnect the vehicle battery before carrying out dismantling or draining work on a fuel system.

Whenever fuel is being handled, drained or stored, or when fuel systems are being dismantled, all forms of ignition must be extinguished or removed; any leadlamps must be flameproof and kept clear of spillage.

 WARNING: No one should be permitted to repair components associated with fuel without first having specialist training.

 WARNING: Do not remove fuel system components while the vehicle is over a pit.

Fuel tank draining

Fuel tank draining should be carried out in accordance with the procedure outlined in the 'FUEL DELIVERY'section of this manual and observing the following precautions:

 WARNING: Fuel must not be extracted or drained from any vehicle whilst it is over a pit.

Draining or extraction of fuel must be carried out in a well ventilated area.

The capacity of containers for fuel must be more than adequate for the full amount of fuel to be extracted or drained. The container should be clearly marked with its contents and placed in a safe storage area which meets the requirements of local authority regulations.

⚠ **CAUTION: When fuel has been extracted or drained from a fuel tank the precautions governing naked lights and ignition sources should be maintained.**

Fuel tank removal

When the fuel line is secured to the fuel tank outlet by a spring steel clip, the clip must be released before the fuel line is disconnected or the fuel tank is removed. This procedure will avoid the possibility of residual fumes in the fuel tank being ignited when the clip is released.

As an added precaution fuel tanks should have a 'FUEL VAPOUR' warning label attached to them as soon as they are removed from the vehicle.

Fuel tank repairs

No attempt should be made to repair a plastic fuel tank. If the structure of the tank is damaged, a new tank must be fitted.

Body repairs

Plastic fuel pipes are particularly susceptible to heat, even at relatively low temperature, and can be melted by heat conducted from some distance away.

When body repairs involve the use of heat, all fuel pipes which run in the vicinity of the repair area must be removed, and the tank outlet plugged, BEFORE HEAT IS APPLIED. If the repair is in the vicinity of the fuel tank, the tank must be removed.

⚠ **WARNING: If welding is to be carried out in the vicinity of the fuel tank, the fuel system must be drained and the tank removed before welding commences.**

Having confirmed a component to be faulty:

- Switch off the ignition and disconnect the battery.
- Remove the component and support the disconnected harness.
- When replacing the component keep oily hands away from electrical connection areas and push connectors home until any locking tabs fully engage.

Battery disconnection

Before disconnecting the battery, disable the alarm system and switch off all electrical equipment. If the radio is to be serviced, ensure the security code has been deactivated.

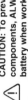 **CAUTION: To prevent damage to electrical components, ALWAYS disconnect the battery when working on the vehicle's electrical system. The ground lead must be disconnected first and reconnected last. Always ensure that battery leads are routed correctly and are not close to any potential chafing points.**

Battery charging

Only recharge the battery with it removed from the vehicle. Always ensure any battery charging area is well ventilated and that every precaution is taken to avoid naked flames and sparks.

Ignition system safety precautions

The vehicle's ignition system produces high voltage and the following precautions should be observed before carrying out any work on the system.

 WARNING: Before commencing work on an ignition system, ensure all high tension terminals, adapters and diagnostic equipment are adequately insulated and shielded to prevent accidental personal contacts and minimise the risk of shock.

WARNING: Wearers of surgically implanted pacemaker devices should not be in close proximity of ignition circuits or diagnostic equipment.

ELECTRICAL PRECAUTIONS

General

The following guidelines are intended to ensure the safety of the operator whilst preventing damage to the electrical and electronic components fitted to the vehicle. Where necessary, specific precautions are detailed in the relevant sections of this Manual which should be referred to prior to commencing repair operations.

Equipment

Prior to commencing any test procedure on the vehicle, ensure that the relevant test equipment is working correctly and any harness or connectors are in good condition. It is particularly important to check the condition of the lead and plugs of mains operated equipment.

Polarity

Never reverse connect the vehicle battery and always ensure the correct polarity when connecting test equipment.

High Voltage Circuits

Whenever disconnecting live ht circuits, always use insulated pliers and never allow the open end of the ht lead to contact other components, particularly ECU's. Exercise caution when measuring the voltage on the coil terminals while the engine is running, high voltage spikes can occur on these terminals.

Connectors and Harness

The engine compartment of a vehicle is a particularly hostile environment for electrical components and connectors:

- Always ensure electrically related items are dry and oil free before disconnecting and connecting test equipment.
- Ensure disconnected multiplugs and sensors are protected from being contaminated with oil, coolant or other solutions. Contamination could impair performance or result in catastrophic failure.
- Never force connectors apart using tools to prise apart or by pulling on the wiring harness.
- Always ensure locking tabs are disengaged before disconnection, and match orientation to enable correct reconnection.
- Ensure that any protection (covers, insulation etc.) is replaced if disturbed.

Quick fit fuel hose connectors

 WARNING: Hose connections between the fuel pump and the fuel rail contain fuel under pressure, which MUST be relieved prior to disconnection of the hoses. See *ENGINE MANAGEMENT SYSTEM - MEMS, Adjustments.*

1. Wipe connection and surrounding area using a lint free cloth.

 NOTE: If the connection is heavily soiled with road salt and dirt, gently twist connector while spraying with WD40.

2. If necessary use an air line to remove contaminates from the retainer area of the connector.
3. Depress collar and disconnect hose.
4. Ensure pipe end is clean and free from corrosion.
5. Lubricate pipe end with clean engine oil.
6. Connect hose to pipe and push firmly into position until a click is heard.
7. Check security of connection by pulling on connector.

 CAUTION: When checking security of connector pull on connector body NOT on the hose.

CONTENTS

GENERAL INFORMATION

Disciplines

Switch off the ignition prior to making any connection or disconnection in the system to prevent electrical surges caused by disconnecting 'live' connections damaging electronic components.

Ensure hands and work surfaces are clean and free of grease, swarf, etc. Grease collects dirt which can cause electrical tracking (short-circuits) or high-resistance contacts.

When handling printed circuit boards, treat with care and hold by the edges only; note that some electronic components are susceptible to body static.

Connectors should never be subjected to forced removal or refit, especially inter-board connectors. Damaged contacts can cause short- circuit and open-circuit fault conditions.

Prior to commencing test, and periodically during a test, touch a good vehicle body earth to discharge static. Some electronic components are vulnerable to static electricity that may be generated by the operator.

Grease for electrical connectors

Some under bonnet and under body connectors may be protected against corrosion by the application of a special grease during vehicle production. Should connectors be disturbed in service, repaired or replaced, additional grease should be applied: Part No. BAU 5811, available in 150 g tubs.

⚠ NOTE: The use of greases other than BAU 5811 must be avoided as they can migrate into relays, switches etc. contaminating the contacts and leading to intermittent operation or failure.

CONTENTS

ENGINE - K SERIES

1.6 MPi

Type	16 valve DOHC
Cylinder arrangement	4 in line - transverse, NO.1 cylinder at front of engine
Bore - liner	80.00 mm
Stroke	79.00 mm
Capacity	1588 cm^3
Firing order	1 - 3 - 4 - 2
Rotation	Clockwise, viewed from the front of the engine
Compression ratio	10.5 : 1
Idle speed	
1.6 MPi MEMS 3	825 ± 50 rpm

1.8 MPi

Type	16 valve DOHC
Cylinder arrangement	4 in line - transverse, No.1 cylinder at front of engine
Bore - liner	80.00 mm
Stroke	89.30 mm
Capacity	1796 cm^3
Firing order	1 - 3 - 4 - 2
Rotation	Clockwise, viewed from the front of the engine
Compression ratio	10.5 : 1
Idle speed	
1.8 MPi MEMS 1.9 (Manual)	875 ± 50 rpm
1.8 MPi MEMS 3 (Manual and Steptronic)	825 ± 50 rpm

Valve timing

Inlet	
opens	12° BTDC
closes	52° ABDC
Exhaust	
opens	52° BBDC
closes	12° ATDC
Valve open period	244°
Valve lift	8.8 mm - inlet
	8.8 mm - exhaust

1.8 VVC

Type	16 valve
Cylinder arrangement	4 in line - transverse, No.1 cylinder at front of engine
Bore - liner	80.00 mm
Stroke	89.30 mm
Capacity	1796 cm^3
Firing order	1 - 3 - 4 - 2
Rotation	Clockwise, viewed from the front of the engine
Compression ratio	10.5 : 1
Idle speed	
1.8 VVC MEMS2J	875 ± 50 rpm
1.8 VVC MEMS3	825 ± 50 rpm

Valve timing

Inlet	
opens	0° ATDC at minimum period
closes	40° ABDC at minimum period

ENGINE - LUBRICATION

System type . . . . Wet sump, crankshaft driven eccentric rotor pump
Relief valve opening pressure . . . . 4.1 bar
Oil pressure at idle . . . . 1.7 to 3.5 bar
Maximum oil pressure at 6500 rev/min . . . . 7.0 bar (below 40° C)
Oil pressure warning light switch opens . . . . 0.3 - 0.5 bar
Oil filter . . . . Full flow with renewable element cartridge

FUEL SYSTEM

Electronic fuel injection data . . . . ***See Engine tuning data.***
Fuel pump
Type . . . . Continuous flow, electrically driven roller vane
Pump maximum pressure at 13.5 V . . . . 3.5 bar
Regulated injection pressure . . . . 3.0 ± 0.2 bar

COOLING SYSTEM

Pressure cap opens . . . . 1.03 bar
Thermostat
starts to open . . . . 86 to 90° C
fully open . . . . 102° C
Cooling fan switch, operating temperature . . . . ON - 102° C, OFF - 96° C
Second cooling fan switch, operating temperature . . ON - 108° C, OFF - 103° C
Engine bay fan switch, operating temperature . . . . . ON - 75° C, OFF - ***See COOLING SYSTEM, Information.***
Engine bay ambient air, warning light switch . . . . . . ON - 90° C

Exhaust
opens . . . . 51° BBDC
closes . . . . 21° ATDC
Valve open period
Variable period - inlet . . . . 220° to 295°
Valve period - exhaust . . . . 252°
Variable overlap . . . . 21° to 58°
Valve lift . . . . 9.5 mm - inlet
9.2 mm - exhaust

CLUTCH

Type	Single plate diaphragm spring, hydraulically operated
Clutch plate diameter	
1.6 MPi	200 mm
1.8 MPi	215 mm
Diaphragm finger clearance	1.00 mm
Diaphragm finger height	
New	37.5 - 32.1 mm
Service limit	42.75 mm
Clutch plate thickness	
New	7.40 - 6.90 mm
Service limit	5.60
Rivet depth	
New	1.00 mm
Service limit	0.20 mm
Clutch plate run-out	
New	0.80 mm
Service limit	1.00 mm
Pressure plate warping - service limit	0.15 mm

MANUAL GEARBOX

1.6 MPi

Gearbox code	G4 BP
Gear ratios	
Fifth	0.765 : 1
Fourth	1.033 : 1
Third	1.307 : 1
Second	1.842 : 1
First	3.167 : 1
Reverse	3.000 : 1

1.8 MPi

Gearbox code	C6 BP
Gear ratios	
Fifth	0.765 : 1
Fourth	1.033 : 1
Third	1.307 : 1
Second	1.842 : 1
First	3.167 : 1
Reverse	3.000 : 1

1.8 VVC

Gearbox code	C4 BP
Gear ratios	
Fifth	0.765 : 1
Fourth	1.033 : 1
Third	1.307 : 1
Second	1.842 : 1
First	3.167 : 1
Reverse	3.000 : 1

STEPTRONIC (EM-CVT) GEARBOX

1.8 MPi

Gearbox code	VT1-11A
Gear ratios (manual mode only)	
Sixth	2.99 : 1
Fifth	3.92 : 1
Fourth	4.87 : 1
Third	6.48 : 1
Second	8.76 : 1
First	13.92 : 1
Reverse	15.32 : 1
Gear ratios ('D' drive mode only)	
Over drive	2.553 : 1
First	13.92 : 1
Reverse	15.32 : 1

GEARBOX - LUBRICATION

Manual Gearbox

Capacities	
Refill	2.2 litres
Dry	2.4 litres
Fluids and Lubricants	
Gearbox oil specification	Texaco MTF 94
Gear linkage grease specification	Unipart multi-purpose lithium grease or equivalent.

Steptronic (EM-CVT)

Capacities	
Refill - gearbox only	4.5 litres
Fluid cooler and lines	1.0 litre
Fluids and Lubricants	
Gearbox fluid specification	Esso EZL799 / Unipart CVT

INFORMATION

FINAL DRIVE

Manual gearbox - MPi

Gearbox code
1.6 MPi G4 BP
1.8 MPi C6 BP

Ratio	3.938 : 1	
Road speed at 1000 rev/min		
Fifth	35.6 km/h	22.2 mph
Fourth	26.4 km/h	16.4 mph
Third	20.8 km/h	13.0 mph
Second	14.8 km/h	9.2 mph
First	8.6 km/h	5.4 mph

Manual gearbox - VVC

Gearbox code C4 BP

Ratio	4.200 : 1	
Road speed at 1000 rev/min (Vehicles with 205 tyres)		
Fifth	33.4 km/h	20.8 mph
Fourth	24.8 km/h	15.4 mph
Third	19.5 km/h	12.1 mph
Second	13.9 km/h	8.6 mph
First	8.1 km/h	5.0 mph
Road speed at 1000 rev/min (Vehicles with 215 tyres)		
Fifth	32.9 km/h	20.5 mph
Fourth	24.4 km/h	15.1 mph
Third	19.2 km/h	12.0 mph
Second	13.7 km/h	8.5 mph
First	7.9 km/h	4.9 mph

Steptronic (EM-CVT) - MPi

Gearbox code VT1-11A

Ratio (Manual mode)	4.05 : 1	
Road speed at 1000 rev/min (manual mode only)		
Sixth	35.2 km/h	22.0 mph
Fifth	26.8 km/h	16.75 mph
Fourth	21.6 km/h	13.5 mph
Third	16.24 km/h	10.15 mph
Second	12.0 km/h	7.5 mph
First	7.36 km/h	4.6 mph

INFORMATION

⚠ NOTE: The following steering geometry settings are given in degrees and minutes, decimal parts of a degree and millimetres. Steering and suspension geometry settings are for a vehicle at unladen weight.

STEERING

Front wheel alignment - toe out - per side	0° 10' ± 6'	0.21° ± 0.1° / 1.105 mm ± 0.651 mm
Front wheel camber - negative	0° 30' ± 0° 30'	0.50° ± 0.50° / 3.315 mm ± 0.315 mm
Front wheel caster - positive	4° 50' ± 1°	4.83° ± 1.0° / 29.98 mm ± 6.71 mm
King pin inclination	11° 40'	11.71° / 78.71 mm
Overall steering ratio		
Manual steering	20.8 : 1	
Power steering	19.1 : 1	
Rear suspension geometry		
Rear wheel alignment - toe-in - per side	0° 10' to ± 0° 7'	0.21° ± 0.12° / 1.105 mm ± 0.76 mm
Rear wheel camber - negative	1° 0' ± 0° 30'	1.0° ± 0.50° / 6.71 mm ± 0.315 mm

SUSPENSION

Front
Type .... Double wishbone with Hydragas springs, separate dampers and anti roll bar.

Rear
Type .... Double wishbone with forward fitting tie bar. Hydragas springs, separate dampers and anti roll bar.

Trim height
Height to wheel arch from hub centre at unladen weight:

Front height	368 ± 10 mm
Rear height	363 ± 10 mm

BRAKES

Front brakes
Disc diameter . . . . 240 mm
Disc thickness new . . . . 22 mm
Disc minimum thickness . . . . 20 mm
Pad minimum thickness . . . . 3 mm

Front brakes (Trophy)
Disc diameter . . . . 304 mm
Disc thickness new . . . . 24 mm
Disc minimum thickness . . . . 22 mm
Pad minimum thickness . . . . 2.5 mm

Rear brakes
Disc diameter . . . . 240 mm
Disc thickness new . . . . 10 mm
Disc minimum thickness . . . . 8 mm
Pad minimum thickness . . . . 3 mm

Brake servo
Servo boost ratio . . . . 4.6 : 1
Anti-lock brake system (up to 2000MY) . . . . Bosch ABS5
Anti-lock brake system (from 2000MY) . . . . . Bosch ABS5.3

Brake master cylinder
Bore diameter . . . . 23.8 mm

WHEELS
Front . . . . 6 x 15 alloy
 . . . . 7 x 16 alloy
Rear . . . . 6 x 15 alloy
 . . . . 7 x 16 alloy
Spare . . . . 5.5 x 14 steel

Road wheel nut torque . . . . 70 Nm

TYRE SIZES
Front . . . . 185/55 R15 82V Goodyear NCT3
 . . . . 195/45 R16 84V Goodyear Eagle F1
 . . . . 195/45 R16 80V Yokohama A539 type
Rear . . . . 205/50 R15 86V Goodyear NCT3
 . . . . 215/40 ZR16 82W Goodyear Eagle F1
 . . . . 215/40 R16 86V Yokohama A539 type
Spare 175/65 R14 82T

TYRE PRESSURES

Pressures (cold):

Tyre Sizes	bar	lbf/in^2
185/55 R15 82V (front)	1.8	26
195/45 R16 84V (front)	1.7	24
195/45 R16 80V (front)	1.7	24
205/50 R15 86V (rear)	1.9	28
215/40 ZR16 82W (front)	1.7	24
215/40 ZR16 82W (rear)	2.5	36
215/40 R16 86V (rear)	2.5	36
175/65 R14 82T (spare) See Warning	2.1	30

⚠ **WARNING: The steel spare wheel supplied with cars fitted with alloy wheels is for temporary use only and must be changed as soon as possible after fitting. The car MUST be driven with caution and speed MUST NOT exceed 50 mph (80 km/h) with the spare wheel fitted. No more than one temporary spare wheel may be fitted at any one time. Replacement tyres fitted to the temporary use spare wheel must be of the same make and specification as those originally fitted.**

ELECTRICAL

System .... 12volt, negative earth

Battery | **Manual Steer** | **Power Steer**
Type - Maintenance free .... YGD 10003 | YGD 10012
Cold crank .... 405 amps | 480 amps
Reserve capacity .... 70 amps | 90 amps

Alternator
Type .... Magnetti Marelli 11 5i 85
Maximum output .... 85 amp

Starter motor | **MPi MEMS 1.9** | **VVC / MPI MEMS 3**
Type .... E80E | M79
Power .... 1.0 kW | 1.4 kW

DIMENSIONS

Overall length	3.913 m	12 ft 10 in
Overall width (includes mirrors)	1.628 m	5 ft 4 in
Overall height		
Cabriolet	1.268 m	4 ft 2 in
Hard Top	1.273 m	4 ft 2 in
Ground clearance	120 mm	4^1/$_2$ in
Trophy	100 mm	3^3/$_4$ in
Wheelbase	2.376 m	7 ft 9^1/$_4$ in
Turning circle, kerb to kerb	10.54 m	34 ft 7 in
Track		
Front	1.394 m	4 ft 6^1/$_2$ in
Rear	1.394 m	4 ft 6^1/$_2$ in

WEIGHTS

1.6 MPi and 1.8 MPi
Cabriolet .... 1075 kg | 2370 lb
Hard Top .... 1095 kg | 2414 lb

1.8 VVC and Trophy
Cabriolet .... 1090 kg | 2403 lb
Hard Top .... 1110 kg | 2447 lb

1.8 MPi Steptronic (EM-CVT)
Cabriolet .... 1100 kg | 2425 lb
Hard Top .... 1120 kg | 2469 lb

Maximum gross weight .... 1320 kg | 2910 lb
Maximum rear axle load (Steptronic EM-CVT) ...... 755 kg | 1664 lb

---

BULBS

Bulb location	Bulb specification	Bulb part number
Headlamp dip beam	12V 55W	GLB 448
Head lamp main beam	12V 55W	GLB 448
Side light	12V 5W	GLB 501
Front direction indicator	12V 21W	GLB 382
Rear direction indicator	12V 21W	GLB 344
Licence plate	12V 5W	GLB 239
Brake light	12V 21W	GLB 382
Fog light	12V 21W	GLB 382
Reverse light	12V 21W	GLB 382
Tail light	12V 5W	GLB 380
Footwell	12V 5W	GLB 239
Glovebox	12V 5W	GLB 239
Front load space	12V 10W	GLB 245
Rear load space	12V 10W	GLB 245
Repeater lamp	12V 5W	GLB 501

ENGINE TUNING DATA

Model: 1.8 MPi MEMS 1.9

Year: 1995 to 2000MY

Engine

Type/capacity:	1.8 K16 / 1796 cm^3
Firing order	1-3-4-2
Compression ratio	10.5 : 1 ± 0.5
Exhaust gas CO content at idle	0.5 % - maximum
Ignition timing at idle *	
vacuum connected	10° BTDC

Igniton Coil

Type	NEC 100630
Primary resistance at 20°C	0.63 to 0.77 Ω
Current consumption at idle	Variable - 5.5 peak

Spark Plugs

Type	Double platinum
	Champion RC8 PYP
	Unipart GSP 9652
Gap	0.9 ± 0.1 mm

Engine Management System

Type	MEMS 1.9
Fuel injection	Indirect multi-port fuel injection
MEMS ECM	Rover/ Motorola
to - VIN 009461	MKC 103730
from - VIN 009462	MKC 104110
Fuel injectors	MJY 100430
Fuel pump	WFX 100670
Fuel pressure regulator	MKW 10016
fuel pressure	3.0 ± 0.2 bar constant
Throttle position sensor	MHB 101440
TP sensor voltages:	
throttle open	4.1 to 4.4 volts
throttle closed	0.6 to 0.9 volts
Intake air temperature sensor	NNK 10001
Engine coolant temperature sensor	MEK 100060
Oxygen sensor	MHK 10006
Distributor cap	NJD 10010
Rotor arm	NJE 10003
direction of rotation	Anti-clockwise
Crankshaft position sensor	NSC 100390
Ambient air temperature sensor	MHK 100520
Fuel grade	95 RON minimum - UNLEADED fuel

⚠ **CAUTION: Serious damage to the engine may occur if a lower octane number fuel than recommended is used. Serious damage to the catalyst will occur if LEADED fuel is used.**

This page is intentionally left blank

INFORMATION

Model: 1.8 VVC MEMS 2J — Year: 1995 to 2001 MY

Engine

Type/Capacity	1.8 K16 / 1796 cm³
Firing order	1-3-4-2
Compression ratio	10.5 : 1 ± 0.5
Exhaust gas CO content at idle *	0.5 % - maximum
Ignition timing at idle * vacuum connected	10° BTDC

Ignition Coil

Type	H type twin coil
Part number	NEC 100690
Primary resistance at 20° C	0.4 to 0.61 Ω

Spark Plugs

Type	Double platinum Champion RC8 PYP Unipart GSP 9652
Gap	0.9 ± 0.1 mm

Engine Management System

Type	MEMS 2J
Fuel injection	Indirect multi-port fuel injection
MEMS ECM	Rover/Motorola
to VIN 010517	MKC 103720
from VIN 010518	MKC 104000
Injectors	MJY 100430
	WFX 100670
Fuel pump	MKW 10016
Fuel pressure regulator	
fuel pressure	3.0 ± 0.2 bar constant
Throttle position sensor	MJC 10020
Intake air temperature sensor	NNK 10001
Engine coolant temperature sensor	MEK 100060
Crankshaft position sensor	NSC 100390
Camshaft position sensor	NSC 100380
Oxygen sensor	MHK 10006
Manifold absolute pressure sensor	MHK 100490
Oil temperature sensor (HCU)	MEK 100060
Ambient air temperature sensor	MHK 100520
Fuel grade	95 RON minimum - **UNLEADED** fuel

⚠ **CAUTION: Serious damage to the engine may occur if a lower octane number fuel than recommended is used. Serious damage to the catalyst will occur if LEADED fuel is used.**

* = Ignition timing in crankshaft degrees.

INFORMATION

Model: 1.6 MPi, 1.8 MPi and VVC MEMS 3 — Year: 1.8 MPi 2000MY on / VVC 2001MY on

Engine

Type/Capacity	
1.6 MPi	1.6 K16 / 1588 cm³
1.8 MPi	1.8 K16 / 1796 cm³
Firing order	1-3-4-2
Compression ratio	10.5 : 1 ± 0.5
Exhaust gas CO content at idle	0.5 % - maximum
Ignition timing at idle * vacuum connected	12° BTDC

Ignition Coil

Type	Nippon Denso
Part number	NEC 100730
Trophy	NEC 100870
Primary resistance	0.7 Ω
Secondary resistance	10 kΩ

Spark Plugs

Type	Unipart GSP 66527
Gap	1.0 ± 0.05 mm

Engine Management System

Type	MEMS 3
Fuel injection	Indirect multi-port fuel injection
MEMS ECM	Rover/Motorola NNN 100901
Entry	Rover/Motorola NNN 000060
Trophy	Rover/Motorola NNN 000100
Injectors	MJY 100550
	WFX 100670
Fuel pump	MKW 10016
Fuel pressure regulator	
fuel pressure	3.0 ± 0.2 bar
Throttle position sensor	MJC 100020
Sensor Values:	
Total track resistance	4 kΩ ± 20%
Sensor supply	5 Volts ± 4%
Intake air temperature sensor	NNK 10001
Engine coolant temperature sensor	MEK 100170
Crankshaft position sensor	NSC 100630
Entry and Trophy	NSC 100760
Camshaft position sensor	NSC 100610+0
Trophy	NSC 000010
Oxygen sensor	MHK 100720
Entry and Trophy	MHK 100840
Manifold absolute pressure sensor	MHK 100820
Oil temperature sensor	
MPi MEMS3	MEK 100170
VVC MEMS3 (HCU)	MEK 100160
Ambient air (engine bay) temperature sensor	MHK 100520
Fuel grade	95 RON minimum - **UNLEADED** fuel

⚠ **CAUTION: Serious damage to the engine may occur if a lower octane number fuel than recommended is used. Serious damage to the catalyst will occur if LEADED fuel is used.**

* = Ignition timing in crankshaft degrees.

Refer to appropriate section heading for component torque figures, e.g.

Road wheel nuts - refer to **SUSPENSION**

Exhaust front pipe to manifold - refer to **MANIFOLD AND EXHAUST**

ENGINE

Camshaft cover, bolts	9 Nm *
Camshaft Cover Plate (except MPi MEMS3 2000MY on and VVC MEMS3 2001MY on)	5 Nm
Camshaft Cover Plate (MPi MEMS3 2000MY on and VVC MEMS3 2001MY on)	10 Nm
Camshaft gear bolt	
8 mm bolts	33 Nm
10 mm bolts	65 Nm
Crankshaft pulley bolt	205 Nm
Cylinder head bolts, tighten progressively	
1st stage	20 Nm *
2nd stage	180°*
3rd stage	180°*
Dipstick/filler tube mounting bracket	10 Nm
Engine harness to oil pump bolt	10 Nm
Flywheel to crankshaft bolts	85 Nm *
Flywheel cover plate	9 Nm
Lifting bracket	9 Nm
Oil pressure relief valve sealing plug	25 Nm
Oil pressure switch	12 Nm
Oil pump to cylinder block bolts	10 Nm +
Sump bolts	25 Nm *
Sump to gearbox, bolts	45 Nm
Sump drain plug	25 Nm
Tensioner pulley backplate bolt - Manual	10 Nm
Tensioner pulley Allen screw - Manual	
timing belt tensioner	45 Nm
Timing belt tensioner bolt - Automatic	
Timing belt tensioner	25 Nm +
Timing belt, front top cover	9 Nm
Timing belt, front lower cover	9 Nm
Timing belt, rear cover to coolant pump	10 Nm
Timing belt rear cover upper bolts	9 Nm
Torsion damper to flywheel	22 Nm *

This page is intentionally left blank

Engine Mountings

Bridge bracket assembly to upper tie bar	88 Nm
Bridge bracket to RH mounting bracket	155 Nm
Buttress LH to subframe	45 Nm
Engine LH mounting to bracket bolts	45 Nm
Engine LH mounting bracket to gearbox bolts (manual gearbox models)	45 Nm
Engine LH mounting centre bolt (manual gearbox models)	82 Nm
Gearbox mounting to RH buttress nut and bolt (EM-CVT only)	82 Nm
LH mounting to engine	45 Nm
LH mounting to gearbox screws (EM-CVT only)	48 Nm
LH mounting to LH upper longitudinal	80 Nm
Lower RH mounting bracket to engine	60 Nm
Lower tie bar to rear subframe	100 Nm
Lower tie bar to sump bracket	100 Nm
Rear engine steady to bracket on sump	85 Nm
Rear engine steady to subframe	85 Nm
Rear mount to subframe bolts	80 Nm
Rear mount to sump	45 Nm
RH buttress to subframe	82 Nm
RH mounting to buttress	45 Nm
RH mounting to RH upper longitudinal	60 Nm
Upper RH mounting bracket to engine	88 Nm
Upper tie bar to RH upper longitudinal	88 Nm

* Tighten in sequence
+ New Patchlok bolt must be fitted.

MODULAR ENGINE MANAGEMENT SYSTEM - MEMS

Air cleaner mounting bracket	10 Nm
Camshaft position sensor - VVC and MEMS 3	6 Nm
Crankshaft position sensor	6 Nm
Distributor cap screws	2 Nm
ECM bracket bolts	8 Nm
Engine coolant temperature sensor	6 Nm
Fuel filter to bracket	10 Nm
Fuel filter, inlet and outlet union	30 Nm
Fuel pipe bracket to body	10 Nm
Fuel pump cover bolts	
Up to 2001MY	17 Nm
2001MY on	10 Nm
Fuel pump locking ring	
Up to 2001MY	45 Nm
2001MY on	35 Nm
Fuel rail to inlet manifold	10 Nm
Fuel rail to fuel feed pipe	8 Nm
HO$_2$ Sensor MEMS 1.9 and 2J	55 Nm
HO$_2$ Sensors MEMS 3 (pre and post catalyst)	55 Nm
ht lead cover screws (MPi MEMS 1.9 & VVC 2J)	2 Nm
Hydraulic Control Unit Solenoid nuts (VVC)	12 Nm
Idle air control valve	1.5 Nm
Ignition coil bracket to engine	25 Nm
Ignition coil bolt - MPi MEMS 1.9	9 Nm
Ignition coil bolt - VVC MEMS 2J	25 Nm
Ignition coil bolts - MPi and VVC MEMS 3	8 Nm
Ignition coil and ht lead cover bolts - MEMS 3	8 Nm
Intake air temperature sensor	7 Nm
Manifold absolute pressure sensor	
VVC (up to 2000MY) and MEMS 3	9 Nm
VVC (2001MY on)	3 Nm
Oil temperature sensor - VVC	15 Nm
Resonator to body	8 Nm
Rotor arm to camshaft	10 Nm
Spark plugs	
MPi MEMS 1.9	25 Nm
VVC MEMS3	25 Nm
MPi MEMS3	27 Nm
VVC MEMS3	27 Nm
Throttle body	7 Nm
Throttle position sensor screws	1.5 Nm

Catalytic Converter

Catalyst overheat sensor	30 Nm
Catalytic converter to front pipe	50 Nm
Catalytic converter to silencer	50 Nm

Fuel Tank

Bulkhead closing panel	9 Nm
Filler hose to tank	3 Nm
Filler neck to wing	3 Nm
Fuel pump cover to body	17 Nm
Fuel pump lock ring	45 Nm
Fuel tank retaining strap	10 Nm

Throttle Cable

Throttle pedal to bulkhead fixing	6 Nm
Throttle pedal bracket to pedal box	22 Nm

COOLING

Coolant pump to cylinder block	10 Nm
Coolant pump to timing belt rear cover	10 Nm
Coolant rail to cylinder block	9 Nm
Engine bay cooling fan to body	9 Nm
Expansion tank to mounting bracket	5 Nm
Radiator to fan motor	3 Nm
Thermostat housing cover	9 Nm
Thermostat housing to cylinder block	9 Nm

Bleed points

Radiator bleed screw	5 Nm
Heater bleed screw	7 Nm
Radiator return line, bleed screw	9 Nm

MANIFOLD AND EXHAUST

Alternator heat shield	9 Nm
Catalyst to silencer	50 Nm
Coolant hose heat shield	9 Nm
Exhaust manifold heat shield	
top bolt	25 Nm
bottom bolt	10 Nm
Exhaust manifold to cylinder head	45 Nm *
Exhaust manifold to front pipe flange nuts	50 Nm
Exhaust mountings to body	25 Nm
Inlet manifold to cylinder head nuts and bolts	
MPi	17 Nm *
VVC	25 Nm *
Inlet manifold support bracket - VVC	25 Nm
Inlet manifold to manifold chamber - VVC	25 Nm
Silencer clamp, nut	30 Nm
Silencer clamp to flange studs	50 Nm
Silencer RH mounting bracket	15 Nm
Silencer heat shield	10 Nm
Stepper motor to inlet manifold	1.5 Nm
Throttle housing to manifold chamber - VVC	9 Nm

* Tighten in sequence

CLUTCH

Clutch damper to bracket (VVC only)	15 Nm
Master cylinder to pedal box	25 Nm
Master cylinder pipe union	18 Nm
Pressure plate to flywheel	25 Nm *
Slave cylinder to mounting bracket	25 Nm
Slave cylinder pipe union	18 Nm
Slave cylinder bleed screw	7 Nm

* Tighten in sequence

MANUAL GEARBOX

Drain plug	45 Nm
Filler plug	35 Nm
Flywheel closing panel	80 Nm
Gear lever assembly to body	9 Nm
Gearbox to engine	80 Nm
Gearbox to sump	45 Nm
Selector cable abutment bracket to gearbox lower bracket	45 Nm
Speedometer cable to gearbox (up to 2000MY)	10 Nm
Road speed transducer (from 2000MY)	12 Nm

STEPTRONIC (EM-CVT) GEARBOX

Connecting rod to selector lever nut	6 Nm
Differential speed sensor	9 Nm
Dipstick tube retaining bolt	25 Nm
Drain plug	30 Nm
Fluid cooler pipe clamp bolt	10 Nm
Fluid cooler pipe to cooler bolt	10 Nm
Fluid cooler unions	14 Nm
Fluid pan bolts	10 Nm *
Fluid pump bolts	10 Nm *
Flywheel closing panel bolts	9 Nm
Gear selector lever assembly to body	10 Nm
Gear shaft speed sensor retaining bolt	9 Nm
Gearbox to engine	80 Nm
Gearbox mounting to gearbox	48 Nm
Hydraulic control unit mounting bolts	10 Nm
Lever to support bracket bolts	10 Nm
Park/Neutral switch	12 Nm
Park solenoid bolts	15 Nm
Pitot chamber bolts	10 Nm
Primary bearing nut	180 Nm
Primary cover bolts	10 Nm
Ratio control motor harness connector nut	9 Nm
Road speed transducer retaining bolt	12 Nm
Secondary cover bolts	10 Nm
Selector cable bracket to gearbox	25 Nm
Selector quadrant detent lever bolt	10 Nm
Selector valve bolts	10 Nm
Sequential gear change microswitch bolts	12 Nm
Shift lock solenoid	15 Nm
Speed Sensor	9 Nm
Starter/Inhibitor/Reverse switch	12 Nm
Valve body bolts	10 Nm +

* Tighten in sequence
+ Fit new bolts/nuts

DRIVE SHAFTS

Drive shaft nut	210 Nm, stake nut

STEERING

EPAS ECU to bracket	10 Nm
EPAS ECU bracket to fascia rail	25 Nm
Ignition lock to steering column	Shear bolts
Pinion cover	8 Nm
Steering rack clamp	22 Nm
Steering rack 'U' bolt	22 Nm
Steering rack to intermediate shaft	22 Nm
Steering column to intermediate shaft	22 Nm
Steering column mounting bracketts	22 Nm
Steering wheel to column	
Up to 2001 My	50 Nm
2001MY on	63 Nm
Track-rod end to steering arm	30 Nm
Track-rod end lock nut	50 Nm
Universal joint to steering rack pinion	20 Nm

INFORMATION

SUSPENSION

Front Suspension

Anti-roll bar clamp bracket	22 Nm
Anti-roll bar link	35 Nm **
Damper upper mounting	37 Nm
Damper lower mounting	45 Nm **
Hub nut	210 Nm
Hydragas unit retaining plate	25 Nm
Hydragas pipe, unions	20 Nm
Lower arm to subframe	85 Nm **
Lower ball joint nut	45 Nm
Lower ball joint to lower arm	40 Nm
Upper arm pivot shaft retaining plate	10 Nm
Upper arm pivot shaft	74 Nm
Upper ball joint nut	54 Nm
Upper ball joint to hub	105 Nm

Rear Suspension

Anti-roll bar bracket to hub	45 Nm
Anti-roll bar to mounting bracket	13 Nm **
Anti-roll bar to link	35 Nm **
Damper upper mounting	50 Nm
Damper lower mounting to upper arms	45 Nm **
Hydragas unit retaining plate	25 Nm
Hydragas pipe, unions	20 Nm
Lower arm to hub	100 Nm **
Lower arm to subframe	85 Nm **
Track control arm adjuster	50 Nm
Track control arm to hub	30 Nm
Track control arm to subframe	80 Nm
Tie bar to subframe	45 Nm **
Tie bar to lower arm	80 Nm **
Upper arm pivot shaft retaining plate	10 Nm
Upper arm pivot shaft	74 Nm
Upper ball joint nut	54 Nm
Upper ball joint to hub	105 Nm

** = Tighten with suspension at nominal trim height

Front Subframe

Clamp plate to subframe	26 Nm
Crush member to subframe	45 Nm
Front mounting to body	30 Nm
Front mounting to subframe	100 Nm
Rear mounting to body	45 Nm
Rear mounting to subframe	100 Nm

Rear Subframe

Clamp plate to subframe	26 Nm
Front mounting to body	30 Nm
Front mounting to subframe	100 Nm
Rear mounting to body	45 Nm
Rear mounting to subframe	100 Nm
LH & RH upper longitudinal bolts	45 Nm

Wheel Nuts

Alloy wheel, nuts	70 Nm *
Spare wheel, nuts	70 Nm *

* = Tighten in sequence

BRAKES

ABS ECU to modulator	8 Nm
ABS ECU to mounting spigot	15 Nm
ABS hydraulic modulator to bracket	10 Nm
ABS sensor bolts	10 Nm
Master cylinder to servo	20 Nm
Master cylinder to pipe union	14 Nm
Pedal box mounting bracket to top plate nuts and bolts	22 Nm
Pedal box mounting bracket to bulkhead bolts	22 Nm
Pedal crosstube bracket to bulkhead nut	22 Nm
Pedal pivot shaft to pedal box end bracket nut	22 Nm
Proportioning valve to body	10 Nm
Proportioning valve to pipe union	14 Nm
Servo to bracket	20 Nm
Servo bracket to body	20 Nm
Servo bracket to body bracket	30 Nm

Front Brakes

ABS speed sensor to hub	10 Nm
Bleed nipple	10 Nm
Brake pipe unions	14 Nm
Caliper body to carrier guide pin	45 Nm
Caliper carrier to hub	85 Nm
Disc to drive flange	7 Nm
Hose to caliper	35 Nm
Hose to upper arm bracket	45 Nm

Rear Brakes

ABS speed sensor to hub	10 Nm
Bleed nipple	10 Nm
Brake pipe unions	14 Nm
Caliper to hub	85 Nm
Caliper body to carrier guide pin	45 Nm
Disc to drive flange	7 Nm
Hose to caliper	35 Nm
Hose to upper arm bracket	45 Nm

Handbrake

Handbrake lever bracket to body	25 Nm
Handbrake assembly to bracket	25 Nm
Handbrake abutment bracket to mounting bracket	25 Nm
Handbrake cable to luggage bay bulk head	10 Nm

SUPPLEMENTARY RESTRAINT SYSTEM

SRS DCU bracket to body	10 Nm
SRS DCU to bracket	10 Nm

Airbags

Passenger airbag to fascia bracket	8 Nm
Drivers airbag to steering wheel	8 Nm
Passenger airbag module bracket to fascia	9 Nm

Seat Belts

Seat belt assembly to body	35 Nm
Seat belt assembly to seat	30 Nm
Seat belt pre-tensioner to seat	45 Nm

BODY

'A' post trim	6 Nm
Crossmember to floorpan	22 Nm
Header trim	6 Nm
Headlamp to body	6 Nm
Underbelly panel	22 Nm

Bonnet

Bonnet locking platform	10 Nm
Bonnet to hinges	9 Nm
Bonnet lock plate to body	25 Nm
Bonnet release lever to bulkhead	9 Nm

Boot

Boot lid to hinges	9 Nm
Boot lid striker to body	10 Nm
Boot latch to boot lid	10 Nm

Bumpers

Crash can to body	25 Nm
Front bumper armature to body	25 Nm
Front bumper valance to bumper armature	25 Nm
Front bumper to crash can	25 Nm
Rear bumper armature to body	22 Nm
Rear bumper valance to armature	25 Nm

Doors

Door finishers	10 Nm
Door glass regulator to door	7 Nm
Door handle to door	2.5 Nm
Door striker screws	18 Nm
Latch assembly to door	5 Nm

Hood

Soft Top

Hood frame hinge to body	45 Nm
Hood catch to header rail	20 Nm
Hood header strikers	6 Nm

Hard Top

Front top catch to hard top	10 Nm

Seats

Seat runners	45 Nm
Squab frame to cushion frame	45 Nm

HEATING AND VENTILATION

Fascia rail support bracket	10 Nm
Heater mountings	10 Nm
Intake duct to body	10 Nm

AIR CONDITIONING

Compressor

Compressor to mounting bracket	45 Nm
Compressor to pipe union	25 Nm

Condenser

Mounting bracket to striker plate panel	17 Nm
Air conditioning pipe to condenser	5 Nm

Evaporator

Evaporator to heater - clamp	3 Nm
Evaporator to lower dash panel	9 Nm

Receiver Drier

Air conditioning pipe to receiver drier	5 Nm

Thermostatic Expansion Valve

Evaporator pipe clamp to expansion valve	5 Nm
Evaporator pipe, bracket	7 Nm

Trinary switch	10 Nm

WIPERS AND WASHERS

Wiper arm to spindle	20 Nm
Motor and linkage assembly to scuttle	10 Nm
Motor to linkage bracket	12 Nm
Crank to motor spindle	18 Nm

ELECTRICAL

Aerial locking nut	3 Nm
Alarm ECU	4 Nm
Alternator to pulley	25 Nm
Alternator to engine mounting clamp bolts	45 Nm
Alternator adjustment tensioner bracket bolts	25 Nm
Alternator tensioner pulley nut (A/C models only)	25 Nm
Central locking motor to door	5 Nm
Fusebox to body	10 Nm
EPAS ECU to mounting	10 Nm
Headlamp lower retaining bolts	6 Nm
Headlamp upper retaining bolts	6 Nm
Horn to valance	8 Nm
Starter motor securing bolts	80 Nm
Tail Lamp to body	2 Nm

INSTRUMENTS

Speedometer cable to gearbox union	19 Nm

JACKING, SUPPORTING AND TOWING

1M0064

1. Central jacking point - front
2. Central jacking point - rear
3. RH sill reinforced bracket - front
4. LH sill reinforced bracket - front
5. LH sill reinforced bracket - rear
6. RH sill reinforced bracket - rear
7. Subframe longitudinal members - front
8. Subframe longitudinal members - rear
9. Front towing eyes

⚠ **WARNING:** In accordance with normal workshop practice, and to avoid the possibility of damage or personal injury, work must not be carried out, on or under a vehicle when it is supported solely on a jack. Place safety supports under the sill reinforced jacking areas (3, 4, 5 or 6).

⚠ **WARNING:** Do not position a jack, jack stand or wheel free support under the suspension attachment points.

⚠ **WARNING:** Do not attempt to jack under suspension attachment points.

This page is intentionally left blank

INFORMATION

⚠ CAUTION: When lifting the side of the vehicle with a workshop jack, ensure that the jack head is positioned under the reinforced area of the sill, as shown.

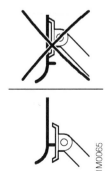

1M0065

WORKSHOP JACK

Front: Locate the jack head under the central location bracket(1).
Position safety supports under both front sill reinforced brackets (3 and 4).

Rear: Locate the jack head under the central location bracket (2).
Position safety supports under both rear sill reinforced brackets (5 and 6).

Side Front: Locate the jack head under the sill reinforced bracket (3 or 4) and position safety support under front subframe longitudinal member (7).

Side rear: Locate the jack head under the sill reinforced bracket (5 or 6) and position safety support under rear subframe longitudinal member (8).

WHEEL-FREE LIFT

If crossbeams are available, locate the pads under the sill reinforced jacking brackets (3, 4) and (5, 6).

If longitudinal beams are available, locate the beams under the subframe longitudinals with lifting pads at the front and rear positions (7 and 8). Raise the lift a few inches and ensure the vehicle is firmly supported. Raise the lift to full height and inspect the lifting points for security.

RECOVERY

Manual gearbox models

It is recommended that a recovery trailer or two wheel car ambulance be used. In an emergency, the car may be towed on its own wheels using the front lashing/towing eyes (9).

Automatic (EM-CVT) gearbox models

It is recommended that a recovery trailer or a two wheel car ambulance is used on the rear wheels. In an emergency, the car may be towed a short distance on its own wheels using the front lashing/towing eyes (9).

Suspended tow

⚠ CAUTION: A front suspended tow must not be attempted on a vehicle with an automatic gearbox. Serious damage to the transmission will occur.

A suspended tow cannot be carried out without incurring damage. If additional damage is immaterial because of existing crash damage, lifting chains can be attached to the towing eyes.

Before towing commences release the handbrake, place the gear lever in neutral and the ignition switch at 'I'. Do not tow at a greater speed than 30 mph, 50 km/h.

On no account should the vehicle be towed with the rear wheels on the ground if the transmission is faulty, the transmission fluid level is low, or the towing distance exceeds 30 miles or 50 km.

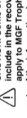 WARNING: Trophy models have a lower ground clearance than most other cars, vehicle recovery should ONLY be carried out by a qualified recovery specialist using a transporter or trailer. Other methods of vehicle recovery, including the use of wheel lift equipment to suspend the front or rear wheels, and towing with rope, bar or chain , will cause damage to the front of the vehicle and are not recommended.

INFORMATION

Transporter or trailer lashing

Use the front towing eyes, and specific lashing points for rear of car. DO NOT secure lashing hooks or trailer fixings to other parts of the car.

⚠ CAUTION: Some of the information include in the recovery section DOES NOT apply to MGF Trophy models. Please take note of the information below.

Because the Trophy model has a lower ground clearance than most other cars, vehicle recovery should ONLY be carried out by a qualified recovery specialist using a transporter or trailer.

Other methods of vehicle recovery, including the use of wheel lift equipment to suspend the front or rear wheels, and towing with rope, bar or chain, will cause damage to the front of the vehicle and are NOT recommended.

TOWING

General

Use the front lashing/towing eyes (9) for towing the vehicle on all four wheels from the front.

 WARNING: To ensure that the steering does not lock when the vehicle is being towed, it is essential that the ignition key is turned to position 'I', and remains there while the vehicle is moving.
Ensure the following precautions are observed:
Do not tow if the gearbox or a drive shaft is faulty.
Do not tow if a wheel or drive shafts are touching the body or frame.
Ensure the gear lever is in neutral and the handbrake is released.
Remember that greater effort than normal will be necessary to apply the brakes if the vehicle is being towed without the engine running.

Automatic (EM-CVT) gearbox models

When a car with automatic gearbox is to be towed on four wheels from the front, the following precautions must be observed:

The gearbox fluid level must be correct before starting to tow.

The selector must be at 'N'.

The car must not be towed at speeds greater than 30 mph, 50 km/h or for distances which exceed 30 miles, 50 km.

⚠ CAUTION: A front suspended tow must not be attempted as serious damage will be caused to the automatic transmission.

△ NOTE: A vehicle fitted with an automatic gearbox cannot be started by towing or pushing.

CAPACITIES

Fuel tank	50 litres
Engine oil refill and filter change:	4.5 litres
Engine oil refill from dry:	5 litres
Manual gearbox:	
Refill	2.2 litres
From dry	2.4 litres
Steptronic (EM-CVT) Gearbox:	
Refill - Gearbox only	4.5 litres
Fluid cooler and lines	1.0 litre
Cooling system from dry:	10.5 litres
Washer reservoir:	2.3 litres

FLUIDS

Brake Fluid

Use only AP New Premium Super DOT 4 brake fluid or Castrol Universal DOT 4 brake/clutch fluid. DO NOT use any other type of fluid.

Anti-Freeze Solutions

The overall anti-freeze concentration should not fall, by volume, below 50% to ensure that the anti-corrosion properties of the coolant are maintained. Anti-freeze concentrations greater than 60% are not recommended as cooling efficiency will be impaired.

Conventional ethylene glycol anti-freeze

Vehicles using conventional anti-freeze are identified by not having a label attached around the expansion tank filler neck or a black filler ring label.

Early vehicles up to **VIN No: RD512771** use **UNIPART Superplus 3 Anti-freeze and Summer Coolant** to protect the cooling system. The coolant is **yellow/green** in colour.

 CAUTION: No other 'universal' or Organic Acid Technology (OAT) anti-freeze should be used with UNIPART Superplus 3 Anti-freeze and Summer Coolant.

If **UNIPART Superplus 3 Anti-freeze and Summer Coolant** is not available, use an ethylene glycol based anti-freeze containing no methanol with non-phosphate corrosion inhibitors which meet specifications BS6580 and BS5117 suitable for use in mixed metal engines. To ensure the protection of the cooling system against corrosion, these anti-freezes must be renewed every 12 months.

Vehicles from **VIN No: RD512772 to Vin No: RD520012** use **UNIPART AFC Longlife Anti-freeze and Summer Coolant** to protect the cooling system. The coolant is **blue** in colour.

CAUTION: No other 'universal' or Organic Acid Technology (OAT) anti-freeze should be used with UNIPART AFC Longlife Anti-freeze and Summer Coolant.

If **UNIPART AFC Longlife Anti-freeze and Summer Coolant** is not available, use an ethylene glycol based anti-freeze containing no methanol with non-phosphate corrosion inhibitors which meet specifications BS6580 and BS5117 suitable for use in mixed metal engines. To ensure the protection of the cooling system against corrosion, these anti-freezes must be renewed every 12 months.

This page is intentionally left blank

Organic Acid Technology (OAT) anti-freeze

Vehicles from Vin No: RD520013 use Unipart OAT (XLC) coolant which is **Orange/Pink** in colour. Vehicles using OAT anti-freeze are identified by a label attached around the expansion tank filler neck - see illustration.

CAUTION: The anti-freeze used in the cooling systems of later cars contains OAT corrosion inhibitors. This anti-freeze must not be used with any other anti-freeze and must not be used as a replacement in cooling systems which previously contained anti-freeze not of this type.

M26 0680

Use UNIPART OAT Anti-freeze and Summer Coolant or any ethylene glycol based anti-freeze (containing no methanol) with only OAT corrosion inhibitors, to protect the cooling system.

Only anti-freeze containing OAT corrosion inhibitors should be used. Do not top-up or refill cooling system with any other type of anti-freeze.

In an emergency, if anti-freeze to this specification is not available, top-up the cooling system with clean water only, but be aware of the resultant reduction in frost protection. The correct anti-freeze concentration must be restored as soon as possible.

Upgrading coolant

For future servicing convenience, it may be desirable to update the specified coolant in an earlier vehicle by replacing it with Unipart OAT (XLC). This is permissible, provided that the cooling system is first drained and flushed at low pressure as described in the Workshop Manual - Repair No: 26.10.01.

When Unipart OAT (XLC) coolant has been added to such a vehicle, it will be necessary to replace the existing black filler neck label with the OAT warning label (part No: PAK100410A), to indicate the coolant specification has been changed.

All vehicles

The cooling system should be drained, flushed and refilled with the correct amount of anti-freeze solution at the intervals given on the Service Maintenance Check Sheet.

After filling with anti-freeze solution, attach a warning label to a prominent position on the vehicle stating the type of anti-freeze contained in the cooling system to ensure that the correct type is used for topping-up.

The recommended quantities of anti-freeze for different degrees of frost protection are:

Solution	Amount of anti-freeze Litres	Commences freezing °C	Commences freezing °F	Frozen solid °C	Frozen solid °F
50%	5.25	-36	-33	-48	-53

Manual gearbox

Use Texaco MTF 94, Unipart MTF94 or Caltex MTF94 for refill and topping-up.

Steptronic (EM-CVT) gearbox

Use (EZL799) Esso CVT or Unipart CVT for refilling or topping up.

Gear linkage

Use Unipart Multi-purpose Lithium Grease or equivalent.

General greasing

Use Unipart Multi-purpose Lithium Grease or equivalent.

Boot hinges

Lubricate with Rocol Ultralube.

Locks, latches and hinges

Use Door Lock and Latch Lubricant, Part No. CYL 100020.

LUBRICATION

The engine and other lubricating systems are filled with high performance lubricants giving prolonged life.

CAUTION: You should always use a high quality oil of the correct viscosity range in the engine and gearbox during maintenance and when topping-up. The use of oil not to the correct specification can lead to high oil and fuel consumption and ultimately to damaged components.

Oil to the correct specification contains additives which disperse the corrosive acids formed by combustion and prevent the formation of sludge which can block the oil ways. Additional oil additives should not be used.
Always adhere to the recommended servicing intervals.

Engine oil

Use oil meeting specification ACEA A2 and having a viscosity band recommended for the temperature range of your locality. Where oils to these Rover and European specifications are not available, well known brands of oils meeting API SH or SJ quality should be used.

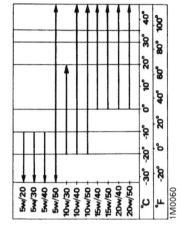

1M0060

CONTENTS

Page

MAINTENANCE

This page is intentionally left blank

CONTENTS

ENGINE COMPARTMENT LOCATIONS - MPi MEMS 1.9

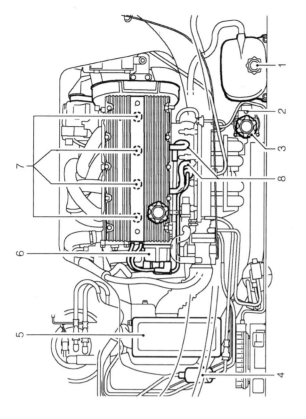

10M0389

1. Coolant expansion tank and cap
2. Engine oil dipstick
3. Engine oil filler cap
4. Fuel filter

5. Air cleaner
6. Distributor cap
7. Spark plugs
8. Crankcase ventilation hoses

ENGINE COMPARTMENT LOCATIONS - VVC
MEMS 2J

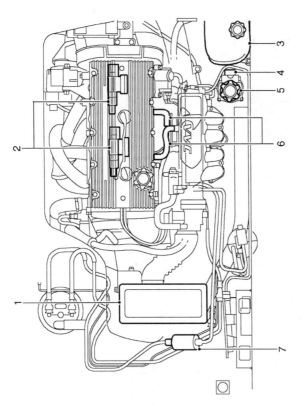

10M0483

1. Coolant expansion tank and cap
2. Engine oil dipstick
3. Engine oil filler cap
4. Fuel filter

5. Air cleaner
6. Ignition coil
7. Spark plugs
8. Crankcase ventilation hoses

ENGINE COMPARTMENT LOCATIONS - VVC
MEMS 3

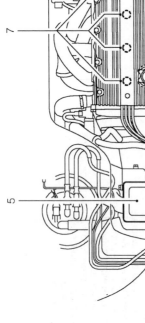
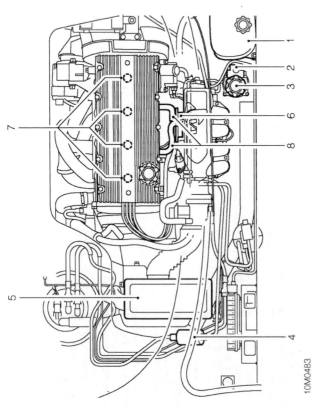

M10 0778

1. Air cleaner
2. Ignition coils
3. Coolant expansion tank and cap
4. Engine oil dipstick

5. Engine oil filler cap
6. Crankcase ventilation hoses
7. Fuel filter

ENGINE COMPARTMENT LOCATIONS - MPi
MEMS 3

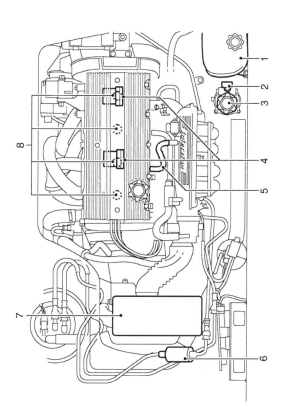

M10 0713

1. Coolant expansion tank and cap
2. Engine oil dipstick
3. Engine oil filler cap
4. Ignition coils

5. Crankcase ventilation hoses
6. Fuel filter
7. Air cleaner
8. Spark plugs

UNDERBONNET LOCATIONS

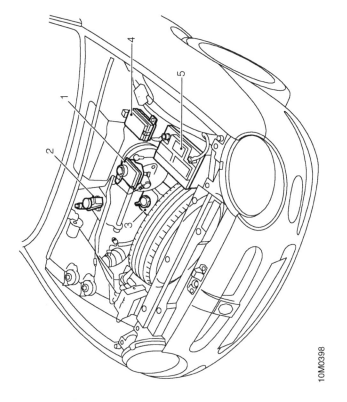

10M0398

1. Brake fluid reservoir
2. Clutch fluid reservoir
3. Windscreen washer reservoir
4. Fusebox
5. Battery

MAINTENANCE

ENGINE OIL

Oil level check

Always check oil level and drain oil with vehicle standing on level ground and use engine oil of specification 10W/40 for topping up and refilling.

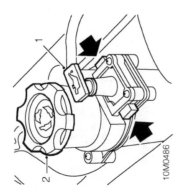

10M0486

1. Pull the dipstick out, wiping the blade clean as it is withdrawn by squeezing the dipstick wiping mechanism (arrowed) between finger and thumb. Re-insert dipstick fully and withdraw again, this time releasing the dipstick wiping mechanism. Check the oil level which must be maintained between minimum mark **'MIN'** and maximum mark **'MAX'** on dipstick.
2. If required, remove filler cap, REMOVE DIPSTICK and top-up with new engine oil to specification 10W/40. *See INFORMATION, Capacities, fluids and lubricants.*

Oil drain and refill

The oil should be drained when engine is warm. The oil filter can be renewed while oil is being drained.

⚠ WARNING: Observe due care when draining engine oil as the oil can be very hot.

Prolonged and repeated contact with used engine oil may cause serious skin disorders. Wash thoroughly after contact. keep out of reach of children.

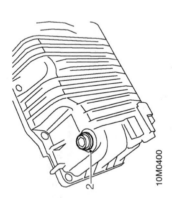

10M0400

1. Place a container under sump.
2. Remove drain plug and sealing washer, allow oil to drain.
3. Clean the drain plug, fit NEW sealing washer and refit drain plug. Tighten to 25 Nm.
4. Remove filler cap, REMOVE DIPSTICK refill with new engine oil to specification 10W/40. Re-check oil level.

CRANKCASE VENT HOSES

10M0355

1. Check crankcase ventilation hoses for signs of splitting and general condition.
2. Check hoses are routed correctly, secure and serviceable.

OIL FILTER RENEWAL

See ENGINE, Repairs.

CAMSHAFT TIMING BELT MPi & VVC

See ENGINE, Adjustments.

FUEL FILTER

See ENGINE MANAGEMENT SYSTEM - MEMS, Repairs.

AIR CLEANER ELEMENT

See ENGINE MANAGEMENT SYSTEM - MEMS, Repairs.

ENGINE TUNING

Tuning must be carried out using TestBook.

SPARK PLUGS

See ENGINE MANAGEMENT SYSTEM - MEMS, Repairs.

FUEL SYSTEM HOSES, PIPES AND UNIONS

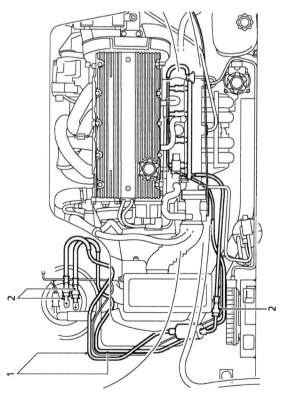

10M0418A

1. Check fuel pipes and connections for chafing and leakage.
2. Check pipes are securely clipped.
3. Check fuel tank is free from leaks.

IGNITION COILS - VVC MEMS 2J

10M0484

1. Check h.t. cables and multiplugs for security.
2. Clean each coil tower.

DISTRIBUTOR CAP, h.t. CABLES AND COIL TOWER - MPi MEMS 1.9

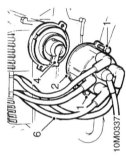

10M0337

1. Release 2 screws.
2. Lift off distributor cap.
3. Check cap for cracks, warping and burns.
4. Check rotor arm for damage.
5. Clean interior and exterior of distributor cap.
6. Check that h.t. cables are free from damage, routed correctly and all connections are tight.
7. Clean ignition coil tower.
8. Refit distributor cap.
9. Tighten distributor cap screws to 2 Nm.

IGNITION COILS - MPi / VVC MEMS 3

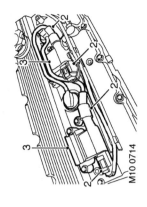

M10 0714

1. Remove coil cover.
2. Check h.t. cables and multiplugs for security.
3. Clean each coil.

DRIVE SHAFT GAITERS

10M0403

1. Check that drive shaft gaiters are not twisted, split or damaged.
2. Check clips are secure.

COOLING SYSTEM

⚠ **WARNING: To prevent injury such as scalding caused by escaping steam or coolant, do not remove pressure relief cap from expansion tank while system is hot.**

Check level and top-up

⚠ **CAUTION: The coolant level should only be checked when the system is cold.**

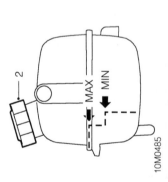

MAX

MIN

10M0485

1. Visually check that coolant level is between the two steps of the level marker inside the expansion tank. If level is appreciably low, suspect leakage or overheating.

⚠ **CAUTION: If coolant is not visible in expansion tank, the system must be refilled in accordance with Refilling procedure.**

2. If required, remove coolant expansion tank cap and top-up with anti-freeze mixture. *See INFORMATION, Capacities, fluids and lubricants.*

⚠ **CAUTION: The coolant must not exceed the expansion tank flange.**

3. Check specific gravity of coolant. The overall anti-freeze concentration must not be below 50% by volume and must not exceed 60% by volume.
4. Refit expansion tank cap.
5. For cooling system drain and refill. *See COOLING SYSTEM, Adjustments.*

GEARBOX FLUID - MANUAL MODELS

Fluid level check and top-up

10M0402

1. Ensure vehicle is standing on level surface.
2. Wipe clean area around filler/level plug and remove plug and sealing washer. Discard sealing washer.
3. Check that fluid is level with bottom of level plug hole.

⚠ **CAUTION: Fluid lodged behind level plug will trickle out when plug is removed and can give impression that level is correct.**

4. Top-up, if required, until fluid just runs from hole. Allow sufficient time for fluid to flow and reach a common level within gearbox. Use Texaco MTF 94 transmission oil. *See INFORMATION, Capacities, fluids and lubricants.*
5. Refit filler/level plug and new sealing washer and tighten to 35 Nm.

EXHAUST SYSTEM

1. Check for damage and signs of leakage.
2. Check security of system.
3. Check mountings and correct alignment.
4. Check security of heat shields.

MAINTENANCE

GEARBOX FLUID - STEPTRONIC (EM-CVT) MODELS

Fluid level check and top-up

⚠ NOTE: Always check fluid level with vehicle standing on level ground and gearbox at operating temperature.

M10 0712

1. With engine running at idle speed and handbrake applied, select 'P' or 'N'. Withdraw dipstick and wipe blade with clean cloth.
2. Re-insert dipstick fully, withdraw and check fluid level which must be maintained between minimum and maximum marks on dipstick.
3. Switch off engine and top-up to maximum mark if required. See AUTOMATIC GEARBOX - 'EM-CVT', Adjustments.
4. Refit dipstick.

CLUTCH FLUID

⚠ WARNING: Do not allow dirt or foreign liquids to enter reservoir when topping up. Use only AP New Premium Super DOT 4 or Castrol Universal DOT 4 clutch fluid from airtight containers.

⚠ CAUTION: Do not allow clutch fluid to contact paint finished surfaces as paint may be damaged. If spilled, remove fluid and clean area with warm water.

Level check

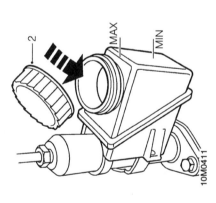

MAX
MIN

10M0411

1. Wipe reservoir body and filler cap, and check level visually.
2. Remove filler cap and top-up, until fluid reaches bottom of reservoir filler neck.
3. The baffle plate halfway up the reservoir acts as the clutch fluid minimum level.

STEERING

Steering column, rack, joints and gaiters

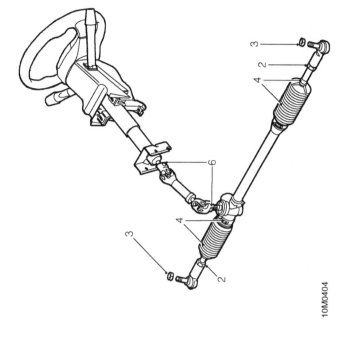

10M0404

1. Check security of steering rack, two mounting fixings, tighten nuts to 22 Nm.
2. Restrain ball joint movement and check that steering track rod, locknuts are tightened to 50 Nm.
3. Check security of 2 track rod end nuts, tighten to 30 Nm.
4. Visually check that the rack sealing gaiters are not twisted or damaged and clips are secure.
5. Check for signs of lubricant leakage.
6. Check intermediate shaft bolts are tightened to 22 Nm.

MAINTENANCE

SUSPENSION DAMPERS, BALL JOINTS, FIXINGS AND GAITERS

Front suspension

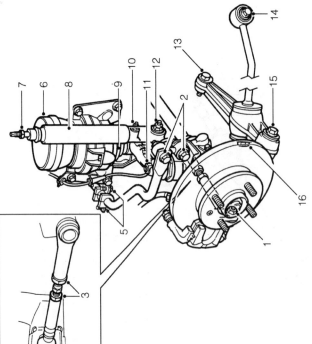

10M0390

1. Check upper ball joint nut - 54 Nm.
2. Check anti-roll bar clamp, bushes and bolts - 22 Nm.
3. Check radius shaft to subframe, fixing bolts - 10 Nm.
4. Check suspension dampers for oil leaks.
5. Check suspension damper top mounting, bushes and nuts - 37 Nm
6. Check hydragas units and pipe connections for fluid leaks.

7. Check condition of hydragas gaiters for splits and fluid leaks.
8. Check radius shaft, bushes and nuts - 74 Nm.
9. Check suspension damper, lower mounting bushes and bolts - 45 Nm.
10. Check lower arm to subframe, mounting bushes and bolts - 85 Nm.
11. Check anti-roll bar to lower arm, link bushes and bolts - 45 Nm.
12. Check lower ball joint, clamp bolt - 45 Nm.

Rear suspension

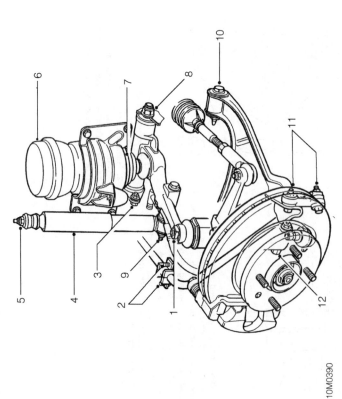

10M0391

1. Check rear link to hub nut - 30 Nm.
2. Check anti-roll bar to hub, link bushes and bolts - 35 Nm.
3. Check track control arm, adjuster nuts - 50 Nm. Ensure that the track control arm has rotational movement, this can be checked by grasping the track control arm and rotating it backwards and forwards on the ball joints.
4. Check rear link to subframe, bushes and bolts - 80 Nm.
5. Check anti-roll bar clamp, bushes and bolts - 13 Nm.
6. Check hydragas units and pipe connections for leaks.
7. Check suspension damper, top mounting bushes and nuts - 37 Nm.
8. Check suspension dampers for oil leaks.

9. Check condition of hydragas gaiters for splits and fluid leaks.
10. Check suspension upper arm, pivot shaft bushes and nuts - 74 Nm.
11. Check upper ball joint nut - 54 Nm.
12. Check suspension damper, lower mounting bushes and bolts - 45 Nm.
13. Check lower arm to subframe, bushes and bolts - 85 Nm.
14. Check tie bar to subframe, bushes and bolts - 45 Nm.
15. Check lower arm to hub, bushes and bolts - 100 Nm.
16. Check tie bar to lower arm, bushes and bolts - 80 Nm.

MAINTENANCE

ROAD WHEELS AND FASTENINGS

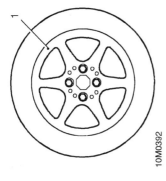

10M0392

1. Check condition of road wheels including spare for signs of buckling and rim damage.

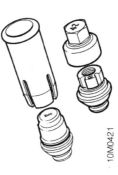

10M0421

2. Push extractor tool over head of nut cover and pull to remove.

3. Fit key socket over locking wheel nut, then fit wheel nut spanner over key socket and unscrew.

4. Working in a diagonal sequence slacken each nut ¹/₂ turn and then tighten to 70 Nm.

TYRE PRESSURES AND CONDITION

1. Check for signs of tyre wear indicator in tread pattern.

2. Check all tyres including spare for uneven wear, external cuts in fabric, exposure of ply or cord structure, lumps and bulges.

3. Check and adjust tyre pressures. *See INFORMATION, General data.*

FOOTBRAKE

10M0338

1. Press brake pedal and check for firm resistance after short pedal movement.

HANDBRAKE

Check

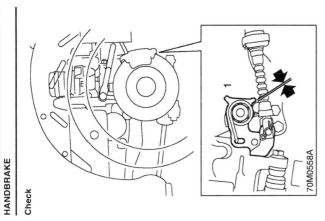

70M0558A

1. Check caliper clearance is between 1 and 2 mm, each side.

2. If the handbrake requires adjustment. *See BRAKES, Adjustments.*

MAINTENANCE

BRAKE FLUID

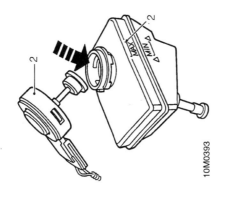

⚠ **WARNING:** Do not allow dirt or foreign liquids to enter reservoir when topping-up. Use only new AP New Premium Super DOT 4 or Castrol Universal DOT 4 brake fluid from airtight containers.

⚠ **CAUTION: Do not allow brake fluid to contact paint finished surfaces as paint may be damaged. If spilled, remove fluid and clean area with clean warm water.**

Level check

10M0393

1. Wipe reservoir body and filler cap clean and check level visually.

2. Remove filler cap and top-up to 'MAX' mark, if required.

MAINTENANCE

Renew fluid, ABS and Non-ABS brake systems.

1. Raise vehicle on four post lift.

⚠ **CAUTION: Ensure that fluid level in reservoir is maintained during the complete operational sequence using new brake fluid.**

⚠ **CAUTION: Never re-use fluid that has been bled from system.**

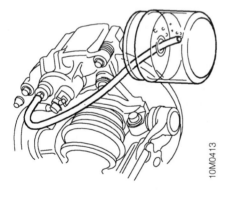

10M0414

Bleed sequence - non ABS and ABS systems
LH rear to RH rear.
RH front to LH front.

⚠ **CAUTION: Braking efficiency may be seriously impaired if wrong bleed sequence is used.**

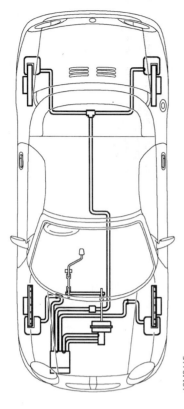

10M0413

2. Attach a bleed tube to LH rear bleed nipple. Submerge free end of tube into jar containing brake fluid.

⚠ **WARNING: Ensure vehicle is in neutral before starting engine.**

3. Start engine to build up vacuum in the brake servo, keep engine running while carrying out bleeding procedure.
4. Open bleed nipple, use an assistant to press brake pedal to the floor and hold.
5. Close bleed nipple, and then release brake pedal.
6. Repeat procedures 4 and 5 until no more air bubbles can be seen flowing from the bleed hose.
7. Hold pedal to floor and tighten bleed screw to 10 Nm.
8. Release brake pedal.
9. Repeat forgoing procedure at each wheel in sequence illustrated, until clean, bubble free fluid flows from the bleed hose at each sequence stage.
10. Remove bleed tube. Apply brakes and check for leakage.
11. Lower vehicle.
12. Check brake pedal for short firm travel when brakes are applied.

BRAKE HOSES AND PIPES

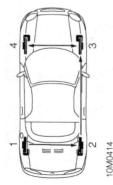

10M0415

1. Visually check all brake fluid pipes, hoses and connections for correct routing and security.
2. Check for signs of chafing, leakage and corrosion.

MAINTENANCE

Renew brake hose - front

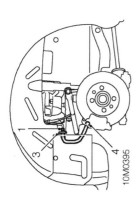

10M0394

Remove

NOTE: Disconnect hose at end nearest to master cylinder first.

1. Release brake pipe union from hose using correct union spanner.
2. Fit plug to pipe end to prevent excessive fluid loss.
3. Withdraw brake hose clip from upper bracket.
4. Remove lower damper nut and bolt to release hose bracket, collect spacer and two washers.
5. Remove banjo bolt at caliper end of hose and discard 2 sealing washers.
6. Remove hose and discard.

Refit

1. Fit banjo end of hose to caliper with banjo bolt and 2 new sealing washers and tighten to 36 Nm.
2. Fit union end of hose to top bracket and secure with clip.
3. Remove plug from pipe end, connect brake pipe to hose and tighten union to14 Nm.
4. Fit lower damper bolt.
5. Position hose bracket, damper, spacer and washers.
6. Fit nut and tighten to 45 Nm.
7. Bleed brake system. See BRAKES, Adjustments.

Renew brake hose - rear

10M0395

Remove

NOTE: Disconnect hose at end nearest to master assembly first.

1. Release brake pipe union from hose using correct union spanner.
2. Fit plug to pipe end to prevent excessive fluid loss.
3. Withdraw brake hose clip from bracket.
4. Remove banjo bolt at caliper end of hose and discard 2 sealing washers.
5. Remove hose and discard.

Refit

1. Fit banjo end of hose to caliper with banjo bolt and 2 new sealing washers and tighten to 36 Nm.
2. Fit union end of hose to rear bracket and secure with clip.
3. Remove plug from pipe end, connect brake pipe to hose and tighten union to 14 Nm.
4. Bleed brake system. See BRAKES, Adjustments.

MAINTENANCE

10M0396

Minimum brake pad thickness:
Dimension A = 3 mm.

NOTE: Measurement does not include pad backing thickness.

4. If the brake pads need to be renewed. See BRAKES, Repairs.
5. Fit road wheels and tighten nuts to 70 Nm.
6. Remove stands and lower vehicle.
7. Depress footbrake several times in order to give correct pad to disc clearance before road testing.

FRONT DISC BRAKES

Check

1. Raise front of vehicle.

WARNING: Support on safety stands.

2. Remove both front road wheels.

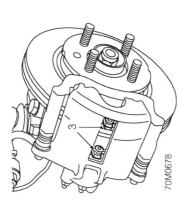

70M0678

3. Check brake pads visually and assess lining thickness.

REAR DISC BRAKES

Check

1. Raise rear of vehicle.

⚠️ **WARNING: Support on safety stands.**

2. Remove both rear road wheels.

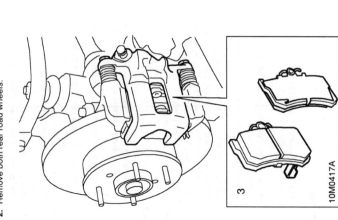

10M0417A

3. Check brake pads visually and assess pad thickness.

10M0397

Minimum brake pad thickness:
Dimension A = 3 mm.

⚠️ NOTE: Measurement does not include pad backing thickness.

4. If the brake pads need to be renewed. *See BRAKES, Repairs.*
5. Fit road wheels and tighten nuts to 70 Nm.
6. Remove stands and lower vehicle.
7. Depress footbrake several times in order to give correct pad to disc clearance before road testing.

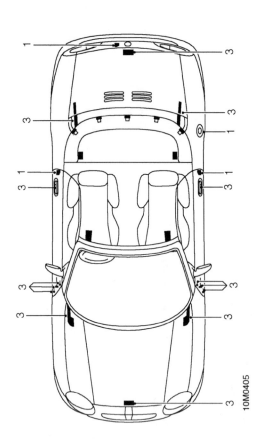

10M0405

BODY

Locks, hinges and latch mechanism (not steering lock)

Exterior paintwork and body panels

1. Visually check paintwork and body panels for damage and corrosion.

Underbody sealer

1. Visually check underbody sealer for damage and continuity.

1. Functionally check operation of all locks.
2. Operate driver's door lock and check that electric central door locking operates.
3. Ensure that all locks, hinges and latch mechanisms are lubricated using Door Lock and Latch Lubricant, Part No. CYL 100020. Inject grease sparingly into lock barrels. Clean off any surplus grease.
DO NOT lubricate the steering lock.

⚠️ NOTE: Use Rocol Ultralube on the boot hinges.

DRIVER AIR BAG MODULE

1. Visually check for signs of damage.
2. To renew an air bag. *See RESTRAINT SYSTEMS, Repairs.*

PASSENGER AIR BAG MODULE

1. Visually check for signs of damage.
2. To renew an air bag. *See RESTRAINT SYSTEMS, Repairs.*

AIR BAG ROTARY COUPLER

See RESTRAINT SYSTEMS, Repairs.

SCREEN WIPERS AND BLADES

1. Operate front screen wiper.
2. Check that blades wipe screen without smearing.
3. Check that wipers park correctly.
4. Operate wiper switch in all modes.
5. Check that wipers operate at speeds selected.

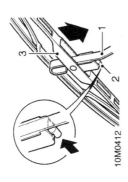

10M0412

Renew blade

1. Lift wiper arm.
2. Press retaining lever.
3. Slide blade down arm.
4. Withdraw blade assembly from arm.
5. Position new blade to wiper arm.
6. Push blade into engagement with arm.
7. Check that it is retained.

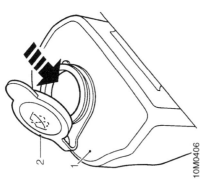

WINDSCREEN WASHERS

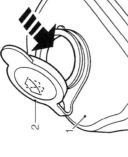

10M0406

1. Visually check mixture level in reservoir.
2. Top-up by removing filler cap and adding required concentration mixture of water and 'Screenwash'.
3. Clean windscreen washer jets using thin wire as a probe.

10M0407

4. Operate windscreen washer and check that jets strike top and centre of area to be wiped.
5. Adjust jet by inserting a needle into jet hole and repositioning.
6. Check operation of wash/wipe.
7. Observe that washer and wipers operate correctly.
8. Recheck level in reservoir after adjustments.

LAMPS, HORNS AND WARNING INDICATORS

1. Switch on sidelamps, and check that sidelamps, tail lamps, rear number plate lamps, and instrument lights illuminate.
2. Switch on headlamps, operate dip switch and check that headlamps function in both dip and main beam, and panel main beam indicator operates.
3. Operate flash switch and check that headlamps flash.
4. Open doors and check interior lamps illuminate.
5. Open bonnet, and rear luggage compartment and check lights illuminate.
6. Press horn and check that horn operates.
7. Switch on ignition and depress brake pedal, check brake lights illuminate.
8. Switch on ignition and operate direction indicator switch to right and left and check that the relative warning indicators flash at front and rear.
9. Operate hazard warning switch and check that all warning indicators flash.

BATTERY CONNECTIONS

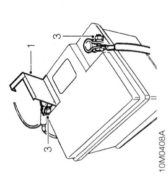

10M0408A

1. Lift flap covering positive terminal.
2. Wipe battery top clean and dry, smear terminal posts with petroleum jelly.
3. Ensure terminals are tight.
4. Replace flap.

FUSEBOX

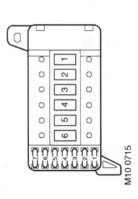

M10 0715

Underbonnet fuse box

1. Release and lift off cover.
2. Check security of fusible link and power lead connections.
3. Refit cover and secure.

ROAD TEST

Park/Neutral (inhibitor) switch - Steptronic (EM-CVT)

1. Select 'D' selector lever position.
2. Check that engine will not start.
3. Select 'R' selector lever position and repeat start check.
4. Check that engine will start with the selector lever in the 'P' and 'N' positions.

Selector cable - Steptronic (EM-CVT)

1. Move selector lever through positions P R N and D and check for correct setting of selector cable

Engine start and fast idle speed

1. Start engine from cold and check that fast engine idle speed is maintained until normal engine temperature is reached.

Engine performance and throttle operation

1. Start engine and check that it starts easily.
2. Check that 'oil pressure' and 'no charge' warning lamps extinguish.
3. Check that throttle pedal movement is free and unrestricted.
4. Check that engine is responsive to throttle movement.

Clutch and gear selection - manual transmission. Normal driving conditions

1. Check that clutch engages smoothly without judder, slipping or noise.
2. Check for abnormal transmission noise.
3. Check for smooth quiet gear change and that gear selected engages easily.

Gear selector and parking pawl engagement - Steptronic (EM-CVT). Normal driving conditions.

1. Select position 'R' and check for smooth take-up.
2. Select 'D', drive away and check for smooth ratio change from rest.
3. Check for abnormal transmission noise.
4. Slow vehicle down and check for smooth ratio change.

5. Select 'Sport', drive away and operate selector lever and steering wheel switches in plus (+) position from rest. Check for smooth up-changes of ratio from rest.
6. Slow vehicle down and operate selector lever and steering wheel switches in minus (-) position. Check for smooth down-changes of ratio.
7. Stop the vehicle on a slope.
8. Select position 'P' and release handbrake.
9. Check that vehicle does not move and selector lever does not slip from 'P' position.
10. Complete the above check with the vehicle facing in the opposite direction.

Steering

1. Check for noise, effort required, free play and self-centering.

Suspension

1. Check for noise, irregularity in ride (e.g dampers) and wheel imbalance.

Footbrake

1. Check for pedal effort, travel, braking efficiency, pulling and binding.

Instruments

1. Check that all instruments operate.
2. Check speedometer for steady operation, noise and operation of distance recorder.

Body

1. Check for abnormal body noise.

Seat belts

1. Check for operation of inertia reels and condition of belt webbing.

Handbrake

1. Apply handbrake firmly, check ratchet travel is less than 5 clicks. Check handbrake is not binding when released.

CONTENTS

This page is intentionally left blank

CONTENTS

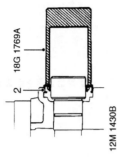

ENGINE

CAMSHAFT FRONT OIL SEAL - EXHAUST - MPi MEMS 1.9 (UP TO 2000MY); VVC MEMS 2J (UP TO 2001MY)

Service repair no - 12.13.07

Remove

1. Remove camshaft timing belt gear. *See this section.*
2. Support engine with jack.

 CAUTION: Place a block of wood between sump and jack to avoid damage.

3. Remove 2 bolts securing RH engine mounting bracket to engine.
4. Lower engine slightly to gain access to exhaust camshaft oil seal.

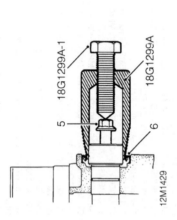

12M1429

5. Fit camshaft timing belt, gear bolt to camshaft and screw tool **18G 1299A** into seal.
6. Remove oil seal by tightening centre bolt of tool **18G 1299A-1**.
7. Remove bolt from camshaft.

Refit

1. Clean sealing area of head and camshaft, ensuring all traces of rubber are removed. Do not scrape sealing surfaces.

12M 1430B

2. Using tool **18G 1769A**, fit new camshaft oil seal.

NOTE: This oil seal is coloured BLACK.

 CAUTION: Oil seal must be fitted dry. Do not use tool 18G 1769.

3. Raise engine, fit and tighten engine mounting bolts to 60 Nm.
4. Fit camshaft timing belt gear. *See this section.*

CAMSHAFT FRONT OIL SEAL - EXHAUST - MPi MEMS 3 (2000MY ON); VVC MEMS 3 (2001MY ON)

Service repair no - 12.13.07

Remove

1. Disconnect battery earth lead.
2. Remove timing belt. *See this section.*
3. Remove **18G 1570** from camshaft gears.

M12 5757

4. Using **12-182** to restrain camshaft gear, remove bolt and plain washer securing camshaft gear to camshaft.
5. Remove camshaft gear.

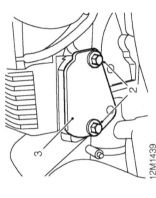

18G1299A-1 18G1768
M12 5752

6. Fit camshaft gear bolt back into end of camshaft.
7. Remove camshaft oil seal using **18G 1768** and centre bolt **18G 1299A-1**.
8. Discard camshaft oil seal.
9. Remove bolt from camshaft.

Refit

1. Clean sealing area of cylinder head and camshaft carrier.

⚠ **CAUTION: Do not use a metal scraper or the machined surfaces may be damaged.**

18G 1749 **18G 1769A**
M12 5753

2. Fit **18G 1749** to end of camshaft to protect seal and fit new seal **18G 1769A.**

⚠ **CAUTION: Oil seal must be fitted dry. DO NOT use 18G 1769.**

△ NOTE: Front oil seals are black.

3. Clean gears and camshaft mating faces.

⚠ **CAUTION: Do not use a metal scraper or the machined surfaces may be damaged.**

⚠ **CAUTION: If the sintered gears have been subjected to prolonged oil contamination, they must be soaked in a solvent bath before refitting. Because of the porous construction of sintered material, oil impregnated in the gears will emerge and contaminate the belt.**

4. Remove camshaft gear bolt.
5. Fit gear to camshaft.
6. Restrain camshaft gear using **12-182**, fit plain washer and tighten bolt to 65 Nm.
7. Align camshaft gears and fit **18G 1570.**
8. Fit timing belt. *See this section.*
9. Connect battery earth lead.

Refit

1. Clean sealing area of cylinder head and camshaft, ensuring all traces of rubber are removed.
Do not scrape sealing surfaces.

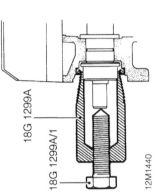

18G 1769A
12M1441A

2. Fit new camshaft oil seal using tool **18G 1769A.**

NOTE: This oil seal is coloured RED.

△ **CAUTION: Oil seal must be fitted dry. Do not use tool 18G 1769.**

3. Fit cover plate and tighten bolts to 5 Nm.
4. Fit engine cover. *See this section.*

CAMSHAFT REAR OIL SEAL - EXHAUST - MPi MEMS 1.9 (UP TO 2000MY)

Service repair no - 12.13.08

Remove

1. Remove engine cover. *See this section.*

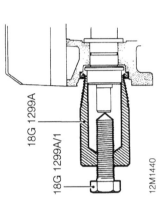

12M1439

2. Remove 2 bolts securing camshaft cover plate to cylinder head.
3. Remove cover plate.

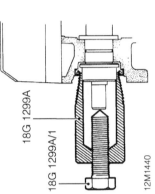

18G 1299A
18G 1299A/1
12M1440

4. Fit camshaft timing belt, gear bolt to camshaft and screw tool **18G 1299A** into seal.
5. Remove oil seal by tightening centre bolt of tool **18G 1299A-1.**
6. Remove bolt from camshaft.

CAMSHAFT REAR OIL SEAL - EXHAUST - VVC MEMS 2J (UP TO 2001MY)

Service repair no - 12.13.08

Remove

1. Remove and discard camshaft rear timing belt. *See this section.*

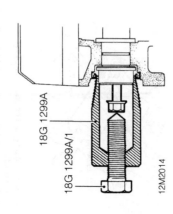

12M2014

18G 1299A
18G 1299A/1

2. Fit camshaft timing belt gear bolt to camshaft and screw tool **18G 1299A** into seal.
3. Remove oil seal by tightening centre bolt of tool **18G 1299A-1**.

Refit

1. Clean sealing area of cylinder head and camshaft, ensuring all traces of rubber are removed. Do not scrape sealing surfaces.

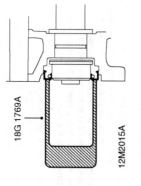

18G 1769A

12M2015A

2. Fit new camshaft oil seal using tool **18G 1769A**.

NOTE: This oil seal is coloured RED.

CAUTION: Oil seal must be fitted dry. Do not use tool 18G 1769.

3. Fit new camshaft rear timing belt. *See this section.*

CAMSHAFT REAR OIL SEAL - EXHAUST - MPi MEMS 3 (2000MY ON); VVC MEMS 3 (2001MY ON)

Service repair no - 12.13.08

Remove

1. Disconnect battery earth lead.
2. Remove engine cover. *See this section.*
3. Position absorbent cloth beneath vehicle to catch any oil spillage.

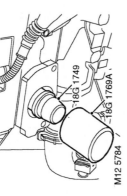

M12 5775

4. Remove 2 bolts securing oil seal cover to cylinder head and remove cover.

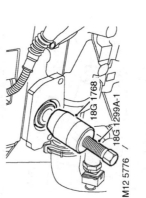

18G 1768
18G 1299A-1

M12 5776

5. Remove camshaft oil seal using **18G 1768** and centre bolt **18G 1299A-1**.
6. Discard camshaft oil seal.

Refit

1. Clean oil seal recess, ensuring all traces of rubber are removed.

CAUTION: Do not use a metal scraper or the machined surfaces may be damaged.

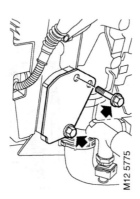

18G 1749
18G 1769A

M12 5784

2. Fit **18G 1749** to end of camshaft to protect seal and fit new camshaft oil seal using **18G 1769A**.

CAUTION: Oil seal must be fitted dry. DO NOT USE 18G 1769.

NOTE: Rear oil seals are red.

3. Ensure area around camshaft oil seal is clean and free from oil.
4. Position cover plate, fit bolts and tighten to 10 Nm.
5. Fit engine cover. *See this section.*
6. Connect battery earth lead.

CAMSHAFT FRONT OIL SEAL - INLET - MPi MEMS 1.9 (UP TO 2000MY)

Service repair no - 12.13.09

Remove

1. Remove camshaft timing belt gear. *See this section.*

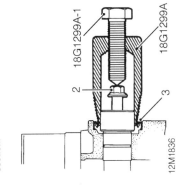

12M1836

2. Fit camshaft timing belt, gear bolt to camshaft and screw tool **18G 1299A** into seal.
3. Remove oil seal by tightening centre bolt of tool **18G 1299A-1**.
4. Remove bolt from camshaft.

Refit

1. Clean sealing area of head and camshaft, ensuring all traces of rubber are removed. Do not scrape sealing surfaces.

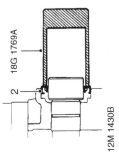

12M 1430B

2. Using tool **18G 1769A** , fit camshaft oil seal.

   NOTE: This oil seal is coloured BLACK.

   ⚠ **CAUTION: Oil seal must be fitted dry. Do not use tool 18G 1769.**

3. Fit camshaft timing belt gear. *See this section.*

CAMSHAFT FRONT OIL SEAL - INLET - VVC MEMS 2J (UP TO 2001MY)

Service repair no - 12.13.09

Remove

1. Remove inlet camshaft timing belt gear. *See this section.*

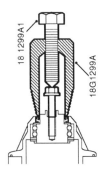

M12 7289

2. Fit camshaft timing belt gear bolt to camshaft and screw tool **18G 1299A** into seal.
3. Remove oil seal by tightening centre bolt of tool **18G 1299A-1**.
4. Remove bolt from camshaft.

Refit

1. Clean sealing area of cylinder head and camshaft, ensuring all traces of rubber are removed. Do not scrape sealing surfaces.

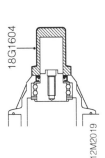

12M2019

2. Fit new camshaft oil seal using tool **18G 1604** until seal is flush with mechanism face.

   ⚠ **CAUTION: Oil seal must be fitted dry.**

3. Fit inlet camshaft timing belt gear. *See this section.*

CAMSHAFT FRONT OIL SEAL - INLET - MPi MEMS 3 (2000MY ON); VVC MEMS 3 (2001MY ON)

Service repair no - 12.13.09

Remove

1. Disconnect battery earth lead.
2. Remove timing belt. *See this section.*
3. Remove **18G 1570** from camshaft gears.

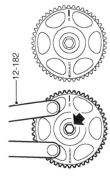

M12 5743

4. Using **12-182** to restrain camshaft gear, remove bolt and plain washer securing camshaft gear to camshaft.
5. Remove camshaft gear.
6. Refit camshaft gear bolt to camshaft.

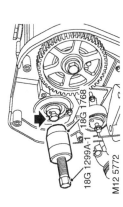

M12 5772

7. Remove camshaft oil seal using **18G 1768** and centre bolt **18G 1299A-1**.
8. Discard camshaft oil seal.
9. Remove bolt from camshaft.

Refit

1. Clean sealing area of cylinder head and camshaft carrier.

⚠ **CAUTION: Do not use a metal scraper or machined surfaces may be damaged.**

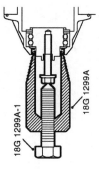

M12 5773

18G 1769A
18G 1749

2. Fit **18G 1749** to end of camshaft to protect seal and fit new camshaft oil seal using **18G 1769A**.

⚠ **CAUTION: Oil seal must be fitted dry. DO NOT USE 18G 1769.**

◁ NOTE: Front oil seals are black.

3. Clean gear and camshaft mating faces.

⚠ **CAUTION: If the sintered gears have been subjected to prolonged oil contamination, they must be soaked in a solvent bath before refitting. Because of the porous construction of sintered material, oil impregnated in the gears will emerge and contaminate the belt.**

4. Remove camshaft gear bolt.
5. Fit gear to camshaft, fit plain washer and using **12-182** to restrain camshaft gear, tighten bolt to 65 Nm.
6. Align camshaft gears and fit **18G 1570**.
7. Fit timing belt. *See this section.*
8. Connect battery earth lead.

CAMSHAFT REAR OIL SEAL - INLET - MPi MEMS 1.9 (UP TO 2000MY)

Service repair no - 12.13.10

Remove

1. Remove rotor arm. *See ENGINE MANAGEMENT SYSTEM - MEMS, Repairs.*

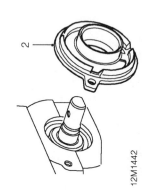

12M1442

2. Remove flash shield.

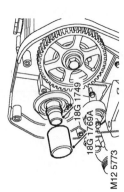

18G 1299A
18G 1299A-1
12M1443

3. Fit camshaft timing belt, gear bolt to camshaft and screw tool **18G 1299A** into seal.
4. Remove oil seal by tightening centre bolt of tool **18G 1299A-1**.
5. Remove bolt from camshaft.

Refit

1. Clean sealing area of cylinder head and camshaft, ensuring all traces of rubber are removed.
Do not scrape sealing surfaces.

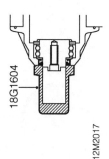

18G 1769A
12M 1444B

2. Fit oil seal using tool **18G 1769A**.

◁ NOTE: This oil seal is coloured RED.

⚠ **CAUTION: Oil seal must be fitted dry. Do not use tool 18G 1769.**

3. Fit flash shield to camshaft.
4. Fit rotor arm. *See ENGINE MANAGEMENT SYSTEM - MEMS, Repairs.*

CAMSHAFT REAR OIL SEAL - INLET - VVC MEMS 2J (UP TO 2001MY)

Service repair no - 12.13.10

Remove

1. Remove and discard camshaft rear timing belt. *See this section.*

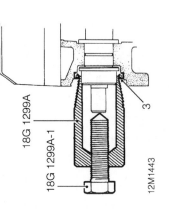

18G 1299A-1
18G 1299A

M12 7288

2. Fit camshaft timing belt gear bolt to camshaft and screw tool **18G 1299A** into seal.
3. Remove oil seal by tightening centre bolt of tool **18G 1299A-1**.
4. Remove bolt from camshaft.

Refit

1. Clean sealing area of cylinder head and camshaft, ensuring all traces of rubber are removed. Do not scrape sealing surfaces.

18G1604

12M2017

2. Fit new camshaft oil seal using tool **18G 1604**, until seal is flush with mechanism face.

⚠ **CAUTION: Oil seal must be fitted dry.**

3. Fit new camshaft rear timing belt. *See this section.*

CAMSHAFT REAR OIL SEAL - INLET - MPi MEMS 3 (2000MY ON); VVC MEMS 3 (2001MY ON)

Service repair no - 12.13.10

Remove

1. Disconnect battery earth lead.
2. Remove engine cover. *See this section.*
3. Position absorbent cloth beneath vehicle to catch any oil spillage.

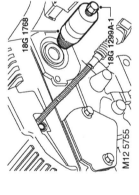

M12 5774

4. Disconnect CMP sensor multiplug and release CMP harness from oil seal cover.

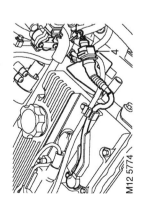

M12 5754

5. Remove 2 bolts securing oil seal cover to cylinder head and position cover aside.

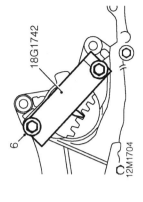

18G 1768
18G 1299A-1
M12 5755

6. Remove camshaft oil seal using **18G 1768** and centre bolt **18G 1299A-1**.
7. Discard camshaft oil seal.

Refit

1. Clean oil seal recess, ensuring all traces of rubber are removed.

⚠ **CAUTION: Do not use a metal scraper or machined surfaces may be damaged.**

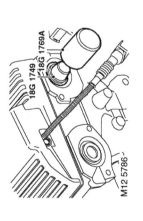

18G 1749
18G 1769A
M12 5786

2. Fit **18G 1749** to end of camshaft to protect seal and fit new camshaft oil seal using **18G 1769A**. DO NOT USE **18G 1769**.

△ NOTE: Oil seals are red.

---

3. Ensure area around camshaft oil seal is clean and free from oil.
4. Position cover plate, fit bolts and tighten to 10 Nm.
5. Secure CMP harness to cover plate and connect CMP multiplug.
6. Fit engine cover. *See this section.*
7. Connect battery earth lead.

CRANKSHAFT PULLEY - MANUAL GEARBOX

Service repair no - 12.21.01

Remove

1. Disconnect battery earth lead.
2. Raise rear of vehicle.

⚠ **WARNING: Support on safety stands.**

3. Remove road wheel(s).
4. Remove alternator drive belt. *See ELECTRICAL, Repairs.*
5. Remove starter motor. *See ELECTRICAL, Repairs.*

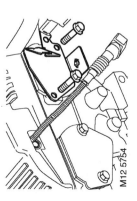

18G1742
6
12M1704

6. Lock crankshaft using tool **18G 1742**.

ENGINE

CRANKSHAFT PULLEY - SEQUENTIAL AUTO (EM-CVT)

Service repair no - 12.21.01

Remove

1. Disconnect battery earth lead.
2. Raise rear of vehicle.

⚠ **WARNING: Support on safety stands.**

3. Remove road wheel(s).
4. Remove alternator drive belt. **See ELECTRICAL, Repairs.**
5. Remove starter motor. **See ELECTRICAL, Repairs.**

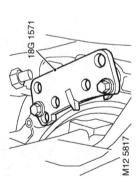

18G 1571

M12 5817

6. Lock crankshaft using tool **18G 1571.**

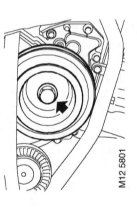

M12 5801

7. Remove crankshaft pulley bolt and washer.
8. Remove crankshaft pulley.

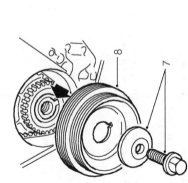

12M1703

7. Remove crankshaft pulley bolt and washer.
8. Remove crankshaft pulley.

Refit

1. Clean crankshaft to pulley mating faces.
2. Fit crankshaft pulley.
3. Fit crankshaft washer and tighten centre bolt to 205 Nm.
4. Remove crankshaft locking tool **18G 1742.**
5. Fit starter motor. **See ELECTRICAL, Repairs.**
6. Fit alternator drive belt. **See ELECTRICAL, Repairs.**
7. Fit road wheel(s) and tighten nuts to correct torque. **See INFORMATION, Torque wrench settings.**
8. Remove stand(s) and lower vehicle.
9. Connect battery earth lead.

CRANKSHAFT FRONT OIL SEAL

Service repair no - 12.21.14

Remove

1. Remove crankshaft timing belt gear. **See this section.**

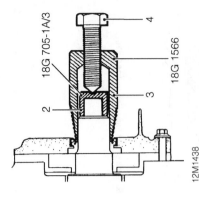

18G 705-1A/3
18G 1566
4
3
2

12M1438

2. Fit thrust button tool **18G 705-1A/3** to crankshaft.
3. Ensure bore of tool is burr free, fit and tighten tool **18G 1566** into crankshaft front oil seal.
4. Tighten centre screw of tool to remove oil seal.
5. Remove thrust button from crankshaft.

Refit

1. Clean crankshaft to pulley mating faces.
2. Fit crankshaft pulley.
3. Fit crankshaft washer and tighten centre bolt to 205 Nm.
4. Remove crankshaft locking tool **18G 1571.**
5. Fit starter motor. **See ELECTRICAL, Repairs.**
6. Fit alternator drive belt. **See ELECTRICAL, Repairs.**
7. Fit road wheel(s) and tighten nuts to correct torque. **See INFORMATION, General data.**
8. Remove stand(s) and lower vehicle.
9. Connect battery earth lead.

Refit

1. Use lint free cloth to thoroughly clean seal recess in oil pump and running surface on crankshaft.
   Clean crankshaft pulley and gear.

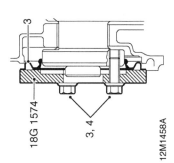

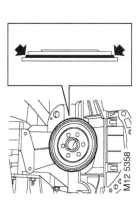

12M1702

2. Fit protector, from oil seal kit, over crankshaft end.

3. Fit new oil seal to crankshaft using tool **18G 1587**. Remove protector.

   ⚠ **CAUTION: Oil seal must be fitted dry.**

4. Fit crankshaft timing belt gear. *See this section.*

CRANKSHAFT REAR OIL SEAL

Service repair no - 12.21.20

Remove

1. Remove flywheel. *See this section.*

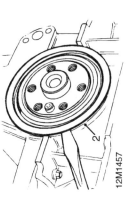

12M1457

2. Using a burr free flat ended screwdriver, ease crankshaft rear oil seal from cylinder block, remove and discard seal.

   ⚠ **CAUTION: Do not mark sealing surface on crankshaft.**

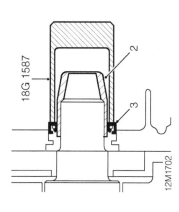

18G 1574

3, 4

12M1458A

Refit

1. Remove all traces of oil and sealant from cylinder block, oil seal recess and running surface of crankshaft.

M12 5358

2. Apply a continuous bead of sealant, Part No. GAC 8000 to replacement oil seal as shown.

   ⚠ **CAUTION: Do not apply oil or grease to any part of oil seal or running surface of crankshaft. Seal must be fitted immediately after applying sealant.**

3. Position oil seal to cylinder block and fit oil seal replacer tool **18G 1574**, retain tool using 3 slave bolts.

4. Evenly tighten oil seal replacer bolts to press oil seal squarely into cylinder block.

5. Leave oil seal replacer tool and oil seal in clamped position for one minute to allow oil seal to relax.

6. Remove oil seal replacer tool.

7. Allow sealant to cure for a minimum of 30 minutes before topping-up oil or rotating crankshaft.

8. Fit flywheel. *See this section.*

CYLINDER HEAD GASKET - MPi MEMS 1.9 (UP TO 2000MY)

Service repair no - 12.29.02

Remove

1. Remove and discard camshaft timing belt. **See this section.**
2. Remove camshaft cover gasket. **See this section.**
3. Remove inlet manifold gasket - MPi. **See MANIFOLD & EXHAUST SYSTEMS, Repairs.**

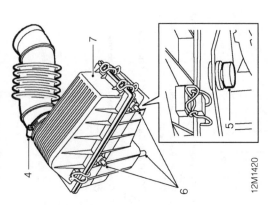

12M1420

4. Loosen clip screw and remove air intake hose from air cleaner.
5. Remove 2 clips securing air cleaner to mounting bracket.
6. Release 3 air cleaner studs from mounting bracket and release air cleaner from resonator duct.
7. Remove air cleaner.

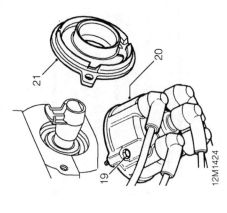

18G 1570

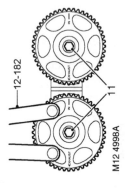

12-182

M12 4998A

NOTE: Manual timing belt tensioner illustrated.

Manual timing belt tensioner :- Remove camshaft belt tensioner spring.
9. Mark camshaft gears for fitting reference.
10. Remove tool **18G 1570**.
11. Restrain camshaft gears using tool **12-182** and remove 2 bolts and plain washers from camshaft gears.

Engines fitted with manual timing belt tensioner

12. Remove tensioner backplate screw and tensioner pulley Allen bolt.
13. Remove tensioner pulley assembly.

All engines

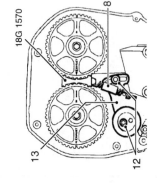

M12 5001

14. Remove bolts from upper part of timing belt rear cover, remove cover.

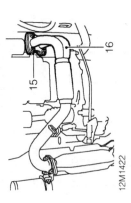

12M1422

15. Remove 4 flange nuts securing exhaust front pipe to manifold.
16. Release front pipe from manifold, remove gasket and discard.

17. Loosen clips and disconnect 2 coolant hoses from cylinder head.
18. Disconnect 2 multiplugs from coolant sensors.

12M1423

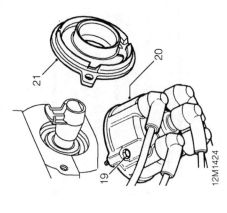

19. Loosen 2 captive bolts securing distributor cap to cylinder head.
20. Release distributor cap and position aside.
21. Remove flash shield from rotor arm.

12M1424

Engines fitted with manual timing belt tensioner

13. Fit camshaft belt tensioner pulley assembly to cylinder head.
14. Fit but do not tighten tensioner pulley Allen bolt.
15. Fit but do not tighten tensioner backplate bolt, connect spring to pillar bolt and tensioner.

△ NOTE: This spring is fitted with a sleeve.

16. Hold tensioner in the OFF position and tighten back plate bolt to 10 Nm.

All engines

17. Fit bolts to upper part of timing belt rear cover and tighten to 9 Nm.
18. Clean mating faces of camshaft and gears.
19. Fit camshaft gears to camshaft.

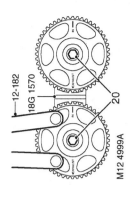

M12 4999A

20. Fit bolts and plain washers securing camshaft gears, restrain gears using tool **12-182** and tighten bolts to:
8 mm bolts to 33 Nm.
10 mm bolts to 65 Nm.
21. Align camshaft gear timing marks using tool **12-182** and fit camshaft gear locking tool **18G 1570** to camshaft gears.

Refit

1. Remove head bolts and tools **18G 1736/1** from cylinder block.
2. Clean joint surfaces on cylinder head and block.
Clean oil and coolant passages.
Clean exhaust manifold and front pipe joint surfaces.
De-carbonise piston crowns and cylinder head if necessary.
3. Wash cylinder head bolts and wipe dry. Oil threads and under head of bolts.
4. Fit NEW cylinder head gasket onto cylinder block.
5. Fit cylinder head onto cylinder block carefully locating dowels.
6. Carefully enter cylinder head bolts. **DO NOT DROP**. Screw bolts into place by hand.

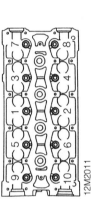

12M2011

7. Tighten cylinder head bolts progressively in sequence shown, using the following procedure:
i. All bolts to 20 Nm.
Use a felt tip pen and mark position of radial mark on each bolt head.
ii. Turn all bolts through 180°.
iii. Turn all bolts through another 180° and align mark.

△ **CAUTION: If bolt is overtightened, back off 90° and realign.**

8. Clean distributor cap to cylinder head mating faces.
9. Fit distributor flash shield, align cap and tighten captive bolts to 2 Nm.
10. Connect multiplugs to coolant sensors.
11. Connect coolant hoses to cylinder head and tighten clips.
12. Fit NEW exhaust manifold to front pipe gasket, align flanges and tighten nuts to 70 Nm.

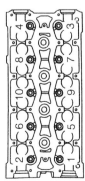

12M1425

22. Loosen 10, E12 cylinder head to oil rail bolts in sequence shown. Remove bolts and store in fitted order.
23. Using assistance, remove cylinder head assembly from cylinder block.
24. Remove cylinder head gasket from cylinder block and discard.

△ **CAUTION: Do not rotate crankshaft with cylinder head removed.**

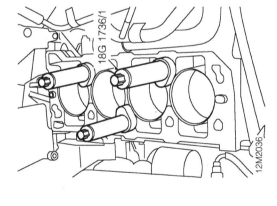

12M2036

25. Fit tools **18G 1736/1** to cylinder block and secure using head bolts as shown.

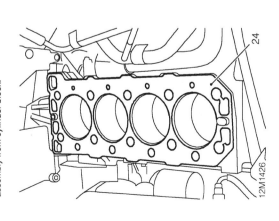

12M1426

22. Fit air cleaner, align to mounting bracket and resonator duct and secure clips.
23. Fit air intake hose to air cleaner and tighten clip.
24. Fit inlet manifold gasket - MPi. *See MANIFOLD & EXHAUST SYSTEMS, Repairs. See this section.*
25. Fit camshaft cover gasket. *See this section.*
26. Fit new camshaft timing belt. *See this section.*

CYLINDER HEAD GASKET - AIR CON - VVC MEMS 2J (UP TO 2001MY); VVC MEMS 3 (2001 MY ON)

Service repair no - 12.29.02/20

Remove

1. Remove inlet manifold gasket. *See MANIFOLD & EXHAUST SYSTEMS, Repairs.*
2. Remove and discard camshaft timing belt. *See this section.*

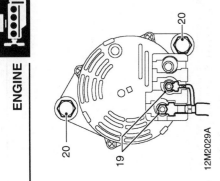

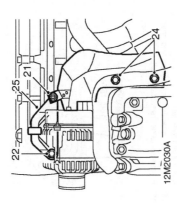

18G 1570   12-182

3. Check correct alignment of timing marks on camshaft gears.
4. Use tool **12-182** to brace camshaft gears.
5. Remove 2 bolts and plain washers from camshaft gears, remove tool **18G 1570**.
6. Mark camshaft gears for fitting reference and remove 2 camshaft gears.
7. Remove timing belt tensioner backplate bolt and tensioner pulley backplate Allen screw.

M12 5000A

8. Remove tensioner pulley assembly.
9. Remove bolts from upper part of timing belt rear cover.
10. Remove rear cover.

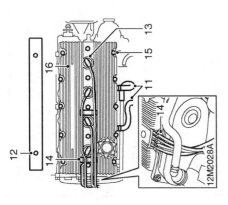

12M2028A

11. Release 2 clips and disconnect 2 breather hoses from camshaft cover.
12. Remove 2 screws securing spark plug cover and remove cover. *VVC MEMS 3 (2001MY ON) only:* remove plug top coils *See ENGINE MANAGEMENT SYSTEM - MEMS, Repairs.*.
13. Disconnect 4 plug tubes from spark plugs.
14. Lift clip plate and grommet and position h.t. leads aside.
15. Progressively slacken then remove 15 bolts from camshaft cover.
16. Remove camshaft cover assembly.

⚠ NOTE: The gasket is reusable and should remain attached to the camshaft cover unless it is to be renewed.

17. Check condition of sealing path, it should be complete and attached to the camshaft cover.
18. Remove gasket from camshaft cover only if sealing path is damaged or detached from gasket. *VVC MEMS 3 (2001MY ON) only:* remove 3 bolts securing A/C compressor, and tie compressor aside. *See AIR CONDITIONING, Repairs.*

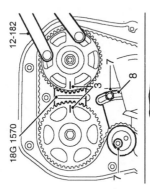

12M2029A

19. Remove 2 nuts securing leads to alternator and position aside.
20. Remove 2 bolts securing alternator to brackets and position alternator forward.

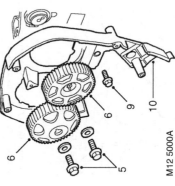

12M2030A

21. Remove nut securing alternator top bracket to cylinder head.
22. Remove bolt securing alternator top bracket to cylinder head.
23. Position top bracket aside and remove alternator.
24. Remove 2 bolts securing exhaust heat shield to bracket and remove heat shield.
25. Collect alternator top bracket.

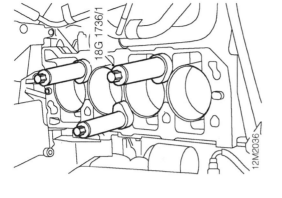

12M2031A

26. Remove 5 flange nuts securing exhaust manifold to cylinder head.

27. Position manifold aside, remove gasket and discard.

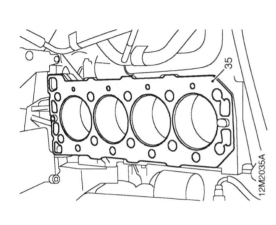

12M2032A

28. Loosen clips and disconnect 2 coolant hoses from cylinder head.

29. Disconnect 2 multiplugs from coolant sensors.

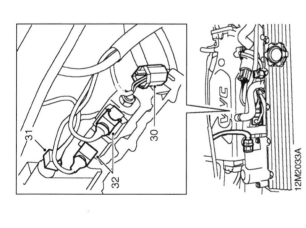

12M2033A

30. Disconnect camshaft sensor multiplug.

31. Disconnect oil temperature sensor multiplug.

32. Disconnect 2 multiplugs from control solenoids.

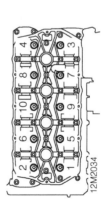

12M2034

33. Loosen 10 E12 cylinder head to oil rail bolts in sequence shown. Remove bolts and store in fitted order.

34. Remove cylinder head assembly from cylinder block, use assistance.

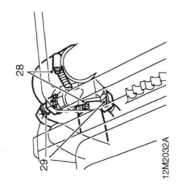

12M2035A

35. Remove cylinder head gasket from cylinder block and discard.

⚠ CAUTION: Do not rotate crankshaft with cylinder head removed.

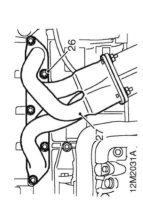

12M2036

36. Fit tools **18G 1736/1** to cylinder block and secure using head bolts as shown.

ENGINE

Refit

1. Remove head bolts and tools 18G 1736/1 from cylinder block.
2. Clean joint surfaces on cylinder head and block.
   Clean oil and coolant passages.
   Clean exhaust manifold and cylinder head joint surfaces.
   De-carbonise piston crowns and cylinder head if necessary.
3. Wash cylinder head bolts and wipe dry. Oil threads and under head of bolts.
4. Fit NEW cylinder head gasket to cylinder block.
5. Fit cylinder head to cylinder block carefully locating dowels, use assistance.
6. Carefully enter cylinder head bolts. **DO NOT DROP.** Screw bolts into place by hand.

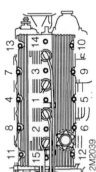

12M2037

7. Tighten cylinder head bolts progressively in sequence shown, using the following procedure:
   i All bolts to 20 Nm. Use a felt tip pen and mark position of radial mark on each bolt head.
   ii Turn all bolts through 180°.
   iii Turn all bolts through another 180° and align mark.

⚠️ **CAUTION: If bolt is overtightened, back off 90° and realign.**

8. Connect multiplugs to control solenoids.
9. Connect multiplug to camshaft sensor.
10. Connect multiplug to oil temperature sensor.
11. Connect multiplugs to coolant sensors.
12. Position coolant hoses to cylinder head and tighten clips.
13. Fit NEW exhaust manifold to cylinder head gasket.

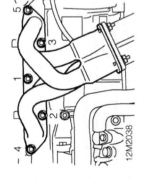

12M2038

14. Position manifold and working in the sequence shown, tighten nuts to 45 Nm.
15. Position camshaft belt tensioner pulley assembly to cylinder head.
16. Fit but do not tighten tensioner pulley Allen screw.
17. Fit tensioner backplate bolt. Hold tensioner in OFF position and tighten tensioner backplate bolt to 10 Nm.

△ NOTE: Do not fit tensioner spring or pillar bolt at this stage.

18. Position alternator top bracket to stud.
19. Fit exhaust heat shield and tighten bolts to 10 Nm.
20. Position alternator and loosely fit lower bolt.
21. Position top bracket and tighten bolt to 25 Nm.
22. Tighten nut to 25 Nm.
23. Align alternator and tighten bolts to 45 Nm.
24. Connect leads to alternator and secure nuts.
25. VVC MEMS 3 (2001MY ON) only: refit 3 bolts securing A/C compressor and tighten bolts to 45 Nm. See **AIR CONDITIONING, Repairs.**
26. Clean mating surfaces and inside of camshaft cover. If necessary, wash oil separator elements in solvent and blow dry.
27. Fit NEW camshaft cover gasket to camshaft cover if required with 'TOP' mark towards the inlet manifold.
28. Fit camshaft cover onto camshaft carrier.

ENGINE

GASKET - CYLINDER HEAD - A/C - MPi MEMS3 - (2000MY ON)

Service repair no - 12.29.02/20

Remove

1. Drain cooling system. See **COOLING SYSTEM, Adjustments.**
2. Remove camshaft timing belt. See this section.
3. Remove inlet manifold gasket. See **MANIFOLD & EXHAUST SYSTEMS, Repairs.**

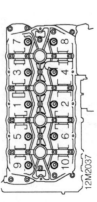

12-182

M12 5758

4. Using **12-182** to restrain camshaft gears, remove bolts securing camshaft gears and collect washers.
5. Remove camshaft gears.

M12 5686

6. Remove 5 bolts from timing belt rear cover.
7. Remove rear cover.
8. Remove camshaft cover gasket. **See this section.**

12M2039

29. Tighten camshaft cover bolts to 9 Nm in the sequence illustrated.
30. Fit clip plate and grommet and press plug tubes onto spark plugs.
31. VVC MEMS 3 (2001MY ON) only: refit plug top coils See **ENGINE MANAGEMENT SYSTEM - MEMS, Repairs..**
32. Fit spark plug cover to camshaft cover and secure screws.
33. Connect breather hose to camshaft cover and secure with clip.
34. Fit camshaft gear rear cover and tighten bolts to 9 Nm.
35. Clean mating surfaces of camshaft and gears.
36. Fit gears to camshafts.
37. Using tool **12-182** to restrain gears, fit bolts and washers and tighten
    8 mm bolts to 33 Nm.
    10 mm bolts to 65 Nm.
38. Check that camshaft gear timing marks are aligned, adjust if necessary using tool **12-182.**
39. Fit tool **18G 1570** to gears.
40. Lower engine to allow camshaft belt to be fitted.
41. Fit a new camshaft timing belt. **See this section.**
42. Fit inlet manifold gasket. See **MANIFOLD & EXHAUST SYSTEMS, Repairs.**

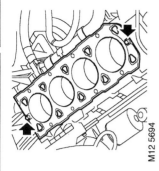

M12 5689

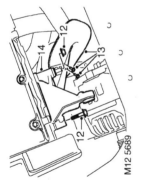

M12 5691

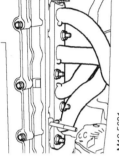

M12 5694

9. Remove nut securing alternator lead and release lead, disconnect alternator multiplug.

12. Remove nut and bolt securing alternator bracket.
13. Remove 2 bolts securing exhaust heat shield and remove heat shield.
14. Collect alternator bracket.

16. Remove 5 flange nuts securing exhaust manifold to cylinder head.
17. Position manifold aside, remove and discard gasket.

22. Remove cylinder head gasket from cylinder block and discard.

⚠ **CAUTION: Do not rotate crankshaft with cylinder head removed.**

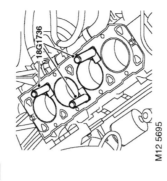

M12 5688

M12 5690

M12 5692

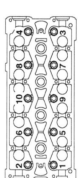

18G1736

M12 5695

10. Remove alternator top bolt and loosen lower bolt.
11. Position alternator forwards to access alternator bracket.

15. Remove 3 bolts securing coolant hose heat shield and remove heat shield.

18. Loosen clips and disconnect 2 coolant hoses from cylinder head.
19. Disconnect 2 multiplugs from coolant sensors.

23. Fit tool **18G 1736** to cylinder block and secure using head bolts as shown.

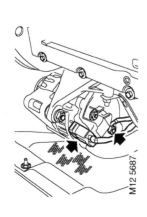

M12 5687

M12 5693

20. Loosen 10 E12 cylinder head to oil rail bolts in sequence shown. Remove bolts and store in fitted order.
21. Remove cylinder head assembly from cylinder block, use assistance.

Refit

1. Remove head bolts and tools 18G 1736 from cylinder block.
2. Clean joint surfaces on cylinder head and block, clean oil and coolant passages. Clean exhaust manifold and cylinder head joint surfaces. De-carbonise piston crowns and cylinder head if necessary.
3. Inspect cylinder head bolts, *See this section.*
4. Wash cylinder head bolts and wipe dry. Oil threads and under head of bolts.
5. Fit new cylinder head gasket to cylinder block.
6. Fit cylinder head to cylinder block carefully locating dowels, use assistance.
7. Carefully enter cylinder head bolts, **DO NOT DROP.** Screw bolts into place by hand.

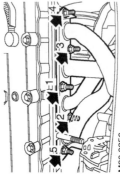

M12 5696

8. Tighten cylinder head bolts progressively in sequence shown, using the following procedure:
i. All bolts to 20 Nm. Use a felt tip pen and mark position of radial mark on each bolt head.
ii. Turn all bolts through 180°
iii. Turn all bolts through another 180° and align mark.

⚠ **CAUTION: If bolt is overtightened, back off 90° and realign.**

9. Connect multiplugs to coolant sensors.
10. Position coolant hoses to cylinder head and tighten clips.
11. Fit new exhaust manifold gasket to cylinder head.

M30 0856

12. Position manifold and working in the sequence shown, tighten nuts to 45 Nm.
13. Position coolant hose heat shield, fit bolts and tighten to 9 Nm.
14. Position alternator bracket.
15. Position exhaust heat shield, fit bolts and tighten to 9 Nm.
16. Tighten alternator bracket nut and bolt to 25 Nm.
17. Align alternator to bracket, fit top bolt, tighten both bolts to 45 Nm.
18. Connect alternator multiplug and lead, secure lead with nut.
19. Fit timing belt rear cover and secure with bolts.
20. Fit camshaft cover gasket. *See this section.*
21. Clean mating surfaces of camshafts and gears.
22. Fit gears to camshafts.
23. Using tool 12-182 to restrain gears, fit bolts and washers and tighten to 65 Nm.
24. Check timing of gears and adjust if necessary. *See MANIFOLD & EXHAUST SYSTEMS, Repairs.*
25. Fit tool 18G 1570 to gears.
26. Fit inlet manifold gasket. *See MANIFOLD & EXHAUST SYSTEMS, Repairs.*
27. Fit camshaft timing belt. *See this section.*
28. Refill cooling system. *See COOLING SYSTEM, Adjustments.*

Refit

1. Clean mating surfaces and inside of camshaft cover.
If necessary, wash oil separator elements in solvent and blow dry.
2. Fit NEW camshaft cover gasket to camshaft carrier with 'TOP' mark towards the inlet manifold.
3. Fit camshaft cover onto camshaft carrier.

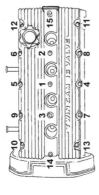

12M1475

4. Tighten camshaft cover bolts to 9 Nm, in the sequence shown.
5. Fit clip plate and grommet and press plug tubes onto spark plugs.
6. Fit spark plug cover to camshaft cover and secure screws.
7. Connect 2 breather hoses to camshaft cover and secure with clips.
8. Fit engine cover. *See this section.*

CAMSHAFT COVER GASKET - MPi MEMS 1.9 (UP TO 2000MY); VVC MEMS 2J (UP TO 2001MY)

Service repair no - 12.29.40

Remove

1. Remove engine cover. *See this section.*

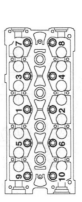

M12 7286

2. Release clips and disconnect 2 breather hoses from camshaft cover.
3. Remove 2 screws securing spark plug cover.
4. Remove spark plug cover.
5. Disconnect 4 plug tubes from spark plugs.
6. Lift clip plate and grommet and position h.t. leads aside.
7. Progressively slacken then remove 15 bolts from cover.
8. Remove camshaft cover assembly.

⚠ NOTE: The gasket is reusable and should remain attached to the camshaft cover unless it is to be renewed.

9. Check condition of sealing path, it should be complete and attached to the gasket.
10. Remove gasket from camshaft cover only if sealing path is damaged or detached from gasket.

GASKET - CAMSHAFT COVER - MPi MEMS3 (2000MY ON); VVC MEMS 3 (2001MY ON)

Service repair no - 12.29.40

Remove

1. Disconnect battery earth lead.
2. Remove coil set. See *ENGINE MANAGEMENT SYSTEM - MEMS, Repairs.*
3. Release 2 clips and disconnect 2 breather hoses from camshaft cover.

M12 5777

4. Release coil harness from support bracket and position aside.

M12 5778

5. Remove bolt securing CMP sensor to cylinder head and position aside.

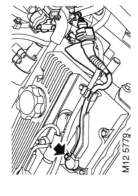

M12 5779

6. Progressively loosen and remove 15 bolts securing camshaft cover.
7. Remove camshaft cover.
8. Remove gasket.

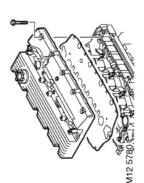

M12 5780

VALVE STEM OIL SEAL - MPi MEMS 1.9 (UP TO 2000MY); VVC MEMS 2J (UP TO 2001MY)

Service repair no - 12.30.26

Remove

1. Disconnect battery earth lead.
2. Remove camshaft cover. *See this section.*
3. Remove inlet and exhaust camshafts. See 'K' Series Engine Overhaul Manual - Overhaul.

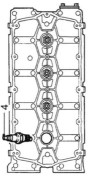

12M1631

4. Using a 16 mm spark plug socket, remove 4 spark plugs.

MS 1567

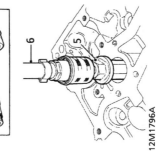

12M1796A

5. Fit and tighten air line adaptor tool **MS 1567** into spark plug hole.
6. Connect an airline to adaptor and apply air pressure.

Refit

1. Clean mating surfaces of camshaft cover and carrier.
2. Clean inside of camshaft cover. If necessary, wash oil separator elements in solvent and blow dry.
3. Fit new gasket with '**EXHAUST MAN SIDE**' mark towards exhaust manifold.
4. Fit camshaft cover to camshaft carrier.

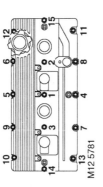

M12 5781

5. Fit bolts and working in sequence illustrated, tighten progressively to 9 Nm.
6. Fit CMP sensor, fit bolt tighten bolt to 9 Nm.
7. Fit coil set. See *ENGINE MANAGEMENT SYSTEM - MEMS, Repairs.*
8. Fit coil harness to support bracket.
9. Connect breather hoses and secure with clips.
10. Connect battery earth lead.

VALVE STEM OIL SEAL - MPi MEMS3 (2000MY ON); VVC MEMS3 (2001MY ON)

Service repair no - 12.30.26

Remove

1. Disconnect battery earth lead.
2. Remove inlet and exhaust camshafts. See 'K' Series Engine Overhaul Manual - Overhaul.

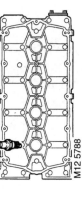

M12 5788

3. Using a 16 mm spark plug socket, remove 4 spark plugs.

MS-1567

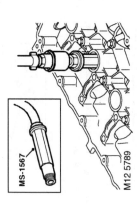

M12 5789

4. Fit and tighten air line adaptor tool **MS 1567** into spark plug hole.
5. Connect an airline to adaptor and apply air pressure.
6. Remove hydraulic tappet from each exhaust valve.

⚠ **CAUTION: Retain tappets in fitted order and store inverted to prevent oil loss.**

Refit

1. Lubricate NEW valve stem oil seal with engine oil.
2. Use tool **18G 1577** to fit NEW oil seals.
3. Fit valve spring and spring cap to each valve.

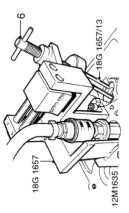

6
18G 1657/13
18G 1657
12M1635

4. Assemble tool **18G 1657** to exhaust valve.
5. Locate valve spring cap with compressor tool **18G 1657/13**.
6. Screw down valve spring compressor until valve stem collet groove is level with top face of spring cap.
7. Attach collets to end of a small flat screwdriver with grease and locate collets in valve stem groove.
8. Unscrew valve spring compressor ensuring collets are correctly located in valve spring cap.
9. Slide head of tool **18G 1657** along to second exhaust valve position.
10. Repeat refit operations on second valve.
11. Remove valve spring compressor tool **18G 1657**.
12. Lubricate tappets with clean unused engine oil and refit in original positions.
13. Repeat oil seal remove and refit operation sequence on inlet valves.
14. Disconnect air line from adaptor tool **MS 1567**.
15. Remove air line adaptor tool **MS 1567**.
16. Clean spark plugs and set gaps to 0.9 ± 0.1 mm.
17. Fit inlet and exhaust camshafts. See 'K' Series Engine Overhaul Manual - Overhaul. *See this section*.
18. Fit camshaft cover.
19. Connect battery earth lead.

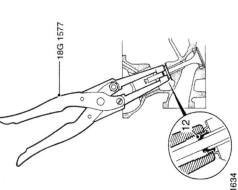

18G 1577
12
12M1634

12. Use tool **18G 1577** to remove valve stem oil seal.
13. Repeat operations to remove second exhaust valve oil seal.

7. Remove hydraulic tappet from each exhaust valve.

⚠ **CAUTION: Retain tappets in fitted order and store inverted to prevent oil loss.**

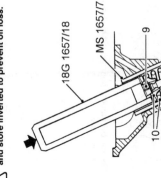

18G 1657/18
MS 1657/7
9
10
12M1797B

8. Fit tool **18G 1657/18** and tool **MS 1657/7** to valve spring cap.
9. Strike head of tool firmly with hammer to release valve spring collets.
10. Remove collets from magnetic end of tool.
11. Remove valve spring cap and spring.

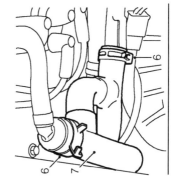
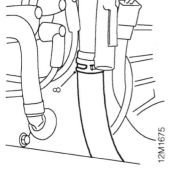

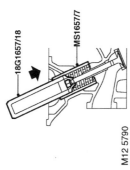

M12 5790

7. Fit tool **18G 1657/18** and tool **MS 1657/T** to valve spring cap.
8. Strike head of tool firmly with hammer to release valve spring collets.
9. Remove collets from magnetic end of tool.
10. Remove valve spring cap and spring.

M12 5820

11. Use tool **18G 1577** to remove valve stem oil seal.
12. Repeat operations to remove second exhaust valve oil seal.

Refit

1. Lubricate new valve stem oil seal with engine oil.
2. Use tool **18G 1577** to fit new oil seals.
3. Fit valve spring and spring cap to each valve.

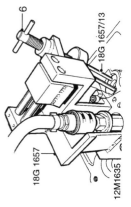

18G 1657

12M1635

4. Assemble tool **18G 1657** over exhaust valve.
5. Locate valve spring cap with compressor tool **18G 1657/13**.
6. Screw down valve spring compressor until valve stem collet groove is level with top face of spring cap.
7. Attach collets to end of a small flat screwdriver with grease and locate collets in valve stem groove.
8. Unscrew valve spring compressor ensuring collets are correctly located in valve spring cap.
9. Slide head of tool **18G 1657** along to second exhaust valve position.
10. Repeat refit operations on second valve.
11. Remove valve spring compressor tool **18G 1657**.
12. Lubricate tappets with clean engine oil and refit in original positions.
13. Disconnect air line from adaptor tool **MS 1567**.
14. Remove air line adaptor tool **MS 1567**.
15. Clean spark plugs and set gaps to 1.00 mm.
16. Fit inlet and exhaust camshafts. **See this section.**
17. Connect battery earth lead.

ENGINE AND MANUAL GEARBOX ASSEMBLY

Service repair no - 12.37.01/99

Remove

1. Disconnect battery earth lead.
2. Remove engine compartment access panel. **See BODY, Exterior fittings. See this section.**
3. Remove engine cover. **See this section.**
4. Drain cooling system. **See COOLING SYSTEM, Adjustments.**

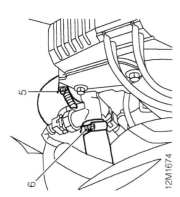

12M1674

5. Release clip securing coolant hose to coolant outlet elbow on cylinder head.

12M1675

6. Release 3 clips securing coolant hose assembly between coolant outlet elbow, heater coolant rail, and feed hose to reservoir.
7. Disconnect hose assembly and position aside.
8. Release clip and hose from coolant rail.

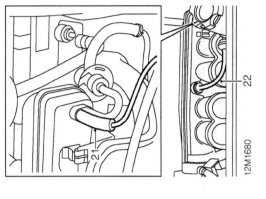

12M1676

9. Release clips securing air intake pipe between air cleaner and throttle body.
10. Remove air intake pipe.

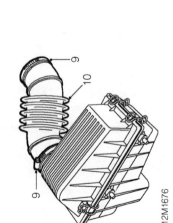

12M1677

11. Remove 'R' clip, washer and clevis pin securing clutch slave cylinder push rod to release lever.
12. Remove clutch slave cylinder push rod.
13. Remove 2 bolts securing clutch slave cylinder to mounting bracket.
14. Position clutch slave cylinder aside.

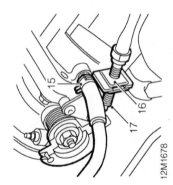

12M1678

15. Release clip and pipe running from cannister purge valve to throttle body.
16. Disconnect throttle cable from throttle body abutment and throttle cam.
17. Release throttle cable from inlet manifold clip and position cable aside.

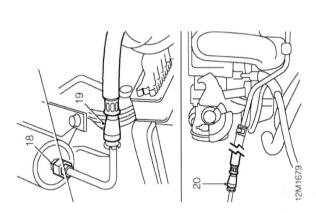

12M1679

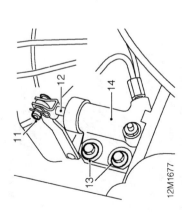

12M1680

18. Position absorbent cloth around fuel filter union. Loosen union to relieve fuel pressure, retighten to 30 Nm.
19. Release fuel feed hose from fuel filter.
20. Release fuel return hose from pipe.
21. Disconnect ECM vacuum pipe from inlet manifold.
22. Release vacuum pipe from inlet manifold.

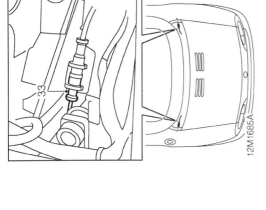

12M1685A

33. Release LH and RH, rear ABS sensor leads from clips and disconnect.

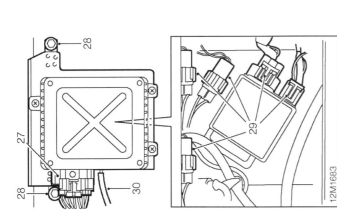

12M1684

31. Disconnect cannister purge valve, multiplug.
32. Remove engine harness earth bolt from body and release 3 earth leads.

12M1683

27. Disconnect multiplug from ECM.
28. Remove inner bolt and loosen outer bolt securing ECM bracket.
29. Disconnect engine harness and relay unit multiplugs.
30. Disconnect vacuum pipe from ECM.

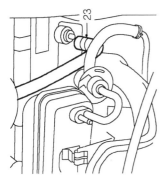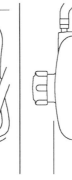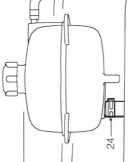

12M1681

23. Release clip and coolant hose from inlet manifold.
24. Release clip and coolant hose from underside of coolant reservoir.

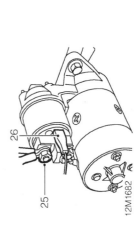

12M1682

25. Remove nut securing starter motor feed lead.
26. Disconnect Lucar from starter motor solenoid and release cable tie from solenoid body.

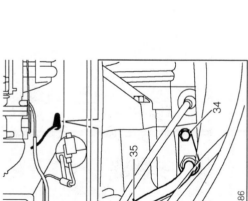

12M1686

34. Remove bolt securing speedometer cable to gearbox.
35. Release speedometer cable from gearbox.
36. Depressurise Hydragas system. **See FRONT SUSPENSION, Adjustments.**
37. Raise vehicle on a 2 post ramp.
38. Remove road wheel(s).

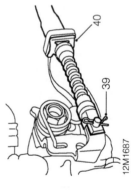

12M1687

39. Remove and discard 'R' clip and remove clevis pin securing LH handbrake cable to caliper.
40. Remove and discard clip securing LH handbrake cable to caliper abutment bracket, release cable and position aside.
41. Remove and discard 'R' clip and remove clevis pin securing RH handbrake cable to caliper.
42. Remove and discard clip securing RH handbrake cable to caliper abutment bracket, release cable and position aside.

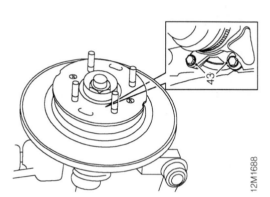

12M1688

43. Remove 2 bolts securing rear LH brake caliper to hub. Release caliper and tie aside.
44. Remove 2 bolts securing rear RH brake caliper to hub. Release caliper and tie aside.
45. Remove silencer heat shield. **See MANIFOLD & EXHAUST SYSTEMS, Repairs.**

12M1689

46. Remove 4 nuts securing anti-roll bar, mounting brackets.

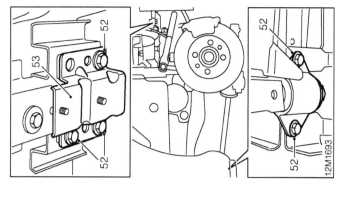

52

53

52

52

52

12M1693

52. Place engine table underneath rear of car, and lower ramp. When engine and rear subframe is supported by table, remove 4 front bolts, and 6 rear bolts securing subframe to body.
53. Collect rear anti-roll bar, mounting brackets.
54. Carefully raise ramp and guide engine and subframe from body.

⚠ **CAUTION: Ensure subframe is securely held on engine table.**

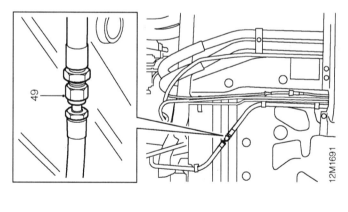

50

50

51

12M1692

50. Release clips securing coolant hoses to coolant rail under vehicle.
51. Release coolant hoses.

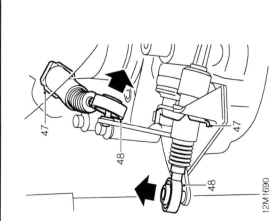

47

48

48

48

12M1690

47. Remove and discard clips securing selector cables to gearbox abutment brackets.
48. Release selector cables from selector linkage and position cables aside.

49

12M1691

49. Disconnect both sides of Hydragas system by breaking union joints under floor pan.

⚠ **CAUTION: Plug the connections.**

Refit

1. Position engine table under body, and carefully lower body onto engine and gearbox assembly.
2. Align subframe to body and loosely fit subframe bolts.

   NOTE: Fit rear anti-roll bar mounting brackets to subframe rear mounting bolts.

3. Carefully lower body remaining distance onto subframe and tighten bolts to;
   Subframe front bolts = 30 Nm.
   Subframe rear bolts = 45 Nm.
4. Raise vehicle and remove engine table.
5. Fit nuts securing anti-roll bar to mounting brackets and tighten to 13 Nm.
6. Fit rear RH brake caliper to hub, fit bolts and tighten to 85 Nm.
7. Fit rear LH brake caliper to hub, fit bolts and tighten to 85 Nm.
8. Position RH handbrake cable to caliper and secure with clevis pin and NEW 'R' clip.
9. Fit NEW spring clip securing RH handbrake cable to caliper abutment bracket.
10. Position LH handbrake cable to caliper and secure with clevis pin and NEW 'R' clip.
11. Fit NEW spring clip securing LH handbrake cable to caliper abutment bracket.
12. Fit silencer heat shield. **See MANIFOLD & EXHAUST SYSTEMS, Repairs.**
13. Fit selector cables to gearbox abutment brackets and secure with NEW spring clips.
14. Clean Hydragas pipe unions.
15. Lubricate NEW 'O' rings and fit to Hydragas pipe unions.
16. Connect Hydragas pipes under floorpan and tighten to 20 Nm.
17. Fit pipes to coolant rail on underside of vehicle and secure with clips.
18. Fit road wheel(s) and tighten nuts to correct torque. *See INFORMATION, Torque wrench settings.*
19. Lower vehicle.
20. Lubricate NEW 'O' ring and fit to speedometer cable.
21. Fit speedometer cable to gearbox and tighten bolt to 19 Nm.
22. Connect LH and RH ABS sensor leads.
23. Position engine harness earth leads to body, fit earth bolt and tighten.
24. Connect cannister purge valve multiplug.
25. Connect vacuum pipe to ECM.
26. Connect engine harness and relay unit multiplugs.
27. Fit ECM bracket and tighten bolts to 8 Nm.
28. Connect ECM multiplug.

29. Fit Lucar and starter motor feed lead to solenoid and tighten nut.
30. Secure cables to solenoid body with cable tie.
31. Connect coolant hose to underside of reservoir and secure with clip.
32. Connect coolant hose to inlet manifold and secure with clip.
33. Connect vacuum pipe to inlet manifold.
34. Connect vacuum pipe between inlet manifold and ECM.
35. Connect fuel return hose to fuel pipe.
36. Connect fuel feed hose to fuel filter.
37. Connect throttle cable to throttle cam and abutment.
38. Secure throttle cable to clip on inlet manifold.
39. Connect pipe from cannister purge valve to throttle body and secure with clip.
40. Fit bolts securing clutch slave cylinder to mounting bracket.
41. Fit push rod to clutch slave cylinder.
42. Fit clevis pin and washer between push rod and release lever and secure with 'R' clip.
43. Fit air intake pipe and secure with clips.
44. Connect hose to coolant rail and secure with clip.
45. Connect hose assembly between coolant outlet elbow, heater coolant rail, and feed hose to coolant reservoir, and secure with clips.
46. Connect hose to coolant outlet elbow and secure with clip.
47. Refill coolant system. **See COOLING SYSTEM, Adjustments.**
48. Fit engine cover. **See this section.**
49. Fit engine compartment access panel. **See BODY, Exterior fittings.**
50. Connect battery earth lead.
51. Pressurise Hydragas system and set correct trim height. *See FRONT SUSPENSION, Adjustments.*

ENGINE AND GEARBOX ASSEMBLY - SEQUENTIAL AUTO (EM-CVT)

Service repair no - 12.37.01/99

Remove

1. Disconnect battery earth lead.
2. Remove engine compartment access panel. **See BODY, Exterior fittings. See this section.**
3. Remove engine cover. **See this section.**
4. Drain transmission fluid. **See AUTOMATIC GEARBOX - 'EM-CVT', Adjustments.**
5. Drain cooling system. **See COOLING SYSTEM, Adjustments.**
6. Models with A/C: Evacuate A/C system. **See AIR CONDITIONING, Adjustments.**
7. Release clips securing air intake pipe between air cleaner and throttle body.
8. Remove air intake pipe.

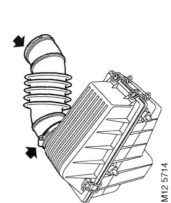

M12 5714

9. Release clip and pipe running from evaporative emission cannister purge valve to throttle body.
10. Disconnect throttle cable from throttle body abutment and throttle cam.
11. Release throttle cable from inlet manifold clip and position cable aside.

M12 5715

12. Position absorbent cloth around fuel filter, loosen union to relieve fuel pressure, retighten to 30 Nm.
13. Release quick release connector securing fuel pipe to injector rail hose.
14. Evacuate hydragas system. *See SUSPENSION, Adjustments.*

M12 5716

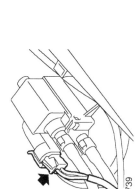

M12 5717

15. Loosen unions on hydragas units and release pipes, remove and discard 'O' rings.

⚠ **CAUTION: Plug the connections.**

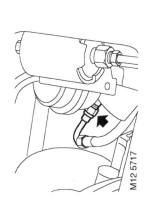

M12 5718

16. Release vacuum pipe from inlet manifold.
17. Release clip and coolant hose from inlet manifold.
18. Release clip and coolant hose from coolant rail.

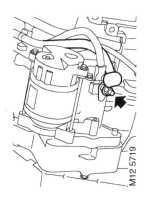

M12 5719

19. Remove nut securing starter motor feed lead.

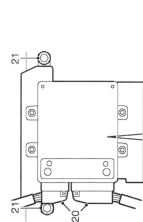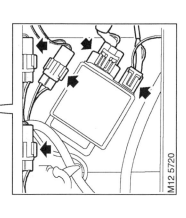

M12 5720

20. Disconnect multiplugs from ECM.
21. Remove inner bolt and loosen outer bolt securing ECM bracket.
22. Disconnect engine harness and relay unit multiplugs.

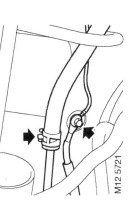

M12 5739

23. Disconnect cannister purge valve multiplug.

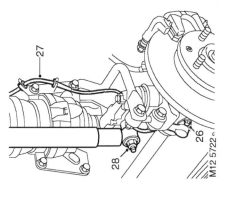

M12 5721

24. Remove engine harness earth bolt from body and release 2 earth leads.
25. Disconnect fuel return hose.

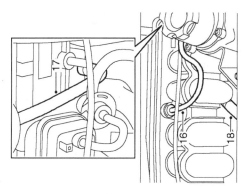

M12 5722

26. Raise vehicle on a 2 post ramp.
27. Remove road wheel(s).
28. Remove 2 bolts securing ABS sensors, release sensors and collect sensor spacers.
29. Release LH and RH rear ABS sensor leads from clips.
30. Remove nuts and bolts securing dampers to upper arms.

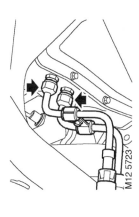

M12 5723

31. Loosen unions and disconnect fluid cooler pipes from gearbox.

⚠ **CAUTION: Plug the connections.**

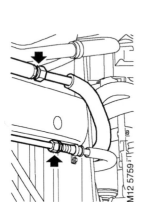

M12 5724

32. Remove 2 bolts securing rear LH brake caliper to hub. Release caliper and tie aside.
33. Remove 2 bolts securing rear RH brake caliper to hub. Release caliper and tie aside.
34. Remove tail pipe heat shield. **See MANIFOLD & EXHAUST SYSTEMS, Repairs.**

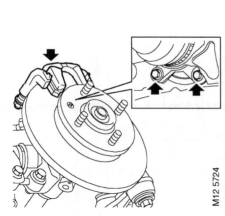

M12 5725

35. Remove 4 nuts securing anti-roll bar bushes to body.

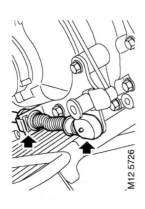

M12 5726

36. Release selector cable from selector linkage.
37. Release selector cable from abutment bracket and position cable aside.

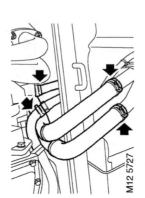

M12 5727

38. Release clips securing coolant hoses to coolant rail under vehicle, and release hoses.
39. Release clips securing heater hoses under vehicle and release hoses.

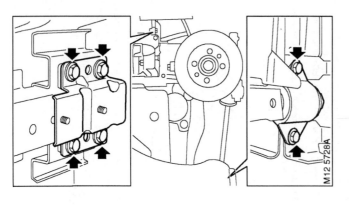

M12 5759

40. **Models with A/C:** Loosen A/C pipe unions under vehicle and release pipes.

CAUTION: Immediately cap all air conditioning pipes to prevent ingress of dirt and moisture into the system.

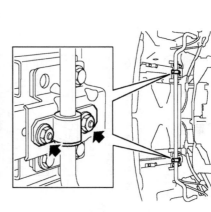

M12 5728A

41. Place engine table underneath rear of car, and lower ramp. When engine and rear subframe are supported by table, remove 4 front bolts, and 6 rear bolts securing subframe to body.
42. Collect rear anti-roll bar mounting brackets.
43. Carefully raise ramp and guide engine and subframe from body.

CAUTION: Ensure subframe is securely held on engine table.

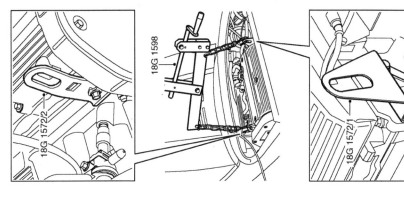

18G 1598

18G 1572/2

18G 1572/1

M12 5735

58. Fit lifting brackets **18G 1572/1** and **18G 1572/2** to cylinder head and tighten bolts to 9 Nm.

59. Fit adjustable lifting equipment **18G 1598** to lifting brackets.

60. Connect hoist to **18G 1598** and raise hoist to take weight of engine and gearbox.

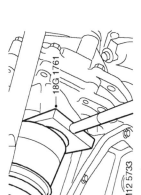

18G 1761

M12 5733

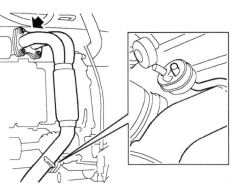

M12 5734

53. Using tool **18G 1761**, release drive shaft from differential.

54. Remove hub assembly and drive shaft.

55. Repeat hub assembly and drive shaft removal for opposite hand.

56. Remove nuts securing exhaust manifold to front pipe.

57. Release front pipe from exhaust manifold and support rubber and remove front pipe. Collect gasket.

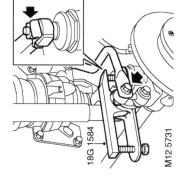

18G 1584

M12 5731

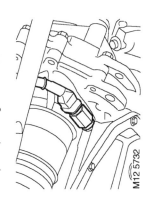

M12 5732

47. Remove bolt securing anti-roll bar link to anti-roll bar.

48. Bend back tab washer on upper ball joint.

49. Remove nut and tab washer securing upper ball joint to hub, discard tab washer.

50. With the hub assembly supported, break upper ball joint taper using tool **18G 1584.**

51. Disconnect multiplug from starter inhibitor/reverse switch and release lead from clip.

52. Remove inhibitor/reverse switch from gearbox.

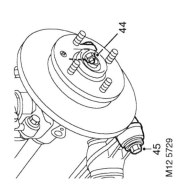

44

45

M12 5729

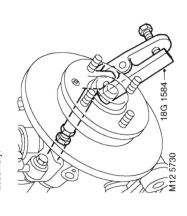

18G 1584

M12 5730

44. Remove bolt securing lower arm to hub assembly.

45. Release nut securing track control rod to hub assembly.

46. Release taper joint using tool **18G 1584.**

M12 5736

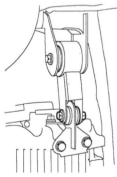

61. Remove nut and bolt securing gearbox mounting to buttress.

M12 5737

62. Remove 4 bolts securing RH buttress to sub frame.

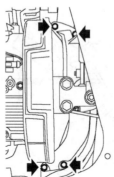

M12 5738

63. Remove bolt securing rear engine steady to bracket on sump.

64. With assistance, raise and remove engine and gearbox assembly, from subframe.

65. Lower engine and gearbox assembly, disconnect hoist from **18G 1598.**

Refit

1. Connect hoist to **18G 1598** and raise engine assembly.

2. Position subframe assembly under engine.

3. Lower engine assembly onto subframe, align RH buttress and LH engine mounting.

4. Fit RH buttress bolts and tighten to 45 Nm.

5. Fit nut and bolt securing gearbox mounting to RH buttress and tighten to 82 Nm.

6. Position rear engine steady to bracket on sump and tighten bolt to 85 Nm.

7. Lower hoist and remove **18G 1598**, remove lifting brackets **18G 1572/1** and **18G 1572/2.**

8. Using a new gasket, position exhaust front pipe, engage front pipe to support rubber, fit exhaust manifold to front pipe flange nuts and tighten to 70 Nm.

9. Clean end of both drive shafts.

10. Lubricate differential oil seals.

11. Wipe taper joints of both hub ball joints and upper arms.

12. Fit both hub assemblies to upper arms and engage both drive shafts to differential.

13. Fit lock washers to upper ball joint pins and tighten nuts to 54 Nm.

14. Bend lock washers upward to lock nuts.

NOTE: Pull outwards on drive shaft inboard joints to check for full engagement.

15. Align both hubs to lower arms and tighten bolts to 100 Nm.

16. Wipe tapers and seats of track control arms and hubs.

17. Fit track control arms to hubs and tighten nuts to 30 Nm.

18. Fit inhibitor/reverse switch and tighten to 12 Nm.

19. Connect multiplug to inhibitor/reverse switch and secure lead to clip.

20. Position engine table under body, and carefully lower onto engine and gearbox assembly.

21. Align subframe to body and loosely fit bolts.

NOTE: Fit rear anti-roll bar mounting brackets to subframe rear mounting bolts.

22. Carefully lower body remaining distance onto subframe and tighten bolts to;
Subframe front bolts = 30 Nm.
Subframe rear bolts = 45 Nm.

23. Raise vehicle and remove engine table.

24. Fit bolts securing anti-roll bar to mounting brackets and tighten to 22 Nm.

25. Fit rear anti-roll bar to anti-roll bar links, fit bolts and tighten to 35 Nm.

26. Connect dampers to upper arms, fit bolts and tighten to 45 Nm.

27. Clean brake caliper mating faces.

28. Fit rear RH brake caliper to hub, fit bolts and tighten to 85 Nm.

29. Fit rear LH brake caliper to hub. fit bolts and tighten to 85 Nm.

30. Clean ABS sensors and mating faces.

31. Fit ABS sensors and spacers, fit bolts and tighten to 10 Nm.

32. Secure ABS leads in clips.

33. Fit tail pipe heat shield. *See MANIFOLD & EXHAUST SYSTEMS, Repairs.*

34. Clean oil cooler pipe ends and mating faces.

35. Connect and tighten oil cooler pipe unions.

36. Fit selector cables to gearbox abutment brackets and secure with spring clips.

37. Clean hydragas pipe unions.

38. Fit new 'O' ring seals to hydragas pipe unions.

39. Connect hydragas pipes to hydragas units and tighten to 20 Nm.

40. **Models with A/C:** Connect A/C pipes and tighten unions.

41. Fit hoses to coolant rail on underside of vehicle and secure with clips.

42. Connect heater hoses and secure with clips.

43. Fit road wheel(s) and tighten nuts to correct torque. *See INFORMATION, Torque wrench settings.*

44. Lower vehicle.

45. Fit road speed transducer multiplug.

46. Position engine harness earth leads to body, fit and tighten earth lead bolt.

47. Connect fuel return hose.

48. Connect EVAP cannister purge valve multiplug.

49. Connect engine harness and relay unit multiplugs.

50. Fit ECM bracket and tighten bolts to 8 Nm.

51. Connect ECM multiplugs.
52. Fit starter motor feed lead to starter motor and tighten nut.
53. Connect coolant hose to inlet manifold and secure with clip.
54. Connect vacuum pipe to inlet manifold.
55. Connect fuel pipe to injector rail.
56. Connect throttle cable to throttle cam and abutment.
57. Secure throttle cable to clip on inlet manifold.
58. Connect pipe from EVAP cannister purge valve to throttle body and secure with clip.
59. Fit air intake pipe and secure with clips.
60. Connect hose to coolant rail and secure with clip.
61. Refill cooling system. **See COOLING SYSTEM, Adjustments.**
62. **Models with A/C:** Recharge A/C system. **See AIR CONDITIONING, Adjustments.**
63. Refill transmission with fluid. **See AUTOMATIC GEARBOX - 'EM-CVT', Adjustments.**
64. Fit engine cover. **See this section.**
65. Fit engine compartment access panel. **See BODY, Exterior fittings.**
66. Connect battery earth lead.
67. Pressurise hydragas system and set correct trim height. **See SUSPENSION, Adjustments.**

ENGINE COVER

Service repair no - 12.37.04/99

Remove

1. Remove hoodwell trim. **See BODY, Interior trim components.**
2. Remove sound deadener pad.

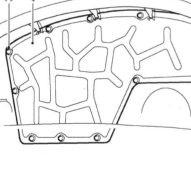

12M1394

3. Remove 11 bolts securing engine cover.
4. Remove engine cover.

Refit

1. Position cover and secure with bolts.
2. Fit sound deadener pad.
3. Fit hoodwell trim. **See BODY, Interior trim components.**

ENGINE MOUNTING - REAR

Service repair no - 12.45.17

Remove

1. Raise rear of vehicle.

   WARNING: Support on safety stands.

2. Support engine on jack.

   CAUTION: Place block of wood between sump and jack to avoid damage occurring.

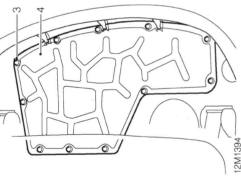

12M1516

3. Remove nut and bolt securing mounting to sump.
4. Remove bolt securing mounting to subframe.
5. Remove mounting.

Refit

1. Position mounting to subframe, fit bolt but do not tighten.
2. Align mounting to sump bracket, fit bolt and tighten to 85 Nm.
3. Tighten bolt securing mounting to subframe to 85 Nm.
4. Remove jack.
5. Remove stand(s) and lower vehicle.

ENGINE MOUNTING - LH - MANUAL GEARBOX MODELS

Service repair no - 12.45.11

Remove

1. Support engine with jack.

   CAUTION: Place a piece of wood between engine and jack to avoid damage.

2. If fitted, remove air intake resonator. **See ENGINE MANAGEMENT SYSTEM - MEMS, Repairs.**

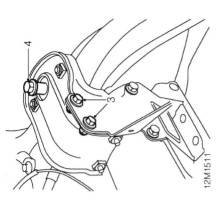

12M1511

3. Remove 2 upper bolts securing clutch slave cylinder bracket to engine mounting bracket.
4. Remove centre bolt from engine mounting.

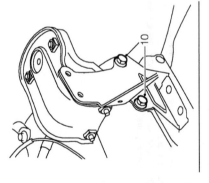

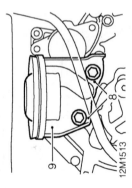

12M1513

8. Remove 2 bolts securing engine mounting bracket to gearbox.
9. Remove engine mounting and bracket.
10. Remove 2 bolts securing mounting to bracket.

Refit

1. Fit engine mounting to bracket and tighten bolts to 45 Nm.
2. Fit engine mounting and bracket to gearbox, fit bolts and tighten to 45 Nm.
3. Fit buttress to subframe and tighten bolts to 45 Nm.
4. Lower engine onto buttress, fit centre bolt and tighten to 82 Nm.
5. Fit bolts securing clutch slave cylinder bracket to engine mounting bracket.
6. Fit air intake resonator (if fitted). *See ENGINE MANAGEMENT SYSTEM - MEMS, Repairs.*
7. Remove jack.

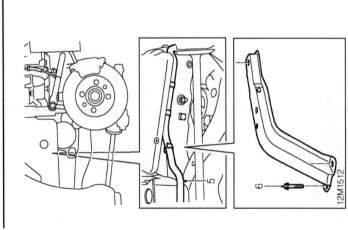

12M1512

5. Release Hydragas pipe from buttress.
6. Remove 4 bolts securing buttress to subframe.
7. Raise height of engine to remove buttress.

ENGINE MOUNTING - LH - STEPTRONIC (EM-CVT) MODELS

Service repair no - 12.45.11

Remove

1. Raise vehicle on a 2 post ramp.
2. Remove LH rear road wheel.
3. Support weight of engine with hydraulic jack.

⚠ NOTE: Place a piece of wood between engine and jack to avoid damage.

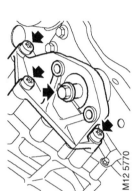

M12 5767

4. If fitted, remove 2 bolts securing air intake resonator to body and release resonator. Collect metal inserts
5. Remove air cleaner. *See ENGINE MANAGEMENT SYSTEM - MEMS, Repairs.*

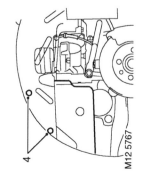

M12 5768

6. Release 3 cables from air cleaner support bracket.

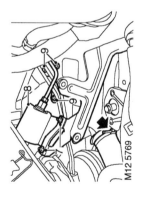

M12 5769

7. Remove 2 nuts securing fuel filter to air cleaner support bracket.
8. Release fuel filter from support bracket and position aside.
9. Remove 3 bolts securing air cleaner support bracket to body and remove bracket.
10. Loosen clip securing air intake hose to resonator and release hose from resonator.
11. Depressurise LH side of hydragas system. *See SUSPENSION, Adjustments.*

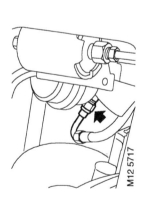

M12 5717

12. Loosen union on hydragas unit, release pipe, remove and discard 'O' ring.

⚠ CAUTION: Plug the connections.

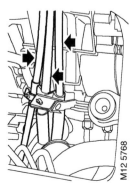

M12 5770

13. Remove nut and bolt securing engine mounting to buttress.
14. Raise engine on jack to access engine mounting bolts.
15. Remove 3 Torx bolts securing engine mounting to gearbox and remove mounting.

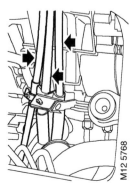

M12 5771

16. Remove 2 bolts securing mounting to bracket.

Refit

1. Fit engine mounting to bracket and tighten bolts to 45 Nm.
2. Fit engine mounting to gearbox and tighten Torx bolts to 48 Nm.
3. Lower engine and align engine mounting to buttress.
4. Fit and tighten nut and bolt securing LH mounting to buttress to 82 Nm.
5. Fit new 'O' ring to pipe and connect to hydragas unit.
6. Tighten hydragas union to 20 Nm.
7. Connect air intake hose to resonator and secure with clip.
8. Position air cleaner support bracket, fit and tighten bolts.
9. Connect cables to clips.
10. Fit fuel filter to support bracket and secure with nuts.
11. If fitted, position resonator to fixing holes, fit spacers and secure with bolts.
12. Fit air cleaner. *See ENGINE MANAGEMENT SYSTEM - MEMS, Repairs.*
13. Fit road wheel(s) and tighten nuts to correct torque. *See INFORMATION, General data.*
14. Remove stand(s) and lower vehicle.
15. Pressurise hydragas system and set correct trim height. *See SUSPENSION, Adjustments.*

23. Remove engine mounting.
24. Collect arm from mounting.

Refit

1. Position arm on engine mounting.
2. Fit engine mounting and restraining loop to buttress. Tighten bolts to 45 Nm.
3. Position buttress assembly to subframe and manoeuvre into position.
4. Fit bolts securing buttress assembly and tighten to 45 Nm.
5. Secure hydragas pipe to clips.
6. Fit nut to engine mounting centre bolt but do not tighten.
7. Fit nut and bolt securing tie rod to buttress but do not tighten.
8. Fit bolts securing arm assembly to engine and tighten to 45 Nm.
9. Tighten engine mounting centre bolt nut to 82 Nm.
10. Tighten bolt securing tie rod to buttress to 85 Nm.
11. Secure vacuum pipe to clips.
12. Fit alternator drive belt and adjust tension. *See ELECTRICAL, Adjustments.*
13. **Models with A/C:** Position compressor and tighten bolts to 45 Nm.
14. Fit alternator drive belt. *See ELECTRICAL, Repairs.*
15. **All models:** Remove jack.
16. Position closing panel, secure with scrivets and Torx screw.
17. Fit road wheel(s) and tighten nuts to correct torque.
18. Remove stand and lower vehicle.
19. Fit engine cover. *See this section.*

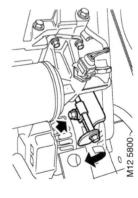

M12 5765

14. **All models:** Release vacuum pipe from clips on body.
15. Remove nut from engine mounting centre bolt.
16. Remove 2 bolts securing arm assembly to engine.
17. Remove nut and bolt securing tie rod to buttress.
18. Remove 4 bolts securing buttress to subframe.

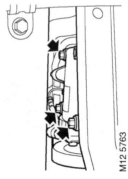

M12 5764

19. Release hydragas pipe from buttress clips and position pipe aside.
20. Manoeuvre buttress and engine mount assembly from wheel arch.

M12 5766

21. Remove 2 bolts securing engine mounting to buttress.
22. Collect restraining loop.

ENGINE MOUNTING - RH

Service repair no - 12.45.12

Remove

1. Raise RH rear of vehicle.

⚠️ **WARNING: Support on safety stand.**

2. Remove RH rear road wheel.
3. Remove 2 scrivets and 1 Torx screw securing closing panel.
4. Remove closing panel.
5. Support engine on jack.

⚠️ NOTE: Place block of wood between jack and engine sump to avoid damage occurring.

6. Remove engine cover. *See this section.*

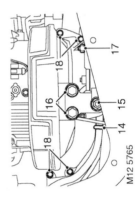

M12 5807

7. Loosen alternator pivot nut and bolt.

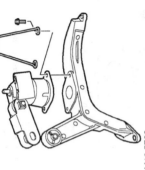

M12 5808

8. Loosen bolt securing alternator adjustment bracket.

M12 5800

9. Loosen bolt securing alternator to adjustment bracket.
10. Rotate alternator drive belt adjustment bolt anti-clockwise to release tension from belt.
11. Release and remove drive belt from pulleys.
12. **Models with A/C:** Remove alternator drive belt. *See ELECTRICAL, Repairs.*

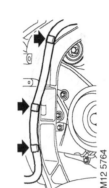

M12 5763

13. Loosen 3 bolts securing A/C compressor to mounting bracket and position compressor aside.

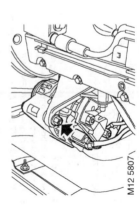

FLYWHEEL - MANUAL GEARBOX MODELS

Service repair no - 12.53.07

Remove

1. Remove gearbox. **See MANUAL GEARBOX, Repairs.**
2. Fit flywheel locking tool **18G 1571** to cylinder head and secure with bolts.
3. Remove crankshaft position sensor. **See ENGINE MANAGEMENT SYSTEM - MEMS, Repairs.**

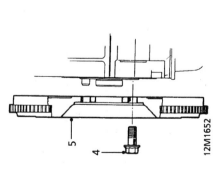

12M1652

4. Remove and discard 6 bolts securing flywheel to crankshaft.
5. Remove flywheel from crankshaft.

Refit

1. Using a tap, clean adhesive from threads of flywheel bolt holes in crankshaft.
2. Clean flywheel and mating face of crankshaft.
3. Fit flywheel to crankshaft.
4. Fit NEW bolts securing flywheel to crankshaft and working in a diagonal sequence tighten bolts to 85 Nm.
5. Fit crankshaft position sensor. **See ENGINE MANAGEMENT SYSTEM - MEMS, Repairs.**
6. Remove bolts securing flywheel locking tool **18G 1571**, remove tool.
7. Fit gearbox. **See MANUAL GEARBOX, Repairs.**

FLYWHEEL - STEPTRONIC (EM-CVT) MODELS

Service repair no - 12.53.07

Remove

1. Remove torsion damper. **See this section.**

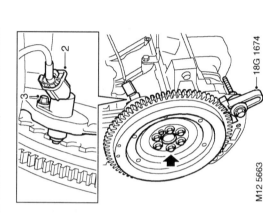

M12 5663

2. Disconnect multiplug from CKP sensor.
3. Remove bolt securing CKP sensor to cylinder block and remove sensor.
4. Fit flywheel locking tool **18G 1674** to sump and secure with bolt.
5. Remove and discard 6 bolts securing flywheel to crankshaft.
6. Remove flywheel locking tool **18G 1674.**
7. Remove flywheel from crankshaft.

Refit

1. Clean bolt holes in crankshaft using an old flywheel bolt with two saw cuts at an angle of 45° to the bolt shank.
2. Clean flywheel and mating face of crankshaft.
3. Fit flywheel to crankshaft.
4. Fit new bolts, but do not tighten at this stage.
5. Fit flywheel locking tool **18G 1674** and secure with bolt.
6. Working in a diagonal sequence tighten flywheel bolts to 85 Nm.
7. Remove flywheel locking tool **18G 1674.**
8. Fit CKP sensor to cylinder block, fit bolt and tighten to 6 Nm.
9. Connect multiplug to CKP sensor.
10. Fit torsion damper. **See this section.**

TORSION DAMPER - STEPTRONIC (EM-CVT) MODELS

Service repair no - 12.53.13

Remove

1. Remove automatic gearbox assembly. *See AUTOMATIC GEARBOX - 'EM-CVT', Repairs.*

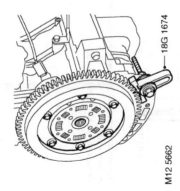

M12 5662

2. Fit flywheel locking tool 18G 1674 to sump and tighten bolt.
3. Progressively loosen and then remove 6 bolts securing torsion damper to flywheel.
4. Remove torsion damper.

Refit

1. Clean torsion damper and flywheel mating faces.
2. Position torsion damper to flywheel, fit bolts but do not tighten at this stage.
3. Working in a diagonal sequence, progressively tighten bolts to 22 Nm.
4. Remove bolt securing flywheel locking tool and remove tool.
5. Refit automatic gearbox assembly. *See AUTOMATIC GEARBOX - 'EM-CVT', Repairs.*

FLYWHEEL STARTER RING GEAR

Service repair no - 12.53.19

Remove

1. Remove flywheel. *See this section.*

12M1460

2. Apply a cold chisel in root of one of ring gear teeth, strike chisel with hammer to break ring gear.
3. Remove starter ring gear.

Refit

1. Clean flywheel and NEW starter ring gear.
2. Heat new starter ring gear evenly to approximately 350°C, indicated when the ring is a light blue colour.
3. Locate ring gear on flywheel and press ring gear hard against flange on flywheel.
4. Ensure ring gear is correctly seated around the complete circumference of flywheel and allow to cool.
5. Fit flywheel. *See this section.*

TORSION DAMPER - STEPTRONIC (EM-CVT) MODELS

Service repair no - 12.60.25

Remove

1. Remove camshaft timing belt. *See this section.*

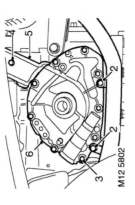

M12 5802

2. Remove 2 bolts securing engine harness to oil pump and move harness clear of pump.
3. Remove 9 bolts securing oil pump to cylinder block.
4. Remove lower bolt from timing belt rear cover.
5. Release rear cover to facilitate pump removal.
6. Remove pump and discard gasket.

Refit

1. Clean oil pump bolt holes in cylinder block.
2. Clean oil seal running surface on crankshaft.
3. Fit new oil pump gasket to cylinder block, align and fit oil pump.

⚠ **CAUTION: Do not lubricate crankshaft front oil seal or running surface of crankshaft.**

OIL FILTER

Service repair no - 12.60.04

Remove

1. Raise rear of vehicle.

⚠ **WARNING: Support on safety stands.**

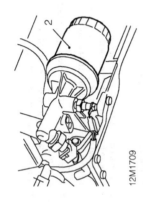

12M1709

2. Clean area around filter head and place a container beneath engine.
3. Using a strap wrench, unscrew and discard filter.

Refit

1. Clean mating face of filter head.
2. Lubricate sealing ring of new filter with clean engine oil.
3. Fit NEW filter and tighten by hand until it seats then tighten a further half turn.
4. Remove stand(s) and lower vehicle.
5. Top up engine with oil to specification 10w/40 until level is correct.
6. Start and run engine and check for oil leaks.
7. Stop engine, wait a few minutes, then check oil level. Top up if necessary.

OIL SUMP

Service repair no - 12.60.38

Remove

1. Remove exhaust front pipe. **See MANIFOLD & EXHAUST SYSTEMS, Repairs.**
2. Drain engine oil. **See MAINTENANCE.**

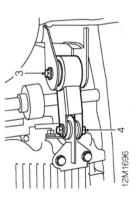

12M1696

3. Loosen bolt securing engine rear mount to subframe.
4. Remove nut and bolt securing engine rear mount to engine.

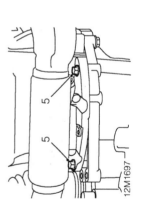

12M1697

5. Remove 2 bolts securing oil sump to gearbox.

12M1698

6. Remove 14 bolts securing oil sump to bearing ladder noting the fitted positions of 2 longest bolts.
7. Using a mallet, gently tap sump sideways to release sealant bond; remove sump.

> **CAUTION: Do not lever between sump flange and bearing ladder.**
>
> *Do not carry out further dismantling if component is removed for access only.*

Refit

1. Clean inside of sump. Remove all traces of sealant using a suitable solvent.
2. Apply sealant from kit, Part No. GUG 705963GM to sump joint face and spread to an even film using a brush or roller.

> **CAUTION: To avoid contamination, assembly should be completed immediately after application of sealant. Do not use RTV or any sealant other than that supplied with kit.**

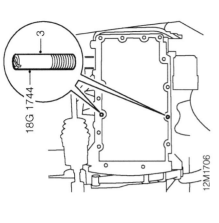

12M1706

3. Fit sump alignment pins **18G 1744** to bearing ladder as shown.

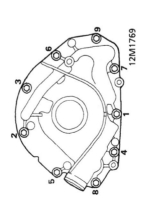

12M1769

4. Fit new Patchlok bolts and tighten in sequence shown to 10 Nm.
5. Fit and tighten bolt securing timing belt rear cover to 9 Nm.
6. Align engine harness to oil pump, fit bolts and tighten to 10 Nm.
7. Fit camshaft timing belt. **See this section.**

8. Remove 4 bolts securing engine rear mount to sump, remove mount.
9. Fit mount to sump, fit bolts and tighten to 80 Nm.

12M1699

4. Position sump to alignment pins, fit 2 bolts at positions 5 and 6, tighten bolts to 4 Nm.
5. Fit 10 bolts into remaining holes ensuring that 2 longest bolts are in original fitted positions, finger tighten bolts.
6. Remove alignment pins **18G 1744,** fit and finger tighten remaining 2 bolts.
7. Progressively tighten sump bolts in sequence shown to 25 Nm.
   Tighten sump to gearbox bolts to 45 Nm.
8. Position engine rear mount to subframe, fit bolt and tighten to 85 Nm.
9. Tighten engine rear mount to oil sump bolt to 80 Nm.
10. Fit exhaust front pipe. **See MANIFOLD & EXHAUST SYSTEMS, Repairs.**
11. Fill engine with oil. **See MAINTENANCE.**

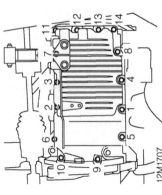

12M1707

SWITCH - OIL PRESSURE

Service repair no - 12.60.50

Remove

1. Disconnect battery earth lead.
2. Raise rear of vehicle.

 WARNING: Support on safety stands.

3. Position container below engine oil filter to collect spillage.

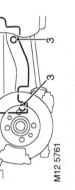

12M1705

4. Disconnect multiplug from oil pressure switch.
5. Remove oil pressure switch.

Refit

1. Clean oil pressure switch threads.
2. Fit oil pressure switch and tighten to 12 Nm.
3. Connect multiplug to oil pressure switch.
4. Remove stand(s) and lower vehicle.
5. Top-up engine oil. **See MAINTENANCE.**
6. Connect battery earth lead.

OIL PRESSURE RELIEF VALVE

Service repair no - 12.60.56

Remove

1. Raise rear of vehicle.

WARNING: Support on safety stands.

2. Remove road wheel(s).

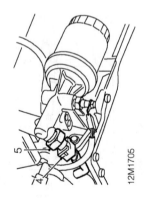

M12 5761

3. Remove 2 scrivets and Torx screw securing closing panel to subframe.
4. Remove closing panel.

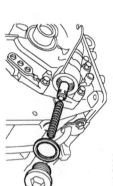

M12 5804

5. Remove relief valve sealing plug and sealing washer.
6. Remove spring and relief valve.

Refit

1. Clean oil pump housing.
2. Clean valve spring, valve and sealing washer.
3. Lubricate relief valve. Fit valve and spring.
4. Fit new sealing washer, fit and tighten sealing plug to 25 Nm.
5. Fit closing panel and secure with fixings.
6. Fit road wheel(s) and tighten nuts to correct torque. **See INFORMATION, General data.**
7. Remove stand(s) and lower vehicle.
8. Check and top up oil level **See MAINTENANCE.**

SENSOR - OIL TEMPERATURE

Service repair no - 12.60.65

Remove

1. Disconnect battery earth lead.
2. Raise rear of vehicle.

WARNING: Support on safety stands.

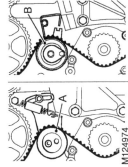

M12 5782

3. Disconnect multiplug from oil temperature sensor.
4. Position drain tin below switch to catch oil spillage.
5. Remove oil temperature sensor.

Refit

1. Clean oil temperature sensor threads.
2. Fit oil temperature sensor and tighten to 15 Nm.
3. Connect multiplug to oil temperature sensor.
4. Remove stand(s) and lower vehicle.
5. Connect battery earth lead.
6. Check and if necessary top up engine oil.

CAMSHAFT TIMING BELT - MPi MEMS 1.9 (UP TO 2000MY)

Service repair no - 12.65.18

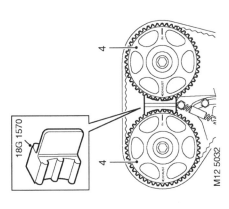

M124974

NOTE: Two types of timing belt tensioner are fitted, type A is a manual tensioner, type B is an automatic tensioner. The tensioners and their timing belts are not interchangeable.

⚠ **CAUTION: Timing belts must be replaced if cylinder head is to be removed or new timing gears, tensioner or coolant pump are to be fitted.**
Timing belts must be stored and handled with care.
Always store a timing belt on its edge with a bend radius greater than 50 mm.
Do not use a timing belt that has been twisted or bent double as this can damage the reinforcing fibres.
Do not use a timing belt if debris other than belt dust is found in timing cover.
Do not use a timing belt if partial engine seizure has occurred.
Do not use a timing belt if belt mileage exceeds 48,000 (77,000 km).
Do not use an oil or coolant contaminated timing belt.

⚠ NOTE: The cause of contamination MUST be rectified.

ENGINE

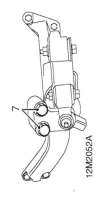

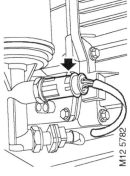

12M2052A

7. Remove 2 bolts securing RH mounting bracket to engine.

Removal - Engines fitted with manual timing belt tensioner

1. Disconnect battery earth lead.
2. Raise front of vehicle.

⚠ **WARNING: Support on safety stands.**

3. Remove timing belt upper front cover. *See this section.*

18G 1570

M12 5032

4. Using a socket and extension bar on crankshaft pulley bolt, rotate crankshaft clockwise and align camshaft gear timing marks with mark on backplate - 90° BTDC.

⚠ **CAUTION: Do not use camshaft gears, gear retaining bolts or timing belt to rotate crankshaft.**

5. Fit camshaft gear locking tool 18G 1570.
6. Support engine on a jack.

⚠ **CAUTION: Place a block of wood between engine and jack to avoid damaging sump.**

8. Remove camshaft timing belt lower front cover. *See this section.*

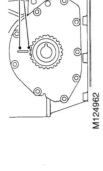

M12 5031

9. If camshaft timing belt is to be reused, mark position of tensioner backplate to cylinder head. Mark direction of rotation on belt using chalk.

10. Loosen tensioner pulley Allen screw ½ turn.
11. Loosen tensioner backplate bolt ½ turn.
12. Push tensioner pulley down to fully OFF position and tighten backplate bolt to 10 Nm.
13. Lower engine to allow clearance between RH mounting bracket and engine.
14. Remove camshaft timing belt.

> CAUTION: **Ease timing belt from the gears using the fingers only, metal levers may damage the belt and gears.**
>
> **Do not rotate the crankshaft with the timing belt removed and the cylinder head fitted.**

Refit - Engines fitted with manual timing belt tensioner

1. Clean crankshaft pulley, timing belt gears, coolant pump drive gear and tensioner pulley.

> CAUTION: **If the sintered gears have been subjected to prolonged oil contamination, they must be soaked in a solvent bath and then thoroughly washed in clean solvent before refitting. Because of the porous construction of sintered material, oil impregnated in the gears will emerge and contaminate the belt.**

18G 1570

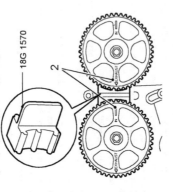

M124961

2. Check correct alignment of camshaft timing marks for 90° BTDC and that tool **18G 1570** is locking camshaft gears.

Tensioning replacement timing belt

18. Loosen tensioner backplate bolt and tension timing belt by applying finger pressure to backplate and pushing tensioner pulley against belt.
19. Hold tensioner in this position and tighten backplate bolt to 10 Nm.
20. Rotate crankshaft clockwise 2 complete revolutions and align camshaft timing gear marks.

> CAUTION: **Do not use camshaft gears, gear retaining bolts or timing belt to rotate crankshaft.**

21. Loosen backplate bolt and check that belt tension is being applied by tensioner spring.
22. Tighten tensioner backplate bolt to 10 Nm.
23. Tighten tensioner pulley Allen bolt to 45 Nm.

All timing belts

24. Fit camshaft timing belt upper front cover. *See this section.*
25. Remove stand(s) and lower vehicle.
26. Connect battery earth lead.

M124962

3. Ensure dots on crankshaft gear are aligned with flange on oil pump and that tool is locking flywheel.
4. Loosen tensioner backplate bolt and ensure tensioner moves freely through its adjustment range and returns under spring tension.
5. Push tensioner down to OFF position and tighten backplate bolt to 10 Nm.
6. Using fingers only, fit timing belt, ensure belt run between the crankshaft gear and the exhaust camshaft gear is kept taut during the fitting procedure.

> CAUTION: **If the original belt is to be refitted, ensure the direction of rotation mark is facing the correct way.**

7. Check that timing belt is positioned centrally around all gears and tensioner pulley.
8. Fit timing belt lower front cover. *See this section.*

> NOTE: Do not fit timing belt upper front cover at this stage.

9. Raise engine on jack, fit RH mounting bolts and tighten to 155 Nm.
10. Lower jack supporting power unit and remove from beneath vehicle.
11. Remove camshaft gear locking tool **18G 1570.**

Tensioning existing timing belt

12. Unhook tensioner spring from pillar bolt.
13. Loosen tensioner backplate bolt.
14. Position tensioner to align mark on backplate with mark on cylinder head.
15. Tighten tensioner backplate bolt to 10 Nm.
16. Tighten tensioner pulley Allen bolt to 45 Nm.
17. Connect tensioner spring to pillar bolt.

Removal - Engines fitted with automatic timing belt tensioner

1. Disconnect battery earth lead.
2. Raise front of vehicle.

⚠ WARNING: Support on safety stands.

3. Remove camshaft timing belt upper front cover. **See this section.**

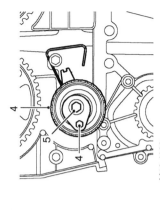

18G 1570

M12 5033

4. Using a socket and extension bar on the crankshaft pulley bolt, rotate crankshaft clockwise to align camshaft gear timing marks with mark on backplate - 90° BTDC.

⚠ CAUTION: Never use camshaft gears, gear retaining bolts or timing belt to rotate crankshaft.

5. Fit camshaft gear locking tool **18G 1570.**
6. Support engine on a jack.

⚠ CAUTION: Place a block of wood between engine and jack to avoid damaging sump.

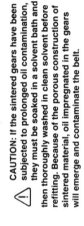

12M2052A

7. Remove and discard 2 nuts securing RH mounting bracket to engine.
8. Remove camshaft timing belt lower front cover. **See this section.**
9. If camshaft timing belt is to be re-used, mark direction of belt rotation using chalk.

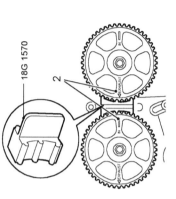

M12 5002

10. Remove and discard timing belt tensioner bolt.
11. Disengage index wire from its fitted position whilst at the same time removing the timing belt tensioner.
12. Lower engine to allow clearance between RH mounting bracket and engine.
13. Remove camshaft timing belt.

⚠ CAUTION: Ease timing belt off timing gears using fingers only. Metal levers may damage the belt and gears.
Do not rotate the crankshaft with the timing belt removed and the cylinder head fitted.

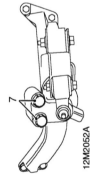

M12 4992

Refit - Engines fitted with automatic timing belt tensioner

1. Clean crankshaft pulley, timing belt gears, coolant pump drive gear and tensioner pulley.

⚠ CAUTION: If the sintered gears have been subjected to prolonged oil contamination, they must be soaked in a solvent bath and then thoroughly washed in clean solvent before refitting. Because of the porous construction of sintered material, oil impregnated in the gears will emerge and contaminate the belt.

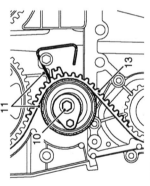

18G 1570

M124961

2. Check correct alignment of camshaft timing marks for 90° BTDC and that tool **18G 1570** is locking camshaft gears.

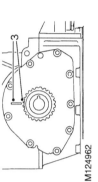

M124962

3. Ensure dots on crankshaft gear are aligned with flange on oil pump and that tool is locking flywheel.

4. Fit timing belt tensioner ensuring that index wire is positioned over pillar bolt and that tensioner lever is at 9 o'clock position.
5. Fit a new tensioner Patchlok bolt and tighten bolt until it is just possible to move tensioner lever.
6. Using the fingers only, fit the timing belt over crankshaft timing gear, then over camshaft gears, coolant pump drive gear and tensioner pulley ensuring that the belt run is kept taut between the crankshaft timing gear and exhaust camshaft gear.

⚠ CAUTION: If original belt is being refitted, ensure that direction of rotation mark is facing correct way.

7. Check that timing belt is positioned centrally around all gears and tensioner pulley.
8. Fit timing belt lower front cover. **See this section.**

▽ NOTE: Do not fit timing belt upper front cover at this stage.

9. Raise engine on jack, fit RH engine mounting bolts and tighten to 155 Nm.
10. Remove jack.
11. Remove camshaft gear locking tool **18G 1570.**

Tensioning timing belt

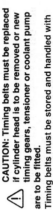

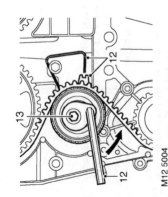

M12 5004

12. Using a 6 mm Allen key, rotate tensioner anti-clockwise and align the tensioner pointer to the index wire.

△ NOTE: If original belt is being refitted, align index wire to lower land of pointer.

△ CAUTION: Ensure that pointer approaches the index wire from above. Should pointer go past index wire, release tension completely and repeat tensioning procedure.

13. Ensuring that pointer maintains correct position, tighten tensioner bolt to 25 Nm.

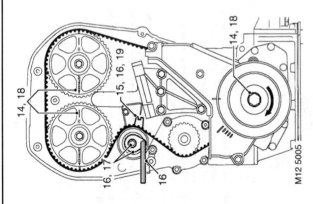

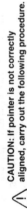

14, 18

15, 16, 19

16, 17

16

M12 5005

14. Using crankshaft pulley bolt, rotate crankshaft 2 turns clockwise and align camshaft gear timing marks.

△ CAUTION: Do not use camshaft gears, gear retaining bolts or timing belt to rotate crankshaft.

15. Check that pointer is still correctly aligned with index wire.

△ CAUTION: If pointer is not correctly aligned, carry out the following procedure.

16. Loosen tensioner bolt until it is just possible to move the tensioner lever and using a 6 mm Allen key, rotate tensioner lever clockwise until pointer is just above the index wire then rotate the lever anti-clockwise until pointer is correctly aligned with index wire.

17. Ensuring that pointer maintains correct position, tighten tensioner bolt to 25 Nm.

18. Using crankshaft pulley bolt, rotate crankshaft 2 turns clockwise and align camshaft gear timing marks.

19. Check that pointer is still correctly aligned with index wire.

20. Fit camshaft timing belt upper front cover. *See this section.*

21. Remove stand(s) and lower vehicle.

22. Connect battery earth lead.

CAMSHAFT TIMING BELT - AIR CON - VVC ENGINES

Service repair no - 12.65.18/20

Remove

△ **CAUTION: Timing belts must be replaced if cylinder head is to be removed or new timing gears, tensioner or coolant pump are to be fitted.**

Timing belts must be stored and handled with care.

Always store a timing belt on its edge with a bend radius greater than 50 mm.

Do not use a timing belt that has been twisted or bent double as this can damage the reinforcing fibres.

Do not use a timing belt if debris other than belt dust is found in timing cover.

Do not use a timing belt if partial engine seizure has occurred.

Do not use a timing belt if belt mileage exceeds 48,000 (77,000 km).

Do not use an oil or coolant contaminated timing belt.

△ NOTE: The cause of contamination MUST be rectified.

1. Disconnect battery earth lead.
2. Raise front of vehicle.

⚠ WARNING: Support on safety stands.

3. Remove timing belt upper front cover. *See this section.*

ENGINE

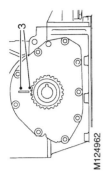

12M2161A

4. Using a socket and extension bar on crankshaft pulley bolt, rotate crankshaft clockwise to align camshaft gear timing marks - 90° BTDC.

5. Fit camshaft gear locking tool **18G 1570**.

6. Support engine on jack.

⚠️ **CAUTION: Place a block of wood between sump and jack to prevent damaging the sump.**

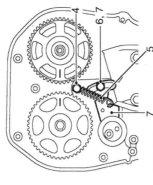

12M2165A

7. Remove 2 bolts securing RH engine mounting to engine.

8. Remove camshaft timing belt lower front cover. **See this section.**

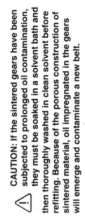

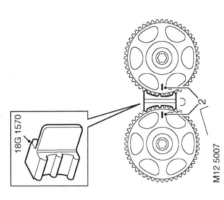

M12 5006

9. If camshaft timing belt is to be reused, mark position of tensioner backplate to cylinder head for belt tensioning reference. Mark direction of rotation on belt using chalk.

10. Loosen tensioner pulley Allen screw ¹/₂ turn.

11. Loosen tensioner backplate bolt ¹/₂ turn.

12. Push tensioner pulley down to fully OFF position.

13. Tighten tensioner backplate screw to 10 Nm.

14. Lower engine to allow clearance between RH mounting bracket and engine.

15. Ease timing belt from camshaft gears and crankshaft gear, remove timing belt.

⚠️ **CAUTION: Ease timing belt from the gears using the fingers only, metal levers may damage the belt and gears.**
Do not rotate the crankshaft with the timing belt removed and the cylinder head fitted.

ENGINE

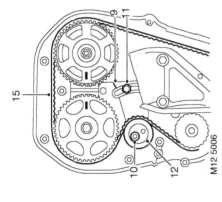

M124962

Refit

1. Clean crankshaft pulley, timing belt gears, coolant pump drive gear and tensioner pulley.

⚠️ **CAUTION: If the sintered gears have been subjected to prolonged oil contamination, they must be soaked in a solvent bath and then thoroughly washed in clean solvent before refitting. Because of the porous construction of sintered material, oil impregnated in the gears will emerge and contaminate a new belt.**

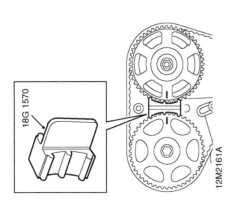

18G 1570

M12 5007

2. Check correct alignment of camshaft gear timing marks for 90° BTDC and that tool **18G 1570** is locking camshaft gears.

3. Ensure dots on crankshaft gear are aligned with flange on oil pump and that tool is locking flywheel.

Replacement timing belt

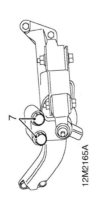

M12 5008

4. Fit pillar bolt supplied with replacement belt to cylinder head.

5. Connect spring supplied with replacement belt to pillar bolt and tensioner.

△ NOTE: This spring is not fitted with a sleeve.

6. Loosen backplate bolt and ensure tensioner moves fully through its adjustment range and returns under spring tension.

7. Push tensioner down to fully OFF position and tighten backplate bolt to 10 Nm.

All timing belts

8. Using fingers only, fit timing belt over crankshaft gear and then over camshaft gears, keeping belt taut between crankshaft gear and exhaust camshaft gear.
9. Position belt using fingers only over tensioner and coolant pump drive gear.

> **CAUTION: If original belt is being refitted, ensure direction of rotation mark is facing correct way.**

10. Check that timing belt is positioned centrally around all gears and pulley.
11. Fit timing belt lower front cover. **See this section.**

> NOTE: Do not fit timing belt upper front cover at this stage.

12. Raise engine on jack and tighten bolts securing engine to mounting to 155 Nm.
13. Remove jack.
14. Remove locking tool **18G 1570**.

Adjust

Tensioning an existing camshaft timing belt

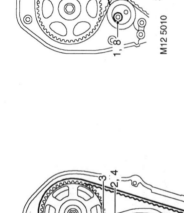

M12 5009

1. Loosen tensioner pulley Allen screw ¹/₂ turn.
2. Loosen tensioner backplate bolt ¹/₂ turn.
3. Position tensioner to align reference mark on backplate and cylinder head.
4. Tighten tensioner backplate bolt to 10 Nm.
5. Tighten tensioner pulley Allen screw to 45 Nm.

Tensioning a new camshaft timing belt

M12 5010

1. Loosen tensioner pulley Allen screw ¹/₂ turn.
2. Loosen tensioner backplate bolt ¹/₂ turn.
3. Apply tension to belt by applying finger pressure to tensioner backplate.
4. With tensioner pulley against timing belt and backplate held in position, tighten tensioner backplate bolt to 10 Nm.
5. Rotate crankshaft clockwise two complete revolutions and align camshaft gear timing marks.

> **CAUTION: Do not use camshaft gears, gear retaining bolts or timing belt to rotate crankshaft.**

6. Loosen tensioner backplate bolt and check that belt is being tensioned by tensioner spring.
7. Tighten tensioner backplate bolt to 10 Nm.
8. Tighten tensioner pulley Allen screw to 45 Nm.
9. Release tensioner spring from pillar bolt and tensioner
10. Remove pillar bolt from cylinder head, discard pillar bolt.

All timing belts

11. Fit timing belt upper front cover. **See this section.**
12. Remove stand(s) and lower vehicle.
13. Connect battery earth lead.

CAMSHAFT TIMING BELT - MPi MEMS3 (2000MY ON)

Service repair no - 12.65.18 - without A/C
Service repair no - 12.65.18/20 - with A/C

Remove

1. Disconnect battery earth lead.
2. Raise rear of vehicle.
3. Remove road wheel(s).

> ⚠ **WARNING: Support on safety stands.**

4. Remove engine cover. **See this section.**

12M 5805

5. Loosen lower fixing bolt securing timing belt upper cover.
6. Remove 5 bolts securing timing belt upper cover.
7. Remove timing belt upper cover and seal.

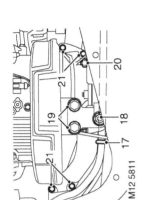

M12 5806

8. Remove 2 scrivets and 1 Torx screw securing closing panel.
9. Remove closing panel.

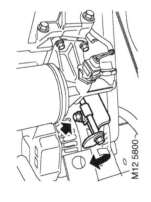

M12 5800

12. Rotate alternator drive belt adjustment bolt anti-clockwise to release tension from belt.
13. Release and remove drive belt from pulleys.
14. **Models with A/C**: Remove alternator drive belt. **See ELECTRICAL, Repairs.**

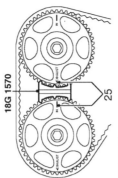

M12 5807

10. Loosen alternator pivot nut and bolt.

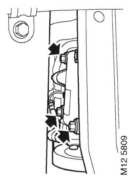

M12 5809

15. Loosen 3 bolts securing A/C compressor to mounting bracket, tie compressor aside.
16. **All models:** Support engine on a jack.

⚠ **CAUTION: Place block of wood between jack and engine sump to avoid damage occurring.**

M12 5808

11. Loosen bolt securing alternator adjustment bracket.

M12 5810

22. Release hydragas pipe from buttress clips and position pipe aside.
23. Manoeuvre buttress and engine mount assembly from wheel arch.
24. Collect arm from mounting.

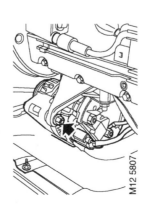

18G 1570

25

M12 5812

25. Rotate crankshaft clockwise to align camshaft gear timing marks.
26. Fit camshaft gear locking tool **18G 1570**.

⚠ NOTE: If necessary, use a small mirror to ensure camshaft gear timing marks are aligned correctly.

27. If camshaft timing belt is to be reused, mark direction of rotation of belt with chalk.

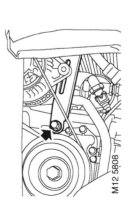

20
21
19
17   18
21

M12 5811

17. Release vacuum pipe from clips on body.
18. Remove nut from engine mounting centre bolt.
19. Remove 2 bolts securing arm assembly to engine.
20. Remove nut and bolt securing tie rod to buttress.
21. Remove 4 bolts securing buttress to subframe.

M12 5787

40. Remove 3 bolts securing lower timing belt cover and remove cover.
41. Remove and discard timing belt.

M12 5819

42. Remove gear from crankshaft.

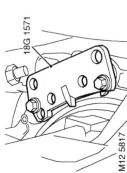

18G 1571

M12 5817

37. Lock crankshaft using tool **18G 1571** and secure with 2 bolts.

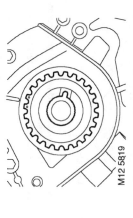

M12 5818

38. Remove crankshaft pulley bolt and washer.
39. Remove crankshaft pulley.

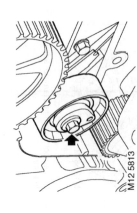

M12 5813

28. Remove and discard timing belt tensioner bolt.

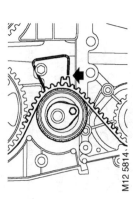

M12 5814

29. Disengage index wire from its fitted position, at the same time removing timing belt tensioner.
30. Ease timing belt from camshaft gears using fingers only.

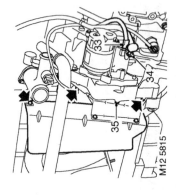

M12 5815

31. Remove bolt securing coolant hose heat shield to bracket on exhaust manifold.
32. Remove 2 bolts securing coolant hose heat shield to cylinder block and remove heat shield.
33. Disconnect Lucar from starter solenoid.
34. Remove nut from starter motor solenoid and release 2 leads.
35. Remove 1 bolt and remove flywheel cover plate.

M12 5816

36. Remove 2 bolts securing starter motor and remove starter motor.

Refit

1. Clean timing gears and pulleys.
2. Check correct alignment of dots on crankshaft gear with flange on oil pump.
3. Check correct alignment of timing marks on crankshaft and camshaft gears.
4. Fit timing belt tensioner ensuring that index wire is positioned over pillar bolt and that tensioner lever is at 9 o'clock position.
5. Fit new Patchlok bolt and tighten bolt until it is just possible to move tensioner lever.
6. Fit timing belt over crankshaft gear and then over camshaft gears, keeping belt taut between crankshaft gear and exhaust camshaft gear.
7. Position belt using fingers only over tensioner and coolant pump drive gear.
8. Check that timing belt is positioned centrally around all gears and pulley.
9. Fit and align lower timing belt cover, ensuring correct position of rubber seal.
10. Fit lower timing belt cover screws and tighten to 9 Nm.
11. Fit crankshaft pulley to crankshaft gear ensuring that indent on pulley locates over lug on gear.
12. Fit crankshaft pulley bolt with washer and tighten to 205 Nm.
13. Remove camshaft and flywheel locking tools.
14. Clean mating faces of starter motor and gearbox.
15. Fit starter motor.
16. Fit bolts and tighten to 80 Nm.
17. Fit leads to starter solenoid and tighten terminal nut.
18. Connect Lucar to starter solenoid.
19. Fit flywheel cover and tighten bolt to 9 Nm.
20. Fit exhaust manifold heat shield and tighten bolts to 9 Nm.
21. Position buttress assembly to subframe and manoeuvre into position.
22. Secure buttress assembly with bolts.
23. Fit nut to engine mounting centre bolt but do not tighten.
24. Fit nut and bolt securing tie rod to buttress but do not tighten.
25. Fit bolts securing arm assembly to engine and tighten to 45 Nm.

26. Tighten engine mounting centre bolt nut to 82 Nm.
27. Tighten bolt securing tie rod to buttress to 85 Nm.
28. Secure hydragas pipe to buttress clips.
29. Remove jack.
30. Fit drive belt to alternator and crankshaft pulleys and adjust tension. See **ELECTRICAL, Adjustments.**
31. **Models with A/C:** Position A/C compressor, tighten bolts to 45 Nm.
32. Fit alternator drive belt. See **ELECTRICAL, Repairs.**

M124918

33. **All models:** Using a 6 mm Allen key, rotate tensioner anti-clockwise and align the pointer to the index wire.

34. Ensuring that the pointer maintains correct position, tighten tensioner bolt to 25 Nm.
35. Using crankshaft pulley bolt, rotate crankshaft 2 turns and align camshaft gear timing marks.
36. **CAUTION: Do not use camshaft gears, camshaft gear retaining bolts or timing belt to rotate crankshaft.**
37. Check that pointer is correctly aligned with index wire.

⚠ **CAUTION: If pointer is not correctly aligned, carry out the following procedure.**

▷ NOTE: If original belt is being refitted align index wire to lower land of pointer.

⚠ **CAUTION: Ensure that the pointer approaches the index wire from above. Should pointer go past index wire, release tension completely and repeat tensioning procedure.**

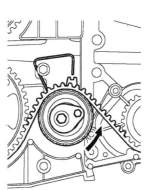

M124919

38. Loosen tensioner bolt until it is just possible to move the tensioner lever, using a 6 mm Allen key, rotate tensioner lever clockwise until pointer is just above the index wire then rotate the lever anti-clockwise until pointer is correctly aligned with index wire.
39. Ensuring pointer maintains correct position, tighten tensioner bolt to 25 Nm.
40. Using the crankshaft pulley bolt rotate crankshaft 2 turns clockwise and align camshaft gear timing marks.
41. Check that the pointer is correctly aligned with index wire.
42. Fit timing belt upper cover and seal, ensure seal is correctly positioned, fit bolts and tighten to 9 Nm.
43. Fit closing panel and secure with screw and scrivets.
44. Fit engine cover. **See this section.**
45. Connect battery earth lead.
46. Fit road wheel(s) and tighten nuts to correct torque. See **INFORMATION, Torque wrench settings.**
47. Remove stand(s) and lower vehicle.

CAMSHAFT TIMING BELT MANUAL TENSIONER

Service repair no - 12.65.19

Remove

▷ NOTE: Automatic timing belt tensioner is removed and refitted during timing belt remove and refit.

1. Remove and discard camshaft timing belt. *See this section.*

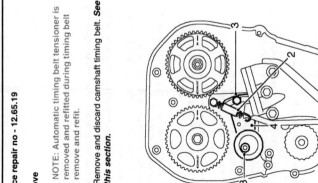

M12 5011

▷ NOTE: MPi tensioner and timing gears illustrated

2. *MPi engines* :- Disconnect tensioner spring from pillar bolt and tensioner.
3. Remove Allen screw and backplate bolt.
4. Remove tensioner.

Refit

1. Fit timing belt tensioner to cylinder head, fit but do not tighten Allen screw and backplate bolt.
2. *MPi engines* :- Connect spring to pillar bolt and tensioner.

▷ NOTE: This spring is fitted with a sleeve.

3. Secure tensioner in the OFF position with backplate bolt, tighten bolt to 10 Nm.
4. Fit new camshaft timing belt. *See this section.*

CAMSHAFT TIMING BELT GEAR

Service repair no - 12.65.20

Remove

1. Remove and discard camshaft timing belt. *See this section.*

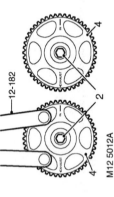

M12 5012A

▷ NOTE: MPi timing gears illustrated.

2. Restrain camshaft gear using tool **12-182**, remove bolt and plain washer from camshaft gear.
3. Remove tool **18G 1570**.
4. Remove camshaft gear.

Refit

1. Clean gear to camshaft mating faces.
2. Fit camshaft gear and align timing marks using **12-182**.
3. Fit plain washer and bolt to camshaft gear, restrain gear using tool **12-182** and tighten bolt to:
   - M8 bolt - 33 Nm.
   - M10 bolt - 65 Nm.
4. Fit camshaft locking tool **18G 1570**.
5. Fit new camshaft timing belt. *See this section.*

CRANKSHAFT TIMING BELT GEAR

Service repair no - 12.65.25

Remove

1. Remove and discard camshaft timing belt. **See this section.**

12M1437

2. Remove crankshaft timing belt gear.

Refit

1. Clean timing gear mating faces.
2. Fit crankshaft timing belt gear.
3. Fit new camshaft timing belt. **See this section.**

TIMING BELT UPPER FRONT COVER

Service repair no - 12.65.41

Remove

1. Remove engine cover. **See this section.**

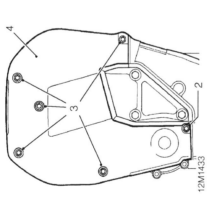

12M1433

2. Loosen lower fixing bolt securing timing belt upper front cover.
3. Remove 5 bolts from timing belt upper front cover.
4. Remove timing belt upper front cover and seal.

Refit

1. Fit timing belt upper front cover, ensuring seal is located correctly.
2. Fit bolts and tighten to 9 Nm.
3. Fit engine cover. **See this section.**

CAMSHAFT TIMING BELT REAR COVER - MPi AND VVC - MANUAL MODELS

Service repair no - 12.65.42

Remove

1. Remove camshaft timing belt gear. **See this section.**
2. Remove bolt securing second cam gear to camshaft and remove gear.
3. Remove alternator drive belt. **See ELECTRICAL, Repairs.**
4. Remove starter motor. **See ELECTRICAL, Repairs.**

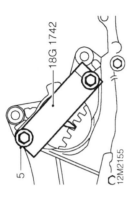

18G 1742

12M2155

5. Fit tool **18G 1742**, and secure with starter motor bolts.

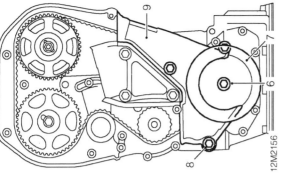

12M2156

6. Remove bolt and plain washer securing crankshaft pulley to crankshaft.
7. Remove crankshaft pulley.
8. Remove 3 bolts securing timing belt lower front cover to engine.
9. Remove lower front cover.

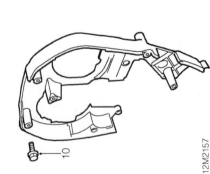

12M2157

10. Remove 3 bolts securing rear cover to engine.
11. Remove timing belt rear cover.

Refit

1. Fit timing belt rear cover.
2. Fit bolts and tighten to 9 Nm.
3. Fit lower front cover and tighten bolts to 9 Nm.
4. Fit crankshaft pulley and tighten bolt to 205 Nm.
5. Fit alternator drive belt. *See ELECTRICAL, Repairs.*
6. Remove crankshaft locking tool.
7. Fit starter motor. *See ELECTRICAL, Repairs.*
8. Fit camshaft gear and tighten bolt to 33 Nm.
9. Fit camshaft timing belt gear. *See this section.*
10. Connect battery earth lead.

TIMING BELT LOWER FRONT COVER

Service repair no - 12.65.43

Remove

1. Disconnect battery earth lead.
2. Remove timing belt upper front cover. *See this section.*
3. Remove alternator drive belt. *See ELECTRICAL, Repairs.*
4. Rotate crankshaft to align camshaft gear timing marks.
5. Remove starter motor. *See ELECTRICAL, Repairs.*

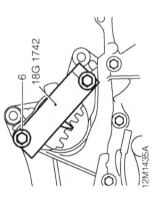

18G 1742

12M1435A

6. Fit crankshaft locking tool **18G 1742** and secure with starter motor bolts.

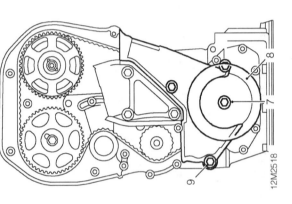

12M2518

7. Remove crankshaft pulley bolt and washer.
8. Remove crankshaft pulley.
9. Remove 3 bolts securing lower front cover.
10. Remove lower cover.

Refit

1. Fit lower cover and tighten bolts to 9 Nm.
2. Clean crankshaft and pulley mating faces.
3. Fit crankshaft pulley to crankshaft gear ensuring that indent on pulley locates over lug on gear.
4. Fit crankshaft pulley bolt with washer and tighten to 205 Nm.
5. Remove crankshaft locking tool **18G 1742.**
6. Fit starter motor. *See ELECTRICAL, Repairs.*
7. Fit alternator drive belt. *See ELECTRICAL, Repairs.*
8. Fit timing belt upper front cover. *See this section.*
9. Connect battery earth lead.

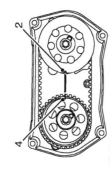

COVER - TIMING BELT LOWER FRONT - MPi MEMS3 (2000MY ON)

Service repair no - 12.65.43

Remove

1. Disconnect battery earth lead.
2. Remove timing belt upper front cover. *See this section.*
3. Remove crankshaft pulley. *See this section.*

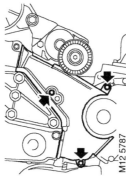

M12 5787

4. Remove 3 bolts securing lower front cover.
5. Remove lower cover.

Refit

1. Fit lower cover and tighten bolts to 9 Nm.
2. Fit crankshaft pulley. *See this section.*
3. Fit timing belt upper front cover. *See this section.*
4. Connect battery earth lead.

CAMSHAFT REAR TIMING BELT - VVC ENGINES

Service repair no - 12.65.56

Remove

⚠ **CAUTION: Timing belts must be replaced if cylinder head is to be removed or new timing gears are to be fitted.**
Timing belts must be stored and handled with care.
Always store a timing belt on its edge with a bend radius greater than 50 mm.
Do not use a timing belt that has been twisted or bent double as this can damage the reinforcing fibres.
Do not use a timing belt if debris other than belt dust is found in timing cover.
Do not use a timing belt if partial engine seizure has occurred.
Do not use a timing belt if belt mileage exceeds 48,000 (77,000 km).
Do not use an oil contaminated timing belt.

⚠ NOTE: The cause of contamination MUST be rectified.

1. Disconnect battery earth lead.
2. Remove timing belt upper front cover. *See this section.*

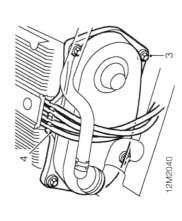

12M2040

3. Remove 4 bolts securing rear timing belt cover.
4. Release h.t. leads from cover clips and remove cover.

18G 1570

12M2161A

5. Rotate crankshaft clockwise to align front camshaft gear timing marks.
6. Fit camshaft locking tool **18G 1570.**

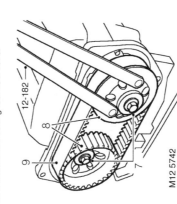

M12 5742

7. Using tool **12-182** to restrain rear camshaft gear, remove bolts securing each camshaft gear.
8. Remove both gears from camshafts.
9. Remove and discard belt.

Refit

1. Clean gear to camshaft mating faces.

12M3434

2. Fit inlet cam gear and align timing mark on cam gear with timing mark on back plate.
3. Using fingers only, fit exhaust cam gear and NEW timing belt together. Ensuring cam gear is located correctly on cam dowel.
4. Align timing mark on exhaust cam gear with timing mark on back plate.
5. Use a straight edge to check alignment of timing marks on camshaft gears and backplate.
6. Use tool **12-182** to restrain gears.
7. Fit bolts to camshaft gears and tighten to 65 Nm.
8. Check that timing belt is positioned centrally around both gears.
9. Using a straight edge, check timing of camshaft rear gears.
10. Remove camshaft locking tool from front camshaft gears.
11. Fit camshaft rear cover and tighten bolts to 9 Nm.
12. Engage h.t. leads to clips.
13. Fit timing belt upper front cover. *See this section.*
14. Connect battery earth lead.

CONTENTS

Page

This page is intentionally left blank

CONTENTS

ENGINE COMPARTMENT COMPONENT LOCATIONS - MPi MEMS 1.9 (UP TO 2000MY)

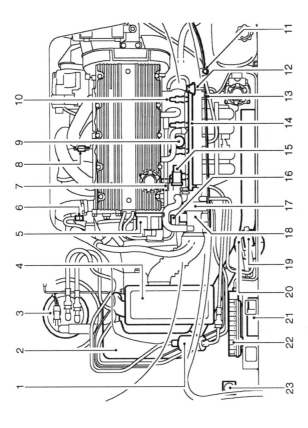

18M 0078B

1. Fuel filter
2. Resonator
3. Fuel pump
4. Air filter
5. Distributor
6. Engine coolant temperature sensor
7. Intake air temperature sensor
8. Oxygen sensor
9. Ignition coil
10. Injector
11. Ambient air temperature sensor
12. Fuel pressure regulator

13. Throttle cable
14. Fuel rail
15. Idle air control valve
16. Throttle position sensor
17. Crankshaft position sensor
18. Throttle body
19. Evaporative emission cannister, purge valve
20. Evaporative emission cannister
21. Engine management relay module
22. Engine control module
23. Inertia fuel shut-off switch

ENGINE MANAGEMENT SYSTEM - MEMS

ENGINE COMPARTMENT COMPONENT LOCATIONS - VVC MEMS 2J (UP TO 2001MY)

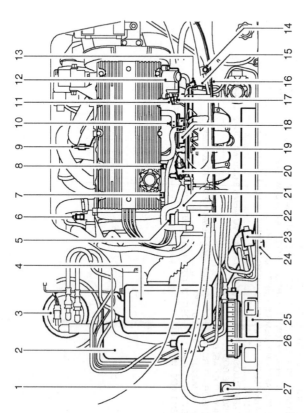

18M 0131B

1. Fuel filter
2. Resonator
3. Fuel pump
4. Air filter
5. Throttle position sensor
6. Engine coolant temperature sensor
7. Intake air temperature sensor
8. Camshaft position sensor
9. Oxygen sensor
10. Injector
11. Hydraulic control solenoid
12. Hydraulic control unit
13. Fuel pressure regulator
14. Ambient air temperature sensor

15. Manifold absolute pressure sensor
16. Throttle cable
17. Oil temperature sensor
18. Ignition coil
19. Fuel rail
20. Idle air control valve
21. Crankshaft position sensor
22. Throttle housing
23. Evaporative emission cannister, purge valve
24. Evaporative emission cannister
25. Engine management relay module
26. Engine control module
27. Inertia fuel shut-off switch

ENGINE MANAGEMENT SYSTEM - MEMS

ENGINE COMPARTMENT COMPONENT LOCATIONS - VVC MEMS 3 (2001MY ON)

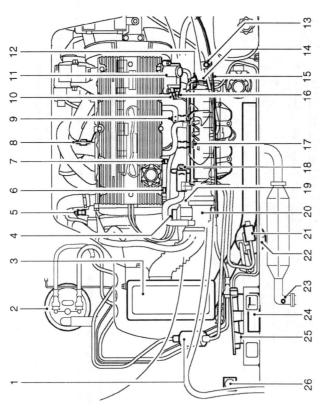

M18 0696

1. Fuel filter
2. Fuel pump
3. Air filter
4. Throttle position sensor
5. Engine coolant temperature sensor
6. Intake air temperature sensor
7. Camshaft position sensor
8. Upstream heated oxygen sensor
9. Injector
10. Hydraulic control solenoid
11. Hydraulic control unit
12. Fuel pressure regulator
13. Ambient air temperature sensor

14. Manifold absolute pressure sensor
15. Throttle cable
16. Oil temperature sensor
17. Fuel rail
18. Idle air control valve
19. Crankshaft position sensor
20. Throttle housing
21. Evaporative emission cannister, purge valve
22. Evaporative emission cannister
23. Downstream heated oxygen sensor
24. Engine management relay module
25. Engine control module
26. Inertia fuel shut-off switch

ENGINE MANAGEMENT SYSTEM - MEMS

ENGINE COMPARTMENT COMPONENT LOCATIONS - MPi MEMS 3 (UP TO 2001MY)

M18 0442A

1. Fuel filter
2. Fuel pump
3. Resonator
4. Air filter
5. Throttle Position (TP) sensor
6. Engine Coolant Temperature (ECT) sensor
7. Intake Air Temperature (IAT) sensor
8. Camshaft Position (CMP) sensor
9. Oxygen sensor (HO2S)
10. Injector
11. Engine oil temperature sensor
12. Fuel pressure regulator
13. Ambient air temperature sensor
14. Manifold Absolute Pressure (MAP) sensor
15. Fuel rail
16. Idle Air Control (IAC) valve
17. Crankshaft Position (CKP) sensor
18. Throttle housing
19. Evaporative emission cannister, purge valve
20. Evaporative emission cannister
21. Engine management relay module
22. Engine Control Module (ECM)
23. Inertia fuel shut-off switch

ENGINE COMPARTMENT COMPONENT LOCATIONS - MPi MEMS 3 (2001MY ON)

M18 0704

1. Fuel filter
2. Fuel pump
3. Air filter
4. Throttle Position (TP) sensor
5. Engine Coolant Temperature (ECT) sensor
6. Intake Air Temperature (IAT) sensor
7. Camshaft Position (CMP) sensor
8. Upstream Heated Oxygen Sensor (HO2S)
9. Injector
10. Engine oil temperature sensor
11. Fuel pressure regulator
12. Ambient air temperature sensor
13. Manifold Absolute Pressure (MAP) sensor
14. Fuel rail
15. Idle Air Control (IAC) valve
16. Crankshaft Position (CKP) sensor
17. Throttle housing
18. Evaporative emission cannister, purge valve
19. Evaporative emission cannister
20. Downstream H02S
21. Engine management relay module
22. Engine Control Module (ECM)
23. Inertia fuel shut-off switch

ENGINE MANAGEMENT SYSTEM - MEMS

23. Heated oxygen sensor (HO2S)
24. Gearbox Interface Unit (GIU)
25. Engine management relay module
26. Ambient Air Temperature (AAT) (engine bay) sensor
27. Engine Control Module (ECM)
28. Cooling fan relay (Non A/C vehicles only)
29. Fusible link FL6 (60A)
30. Fusible link FL4 (40A) Ignition switch
31. Fusible link FL3 (30A) Engine bay cooling fan relay
32. Under bonnet fusebox
33. Fuse 2 (30A) ECM and A/C relay pack
34. Fuse 6 (15A) Cooling fan relay (non A/C vehicles only)
35. A/C relay pack (A/C vehicles only)
36. Fuse 6 (10A) Engine bay cooling fan relay
37. Fuse 15 (20A) Cooling fan relay (non A/C vehicles only)
38. Fuse 1 (10A) Instrument pack
39. Fuse 14 (15A) ECM and A/C relay pack

1. Passenger compartment fusebox
2. Engine bay cooling fan relay
3. A/C trinary switch
4. Alternator
5. ABS ECU
6. Gearbox differential speed sensor (EM-CVT)
7. MAP Sensor
8. Ignition switch
9. IAT sensor
10. Alarm ECU
11. ECT sensor
12. TP sensor
13. IAC valve
14. Diagnostic socket
15. Instrument pack
16. Ignition coils
17. Engine oil temperature sensor
18. CKP sensor
19. CMP sensor
20. Park/Neutral switch (EM-CVT)
21. Injectors (4 off)
22. Purge valve

ENGINE MANAGEMENT SYSTEM - MEMS

MPi MEMS 3 CONTROL DIAGRAM - (UP TO 2001 MY)

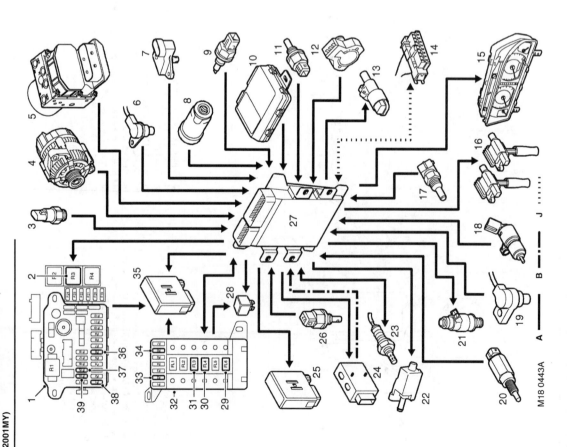

M18 0443A

A = Hardwired connection; B = Serial link; J = Diagnostic ISO 9141 K line bus

ENGINE MANAGEMENT SYSTEM - MEMS

MPi/VVC MEMS 3 CONTROL DIAGRAM - (2001MY ON)

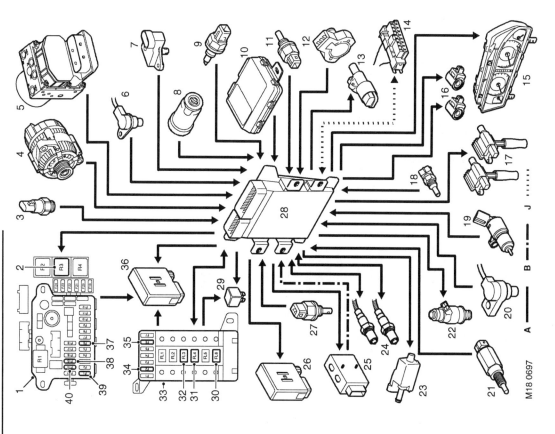

M18 0697

A = Hardwired connection; B = Serial link; J = Diagnostic ISO 9141 K line bus

1. Passenger compartment fusebox
2. Engine bay cooling fan relay
3. A/C trinary switch
4. Alternator
5. ABS ECU
6. Gearbox differential speed sensor (EM-CVT)
7. MAP Sensor
8. Ignition switch
9. IAT sensor
10. Alarm ECU
11. ECT sensor
12. TP sensor
13. IAC valve
14. Diagnostic socket
15. Instrument pack
16. Hydraulic control solenoids (VVC)
17. Ignition coils
18. Engine oil temperature sensor
19. CKP sensor
20. CMP sensor
21. Park/Neutral switch (EM-CVT)
22. Injectors (4 off)

23. Purge valve
24. Heated oxygen sensors (HO2S)
25. Gearbox Interface Unit (GIU)
26. Engine management relay module
27. Ambient Air Temperature (AAT) (engine bay) sensor
28. Engine Control Module (ECM)
29. Cooling fan relay (Non A/C vehicles only)
30. Fusible link FL6 (60A)
31. Fusible link FL4 (40A) Ignition switch
32. Fusible link FL3 (30A) Engine bay cooling fan relay
33. Under bonnet fusebox
34. Fuse 2 (30A) ECM and A/C relay pack
35. Fuse 6 (15A) Cooling fan relay (non A/C vehicles only)
36. A/C relay pack (A/C vehicles only)
37. Fuse 6 (10A) Engine bay cooling fan relay (non A/C vehicles only)
38. Fuse 15 (20A) Cooling fan relay (non A/C vehicles only)
39. Fuse 1 (10A) Instrument pack
40. Fuse 14 (15A) ECM and A/C relay pack

ENGINE MANAGEMENT SYSTEM - MPi MEMS 1.9

The Engine Control Module (ECM) monitors the conditions required for optimum combustion of fuel in the cylinder through sensors located at strategic points around the engine. From these sensor inputs, the engine control module can adjust the fuel quantity and timing of the fuel being delivered to the cylinders.

The main features are as follows:

- A single ECM controls the fuel injection system and the ignition system. The ECM incorporates short circuit protection and can store intermittent faults on certain inputs. TestBook can interrogate the ECM for these stored faults.

- The ECM is electronically immobilised preventing the engine from being started unless it receives a coded signal from the anti-theft control unit.

- In conjunction with the throttle position sensor the ECM uses the speed/density method of air flow measurement to calculate fuel delivery. This method measures the inlet air temperature and inlet manifold pressure and assumes that the engine is a calibrated vacuum pump, with its characteristics stored in the ECM, it can then determine the correct amount of fuel to be injected.

- A separate diagnostic connector, located on the passenger compartment fusebox, allows engine tuning or fault diagnosis to be carried out using TestBook without disconnecting the ECM harness multiplug.

- The ECM harness multiplug incorporates specially plated pins to minimise oxidation and give improved reliability.

- The ECM controls the operation of the radiator and air conditioning cooling fans, based on signals received from the engine coolant temperature sensor and trinary switch. The engine compartment cooling fan receives signals from the ambient air temperature sensor. If a high engine coolant temperature is detected the ECM will prevent the air conditioning system from operating.

- If certain system inputs fail, the ECM implements a back-up facility to enable the system to continue functioning, although at a reduced level of performance.

BASIC IGNITION TIMING - MPi

Crankshaft position sensor

19M2031

IGNITION SYSTEM - MPi MEMS 1.9

The ECM determines the optimum ignition timing based on the signals from the following sensors:

1. Crankshaft position sensor - Engine speed and crankshaft position
2. Manifold absolute pressure sensor - Engine load
3. Engine coolant temperature sensor - Engine temperature
4. Manifold absolute pressure sensor - Throttle pedal released

The engine management system uses no centrifugal or vacuum advance. Timing is controlled by the ECM which is energised by the main relay within the relay module.

Spark distribution is achieved by means of a rotor arm and distributor mounted at the No.4 cylinder end of the inlet camshaft.

ENGINE MANAGEMENT SYSTEM - MEMS

Manifold absolute pressure sensor

The manifold absolute pressure (MAP) sensor is located within the ECM and detects manifold pressure via a hose connected to the inlet manifold. The MAP sensor converts pressure variations into graduated electrical signals which can be read by the ECM. Increases and decreases in the manifold pressure provide the ECM with an accurate representation of the load being placed on the engine allowing the ECM to adjust the quantity of fuel being injected and the ignition timing to achieve optimum fuelling of the engine.

The speed and position of the engine is detected by the crankshaft position (CKP) sensor which is bolted to, and projects through, the engine adapter plate adjacent to the flywheel.

The CKP sensor is an inductive sensor consisting of a bracket mounted body containing a coil and a permanent magnet which provides a magnetic field. The CKP sensor is situated so that an air gap exists between it and the flywheel. Air gap distance is critical for correct operation.

The flywheel incorporates a reluctor ring which consists of 32 poles spaced at 10° intervals, with 4 missing poles at 0°, 120°, 180° and 310°. The missing poles inform the ECM when to operate the groups of injectors. When the flywheel rotates, as a pole passes the CKP sensor it disturbs the magnetic field inducing a voltage pulse in the coil. This pulse is transmitted to the ECM.

By calculating the number of pulses that occur within a given time, the ECM can determine the engine speed. The output from the CKP sensor when used in conjunction with that from the manifold absolute pressure sensor provides idle stabilisation and reference for injection timing.

ENGINE MANAGEMENT SYSTEM - MEMS

IGNITION TIMING COMPENSATION - MPi

Engine coolant temperature sensor

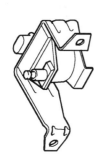

19M0847

The engine coolant temperature (ECT) sensor is a 'thermistor' (a temperature dependent resistor), i.e. the voltage output varies in proportion to temperature. The ECT sensor is located in the front of the coolant outlet elbow and can be distinguished from the gauge sensor by its brown colour. The ECM constantly monitors this signal and uses the information to provide optimum driveability and emissions by advancing or retarding the ignition timing.

Idle speed control

With the throttle pedal released and the engine at idle, the ECM uses the fast response of ignition timing to maintain idle stabilisation.

When loads are placed on or removed from the engine, the ECM senses the change in engine speed, and in conjunction with adjusting the idle air control (IAC) valve, advances or retards the ignition timing to maintain a specified idle speed. When load is removed from the engine, the IAC valve returns to its original position and the ignition timing returns to the idle setting.

◁ NOTE: Due to the sensitivity of this
   system the ignition timing will be
   constantly changing at idle speed.

IGNITION COMPONENTS -MPi

Ignition coil

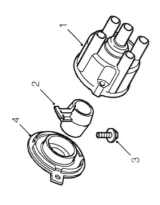

19M0848

The coil for the programmed ignition system is mounted on the back of the engine. The coil has a lower primary winding resistance (0.63 to 0.77 ohms at 20°C) than a coil in a conventional ignition system. This allows the full h.t. output to be reached faster and so makes the coil operation more consistent throughout the engine speed range.

Distributor cap and rotor arm

19M0857

1. Distributor cap
2. Rotor arm
3. Retaining screw
4. Anti-flash shield

The distributor cap, carrying a central carbon brush and four h.t. lead pick-ups, is located at the No.4 cylinder end of the inlet camshaft and surrounds the rotor arm. The rotor arm is secured by a retaining screw to a 'D' shaped stub shaft, which is press fitted into a vibration absorbing bush in the camshaft, and is protected from oil contamination by an anti-flash shield which incorporates an oil drain.

ENGINE MANAGEMENT SYSTEM - MEMS

FUEL SYSTEM - MPi

Engine Control Module (ECM)

19M0849

The Modular Engine Management System (MEMS) is controlled by an ECM mounted on the bulkhead in the engine compartment.

The ECM is an adaptive unit which over a period of time learns the load and wear characteristics of the engine it controls.

The ECM remembers and updates two main engine requirements when the engine is running at normal operating temperature:

1. The position of the idle air control (IAC) valve required to achieve a specified idle speed. This is then used as a reference for IAC valve movement to achieve idle speed under all load conditions.

2. The fuelling change or offset required to achieve a set oxygen sensor output indicating an air fuel ratio of 14.7:1. This allows the system to provide the correct fuelling without having to apply excessive adjustments to the fuelling which can adversely affect the emissions and driveability.

⚠ NOTE: After fitting a different ECM, TestBook will be required to reprogram the ECM with the code from the anti-theft control unit and to perform a full engine tune procedure.

The ECM inputs and outputs are shown in the following table.

INPUTS
Crankshaft position sensor
Ambient air temperature sensor
Manifold absolute pressure sensor
Engine coolant temperature sensor
Intake air temperature sensor
Heated oxygen sensor
Throttle position sensor
Diagnostic input
Battery supply
Starter signal
Earth supply
Anti-theft control unit
A/C Trinary switch

ECM

OUTPUTS
Ignition coil
Injectors
Idle air control valve
Fuel pump relay
Diagnostic connector
Heated oxygen sensor relay
Main relay
Cooling fans
Air conditioning fans
Engine bay fans
Purge valve

ENGINE MANAGEMENT SYSTEM - MEMS

The ECM provides an earth signal for the period the injectors are required to be open, the injector solenoids are energised and fuel is sprayed into the inlet manifold onto the back of the inlet valves. The ECM carefully meters the amount of fuel injected by adjusting the injector opening period (pulse width). During cranking, when the engine speed is below approximately 400 rev/min, the ECM increases the injector pulse width to aid starting. The amount of increase depends upon engine coolant temperature. To prevent flooding, the ECM periodically inhibits the operation of the injectors.

Intake air temperature sensor

19M0850

The intake air temperature (IAT) sensor is located in the side of the inlet manifold. The IAT sensor is of the negative temperature coefficient (NTC) type, designed to reduce its resistance with increasing temperature.

The ECM receives a signal from the IAT sensor proportional to the temperature of the intake air. When this signal is used in conjunction with the signal from the manifold absolute pressure sensor. The ECM calculates the volume of oxygen in the air and adjusts the quantity of fuel being injected, to achieve optimum fuelling of the engine.

Throttle housing

The throttle housing is located between the inlet manifold and air intake hose and is sealed to the throttle housing by an 'O' ring. The throttle housing incorporates a throttle disc which is connected to the throttle pedal via the throttle lever and a cable.

There are two breather pipes connected to the throttle housing, one either side of the throttle disc. When the engine is running with the throttle disc open, both pipes are subject to manifold depression and draw crankcase fumes into the manifold. When the throttle disc is closed, only the pipe on the inlet manifold side of the disc is subject to manifold depression. This pipe incorporates a restrictor to prevent engine oil being drawn into the engine by the substantially greater manifold depression.

Mounted on the throttle housing are the throttle position sensor and idle air control valve.

Injectors

19M0851

The four fuel injectors are fitted between the pressurised fuel rail and inlet manifold. Each injector comprises a solenoid operated needle valve and a specially designed nozzle to ensure good fuel atomisation.

The injectors are controlled in grouped mode with 2 & 3 being grouped and 1 & 4 being grouped, with the injectors in each group being operated alternatively. The ECM determines when to operate the injectors based on the signal it receives from the crankshaft position sensor.

Throttle position sensor

19M2145

The throttle position (TP) sensor is a potentiometer attached to the throttle housing and is directly coupled to the throttle disc. The TP sensor is non-adjustable. Closed throttle is detected by the TP sensor which initiates idle speed control via the idle air control valve.

The ECM supplies the TP sensor with a 5 volt supply and an earth path. The TP sensor returns a signal proportional to throttle disc position.

Throttle disc movement causes voltage across the TP sensor to vary. The ECM calculates the rate of change of the voltage signal in positive (acceleration) or negative (deceleration) directions. From this the ECM can determine the required engine speed, rate of acceleration or rate of deceleration and apply acceleration enrichment, deceleration fuel metering or over-run fuel cut-off.

Idle air control valve

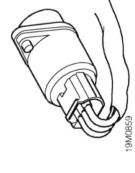

19M0859

The idle air control (IAC) valve is mounted on the inlet manifold and controlled by the ECM. The IAC valve opens a pintle valve situated in an air passage in the throttle housing, allowing air to bypass the throttle disc and flow straight into the inlet manifold.

By changing the amount the IAC valve is open the ECM can control engine idle speed and cold start air flow requirements by adjusting the flow of air in the passage.

During cold starting the ECM indexes the IAC valve open slightly to provide a level of fast idle, dependent on engine coolant temperature. As the engine warms, fast idle is gradually decreased until normal operating temperature is reached. The position of the IAC valve can be checked using TestBook and should be within the range of 20 to 40 steps when the engine is running. If it is identified as being outside this range it can be adjusted to within range using TestBook. This ensures that the IAC valve is at the optimum position within its range for providing further movement to compensate for changes in engine load or temperature in accordance with signals from the ECM.

△ NOTE: The position of the throttle disc is preset during manufacture and the throttle position setting screw MUST NOT be adjusted.

Engine management relay module

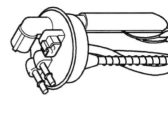

19M0855

The relay module is located on the bulkhead in the engine compartment behind the engine control module. The relay module contains the following relays:

• Main relay - energised when the ignition is switched on and supplies power to the ECM.
• Fuel pump relay - energised by the ECM for a short period when the ignition is switched on, during cranking and while the engine is running.
• Starter relay - energised by the cranking signal from the ignition switch.
• Heated oxygen sensor relay - energised by the ECM and supplies current to the heated oxygen sensor element.

Fuel pump

19M0856

The electric fuel pump is located inside the fuel tank and is energised by the ECM via the fuel pump relay in the relay module and the fuel cut-off inertia switch.

The fuel pump delivers more fuel than the maximum load requirement for the engine, pressure is therefore maintained in the fuel system under all conditions.

Fuel pressure regulator

19M0860

The pressure regulator is a mechanical device controlled by manifold depression and is mounted on one end of the fuel rail. The regulator ensures that fuel rail pressure is maintained at a constant pressure difference to that in the inlet manifold, as manifold depression increases the regulated fuel pressure is reduced in direct proportion.

When pressure exceeds the regulator setting, excess fuel is returned to the fuel tank swirl pot which contains the fuel pump pick-up.

Inertia fuel shut-off switch

19M0852

The electrical circuit for the fuel pump incorporates an inertia fuel shut-off (IFS) switch which, in the event of a sudden deceleration, breaks the circuit to the fuel pump preventing fuel being delivered to the engine. The IFS switch is situated in the engine compartment next to the ECM, and must be reset by pressing the rubber top before the engine can be restarted.

 WARNING: ALWAYS check for fuel leaks and the integrity of fuel system connections before resetting the switch.

Diagnostic connector

19M0853

A diagnostic connector, located on the passenger compartment fusebox, allows engine tuning or fault diagnosis to be carried out using TestBook without disconnecting the ECM harness multiplug.

Heated oxygen sensor

19M0854

The modular engine management system operates a closed loop emission system to ensure the most efficient level of exhaust gas conversion. Amend text and include subscript commands

A heated oxygen sensor (HO$_2$S) fitted in the exhaust manifold monitors the exhaust gases. It then supplies a small voltage proportional to exhaust oxygen content to the ECM. As the air/fuel mixture weakens, the exhaust oxygen content increases and so the voltage to the ECM decreases. If the mixture becomes richer so the oxygen content decreases and the voltage increases.

From this signal the ECM can determine the air/fuel mixture being delivered to the engine, and can adjust the duration the injectors are open to maintain the ratio necessary for efficient gas conversion by the catalyst.

The HO$_2$S has an integral heating element to ensure an efficient operating temperature is quickly reached from cold. The electrical supply to the heater element is controlled by the ECM via the HO$_2$S relay in the relay module.

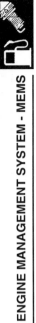

Acceleration enrichment

When the throttle pedal is depressed, the ECM receives a rising voltage from the throttle position sensor and detects a rise in manifold pressure from the manifold absolute pressure sensor. The ECM provides additional fuel by increasing the normal injector pulse width and also provides a small number of extra additional pulses on rapid throttle openings.

Over-run fuel cut-off

The ECM implements over-run fuel cut-off when the engine speed is above 2000 rev/min with engine at normal operating temperature and the throttle position sensor in the closed position, i.e. the vehicle is 'coasting' with the throttle pedal released. The ECM indexes the idle air control valve open slightly to increase the air flow through the engine to maintain a constant manifold depression to keep emissions low.

Fuel is progressively reinstated as the throttle position sensor is opened.

Over-speed fuel cut-off

To prevent damage at high engine speeds the ECM will implement fuel cut-off at engine speeds above 7000 rev/min by inhibiting the earth path for the injectors, as engine speed falls to 6990 rev/min, fuel is progressively reinstated.

Ignition switch off

When the ignition is switched off, the ECM will keep the main relay energised for approximately 30 seconds while it drives the idle air control valve to its power down position, ready for the next engine start.

The ECM then monitors the engine bay temperature using the ambient air temperature sensor. If the temperature is above a certain limit, the ECM will drive the engine bay fan for 8 minutes, and will then power down. If the engine bay temperature is below the limit the ECM will power down after 10 seconds.

Engine compartment ambient air temperature sensor

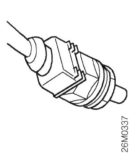

26M0337

The ECM monitors the engine compartment temperature using the ambient air temperature sensor. When the temperature exceeds a certain limit, the engine bay fan relay is energised to run the fan. If the temperature continues to rise, and exceeds another higher limit, the engine bay warning lamp (in the instrument pack) is illuminated.

If the ambient air temperature sensor fails, the engine bay fan will run while the ignition is on and the warning lamp will be permanently lit.

AIR INTAKE SYSTEM - MPi

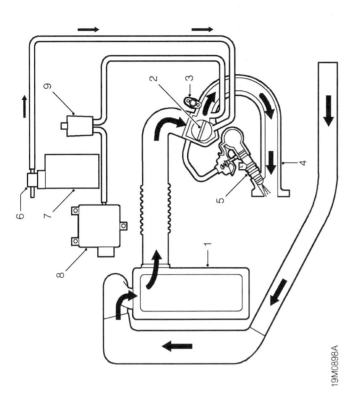

19M0898A

1. Air cleaner element
2. Throttle disc
3. Idle air control valve
4. Inlet manifold
5. Injector
6. Evaporative emission cannister, purge valve
7. Evaporative emission cannister
8. Engine Control Module (ECM)
9. Fuel trap - green connection to ECM

Intake air is drawn into the throttle body through an air filter element. Incorporated in the throttle body are the throttle disc and the throttle position sensor.

Air passes from the throttle body to the inlet manifold where it is mixed with fuel injected by the injectors before the mixture is drawn into the combustion chamber.

Inlet manifold depression is measured via a hose, by the MAP sensor which is incorporated in the ECM. A signal from the MAP sensor is used by the ECM to calculate the amount of fuel delivered by the injectors.

ENGINE MANAGEMENT SYSTEM - MEMS

ENGINE MANAGEMENT SYSTEM - VVC - MEMS 2J

The Engine Control Module (ECM) monitors the conditions required for optimum combustion of fuel in the cylinder through sensors located at strategic points around the engine. From these sensor inputs, the engine control module can adjust the fuel quantity and timing of the fuel being delivered to the cylinders. The ECM also controls the valve period, by driving the variable valve control (VVC) mechanism, to produce the optimum engine torque characteristic.

The main features are as follows:

- A single ECM controls the fuel injection system and the ignition system. The ECM incorporates short circuit protection and can store intermittent faults on certain inputs. TestBook can interrogate the ECM for these stored faults.

- The ECM measures the cam period via the cam sensor, and controls the VVC mechanism via two solenoids: one which increases the cam period and one which reduces it.

- The ECM is electronically immobilised preventing the engine from being started unless it receives a coded signal from the anti-theft control unit.

- The ECM uses the speed/density method of air flow measurement to calculate fuel delivery. This method calculates the density of intake air by measuring its pressure and temperature. The density signal, along with engine speed, allows the ECM to make a calculation of the air volume being inducted, and hence determine how much fuel should be injected to give the correct air/ fuel ratio.

- A separate diagnostic connector allows engine tuning or fault diagnosis to be carried out using TestBook without disconnecting the ECM harness multiplug. The multiplug is located on the passenger compartment fusebox.

- The ECM harness multiplug incorporates specially plated pins to minimise oxidation and give improved reliability.

- The ECM controls the operation of the radiator, air conditioning and engine compartment fans based on signals received from engine coolant temperature and engine bay temperature sensors. If a high engine temperature is detected, the ECM will prevent the air conditioning system from operating.

- If certain system inputs fail, the ECM implements a back-up facility to enable the system to continue functioning, although at a reduced level of performance.

- The ECM used on the VVC engine implements tune select. This means that each ECM may contain one or more vehicle's engine calibration. When first supplied, the ECM has no calibration selected and will not run the engine. When fitted to a vehicle, the ECM calibration for that vehicle must be selected using TestBook. This is to prevent ECM's being fitted to vehicles with the wrong calibration selected. It is an additional action to programming the ECM security code.

IGNITION SYSTEM - VVC

The engine control module determines the optimum ignition timing based on the signals from the following sensors:

1. Crankshaft position sensor - Engine speed and crankshaft position
2. Camshaft position sensor - Camshaft position
3. Manifold absolute pressure sensor - Engine load
4. Engine coolant temperature sensor - Engine temperature
5. Throttle position sensor - Throttle pedal position

The VVC engine employs a direct ignition system which consists of two twin-ignition coils driven directly from the ECM. Each twin-ignition coil supplies two cylinders.

BASIC IGNITION TIMING - VVC

Crankshaft position sensor

19M2031

The speed and position of the engine is detected by the crankshaft position sensor which is bolted to, and projects through, the engine adapter plate adjacent to the flywheel.

The crankshaft position sensor is an inductive sensor consisting of a bracket mounted body containing a coil and a permanent magnet which provides a magnetic field. The sensor is situated such that an air gap exists between it and the flywheel. Air gap distance is critical for correct operation.

The flywheel incorporates a reluctor ring which consists of 32 poles spaced at 10° intervals, with 4 missing poles at 30°, 60°, 210°and 250°. When the flywheel rotates, as a pole passes the CKP sensor, it disturbs the magnetic field, inducing a voltage pulse in the coil, which is transmitted to the ECM.

By calculating the number of pulses that occur within a given time, the ECM can determine the engine speed. The output from this sensor when used in conjunction with that from the manifold absolute pressure sensor provides idle stabilisation and reference for both ignition and injection timing.

Camshaft position sensor

19M2063

The camshaft position sensor has two functions. The first is to enable the ECM to run a sequential fuelling mode. The second is to measure the actual cam period, this measurement is achieved using teeth on the camshafts to indicate when the valve opens and closes.

If the camshaft position sensor fails when the engine is running, the engine will continue to run normally in sequential fuelling mode. If the sensor fails before the engine is started, the engine will start but run in grouped fuelling mode. The engine running in grouped fuelling mode can be detected by a reduced rev limit: 5500/5800 rpm in comparison to the normal rev limit of 7000/7300 rpm. Camshaft position sensor failure can be identified using TestBook.

ENGINE MANAGEMENT SYSTEM - MEMS

Manifold absolute pressure sensor

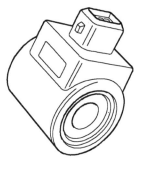

19M2062

The manifold absolute pressure (MAP) sensor is fixed directly to the inlet manifold. The ECM provides a 5 volt supply and earth path to the sensor. The sensor then returns a voltage output which represents the pressure. Increases and decreases in the manifold pressure provide the ECM with an accurate representation of the load being placed on the engine. Allowing the ECM to calculate both the ignition timing and quantity of fuel to be injected to achieve optimum fuelling of the engine. The voltage supply for this sensor is provided directly from the ECM.

IGNITION TIMING COMPENSATION - VVC

Engine coolant temperature sensor

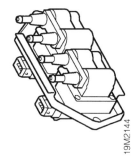

19M0847

The engine coolant temperature sensor is a 'thermistor' (a temperature dependent resistor), i.e. the voltage output varies in proportion to temperature. The sensor is located in the front of the coolant outlet elbow. The ECM constantly monitors this signal and uses the information to provide optimum driveability and emissions by advancing or retarding the ignition timing.

Idle speed control

With the throttle pedal released and the engine at idle, the ECM uses the fast response of the engine ignition timing to maintain idle stabilisation.

When loads are placed on or removed from the engine, the ECM senses the change in engine speed and in conjunction with adjusting the idle air control valve, advances or retards the ignition timing to maintain a specified idle speed. When load is removed from the engine, the idle air control valve returns to its original position and the ignition timing returns to the idle setting.

> NOTE: Due to the sensitivity of this system, the ignition timing will be constantly changing at idle speed.

IGNITION COMPONENTS - VVC

Ignition coil

19M2144

The coils for the programmed ignition system are mounted on the rear face of the engine block. Each coil has a low primary winding resistance (0.71 to 0.81 ohms at 20°C). This allows the full h.t. output to be reached faster and so makes the coil operation more consistent throughout the engine speed range.

VVC MECHANISM CONTROL

Hydraulic control solenoid

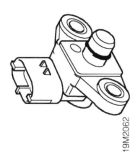

19M2356

The ECM controls two solenoids in order to control the VVC mechanism. Only one solenoid will be energised at a time to either drive the VVC mechanism towards minimum cam period, or towards maximum cam period. The desired cam period is calculated by the ECM using engine speed and manifold pressure (engine load). The current cam period is measured by the ECM using the camshaft position sensor. The ECM then energises the correct solenoid in order to move the mechanism towards the desired position.

Oil Temperature sensor

19M2061

An oil temperature sensor is mounted in the hydraulic control unit (HCU). The oil temperature measured by the ECM is used to derive the viscosity of the oil passing through the HCU which indicates how quickly the VVC mechanism will respond.

ENGINE MANAGEMENT SYSTEM - MEMS

FAULT DETECTION - VVC

If the ECM detects any faults with cam period measurement during start up and initial running, the ECM will try and drive the mechanism to minimum cam period.

If the ECM loses the cam period signal during running, the cam period will remain frozen at the last valid period. Engine speed may be limited as low as 5500 rpm depending on cam period when the fault occurred. The engine idle speed will be raised and will remain raised for the rest of the journey.

△ NOTE: A camshaft period measurement fault will only be recorded by the ECM if the fault is detected at start-up or during initial running. Camshaft period measurement faults are identified using TestBook.

ENGINE MANAGEMENT SYSTEM - MEMS

The ECM remembers and updates two main engine requirements when the engine is running at normal operating temperature:

1. The position of the idle air control valve required to achieve a specified idle speed. This is then used as a reference for idle air control valve movement to achieve idle speed under all load conditions.

2. The fuelling change or offset required to achieve an oxygen sensor output indicating an air-fuel ratio of 14.7:1. This allows the system to provide the correct fuelling without having to apply excessive adjustments to the fuelling which can adversely affect the emissions and driveability.

△ NOTE: After fitting a different ECM, TestBook will be required to reprogram the ECM with the code from the anti-theft control unit; to select the correct vehicle tune, and to perform a full engine tune procedure.

The ECM inputs and outputs are shown in the following table.

FUEL SYSTEM - VVC

Engine Control Module (ECM)

19M2130

The Modular Engine Management System (MEMS) is controlled by an ECM mounted on the bulkhead in the engine compartment. The ECM is an adaptive unit which over a period of time learns the load and wear characteristics of the engine.

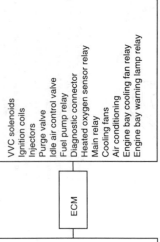

INPUTS
Crankshaft position sensor
Camshaft position sensor
Manifold absolute pressure sensor
Engine oil temperature
Engine coolant temperature sensor
Intake air temperature sensor
Heated oxygen sensor
Throttle position sensor
Diagnostic input
Battery supply
Starter signal
Earth supply
Anti-theft control unit
Engine bay temperature sensor

ECM

OUTPUTS
VVC solenoids
Ignition coils
Injectors
Purge valve
Idle air control valve
Fuel pump relay
Diagnostic connector
Heated oxygen sensor relay
Main relay
Cooling fans
Air conditioning
Engine bay cooling fan relay
Engine bay warning lamp relay

Intake air temperature sensor

19M0850

The intake air temperature sensor is located in the side of the inlet manifold. The sensor is of the negative temperature coefficient (NTC) type, designed to reduce its resistance with increasing temperature.

The ECM receives a signal from the IAT sensor proportional to the temperature of the intake air. When this signal is used in conjunction with the signal from the manifold absolute pressure sensor. The ECM calculates the volume of oxygen in the air and adjusts the quantity of fuel being injected, to achieve optimum fuelling of the engine.

Injectors

19M0851

The four fuel injectors are fitted between the pressurised fuel rail and inlet manifold. Each injector comprises of a solenoid operated needle valve and a specially designed nozzle to ensure good fuel atomisation.

After the engine has started the injectors are controlled individually. The ECM determines when to operate the injectors based on the signal it receives from the crankshaft and camshaft position sensors.

The ECM provides an earth signal for the period the injectors are required to be open, the injector solenoids are energised and fuel is sprayed into the inlet manifold onto the back of the inlet valves. The ECM carefully meters the amount of fuel injected by adjusting the injector opening period (pulse width). During cranking, when the engine speed is below approximately 400 rev/min, the ECM increases the injector pulse width to aid starting. The amount of increase depends upon engine coolant temperature. To prevent flooding, the ECM periodically inhibits the operation of the injectors during extended cranking.

Throttle housing

The throttle housing is located between the inlet manifold and air intake hose and is sealed to the manifold by an 'O' ring. The throttle housing incorporates a throttle disc which is connected to the throttle pedal via the throttle lever and a cable.

There are two breather pipes connected to the throttle housing, one on either side of the throttle disc. When the engine is running with the throttle disc open, both pipes are subject to manifold depression and draw crankcase fumes into the manifold. When the throttle disc is closed, only the pipe on the inlet manifold side of the disc is subject to manifold depression. This pipe incorporates a restrictor to prevent engine oil being drawn into the engine by the substantially greater manifold depression.

The throttle body also houses the throttle position sensor which provides signals to the ECM relative to the throttle disc position and rate of movement.

Throttle position sensor

19M2145

The throttle position (TP) sensor is a potentiometer attached to the throttle housing and is directly coupled to the throttle disc, the TP sensor is non adjustable. The TP sensor is used to detect closed throttle, allowing the ECM to initiate idle speed control.

The ECM supplies the TP sensor with a 5 volt feed and an earth path. The TP sensor returns a signal proportional to throttle disc position.

Throttle disc movement causes voltage across the TP sensor to vary. The control module calculates the rate of change of the voltage signal in positive (acceleration) or negative (deceleration) directions. From this, the ECM can determine the rate of movement and apply acceleration enrichment, deceleration fuel metering or over-run fuel cut-off.

Idle air control valve

19M0859

The idle air control valve is mounted on the inlet manifold and controlled by the ECM. The idle air control valve opens a pintle valve situated in an air passage in the throttle housing. Air is allowed to bypass the throttle disc and flow straight into the inlet manifold.

By changing the amount the idle air control valve is open the ECM can control engine idle speed and cold start air flow requirements by adjusting the flow of air in the passage.

During cold starting the ECM indexes the idle air control valve open slightly to provide a level of fast idle, dependent on engine coolant temperature. As the engine warms, fast idle is gradually decreased until normal operating temperature is reached.

The position of the idle air control valve should be within the range of 20 to 40 steps when the engine is idling at normal engine temperature. This ensures that the idle air control valve is able to supply varying amounts of by-pass air to compensate for all loads and temperature conditions. If the valve is identified as being outside the specified range a fault may exist. Faults should be investigated and rectified before using TestBook to adjust the idle air control valve.

ENGINE MANAGEMENT SYSTEM - MEMS

ENGINE MANAGEMENT SYSTEM - MEMS

Engine management relay module

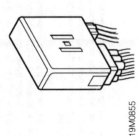

19M0855

The relay module is located on the bulkhead in the engine compartment behind the engine control module. The relay module contains the following relays:

- Main relay - energised when the ignition is switched on and supplies power to the ECM.
- Fuel pump relay - energised by the ECM for a short period when the ignition is switched on, during cranking and while the engine is running.
- Starter relay - energised by the cranking signal from the ignition switch.
- Heated oxygen sensor relay - energised by the ECM and supplies current to the heated oxygen sensor element.

Fuel pump

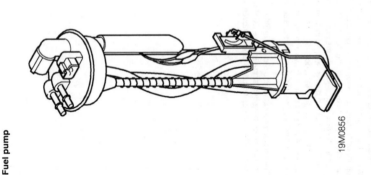

19M0856

The electric fuel pump is located inside the fuel tank and is energised by the ECM via the fuel pump relay in the relay module and the fuel cut-off switch.

The fuel pump delivers more fuel than the maximum load requirement for the engine, pressure is therefore maintained in the fuel system under all conditions.

Fuel pressure regulator

19M0860

The pressure regulator is a mechanical device mounted on one end of the fuel rail. Pressure is controlled by diaphragm spring pressure and modified by the vacuum signal. The regulator ensures that fuel rail pressure is maintained at a constant pressure difference to that in the inlet manifold, as manifold depression increases the regulated fuel pressure is reduced in direct proportion.

When pressure exceeds the regulator setting, excess fuel is returned to the fuel tank swirl pot which contains the fuel pump pick-up.

Inertia fuel shut-off switch

19M0852

The electrical circuit for the fuel pump incorporates an inertia switch which, in the event of a sudden deceleration, breaks the circuit to the fuel pump preventing fuel being delivered to the engine. The switch is situated next to the ECM and can be reset by pressing the rubber top.

 WARNING: ALWAYS check for fuel leaks and the integrity of fuel system connections before resetting the switch.

ENGINE MANAGEMENT SYSTEM - MEMS

Diagnostic connector

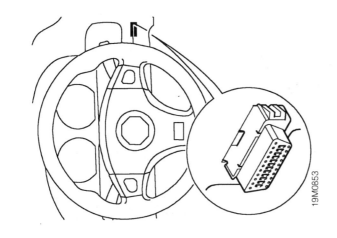

19M0853

A diagnostic connector, located on the passenger compartment fusebox, allows engine tuning or fault diagnosis to be carried out using TestBook without disconnecting the ECM harness multiplug.

Heated oxygen sensor

19M0854

The engine management system operates a closed loop emission system to ensure the most efficient level of exhaust gas conversion.

A heated oxygen sensor, fitted in the exhaust down pipe, monitors the oxygen content of exhaust gases. The sensor generates a voltage related to the oxygen content of the exhaust. As the air/fuel mixture weakens, the exhaust oxygen content increases and so the voltage to the ECM decreases. If the mixture becomes richer, so the oxygen content decreases and the voltage increases.

From this signal the ECM can determine if the air/fuel mixture being delivered to the engine is rich or lean. The ECM can adjust the duration that the injectors are open to maintain the air/fuel ratio necessary for efficient gas conversion by the catalyst.

The heated oxygen sensor has an integral heating element to ensure an efficient operating temperature is quickly reached from cold. The electrical supply to the heater element is controlled by the ECM via the heated oxygen sensor relay in the relay module.

ENGINE MANAGEMENT SYSTEM - MEMS

Acceleration enrichment

When the throttle pedal is depressed, the ECM receives a rising voltage from the throttle position sensor and detects a rise in manifold pressure from the manifold absolute pressure sensor. The ECM provides additional fuel by increasing the normal injector pulse width and also provides a number of extra additional pulses on rapid throttle openings.

Over-run fuel cut-off

The ECM implements over-run fuel cut-off when the engine speed is above 1600 rpm with engine at normal operating temperature and the throttle position sensor in the closed position, i.e. when ECM senses that the vehicle is 'coasting' with the throttle pedal released. The ECM indexes the idle air control valve open slightly to increase the air flow through the engine to maintain a constant manifold depression to keep emissions low.

Fuel is immediately reinstated if the throttle is opened. If engine speed drops below 1600 rpm on over-run, fuel is progressively reinstated.

Over-speed fuel cut-off

To prevent damage at high engine speeds the ECM will implement fuel cut-off at engine speeds above approximately 7000 rpm. Fuel is reinstated as engine speed falls.

Ignition switch off

In the first 10 seconds after ignition is switched off, the ECM drives the idle air control valve to its power down position (ready for the next engine start), and stores any required information.

The ECM then monitors the engine bay temperature using the ambient air temperature sensor. If the temperature is above a certain limit, the ECM will drive the engine bay fan for 8 minutes, and will then power down. If the engine bay temperature is below the limit the ECM will power down after 10 seconds.

Engine compartment ambient air temperature sensor

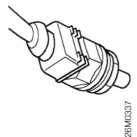

26M0337

The ECM monitors the engine compartment temperature using the ambient air temperature sensor. When the temperature exceeds a certain limit, the engine bay fan relay is energised to run the fan. If the temperature continues to rise, and exceeds another higher limit, the engine bay warning lamp (in the instrument pack) is illuminated.

If the ambient air temperature sensor fails, the engine bay fan will run while the ignition is on and the warning lamp will be permanently lit.

ENGINE MANAGEMENT SYSTEM - MEMS

AIR INTAKE SYSTEM - VVC

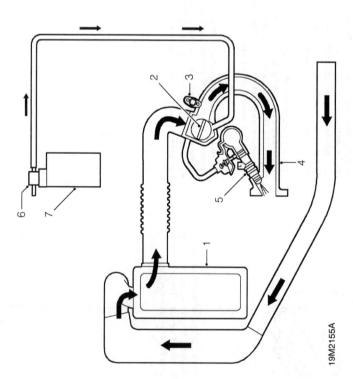

19M2155A

1. Air cleaner element
2. Throttle disc
3. Idle air control valve
4. Inlet manifold

Intake air is drawn into the throttle housing through an air filter element. Incorporated in the throttle housing are the throttle disc and the throttle position sensor.

Air passes from the throttle housing via the manifold chamber into the inlet tracts. Fuel is sprayed into the inlet manifold by the injectors and the air/fuel mixture is drawn into the combustion chamber.

5. Injector
6. Evaporative emission cannister, purge valve
7. Evaporative emission cannister

Inlet manifold depression is measured by the MAP sensor which is mounted on the end of the manifold chamber. A signal from the MAP sensor is used by the ECM to calculate the amount of fuel to be delivered by the injectors.

ENGINE MANAGEMENT SYSTEM - MEMS

ENGINE MANAGEMENT SYSTEM - MPi/VVC MEMS 3

DESCRIPTION

General

The Modular Engine Management System Version 3 (MEMS 3) is a sequential, multipoint fuel injection system controlled by the Engine Control Module (ECM).

The ECM uses the components shown in the control diagram to control the operation of the:

- Fuel system
- Ignition system
- Variable Valve Control (VVC) system (where applicable)
- Evaporative Emissions (EVAP) system
- Engine cooling fan(s)
- Air Conditioning (A/C) (where applicable)
- Steptronic Electro Mechanical Constantly Variable Transmission (EM-CVT) (where applicable)

The ECM uses the speed/density method of air flow measurement to calculate fuel delivery. This method calculates the density of intake air by measuring its pressure and temperature. The density signal, combined with the engine speed signal, allows the ECM to make a calculation of the air volume being inducted and determine the quantity of fuel to be injected to give the correct air/fuel ratio.

Engine Control Module (ECM)

The ECM is located on a bracket on the rear bulkhead in the engine compartment. Two harness connectors are used to connect the ECM to the main harness.

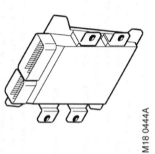

M18 0444A

The ECM electronic components are housed in an aluminium case for heat dissipation and protection from electro-magnetic interference.

The ECM is connected to earth via pins 59, 66 and 73. With the ignition off, the ECM is supplied with battery voltage to power the memory. The voltage is supplied from the battery positive terminal via the under bonnet fusebox fuse 2 to pin 80 of the ECM.

When the ignition switch is in position II (ignition on), the ECM also receives battery voltage, via the passenger compartment fusebox fuse 14, at pin 61. The ECM energises the main relay by completing the earth path for the relay coil which is connected to the ECM at pin 54. The main relay provides battery voltage to various peripheral components and also to the ECM at pin 19.

When the ignition switch is turned to position II, the ECM primes the fuel system by running the fuel pump for approximately two seconds. This is achieved by completing the earth path for the fuel pump relay coil. The fuel pump relay coil is connected to battery voltage at the ignition switch, the earth being supplied by the ECM at pin 68. The ECM references the sensors and the IAC valve stepper motor prior to start up.

Security code information is exchanged between the ECM and the alarm ECU via a wire connected between pin 72 of the ECM and the alarm ECU.

ENGINE MANAGEMENT SYSTEM - MEMS

When the ignition is turned to position III (crank,) the ECM communicates with the alarm ECU. If it receives authority to start, the ECM begins ignition and fuelling when CKP and CMP sensor signals are detected. The ECM will run the fuel pump continuously when CKP sensor signals are received (crank turning). When the ignition switch is turned to position 0 (off), the ECM switches off ignition and fuelling to stop the engine. The ECM continues to hold the main relay in the on position until it has completed the power down functions. Power down functions include engine cooling and referencing the IAC valve stepper motor and includes memorising data required for the next start up. When the power down process is completed, the ECM switches off the main relay and enters a low power mode. During low power mode the ECM will consume less than 1mA.

If the ECM suffers an internal failure, such as a break down of the processor or driver circuits, there are no back up systems or limp home capability. If a sensor circuit fails to supply an input, this will result in a substitute or default value being adopted where possible. This enables the vehicle to function, but with reduced performance.

Heated Oxygen Sensor (H0₂S)

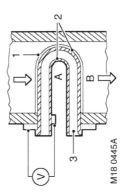

M18 0703

A HO₂S is located upstream of the catalytic converter, in the exhaust manifold (up to 2001 MY) or the twin pipe section of the exhaust front pipe (from 2001 MY). From 2001 MY, a HO₂S is also installed in the downstream side of the catalytic converter. The upstream HO₂S provides a feedback signal to the ECM to enable closed loop fuelling control. Where fitted, the downstream HO₂S provides a feedback signal to enable the ECM to monitor the efficiency of the catalytic converter, by comparing the signals from the upstream and downstream HO₂S.

If the upstream HO₂S fails, the ECM adopts an open loop fuelling strategy. If the downstream HO₂S fails, the ECM suspends catalytic converter monitoring.

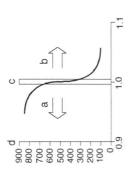

M18 0445A

A. Ambient Air.
B. Exhaust Gases.

1. Protective ceramic coating.
2. Electrodes.
3. Zirconium Oxide.

⚠ **CAUTION: HO₂ sensors are easily damaged by dropping, excessive heat or contamination. Care must be taken not to damage the sensor housing or tip.**

- **The HO₂S becomes very hot, take care when working near it.**
- **Do not measure the resistance of the sensing element.**
- **Observe the correct torque tightening value when installing the H0₂S.**
- **Do not subject the H0₂S to mechanical shocks.**
- **The HO₂S may be contaminated if fuel with added lead is used.**

The HO₂S consists of a sensing element, the outer surface of which is exposed to exhaust gases, whilst the inner surface is exposed to ambient air. The sensor has a ceramic coating to protect the sensing element from contamination and heat damage.

The amount of oxygen in ambient air is constant at approximately 20%. The oxygen content of the exhaust gases varies with the AFR with a typical value for exhaust gas of around 2%.

The difference in oxygen content of the two gases produces an electrical potential difference across the sensing element. Rich mixtures, which burn almost all of the available oxygen, produce high sensor voltages. During lean running, there is an excess of oxygen in the mixture and some of this oxygen leaves the combustion chamber unburnt.

In these conditions, there is less difference between the oxygen content of the exhaust gas and the ambient air, and a low potential difference (voltage) is output by the HO₂S.

M18 0446A

a. Rich AFR
b. Lean AFR
c. Lambda window
d. HO₂S Output in mV.

The material used in the sensing element only becomes active at a temperature of 300 °C (572 °F), therefore it is necessary to provide additional heating via an electrical resistive element. The element uses a 12V supply provided by the ECM and allows a short warm up time and minimises emissions from start-up. The resistance of the heating element can be measured using a multimeter and should be 6 Ω at 20 °C (68 °F).

Crankshaft Position (CKP) Sensor

The variable reluctance CKP sensor is mounted at the rear of the engine with the sensor tip facing the engine face of the flywheel and is secured in the casting with a single screw. The sensor tip of the CKP sensor is adjacent to a profiled target ring formed on the inner face of the flywheel.

19M2031

The signal produced by the CKP sensor allows the ECM to calculate the rotational speed and angular position of the crankshaft. This information is required by the ECM to calculate ignition timing, fuel injection timing and fuel quantity during all conditions when the engine is cranking or running. If the CKP sensor signal is missing, the vehicle will not run as there is no substitute signal or default.

ENGINE MANAGEMENT SYSTEM - MEMS

The CKP sensor is variable reluctance sensor and provides an analogue voltage output to the ECM relative to the speed and position of the target on the flywheel. A permanent magnet inside the sensor applies a magnetic flux to a sensing coil winding. This creates an output voltage which is read by the ECM.

As the gaps between the poles of the target pass the sensor tip, the magnetic flux is interrupted and this causes a change to the output voltage (e.m.f.).

It is important to note that the ECM is unable to determine the exact position of the engine with its four stroke cycle from the CKP sensor alone: the CMP sensor must also be referenced to provide sufficient data for ignition control and sequential injection.

M18 0447B

The 'spaces' on the target are spaced at a rate of one hole per 10°. There are only 32 holes, this leaves four 'spaces' where a single hole is missing. When the crankshaft is positioned at TDC (cylinder number one firing position) the CKP sensor is positioned at 55° BTDC. The 'missing' holes are positioned at 80°, 110°, 260° and 300° before the CKP sensor position.

Camshaft Position (CMP) Sensor

The CMP sensor provides a signal which enables the ECM to determine the position of the camshaft relative to the crankshaft. This allows the ECM to synchronise fuel injection and, on VVC engines, monitor valve timing.

CMP Sensor - MPi Engines

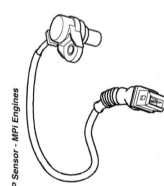

M18 0701

The CMP sensor on MPi engines is located on the camshaft cover (under the plastic cover) at the opposite end to the camshaft drive and reads off a reluctor on the exhaust camshaft.

The sensor is a hall effect sensor which detects the reluctor mounted on the exhaust camshaft. The sensor receives a battery supply from the main relay. The sensor operates on the principle of a voltage generated when the sensor is exposed to a magnetic flux. This causes a potential difference in voltage as the reluctor passes the sensor which is detected as a digital signal by the ECM.

ENGINE MANAGEMENT SYSTEM - MEMS

The half moon cam wheel reluctor enables the ECM to provide sequential fuel injection at start up, but it cannot provide a back-up signal in cases of CKP sensor failure.

If the CMP sensor signal is missing, the engine will still start and run, but the fuel injection may be out of phase. This will be noticeable by a reduction in performance and driveability, together with an increase in fuel consumption and emissions.

As the camshaft rotates the signal will switch between the high and low voltages. The position of the half moon cam wheel relative to the camshaft is not adjustable. The air gap between the CMP sensor tip and the half moon cam wheel is not adjustable.

CMP Sensor - VVC Engines

19M2063

The CMP sensor on VVC engines is located on the rear face of the cylinder head and reads off a reluctor on the inlet camshaft.

The CMP sensor is a variable reluctance sensor which does not require a power supply. The sensor consists of a permanent magnet and a sensing coil winding.

The signal is generated by changes which occur in the magnetic flux of the magnet. As the reluctor passes the sensor, an electromotive force (e.m.f.) is generated in the coil winding. The amplitude of the e.m.f. is proportional to the frequency of the change of magnetic flux which is detected by the ECM as an analogue signal.

CMP Reluctor - MPi and VVC Engines

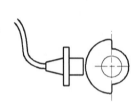

M18 0448

The reluctor consists of a single 'tooth' design which extends over 180° of the camshaft's rotation, for this reason it is known as a half moon cam wheel.

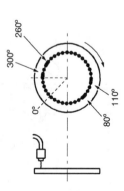

ENGINE MANAGEMENT SYSTEM - MEMS

Manifold Absolute Pressure (MAP) Sensor

The output signal from the MAP sensor, together with the CKP and IAT sensors, is used by the ECM to calculate the amount of air induced into the cylinders. This enables the ECM to determine ignition timing and fuel injection duration values.

The MAP sensor receives a 5V ± 4% supply voltage from the ECM and provides the ECM with an analogue signal which relates to the absolute manifold pressure and allows the ECM to calculate engine load.

19M2062

If the MAP signal is missing, the ECM will substitute a default manifold pressure reading based on crankshaft speed and throttle angle. The engine will continue to run with reduced driveability and increased emissions, although this may not be immediately apparent to the driver. The ECM will store fault codes which can be retrieved using TestBook.

Engine Coolant Temperature (ECT) Sensor

19M0847

The ECT sensor is located in the cooling system outlet elbow from the cylinder head and provides a signal to the ECM which allows the engine temperature to be determined.

The ECT sensor consists of an encapsulated negative temperature coefficient (NTC) thermistor which is in contact with the engine coolant. The ECM uses engine temperature to calculate fuelling and ignition timing parameters during start up. It is also used to provide a temperature correction for fuelling and ignition timing when the engine is warming up, running normally or overheating. The ECT signal is used by the ECM to control the engine cooling fans.

If the ECT sensor fails or becomes disconnected, the ECM will use a default value which is based on values from the engine oil temperature sensor. The driver may not notice that a fault is present although a fault code will be stored in TestBook. The default value will also include operation of the cooling fans in fast mode when the engine is running.

ENGINE MANAGEMENT SYSTEM - MEMS

Intake Air Temperature (IAT) Sensor

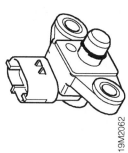

19M0850

The IAT sensor is located in the intake manifold near cylinder number four fuel injector. The sensor consists of an NTC thermistor mounted in an open housing to allow air flow over the sensing element. The IAT sensor provides a signal which enables the ECM to adjust ignition timing and fuelling quantity according to the intake air temperature, thus ensuring optimum performance, driveability and low emissions.

The IAT sensor is part of a voltage divider circuit which consists of a regulated 5 volt supply, and a fixed resistor (both are inside the ECM) and a temperature dependent variable resistor (the IAT sensor).

The IAT sensor operates in a similar manner to the ECT sensor. Refer to ECT sensor diagram and description for method of IAT sensor operation.

If the IAT sensor fails, or is disconnected, the vehicle will continue to run. The ECM will substitute a default value using the information from the speed/load map to run the engine, but adaptive fuelling will be disabled.

This condition would not be immediately apparent to the driver, but the ECM will store fault codes which can be retrieved using TestBook.

Engine Oil Temperature Sensor

19M2061

The engine oil temperature sensor is located in the oil filter housing on MPi engines and in the Hydraulic Control Unit (HCU) on VVC engines. The sensor provides a signal which allows the ECM to adjust fuelling values according to engine oil temperature, to produce optimum engine performance and minimum emissions during the engine warm up phase. On VVC engines, the ECM also uses the oil temperature to derive the viscosity of the oil passing through the HCU, which indicates how quickly the VVC mechanism will respond.

The engine oil temperature sensor consists of an encapsulated Negative Temperature Coefficient (NTC) thermistor which is in contact with the engine oil.

The engine oil temperature sensor operates in a similar manner to the ECT sensor.

If the engine oil temperature sensor fails, the ECM will substitute a default value which is ramped up to 80°C (176°F). This condition will not be apparent to the driver, with the exception of the temperature gauge which will display incorrect readings depending on the sensor failure.

The vehicle will run but may suffer from reduced engine performance and increased emissions as adaptive fuelling is disabled. The ECM will store fault codes which can be retrieved using TestBook.

ENGINE MANAGEMENT SYSTEM - MEMS

Throttle Position (TP) Sensor

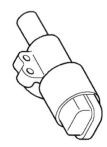

19M2145

The TP sensor is mounted on the throttle body and is driven from the end of the throttle spindle. The TP sensor consists of a potentiometer which provides an analogue voltage that the ECM converts to throttle position information. The TP sensor signal is required for the following vehicle functions:

- Idle speed control
- Throttle damping
- Deceleration fuel cut off
- Engine load calculations
- Acceleration enrichment
- Full load enrichment
- Automatic gearbox shift points.

The TP sensor is a potentiometer which acts as a voltage divider in an external ECM circuit. The potentiometer consists of a 4kΩ ± 20% resistive track and a wiper arm, driven by the throttle spindle, which sweeps over the track.

The track receives a regulated 5 V ± 4% supply from the ECM, together with an earth path. As the wiper arm moves over the track it will connect to areas of different voltage ranging from 0 to 5 volts. The 'output' from the wiper arm is connected to the ECM to provide an analogue voltage signal.

The TP sensor requires no adjustment as the ECM will learn the lower voltage limit which correspond to closed throttle.

If the TP sensor signal is missing the vehicle will continue to run but may suffer from poor idle control and throttle response. The ECM will store fault codes which can be retrieved using TestBook.

Idle Air Control (IAC) Valve

M19 2984

The IAC valve is located on the inlet manifold. It allows the ECM to control the engine idling speed by regulating the amount of air which by-passes the throttle valve. It also allows the ECM to provide a damping function when the throttle is closed under deceleration, this reduces hydrocarbon (HC) emissions.

The IAC valve is controlled by the ECM using a stepper motor. This consists of a core which is rotated by magnetic fields produced by two electro-magnet bobbins set at 90° to each other.

The stepper motor controls the volume of air passing through a duct which leads from the inlet manifold to a pipe connected to the throttle body. The bobbins are connected to the ECM driver circuits. Each of the four connections can be connected to 12 volts or earth, enabling four 'phases' to be obtained. The ECM drives the four phases to obtain the desired idle speed.

When the ignition is switched off the ECM enters a power down routine which includes 'referencing' the stepper motor. This means that the ECM will rotate the motor so that it can memorise the position when it next needs to start the engine.

The stepper motor referencing procedure can take from three to five seconds. If the ECM cannot reference the stepper motor during power down, it will do so at ignition on. If the stepper motor fails, there are no back up idle control systems. The idle speed may be too high or too low and if a load is placed on the engine it may stall. The ECM will store fault codes which can be retrieved by TestBook.

Ignition Coils

Two ignition coils are mounted on the camshaft cover above the spark plugs for cylinders 1 and 3 and secured with screws.

Each coil operates a pair of spark plugs using the wasted spark principle. The coil has a plug connection on its lower face and an ht lead which connects to the second plug.

M18 0449A

The coil fitted above cylinder 1 is attached to the spark plug for cylinder 1 and the ht lead connects to the spark plug for cylinder 4.

The coil fitted above cylinder 3 is attached to the spark plug for cylinder 3 and the ht lead connects to the spark plug for cylinder 2.

⚠ **WARNING: The ht voltage of the ignition system is in excess of 50 kV and the lt voltage is in excess of 400 volts. Voltages this high can cause serious injury and may even be fatal. Never touch any ignition components while the engine is running or being cranked.**

⚠ **CAUTION: Never crank or run the engine with the ht leads disconnected from the ignition coils; failure of the ECM and/or the coil will result. Always disable the ignition system by disconnecting the lt connectors from the coil.**

Each ignition coil consists of a pair of windings wrapped around a laminated iron core. The primary winding has a resistance of 0.7Ω and the secondary winding has a resistance of 10 kΩ.

Fuel Injectors

The fuel injectors are located directly under the fuel rail and connect to the intake manifold runners. Each injector delivers fuel to the engine in a targeted, atomised spray (onto the intake valve heads) which takes place once per cycle. Each injector opens during the intake stroke of the cylinder it supplies.

M18 0702

An injector consists of a pintle type needle and seat, and a solenoid winding which lifts the needle against a return spring. The injector nozzle delivers the fuel spray to precise areas of the intake ports to maximise the benefits of the swirl and turbulence in the manifold and head ports.

ENGINE MANAGEMENT SYSTEM - MEMS

The solenoid winding has a resistance of 13 - 16Ω at 20°C (68°F). The fuel injectors operate at a regulated pressure of 3.5 bar (50 lbf/in²). The regulator is located on the end of the fuel rail and excess fuel is returned to the swirl pot via a return line to the tank.

The injectors receive fuel under pressure from the fuel rail and a 12 volts supply from the main relay. To deliver fuel to the engine, the ECM has to lift the needle off the injector seat by energising the solenoid. To energise the solenoid the ECM supplies an earth path to the injector winding.

If an injector fails, the engine may lose power and driveability. The ECM will store fault codes which can be retrieved using TestBook.

Evaporative Emissions (EVAP) Cannister Purge Valve

The EVAP cannister purge valve is located in the engine compartment on the rear bulkhead. The purge valve is connected via a flexible pipe to the inlet manifold.

The cannister purge valve consists of a solenoid operated valve which is controlled by the ECM using a 12 volts PWM signal. The EVAP cannister purge valve controls the flow of fuel vapours from the EVAP cannister to the intake manifold of the engine.

When the vehicle is being driven the ECM will purge the EVAP cannister by opening the cannister purge valve, this allows the vacuum present in the intake manifold to draw fuel vapour from the cannister into the cylinders for combustion.

When fuel vapour is being removed from the cannister, fresh air is allowed to enter via an automatic one-way valve, this makes the cannister ready for the next 'absorption' phase.

The amount of fuel vapour which enters the cylinders can affect the overall AFR, therefore the ECM must only open the cannister purge valve when it is able to compensate by reducing fuel injector duration. The cannister purge valve will only operate under the following conditions:

- Engine at normal operating temperature
- Adaptive fuelling enabled
- Closed loop fuelling enabled.

Alternator

The alternator is located on a bracket which is attached to the cylinder block on the front RH side of the engine. The alternator is driven by a Polyvee belt from the crankshaft pulley. The alternator converts mechanical energy into electrical energy to power the electrical systems and maintain the battery charge.

The alternator outputs a signal to the ECM which represents the electrical load on the vehicle systems and the mechanical load exerted on the engine by the alternator. The signal output from the alternator is a variable PWM signal which is proportional to the load applied to the engine.

The ECM uses the load signal to provide idle speed compensation and to reduce engine speed fluctuations. If the load signal fails, the ECM uses a default value and stores a fault code which can be retrieved using TestBook.

Air Conditioning (A/C) Trinary Switch

The A/C trinary switch is located on the receiver/drier at the rear of the under bonnet compartment. It contains three pressure switches; high, low and medium. The medium switch completes an earth path between the ECM and an earth header joint. The high and low switches are connected between the A/C switch and the ECM.

M18 0451A

The trinary switch has three functions:

1. To disengage the A/C compressor clutch if the refrigerant pressure falls below the 'minimum' specified value.
2. To disengage the A/C compressor clutch if the refrigerant pressure exceeds the 'maximum' specified value.
3. To switch the cooling fan to high speed if the refrigerant pressure exceeds the 'high' specified value.

A/C Trinary Switch Pressure Settings

Switch	Opening Pressure bar (lbf/in²)	Closing Pressure bar (lbf/in²)
Low	1.96 (28) pressure decreasing	2.35 (34) pressure increasing
Medium	13.7 (198) pressure decreasing	18.6 (270) pressure increasing
High	28.4 (412) pressure increasing	22.6 (328) pressure decreasing

Functions 1 and 2 are performed by a single series circuit containing both minimum and maximum pressure switches. The switches are both normally closed, so if either threshold is exceeded the continuity of the earth path to the ECM is broken. This causes the ECM strategy to disengage the A/C compressor clutch on safety grounds.

Function 3 is performed by a separate circuit containing a single normally open pressure switch. This switch opens when the pressure exceeds a specified value indicating that extra cooling is required to reduce refrigerant pressure, this will cause the ECM to energise the condenser fan relay and start the fan.

ENGINE MANAGEMENT SYSTEM - MEMS

VVC Mechanism Control (Where Applicable)

Hydraulic Control Solenoid

19M2356

The ECM controls two solenoids in order to control the VVC mechanism. Only one solenoid will be energised at a time to either drive the VVC mechanism towards minimum cam period, or towards maximum cam period. The desired cam period is calculated by the ECM using engine speed and manifold pressure (engine load). The current cam period is measured by the ECM using the camshaft position sensor. The ECM then energises the correct solenoid in order to move the mechanism towards the desired position.

Fault Detection

If the ECM detects any faults with cam period measurement during start up and initial running, the ECM will try and drive the mechanism to minimum cam period.

If the ECM loses the cam period signal during running, the cam period will remain frozen at the last valid period. Engine speed may be limited as low as 5500 rpm depending on cam period when the fault occurred. The engine idle speed will be raised and will remain raised for the rest of the journey.

Steptronic (EM-CVT) Gearbox (Where Applicable)

The MEMS 3 ECM controls the EM-CVT unit in conjunction with the Gearbox Interface Unit (GIU) and several peripheral gearbox switches and sensors.

The GIU outputs gear selector lever position status, manual/sport selection and snow mode selection to the ECM. The ECM then provides an output to the instrument pack to display the appropriate gear position information in the LCD or illuminate the snow mode or gearbox fault warning lamps.

For further information on EM-CVT (Steptronic) gearbox See AUTOMATIC GEARBOX - 'EM-CVT', Description and operation.

Gearbox Interface Unit (GIU)

Electronic control of the EM-CVT Steptronic gearbox operates as an integral part of the MEMS 3 system software. The ECM accepts inputs from the GIU, communicates with the GIU for gearbox control, accepts driver inputs for gear selection and communicates information to the driver via the instrument pack.

The GIU connection which supplies information to the ECM is a serial communication link. This supplies the ECM with all the driver inputs from the gearbox switches.

The ECM output to the GIU is a hardwired connection which instructs the GIU of the required ratio control motor position. This information is output in the form of 500 Hz PWM signals.

Gearbox Shaft Speed Sensor

The ECM receives an input from the EM-CVT gearbox differential speed sensor which is located at the rear of the gearbox. The sensor is a Hall effect sensor which reads off the differential crown wheel teeth to provide a road speed signal. This signal is used by the ECM to determine when the vehicle is stationary and to allow accurate calculation of the true gearbox ratio.

Park/Neutral Switch

The park/neutral switch is located at the rear of the gearbox and is operated by a cam which moves via a cable with the gear shift selector lever position. An output from the park/neutral switch is connected to the ECM to enable gearbox load compensation. The ECM will adjust the IAC valve stepper motor to the appropriate position to maintain the idle speed when the gearbox is moved into and out of drive or reverse.

The park/neutral switch also operates the reverse lamps via a hardwired connection and controls a shift interlock solenoid which is fitted in selected markets only.

Ignition Switch Signal

A hardwired digital input to ECM pin 61 provides an ignition on signal. When the ECM has been idle for a period of time, it goes into 'sleep' (power saving) mode.

When the ECM receives an ignition on signal from the ignition switch, the ECM 'wakes up' and energises the main relay.

Main Relay

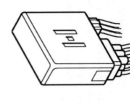

19M0855

The main relay is located in the engine management relay module which is positioned behind the ECM mounting bracket. The relay module contains the main relay, the fuel pump relay and the starter relay.

The relay is normally open when the ignition is off. When the ignition is switched on to position II, the ECM provides an earth path for the relay coil which energises, closing the contacts.

A permanent battery supply is provided to the relay contacts from fuse 2 in the under bonnet fusebox. The relay supplies battery voltage to the following components:

- ECM pin 19
- HO$_2$S
- CMP sensor
- Purge valve
- Fuel injectors
- Ignition coils
- Gearbox Interface Unit (GIU) via an in-line 10A fuse.

If the main relay fails, power will not be supplied to the above components and the engine will not start. The ECM will store fault codes which can be retrieved using TestBook.

Fuel Pump Relay

The fuel pump relay is located in the engine management relay module which is positioned behind the ECM mounting bracket. The relay is normally open when the ignition is off.

When the ignition is switched on to position II, the ECM provides an earth path for the relay coil. With the ignition on the relay receives a feed, via the ignition switch, from fuse 14 in the passenger compartment fusebox which energises the relay coil, closing the contacts.

A permanent battery supply is provided to the relay contacts from fuse 2 in the under bonnet fusebox, via the inertia switch. The feed passes through the relay contacts and operates the fuel pump to pressurise the fuel system. The relay will be energised for a short time only to pressurise the fuel system.

When the ignition switch is moved to the crank position III, the ECM will energise the relay when the engine starts cranking and will remain energised until the engine stops.

If the engine stalls and the ECM stops receiving a signal from the CKP sensor, the ECM will remove the earth path for the relay, stopping the fuel pump.

WARNING: ALWAYS check for fuel leaks and the integrity of the fuel system before resetting the inertia switch.

The inertia switch, when tripped, cuts off the power supply to the relay contacts, disabling the fuel pump in the event of a sudden deceleration. If the fuel pump fails to operate, check that the inertia switch is not tripped. The switch is reset by depressing the rubber cap on the top of the switch.

If the fuel pump relay fails, power will not be supplied to the fuel pump and the engine will not start or will stop if already running due to fuel starvation. The ECM will store fault codes which can be retrieved using TestBook.

A/C Compressor Clutch Relay (Where Applicable)

On vehicles fitted with air conditioning, an A/C relay module is located under the bonnet adjacent to the under bonnet fusebox. When the engine is running and the driver requests A/C on, the ECM receives a signal from the A/C switch to pin 56.

If conditions are correct, the ECM grants the A/C request by completing an earth path from pin 54 to the A/C clutch relay coil. The A/C clutch relay coil receives a battery feed from the ignition switch position II. The feed is supplied via fuse 15 in the passenger compartment fusebox to the relay coil. The coil will energise closing the relay contacts.

A permanent battery supply, via fuse 5 in the under bonnet fusebox, passes through the relay contacts and operates the compressor clutch.

The ECM will disengage the A/C compressor clutch if the coolant temperature exceeds 118°C (244°F) and will re-engage the A/C compressor clutch when the coolant temperature falls to less than 114°C (237°F).

If the A/C clutch relay fails, the A/C will be inoperative and the ECM will store fault codes which can be retrieved using TestBook.

Cooling Fans

The cooling system comprises an engine coolant cooling fan which is located behind the radiator and an engine bay cooling fan located in the engine bay. On vehicles fitted with A/C, an additional cooling fan is located behind the radiator and A/C condenser.

An engine bay cooling fan is located in the engine bay. The fan is used to reduce engine bay temperatures especially when the vehicle is stationary. The fan draws air through the RH air intake into the engine bay.

On all vehicles the engine bay cooling fan relay is located adjacent to the passenger compartment fusebox.

On vehicles without A/C, the engine cooling fan relay is located behind the under bonnet fusebox. On vehicles with A/C, the engine cooling fan relay and the condenser fan relay are located in the A/C relay module which is located adjacent to the under bonnet fusebox.

Engine Coolant Cooling Fan

The engine cooling fan relay is energised by the ECM on receipt of an appropriate coolant temperature signal from the ECT sensor.

When the engine is running, the ECM will energise the relay to operate the fan at a coolant temperature of 104°C (219°F) and will go off when the coolant temperature decreases to less than 98°C (208°F).

When A/C is fitted, the engine cooling fan and the condenser fan can operate at two speeds, being operated in series or parallel by the ECM. Refer to the Air Conditioning section for condenser fan details.

Engine Bay Cooling Fan

The engine bay cooling fan relay is energised by ECM on receipt of an appropriate engine bay temperature signal from the ambient air temperature sensor.

When the engine is running, the ECM will energise the relay to operate the fan when an engine bay temperature of 75°C (167°F) is reached. The ECM has a timer which energises the relay for a predetermined period. If the temperature decreases to less than 60°C (140°F) before the timer has expired, the ECM will de-energise the relay.

If the engine bay temperature exceeds 130°C (266°F), the ECM will illuminate the engine bay overheat warning lamp in the instrument pack. The warning lamp informs the driver that the engine bay temperature is abnormally high or that a system fault has occurred. When the engine bay temperature falls below 110°C (230°F) the ECM will extinguish the warning lamp.

When the engine is off, the fan remains active for a predetermined period after the engine is switched off.

Ambient Air Temperature (AAT) Sensor (Engine Bay)

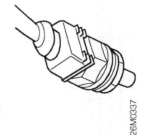

26M0337

The AAT sensor is located in the engine bay on the header panel directly above the inlet manifold.

The AAT sensor receives a supply from ECM pin 21 and is connected to ECM pin 34 which is a common earth. The AAT sensor operates the engine bay cooling fan as described in Cooling Fans.

If the AAT sensor fails, the engine bay cooling fan will operate at all times when the ignition is on and the engine bay overheat warning lamp in the instrument pack will be illuminated.

Engine Bay Cooling Fan Relay

The engine bay cooling fan relay is located adjacent to the passenger compartment fusebox and is the central relay in a block of three.

The relay coil and contacts receive a permanent battery feed from fusible link 3 in the under bonnet fusebox and fuse 6 in the passenger compartment fusebox. The relay coil is connected to ECM pin 74 which provides an earth path when cooling fan operation is required.

If the cooling fan relay fails, the cooling fan will not operate and engine bay overheat may occur. The ECM will store fault codes which can be retrieved using TestBook.

Engine Bay Overheat Warning Lamp

The engine bay overheat warning lamp is located in the centre warning lamp cluster in the instrument pack. If the engine bay temperature exceeds 130°C (275°F), the ECM will illuminate the warning lamp to inform the driver that the engine bay temperature is abnormally high. When the engine bay temperature falls below 110°C (230°F) the ECM will extinguish the warning lamp.

The ECM will also illuminate the warning lamp if a cooling fan, relay or AAT sensor fault is detected.

The warning lamp receives a feed from the ignition switch when the switch is in position II. When the ECM requires the warning lamp to be illuminated, it completes an earth path from the warning lamp to ECM pin 62.

Tachometer Drive

The ECM provides an output signal on pin 55 for engine speed, derived from the CKP sensor. The signal is passed to the instrument pack for tachometer operation and is also used by the EPAS ECU pin 15 for an engine speed signal.

Failure of this output will be shown by the tachometer not functioning. The ECM will record fault codes which can be retrieved using TestBook.

Fuel Pump

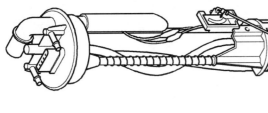

M18 0698

Vehicle Immobilisation

The vehicle immobilisation system operates by the alarm ECU transmitting a unique code to the ECM when the ignition is switched on. If the code is recognised by the ECM it will energise the injectors and allow the engine to start.

If no code is received or the code is incorrect, the ECM will disable the vehicle by not energising the fuel injectors.

The alarm ECU also controls the starter relay and will passively disarm the starter relay when the key is removed from the ignition switch. Rearming is performed by turning the ignition on which activates a coil around the ignition key barrel.

The coil transmits a waveform signal which excites the remote handset to transmit a re-mobilisation signal. When the signal is received by the alarm ECU, the starter relay will be enabled.

Replacement ECM's are supplied blank and must learn the alarm ECU security code for the vehicle to which it is fitted. When the ECM is connected to the vehicle, TestBook is required to enable the ECM to learn the alarm ECU code. If a new alarm ECU is fitted, the ECM will need to learn the new security code using TestBook.

Rough Road Detection

MEMS 3 has a misfire detection facility which is part of the On-Board Diagnostics (OBD) system. Misfire detection is disabled when the ECM senses that the vehicle is on a 'rough road'. The system software can detect variations in the signal output and disable misfire detection to prevent incorrect faults being logged by the ECM.

The 'rough road' signal is passed from the ABS ECU on a hardwired output to the ECM pin 78. The signal is in the form of a square wave digital pulse train of between 0 and 5 V at 8000 pulses per mile.

On vehicles without ABS, an ABS reluctor ring is fitted to the LH rear wheel and provides 48 pulses per rotation of the wheel to a variable reluctance sensor. The output from the sensor is received by the GIU which passes a buffered version of the signal to the ECM pin 78.

The electric fuel pump is located inside the fuel tank and is energised by the ECM via the fuel pump relay in the engine management relay module and the inertia switch.

The fuel pump delivers more fuel than the maximum load requirement for the engine, maintaining pressure in the fuel system under all conditions.

Fuel Pressure Regulator

M18 0699

The fuel pressure regulator is a mechanical device mounted on the end of the fuel rail. Pressure is controlled by diaphragm spring pressure and is modified by a vacuum signal from the inlet manifold.

The regulator ensures that fuel pressure is maintained at a constant pressure difference to that in the inlet manifold. As manifold depression increases, the regulated fuel pressure is reduced in direct proportion.

When pressure exceeds the regulator setting, excess fuel is returned to the fuel tank swirl pot which contains the fuel pump pick-up.

Inertia Fuel Cut-Off Switch

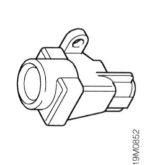

19M0852

The electrical circuit for the fuel pump incorporates an inertia switch which, in the event of a sudden deceleration, breaks the circuit to the fuel pump preventing fuel being delivered to the engine. The switch is located adjacent to the ECM and can be reset by pressing the rubber top.

⚠ **WARNING: ALWAYS check for fuel leaks and the integrity of the fuel system connections before resetting the switch.**

ENGINE MANAGEMENT SYSTEM - MEMS

Diagnostic socket

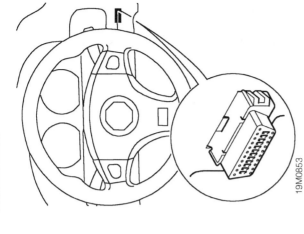

19M0853

Diagnostics

A diagnostic socket allows the exchange of information between the ECM and TestBook or a diagnostic tool using Keyword 2000 protocol.

The diagnostic socket is located in the passenger compartment fusebox which is located below the fascia on the driver's side.

A dedicated diagnostic (ISO 9141 K Line) bus is connected between the ECM and the diagnostic socket and allows the retrieval of diagnostic information and the programming of certain functions using TestBook.

The ECM uses a 'P' code diagnostic strategy and can record faults relating to the engine management and EM-CVT gearbox interface unit functions.

The 'P' codes are qualified by one of the following failure types:

- Min - the minimum expected value has been exceeded
- Max - the maximum expected value has been exceeded
- Signal - the signal is not present
- Plaus - an implausible condition has been detected

From 2001 MY, after detecting a fault which causes an increase of emissions above the legislated threshold, in addition to storing a 'P' code the ECM also illuminates a Malfunction Indicator Lamp (MIL) in the instrument pack. The ECM performs a 2 seconds bulb check of the MIL each time the ignition is switched on.

Malfunction Indicator Lamp

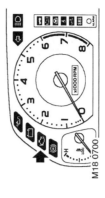

M18 0700

ENGINE MANAGEMENT SYSTEM - MEMS

ECM Harness Connector Details

The following tables give input/output information for the two harness connectors used on the ECM.

Connector C0635 (Up to 2001 MY)/C0914 (From 2001 MY) - Black, 52 Pin

Pin No.	Description	Input/Output
1	Upstream HO$_2$S heater	Output
2	Downstream HO$_2$S screened earth (from 2001MY only)	Input
3	Downstream HO$_2$S positive (from 2001 MY only)	Output
4	CKP sensor positive	Output
5	CMP sensor screen earth (non EM-CVT gearbox only)	Input
6	Oil temperature sensor earth	Input
7	ECT sensor earth	Input
8	MAP sensor supply +5V	Output
9	Differential speed sensor signal - (EM-CVT gearbox only)	Input
10	Oil temperature unit (VVC only)	Output
11	Not used	-
12	Decrease solenoid valve (VVC only)	Output
13	IAC valve stepper motor phase B	Input/Output
14	Injector 3 earth	Input
15	Upstream HO$_2$S positive	Output
16	CMP sensor signal	Input
17	CKP sensor screened earth	Input
18	IAT sensor earth	Input
19	Main relay supply signal	Input
20	TP sensor signal	Input
21	Engine bay temperature sensor signal	Input
22	Not used	-
23	Not used	-
24	IAC valve stepper motor phase D	Input/Output
25	Injector 1 earth	Input
26	Ignition coil 2 earth	Input

Connector C0635 (Up to 2001 MY)/C0914 (From 2001 MY) - Continued

Pin No.	Description	Input/Output
27	Downstream HO$_2$S heater (from 2001 MY only)	Output
28	Upstream HO$_2$S screened earth	Input
29	Downstream HO$_2$S negative (from 2001 MY only)	Input
30	CKP sensor negative	Input
31	MAP sensor earth	Input
32	Engine oil temperature sensor signal	Input
33	ECT sensor signal	Input
34	TP sensor earth	Input
35	Alternator load signal	Input
36	Not used	-
37	Sensor earth	Input
38	EVAP purge valve drive	Output
39	IAC valve stepper motor phase A	Input/Output
40	Injector 4 earth	Input
41	Upstream HO$_2$S negative	Input
42	CMP sensor earth	Input
43	Not used	-
44	IAT sensor signal	Input
45	MAP sensor signal	Input
46	TP sensor supply +5V	Output
47	Not used	-
48	Instrument pack - gearbox position display PWM signal (EM-CVT gearbox only)	Output
49	Increase solenoid valve (VVC only)	Output
50	IAC valve stepper motor phase C	Input/Output
51	Injector 2 earth	Input
52	Ignition coil 1 earth	Input

Connector C0634 (Up to 2001 MY)/C0913 (From 2001 MY) - Black, 28 Pin

Pin No.	Description	Input/Output
53	A/C clutch relay coil earth (A/C vehicles only)	Input
54	Main relay coil earth	Input
55	Instrument pack - tachometer drive	Output
56	A/C trinary switch hi/low (A/C vehicles only)	Input
57	Not used	
58	Diagnostic ISO 9141 K Line	Input/Output
59	Main earth 1	Input
60	Cooling fan relay 2 coil earth (A/C vehicles only)	Input
61	Ignition switch	Input
62	Instrument pack - engine bay overheat warning lamp	Output
63	Park/Neutral switch (EM-CVT gearbox only)	Input
64	Rough road sensor positive (non ABS only)	Input
65	Not used	
66	Main earth 3	Input
67	Cooling fan relay 1 coil earth	Input
68	Fuel pump relay coil earth	Input
69	Malfunction Indicator Lamp (MIL) (from 2001 MY only)	Output
70	Trinary switch A/C fan request (A/C vehicles only)	Input
71	Sensor earth	Input
72	Alarm ECU - immobilisation coded signal	Input
73	Main earth 2	Input
74	Engine bay cooling fan relay coil earth	Input
75	Gearbox Interface Unit (GIU) data transmit (EM-CVT gearbox only)	Output
76	Not used	-
77	Gearbox Interface Unit (GIU) data receive (EM-CVT gearbox only)	Input
78	Road speed signal	Input
79	Not used	-
80	Battery permanent supply - under bonnet fusebox Fuse 2	Input

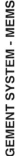

OPERATION

Acceleration Enrichment

When the throttle pedal is depressed, the ECM receives a rising voltage from the TP sensor and detects a rise in manifold pressure from the MAP sensor. The ECM provides additional fuel by increasing the normal injector pulse width and also provides a number of extra additional pulses on rapid throttle openings.

Over-Run Fuel Cut-Off

The ECM implements over-run fuel cut-off when the engine speed is above 1600 rpm with the engine at normal operating temperature and the TP sensor in the closed position, i.e. when ECM senses that the vehicle is 'coasting' with the throttle pedal released. The ECM indexes the IAC valve open slightly to increase the air flow through the engine to maintain a constant manifold depression to keep emissions low.

Fuel is immediately reinstated if the throttle is opened. If the engine speed drops below 1600 rpm on over-run, fuel is progressively reinstated.

Over-Speed Fuel Cut-Off

To prevent damage at high engine speeds the ECM will implement fuel cut-off at engine speeds above approximately 7000 rpm. Fuel is reinstated as the engine speed falls.

Ignition Switch Off

In the first 10 seconds after the ignition is switched off, the ECM drives the IAC valve to its power down position (ready for the next engine start), and stores any required information.

The ECM then monitors the engine bay temperature using the ambient air temperature sensor. If the temperature is above a certain limit, the ECM will drive the engine bay fan for 8 minutes, and will then power down. If the engine bay temperature is below the limit the ECM will power down after 10 seconds.

Fuel Quantity

The ECM controls fuel quantity by providing sequential injection to the cylinder head intake ports. Sequential injection allows each injector to deliver a precise amount of fuel to the cylinder intake ports, during the induction stroke, in cylinder firing order.

The CMP sensor and reluctor allows the ECM to synchronise injection at cranking speed for starting. The precise quantity of fuel delivered is controlled by adjusting the duration of the injector open time.

To achieve optimum performance the ECM is able to 'learn' the individual characteristics of an engine and adapt the fuelling strategy to suit. This capability is known as adaptive fuel strategy.

Adaptive fuel strategy must be maintained under all throttle positions except:

- Cold start
- Hot start
- Wide open throttle.

All of the above throttle positions are deemed to be 'open loop'. Open loop fuelling does not rely on information from the HO_2S, but sets the air/fuel ratio (AFR) according to the stored data in the ECM.

During a cold start, the ECM references the ECT sensor to calculate the appropriate amount of fuel required to support combustion and adjusts the idle speed to the correct 'fast idle' value. This strategy is maintained until the HO_2S is hot enough to provide an accurate feedback signal.

The specific nature of the other open loop conditions means that the HO_2S feedback is unsuitable as a control value for fuelling. Adaptive strategy also allows the ECM to compensate for wear in engine components and allow for production tolerances in mass produced components such as sensors.

To calculate the amount of fuel to be injected into each cylinder, the ECM has to determine the quantity of oxygen available in the cylinder to burn it. This can be calculated by processing information from the following sensors:

- MAP sensor
- CKP sensor
- ECT sensor
- TP sensor.

During one engine revolution, 2 of the 4 cylinders draw in air. The ECM uses the CKP sensor signal to determine the potential air intake volume in the cylinders.

The oxygen content of the air contained in the cylinders can be calculated by the ECM using information from the MAP sensor and the IAT sensor. The pressure of the air in the intake manifold will vary according to the following factors:

- The position of the throttle valve (driver input)
- The atmospheric pressure (altitude and weather conditions)
- The mechanical condition of the engine (volumetric efficiency).

The pressure in the intake manifold, downstream of the throttle valve, indicates how much air has flowed into the cylinders. This will decrease at higher altitudes as the air becomes 'thinner' or less dense. This will also mean that there will be less oxygen contained in the air which will be available for combustion of fuel.

The temperature of the air will also affect the oxygen content. Air which is cool has molecules packed closer together than hot air, therefore; cooler air contains more oxygen for any given volume than hotter air.

From the above information, the ECM can calculate how much air has been induced into the cylinders. By comparing these values to a fuelling map stored in the ECM memory, the amount of oxygen induced into the cylinders can be calculated. The values obtained from the ECT sensor, engine oil temperature sensor and TP sensor provide 'fine tuning' to the calculations.

To deliver the fuel the ECM completes an earth path to the injector coil, opening the injector for the precise amount of time required for the quantity determined. The correct cylinder order is determined by referencing the CMP sensor during start up to synchronise the CMP sensor signal to the CKP sensor signal. The fuel is injected into the inlet ports of the intake manifold and is drawn into the cylinder as an air and fuel mixture.

The ECM ensures that the amount of fuel injected is not affected by the variations in inlet manifold pressure. The ECM corrects the injector duration time, using MAP sensor information.

The ECM references battery voltage to adjust opening times to suit the state of battery charge. This is required because low battery voltage will mean slower response from the injectors, and could give a leaner AFR than intended.

Ignition Timing

The ignition timing is an important part of the ECM adaptive strategy. The ignition system consists of two double ended coils, mounted on the cam cover directly over the spark plugs, which operate using the wasted spark principle. Each coil is connected to a pair of spark plugs, 1 and 4, 2 and 3.

The spark plugs are connected in series with the secondary winding of the coil so a spark occurs in both cylinders at the same time. When a spark occurs in the cylinder which is on the compression stroke the air/fuel charge is ignited. The spark has no effect on the cylinder at the end of the exhaust stroke, hence the term 'wasted spark'.

The major advantage of this system is that a distributor cap and rotor arm are eliminated thereby improving performance and reliability. The timing of the spark will affect the quality of combustion and the power produced.

The ECM will reference all relevant sensors to achieve the optimum timing for any given condition. This electronically increases the primary coil charging time (dwell angle) as engine speed increases to maintain coil ht voltage at high engine speeds.

The ECM calculates ignition timing using inputs from the following:

- CKP sensor
- TP sensor
- ECT sensor
- IAT sensor.

The ECM calculates dwell angle using inputs from the following:

- CKP sensor
- Battery voltage.

At start up the ECM sets ignition timing by referencing the ECT sensor. After start up, the ignition timing will be controlled according to maps stored in the memory and modified according to additional sensor inputs.

The choice of ignition point is critical in maintaining engine power output with low emissions. Advancing the ignition may increase power output under certain conditions, but it also increases the amount of oxides of nitrogen (NOx) and carbon monoxide (CO) produced in the combustion chamber.

There is a narrow range of ignition points for all engine conditions which give an acceptable compromise between power output and emission control.

The ignition mapping contained within the ECM memory keeps the ignition timing within this narrow band. The ignition timing is used to control engine idle speed in conjunction with the IAC valve stepper motor.

As the MEMS 3 system does not have a knock sensor, ignition timing advance is controlled using different mapping at high engine and intake air temperatures in order to avoid detonation (pinking).

Idle Speed Control

The ECM regulates the engine speed at idling. The ECM uses two methods of idle speed control:

- Ignition timing adjustment
- IAC valve stepper motor.

When the engine idle speed fluctuates, and there are no additional loads on the engine, the ECM will vary the ignition timing and the IAC valve to regulate the idle speed.

This allows very rapid correction of out of tolerance idle speeds. When an additional load is placed on the engine, such as when the power steering is turned on full lock, the ECM uses the IAC valve stepper motor to control the idle speed to specification.

The idle speed is determined from the CKP sensor, but there are also inputs to the ECM from the following:

- Alternator
- Park/Neutral switch (EM-CVT)
- A/C system
- Cooling fan status.

If the ECM receives information from the above inputs that an extra load is being placed on the engine, it can immediately compensate and avoid engine poor idle or stall conditions.

The IAC valve stepper motor is mounted on the inlet manifold and controls a throttle valve air by-pass port.

To increase the idle speed, the stepper motor allows more air to by-pass the throttle and enter the cylinders. To decrease the idle speed, the stepper motor allows less air to enter the cylinders.

The stepper motor is a bi-polar type which consists of two windings controlled by pulse width modulated (PWM) signals from the ECM.

The position of the stepper motor is always referenced on power down of the ECM, this may take from three to five seconds. The stepper motor is also used to reduce manifold vacuum during deceleration to control emissions.

ENGINE MANAGEMENT SYSTEM - MEMS

Evaporative Emissions (EVAP) Control System

The hydrocarbon vapour given off by petrol is harmful to health and the environment. Legislation limits the amount of hydrocarbons (HC) which can be emitted to atmosphere by a motor vehicle.

To meet the limits imposed, a charcoal cannister is fitted to the fuel system to absorb fuel vapour from the tank when the vehicle is not in use. The charcoal cannister has a finite capacity and therefore needs to be purged when the vehicle is driven.

This is achieved by drawing the fuel vapours out of the cannister and into the cylinders of the engine. The HC vapours are converted into carbon dioxide (CO_2) and water (H_2O) by the combustion process and catalytic converter.

ENGINE MANAGEMENT SYSTEM - MEMS

AIR INTAKE SYSTEM - MPi/VVC MEMS 3

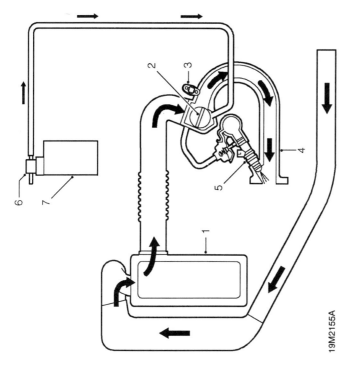

19M2155A

1. Air cleaner element
2. Throttle disc
3. IAC valve
4. Inlet manifold
5. Injector
6. Evaporative emission cannister purge valve
7. Evaporative emission cannister

Intake air is drawn into the throttle housing through the air filter element. Incorporated in the throttle housing is the throttle disc and the TP sensor.

Air passes from the throttle housing via the manifold chamber into the inlet tracts. Fuel is sprayed into the inlet manifold by the injectors and the air/fuel mixture is drawn into the combustion chamber.

Inlet manifold depression is measured by the MAP sensor which is mounted near the end of the inlet manifold chamber. A signal from the MAP sensor is used by the ECM to calculate the amount of fuel to be delivered by the injectors.

FUEL DELIVERY SYSTEM

RECIRCULATING FUEL SYSTEM

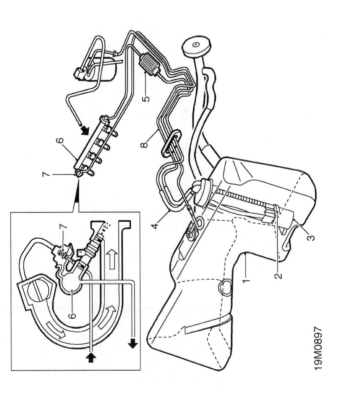

19M0897

1. Fuel tank
2. Fuel pump
3. Swirl pot
4. Feed line

5. Fuel filter
6. Fuel rail
7. Fuel pressure regulator
8. Return line

A recirculating fuel system is used to supply fuel to the injectors at a constant pressure and return excess fuel to the fuel tank.

Fuel pressure is produced by an electric pump immersed in the fuel tank and operating in a swirl pot to maintain a constant fuel level around the pump pick-up.

Pressurised fuel is fed to an in-line fuel filter via a non-return valve which prevents fuel returning to the tank when the pump is not running. Fuel is delivered from the fuel filter to the fuel rail which supplies the injectors. A fuel pressure regulator mounted on the fuel rail controls the pressure of fuel in the rail and returns excess fuel to the swirl pot in the tank. A venturi in the fuel tank causes returning fuel to draw cool fuel into the swirl pot from the tank.

ENGINE MANAGEMENT SYSTEM - MEMS

FUEL TANK BREATHING SYSTEM

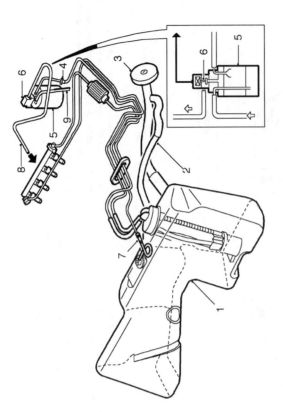

19M0899

1. Fuel tank
2. Filler neck breather pipe
3. Filler cap
4. Two-way breather valve
5. Evaporative emission cannister

6. Evaporative emission cannister, purge valve
7. Vent line
8. Fuel release line
9. Air intake line

When filling the fuel tank, air trapped in the fuel tank by the rising fuel level is allowed to vent to the top of the filler neck by a separate breather pipe.

With the filler cap in place, fuel tank breathing is via a two-way breather valve which allows expanding fumes to exit the tank. From the two-way breather valve, fumes are directed to the evaporative emission cannister where they can be purged into the engine via the evaporative emission cannister purge valve.

ENGINE MANAGEMENT SYSTEM - MEMS

EMISSION CONTROL SYSTEMS

The vehicle is fitted with various items of emission and evaporative control components to comply with emission regulation requirements.

Three control systems are used to reduce harmful emissions released into the atmosphere from the vehicle at all times, and under all conditions. These are:

1. Crankcase emission control
2. Exhaust emission control
3. Fuel vapour evaporative loss control

In many countries it is against the law for a vehicle owner or an unauthorised repair shop to modify or tamper with emission control equipment. In this event the vehicle owner and/or the repairer may be liable for prosecution.

The emission control system fitted to the vehicle is designed to keep the emissions within the legal limits provided that the engine is correctly maintained and is in good mechanical condition.

Crankcase Emission Control System

Gases from the crankcase are drawn into the throttle housing to be burnt in the combustion chambers with the fuel mixture. The system provides effective emission control while the engine is running under all circumstances.

There are two breather pipes connected to the throttle housing, one either side of the throttle disc. When the engine is running with the throttle disc open, both pipes are subject to manifold depression and draw crankcase fumes into the manifold. When the throttle disc is closed, only the pipe on the inlet manifold side of the disc is subject to manifold depression. This pipe incorporates a restrictor to prevent engine oil being drawn into the engine by the substantially greater manifold depression.

Exhaust Emission Control

The engine management system provides accurately metered quantities of fuel to the combustion chambers to ensure the most efficient air to fuel ratio under all conditions of operation. A further improvement to combustion is made by measuring the oxygen content of the exhaust gases to enable the quantity of fuel injected to be varied maintaining the ratio necessary for efficient gas conversion by the catalytic converter.

The catalytic converter is situated between the exhaust front pipe and exhaust silencer. The catalytic converter reduces the emission of Carbon Monoxide, Oxides of Nitrogen and Hydrocarbons released into the atmosphere. The active constituents of the converter are the precious metals Platinum and Rhodium.

The correct operation of the catalytic converter is dependent upon close control of the oxygen concentration in the exhaust gas entering the converter. The quantity of oxygen in the exhaust gas is determined by a heated oxygen sensor situated upstream of the catalytic converter, in the exhaust manifold (up to 2001 MY) or front pipe (from 2001 MY). The heated oxygen sensor provides the engine control module with a signal proportional to the oxygen content. The ECM can then determine whether any adjustment is required to the amount of fuel being injected to achieve the correct exhaust gas content, and implement the required changes.

From 2001 MY, a downstream heated oxygen sensor is installed in the outlet of the catalytic converter. By comparing the inputs from the upstream and downstream heated oxygen sensors, the ECM can monitor the efficiency of the catalytic converter.

⚠ **CAUTION: Serious damage to the catalytic converter will occur if leaded fuel is used. The filler neck is designed to accommodate only unleaded fuel pump nozzles.**

ENGINE MANAGEMENT SYSTEM - MEMS

EVAPORATIVE EMISSION CONTROL

19M0899

1. Fuel tank
2. Filler neck breather pipe
3. Filler cap
4. Two-way breather valve
5. Evaporative emission cannister
6. Evaporative emission cannister, purge valve
7. Vent line
8. Fuel release line
9. Air intake line

Evaporative Emission Cannister

The evaporative emission (EVAP) cannister contains charcoal which absorbs and stores fuel vapour from the fuel tank while the engine is not running. When the engine is running the vapour is purged from the cannister into the engine and burned.

The EVAP cannister is purged when the EVAP cannister purge valve is opened. Manifold depression draws fresh air into the cannister through the charcoal, which releases fuel vapour into the throttle housing.

Evaporative Emission Cannister, Purge Valve

An EVAP cannister, purge valve is operated by the ECM. The purge valve remains closed when the engine is cold or at idling speed, to protect engine tune and catalyst performance. If the EVAP cannister was purged during cold running or at idling speed, the additional enrichment in fuel mixture would delay catalyst light off time and cause erratic idling. When the engine is above 75°C, the purge valve solenoid will become operational (modulated ON and OFF) whenever the engine speed is above approximately 1800 rev/min. When the purge valve is opened, fuel vapour from the EVAP cannister is drawn into the throttle housing for combustion.

ENGINE MANAGEMENT SYSTEM - MEMS

THROTTLE CABLE

Service repair no - 19.20.05

⚠ NOTE: Before adjustment, ensure the cable is correctly routed and located. Do not attempt to adjust the throttle cable or engine idle speed by means of the throttle stop screw.

Adjust

1. Remove the engine compartment access panel. See *BODY, Exterior fittings*.

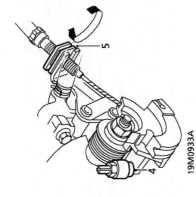

19M0933A

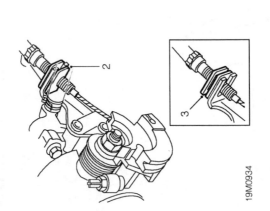

19M0934

2. Release cable adjusting nut from abutment bracket.

3. Position outer cable to abutment bracket so that adjusting nut is in contact with top of abutment bracket.

4. Hold throttle cam in fully closed position, ensure throttle cam contacts throttle stop screw.

5. Rotate cable adjusting nut until all slack is taken out of inner cable. Ensure throttle does not open.

6. Locate throttle cable adjusting nut in abutment bracket.

7. Operate throttle pedal and ensure that full throttle pedal movement is available.

8. Fit engine compartment access panel. *See BODY, Exterior fittings*.

This page is intentionally left blank

ENGINE MANAGEMENT SYSTEM - MEMS

FUEL TANK DRAINING

Service repair no - 19.55.02

> ⚠ **WARNING: The fuel tank must be drained before removing it from the vehicle. Ensure that both sides of the fuel tank are completely drained.**

1. Disconnect battery earth lead.
2. Depressurise fuel system. *See this section.*

Drain

> ⚠ **WARNING: Petrol/gasoline vapour is highly flammable, and in contained spaces is also explosive and toxic. Always have a fire extinguisher containing FOAM, CO₂, GAS OR POWDER close at hand when handling or draining fuel.**

3. Remove fuel pump. *See Repairs.*
4. Using a fuel recovery appliance, drain fuel from the tank into a sealed container. Follow the manufactures instructions for the connnection and safe use of the appliance.
5. Due to the construction of the fuel tank, it will be necessary to drain fuel from each side of the tank separately.

> △ NOTE: Fuel vapour causes the fuel tank to swell, before attempting fuel tank removal ensure fuel is completely drained and the tank is left in the drained condition for at least 2 hours. *See Repairs.*

FUEL SYSTEM DEPRESSURISE

Service repair no - 19.50.02

1. Disconnect battery earth lead.
2. Remove engine compartment access panel. *See BODY, Exterior fittings.*
3. Position absorbent cloth around fuel filter outlet union.

19M0935

4. Loosen fuel filter outlet union to relieve fuel pressure.

> ⚠ **CAUTION: To prevent damage to the fuel system pipes and components, use two spanners when loosening or tightening unions.**

5. Tighten fuel filter outlet union to 30 Nm.
6. Remove absorbent cloth.
7. Fit engine compartment access panel. *See BODY, Exterior fittings.*
8. Connect battery earth lead.

AIR CLEANER

Service repair no - 19.10.01

Remove

1. Disconnect battery earth lead.
2. Remove engine cover. *See ENGINE, Repairs.*
3. Remove engine compartment access panel. *See BODY, Exterior fittings.*

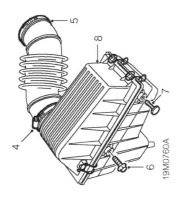

19M0760A

4. Loosen clip screw and release hose from air cleaner.
5. Remove clip and remove hose from throttle body.
6. Remove bolt securing air cleaner to mounting bracket.
7. Remove stud securing air cleaner to mounting bracket.
8. Remove air cleaner from lower mounting and resonator duct. *Do not carry out further dismantling if component is removed for access only.*
9. Release 4 clips securing air cleaner cover.
10. Remove air cleaner cover and element.
11. Clean air cleaner box and cover.
12. Fit air cleaner element and cover and secure with clips.

Refit

1. Fit air cleaner assembly and align to mounting bracket and resonator duct.
2. Fit bolt and stud securing air cleaner to mounting bracket.
3. Fit hose to throttle body and secure clip.
4. Position hose to air cleaner and tighten clip screw.
5. Fit engine compartment access panel. *See BODY, Exterior fittings.*
6. Fit engine cover. *See ENGINE, Repairs.*
7. Connect battery earth lead.

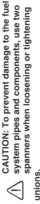

AIR CLEANER - MGF TROPHY

Service repair no - 19.10.01

Remove

1. Remove air cleaner element. *See this section.*

SP19 0003

2. Remove 2 retaining studs securing air cleaner to support bracket.
3. Release air cleaner from lower grommet.
4. Release front air intake hose.
5. Remove screw securing rear air intake hose.
6. Release rear air intake hose and manoeuvre air cleaner from engine bay.

Refit

1. Position air cleaner and align rear air intake hose.
2. Fit and tighten screw securing rear air intake hose.
3. Align and connect front air intake hose.
4. Secure air cleaner in lower grommet.
5. Align air cleaner to support bracket and fit retaining studs.
6. Fit air cleaner element. *See this section.*

AIR CLEANER ELEMENT

Service repair no - 19.10.10

Remove

1. Remove engine compartment access panel. *See BODY, Exterior fittings.*

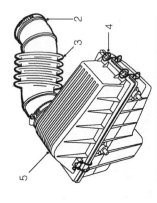
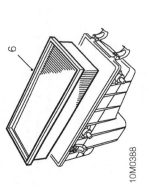

10M0388

2. Remove clip securing air intake hose to throttle body.
3. Release hose from throttle body.
4. Release 4 clips securing cover to air cleaner.
5. Manoeuvre cover from air cleaner to gain sufficient access to element.
6. Remove air cleaner element.

ENGINE MANAGEMENT SYSTEM - MEMS

ELEMENT - AIR CLEANER - MGF TROPHY

Service repair no - 19.10.10

Remove

1. Disconnect battery earth lead.
2. Remove engine cover. *See ENGINE, Repairs.*
3. Remove engine compartment access cover. *See BODY, Exterior fittings.*

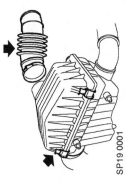

SP19 0001

4. Release clip and disconnect air intake hose from throttle body.
5. Loosen clip securing air intake hose to air cleaner and remove hose.
6. Release 4 clips securing air cleaner cover.

SP19 0002

7. Remove air cleaner cover and remove element.

Refit

1. Fit NEW air cleaner element.
2. Position cover to air cleaner and secure with clips.
3. Connect air intake hose to throttle body and secure with clip.
4. Fit engine compartment access panel. *See BODY, Exterior fittings.*

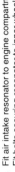

Refit

1. Clean inside of air cleaner.
2. Fit air cleaner element.
3. Fit air cleaner cover and secure clips.
4. Fit air intake hose to air cleaner and secure with clip.
5. Fit air intake hose to throttle body and secure with clip.
6. Fit engine compartment access cover. **See BODY, Exterior fittings.**
7. Fit engine cover. **See ENGINE, Repairs.**
8. Connect battery earth lead.

AIR INTAKE RESONATOR - UP TO 2001MY

Service repair no - 19.70.03

Remove

1. Remove air cleaner. **See this section.**
2. Remove engine compartment access panel. **See BODY, Exterior fittings.**
3. Loosen clip securing air intake pipe to resonator.
4. Disconnect pipe from resonator.
5. Raise rear of vehicle.

⚠ **WARNING: Support on safety stands.**

6. Remove LH rear road wheel.

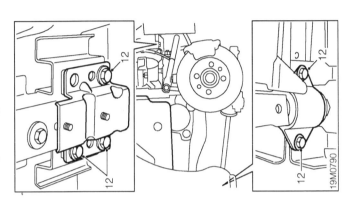

19M0789

7. Remove nut securing top of damper to body.
8. Remove rear anti-roll bar. **See FRONT SUSPENSION, Repairs.**
9. Remove 2 bolts securing resonator to inner wheel arch.
10. Release ABS sensor lead from Hydragas unit bracket.
11. Support LH side of body with jack.

⚠ **CAUTION: Place suitable block of wood between trolley jack and body to prevent damage occurring.**

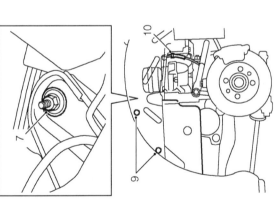

19M0790

12. Remove 5 bolts securing LH side of subframe to body.
13. Raise body away from subframe to gain access to resonator.
14. Remove air intake resonator.

Refit

1. Fit air intake resonator to engine compartment.
2. Fit bolts securing resonator to inner wheel arch.
3. Lower body onto subframe and tighten bolts to:
   Rear mount to body = 45 Nm
   30 Nm.
4. Connect air intake pipe to resonator and tighten clip.
5. Fit ABS wheel speed sensor lead to Hydragas unit bracket.
6. Fit rear anti-roll bar. **See FRONT SUSPENSION, Repairs.**
7. Fit bolt securing damper to body and tighten to 37 Nm.
8. Fit road wheel(s) and tighten nuts to correct torque. **See INFORMATION, Torque wrench settings.**
9. Remove stand(s) and lower vehicle.
10. Fit air cleaner. **See this section.**

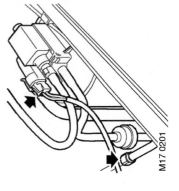

M17 0201

4. Release and disconnect feed hose.
5. Disconnect multiplug from purge valve.
6. Release EVAP cannister from support bracket and remove EVAP cannister.

Refit

1. Position EVAP cannister and secure in support bracket.
2. Connect hose to inlet manifold and secure with clip.
3. Connect feed hose.
4. Connect multiplug to purge valve.
5. Fit engine compartment access panel. *See ENGINE, Repairs.*
6. Connect battery earth lead.

EVAPORATIVE EMISSION CANNISTER

Service repair no - 17.15.13

Remove

1. Disconnect battery earth lead.
2. Remove engine compartment access panel. *See BODY, Exterior fittings.*

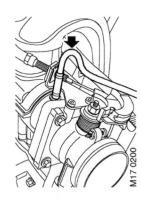

M17 0200

3. Release clip and disconnect hose from inlet manifold.

SENSOR - CAMSHAFT POSITION (CMP) - MPi MEMS3

Service repair no - 18.30.24

Remove

1. Remove engine cover. *See ENGINE, Repairs.*

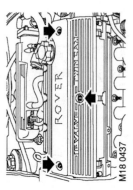

M18 0437

2. Remove three bolts securing coil cover to engine and remove coil cover.

M18 0438

3. Release CMP multiplug from bracket and disconnect multiplug.
4. Release sensor cable from clip.
5. Remove bolt securing camshaft sensor and remove sensor.

Refit

1. Clean camshaft sensor and mating face.
2. Fit camshaft sensor, fit bolt and tighten to 6 Nm.
3. Connect CMP multiplug and secure in bracket.
4. Fit coil cover, fit bolts and tighten to 8 Nm.
5. Fit engine cover. *See ENGINE, Repairs.*

SENSOR - CAMSHAFT POSITION (CMP) - VVC

Service repair no - 18.30.24

Remove

1. Remove engine compartment access panel. *See BODY, Exterior fittings.*

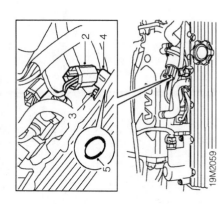

19M2059

2. Disconnect multiplug from CMP sensor.
3. Remove bolt securing CMP sensor to cylinder head.
4. Remove CMP sensor.
5. Remove 'O' ring seal from sensor.

Refit

1. Clean sealing faces of sensor and cylinder head.
2. Fit NEW 'O' ring seal to CMP sensor.
3. Fit sensor to cylinder head and tighten bolt to 6 Nm.
4. Connect multiplug.
5. Fit engine compartment access panel. *See BODY, Exterior fittings.*

ENGINE MANAGEMENT SYSTEM - MEMS

CATALYTIC CONVERTER

Service repair no - 17.50.01

Remove

1. Raise rear of vehicle.

> ⚠ **WARNING: Support on safety stands.**

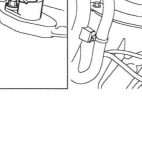

17M0053

2. Remove nut and special washer securing rear silencer clamp.
3. Remove catalyst overheat sensor from catalyst (if fitted).
4. Remove 3 flange nuts securing catalytic converter to front pipe.
5. Remove rear silencer clamp.
6. Remove 3 flange nuts securing catalytic converter to silencer.
7. Remove catalytic converter.
8. Remove and discard gaskets.

Refit

1. Clean flange mating faces of front pipe, silencer and catalytic converter.
2. Fit NEW gaskets to catalytic converter studs.
3. Fit catalytic converter to silencer, fit nuts and tighten to 70 Nm.
4. Clean catalyst overheat sensor and mating faces (if fitted).
5. Fit and tighten catalyst overheat sensor to 30 Nm (if fitted).
6. Position catalytic converter to front pipe.
7. Fit rear silencer clamp.
8. Fit nuts and tighten to 70 Nm.
9. Align rear silencer clamp strap, fit special washer, fit nut and tighten to 30 Nm.
10. Remove stand(s) and lower vehicle.

> ⚠ **CAUTION: Ensure all joints are free from leaks. Exhaust gas leaks upstream of the catalyst could lead to internal failure of the catalyst.**

ENGINE MANAGEMENT SYSTEM - MEMS

SENSOR - CRANKSHAFT POSITION (CKP) - MPi MEMS 1.9 (UP TO 2000MY); VVC MEMS 2J (UP TO 2001MY)

Service repair no - 18.30.12

Remove

1. Disconnect battery earth lead.
2. Remove engine compartment access panel. **See BODY, Exterior fittings.**

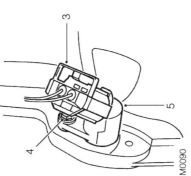

18M0090

3. Release sensor multiplug from harness.
4. Remove bolt securing sensor.
5. Remove sensor.

Refit

1. Clean sensor and location.
2. Position sensor and tighten bolt to 6 Nm.
3. Connect multiplug to harness.
4. Fit engine compartment access panel. **See BODY, Exterior fittings.**
5. Connect battery earth lead.

ENGINE MANAGEMENT SYSTEM - MEMS

SENSOR - CRANKSHAFT POSITION (CKP) - MPi MEMS3 (2000MY ON); VVC MEMS 3 (2001MY ON)

Service repair no - 18.30.12

Remove

1. Disconnect battery earth lead.
2. Raise rear of vehicle.

> ⚠ **WARNING: Support on safety stands.**

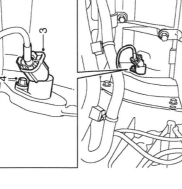

M18 0435

3. Disconnect multiplug from CKP sensor.
4. Remove bolt securing CKP sensor to flywheel housing.
5. Remove CKP sensor.

Refit

1. Clean CKP sensor and mating face of flywheel housing.
2. Position CKP sensor, fit bolt and tighten to 6 Nm.
3. Connect multiplug to CKP sensor.
4. Remove stand(s) and lower vehicle.
5. Connect battery earth lead.

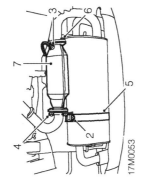

DISTRIBUTOR CAP - MPi MEMS 1.9 (UP TO 2000MY)

Service repair no - 18.20.10

Remove

1. Remove engine cover. *See ENGINE, Repairs.*

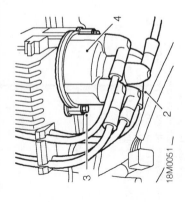

18M0051

2. Disconnect h.t. leads from distributor cap, noting their fitted positions.
3. Remove 2 bolts securing distributor cap.
4. Remove cap.

Refit

1. Fit distributor cap and tighten bolts to 2 Nm.
2. Connect h.t. leads.
3. Fit engine cover. *See ENGINE, Repairs.*

ENGINE CONTROL MODULE (ECM) - MPi MEMS 1.9 (UP TO 2000MY)

Service repair no - 18.30.01

Remove

1. Disconnect battery earth lead.
2. Remove engine compartment access panel. *See BODY, Exterior fittings.*

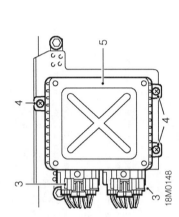

18M0072

3. Disconnect multiplug from ECM.
4. Disconnect vacuum pipe from ECM.
5. Remove 3 screws securing ECM to mounting bracket.
6. Remove ECM.

Refit

1. Locate ECM in engine compartment and tighten screws.
2. Connect vacuum pipe to ECM.
3. Connect multiplug to ECM.
4. Fit engine compartment access panel. *See BODY, Exterior fittings.*
5. Connect battery earth lead.

ENGINE CONTROL MODULE (ECM) - VVC MEMS 2J (UP TO 2001MY)

Service repair no - 18.30.01

Remove

1. Disconnect battery earth lead.
2. Remove engine compartment access panel. *See BODY, Exterior fittings.*

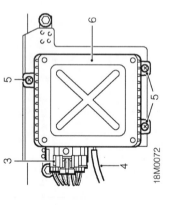

18M0148

3. Disconnect 2 multiplugs from ECM.
4. Remove 3 screws securing ECM to mounting bracket.
5. Remove ECM.

Refit

1. Locate ECM to bracket and tighten screws.
2. Connect multiplugs to ECM.
3. Fit engine compartment access panel. *See BODY, Exterior fittings.*
4. Connect battery earth lead.

ENGINE CONTROL MODULE (ECM) - MPi MEMS3 (2000MY ON); VVC MEMS 3 (2001MY ON)

Service repair no - 18.30.01

Remove

1. Disconnect battery earth lead.
2. Remove engine compartment access panel. *See BODY, Exterior fittings. See ENGINE, Repairs.*

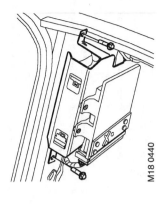

M18 0440

3. Remove 2 bolts securing ECM mounting bracket.
4. Release mounting bracket from support bracket and position to access ECM screws.

SENSOR - ENGINE COOLANT TEMPERATURE (ECT)

Service repair no - 18.30.10

Remove

1. Disconnect battery earth lead.
2. Remove engine cover. *See ENGINE, Repairs.*
3. Raise vehicle on ramp.
4. Position container below sensor.

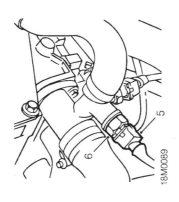

18M0089

5. Disconnect sensor multiplug.
6. Remove sensor from top coolant hose adapter.

Refit

1. Clean sensor threads and mating faces.
2. Fit sensor and tighten to 6 Nm.
3. Connect multiplug to sensor.
4. Remove container, and lower vehicle.
5. Top-up cooling system. *See MAINTENANCE.*
6. Fit engine cover. *See ENGINE, Repairs.*
7. Connect battery earth lead.

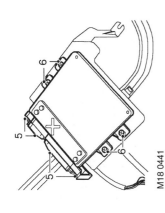

M18 0441

5. Release ECM multiplug catches and disconnect ECM multiplugs.
6. Remove 4 screws securing ECM to mounting bracket.
7. Remove ECM.

Refit

1. Locate ECM to mounting bracket, fit and tighten screws.
2. Connect multiplugs and secure multiplug catches.
3. Position mounting bracket in support bracket, fit bolts and tighten to 8 Nm.
4. Fit engine compartment access panel. *See BODY, Exterior fittings. See ENGINE, Repairs.*
5. Connect battery earth lead.
6. Initiate ECM using TestBook.

ENGINE MANAGEMENT RELAY MODULE

Service repair no - 18.30.06

Remove

1. Remove engine compartment access panel. *See BODY, Exterior fittings.*

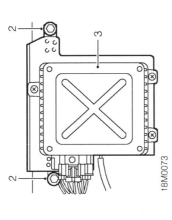

18M0073

◁ NOTE: MPi MEMS 1.9 ECM shown

2. Remove 2 bolts securing ECM mounting bracket.
3. Move bracket aside and release engine management relay module.

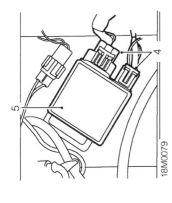

18M0079

4. Disconnect 2 multiplugs from relay module.
5. Remove relay module.

Refit

1. Connect multiplugs to relay module.
2. Secure relay module onto ECM mounting bracket.
3. Fit ECM mounting bracket and tighten bolts. *See BODY, Exterior fittings.*
4. Fit engine compartment access panel. *See BODY, Exterior fittings.*

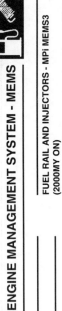

ENGINE MANAGEMENT SYSTEM - MEMS

FUEL FILTER

Service repair no - 19.25.02

Remove

1. Disconnect battery earth lead.
2. Remove engine compartment access panel. **See BODY, Exterior fittings.**
3. Position cloth around fuel outlet union.

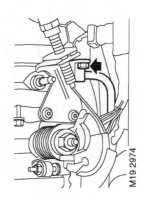

19M2305

4. Loosen union to relieve fuel pressure and disconnect pipe.

⚠️ **CAUTION: Use two spanners when loosening or tightening unions.**

5. Position cloth around fuel filter union.
6. Loosen union and disconnect fuel inlet pipe from fuel filter.
7. Release clip and remove filter from housing.
8. Discard fuel filter.

Refit

1. Clean fuel pipe unions.
2. With arrow on the fuel filter pointing rearwards position NEW filter into housing.
3. Tighten fuel inlet pipe to 30 Nm.
4. Connect fuel outlet pipe to fuel filter and tighten to 30 Nm.
5. Fit engine compartment access panel. **See BODY, Exterior fittings.**
6. Connect battery earth lead.

FUEL INJECTORS - MPi

Service repair no - 19.60.12

Remove

1. Disconnect battery earth lead.
2. Remove fuel rail. **See this section.**
3. Release multiplugs from injectors.

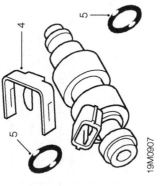

19M0907

4. Release spring clips securing injectors to fuel rail.
5. Remove injectors and discard 2 'O' rings from each injector.
6. Fit protective caps to each injector.

Refit

1. Clean injectors and injector recesses in fuel rail and inlet manifold.
2. Lubricate 8 NEW 'O' rings with silicone grease and fit to injectors.
3. Fit fuel rail to injectors.
4. Fit spring clips to secure injectors to fuel rail.
5. Fit multiplugs to injectors.
6. Fit fuel rail. **See this section.**
7. Connect battery earth lead.

FUEL INJECTORS - VVC

Service repair no - 19.60.12

Remove

1. Disconnect battery earth lead.
2. Remove fuel rail. **See this section.**

19M2102

3. Disconnect multiplugs from injectors.
4. Remove injectors from inlet manifold.
5. Remove and discard 'O' rings from injectors.

Refit

1. Lubricate new 'O' rings with silicone grease and fit to injectors.
2. Fit injectors to fuel rail and connect multiplugs.
3. Fit fuel rail. **See this section.**
4. Connect battery earth lead.

FUEL RAIL AND INJECTORS - MPi MEMS3 (2000MY ON)

Service repair no - 19.60.12
Service repair no - 19.60.04

Remove

1. Disconnect battery earth lead.
2. Remove engine cover. **See ENGINE, Repairs.**

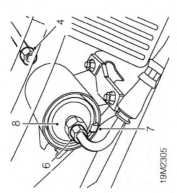

M19 2973

3. Release clip and disconnect vacuum pipe from fuel pressure regulator.
4. Position absorbent cloth beneath fuel rail.

M19 2974

5. Remove 2 bolts securing fuel pipe to fuel rail.
6. Release fuel pipe from fuel rail, remove and discard 'O' ring.

⚠️ **CAUTION: Plug connections.**

18G 1741

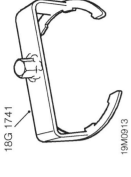

19M0913

FUEL PUMP (UP TO 2001MY)

Service repair no - 19.45.08

Remove

1. Disconnect battery earth lead.
2. Depressurise fuel system. *See **Adjustments**.*
3. Remove engine cover. *See **ENGINE - 'K' SERIES, Repairs**.*

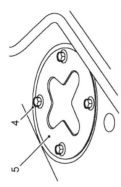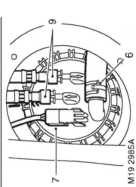

M19 2985A

4. Remove 4 bolts securing fuel pump cover.
5. Remove fuel pump cover.
6. Release clip and hose securing breather hose to fuel pump.
7. Disconnect fuel pump multiplug.
8. Position absorbent cloth around fuel hoses to collect any fuel spillage.
9. Noting their fitted positions, release fuel feed hose (orange connector) and fuel return hose (green connector) from fuel pump.

10. Using tool **18G 1741**, loosen fuel pump to tank retaining ring.
11. Remove tool.
12. Remove fuel pump retaining ring.
13. Remove fuel pump from tank.

⚠ **CAUTION: Do not insert a lever between the fuel tank and fuel pump, as damage to the sealing surface of the fuel tank may occur.**

14. Remove sealing ring from fuel tank and discard.
15. Remove absorbent cloth.

M19 2975

Refit

1. Remove protective caps from each injector.
2. Clean injectors and recesses in fuel rail and inlet manifold.
3. Lubricate new 'O' rings with silicone grease and fit to each end of injectors.
4. Fit injectors to fuel rail.
5. Secure injectors to fuel rail with spring clips.
6. Position fuel rail assembly and connect injector multiplugs.
7. Fit injector spacer.
8. Push each injector into inlet manifold.
9. Fit bolts securing fuel rail to inlet manifold and tighten to 10 Nm.
10. Using a new 'O' ring, connect fuel feed to fuel rail, fit bolts and tighten to 8 Nm.
11. Connect vacuum pipe to fuel pressure regulator and secure with clip.
12. Fit engine cover. *See **ENGINE, Repairs**.*
13. Connect battery earth lead.

7. Remove 2 bolts securing fuel rail to inlet manifold.
8. Release fuel rail and injectors from inlet manifold.
9. Release and remove injector spacer.
10. Disconnect multiplugs from injectors.
11. Remove the fuel rail complete with injectors.

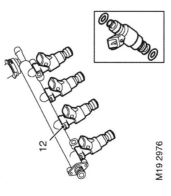

M19 2976

12. Release spring clips securing injectors to fuel rail and remove fuel injectors.
13. Remove and discard 2 'O' rings from each injector.
14. Fit protective caps to each end of injectors.

FILLER NECK

Service repair no - 19.55.07

Remove

1. Disconnect battery earth lead.
2. Remove air cleaner. *See this section.*
3. Drain fuel tank. *See Adjustments.*

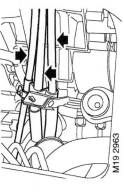

M19 2963

4. Release 3 cables from air cleaner support bracket.

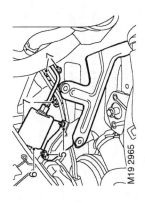

M19 2965

5. Remove 2 nuts securing fuel filter to air cleaner support bracket.
6. Release fuel filter from support bracket and position aside.
7. Remove 3 bolts securing air cleaner support bracket to body and remove bracket.

> **WARNING: Fuel vapour is highly flammable and in confined spaces is also explosive and toxic. Always have a fire extinguisher containing foam, CO$_2$ gas or powder close at hand when handling or draining fuel.**

7. Disconnect fuel pump multiplug.
8. Position absorbent cloth around fuel hoses to collect any fuel spillage.
9. Noting fitted position, release fuel feed and return hoses from pump.

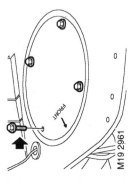

19-009

M19 3338

10. Using tool **19-009** , loosen and remove fuel pump locking ring from tank.
11. Remove fuel pump retaining ring, release fuel pump and remove from tank. Discard fuel tank sealing ring.

Refit

1. Clean fuel pump and mating face.
2. Fit new fuel pump seal to pump body, locate pump assembly through tank opening. Fit seal to tank, push pump fully home taking care not to dislodge the seal.
3. Fit fuel pump locking ring and using tool **19-009** , tighten to 35 Nm.
4. Connect fuel feed and return hoses to pump.
5. Connect multiplug to fuel pump.
6. Connect fuel pump breather hose and secure with clip.
7. Fit fuel pump access cover, fit and tighten bolts to 10 Nm.
8. Fit subwoofer assembly. *See ELECTRICAL, Repairs.*
9. Fit engine cover. *See ENGINE - 'K' SERIES, Repairs.*
10. Connect battery earth lead.

Refit

1. Clean pump to tank mating faces.
2. Fit NEW sealing ring to fuel tank.

PUMP - RENEW (2000MY ON)

Service repair no - 19.45.08

Remove

1. Disconnect battery earth lead.
2. Depressurise fuel system. *See Adjustments.*
3. Remove subwoofer assembly. *See ELECTRICAL, Repairs.*
4. Remove engine cover. *See ENGINE - 'K' SERIES, Repairs.*

> **WARNING: The spilling of fuel is unavoidable during this operation. Ensure that all necessary precautions are taken to prevent fire and explosion.**

19M0914

3. Fit fuel pump to tank ensuring location marker on fuel pump aligns between two markers on fuel tank.

> **CAUTION: To ensure seal does not become dislodged. The fuel pump should be pushed not twisted into place.**

4. Fit fuel pump lock ring and tighten to 45 Nm using tool 18G 1741.
5. Remove tool.
6. Connect fuel feed hose (orange connector) and fuel return hose (green connector) to fuel pump.
7. Connect fuel pump multiplug.
8. Connect breather hose to fuel pump and secure clip.
9. Fit fuel pump cover, fit bolts and tighten to 17 Nm.
10. Fit engine cover. *See ENGINE - 'K' SERIES, Repairs.*
11. Connect battery earth lead.

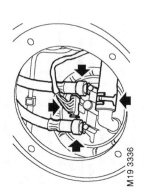

FRONT

M19 2961

5. Remove 4 bolts securing fuel pump access cover to body and remove cover.

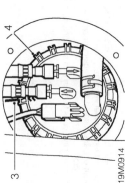

M19 3336

6. Release clip and disconnect hose securing fuel pump breather hose to fuel pump.

HOSE - BREATHER - TANK TO FILLER NECK

Service repair no - 19.55.14

Remove

1. Disconnect battery earth lead.
2. If fitted, remove subwoofer assembly. *See ELECTRICAL, Repairs.*
3. Remove hoodwell trim. *See BODY, Interior trim components.*
4. Remove engine cover. *See ENGINE, Repairs.*

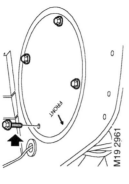

M19 2961

5. Remove 4 bolts securing fuel pump cover and remove cover.

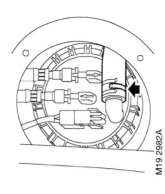

M19 2982A

6. Release clip and disconnect breather hose from fuel pump.

M19 2962

15. Remove 2 bolts securing filler neck to body and remove filler neck.

Refit

1. Position filler neck, fit and tighten 2 bolts securing neck to body.
2. Connect tank hose to filler neck and secure with clip.
3. Connect breather hose to filler neck and secure with clip.
4. Manoeuvre gaiter into position, fit clamping plate and secure with nuts.
5. Fit and tighten 2 bolts securing resonator to body to 8 Nm.
6. Fit air intake elbow to resonator.
7. Connect air intake hose to resonator and secure with clip.
8. Position air cleaner support bracket, fit and tighten bolts.
9. Connect cables to clips.
10. Fit fuel filter to support bracket and secure with nuts.
11. Refill fuel tank. *See Adjustments.*
12. Fit fuel cap.
13. Fit air cleaner. *See this section.*
14. Connect battery earth lead.

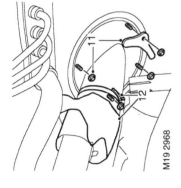

M19 2966

8. Loosen clip securing air intake hose to resonator and release hose from resonator.
9. Remove air intake elbow from resonator.

M19 2967

10. Remove 2 bolts securing air intake resonator to body.

M19 2968

11. Remove 4 nuts securing filler neck gaiter and collect gaiter clamp.
12. Slide gaiter up filler neck, loosen clip and release hose from filler neck.

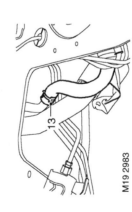

M19 2983

13. Release clip securing breather hose to filler neck and disconnect hose.
14. Remove fuel filler cap.

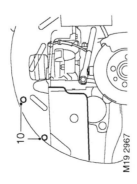

FUEL RAIL - MPi MEMS 1.9 (UP TO 2000MY)

Service repair no - 19.60.04

Remove

1. Disconnect battery earth lead.
2. Remove engine cover. See *ENGINE, Repairs.*
3. Remove engine compartment access panel. See *BODY, Exterior fittings.*
4. Position absorbent cloth around fuel filter union. Loosen union to release fuel pressure.
5. Retighten union to 30 Nm.

M19 2964A

7. Release clip and disconnect breather hose from filler neck.
8. Remove breather hose.

Refit

1. Position hose and fit to filler neck and fuel pump.
2. Secure hose with clips.
3. Fit fuel pump cover and secure with bolts.
4. If fitted, fit subwoofer assembly. See *ELECTRICAL, Repairs.*
5. Fit engine cover. See *ENGINE, Repairs.*
6. Fit hoodwell trim. See *BODY, Interior trim components.*
7. Connect battery earth lead.

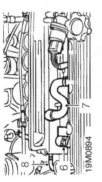

19M0894

6. Release clip and remove breather hose between throttle body and camshaft cover.
7. Remove breather hose between inlet manifold and camshaft cover.
8. Disconnect vacuum pipe from fuel pressure regulator.
9. Loosen clip and disconnect fuel return hose from fuel rail.

⚠ **CAUTION: Plug the connections.**

10. Remove hose running between idle air control valve and throttle body.

19M0895

11. Remove 2 bolts securing fuel feed pipe to fuel rail.
12. Disconnect fuel feed pipe from fuel rail and remove and discard 'O' ring.

⚠ **CAUTION: Plug the connections.**

13. Release injector harness multiplug from bracket on throttle body.
14. Disconnect injector harness multiplug.

19M0896

15. Remove 2 bolts securing fuel rail to inlet manifold.
16. Release fuel injectors and rail assembly from inlet manifold.
17. Remove fuel rail, injectors, injector harness and pressure regulator.

⚠ **CAUTION: Do not attempt to remove fuel pressure regulator from fuel rail, as regulator and fuel rail are only serviced as an assembly.**

18. Fit protective caps to each injector.

Refit

1. Clean injectors and injector recesses in inlet manifold.
2. Fit fuel rail and injector assembly to cylinder head.
3. Fit bolts securing fuel rail to inlet manifold and tighten to 10 Nm.
4. Connect vacuum hose to fuel pressure regulator.
5. Connect fuel return hose to fuel rail and secure with clip.
6. Lubricate NEW 'O' ring with silicone grease and fit to fuel feed pipe.
7. Fit fuel feed pipe to fuel rail and tighten bolts to 8 Nm.
8. Fit hose running between idle air control valve and throttle body.
9. Fit breather hose between inlet manifold and camshaft cover.
10. Fit breather hose between throttle body and camshaft cover, secure with clips.
11. Fit engine cover. See *ENGINE, Repairs.*
12. Fit engine compartment access panel. See *BODY, Exterior fittings.*
13. Connect battery earth lead.

FUEL RAIL - VVC

Service repair no - 19.60.04

Remove

1. Disconnect battery earth lead.
2. Remove inlet manifold chamber. *See MANIFOLD & EXHAUST SYSTEMS, Repairs.*
3. Position absorbent cloth around fuel filter outlet union. Slacken union to relieve fuel pressure. Retighten union to 30 Nm.

⚠ **CAUTION: To prevent damage to fuel system pipes and components, use two spanners when loosening or tightening unions.**

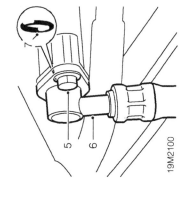

19M2099

4. Release clip and release fuel return pipe from fuel rail.

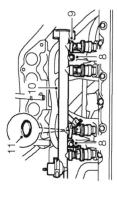

19M2100

5. Remove 2 bolts securing fuel feed pipe to fuel rail.
6. Release fuel feed pipe from fuel rail.
7. Remove and discard 'O' ring.

⚠ **CAUTION: Plug the connections.**

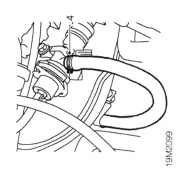

19M2101

8. Remove 2 bolts securing fuel rail to inlet manifold.
9. Remove spring clips securing injectors to fuel rail.
10. Release fuel rail from injectors and remove.
11. Remove and discard 'O' rings from injectors.

Refit

1. Lubricate new 'O' rings with silicone grease and fit to injectors.
2. Position fuel rail and fit to injectors.
3. Fit spring clips securing fuel rail to injectors.
4. Fit bolts securing fuel rail to inlet manifold and tighten to 10 Nm.
5. Connect fuel return pipe to fuel rail and secure with clip.
6. Remove plugs from fuel feed pipe and fuel rail.
7. Lubricate new 'O' ring with silicone grease and fit to fuel feed pipe.
8. Connect fuel feed pipe to fuel rail and tighten bolts to 8 Nm.
9. Fit inlet manifold chamber. *See MANIFOLD & EXHAUST SYSTEMS, Repairs.*
10. Connect battery earth lead.

FUEL TANK

Service repair no - 19.55.01

⚠ **WARNING: See RESTRAINT SYSTEMS, Precautions.**

Remove

1. Make the SRS system safe. *See RESTRAINT SYSTEMS, Precautions.*
2. Remove air cleaner. *See this section.*
3. Drain fuel tank. *See Adjustments.*

△ **NOTE: Fuel vapour causes the fuel tank to swell, before attempting fuel tank removal ensure fuel is completely drained and the tank is left in the drained condition for at least 2 hours.**

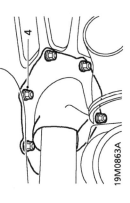

19M0863A

4. Remove 5 nuts securing fuel filler pipe gaiter to bulkhead.
5. Remove fuel filler cap.

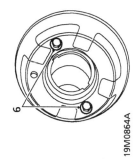

19M0864A

6. Loosen 2 bolts securing filler neck to rear wing.

ENGINE MANAGEMENT SYSTEM - MEMS

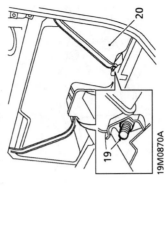

19M0869A

18. Remove and discard plastic fuel tank sealing sheet.

19M0870A

19. Remove 2 nuts securing tank retaining straps to body and position aside.
20. Remove fuel tank.

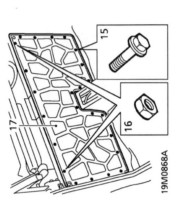

19M0867A

14. Remove 9 retaining studs securing felt pad to rear bulkhead and remove pad.

19M0868A

15. Remove 22 bolts securing closing panel to rear bulkhead.
16. Remove 2 nuts securing closing panel to rear bulkhead.
17. Remove closing panel.

ENGINE MANAGEMENT SYSTEM - MEMS

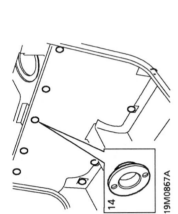

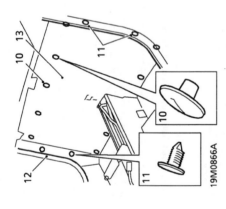

19M0866A

10. Remove 9 retaining studs securing carpet to rear bulkhead.
11. Remove 4 clips securing carpet to 'B' post.
12. Release carpet from door seals and velcro strips.
13. Remove carpet.

19M0865A

7. Release clip securing filler hose to fuel tank and position hose aside.
8. Remove front console. *See BODY, Interior trim components.*
9. Lower hood.

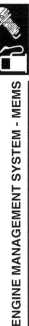
Refit

1. Position fuel tank to body.
2. Align retaining straps to body and tighten nuts to 10 Nm.
3. Align NEW plastic sheet to bulkhead and press seal into place.
4. Fit bulkhead closing panel and tighten nuts and bolts to 9 Nm.
5. Fit felt pad and secure with studs.
6. Fit carpet and secure with studs.
7. Position carpet to velcro and behind door seal.
8. Fit front console. See **BODY, Interior trim components.**
9. Raise rear of hood.

⚠️ **CAUTION: Do not use any lubricants on flexible filler hose to ease assembly.**

10. Position filler hose to tank and tighten clip to 3 Nm.
11. Fit bolts securing filler neck to wing and tighten to 3 Nm.
12. Fit filler cap.
13. Position filler gaiter to body studs and secure with nuts.
14. Fit air cleaner. See **this section.**
15. Fit fuel pump. See **this section.**

h.t. LEADS - SET - MPi MEMS 1.9 (UP TO 2000MY)

Service repair no - 18.20.11

Remove

1. Disconnect battery earth lead.
2. Remove engine cover. See **ENGINE, Repairs.**

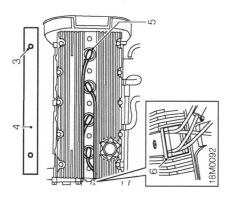

18M0092

3. Remove 2 screws securing h.t. lead cover.
4. Remove cover.
5. Release h.t. leads from spark plugs.
6. Release h.t. leads from retaining plate grommet.

---

ht LEAD - SET - MPi MEMS3 (2000MY ON)

Service repair no - 18.20.11

Remove

1. Remove engine cover. See **ENGINE, Repairs.**

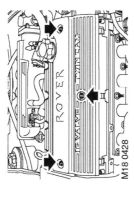

M18 0428

2. Remove screws securing coil cover and remove cover.

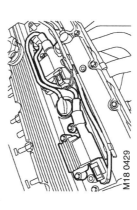

M18 0429

3. Disconnect ht leads from coils, release ht leads from retainers.
4. Disconnect ht leads from plugs and remove ht leads.

Refit

1. Connect ht leads to plugs.
2. Connect ht leads to coils and secure in retainers.
3. Fit coil cover and tighten screws to 8 Nm.
4. Fit engine cover. See **ENGINE, Repairs.**

7. Release h.t. leads from distributor cap.

Refit

1. Fit h.t. leads to distributor cap.

◁ **NOTE:** Ensure cylinder number printed on h.t. lead matches cylinder number embossed on distributor cap.

2. Route h.t. leads correctly through grommet and onto retaining plate.
3. Connect h.t. leads to spark plugs.
4. Fit h.t. lead cover and tighten screws to 2 Nm.
5. Fit engine cover. See **ENGINE, Repairs.**
6. Connect battery earth lead.

18M0093

VALVE - IDLE AIR CONTROL (IAC) - MPi MEMS 1.9 (UP TO 2000MY) ; VVC MEMS 2J (UP TO 2001MY)

Service repair no - 18.30.05

Remove

1. Disconnect battery earth lead.
2. Remove engine cover. *See ENGINE, Repairs.*

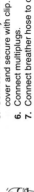

18M0087

3. Disconnect multiplug from valve.
4. Remove 2 Torx screws securing valve to inlet manifold.
5. Remove valve.
6. Remove 'O' ring and discard.

Refit

1. Ensure mating faces of inlet manifold and valve are clean.
2. Lubricate NEW 'O' ring with silicone grease and fit to valve.
3. Fit valve and tighten Torx screws to 1.5 Nm.
4. Connect multiplug to valve.
5. Fit engine cover. *See ENGINE, Repairs.*
6. Connect battery earth lead.

VALVE - IDLE AIR CONTROL (IAC) - MPi MEMS 3 (2000MY ON) ; VVC MEMS 3 (2001MY ON)

Service repair no - 18.30.05

Remove

1. Remove engine cover. *See ENGINE, Repairs.*

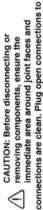

M18 0432

2. Disconnect multiplug from IAC valve.
3. Release bypass hose from IAC valve and remove from throttle body.
4. Release breather hose from throttle body and position aside.
5. Remove 4 Torx screws securing IAC valve to inlet manifold.
6. Remove IAC valve.
7. Remove and discard 'O' ring.

Refit

1. Clean mating faces of IAC valve and inlet manifold.
2. Lubricate new 'O' ring with silicone grease and fit to IAC valve.
3. Fit IAC valve to inlet manifold.
4. Tighten Torx screws to 1.5 Nm.
5. Connect breather hose to throttle body.
6. Connect air bypass hose to IAC valve and throttle body.
7. Connect multiplug to IAC valve.
8. Fit engine cover. *See ENGINE, Repairs.*

HYDRAULIC CONTROL UNIT SOLENOIDS (HCU) - VVC (2001MY ON)

Service repair no - 18.30.39

Remove

1. Disconnect battery earth lead.

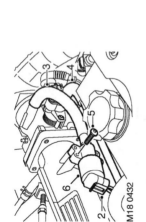
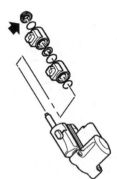

M18 0705

2. Release 2 clips and disconnect breather hose from camshaft cover.

CAUTION: Before disconnecting or removing components, ensure the immediate area around joint faces and connections are clean. Plug open connections to prevent contamination.

3. Remove breather hose between camshaft cover and plenum chamber.
4. Disconnect 5 multiplugs from engine harness and move aside for access.
5. Disconnect breather hose from camshaft cover and move aside for access.
6. Note angle at which each solenoid is positioned relative to HCU.

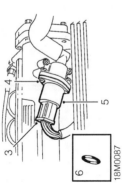

M18 0561

7. Remove nut securing solenoids to HCU.
8. Remove 'O' ring.

9. Remove outer solenoid and 'O' ring.
10. Remove inner solenoid and 'O' ring.

Refit

1. Clean solenoid mounting faces.
2. Fit 'O' ring to inner solenoid, fit solenoid ensuring end lettering faces away from HCU.
3. Fit 'O' ring to outer solenoid.
4. Fit outer solenoid ensuring lettering faces away from HCU, align solenoids, fit and tighten nut to 12 Nm.
5. Connect throttle body breather hose to cam cover and secure with clip.
6. Connect multiplugs.
7. Connect breather hose to cam cover and secure with clip.
8. Connect battery earth lead.

ENGINE MANAGEMENT SYSTEM - MEMS

IGNITION COIL - MPi MEMS 1.9 (UP TO 2000MY)

Service repair no - 18.20.32

Remove

1. Disconnect battery earth lead.
2. Remove engine compartment access panel. **See BODY, Exterior fittings.**

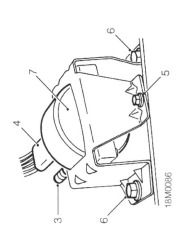

18M0086

3. Disconnect king lead from coil.
4. Disconnect multiplug from coil.
5. Raise rear of vehicle and remove bolt on underside of bracket.

⚠ **WARNING: Support on safety stands.**

6. Remove bolts on either side of bracket.
7. Collect coil and bracket assembly.

Refit

1. Fit 2 bolts securing coil bracket to engine and tighten to 25 Nm.
2. Fit bolt on underside of bracket and tighten to 9 Nm.
3. Remove stand(s) and lower vehicle.
4. Connect harness to side of bracket.
5. Connect multiplug to coil.
6. Connect king lead to coil.

   ⚠ **CAUTION: Ensure that king lead is routed away from CKP sensor lead.**

7. Fit engine compartment access panel. **See BODY, Exterior fittings.**
8. Connect battery earth lead.

ENGINE MANAGEMENT SYSTEM - MEMS

IGNITION COIL - VVC MEMS 2J (UP TO 2001MY)

Service repair no - 18.20.44

Remove

1. Disconnect battery earth lead.
2. Remove engine compartment access panel. **See BODY, Exterior fittings.**

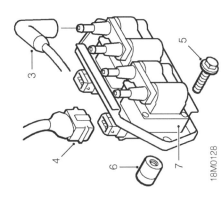

18M0128

3. Disconnect 4 h.t. leads from coils.
4. Disconnect 2 multiplugs from coils.
5. Remove 2 bolts securing coil bracket to cylinder block.
6. Collect spacer.
7. Remove coil assembly.

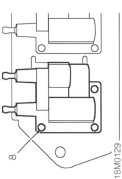

18M0129

8. Drill out 3 rivets securing coil to bracket.
9. Remove coil.

Refit

1. Position coil to bracket and secure with bolts.
2. Position coil assembly to engine and fit bolts and spacer.
3. Tighten bolts to 25 Nm.
4. Fit multiplugs.
5. Fit h.t. leads in position indicated on coil bracket.
6. Fit engine compartment access panel. **See BODY, Exterior fittings.**
7. Connect battery earth lead.

IGNITION COIL - MPi MEMS3 (2000MY ON); VVC MEMS 3 (2001MY ON)

Service repair no - 18.20.44

Remove

1. Remove engine cover. *See ENGINE, Repairs.*

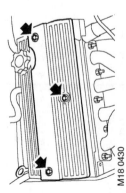

M18 0430

2. Remove 3 screws securing coil cover.
3. Remove cover.

M18 0431

4. Release ht lead from spark plug.
5. Remove 2 bolts securing coil and release coil from spark plug.
6. Disconnect multiplug from coil and remove coil.
7. Remove ht lead from coil.

Refit

1. Fit ht lead to coil.
2. Fit coil and connect multiplug.
3. Fit and tighten bolts securing coil to 8 Nm.
4. Connect ht lead to spark plug and secure lead in clip.
5. Fit coil cover and tighten bolts to 8 Nm.
6. Fit engine cover. *See ENGINE, Repairs.*

SENSOR - INTAKE AIR TEMPERATURE (IAT) - MPi MEMS 1.9 (UP TO 2000MY) ; VVC MEMS 2J (UP TO 2001MY)

Service repair no - 18.30.09

Remove

1. Disconnect battery earth lead.
2. Remove engine compartment access panel. *See BODY, Exterior fittings.*

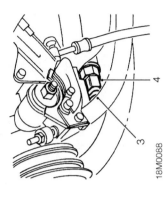

18M0088

3. Disconnect multiplug from IAT sensor.
4. Remove IAT sensor from inlet manifold.

Refit

1. Clean sensor threads and mating face.
2. Fit IAT sensor to inlet manifold and tighten to 7 Nm.
3. Connect multiplug to IAT sensor.
4. Fit engine compartment access panel. *See BODY, Exterior fittings.*
5. Connect battery earth lead.

SWITCH - INERTIA FUEL SHUT-OFF

Service repair no - 19.22.09

Remove

1. Disconnect battery earth lead.
2. Remove engine compartment access panel. *See BODY, Exterior fittings.*

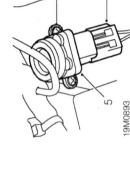

19M0893

3. Disconnect multiplug from switch.
4. Remove 2 Torx screws securing switch to body.
5. Remove switch.

Refit

1. Fit switch and tighten screws.
2. Connect multiplug to switch.
3. To ensure switch is set in correct position, press down on top.
4. Fit engine compartment access panel. *See BODY, Exterior fittings.*
5. Connect battery earth lead.

SENSOR - INTAKE AIR TEMPERATURE (IAT) - MPi MEMS3 (2000MY ON); VVC MEMS 3 (2001MY ON)

Service repair no - 18.30.09

Remove

1. Remove engine compartment access panel. See BODY, Exterior fittings.

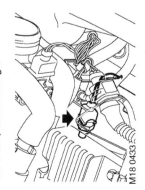

M18 0433

2. Disconnect IAT sensor multiplug.
3. Loosen and remove IAT sensor.

Refit

1. Fit and tighten IAT sensor.
2. Connect IAT sensor multiplug.
3. Fit engine compartment access panel. See BODY, Exterior fittings.

SENSOR - MANIFOLD ABSOLUTE PRESSURE (MAP) - VVC (UP TO 2000MY)

Service repair no - 18.30.56

Remove

1. Remove engine compartment access panel. See BODY, Exterior fittings.

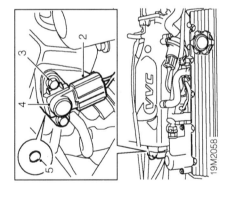

19M2058

Up to 2001MY sensor shown

2. Disconnect multiplug from MAP sensor.
3. Remove 2 bolts securing MAP sensor to manifold chamber.
4. Remove MAP sensor.
5. Remove 'O' ring seal from MAP sensor.

Refit

1. Clean sealing faces of MAP sensor and manifold chamber.
2. Fit NEW 'O' ring seal to MAP sensor.
3. Fit MAP sensor to manifold chamber and tighten bolts to 9 Nm.
4. Connect multiplug to MAP sensor.
5. Fit engine compartment access panel. See BODY, Exterior fittings.

SENSOR - MANIFOLD ABSOLUTE PRESSURE (MAP) VVC (2001MY ON)

Service repair no - 18.30.56

Remove

1. Disconnect battery earth lead.
2. Remove engine compartment access cover. See BODY, Exterior fittings.

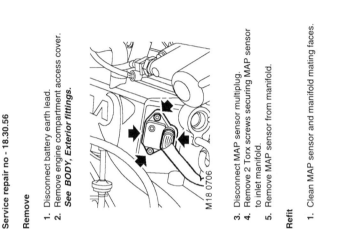

M18 0706

3. Disconnect MAP sensor multiplug.
4. Remove 2 Torx screws securing MAP sensor to inlet manifold.
5. Remove MAP sensor from manifold.

Refit

1. Clean MAP sensor and manifold mating faces.

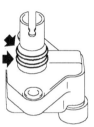

M18 0707

2. Ensure 2 'O' rings are fitted to sensor.
3. Fit sensor to manifold and tighten Torx screws to 3 Nm.
4. Connect multiplug to MAP sensor.
5. Fit engine compartment access cover. See BODY, Exterior fittings.
6. Connect battery earth lead.

SENSOR - MANIFOLD ABSOLUTE PRESSURE (MAP) - MPi MEMS3

Service repair no - 18.30.56

Remove

1. Remove engine cover. See ENGINE, Repairs.

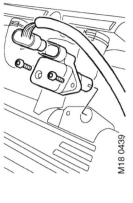

M18 0439

2. Disconnect MAP sensor multiplug.
3. Remove 2 Torx screws securing MAP sensor to inlet manifold.
4. Remove MAP sensor from manifold.

Refit

1. Clean MAP sensor and manifold mating faces.
2. Fit MAP sensor to inlet manifold, fit and tighten Torx screws.
3. Connect MAP sensor multiplug.
4. Fit engine cover. See ENGINE, Repairs.

ENGINE MANAGEMENT SYSTEM - MEMS

SENSOR - OIL TEMPERATURE - VVC

Service repair no - 18.30.41

Remove

1. Remove engine compartment access panel.
   See BODY, Exterior fittings.

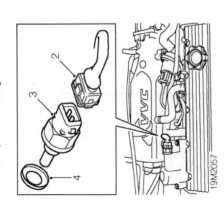

19M2057

2. Disconnect multiplug from oil temperature sensor.
3. Remove temperature sensor from hydraulic control unit.
4. Remove and discard seal.

Refit

1. Clean sealing faces of sensor and hydraulic control unit.
2. Fit seal to sensor.
3. Fit sensor and tighten to 15 Nm.
4. Connect multiplug.
5. Fit engine compartment access panel. *See BODY, Exterior fittings.*

SENSOR - OXYGEN (H02S) (UP TO 2001MY)

Service repair no - 19.22.16

Remove

1. Remove engine cover. *See ENGINE, Repairs.*

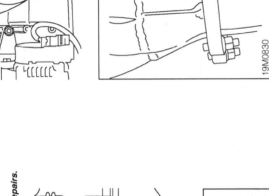

19M0829

2. Disconnect HO₂S multiplug.
3. Release multiplug from bracket.

SENSOR - HEATED OXYGEN (H02S) - PRE CAT (2001MY ON)

Service repair no - 19.22.16

Remove

1. Disconnect battery earth lead.
2. Remove engine cover. *See ENGINE - 'K' SERIES, Repairs.*

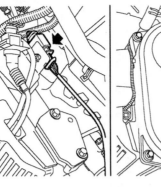 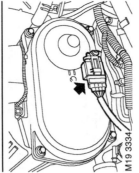

M19 3334

3. Rotate HO₂S sensor multiplug through 90° to release from mounting.
4. Disconnect HO₂S sensor multiplug from harness.
5. Raise rear of vehicle.

⚠ **WARNING: Do not work on or under a vehicle supported only by a jack. Always support the vehicle on safety stands.**

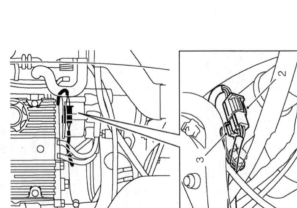

19M0830

4. Using a 22 mm crows foot spanner, remove HO₂S sensor.

Refit

1. Fit HO₂S sensor and tighten to 55 Nm.
2. Secure multiplug to bracket.
3. Connect multiplug to HO₂S sensor.
4. Fit engine cover. *See ENGINE, Repairs.*

⚠ **CAUTION: Ensure oxygen sensor joint does not leak. Exhaust gas leaks upstream of the catalyst could lead to internal failure of the catalyst.**

ENGINE MANAGEMENT SYSTEM - MEMS

SENSOR - HEATED OXYGEN (HO2S) - POST CAT (2001MY ON)

Service repair no - 19.22.71

Remove

1. Disconnect battery earth lead.
2. Remove engine compartment access cover. *See BODY, Exterior fittings.*

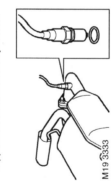

M19 3332

3. Release HO$_2$S sensor multiplug from bracket and disconnect from harness.
4. Raise rear of vehicle.

⚠ **WARNING: Do not work on or under a vehicle supported only by a jack. Always support the vehicle on safety stands.**

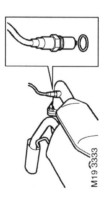

M19 3333

5. Remove HO$_2$S sensor.

Refit

1. Fit HO$_2$S sensor and tighten to 55 Nm.
2. Connect and secure HO$_2$S sensor multiplug.
3. Fit engine compartment access cover. *See BODY, Exterior fittings.*
4. Remove stands and lower vehicle.
5. Connect battery earth lead.

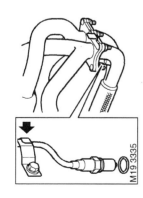

M19 3335

6. Remove HO$_2$S sensor lead from clip.
7. Using a 22 mm crows foot spanner, remove HO$_2$S sensor.

Refit

1. Fit HO$_2$S sensor and tighten to 55 Nm.
2. Fit HO$_2$S sensor lead to clip.
3. Connect multiplug and secure to mounting.
4. Fit engine cover. *See ENGINE - 'K' SERIES, Repairs.*
5. Remove stands and lower vehicle.
6. Connect battery earth lead.

ROTOR ARM - MPi MEMS 1.9 (UP TO 2000MY)

Service repair no - 18.20.23

Remove

1. Remove distributor cap. *See this section.*

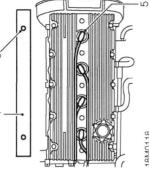

18M0052

2. Remove screw securing rotor arm to camshaft.
3. Remove rotor arm.

Refit

1. Clean rotor arm to camshaft mating faces
2. Fit rotor arm to camshaft and tighten screw to 10 Nm.
3. Fit distributor cap. *See this section.*

SPARK PLUGS - MPi MEMS 1.9 (UP TO 2000MY); VVC MEMS 2J (UP TO 2001MY)

Service repair no - 18.20.02

Remove

1. Disconnect battery earth lead.
2. Remove engine cover. *See ENGINE, Repairs.*

18M0118

3. Remove 2 screws securing h.t. lead cover.
4. Remove cover.
5. Disconnect h.t. leads from spark plugs.
6. Remove all spark plugs using spark plug socket.

SPARK PLUGS - MPi MEMS 3 (2000MY ON); VVC MEMS 3 (2001MY ON)

Service repair no - 18.20.02

Remove

1. Remove coils. *See this section.*
2. Clean area around spark plugs.

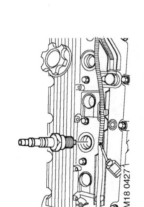

M18 0427

3. Using a 16 mm spark plug socket remove 4 spark plugs.

Refit

1. Fit terminals to new spark plugs.
2. Set gap of each new spark plug to 1.00 ± 0.05 mm.
3. Fit spark plugs and tighten to 27 Nm.
4. Refit coils. *See this section.*

Refit

18M0055

1. Set gap of each new spark plug to 0.9 ± 0.1 mm.
2. Fit spark plugs and tighten to 25 Nm.
3. Connect h.t. leads to spark plugs.
4. Fit h.t. lead cover and tighten screws to 2 Nm.
5. Fit engine cover. *See ENGINE, Repairs.*
6. Connect battery earth lead.

THROTTLE BODY

Service repair no - 19.22.45

Remove

1. Disconnect battery earth lead.
2. Remove engine compartment access panel. *See BODY, Exterior fittings.*

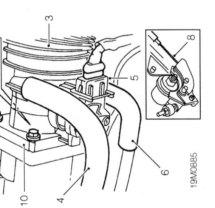

19M0885

3. Release clips and disconnect air hose from throttle body and air cleaner.
4. Disconnect Idle Air Control valve hose from throttle body.
5. Disconnect multiplug from throttle position sensor.
6. Release clip and disconnect breather hose from throttle body.
7. Release throttle cable adjusting nut from abutment bracket.
8. Release throttle cable from cam.
9. Remove 4 bolts securing throttle body to inlet manifold.
10. Remove throttle body and move multiplug mounting bracket aside.
11. Remove 'O' ring and discard.

Refit

1. Clean mating surfaces of throttle body and inlet manifold.
2. Lubricate NEW 'O' ring with silicone grease and fit to throttle body.
3. Position throttle body and multiplug bracket, fit bolts and tighten to 7 Nm.
4. Position throttle cable to cam.
5. Locate throttle cable adjusting nut in abutment bracket.
6. Connect breather hose to throttle body. and secure clip.
7. Connect multiplug to throttle position sensor.
8. Connect Idle Air Control valve to throttle body.
9. Connect air hose to throttle body and air cleaner and secure clips.
10. Fit engine compartment access panel. *See BODY, Exterior fittings.*
11. Connect battery earth lead.
12. Adjust throttle cable. *See Adjustments.*

THROTTLE CABLE

Service repair no - 19.20.06

Remove

1. Remove engine cover. *See ENGINE - 'K' SERIES, Repairs.*
2. Remove engine compartment access panel. *See BODY, Exterior fittings.*

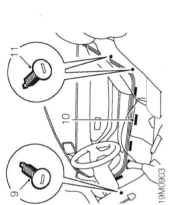

19M0900

3. Disconnect throttle cable abutment from throttle bracket.

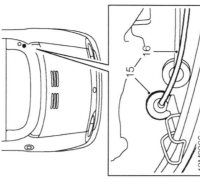

19M0901

4. Remove 2 nuts securing throttle pedal bracket to bulkhead.

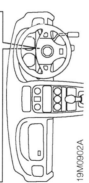
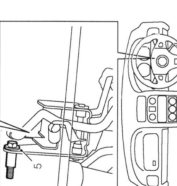

19M0902A

5. Remove bolt securing throttle pedal bracket to pedal box and collect spacer.
6. Position throttle pedal assembly and remove cable retaining clip.
7. Release cable nipple and abutment from throttle pedal.
8. Collect rubber washer.

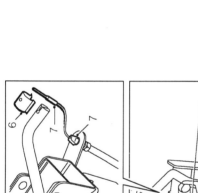

19M0903

9. Remove stud securing carpet to inner wheel arch.
10. Release carpet from door seal and 5 velcro strips.
11. Remove 2 studs securing carpet to 'B' post and release carpet from door seal and velcro to reveal cables.

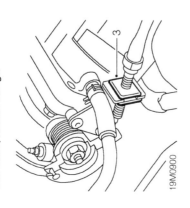

19M0904

12. Release cable from 3 sill clips and 3 'B' post clips.
13. Release cable from floorpan crossmember.

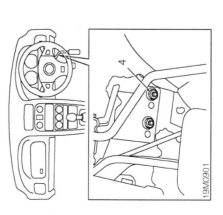

19M0905

14. Release throttle cable from throttle body abutment and cam and position aside.

19M0906

15. Position hoodwell insulation aside and release cable grommet from hoodwell.
16. Remove throttle cable.

Refit

1. Feed cable through hoodwell panel and secure throttle cable to throttle body cam.
2. Engage grommet to hoodwell.
3. Position cable to 'B' post and sill and engage clips.
4. Position cable under insulation.
5. Fit rubber washer to cable abutment.
6. Fit cable abutment to throttle pedal bracket and engage cable nipple to pedal.
7. Fit cable retaining clip to pedal.
8. Align throttle pedal to bulkhead fixings and tighten nuts to 6 Nm.
9. Position harness clip to stud and secure with nut.
10. Fit bolt and spacer and tighten to 22 Nm.
11. Position carpets and secure with studs and velcro.
12. Position carpet beneath door seal.
13. Adjust cable length and fit cable abutment to throttle body.
14. Fit engine compartment access panel. *See BODY, Exterior fittings.*
15. Fit engine cover. *See ENGINE - 'K' SERIES, Repairs.*

SENSOR - THROTTLE POSITION (TP) - MPi MEMS 1.9 (UP TO 2000MY) ; VVC MEMS 2J (UP TO 2001MY)

Service repair no - 18.30.17

Remove

1. Disconnect battery earth lead.
2. Remove engine cover. *See ENGINE, Repairs.*

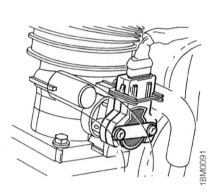

18M0091A

3. Disconnect multiplug from TP sensor.
4. Remove and discard 2 Torx screws and washers securing TP sensor.
5. Remove clamping plate.
6. Pull TP sensor off throttle spindle.

⚠ **CAUTION: Do not twist or apply leverage to TP sensor.**

Refit

1. Clean mating faces of TP sensor and throttle body.
2. Ensure that during fitting, the machined flat on throttle spindle will be aligned with mating portion of TP sensor.

---

6. Fit NEW Torx screws and washers, and tighten screws to 1.5 Nm.
7. Connect multiplug.
8. Operate throttle cable cam 2 or 3 times and ensure that full travel to throttle open and closed positions is available.
9. Fit engine cover. *See ENGINE, Repairs.*

⚠ NOTE: A 'throttle initialisation' procedure MUST be carried out using TestBook whenever the TP sensor is removed or renewed.

10. Connect battery earth lead.

⚠ **CAUTION: The TP sensor can easily be damaged during fitting. When pressing sensor onto throttle body, use fingers only and apply pressure to grey coloured area shown shaded on illustration. Do not use securing screws to pull throttle position sensor into fitted position.**

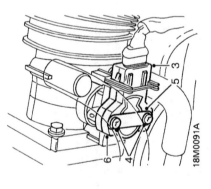

18M0091

3. Fit TP sensor.
4. Rotate TP sensor anti-clockwise to align fixing holes.

⚠ **CAUTION: Do not rotate sensor in a clockwise direction, and ensure it is not rotated beyond its internal stops.**

5. Fit clamping plate.

⚠ **CAUTION: DO not exceed specified torque figure.**

SENSOR - THROTTLE POSITION (TP) - MPi MEMS3 (2000MY ON); VVC MEMS 3 (2001MY ON)

Service repair no - 18.30.17

Remove

1. Remove engine cover. *See ENGINE, Repairs.*

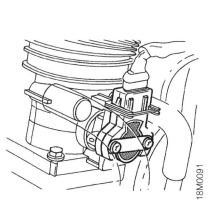

M18 0436

2. Release air bypass hose from IAC valve and remove from throttle body.
3. Disconnect multiplug from TP sensor.
4. Remove and discard 2 Torx screws and wave washers securing TP sensor to inlet manifold.
5. Remove TP sensor specification plate.
6. Pull TP sensor from throttle spindle.

⚠ **CAUTION: DO NOT twist or apply leverage to TP sensor.**

Refit

1. Clean mating faces of throttle housing and TP sensor.
2. Fit TP sensor to throttle spindle. Ensure that during fitting the machined flat on the throttle spindle is aligned with the mating portion of the TP sensor.

⚠ **CAUTION: The TP sensor can easily be damaged during fitting. When pressing the sensor onto throttle spindle, use fingers only and apply pressure only to the area shown shaded in the illustration.**

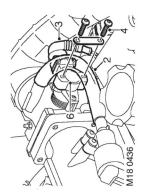

18M0091

3. Rotate TP sensor in an anti-clockwise direction to align fixing holes.

⚠ **CAUTION: Do not rotate TP sensor in a clockwise direction and ensure that it is not rotated beyond it's internal stops.**

4. Fit TP sensor specification plate.
5. Fit new Torx screws and wave washers, tighten Torx screws to 1.5 Nm.

⚠ **CAUTION: Do not exceed specified torque figure.**

6. Connect multiplug to TP sensor.
7. Operate throttle cable cam 2 or 3 times and ensure that full travel to the throttle open and the throttle closed positions is available.
8. Fit air bypass hose to IAC valve and connect to throttle body.
9. Fit engine cover. *See ENGINE, Repairs.*

⚠ NOTE: A 'throttle initialisation' procedure MUST be carried out using Testbook whenever the TP sensor is removed or renewed.

This page is intentionally left blank

COOLING SYSTEM

CONTENTS

Page

DESCRIPTION AND OPERATION

COOLING SYSTEM COMPONENTS

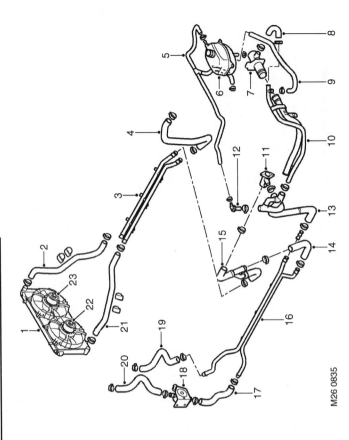

M26 0835

1. Radiator
2. Hose - radiator top
3. Pipe assembly - underfloor
4. Hose - engine inlet
5. Hose - bleed line
6. Expansion tank
7. Adaptor
8. Hose - engine rail to thermostat housing
9. Hose - expansion tank to engine rail
10. Pipe assembly - engine rail/engine inlet
11. Adaptor
12. Jiggle valve
13. Hose assembly - bypass/heater return
14. Hose - engine outlet hose to heater feed pipe
15. Hose - engine outlet
16. Pipe assembly - heater feed and return
17. Hose - heater feed pipe to control valve
18. Control valve
19. Hose - heater matrix to heater return pipe
20. Hose - control valve to heater matrix
21. Hose - radiator bottom
22. Fan - radiator cooling
23. Fan - air conditioning vehicles only

COOLING SYSTEM

COOLING SYSTEM OPERATION

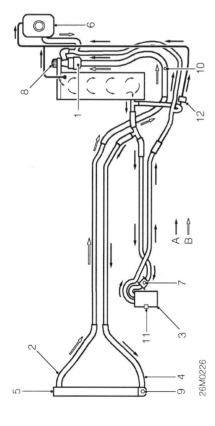

26M0226

A = HOT
B = COLD

1. Thermostat
2. Radiator top hose
3. Heater matrix
4. Radiator bottom hose
5. Radiator
6. Header tank

7. Heater valve
8. Water pump
9. Bleed screw
10. Bleed nipple
11. Bleed screw
12. Jiggle valve

The cooling system employed is the by-pass type, allowing coolant to circulate around the engine while the thermostat is closed. This prevents temperature build up in the cylinder head prior to the thermostat opening.

The siting of the thermostat in the inlet, rather than the outlet side of the system, provides a more stable control of coolant temperature in the engine.

When cold, the thermostat closes off the coolant feed from the radiator outlet. Coolant is able to circulate through the bypass and heater circuits, returning back to the engine via the thermostat bulb.

As temperature increases the thermostat gradually opens, bleeding cool fluid into the cylinder block and allowing hot coolant to flow to the radiator, balancing the flow of hot and cold fluid to maintain temperature. As the thermostat opens further, so the full flow of coolant passes through the radiator.

Any excess coolant created by heat expansion is returned to the expansion tank via the bleed line. A jiggle valve fitted at the start of the bleed line, prevents pressure build-up in the expansion tank by regulating the amount of returning coolant.

The coolant circulating pump is a rotor type drawing coolant directly from the thermostat, the pump is driven by a geared pulley from the camshaft timing belt.

The radiator positioned at the front of the vehicle, is a copper/brass cross - flow type with moulded plastic end tanks. The radiator is mounted in rubber bushes; the bottom of the radiator is located in the front body member, and the top is located in the bonnet locking platform. The hoses connecting the radiator to the engine run underneath the vehicle. Three bleed points are provided for bleeding the system.

For additional air flow through the radiator matrix, usually operational when the vehicle is stationary, an electric cooling fan is fitted to the rear of the radiator. The temperature of the cooling system is monitored by the ECM via signals from an engine coolant temperature sensor, which is mounted in the cylinder block, outlet elbow. When a temperature of 102°C is reached the ECM switches the fan on via a relay. The fan switches off at 96°C.

Vehicles fitted with air conditioning have 2 fans. These operate either in series or parallel according to engine coolant temperature or air conditioning requirements.

The ECM disengages the compressor's clutch when the coolant temperature exceeds 117 °C and re-engages when the coolant temperature drops below 112 °C.

COOLING SYSTEM

ENGINE COMPARTMENT COOLING - Air cooling system.

In addition to the normal water cooling system an air cooling system is provided for the engine compartment. This is achieved by a fan mounted in the right hand side intake ducting, blowing cool air over the engine.

The temperature of the engine compartment is monitored by the ECM via signals from an ambient air temperature sensor. The sensor is mounted on the engine compartment header panel, directly above the inlet manifold.

When a temperature of 75°C (85°C)* is reached in the engine compartment the ECM switches the fan on via a relay. The fan is controlled by a timer and will operate for three minutes. However, if a temperature of 65°C (75°C)* is reached before the pre-set time has elapsed the fan will switch off automatically.

If the engine compartment temperature rises to 130°C, the ECM will illuminate the engine compartment warning light in the instrument panel. This will warn the driver of abnormal engine compartment temperature or that a fault exists in the system. When the temperature drops below 110°C the warning light will extinguish.

The fan will operate for up to eight minutes after the ignition has been switched off to attain the required engine compartment temperature.

* VVC temperatures are shown in brackets.

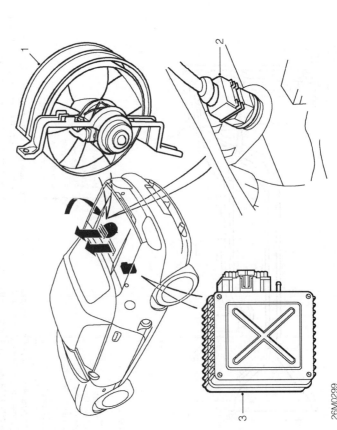

26M0299

1. Engine compartment cooling fan
2. Ambient air temperature sensor
3. ECM

COOLING SYSTEM

DRAIN AND REFILL

Service repair no - 26.10.01

Drain

⚠ **WARNING: Do not remove expansion tank filler cap when the engine is hot. The cooling system is pressurised. Personal scalding could result.**

⚠ **CAUTION: Any coolant split on the vehicle's body must be washed off immediately to prevent damage to the paint work.**

1. Position heater temperature control to maximum heat position.

26M0273

2. Remove expansion tank filler cap.
3. Position container to collect coolant.

26M0274

4. Release clip and disconnect coolant hoses at rear of under floor coolant rail.
5. Allow cooling system to drain.

Refill

6. Flush system with water under low pressure.

⚠ **CAUTION: High pressure water could damage the radiator.**

7. Connect coolant hoses at the rear of the underfloor coolant rail, secure with clips.
8. Prepare coolant to the required concentration. **See INFORMATION, Capacities, fluids and lubricants.**
9. Turn heater temperature control to maximum heat position.

COOLING SYSTEM

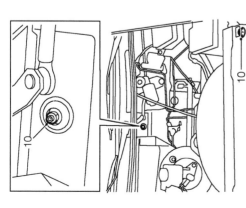

26M0275

10. Remove bleed screw from radiator, and open heater bleed nipple.
11. Fill the system with coolant.

⚠ NOTE: To prevent introducing air into the system, keep the expansion tank filled.

12. When a constant flow of coolant is being emitted from both bleed points, close bleed points and tighten to:
   Radiator bleed screw 5 Nm.
   Heater bleed nipple 7 Nm.
13. Fill expansion tank to the brim.
14. Fit expansion tank filler cap and start the engine.
15. Run the engine until the radiator cooling fan operates.

⚠ NOTE: DO NOT operate the air conditioning (if fitted).

16. Check the cooling system for leaks, and that the heater is emitting heat.
   If the heater is **NOT** emitting heat, see **Additional bleed.**
17. Switch off engine and allow to cool.
18. Check level of coolant, top-up to 'MAX' mark on expansion tank if necessary.

Additional bleed

19. Allow engine to cool.
20. Remove engine compartment access panel. **See BODY, Exterior fittings.**
21. Release clip and remove inlet air hose from throttle housing.
22. Top-up the expansion tank with coolant.

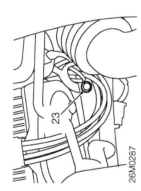

26M0287

23. Remove bleed screw from radiator return rail.
24. When a constant flow of coolant is being emitted from bleed point, fit bleed screw and tighten to 9 Nm.
25. Fit inlet hose to throttle housing and secure with clip.
26. Fit engine compartment access panel. **See BODY, Exterior fittings.**
27. Check level of coolant, top-up to 'MAX' mark on expansion tank if necessary.

COOLING SYSTEM

EXPANSION TANK

Service repair no - 26.15.01

Remove

1. Remove engine compartment access panel. **See BODY, Exterior fittings.**

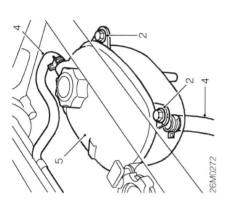

26M0272

2. Remove 2 bolts securing tank to body.
3. Position container to catch spillage.
4. Release 2 hoses from tank and allow to drain.
5. Remove expansion tank.

Refit

1. Fit tank.
2. Connect coolant hoses to tank and secure clips.
3. Position tank to body and secure with bolts.
4. Top-up cooling system. **See MAINTENANCE.**
5. Fit engine compartment access panel. **See BODY, Exterior fittings.**

RADIATOR FAN AND MOTOR

Service repair no - 26.25.23

Remove

1. Remove front bumper valance. **See BODY, Exterior fittings.**

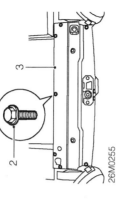

26M0255

2. Remove 9 bolts securing bonnet locking panel.
3. Position panel aside.

26M0256

4. Disconnect multiplug from fan.
5. Remove 3 nuts securing fan cowl to radiator.
6. Remove fan assembly.

Refit

1. Fit fan assembly and tighten nuts to 3 Nm.
2. Connect multiplug.
3. Position bonnet locking panel and tighten bolts to 10 Nm.
4. Fit front bumper valance. **See BODY, Exterior fittings.**

COOLING SYSTEM

ENGINE COMPARTMENT COOLING FAN

Service repair no - 26.25.39
Service repair no - 26.25.39/20 A/C fitted

Remove

1. Disconnect battery earth lead.
2. Remove engine cover. *See ENGINE, Repairs.*
3. **Models with A/C:** Remove alternator. *See ELECTRICAL, Repairs.*

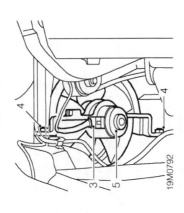

19M0792

4. Disconnect multiplug from motor.
5. Remove 2 nuts securing fan assembly to body.
6. Remove fan assembly.

Refit

1. Fit fan assembly and tighten nuts to 9 Nm.
2. Connect multiplug.
3. **Models with A/C:** Fit alternator. *See ELECTRICAL, Repairs.*
4. Fit engine cover. *See ENGINE, Repairs.*
5. Connect battery earth lead.

ENGINE COMPARTMENT AMBIENT AIR TEMPERATURE (AAT) SENSOR

Service repair no - 26.25.40

Remove

1. Remove engine compartment access panel. *See BODY, Exterior fittings.*

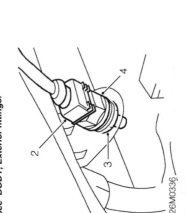

26M0336

2. Disconnect AAT sensor multiplug.
3. Remove nut securing AAT sensor to bracket.
4. Remove AAT sensor.

Refit

1. Fit AAT sensor and secure with nut.
2. Connect multiplug.
3. Fit engine compartment access panel. *See BODY, Exterior fittings.* compartment

---

COOLING SYSTEM

RADIATOR

Service repair no - 26.40.01
Service repair no - 26.40.01/20 A/C fitted

Remove

1. Raise front of vehicle.

⚠️ **WARNING: Support on safety stands.**

2. Remove bonnet locking platform. *See BODY, Exterior fittings.*
3. Drain cooling system. *See Adjustments.*
4. Release clips securing top and bottom hoses to radiator and remove hoses.

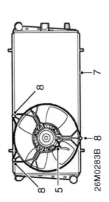

26M0283B

5. Disconnect multiplug from fan.
6. **Models with A/C:** Disconnect multiplugs from fans.
7. **All models:** Remove radiator assembly.
8. Remove 3 nuts securing fan to radiator and remove fan.
9. **Models with A/C:** Remove 6 nuts securing fans to radiator and remove fans.

Refit

1. Fit fan/s to radiator and tighten nuts to 3 Nm.
2. Fit radiator to lower grommets.
3. Fit coolant hoses to radiator and secure with clips.
4. Connect multiplug.
5. **Models with A/C:** Connect multiplugs to fans.
6. Refill cooling system. *See Adjustments.*
7. Fit bonnet locking platform. *See BODY, Exterior fittings.*
8. Remove stand(s) and lower vehicle.

COOLING SYSTEM

THERMOSTAT - MPi MEMS 1.9 (UP TO 2000MY)

Service repair no - 26.45.09

Remove

1. Disconnect battery earth lead.
2. Remove engine compartment access panel. *See BODY, Exterior fittings.*
3. Drain cooling system. *See Adjustments.*
4. Remove ignition coil - MPi. *See ENGINE MANAGEMENT SYSTEM - MEMS, Repairs.*

5. Remove 2 bolts securing expansion tank and position tank aside.

26M0276

6. Remove 2 bolts securing coolant rail to cylinder block.
7. Remove 3 bolts securing thermostat housing cover.
8. Position coolant rail aside and remove thermostat.

26M0277

Refit

1. Clean sealing faces.
2. Fit thermostat.
3. Position housing and tighten bolts to 9 Nm.
4. Position coolant rail and tighten bolts to 9 Nm.
5. Fit ignition coil - MPi. *See ENGINE MANAGEMENT SYSTEM - MEMS, Repairs.*
6. Position expansion tank and secure with bolts.
7. Connect battery earth lead.
8. Refill cooling system. *See Adjustments.*
9. Fit engine compartment access panel. *See BODY, Exterior fittings.*

THERMOSTAT - VVC

Service repair no - 26.45.09

Remove

1. Disconnect battery earth lead.
2. Remove engine compartment access panel. *See BODY, Exterior fittings.*
3. Drain cooling system. *See Adjustments.*

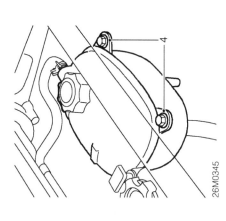

26M0345

4. Remove 2 bolts securing expansion tank and position tank aside.

26M0346

5. Remove 2 bolts securing coolant rail to cylinder block.
6. Remove 3 bolts securing thermostat housing cover.
7. Position coolant rail aside and remove thermostat.

Refit

1. Clean sealing faces.
2. Fit thermostat.
3. Position housing and tighten bolts to 9 Nm.
4. Position coolant rail and tighten bolts to 9 Nm.
5. Position expansion tank and secure with bolts.
6. Connect battery earth lead.
7. Refill cooling system. *See Adjustments.*
8. Fit engine compartment access panel. *See BODY, Exterior fittings.*

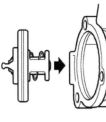

COOLING SYSTEM

THERMOSTAT - MPi MEMS 3 (2000MY ON)

Service repair no - 26.45.09

Remove

1. Disconnect battery earth lead.
2. Drain cooling system. *See Adjustments.*

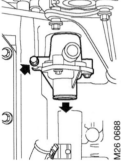

M26 0683

3. Disconnect multiplug from CKP sensor.

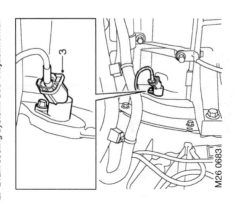

M26 0684

4. Remove 2 bolts securing coolant rail to cylinder block.
5. Release coolant rail from thermostat housing.
6. Lower vehicle.
7. Remove engine compartment access panel. *See BODY, Exterior fittings.*

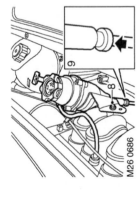

M26 0686

8. Remove bolt securing dipstick tube to inlet manifold.
9. Depress collar and remove upper part of dipstick tube.

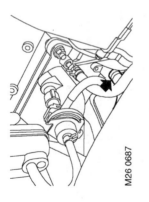

M26 0687

10. Release clip and disconnect heater hose from thermostat housing.

M26 0688

11. Remove bolt securing thermostat housing to cylinder block.
12. Release and remove thermostat housing.

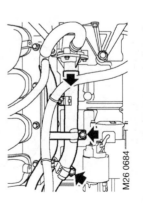

M26 0689

13. Remove and discard 2 'O' rings from thermostat housing outlets.
14. Remove 3 bolts securing thermostat housing cover to thermostat housing.
15. Remove thermostat housing cover.
16. Remove thermostat from housing.
17. Remove rubber seal from thermostat.

Refit

1. Examine thermostat rubber seal for signs of deterioration or damage, renew if necessary.
2. Fit rubber seal to thermostat.
3. Clean mating faces of thermostat and cover.

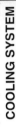

M26 0690

4. Align thermostat to shoulder in thermostat housing.
5. Fit thermostat housing cover and tighten bolts to 9 Nm.
6. Clean 'O' ring grooves on thermostat housing outlets.
7. Lubricate new 'O' rings with rubber grease and fit to thermostat housing outlets.
8. Position thermostat housing to coolant pump and push into place.
9. Fit bolt securing thermostat housing to cylinder block and tighten to 9 Nm.
10. Position upper part of dipstick tube and connect to lower part.
11. Fit engine compartment access panel. *See BODY, Exterior fittings.*
12. Raise vehicle.
13. Connect coolant rail to thermostat housing.
14. Align coolant rail to cylinder block, fit bolts and tighten to 9 Nm.
15. Connect CKP sensor multiplug.
16. Connect heater hose to thermostat housing and secure with clip.
17. Refill cooling system. *See Adjustments.*
18. Connect battery earth lead.

ENGINE COOLANT PUMP

Service repair no - 26.50.01

Remove

1. Disconnect battery earth lead.
2. Remove camshaft timing belt. *See ENGINE, Repairs.*
3. Drain cooling system. *See Adjustments.*
4. Remove bolt securing timing belt rear cover to coolant pump.

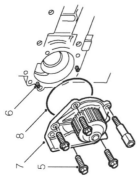

26M0281A

5. Remove 5 bolts securing engine coolant pump to cylinder block.
6. Release pump from 2 dowels.
7. Remove engine coolant pump.
8. Remove 'O' ring seal from pump body and discard.

Refit

1. Clean pump and cylinder block mating faces.
2. Fit NEW 'O' ring seal to pump body and fit pump to cylinder block.
3. Fit bolts securing engine coolant pump to cylinder block and tighten to 10 Nm.
4. Fit bolt securing timing belt rear cover to engine coolant pump and tighten to 10 Nm.
5. Fit camshaft timing belt. *See ENGINE, Repairs.*
6. Refill coolant system. *See Adjustments.*

This page is intentionally left blank

MANIFOLD & EXHAUST SYSTEMS

CONTENTS

Page

DESCRIPTION AND OPERATION

REPAIRS

EXHAUST PIPE - UP TO 2001 MY

30M0267A

1. Exhaust silencer
2. Flange nut - 6 off
3. Gasket - exhaust manifold
4. Exhaust manifold
5. Flange nuts - 5 off
6. Stud - 4 off
7. Gasket - manifold to front pipe
8. Exhaust front pipe
9. Flange nut - 4 off
10. Mounting rubber
11. Gasket - pipe flange - 2 off
12. Catalytic converter
13. Clamp bracket - rear silencer
14. Washer - clamp bracket
15. Nut - clamp bracket
16. Mounting bracket - silencer
17. Nut - mounting bracket - 2 off
18. Mounting bracket - 2 off
19. Mounting rubber - 2 off
20. Heat shield - silencer
21. Bolt M6 - heat shield - 4 off

MANIFOLD & EXHAUST SYSTEMS

EXHAUST PIPE - 2001 MY ON

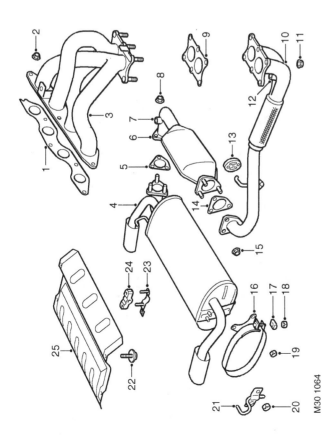

M30 1064

1. Gasket - exhaust manifold
2. Flange nut - exhaust manifold to cylinder head - 5 off
3. Exhaust manifold
4. Exhaust silencer
5. Gasket - silencer to catalytic converter
6. Catalytic converter
7. Downstream HO$_2$S mounting boss
8. Flange nut - catalytic converter to silencer - 3 off
9. Gasket - manifold to front pipe
10. Exhaust front pipe
11. Flange nut - manifold to front pipe - 6 off
12. Upstream HO$_2$S mounting boss
13. Mounting rubber
14. Gasket - catalytic converter to front pipe
15. Flange nut - catalytic converter to front pipe - 3 off
16. Clamp bracket - silencer
17. Washer - clamp bracket
18. Nut - clamp bracket
19. Nut - clamp bracket attachment
20. Nut - silencer mounting bracket - 2 off
21. Mounting bracket - silencer
22. Bolt - heat shield - 4 off
23. Mounting bracket - 2 off
24. Mounting rubber - 2 off
25. Heat shield - silencer

MANIFOLD & EXHAUST SYSTEMS

INLET MANIFOLD - MPi

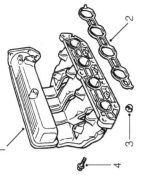

30M0286

Up to 2000MY shown

1. Inlet manifold - plastic
2. Gasket - inlet manifold
3. Nut - inlet manifold - 3 off
4. Bolt - inlet manifold - 4 off

The inlet manifold is a one piece plastic moulding attached to the cylinder head with a gasket interposed between the two components The throttle housing is bolted to the manifold chamber, sealing being effected by means of an 'O' ring. The intake air temperature sensor is inserted above the pipe flange.

EXHAUST MANIFOLD

The 4 branch fabricated steel exhaust manifold terminates in a flange with two outlet ports. Up to 2001 MY, a mounting boss for a Heated Oxygen Sensor (HO$_2$S) is incorporated on the rear of the exhaust manifold, between the branch pipes for cylinders 2 and 3. The exhaust manifold flanges are sealed to the cylinder head and exhaust front pipe by gaskets.

EXHAUST SYSTEM

The exhaust system consists of a twin front pipe, terminating in an expansion chamber, a catalytic converter and a twin tail pipe which incorporates a large capacity silencer. The entire exhaust system is manufactured from stainless steel.

The silencer contains a series of expansion chambers, resonators and baffles designed to give an improved exhaust system, and reduce condensation to increase the life of the system.

> NOTE: Service repair tail pipes are available to allow repair without replacing the silencer.

From 2001 MY, two HO$_2$S are installed in the exhaust system:

- One HO$_2$S is installed upstream of the catalytic converter, in a mounting boss in the front pipe
- The 2nd HO$_2$S is installed downstream of the catalytic converter, in a mounting boss in the catalytic converter outlet pipe

The catalytic converter operates in a closed loop system. The exhaust gases are monitored by the Engine Control Module (ECM) via signals sent from the upsteam HO$_2$S in the exhaust manifold (up to 2001 MY) or exhaust front pipe (from 2001 MY). The ECM adjusts the fueling to maintain emissions acceptable to the catalytic converter. From 2001 Model Year, the ECM uses the signal from the downstream HO$_2$S to monitor the condition of the catalytic converter. For information on the operation of the catalytic converter **See ENGINE MANAGEMENT SYSTEM - MEMS, Information.**

MANIFOLD & EXHAUST SYSTEMS

FRONT PIPE (2001MY ON)

Service repair no - 30.10.09

Remove

1. Disconnect battery earth lead.
2. Remove pre catalyst HO₂S. See *FUEL DELIVERY SYSTEM, Repairs.*

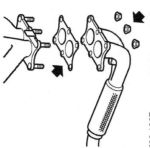

M30 1067

3. Remove 6 nuts, release front pipe from exhaust manifold and discard gasket.

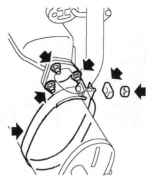

M30 1068

4. Remove nut and washer from silencer clamp.
5. Remove 3 nuts securing front pipe to catalyst.
6. Remove clamp from silencer.

FRONT PIPE (UP TO 2000MY)

Service repair no - 30.10.09

Remove

1. Raise rear of vehicle.

⚠ **WARNING: Support on safety stands.**

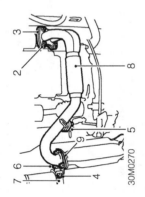

30M0270

2. Remove 4 nuts from manifold flange joint.
3. Remove and discard gasket from flange.
4. Remove nut and special washer securing rear silencer clamp.
5. Disconnect rubber mounting from front pipe.
6. Remove 3 nuts securing front pipe to catalytic converter.
7. Remove rear silencer clamp from flange joint.
8. Remove front pipe from vehicle.
9. Remove and discard gasket, front pipe to catalytic converter.

Refit

1. Clean all mating faces.
2. Position a NEW flange gasket and fit front pipe to manifold, tighten nuts to 50 Nm.
3. Position a NEW gasket and fit front pipe to catalytic converter, position rear silencer clamp bracket to flange studs, fit nuts and tighten to 50 Nm.
4. Connect rubber mounting to front pipe.
5. Align rear silencer clamp, fit special washer, fit nut and tighten to 30 Nm.
6. Remove stand(s) and lower vehicle.

⚠ **CAUTION: Ensure exhaust system is free from leaks. Exhaust gas leaks upstream of the catalyst could cause internal damage to the catalyst.**

MANIFOLD & EXHAUST SYSTEMS

INLET MANIFOLD - VVC

30M0397

Up to 2000MY shown

1. Inlet manifold chamber
2. Inlet manifold
3. Gasket - manifold chamber to inlet manifold
4. Gasket - inlet manifold to cylinder head
5. Bolt - manifold chamber to inlet manifold
6. Bolt - inlet manifold to cylinder head
7. Nut - inlet manifold to cylinder head
8. Vacuum pipe union
9. Inlet manifold support stay

The alloy inlet manifold assembly comprises a manifold chamber bolted to the inlet manifold with a gasket interposed between the two components. The throttle housing is bolted to the manifold chamber and sealed with an 'O' ring.

The manifold chamber incorporates the manifold absolute pressure sensor and brake servo vacuum hose union. The air intake temperature sensor is incorporated in the inlet manifold. The inlet manifold is attached to the cylinder head and sealed with a gasket. A strut between the inlet manifold and the cylinder block supports the inlet manifold assembly.

SILENCER

Service repair no - 30.10.22

Remove

1. Raise rear of vehicle.

⚠ **WARNING: Support on safety stands.**

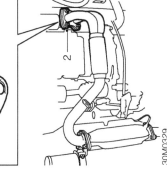

30M0268

2. Remove nut and special washer securing silencer strap clamp.
3. Remove 2 flange nuts securing silencer strap clamp.
4. Remove strap clamp.
5. Remove 2 flange nuts securing silencer RH mounting bracket, remove mounting bracket.
6. Remove 3 flange nuts securing silencer to catalyst.
7. Release catalyst from silencer, remove and discard gasket.
8. Release silencer from LH mounting bracket, remove silencer.

M30 1069

7. Release rubber mounting, remove front pipe and discard gasket.

Refit

1. Clean front pipe and mating faces.
2. Fit new gasket and tighten nuts securing front pipe to manifold to 50 Nm.
3. Fit silencer clamp and tighten nuts securing clamp to front pipe to 50 Nm.
4. Connect mounting to front pipe.
5. Fit washer and tighten silencer clamp nut to 30 Nm.
6. Fit pre catalyst HO_2S. See *FUEL DELIVERY SYSTEM, Repairs.*
7. Connect battery earth lead.

GASKET - EXHAUST MANIFOLD TO FRONT PIPE (UP TO 2000MY)

Service repair no - 30.10.26

Remove

1. Raise rear of vehicle.

⚠ **WARNING: Support on safety stands.**

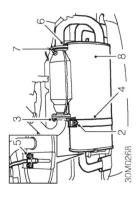

30M0329

2. Remove 4 nuts securing exhaust manifold to front pipe.
3. Release down pipe from exhaust manifold and collect gasket.

Refit

1. Fit gasket to exhaust manifold studs.
2. Fit down pipe to exhaust manifold and secure with nuts.
3. Tighten nuts to 50 Nm.
4. Remove stand(s) and lower vehicle.

Refit

1. Clean mating faces of silencer and catalytic converter.
2. Fit silencer to LH mounting bracket.
3. Fit silencer RH mounting bracket to mounting, fit nuts and tighten to 15 Nm.
4. Fit NEW gasket to catalyst.
5. Position catalyst to silencer, fit nuts and tighten to 50 Nm.
6. Fit rear silencer clamp to flange studs, fit nuts and tighten to 50 Nm.
7. Align rear silencer clamp strap, fit special washer, fit nut and tighten to 30 Nm.
8. Remove stand(s) and lower vehicle.

⚠ **CAUTION: Ensure exhaust system is free from leaks. Exhaust gas leaks upstream of the catalyst could cause internal damage to the catalyst.**

GASKET - EXHAUST MANIFOLD TO FRONT PIPE (2001MY ON)

Service repair no - 30.10.26

Remove

1. Disconnect battery earth lead.
2. Remove engine compartment access cover. **See *BODY, Exterior fittings*.**

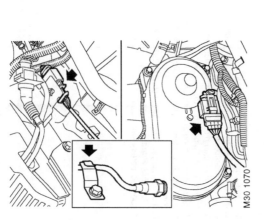

M30 1070

3. Rotate HO$_2$S multiplug through 90° to release from mounting.
4. Raise rear of vehicle.

⚠ **WARNING: Do not work on or under a vehicle supported only by a jack. Always support the vehicle on safety stands.**

5. Release HO$_2$S lead from clip.

M30 1067

6. Remove 6 nuts, release front pipe from exhaust manifold and discard gasket.

Refit

1. Clean front pipe and manifold mating faces.
2. Fit new gasket and tighten nuts securing front pipe to manifold to 50 Nm.
3. Fit HO$_2$S lead to clip.
4. Secure HO$_2$S multiplug to mounting.
5. Remove stand and lower vehicle.
6. Fit engine compartment access cover. **See *BODY, Exterior fittings*.**
7. Connect battery earth lead.

SILENCER HEAT SHIELD

Service repair no - 30.10.44

Remove

1. Remove silencer. **See *this section*.**

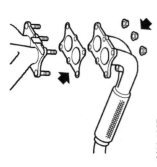

30M0271

2. Remove 4 bolts securing silencer heat shield.
3. Remove heat shield.

Refit

1. Fit heat shield to underside of vehicle, fit bolts and tighten to 10 Nm.
2. Fit silencer. **See *this section*.**

FUEL TANK HEAT SHIELD

Service repair no - 30.10.64

Remove

1. Remove engine cover. **See *ENGINE, Repairs*.**

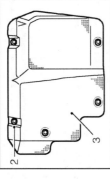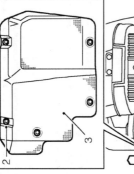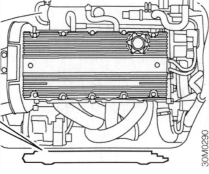

30M0290

2. Remove 5 nuts securing heat shield to bulkhead.
3. Remove heat shield.

Refit

1. Fit heat shield and secure with nuts.
2. Fit engine cover. **See *ENGINE, Repairs*.**

MANIFOLD - INLET - MPi MEMS 1.9 (UP TO 2000MY)

Service repair no - 30.15.02

Remove

1. Remove inlet manifold gasket. *See this section.*
2. Manoeuvre inlet manifold to gain access to bolts securing throttle body to inlet manifold.

30M0283A

3. Release hose from stepper motor.
4. Remove 4 bolts securing throttle body to inlet manifold.
5. Remove throttle body from manifold.
6. Remove and discard 'O' ring from throttle body.

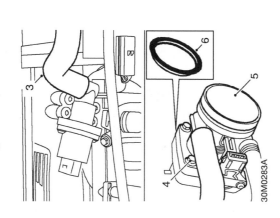

30M0284A

7. Remove 4 Tx30 Torx screws securing stepper motor to inlet manifold.
8. Remove stepper motor from manifold.
9. Remove and discard 'O' ring from stepper motor.

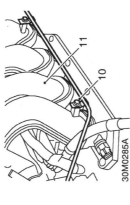

30M0285A

10. Remove 2 screws securing fuel pipe to inlet manifold.
11. Manoeuvre inlet manifold and remove from engine compartment.
    Do not carry out further dismantling if component is removed for access only.

⚠ **CAUTION: Plug the connections.**

12. Remove air intake temperature sensor from manifold.
13. Remove sealing washer from sensor.

14. Release pressure regulator vacuum hose from inlet manifold.
15. Disconnect 4 injector multiplugs.
16. Remove 2 bolts securing fuel rail to inlet manifold.
17. Release 4 injectors from inlet manifold.
18. Remove fuel rail complete with injectors and pressure regulator.
19. Remove and discard lower 'O' rings from injectors.
20. Fit protective caps to each injector.

Rebuild

21. Clean fuel rail and temperature sensor mating surfaces.
22. Fit NEW sealing washer to air intake temperature sensor, fit sensor and tighten to 7 Nm.
23. Remove protective caps from injectors.
24. Fit NEW 'O' ring seals to injectors.
25. Align injectors to inlet manifold and push fuel rail into position.
26. Fit fuel rail retaining bolts and tighten to 9 Nm.
27. Connect injector multiplugs.
28. Connect pressure regulator vacuum hose to inlet manifold.

Refit

1. Position manifold to engine compartment.
2. Clean stepper motor to manifold chamber mating faces.
3. Fit NEW 'O' ring to stepper motor, position to inlet manifold and tighten Torx screws to 1.5 Nm.
4. Clean throttle body to manifold mating faces.
5. Fit NEW 'O' ring to throttle body.
6. Position throttle body and injector harness multiplug bracket to inlet manifold.
7. Fit bolts and tighten to 7 Nm.
8. Fit inlet manifold gasket. *See this section.*

MANIFOLD - INLET - MPi MEMS 3 (2000MY ON)

Service repair no - 30.15.02

Remove

1. Remove inlet manifold gasket. *See this section.*

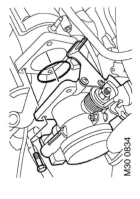

M18 0437

2. Remove 3 bolts securing coil cover and remove coil cover.

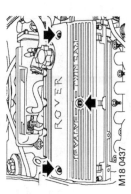

M30 0831

3. Remove bolt securing RH coil, release coil and disconnect coil multiplugs.
4. Release coil harness from harness clips.

5. Disconnect IAC valve and TP sensor multiplugs.
6. Disconnect IAC valve hose.

M30 0832

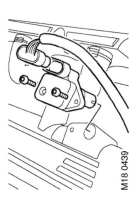

7. Release and disconnect injector multiplug.
8. Manoeuvre inlet manifold to gain access to bolts securing throttle body to inlet manifold.

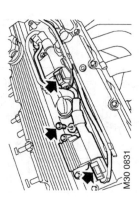

M30 0833

9. Remove 4 bolts securing throttle body to inlet manifold.
10. Remove throttle body from manifold.
11. Remove and discard 'O' ring seal from throttle body.
12. Remove air filter. *See ENGINE MANAGEMENT SYSTEM - MEMS, Repairs.*
13. Manoeuvre inlet manifold and remove from engine compartment.

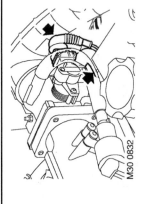

M30 0834

14. Remove air intake sensor from manifold.
15. Remove sealing washer from sensor.

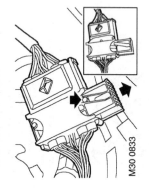

M30 0835

16. Release pressure regulator vacuum hose from inlet manifold.

M30 0836

17. Remove 2 Torx screws securing MAP sensor and remove MAP sensor.

M18 0439

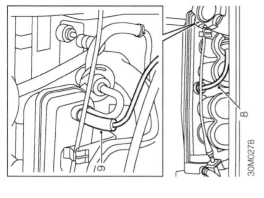

8. Release brake servo vacuum pipe from manifold chamber.
9. Release ECU vacuum hose from manifold chamber.

30M0278

GASKET - INLET MANIFOLD - MPi MEMS 1.9 (UP TO 2000MY)

Service repair no - 30.15.08

Remove

1. Remove engine cover. *See ENGINE, Repairs.*
2. Drain cooling system. *See COOLING SYSTEM, Adjustments.*
3. Remove engine compartment access panel. *See BODY, Exterior fittings.*

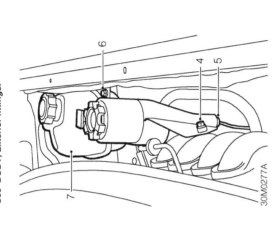

30M0277A

4. Remove bolt securing engine oil level dipstick/filler tube bracket to body.
5. Release clip securing dipstick/filler tube to pipe and remove tube.
6. Remove 2 bolts securing expansion tank to body.
7. Release expansion tank from lower fixing and position aside.

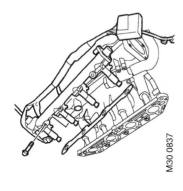

M30 0837

18. Remove 2 bolts securing fuel rail to inlet manifold.
19. Release 4 injectors from inlet manifold.
20. Collect injector spacer.
21. Remove fuel rail complete with injectors pressure regulator and harness.

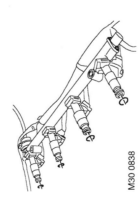

M30 0838

22. Remove and discard lower 'O' rings from injectors.
23. Fit protective caps to each injector.

M30 0839

24. Remove 4 Torx screws securing IAC valve, remove IAC valve and collect 'O' ring.

Refit

1. Using a new 'O' ring, fit IAC valve and tighten Torx screws.
2. Clean fuel rail and temperature sensor mating surfaces.
3. Fit new seal to temperature sensor, fit sensor and tighten to 7 Nm.
4. Fit new 'O' ring seals to injectors.
5. Fit injector spacer.
6. Align injectors to inlet manifold and push fuel rail into position.
7. Fit fuel rail retaining bolts and tighten to 10 Nm.
8. Fit MAP sensor and tighten Torx screws.
9. Connect pressure regulator vacuum hose to inlet manifold.
10. Position manifold to engine compartment.
11. Clean throttle body to manifold mating faces.
12. Fit new seal to throttle body.
13. Position throttle body, fit bolts and tighten to 7 Nm.
14. Fit air filter. *See ENGINE MANAGEMENT SYSTEM - MEMS, Repairs.*
15. Fit stud and bolt securing air cleaner to mounting bracket.
16. Fit hose to throttle body and secure with clip.
17. Position hose to air cleaner and tighten clip screw.
18. Connect hose to IAC valve.
19. Connect and secure injector multiplug.
20. Connect IAC valve and TP sensor multiplugs.
21. Secure coil harness to harness clips.
22. Position coil and connect coil multiplugs, fit bolt and tighten to 8 Nm.
23. Position coil cover, fit bolts and tighten to 9 Nm.
24. Fit inlet manifold gasket. *See this section.*

MANIFOLD & EXHAUST SYSTEMS

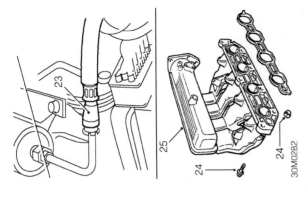

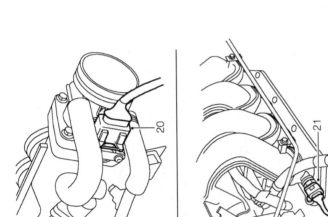

CAUTION: Depressurise fuel pressure before disconnecting fuel pipes. See *ENGINE MANAGEMENT SYSTEM - MEMS, Adjustments.*

20. Disconnect throttle potentiometer multiplug.
21. Disconnect air intake temperature sensor multiplug.
22. Position absorbent cloth to collect any fuel spillage.
23. Release fuel feed hose from fuel filter pipe.
24. Remove 3 nuts and 4 bolts securing inlet manifold to cylinder head.
25. Release inlet manifold from cylinder head studs.
26. Remove and discard gasket from inlet manifold.

30M0282

30M0281

MANIFOLD & EXHAUST SYSTEMS

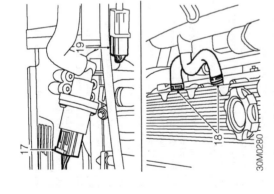

17. Disconnect stepper motor multiplug.
18. Release 2 clips and 2 breather hoses from camshaft cover.
19. Disconnect injector harness multiplug.

30M0280

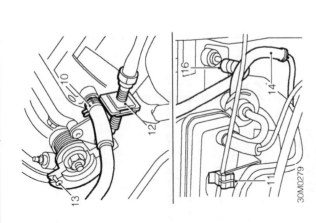

10. Release clip and hose, EVAP cannister to inlet manifold chamber.
11. Release throttle cable from manifold chamber clip.
12. Release throttle cable from abutment bracket.
13. Release inner cable from throttle cam.
14. Release fuel return hose from fuel pressure regulator.
15. Position drainage tray to collect coolant spillage.
16. Loosen clip and disconnect coolant hose from inlet manifold.

30M0279

Refit

1. Clean manifold to cylinder head mating faces.
2. Fit NEW gasket to inlet manifold and position to cylinder head studs.

30M0322

3. Fit nuts and bolts securing inlet manifold to cylinder head and tighten in sequence shown to 17 Nm.
4. Secure fuel feed hose to fuel filter pipe.
5. Connect air intake temperature sensor multiplug.
6. Connect throttle potentiometer multiplug.
7. Connect injector harness multiplug.
8. Connect breather hoses to camshaft cover and secure clips.
9. Connect stepper motor multiplug.
10. Connect coolant hose to inlet manifold and tighten clip.
11. Connect fuel return hose to fuel pressure regulator.
12. Connect throttle inner cable to cam.
13. Secure throttle cable to abutment bracket.
14. Secure throttle cable to manifold clip.
15. Connect EVAP cannister to inlet manifold hose and secure clip.
16. Connect ECU vacuum hose to inlet manifold.
17. Connect brake servo vacuum hose to inlet manifold.
18. Position expansion tank to mounting bracket, fit bolts and tighten to 5 Nm.
19. Fit dipstick/filler tube to pipe.
20. Align dipstick/filler tube mounting bracket, fit bolt and tighten to 10 Nm.
21. Refill cooling system. *See COOLING SYSTEM, Adjustments.*
22. Fit engine compartment access panel. *See BODY, Exterior fittings.*
23. Fit engine cover. *See ENGINE, Repairs.*

GASKET - INLET MANIFOLD - MPi MEMS 3 (2000MY ON)

Service repair no - 30.15.08

Remove

1. Disconnect battery earth lead.
2. Remove engine cover. *See ENGINE, Repairs.*
3. Drain cooling system. *See COOLING SYSTEM, Adjustments.*

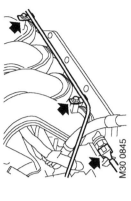

M12 5778

4. Release coil harness from harness support bracket.

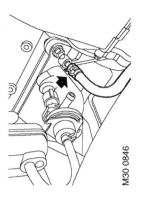

M30 0840

5. Remove dipstick.
6. Release vacuum pipe from dipstick/ oil filler tube.
7. Remove bolt securing engine oil level dipstick/filler tube bracket to manifold.
8. Release clip securing dipstick/filler tube to pipe and remove tube.

M30 0841

9. Release brake servo vacuum pipe from manifold chamber.

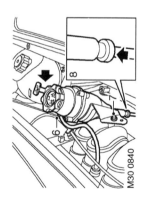

M30 0843

10. Release EVAP cannister hose from inlet manifold chamber.
11. Release EVAP cannister from support bracket and position cannister aside.
12. Release throttle cable from manifold chamber clip.
13. Release throttle cable from abutment bracket.
14. Release inner cable from throttle cam.

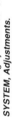

M30 0844

15. Release clip securing fuel return hose to inlet manifold and release hose.

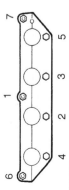

M30 0845

16. Remove 2 bolts securing return pipe to inlet manifold and position pipe aside.
17. Disconnect IAT sensor multiplug.

⚠️ **CAUTION: Plug the connections.**

M30 0846

18. Release clip and disconnect coolant hose from inlet manifold.

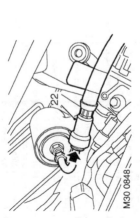

M30 0857

19. Release 2 clips and 2 breather hoses from camshaft cover.
20. Disconnect MAP sensor multiplug.
21. Position absorbent cloth to collect any fuel spillage.

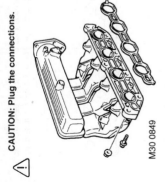

M30 0848

22. Release fuel feed hose from fuel filter pipe.

⚠ **CAUTION: Plug the connections.**

M30 0849

23. Remove 3 nuts and 4 bolts securing inlet manifold to cylinder head.

24. Release inlet manifold from cylinder head studs.
25. Remove and discard gasket seal from inlet manifold.

Refit

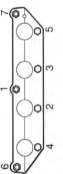

M30 0842

1. Clean manifold to cylinder head mating faces.
2. Fit new gasket seal to inlet manifold and position inlet manifold to cylinder head studs.
3. Fit nuts and bolts securing inlet manifold to cylinder head and tighten in sequence shown to 25 Nm.
4. Secure fuel feed hose to fuel filter pipe.
5. Connect MAP sensor multiplug.
6. Connect breather hoses to camshaft cover and secure clips.
7. Connect coolant hose to inlet manifold and secure with clip.
8. Connect fuel return hose to manifold and secure with clip.

GASKET - INLET MANIFOLD - VVC

Service repair no - 30.15.08

Remove

1. Remove manifold chamber gasket. *See this section.*
2. Drain cooling system. *See COOLING SYSTEM, Adjustments.*

⚠ **CAUTION: Depressurise fuel pressure before disconnecting fuel pipes. See ENGINE MANAGEMENT SYSTEM - MEMS, Adjustments.**

3. Position cloth to catch spillage.

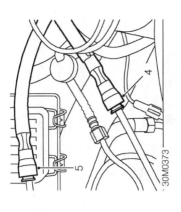

30M0373

4. Release fuel return hose from fuel return pipe.
5. Release fuel feed hose from fuel filter pipe.
6. Position drainage tray to collect coolant spillage.

9. Fit and tighten bolts securing fuel return pipe to manifold.
10. Connect IAT sensor multiplugs.
11. Connect throttle inner cable to cam.
12. Secure throttle cable to abutment bracket.
13. Secure throttle cable to manifold clip.
14. Fit EVAP cannister in support bracket.
15. Connect EVAP cannister to inlet manifold hose and secure clip.
16. Connect brake servo vacuum hose to inlet manifold.
17. Fit dipstick/filler tube to pipe.
18. Align dipstick/filler tube mounting bracket, fit bolt and tighten to 10 Nm.
19. Fit dipstick.
20. Secure coil harness to support bracket.
21. Refill cooling system. *See COOLING SYSTEM, Adjustments.*
22. Fit engine cover. *See ENGINE, Repairs.*
23. Connect battery earth lead.

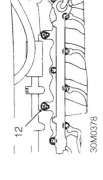

30M0378

12. Remove 2 nuts and 7 bolts securing inlet manifold to cylinder head.
13. Remove inlet manifold from cylinder head studs.
14. Remove and discard gasket seal from inlet manifold.

Refit

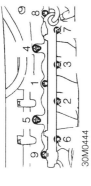

30M0444

1. Clean manifold to cylinder head mating faces.
2. Fit NEW gasket seal to cylinder head.
3. Fit inlet manifold to studs.

4. Fit nuts and bolts securing inlet manifold to cylinder head and tighten in sequence shown to 25 Nm.
5. Align support bracket and tighten bolt to 25 Nm.
6. Secure fuel feed hose to fuel filter pipe.
7. Secure fuel return hose to return pipe.
8. Connect air intake temperature sensor multiplug.
9. Connect injector harness multiplug.
10. Connect coolant hose to inlet manifold and secure clip.
11. Fit manifold chamber gasket. *See this section.*
12. Refill cooling system. *See COOLING SYSTEM, Adjustments.*

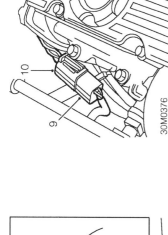

30M0376

9. Disconnect injector harness multiplug.
10. Release injector multiplug from bracket.

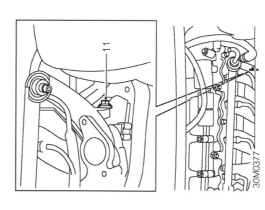

30M0377

11. Remove bolt securing inlet manifold to support bracket.

30M0374

7. Loosen clip and disconnect coolant hose from inlet manifold.

30M0375

8. Disconnect air intake temperature sensor multiplug from manifold.

GASKET - EXHAUST MANIFOLD - MPi MEMS 3 (2000MY ON)

Service repair no - 30.15.12

Remove

1. Disconnect battery earth lead.
2. Remove engine cover. See *ENGINE, Repairs.*
3. Raise rear of vehicle.

⚠ **WARNING: Support on safety stands.**

4. Remove LH road wheel.

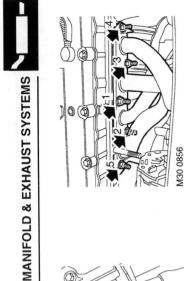

5. Remove 2 scrivets and 1 Torx screw closing splash panel and remove panel.

M30 0850

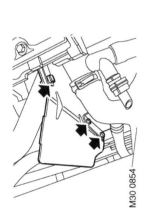

6. Release tension on alternator drive belt tensioner and remove drive belt.

M30 0851

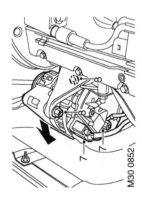

7. Remove nut securing alternator lead and release lead, disconnect alternator multiplug.
8. Remove alternator top bolt and loosen lower bolt.
9. Position alternator forwards to access alternator bracket.

M30 0852

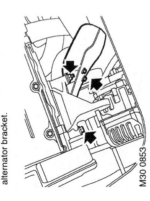

10. Remove nut and bolt securing alternator bracket.
11. Remove 2 bolts securing alternator heat shield and remove heat shield.
12. Collect alternator bracket.

M30 0853

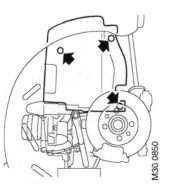

13. Remove 3 bolts securing coolant hose heat shield and remove heat shield.

M30 0854

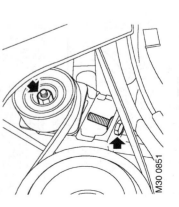

14. Remove 5 flange nuts securing exhaust manifold to cylinder head.
15. Position manifold aside, remove and discard gasket.

M30 0855

Refit

1. Clean exhaust manifold and cylinder head mating faces.
2. Fit new exhaust manifold gasket to cylinder head.

M30 0856

3. Position manifold and working in the sequence shown, tighten nuts to 45 Nm.
4. Position coolant hose heat shield, fit bolts and tighten to 9 Nm.
5. Position alternator bracket.
6. Position alternator heat shield, fit bolts and tighten to 9 Nm.
7. Tighten alternator bracket nut and bolt to 25 Nm.
8. Align alternator to bracket, fit top bolt, tighten both bolts to 45 Nm.
9. Connect alternator multiplug and lead, secure lead with nut.
10. Fit alternator drive belt and engage to tensioner. Ensure drive belt is located correctly on pulleys.
11. Adjust alternator drive belt tension. *See ELECTRICAL, Adjustments.*
12. Position closing panel and secure with scrivets and Torx screw.
13. Fit road wheel.
14. Fit engine cover. *See ENGINE, Repairs.*
15. Remove stand(s) and lower vehicle.
16. Connect battery earth lead.

GASKET - INLET MANIFOLD CHAMBER - VVC

Service repair no - 30.15.37

Remove

1. Remove engine compartment access panel. **See BODY, Exterior fittings.**
2. Remove engine cover. **See ENGINE, Repairs.**

30M0379

3. Remove bolt securing engine oil level dipstick/filler tube bracket to manifold.
4. Release clip securing dipstick/filler tube to pipe and remove tube.
5. Release brake servo vacuum pipe from manifold chamber.

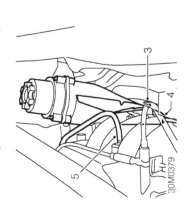

30M0380

6. Release throttle cable from abutment bracket.
7. Release inner cable from throttle cam.
8. Release clip and hose, EVAP cannister to inlet manifold chamber.

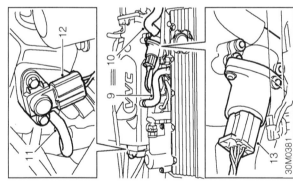

30M0381

9. Release clip and engine breather hose from camshaft cover.
10. Release hose from air by-pass valve.
11. Disconnect vacuum hose connecting fuel pressure regulator to manifold chamber.
12. Disconnect MAP sensor multiplug.
13. Disconnect idle air by-pass valve multiplug.

30M0382

14. Remove 4 bolts securing throttle body to manifold chamber.

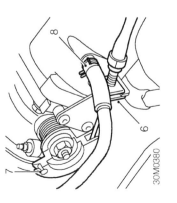

30M0383

15. Remove 5 bolts securing manifold chamber to inlet manifold.
16. Remove manifold chamber.
17. Remove and discard gasket seal from inlet manifold.
18. Remove and discard 'O' ring seal from throttle housing.

Refit

1. Clean inlet manifold and manifold chamber mating faces.
2. Fit NEW 'O' ring seal to throttle housing.
3. Fit NEW gasket seal to inlet manifold and position manifold chamber.
4. Tighten bolts securing manifold chamber to inlet manifold to 25 Nm.
5. Align throttle housing to manifold chamber and bracket to housing.
6. Tighten bolts to 9 Nm.
7. Connect MAP sensor multiplug.
8. Connect idle air valve multiplug.
9. Engage breather hose to manifold chamber and secure with clip.
10. Engage air by-pass hose to valve.
11. Connect throttle inner cable to cam.
12. Secure throttle cable to abutment bracket.
13. Secure throttle cable to manifold clip.
14. Connect EVAP cannister to inlet manifold hose and secure clip.
15. Connect brake servo vacuum hose to inlet manifold.
16. Fit dipstick/filler tube to pipe.
17. Align dipstick/filler tube mounting 10 Nm.
18. Fit engine cover. **See ENGINE, Repairs.**
19. Fit engine compartment access panel. **See BODY, Exterior fittings.**

GASKET - EXHAUST MANIFOLD - MPi MEMS 1.9 (UP TO 2000MY)

Service repair no - 30.15.12

Remove

1. Disconnect battery earth lead.
2. Remove engine cover. *See ENGINE, Repairs.*

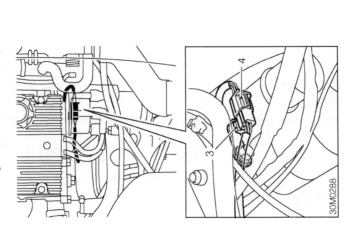

30M0288

3. Release HO₂S sensor multiplug from bracket on gearbox.
4. Disconnect HO₂S sensor multiplug from engine harness.

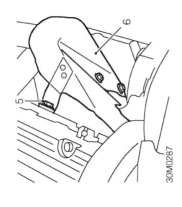

30M0287

5. Remove 3 bolts securing exhaust manifold heat shield.
6. Remove exhaust manifold heat shield.

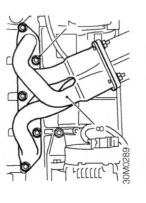

30M0289

7. Remove 5 nuts securing manifold to cylinder head.
8. Move exhaust manifold aside and collect gasket.

GASKET - EXHAUST MANIFOLD - WITH AIR CONDITIONING - MPi MEMS 1.9 (UP TO 2000MY)

Service repair no - 30.15.12/20

Remove

1. Disconnect battery earth lead.
2. Remove engine cover. *See ENGINE, Repairs.*

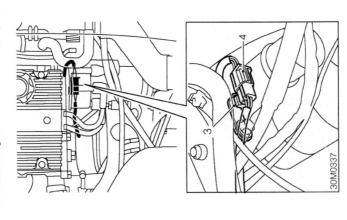

30M0337

3. Release oxygen sensor multiplug from bracket on gearbox.
4. Disconnect oxygen sensor multiplug from engine harness.
5. Remove alternator. *See ELECTRICAL, Repairs.*

Refit

1. Clean mating faces of exhaust manifold and cylinder head.
2. Fit manifold gasket and position manifold to cylinder head.
3. Fit nuts securing manifold to cylinder head.

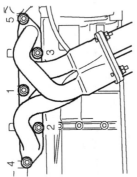

30M0340

4. Working in the sequence illustrated, tighten manifold to cylinder head nuts to 45 Nm.
5. Connect HO₂S sensor multiplug to engine harness.
6. Secure multiplug to bracket.
7. Fit exhaust manifold heat shield and tighten bolts.

   Top bolt = 25 Nm.
   Bottom bolts = 10 Nm.
8. Fit engine cover. *See ENGINE, Repairs.*
9. Connect battery earth lead.

⚠ **CAUTION: Ensure exhaust system is free from leaks. Exhaust gas leaks upstream of the catalyst could cause internal damage to the catalyst.**

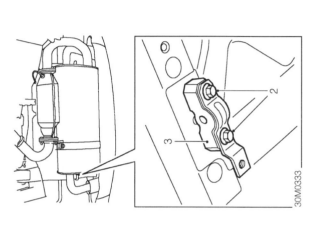

3. Remove brackets and rubbers.

EXHAUST MOUNTINGS

Service repair no - 30.20.06

Remove

1. Remove silencer heat shield. *See this section.*

30M0333

2. Remove 4 bolts securing LH and RH exhaust mountings.

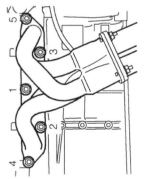

30M0334

4. Remove mounting rubber securing front pipe to subframe.

Refit

1. Fit mounting rubber securing front pipe to subframe.
2. Fit LH and RH mounting rubbers and brackets, fit bolts and tighten to 25 Nm.
3. Fit silencer heat shield. *See this section.*

30M0338

6. Remove 2 bolts and 1 nut securing exhaust manifold heat shield.
7. Remove exhaust manifold heat shield.
8. Remove bolt securing top alternator mounting bracket.
9. Remove top alternator mounting bracket.
10. Remove 5 nuts securing exhaust manifold to cylinder head.
11. Move exhaust manifold aside and collect gasket.

Refit

1. Clean mating faces of exhaust manifold and cylinder head.
2. Fit manifold gasket and position manifold to cylinder head.
3. Fit nuts securing manifold to cylinder head.

30M0340

4. Working in the sequence illustrated, tighten manifold to cylinder head nuts to 45 Nm.
5. Connect oxygen sensor multiplug to engine harness.
6. Secure multiplug to bracket.
7. Fit top alternator mounting bracket and tighten bolt to 25 Nm.
8. Fit exhaust manifold heat shield and tighten fixings:
   Top nut = 25 Nm.
   Bottom bolts = 10 Nm.
9. Fit alternator. *See ELECTRICAL, Repairs.*
10. Fit engine cover. *See ENGINE, Repairs.*
11. Connect battery earth lead.

⚠ **CAUTION: Ensure exhaust system is free from leaks. Exhaust gas leaks upstream of the catalyst could cause internal damage to the catalyst.**

CLUTCH

CONTENTS

CLUTCH

CLUTCH COMPONENTS

33M0186A

1. Flywheel
2. Clutch plate
3. Pressure plate
4. Release bearing
5. Release bearing fork
6. Fork retaining bolt

7. Pressure plate bolts
8. Clutch release shaft
9. Clutch release shaft, washer
10. Clevis pin
11. 'R' clip

HYDRAULIC CLUTCH SYSTEM

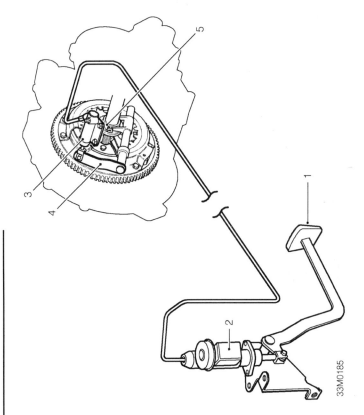

33M0185

1. Clutch pedal
2. Master cylinder
3. Slave cylinder

4. Release arm
5. Release bearing

CLUTCH SYSTEM OPERATION

The diaphragm type clutch is operated via a hydraulic system.

When pressure is applied to the clutch pedal, fluid is pumped from the master cylinder to the slave cylinder causing the slave cylinder piston to apply pressure to the release lever. The release lever rotates the release fork and shaft.

The release fork changes rotary movement of the release lever into linear movement pushing the release bearing against the pressure plate diaphragm fingers, applying pressure to the drive plate springs and dis-engaging the clutch.

When pressure is released from the clutch pedal the master cylinder piston is returned by a spring which causes a pressure decrease. The drop in pressure allows the diaphragm fingers to push the release bearing back, decreasing the pressure on the drive plate springs and re-engaging the clutch.

SLAVE CYLINDER COMPONENTS

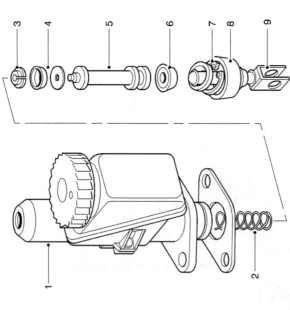

33M0187

1. Bleed screw
2. Slave cylinder
3. Return spring
4. Seal
5. Piston assembly

6. Dust cover
7. Push-rod
8. Clevis pin
9. R-clip

MASTER CYLINDER COMPONENTS

33M0188

1. Master cylinder
2. Spring
3. Spring seat
4. Seal and washer
5. Piston

6. Seal
7. Circlip
8. Boot
9. Push-rod

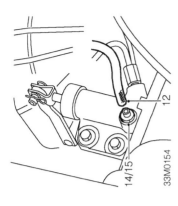

14/15

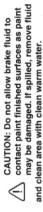

12

33M0154

CLUTCH - BLEED

Service repair no - 33.15.01

⚠ **CAUTION: Do not allow brake fluid to contact paint finished surfaces as paint may be damaged. If spilled, remove fluid and clean area with clean warm water.**

⚠ **CAUTION: Ensure master cylinder is topped up at frequent intervals. Use only NEW fluid.**

1. Open bonnet.
2. Open luggage compartment.
3. Remove engine compartment access panel. **See BODY, Exterior fittings.**
4. Position cloth around master cylinder to catch spillage.
5. Clean area around master cylinder pipe union.
6. Depress clutch pedal to floor and hold.

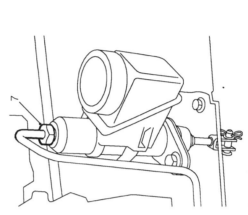

33M0153

7. Loosen master cylinder pipe union and allow air and fluid to escape.
8. Tighten pipe union.
9. Return clutch pedal to released position.
10. Repeat process until bubble free fluid emerges and tighten union to 18 Nm.

11. Clean area around slave cylinder bleed nipple.
12. Position bleed bottle and connect hose to bleed nipple.
13. Depress clutch pedal to floor and hold.
14. Loosen bleed nipple and allow air and fluid to escape.
15. Tighten nipple.
16. Return clutch pedal to released position.
17. Repeat process until bubble free fluid emerges.
18. Depress clutch pedal to floor and hold.
19. Open bleed nipple and by hand, pull clutch lever to fully released position.
20. Tighten nipple to 7 Nm.
21. Return clutch pedal to released position.
22. Remove bleed bottle.
23. Top up master cylinder.
24. Fit engine compartment access cover. **See BODY, Exterior fittings.**

This page is intentionally left blank

8. Measure rivet depth at point 'B', renew plate if less than service limit:

   Rivet depth - NEW = 1.0 mm
   Rivet depth - SERVICE LIMIT = 0.20 mm

33M0180

9. Measure clutch plate run-out using a dial gauge and a gearbox mainshaft; renew plate if outside service limit:

   Run-out - NEW = 0.80 mm
   Run-out - SERVICE LIMIT = 1.0 mm

10. Check clutch plate for signs of wear or damage. Check for signs of overheating on drive straps (deep straw or blue colour); renew pressure plate if necessary.

⚠ **CAUTION: Renew a pressure plate which has been accidentally dropped.**

CLUTCH PLATE AND RELEASE BEARING

Service repair no - 33.10.07

Remove

1. Remove gearbox. *See MANUAL GEARBOX, Repairs.*

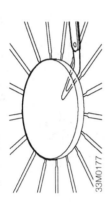

33M0177

2. Place a circular piece of flat plate across diaphragm fingers and insert feeler gauges between plate and fingers; measure finger clearance:

   Diaphragm finger clearance - service limit = 1.0 mm
   Renew pressure plate if clearance obtained is outside service limits.

3. Progressively loosen then remove 6 bolts securing pressure plate to flywheel.

4. Remove pressure plate.

5. Remove clutch plate.

6. Inspect clutch linings for signs of wear or oil contamination. Check for broken or weak springs and signs of cracking of spring apertures; renew components as necessary.

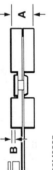

33M0285

7. Measure clutch plate thickness at point 'A', renew plate if less than service limit.

   clutch plate thickness - NEW = 7.40 mm - 6.90 mm
   clutch plate thickness - SERVICE LIMIT = 5.60 mm.

This page is intentionally left blank

33M0181

11. Using a straight edge and feeler gauges, check surface of pressure plate for warping at 4 separate points, renew plate if warping exceeds service limit:

Pressure plate warping - SERVICE LIMIT = 0.15 mm

Release bearing

12. Remove release bearing.
13. Examine release bearing for signs of wear or damage, renew if necessary.

Refit

Release bearing

1. Clean gearbox input shaft and release bearing mating faces.
2. Fit release bearing.

Clutch assembly

3. Clean all components.
4. Clean flywheel.
5. Ensure locating dowels are fitted in flywheel.
6. Smear clutch plate splines with molybdenum disulphide grease.
7. Position clutch plate to flywheel with 'FLYWHEEL SIDE' marking towards flywheel.

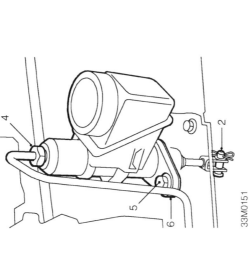

18G 1483

33M0182

8. Position pressure plate to flywheel and fit alignment tool **18G 1483**.
9. Fit 6 bolts securing pressure plate to flywheel, tighten bolts sufficiently until drive plate is held in its central position. Remove **18G 1483** from pressure plate.
10. Working by diagonal sequence, progressively tighten pressure plate bolts to 25 Nm.
11. Fit gearbox. **See MANUAL GEARBOX, Repairs.**

CLUTCH MASTER CYLINDER

Service repair no - 33.20.01

Remove

⚠ **CAUTION: Do not allow brake fluid to contact paint finished surfaces as paint may be damaged. If spilled, remove fluid and clean area with clean warm water.**

1. Remove underbonnet closing panel, **See BODY, Exterior fittings.**

33M0151

2. Remove clevis pin from clutch pedal.
3. Position cloth to catch spillage.
4. Loosen and release union securing fluid pipe to master cylinder, position fluid pipe aside.

⚠ **CAUTION: Plug the connections.**

5. Remove 2 bolts securing master cylinder to pedal box.
6. Remove master cylinder.
7. Remove and discard gasket.

Refit

1. Using NEW gasket, fit master cylinder and tighten bolts to 25 Nm.
2. Position pipe and tighten union to 18 Nm.
3. Position clutch pedal to push rod, fit clevis pin.
4. Fit washer and clip.
5. Bleed clutch. **See Adjustments.**
6. Fit underbonnet closing panel. **See BODY, Exterior fittings.**

CLUTCH SLAVE CYLINDER

Service repair no - 33.35.01

Remove

1. Remove engine cover. *See ENGINE, Repairs.*

33M0152

2. Remove clevis pin from slave cylinder.

⚠ **CAUTION: Do not allow brake fluid to contact paint finished surfaces as paint may be damaged. If spilled, remove fluid and clean area with clean warm water.**

3. Release pipe union from slave cylinder and position aside.

⚠ **CAUTION: Plug the connections.**

4. Remove 2 bolts securing slave cylinder to bracket and remove slave cylinder.

Refit

1. Fit slave cylinder and tighten bolts to 25 Nm.
2. Position pipe and tighten union to 18 Nm.
3. Position cylinder rod to lever and secure with clevis pin.
4. Bleed clutch. *See Adjustments.*
5. Fit engine cover. *See ENGINE, Repairs.*

DAMPER - CLUTCH - VVC

Service repair no - 33.15.05

Remove

1. Remove underbonnet closing panel, *See BODY, Exterior fittings.*

⚠ **CAUTION: Do not allow brake fluid to contact paint finished surfaces as paint may be damaged. If spilled, remove fluid and clean area with clean warm water.**

2. Place container underneath clutch damper to collect fluid spillage.

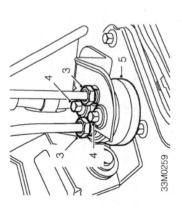

33M0259

3. Release 2 clutch pipe unions from clutch damper.
4. Remove 2 bolts securing clutch damper to bracket.
5. Collect clutch damper.

⚠ **CAUTION: Plug the connections.**

Refit

1. Position clutch damper to bracket.
2. Fit bolts securing clutch damper to bracket and tighten to 15 Nm.
3. Fit clutch pipe unions to clutch damper and tighten to 18 Nm.
4. Bleed clutch hydraulic system. *See Adjustments.*
5. Collect drip tray.
6. Fit underbonnet closing panel. *See BODY, Exterior fittings.*

CONTENTS

GEAR LEVER

Service repair no - 37.16.04

⚠ **WARNING:** *See RESTRAINT SYSTEMS, Precautions.*

Remove

1. Disconnect battery earth lead.
2. Remove front console. *See BODY, Interior trim components.*

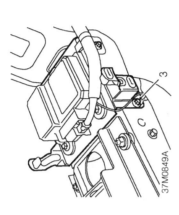

3. Remove 4 Tx30 Torx bolts securing SRS DCU bracket to tunnel, position bracket aside.

37M0849A

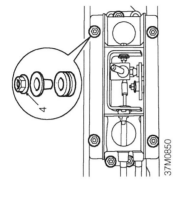

37M0850

4. Remove 4 nuts and 3 bolts securing lever assembly to tunnel.

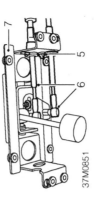

37M0851

5. Remove bolt securing cable abutment clip to lever assembly and release clip.
6. Release 2 cables from ball joints and lever assembly.
7. Remove lever assembly.

Refit

1. Connect cables to lever assembly.
2. Position outer cables and secure with clip.
3. Secure retaining clip with bolt.
4. Position gear lever assembly to body.
5. Fit and tighten nuts and bolts to 9 Nm.
6. Position SRS bracket to body, fit harness earth lead and tighten Torx bolts to 9 Nm.
7. Fit front console. *See BODY, Interior trim components.*
8. Connect battery earth lead.

GEAR CHANGE CABLE

Service repair no - 37.16.16

⚠ **WARNING: See RESTRAINT SYSTEMS, Precautions.**

Remove

1. Position vehicle on a 2 post ramp.
2. Make the SRS system safe. **See RESTRAINT SYSTEMS, Precautions.**
3. Remove engine cover. **See ENGINE, Repairs.**
4. Drain engine coolant. **See COOLING SYSTEM, Adjustments.**
5. Release handbrake to OFF position.

⚠ **CAUTION: To prevent damage to sump place a piece of wood between jack and sump.**

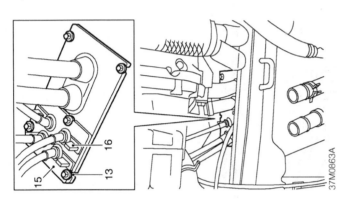

37M0858

6. Release gear change cable from gearbox linkage.
7. Remove and discard clip securing cable to abutment bracket.
8. Release cable from abutment bracket.
9. Place support jack underneath engine sump and support engine weight.

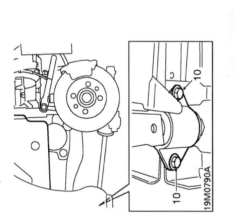

19M0790A

10. Remove 2 bolts securing each front subframe mounting to body brackets.
11. Lower jack carefully, to allow access to closing plate bolts.

⚠ **CAUTION: Care must be taken that no cables or pipes are stretched when lowering front of subframe.**

12. Tie coolant hoses aside to allow access to closing plate.

13. Release 2 upper bolts and remove 3 remaining bolts securing closing plate to bulkhead.
14. Apply soft soap to all four closing plate cables, to ease movement of closing plate.
15. Release closing plate from bulkhead and slide along cables.
16. Release gear change cable grommet from closing plate.
17. Remove front console. **See BODY, Interior trim components.**

37M0863A

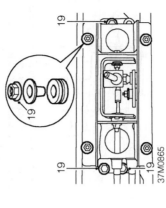

18. Remove 4 Torx bolts securing SRS DCU bracket to tunnel, position bracket aside.

37M0864A

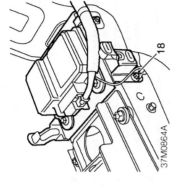

19. Remove 4 nuts and 3 bolts securing gear selector assembly to tunnel.

37M0865

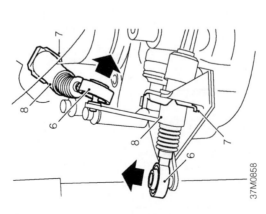

10. Remove nut securing fuel pipe bracket to body.
11. Remove 3 bolts securing air cleaner mounting bracket to body.
12. Remove air cleaner mounting bracket.
13. Remove air cleaner duct from resonator.

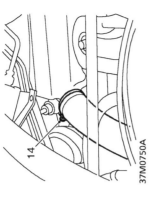

37M0750A

14. Loosen clip and release air intake hose from resonator.

GEARBOX

Service repair no - 37.20.02/99

Remove

1. Disconnect battery earth lead.
2. Raise vehicle on a 2 post ramp.
3. Depressurise LH side of hydragas system. *See FRONT SUSPENSION, Adjustments.*
4. Remove road wheel(s).
5. Remove air cleaner. *See ENGINE MANAGEMENT SYSTEM - MEMS, Repairs.*
6. Remove starter motor. *See ELECTRICAL, Repairs.*
7. Drain gearbox oil. *See MAINTENANCE.*

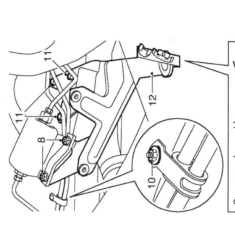

37M0749A

8. Remove 2 nuts securing fuel filter to air cleaner mounting bracket.
9. Release 2 hand brake cables and speedometer cable from clips on air cleaner mounting bracket.

MANUAL GEARBOX

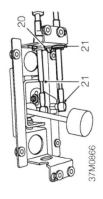

37M0866

20. Position gear selector assembly and remove bolt securing cable abutment clip to assembly.
21. Remove cable abutment clip and release cable from assembly.
22. Remove gear change cable from tunnel and engine compartment.

Refit

1. Position gear change cable to tunnel and feed through rear bulkhead.
2. Position cable in engine compartment.
3. Lubricate all four cables with soft soap to ease grommet movement on cables.
4. Position cable into closing plate slot and secure with grommet.
5. Align closing plate to bulkhead and secure with bolts.
6. Raise subframe on jack, fit subframe mounting bolts and tighten to 30 Nm.
7. Position cable to gear selector abutment bracket.
8. Engage cable to selector ball joint.
9. Fit NEW abutment bracket clip.
10. Fit cable to gear lever selector assembly.
11. Position cable to abutment, fit retaining clip and secure with bolt.
12. Position gear lever assembly to tunnel, fit and tighten nuts and bolts to 9 Nm.
13. Position SRS DCU bracket to tunnel, fit harness earth connector, tighten Torx bolts to 10 Nm.

⚠ **WARNING: The crash sensor is incorporated inside the DCU, therefore it imperative that the DCU bolts are tightened to their correct torque.**

14. Fit front console. *See BODY, Interior trim components.*
15. Untie and position coolant hoses.
16. Fill engine coolant system. *See COOLING SYSTEM, Adjustments.*
17. Fit engine cover. *See ENGINE, Repairs.*

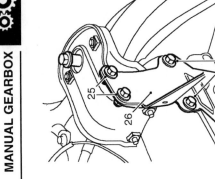

37M0751A

15. Disconnect 2 reverse light switch connections.

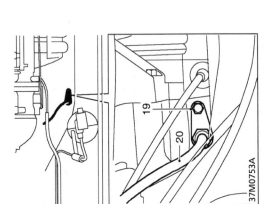

37M0752A

16. Remove 'R' clip and clevis pin securing clutch slave cylinder push rod to release lever. Remove push rod from slave cylinder.
17. Remove 2 bolts securing slave cylinder to mounting bracket.
18. Release slave cylinder pipe from clip under bracket and move cylinder aside.

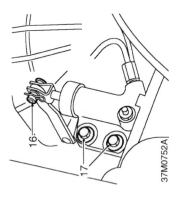

37M0753A

19. **Up to 2000MY:** Remove bolt securing speedometer cable pinion to gearbox.
20. Release speedometer cable from gearbox.
21. Remove and discard 'O' ring seal.
22. **2000MY ON:** Disconnect multiplug from road speed transducer.
23. Remove bolt securing transducer to gearbox, remove transducer and discard 'O' ring.
24. **All models:** Release clip securing starter motor lead to slave cylinder mounting bracket, position lead aside.

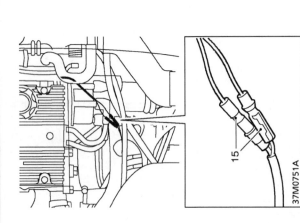

37M0754B

25. Remove 4 bolts securing clutch slave cylinder mounting bracket to gearbox.
26. Remove clutch slave cylinder mounting bracket.

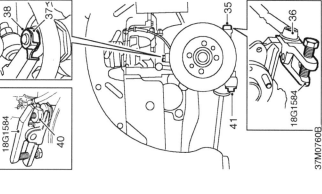

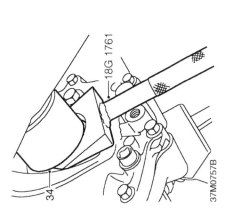

37M0760B

35. Remove nuts securing track control arms to both hubs.
36. Break track control arm joints using tool **18G 1584.**
37. Bend back lock tabs from both ball joint nuts.
38. Remove nuts securing ball joints to upper arms.
39. Remove lock tabs.
40. Release taper joints from upper arms using tool **18G 1584.**
41. Remove bolts securing lower suspension arms to both hubs.
42. Remove both hubs complete with drive shafts.

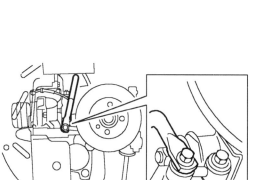

37M0759B

33. Remove nuts and bolts securing anti-roll bar to LH and RH links.

18G 1761

37M0757B

34. Release both drive shafts from gearbox using tool **18G 1761.**

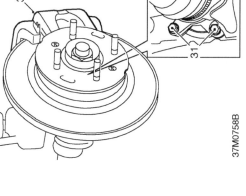

37M0758B

31. Remove 4 bolts securing both caliper carriers to hubs.
32. Move calipers aside. Tie caliper clear of brake discs, ensuring that the weight of the caliper is supported.

CAUTION: Do not allow caliper to hang on brake hose as weight of caliper may damage hose.

37M0756B

27. Remove bolt securing ABS speed sensors to both rear hubs.
28. Release ABS speed sensors from hubs and collect spacers.
29. Release ABS sensor cable from clips on both upper arms.
30. Release ABS sensor cable from 3 clips on LH hydragas unit.

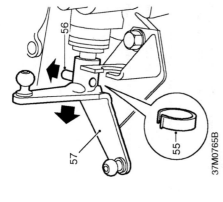

37M0765B

55. Remove clip retaining selector linkage roll pin.
56. Using a suitable punch, drive out selector linkage roll pin.
57. Remove selector linkage from selector shaft.

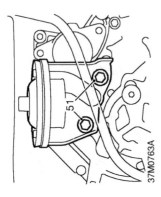

37M0763A

51. Remove 2 bolts securing LH engine mounting to gearbox, remove mounting.

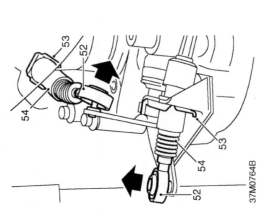

37M0764B

52. Release both gear change cable ball joints from linkage.
53. Remove and discard 2 clips securing gear change cables to abutment brackets and discard clips.
54. Release gear change cables from abutment brackets.

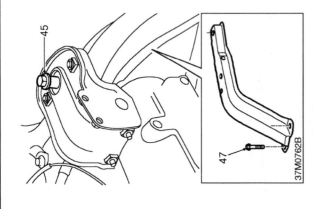

37M0762B

45. With assistance remove nut and bolt securing LH engine mounting to buttress.
46. Raise engine on jack.

⚠ **CAUTION: Use a block of wood or hard rubber pad to protect sump.**

47. Remove 4 bolts securing buttress to subframe.
48. Adjust height of gearbox and remove buttress.
49. Lower engine on jack until gearbox is supported on subframe.
50. Remove resonator.

37M0761B

43. Remove 2 bolts securing resonator to body.
44. Release hydragas pipe from 3 clips on LH buttress.

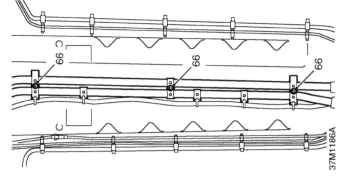

37M1186A

66. Remove 3 bolts securing coolant pipes to floor pan.
67. Remove nut and bolt securing LH rear suspension damper to upper arm.
68. Remove spacer and ABS sensor cable clip.
69. Support LH side of rear subframe on jack.

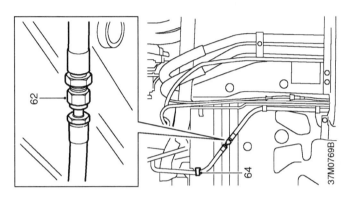

37M0769B

62. Loosen LH rear hydragas unit union joint at rear of floor pan and break joint.
63. Remove and discard 'O' ring seal.

⚠ **CAUTION: Plug the connections.**

64. Remove clip securing hydragas pipe to floor pan.
65. Remove crossmember. **See BODY, Exterior fittings.**

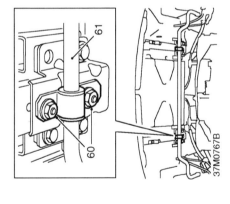

37M0767B

60. Remove 4 nuts securing both rear anti-roll bar bush clamps.
61. Remove rear anti-roll bar.

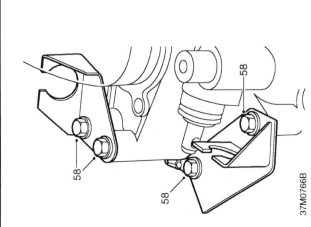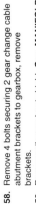

37M0766B

58. Remove 4 bolts securing 2 gear change cable abutment brackets to gearbox, remove brackets.
59. Remove silencer heat shield. **See MANIFOLD & EXHAUST SYSTEMS, Repairs.**

70. Remove 3 LH rear and 2 LH front subframe to body mounting bolts.
71. Remove LH rear anti-roll bar bracket from rear mounting.
72. Lower subframe sufficiently to allow gearbox removal.
73. Raise engine on jack until clear of rear subframe LH longitudinal member.

⚠ **CAUTION: Use a block of wood or hard rubber pad to protect sump.**

74. Remove 7 bolts and 1 nut and bolt securing gearbox to engine.
75. With assistance, release gearbox from engine.
76. Remove gearbox between body and subframe.
77. Remove circlips from end of both drive shafts.

37M0771B

Refit

1. Clean mating faces of gearbox and engine; ensure locating dowels are fitted.
2. With assistance, fit gearbox and locate onto dowels.

⚠ **CAUTION: During the above keep the drive shaft horizontal to avoid damaging oil seal.**

3. Fit 7 bolts and 1 nut and bolt securing gearbox to engine. Tighten:
   - Gearbox to engine 80 Nm
   - Gearbox to sump 45 Nm.
4. Lower engine on jack until gearbox rests on subframe longitudinal member, remove jack.
5. Raise subframe on jack.
6. Fit rear anti-roll bar mounting bracket to subframe rear mounting.
7. Fit bolts securing front and rear subframe mountings and tighten bolts to:
   - Rear mounting 45 Nm
   - Front mounting 30 Nm.
8. Align suspension damper to upper arm, fit ABS sensor lead clip and spacer and tighten nut and bolt to 45 Nm.
9. Fit coolant pipes to floor and tighten bolts to 25 Nm.
10. Fit crossmember. See **BODY, Exterior fittings.**
11. Ensure union of hydragas pipes are clean and fit new 'O' ring seal.
12. Connect hydragas pipe and tighten union to 20 Nm.
13. Fit clip to secure hydragas pipe to floor.
14. Fit rear anti-roll bar and tighten bolts to 13 Nm.
15. Fit gear change cable abutment brackets and tighten bolts to 45 Nm.

⚠ NOTE: Fit earth cable to upper bolt on lower bracket.

16. Ensure selector linkage and shaft are clean, fit linkage to shaft and secure with new roll pin.
17. Fit clip to retain roll pin.
18. Clean gear change linkage and cable sockets.
19. Fit gear change cables to abutment brackets and fit NEW clips.
20. Apply grease to cable socket.
21. Fit cables to linkage.
22. Fit silencer heat shield. See **MANIFOLD & EXHAUST SYSTEMS, Repairs.**
23. Fit LH engine mounting to gearbox and and tighten bolts to 48 Nm.
24. With gearbox raised clear of subframe, fit the resonator but do not fit bolts at this stage.
25. Fit buttress and tighten bolts to 45 Nm.
26. Fit hydragas pipe to clips on buttress.
27. Fit bolts securing resonator to body.
28. Lower LH engine mounting onto buttress and tighten bolt to 80 Nm.
29. Clean end of both drive shaft inboard joints and fit NEW circlips to shafts.
30. Lubricate differential oil seals.
31. Wipe taper joints of both hub ball joints and upper arms.
32. Fit both hub assemblies to upper arms and engage both drive shafts to differential.
33. Fit lock washers to upper ball joint pins and tighten nuts to 54 Nm.
34. Bend lock washers upward to lock nuts.

⚠ NOTE: Pull outwards on drive shaft inboard joints to check for full engagement.

35. Align both hubs to lower arms and tighten bolts to 100 Nm.
36. Wipe tapers and seats of track control arms and hubs.
37. Fit track control arms to hubs and tighten nuts to 30 Nm.
38. Fit bolts securing anti-roll bar to LH and RH links and tighten nuts to 35 Nm.
39. Fit calipers to hubs and tighten bolts to 85 Nm.
40. Clean ABS sensors, sensor spacers and mating faces on hubs.
41. Fit ABS spacers and sensors to hubs and tighten bolts to 10 Nm.
42. Secure ABS sensor cables to clips on upper suspension arms.
43. Fit LH ABS sensor cables to clips on subframe. Fit clutch slave cylinder mounting bracket. Fit and tighten bolts.
44. Fit clutch slave cylinder mounting bracket. Fit and tighten bolts.
45. Secure starter motor lead clip to clutch slave cylinder mounting bracket.

46. **Up to 2000MY:** Fit new 'O' ring seal to speedometer cable pinion housing, fit pinion to gearbox and tighten bolt to 10 Nm.
47. **2000MY ON:** Fit new 'O' ring to road speed transducer, fit transducer to gearbox and tighten bolt to 12 Nm.
48. Connect multiplug to transducer.
49. **All models:** Fit clutch slave cylinder to bracket and secure pipe to clip on under side.
50. Tighten bolts securing slave cylinder to 25 Nm.
51. Clean clutch push rod, and clevis pin.
52. Grease clevis pin and end of push rod.
53. Fit push rod to cylinder, align rod to clutch lever and fit clevis pin.
54. Fit NEW 'R' clip to secure clevis pin.
55. Connect reverse lamp switch wires.
56. Connect air intake hose to resonator and tighten clip.
57. Fit starter motor. See **ELECTRICAL, Repairs.**
58. Fit air cleaner duct to resonator.
59. Fit air cleaner mounting bracket. Fit and tighten bolts.
60. Fit fuel pipe clip to stud on body and tighten nut.
61. Fit hand brake and speedometer cables to clips on air cleaner bracket.
62. Fit fuel filter bracket to air cleaner bracket and tighten nuts.
63. Fit air cleaner. See **ENGINE MANAGEMENT SYSTEM - MEMS, Repairs.**
64. Fill gearbox with oil. See **MAINTENANCE.**
65. Connect battery earth lead.
66. Pressurise LH side of suspension. See **FRONT SUSPENSION, Adjustments.**

SELECTOR SHAFT OIL SEAL

Service repair no - 37.23.10

Remove

1. Raise rear of vehicle.

⚠ **WARNING: Support on safety stands.**

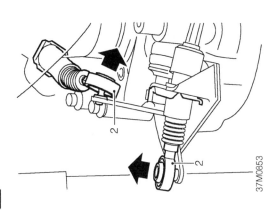

37M0853

2. Release 2 gear change cables from selector linkage.

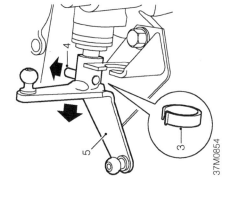

37M0854

3. Remove clip securing selector linkage roll pin.
4. Using a suitable punch, drive out roll pin from selector linkage and discard roll pin.
5. Remove selector linkage from shaft.

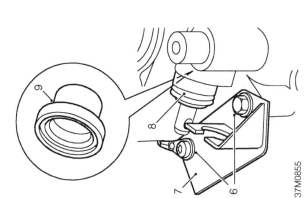

37M0855

6. Remove bolt and Torx screw securing lower gear change cable abutment bracket to gearbox.
7. Remove gear change cable abutment bracket.
8. Remove oil seal cover from selector shaft.
9. Using a flat screwdriver remove oil seal from gearbox and discard oil seal.

Refit

1. Clean oil seal housing and selector shaft.
2. Lubricate NEW seal using clean unused engine oil.
3. Fit oil seal to selector shaft.
4. Secure seal to gearbox using a deep socket.
5. Fit oil seal cover and secure to seal flange.
6. Fit gear change cable abutment bracket, fit bolts and tighten to 45 Nm.

△ NOTE: Position earth lead to abutment bracket retaining bolt.

7. Fit selector linkage to shaft, align holes, fit NEW roll pin and secure clip.
8. Secure gear change cables to selector linkage.
9. Remove stand(s) and lower vehicle.

MANUAL GEARBOX

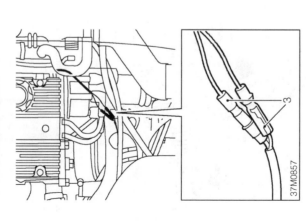

54M0072

6. Fit a wedge between suspension upper arm and subframe. Lower suspension onto wedge and remove jack.

⚠ **CAUTION: Ensure that an appropriate wedge is used to prevent any damage occurring to the suspension components.**

7. Position drain tray to collect oil spillage from gearbox.

DIFFERENTIAL OIL SEAL

Service repair no - 51.20.37

Remove

1. Raise rear of vehicle.

⚠ **WARNING: Support on safety stands**

2. Remove road wheel(s).

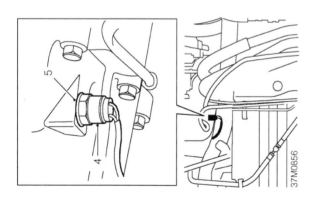

54M0071

3. Remove 2 scrivets and Torx screw securing closing panel.
4. Remove closing panel.
5. Place a jack under vehicle and raise hub.

MANUAL GEARBOX

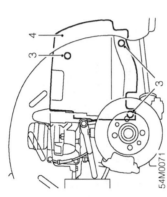

37M0856

4. Remove reverse lamp switch.
5. Collect sealing washer and discard.

Refit

1. Clean threads and mating faces of reverse lamp switch.
2. Fit NEW sealing washer to reverse lamp switch.
3. Fit and tighten reverse lamp switch to gearbox.
4. Connect reverse lamp switch connectors.
5. Fit engine compartment access panel. *See BODY, Exterior fittings.*
6. Remove stand(s) and lower vehicle.

MANUAL GEARBOX

REVERSE LAMP SWITCH

Service repair no - 37.27.01

Remove

1. Raise rear of vehicle.

⚠ **WARNING: Support on safety stands.**

2. Remove engine compartment access panel. *See BODY, Exterior fittings.*

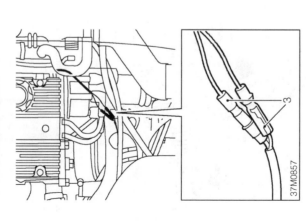

37M0857

3. Disconnect reverse lamp switch connectors.

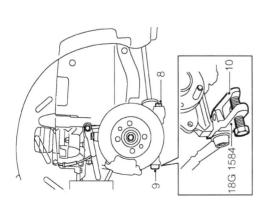

8. Remove bolt securing lower arm to hub.
9. Remove nut securing track control arm to hub.
10. Break taper joint using tool **18G 1584** and release track control arm.

54M0073

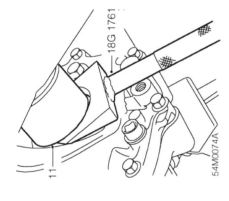

11. Release drive shaft from differential using tool **18G 1761**.
12. Remove and discard circlip from drive shaft.
13. Secure drive shaft clear of gearbox for access.
14. Carefully prise oil seal out of differential housing.

⚠ **CAUTION: Two types of oil seal are fitted to the PG1 gearbox, retain old oil seal for reference.**

54M0074A

⚠ **CAUTION: If a later type gearbox is to be fitted to a vehicle that has early drive shafts fitted. The gearbox must be fitted with early type oil seals.**

Refit

1. Thoroughly clean oil seal recess and splines of drive shaft.
2. Lubricate NEW oil seal with clean unused gearbox oil.
3. Using appropriate tools carefully drift oil seal into differential housing until oil seal is fully seated in recess.
4. Fit RH oil seal using tools:
   18G 1354 and **18G 1354-16.**

Fit LH oil seal using following tools:
Type A oil seal - use tool **18G 1354** and **18G 1354-16.**
Type B oil seal - use tool **18G 134** and **18G 134-12.**

37M1189

A - early type oil seal   B - modified oil seal

⚠ **CAUTION: The differential is fitted with either early type or modified type oil seals. The modified oil seal is fitted to later gearboxes which have machined, seal location faces. Modified oil seals must not be fitted to early gearboxes.**

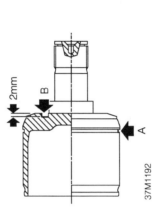

37M1192

◁ NOTE: The drive shaft inboard joint has also been modified for use with the modified oil seal. The modified drive shaft can be identified by the external groove at point 'A' which indicates that additional oil seal clearance has been added at point 'B'.

◁ NOTE: Modified drive shafts can be used with either early type or modified oil seals.

⚠ **CAUTION: Do not attempt to fit a modified oil seal with an early type drive shaft, as the circlip on the drive shaft will not engage in the differential.**

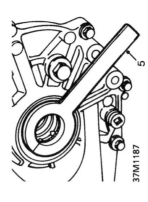

37M1187

5. Fully insert oil seal protector tool (Unipart part number TRV 100060) into differential oil seal so that oil seal lip is protected, ensure split end of seal protector is butted correctly.
6. Fit NEW circlip to drive shaft.
7. Ensuring drive shaft is kept horizontal, insert drive shaft through the seal protector until the drive shaft begins to engage with the differential splines in the housing.
8. Remove seal protector by pulling carefully on the seal protector's tail.

9. Fully engage driveshaft into differential.

 CAUTION: Pull on drive shaft to ensure that circlip has engaged correctly.

10. Locate rear link ball joint to hub and tighten nut to 30 Nm.

11. Fit bolt securing lower arm to hub and tighten to 100 Nm.

12. Raise hub on jack and remove wedge. lower jack and remove.

13. Remove spillage tray.

14. Fit closing panel and secure with scrivets and Torx screw.

15. Fit road wheel(s) and tighten nuts to correct torque. *See INFORMATION, Torque wrench settings.*

16. Remove stand(s) and lower vehicle.

17. Check and top up gearbox oil. *See MAINTENANCE.*

This page is intentionally left blank

STEPTRONIC EM-CVT COMPONENT LOCATION

M44 1303B

1. Fluid cooler
2. Brake switch
3. Instrument pack
4. Steering wheel switches
5. Engine Control Module (ECM)

6. Gearbox Interface Unit (GIU)
7. Steptronic EM-CVT gearbox
8. Selector cable
9. Fluid cooler feed/return pipes
10. Gear selector lever

AUTOMATIC GEARBOX - 'EM-CVT'

CONTENTS

Page

AUTOMATIC GEARBOX - 'EM-CVT'

STEPTRONIC EM-CVT GEARBOX

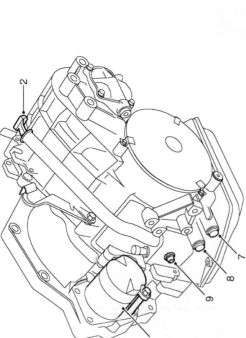
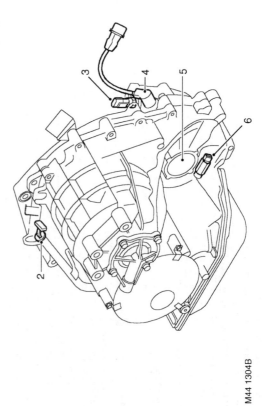

M44 1304B

AUTOMATIC GEARBOX - 'EM-CVT'

1. Starter motor
2. Fluid level dipstick
3. Road speed transducer
4. Gearbox differential speed sensor
5. LH drive shaft connection

6. Park/Neutral switch
7. Fluid cooler return connection
8. Fluid cooler feed connection
9. Ratio control motor connector

DESCRIPTION AND OPERATION   3

2   DESCRIPTION AND OPERATION

AUTOMATIC GEARBOX - 'EM-CVT'

AUTOMATIC GEARBOX - 'EM-CVT'

STEPTRONIC EM-CVT GEARBOX - SECTIONAL VIEW

1. Ratio control motor
2. Fluid sump
3. Hydraulic control unit
4. Primary pulley
5. Fluid pump
6. Secondary pulley
7. Drive belt
8. Differential

9. Road speed transducer
10. Pinion shaft
11. Final drive reduction gear
12. Secondary reduction gear
13. Drive clutch
14. Reverse clutch
15. Planetary gear set
16. Input shaft

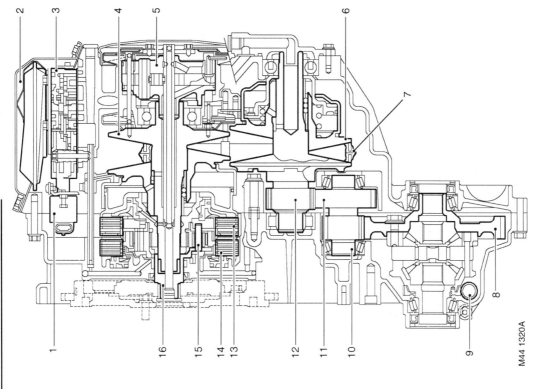

M44 1320A

DESCRIPTION

General

The Electro Mechanical - Continuously Variable Transmission (EM-CVT) is based on a standard CVT unit with electronic components fitted to control the gear ratio. This gives the driver a choice between an automatic gearbox and a semi-automatic Steptronic manual gearbox.

The gearbox can be operated as a conventional CVT unit by selecting P, R, N or D on the selector lever. Moving the selector lever across the gate trips a microswitch and puts the gearbox into manual/sport mode.

In sport mode, the gearbox still operates as a conventional CVT unit, but becomes more responsive to changes in driver demands. Engine speed is higher in this mode which gives improved acceleration.

When in sport mode, if the selector lever or either of the steering wheel switches are moved to the + or - positions, the system changes to operate in manual mode. Manual gear changes can be performed sequentially using either the selector lever or the steering wheel switches. Movement of the selector lever in a forward direction (+) changes the gearbox up the gear ratios and movement in a rearward (-) direction changes the gearbox down the ratios. Either of the + and - switches on the steering wheel perform the same function as the selector lever when in sport mode.

Gearbox operation is controlled by a Gearbox Interface Unit (GIU) and the ECM which communicate via a dedicated serial link and a hardwired connection. The MEMS3 ECM is programmed with an EM-CVT control strategy to operate the gearbox in conjunction with the GIU.

Steptronic EM-CVT unit

When in automatic mode, the EM-CVT provides an infinite number of ratios within its operating range. The stepless shifting pattern of the transmission provides a smooth transfer of power to the road wheels whilst allowing full vehicle performance to be available at all times.

In sport mode, the EM-CVT operates as in automatic mode but with a higher engine speed under all driving conditions which gives improved acceleration.

In manual mode, the EM-CVT provides electronic selection of six predetermined ratios. Selection is made by the driver using the selector lever or the steering wheel switches.

The EM-CVT unit comprises mechanical and electrical components which work together to provide the automatic and manual operation of the gearbox.

The following mechanical components comprise the EM-CVT unit (Refer to EM-CVT sectional view):

- Torsion damper
- Planetary gear set
- Clutches
- Pulleys and steel belt
- Pinion shaft
- Differential unit
- Hydraulic pump.

AUTOMATIC GEARBOX - 'EM-CVT'

STEPTRONIC EM-CVT CONTROL DIAGRAM

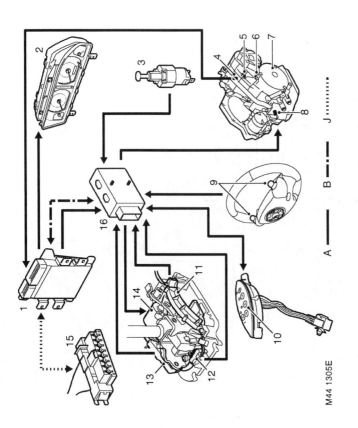

M44 1305E

A = Hardwired; B = Serial link; J = Diagnostic ISO9141 K Line

A ——— B —·—·—· J ··········

1. Engine Control Module (ECM)
2. Instrument pack
3. Brake switch
4. Road speed transducer
5. Gearbox differential speed sensor
6. Park/Neutral switch
7. EM-CVT Steptronic gearbox
8. Ratio control motor
9. Steering wheel switches
10. P R N D S LED module
11. P R N D switch
12. Manual/Sport switch
13. Sport +/- switch
14. Shift lock solenoid (if fitted)
15. Diagnostic socket
16. Gearbox Interface Unit (GIU)

Torsion damper

The transmission is driven from the engine via a torsion damper. The torsion damper is attached to the flywheel with six bolts and is constructed similar to a conventional clutch drive plate, but without the clutch lining. The torsion damper has a splined hub which engages with the gearbox input shaft. The hub is located on an inner plate which contains compression springs. Engine power is transmitted from the flywheel and damper attachment to the hub via the compression springs which absorb torsional vibrations from the engine and provide a smooth power delivery to the gearbox.

Planetary gear set

The planetary gear set enables the gearbox to provide a rotational output to the drive shafts in two directions to provide the vehicle with forward and reverse selections.

Engine torque is transmitted from the engine and the torsional damper to the input shaft which is attached to the planet carrier.

When forward is selected, the carrier is connected directly to the sunwheel by the drive clutch. The epicyclic gear set rotates as one unit and engine torque is passed directly to the primary pulley.

When reverse is selected, the annulus of the planetary gear set is held stationary by the reverse clutch. Three pairs of planet gears then drive the sunwheel in the opposite direction rotating the primary pulley in the reverse direction.

Clutches

Each of the two clutches comprise a multiplate wet clutch pack. Each pack has three friction plates providing six friction surfaces. Hydraulic pressure controls the clutches to allow the vehicle to move away smoothly regardless of the degree of throttle opening. Fluid from the fluid cooler is directed to the clutch plates to prevent overheating of the friction surfaces.

Pulleys and steel belt

The major drive components of the gearbox are a pair of vee shaped pulleys and a steel drive belt. Each pulley comprises one fix sheave and one moveable sheave. Both moveable sheaves are positioned diagonally opposite each other to prevent misalignment of the belt during shift changes. Each moveable sheave is operated by a hydraulic cylinder and piston, with hydraulic pressure controlled by the hydraulic control unit. The moveable sheaves are located on ball splines which prevents them rotating in relation to the fixed sheaves.

Rotation of the planetary gear set rotates the primary pulley. The V-belt transfers the primary pulley rotation to the secondary pulley whose torque and speed is controlled by the position of the V-belt on the two pulleys.

A 24 mm wide steel, push type V-belt is used to transfer engine torque between the two pulleys. The belt is cooled and lubricated by an fluid jet.

The belt comprises two steel bands each constructed from ten steel strips. The steel bands contain approximately 350 steel segments which abut each other to allow the belt to transmit torque by compression. The belt has several different thicknesses of steel segments which reduce the noise of the segments contacting the pulleys by changing the harmonic frequencies.

Pinion shaft

The pinion shaft, which is supported on two tapered bearings, provides location for two gears which provide a two step helical gear reduction between the secondary pulley and the differential crownwheel and provide the correct rotational direction of the drive shafts.

Differential

Drive from the final reduction gear is transferred to the differential crownwheel. The crownwheel is bolted to the differential case with eight bolts. Drive from the crownwheel is transferred via bevel gears to the drive shafts. The differential is supported on tapered bearings.

Hydraulic pump

The hydraulic pump is located on the opposite side of the gearbox to the planetary gear set. The pump is driven directly from the torsion damper via a shaft which is located through the centre of the input shaft. The shaft is splined to the planet carrier which always rotates at engine crankshaft speed.

The pump has a swept volume of 10.32 cc per revolution and can produce a pressure of up to 40 bar (580 lbf/in²) for the highest torque requirement. The pressurized fluid from the pump is used for gearbox lubrication and transmission control.

The following electrical components are used on the EM-CVT unit:

• Ratio control motor
• Gearbox differential speed sensor
• Park/Neutral switch.

Ratio Control Motor

The ratio control motor operates to match the gear ratio to the target engine speed. In any mode, the motor position is varied to provide the 'kickdown' function of a conventional automatic transmission. In manual mode, the position of the motor is varied to control the engine speed, fixing the current gear ratio. The motor operates the hydraulic control unit to adjust the primary pulley.

The ratio control motor is located inside the gearbox, on one side of the hydraulic control unit. The motor is connected to the main harness via a circular seven way connector with four connections used for the motor operation. The connector is screwed into the forward face of the gearbox and is secured with a nut.

The ratio control motor is a linear actuator which is controlled by the GIU in response to PWM signals at 500 Hz from the ECM. The motor itself is a bi-polar stepper motor which contains two bobbins which create magnetic fields to move the motor to the required position.

Gearbox Differential Speed Sensor

The gearbox differential speed sensor is located in the rear face of the gearbox adjacent to the road speed transducer. The sensor is connected to the main harness via a fly lead with a three pin connector.

The gearbox differential speed sensor is a Hall effect sensor which uses a an 81 tooth target wheel which is the teeth of the gearbox differential crown wheel. The sensor output is read directly by the ECM which calculates an accurate vehicle speed. The sensor output is unaffected by locking of the wheels due to the operation of the differential. The ECM vehicle speed calculation allows the EM-CVT system to calculate the current gear ratio.

Park/Neutral Switch

The park/neutral switch is screwed into the rear face of the gearbox below the LH drive shaft. The switch is connected to the main harness by a four pin connector.

The switch is operated by a cam which also operates the hydraulic control unit within the gearbox. The cam is controlled by the selector lever via a cable to the gearbox. The switch has two positions and performs several functions.

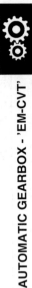

AUTOMATIC GEARBOX - 'EM-CVT'

When the transmission is in any position other than the Park (P) or Neutral (N) positions, the switch interrupts the starter relay coil earth path to the alarm ECU preventing starter motor operation. This signal is also used by the ECM to adjust the stepper motor of the IAC valve to adjust the engine idle speed when Reverse (R) or Drive (D) is selected.

When Reverse (R) is selected, the switch moves to its second position and activates the reverse lamps.

In selected markets, when the selector lever is in the 'P' position and the ignition is switched on, the park/neutral switch input causes the GIU to energise a shift lock solenoid on the selector lever. This locks the lever in the 'P' position.. The selector lever cannot be moved from the 'P' position until the ignition is switched on and the footbrake is applied. The shift lock solenoid is only active when the ignition is on.

Road speed transducer

The road speed transducer is located on the rear face of the gearbox, above the RH drive shaft, adjacent to the gearbox differential speed sensor. The transducer is used by the instrument pack for speedometer drive, the Electronic Power Assisted Steering (EPAS) system and the ECM.

See INSTRUMENTS, Information.
See STEERING, Information.

Gearbox Interface Unit (GIU)

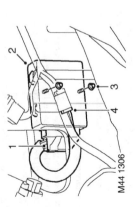

M44 1306

1. Harness connector
2. GIU
3. Mounting nut (2 off)
4. GIU fuse (10A)

The GIU is located in the in the LH side of the luggage compartment behind the trim. The GIU has two captive studs which are secured to the body with two nuts.

Permanent battery voltage is supplied to the GIU from fuse 2 in the engine compartment fusebox via a 10 Amp in-line fuse located on the harness near the GIU connector.

The GIU responds to control messages from the ECM to control the gearbox operation. The GIU also passes messages to the ECM in response to driver input commands enabling the ECM to operate the gearbox accordingly.

The ECM and GIU have a programmed default strategy which is engaged when specific faults are detected. Any condition requiring the default strategy will be relayed to the driver by illumination of the gearbox fault lamp in the instrument pack.

The ECM will need to learn the ratio control motor position when a new ECM is fitted. This is performed automatically by the ECM using a fast adaptation procedure. Refer to Operation section for details.

A 'limp-home mode' is provided if the system detects a fault but is still able to control the gearbox ratio. In addition to the fault lamp illumination, the driver will experience the engine speed being limited to approximately 3000 rev/min.

If the system is unable to control the gearbox ratio, the ECM will be unable to implement the default strategy, the gearbox will remain in a single ratio and the fault lamp will illuminate. If in the lowest gear, the engine speed will increase rapidly to 6000 rev/min and vehicle speed will be limited to a maximum of 30 mph (48.3 km/h). If in the highest gear, the driver will experience very slow acceleration and engine speeds of approximately 2000 to 2250 rev/min at 50 mph (80.5 km/h).

A single multiplug provides all input and outputs connection to and from the GIU. The following table shows the harness connector pin numbers and input/output information.

GIU connector C0932 pin details

Pin No.	Description	Input/Output
1	Shift lock solenoid drive (digital signal)	Output
2	Not used	-
3	12V Battery voltage from ECM relay module	Input
4	Earth	Input
5	Ratio control motor - Phase 1A (digital signal)	Input/Output
6	Ratio control motor - Phase 1B (digital signal)	Input/Output
7	Ratio control motor - Phase 2A (digital signal)	Input/Output
8	Ratio control motor - Phase 2B (digital signal)	Input/Output
9	Not used	-
10	Not used	-
11	Not used	-
12	Not used	-
13	Brake switch	Input
14	Park/Neutral switch	Input
15	Not used	-
16	Not used	-
17	GIU to ECM serial link	Output
18	ECM to GIU (Ratio control motor position)	Input
19	Not used	-
20	Not used	-
21	Not used	-
22	Shift lock solenoid drive (digital signal)	Output
23	Not used	-
24	12V battery voltage from ECM relay module	-

Continued......

Connector C0932 pin details (continued)

Pin No.	Description	Input/Output
25	Earth	Input
26	Park (P) LED (digital)	Output
27	Reverse (R) LED (digital)	Output
28	Neutral (N) LED (digital)	Output
29	Drive (D) LED	Output
30	Manual (M) LED (digital)	Output
31	Park/Neutral switch	Input
32	Reverse switch	Input
33	Neutral switch	Input
34	Drive switch	Input
35	Manual/sport switch	Input
36	Selector lever manual UP (+) switch	Input
37	Steering wheel manual UP (+) switch	Input
38	Selector lever manual DOWN (-) switch	Input
39	Steering wheel manual DOWN (-) switch	Input
40	Not used	-
41	Not used	-
42	Not used	-

 NOTE: Pins 1 and 22, 2 and 23 and. 4 and 25 are connected together inside the GIU.

Engine Control Module - EM-CVT control

All electronic control of the EM-CVT operates as part of the MEMS3 ECM control strategy. The ECM receives an input from the gearbox differential speed sensor and communicates with the GIU to control the gearbox. The ECM also provides driver information via the LCD display in the instrument pack for gear ratio selected and automatic/sport mode selection.

The following input/output signals are used by the ECM for EM-CVT control.

• Crankshaft position (CKP) sensor
• EM-CVT Road speed transducer
• Throttle position (TP) sensor
• Engine coolant temperature (ECT) sensor
• Manifold absolute pressure (MAP) sensor
• Instrument pack gear/mode display
• Park/Neutral switch
• EM-CVT Ratio control motor position
• GIU serial link.

Refer to Engine Management for full ECM pin-out details. **See *ENGINE MANAGEMENT SYSTEM - MEMS, Information*.**

Gear Selector Lever assembly

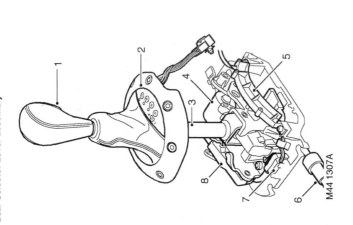

M44 1307A

1. Park/Reverse release button
2. LED module
3. Selector lever
4. Shift lock solenoid (if fitted)
5. PRND switch
6. Selector cable
7. Manual/Sport switch
8. Sport +/- switch

The gear selector lever assembly comprises a shift lock solenoid, LED module, manual/sport switch, sport +/- switch and PRND switch.

A die cast plate provides the attachment for the selector lever components. The plate is secured to a fabricated mounting with bolts, which in turn is secured to the floor pan with bolts and nuts. Rubber mounts between the mounting and the floor pan isolate vibrations from the selector lever.

The selector lever is attached to a gimbal mounting which allows gear selection in automatic and sport mode in a forward and backward direction and selection between automatic and sport in a left and right transverse direction.

Accidental selection of reverse (R) or park (P) is prevented by a locking mechanism on the lever. A button on the lever releases the mechanism allowing the lever to be moved to the 'P' or 'R' positions.

Shift Lock Solenoid (selected markets only)

When fitted, the shift lock solenoid is attached to a plate which is secured to the die cast plate with two screws in front of the selector lever. The solenoid is connected to the main harness by a two pin connector.

The solenoid is powered by the GIU. When the solenoid is energised, a pin is ejected which engages with a hole in the selector lever, locking it in the park position.

When the selector lever is in the 'P' position and the ignition is on, the solenoid will be energised until the footbrake is depressed. When the solenoid is de-energised the pin is retracted allowing the selector lever to be moved.

LED Module

The LED module is located in the selector lever gaiter surround and is secured with two screws. The module is connected to the main harness by an eight pin connector C0245.

The LED module illuminates the selector position display on the selector lever surround for the PRND and S positions. When the side lamps are switched on, all LED's are illuminated at a low intensity, with the selected LED illuminated at a higher intensity.

Manual/Sport Switch

The manual/sport switch is located on the die cast metal plate behind the selector lever and is secured to the plate with a metal strap. The switch is connected to the main harness by a four pin connector C0675 which is shared with the manual +/- switches. The manual/sport switch and the manual +/- switch can only be replaced as a pair.

The manual/sport switch is a cam operated microswitch. A lever with a roller is attached to the switch body. When the selector lever is moved from automatic to the manual/sport position, the roller contacts a cam plate which depresses the lever and operates the switch. The switch contacts remain closed when the selector lever is in the sport position.

The operation of the switch is sensed by the GIU which switches the gearbox operation to manual/sport when 'S' is selected and deselects manual/sport mode when 'D' (automatic operation) is selected.

Steptronic Manual (+/-) Switch

The manual +/- switch is located on the LH side of the selector lever and is secured to a bracket, which is secured to the die cast plate with two cap screws. The switch is connected to the main harness by a four pin connector C0675 which is shared with the manual/sport switch. The manual +/- switch and the manual/sport switch can only be replaced as a pair.

When the selector lever is moved to the manual/sport position, a dog engages with a slotted abutment on the switch. When the lever is moved to the + or - position the dog moves the switch completing a contact. This is sensed by the GIU which initiates the appropriate gear ratio selection.

PRND Switch

The PRND switch is located on the RH side of the selector lever and is secured to the die cast plate with two screws. The switch is connected to the main harness by a six pin connector.

The PRND switch has a sliding contact which moves with the selector lever. The switch has four contacts which correspond to the PRND positions. Each contact is connected to the GIU which then calculates the control strategy for the selection made.

Brake Switch GIU input (selected markets only)

The brake switch is located on the pedal box and is activated by operation of the brake pedal. The switch supplies an input to the GIU in addition to operating the brake lamps.

When the brake switch is operated, a 12V feed is sensed by the GIU. This is used by the GIU to de-energise the shift lock solenoid providing that the ignition is on.

Steering Wheel Switches

Two additional selector switches are located on the steering wheel. Each switch is a three position, spring biased to centre switch. The switches can be pushed in either direction (+/-) to change the gearbox ratio. The switches provide the same functionality as the selector lever +/- switches and are only operative when the selector lever is in the manual/sport position.

Each switch is connected to the GIU via the rotary coupler. When either switch is operated in the +/- position, an earth path from the GIU is completed. This is sensed by the GIU which initiates the appropriate gear ratio selection.

Instrument Pack

The instrument pack displays gearbox selection and illuminates a fault lamp if a gearbox fault is detected.

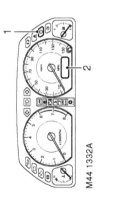

M44 1332A

1. Gearbox fault lamp
2. Liquid crystal display

The gearbox related displays in the instrument pack are controlled by the ECM which transmits PWM signals to operate the lamps and the LCD.

Liquid Crystal Display (LCD)

The LCD is located at the bottom the speedometer. In addition to displaying the odometer, trip meter, the LCD also displays the current gearbox status. The following table shows the characters displayed and their definition.

Character	Description
P	Park
R	Reverse
N	Neutral
D	Drive
D^{Sport}	Sport mode
1	Manual 1st ratio
2	Manual 2nd ratio
3	Manual 3rd ratio
4	Manual 4th ratio
5	Manual 5th ratio
6	Manual 6th ratio
F	Fast adaptation

When the ECM is replaced, the ECM EEPROM re-initialised by TestBook or the gearbox replaced, the LCD alternately flashes 'F' and the selected mode until the fast adaptation cycle is complete.

Gearbox fault lamp

The gearbox fault lamp is located in the instrument pack and is illuminated by the ECM when a gearbox fault is detected.

If a gearbox fault is detected by the ECM, in addition to the gearbox fault lamp being illuminated, the LCD transmission display is extinguished.

Fluid Cooler

The fluid cooler is located at the front of the vehicle behind the bumper, in front of the engine cooling radiator. The fluid cooler comprises eight horizontal cores which allow fluid to flow across from one side of the cooler to the other. Each core is joined by thin fins which aid heat dissipation.

Two fluid lines from the gearbox, comprising alloy pipes and flexible hoses, provide the feed and return to and from the fluid cooler.

Diagnostics

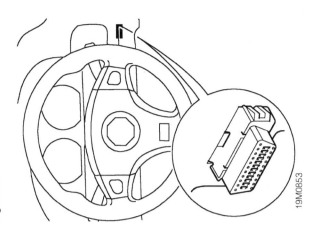

19M0853

A diagnostic socket allows the exchange of information between the ECM and TestBook. The diagnostic socket is located in the passenger compartment fusebox which is below the fascia on the driver's side.

AUTOMATIC GEARBOX - 'EM-CVT'

The diagnostic socket is connected to the ECM on an ISO9141 K Line. The system uses a 'P' code diagnostic strategy and can record faults relating to the gearbox differential speed sensor and the ratio control motor.

The GIU and ECM monitor all inputs and outputs relating to the EM-CVT system. If a fault is detected, a code applicable to that fault is stored in a fault log in the GIU. When TestBook is connected GIU codes are accessed via the ECM diagnostic strategy.

The MEMS3 ECM is a major component in gearbox control. Functionality of engine sensors should be established to eliminate any ECM related faults from the gearbox diagnostics.

OPERATION

General

The transmission is driven from the engine via a torsion damper bolted to the flywheel. The torsion damper drives the input shaft which in turn drives the planet carrier. Depending on whether forward or reverse is selected, the primary pulley will rotate, transferring torque to the secondary pulley causing the vehicle to move in the required direction.

The steel belt is fitted between the primary and secondary pulleys. Each pulley consists of one fixed sheave and one axially moveable sheave. The moveable pulley sheaves are located diagonally opposite to each other to prevent misalignment of the belt during shift changes.

Each moving pulley sheave is connected to a hydraulic cylinder which is controlled by hydraulic pressure generated by the integral pump running at engine speed. Moving the pulley sheaves together increases their effective diameter and moving them apart decreases the diameter due to the conical faces of each pulley. In this way the gear ratios of the EM-CVT unit are achieved.

The EM-CVT unit has two multiplate wet clutch packs; one for forward and one for reverse. Each pack comprises three friction plates. The clutches are hydraulically controlled which enables the vehicle to move smoothly from standstill irrespective of the throttle position. The clutches are fed hydraulic fluid from the fluid cooler to prevent them overheating.

When the selector lever is in the Park (P) position, a spring and cone operated pawl mechanically locks the secondary pulley, consequentially locking the rear wheels. If 'P' is selected when the vehicle is moving, the pawl will not engage until the vehicle speed falls to below 4 mph (7 km/h). A rattling sound may be heard if 'P' is selected when the vehicle is moving.

Driving - Automatic mode

To pull away from a standstill a low ratio is required. The primary pulley is held fully open, reducing its diameter and allowing the belt to seat at the bottom of the pulley. The secondary pulley is held closed, forcing the belt to run in its increased diameter.

As the vehicle speed increases, higher ratios are required. As engine speed increases the fluid pressure generated by the pump increases. This increase in pressure is felt by the primary pulley cylinder which moves to gradually move the pulley sheaves together increasing its effective diameter.

Simultaneously, the secondary pulley sheaves move apart, reducing its diameter and increasing the gearbox ratio. When the primary pulley is closed and the secondary pulley is fully open, the gearbox operates in an overdrive ratio, with the secondary pulley rotating at approximately two and a half times the speed of the primary pulley.

When kickdown is required, the ECM transmits a message to the GIU to control the ratio control motor accordingly. The GIU adjusts the ratio control motor which, in turn, moves the hydraulic control valve to lower the gearbox ratio to achieve the required acceleration.

Driving - Manual/Sport mode

In manual/sport mode the gearbox functions as a conventional CVT unit or a semi-automatic manual transmission. In sport mode, the engine speed is higher under all driving conditions which gives improved acceleration.

By moving the selector lever to the + or - position, or pressing a steering wheel switch, the system is commanded to operate in manual mode. If required, the driver can make sequential gear selections using either the selector lever or the steering wheel mounted switches.

The ratio control motor operates to match the gear ratio to the target engine speed. In any mode, the motor position is varied to provide the 'kickdown' function of a conventional automatic transmission.

In manual mode, the position of the ratio control motor is varied to control engine speed, fixing the current gear ratio. The action of the motor operates the hydraulic control unit to adjust the primary pulley.

The GIU checks if a requested gear change made by the driver is permitted. Gear changes will be ignored if the driver requests a change which is dangerous or could damage the transmission.

If a shift up is required and the driver has not made the required selection using the selector lever or the steering wheel switches, the next higher gear will be selected when the engine speed reaches maximum rev/min.

If the driver does not make a required shift down when the vehicle is slowing, the next lower gear will be selected automatically. The LCD in the instrument pack will always display the current gear.

Manual/sport mode is deselected by moving the selector lever back to the 'D' (automatic) position.

Fast Adaptation Procedure

When a new gearbox is fitted, the ECM replaced or ECM EEPROM re-initialised by TestBook, the ECM needs to learn the positions of the ratio control motor for given engine speeds. The ECM will target twelve engine speeds between 1400 and 4500 rev/min in order to achieve fast adaptation.

Fast adaptation is performed as follows:

 WARNING: Ensure that all road tests are conducted by suitably qualified drivers in a safe and legal manner, and where local traffic conditions allow.

- With the selector lever in position 'D', accelerate the vehicle up to 35 mph (55 km/h), then release the accelerator pedal and allow the vehicle to decelerate without braking.

- As the vehicle decelerates, the ECM will learn the ratio control motor adaptation points. This procedure should be complete before the vehicle stops moving.

- If the gearbox reaches its lowest ratio before the adaptation is complete, the engine speed will drop from the target speed to idle.

- To complete the procedure, accelerate up to a speed of more than 25 mph (40 km/h) and release the accelerator pedal again. Allow the vehicle to decelerate without braking to enable the ECM software to learn the remaining adaptation points.

- Fast adaptation is complete when the 'F' in the instrument pack LCD stops flashing and only the mode is displayed.

The ECM software continuously adapts to account for gearbox wear and fast adaptation errors. The driver will not be aware that any adaptation is taking place and normal driving will be maintained.

FAULT DIAGNOSIS

Before commencing any gearbox fault diagnosis check that:

- The engine is correctly tuned
- The gearbox fluid and fluid level is correct
- The selector cable is correctly adjusted
- All gearbox and GIU connectors are correctly assembled.

The following tables list possible faults and corrective action required. If the fault remains after the corrective action has been applied, then the gearbox must be replaced.

The tables show tests which can be carried out to determine the fault. The tests are detailed at the end of this section.

Fault: Engine will not start in 'P' or 'N'

Fault	Action	Test
Selector cable out of adjustment	Adjust selector cable *See Adjustments.*	
Park/Neutral switch fault	Check switch	Test 2
Park/Neutral switch open circuit	Check harness continuity	

Fault: Park lock does not hold vehicle

Fault	Action	Test
Selector cable out of adjustment	Adjust selector cable *See Adjustments.*	
Gearbox internal damage	Replace gearbox *See Repairs.*	

Fault: Vehicle moves when 'N' is selected

Fault	Action	Test
Selector cable out of adjustment	Adjust selector cable *See Adjustments.*	
Forward or reverse clutch dragging	Check condition of fluid	Test 1

Fault: Engine can be started in 'D' or 'R' positions

Fault	Action	Test
Selector cable out of adjustment	Adjust selector cable *See Adjustments.*	
Park/Neutral switch fault	Check switch	Test 2

Fault: Engine can be started in all selector positions

Fault	Action	Test
Park/Neutral switch fault	Check switch	Test 2
Park/Neutral switch open circuit	Check harness continuity	

Fault: No drive when 'D' or 'R' is selected

Fault	Action	Test
Gearbox fluid level incorrect	Check and top up gearbox with correct fluid *See MAINTENANCE.*	
Selector cable out of adjustment	Adjust selector cable *See Adjustments.*	
Gearbox internal damage	Replace gearbox *See Repairs.*	

Fault: Vehicle moves above 6 mph (10 km/h) when 'D' or 'R' selected

Fault	Action	Test
Engine idle speed too high	Check and correct engine idle speed *See INFORMATION, Engine tuning data.*	

Fault: Vehicle judders when 'D' or 'R' is selected with engine at idle

Fault	Action	Test
Gearbox fluid level incorrect	Check and top up gearbox with correct fluid *See MAINTENANCE.*	
Engine idle speed too high	Check and correct engine idle speed *See INFORMATION, Engine tuning data.*	
Gearbox internal damage	Check condition of fluid	Test 1

Fault: Acceleration poor but engine racing when cold only

Fault	Action	Test
Gearbox fluid level incorrect	Check and top up gearbox with correct fluid *See MAINTENANCE.*	
Gearbox internal damage	Check condition of fluid	Test 1

AUTOMATIC GEARBOX - 'EM-CVT'

Fault: Delayed response when Manual mode is selected from 'D' Sport with vehicle moving

NOTE: Verify this fault by performing Test 5.

Fault	Action	Test
Electrical circuit failure	Check circuit continuity	

Fault: Vehicle moves forward or backward when starting in 'P' or 'N'

Fault	Action	Test
Selector cable out of adjustment	Adjust selector cable *See Adjustments.*	

Fault: Hydraulic cavitation noises from gearbox

Fault	Action	Test
Gearbox fluid level incorrect	Check and top up gearbox with correct fluid *See MAINTENANCE.*	
Fluid filter clogged or dirty	Replace Fluid filter *See Repairs.*	
Air ingress via fluid filter connection	Replace 'O' ring *See Repairs.*	
Gearbox internal damage	Check condition of fluid	Test 1

AUTOMATIC GEARBOX - 'EM-CVT'

Fault: Acceleration poor but engine racing when hot

Fault	Action	Test
Gearbox fluid level incorrect	Check and top up gearbox with correct fluid *See MAINTENANCE.*	
Selector cable out of adjustment	Adjust selector cable *See Adjustments.*	
Gearbox internal damage	Check condition of fluid	Test 1

Fault: Engine stalls during braking

Fault	Action	Test
Engine idle speed too low	Check and correct engine idle speed *See INFORMATION, Engine tuning data.*	

Fault: Kick down delayed or insufficient

NOTE: Verify this fault by performing Test 3.

Fault	Action	Test
Gearbox Interface Unit (GIU) electrical failure	Check harness connections and GIU remote fuse. Check for fault codes using TestBook.	
Ratio control motor failure	Measure resistance at gearbox connector pins. Measure between pins which correspond to the harness connector blue/yellow and blue/grey wires and the blue/red and blue/white wires. The resistance must be between 18 and 30 Ω .	

Fault: Delayed response when Sport selected from 'D' while vehicle moving

NOTE: Verify this fault by performing Test 4.

Fault	Action	Test
Electrical circuit failure	Check circuit continuity	

AUTOMATIC GEARBOX - 'EM-CVT'

Fault: Fluid leaks from gearbox

Fault	Action
Leak from fluid dipstick tube	Replace dipstick 'O' ring
Leak from gearbox fluid pan gasket	Ensure fluid pan bolts are correctly tightened Replace fluid pan gasket
Leak from Park/Neutral switch	Ensure switch is correctly tightened Replace switch 'O' ring
Leak from gearbox drain plug	Ensure plug is correctly tightened Replace drain plug sealing ring
Leak from speed transducer	Ensure transducer is correctly tightened Replace transducer 'O' ring
Leak from gearbox differential speed sensor	Ensure sensor is correctly tightened Replace sensor 'O' ring
Leak from primary cover	Ensure that cover is correctly tightened Replace 'O' ring
Leak from secondary cover	Ensure that cover is correctly tightened Replace cover 'O' rings
Leak from selector shaft lever	Replace selector shaft lever seal
Leak from fluid cooler pipe connections	Ensure that pipes are correctly tightened Replace pipe to gearbox connection 'O' rings
Leak from input shaft	Replace input shaft seal
Leak from differential oil seal(s)	Replace oil seals
Leak from fluid cooler pipe connections	Ensure that pipes are correctly tightened Replace pipe to fluid cooler connection 'O' rings

---

TESTS

TEST 1: Fluid condition check

1. Drain and examine gearbox fluid. *See Adjustments.*
2. If fluid contains metallic particles, replace gearbox and flush fluid cooler and pipes.
3. If fluid is discoloured, burnt or contains water:

   - Fill gearbox with correct fluid to the correct level.
   - Test drive vehicle for at least 10 miles (16 km) using all selector positions.
   - If fault is still present, replace gearbox.

4. If drained fluid is in good condition, re-check selector cable adjustment.
5. If adjustments are correct and the fault is still present, replace the gearbox. *See Repairs.*

TEST 2: Park/Neutral switch check

M44 1360

1. With engine stopped, disconnect multiplug from park/neutral switch.
2. Connect a circuit continuity tester between switch pins 4 and 2.
3. Move gear selector lever through all positions and observe continuity tester. Circuit continuity should only exist with selector in positions 'P' and 'N'.
4. Disconnect continuity tester and reconnect between switch pins 3 and 1.
5. Move gear selector lever through all positions and observe continuity tester. Circuit continuity should only exist with selector in position 'R'.
6. If park/neutral switch does not function as described in steps 3 and 5, replace switch. *See Repairs.*

TEST 3: Kick-down check

A stop watch and the vehicle tachometer is required for this test.

1. With the gear selector lever in position 'D', accelerate the vehicle up to 50 mph (80 km/h).
2. When 50 mph (80 km/h) is reached, release the accelerator pedal and, without using the brakes, allow the vehicle to decelerate to 38 mph (61 km/h).
3. When the vehicle has reached 38 mph (61 km/h) apply full throttle to initiate kick-down.
4. If engine speed is between 3800 and 4200 rev/min within 1 to 2 seconds of reaching 38 mph (61 km/h), kick-down operation is satisfactory.

TEST 4: Delayed shift response

A stop watch and the vehicle tachometer is required for this test.

1. With gear selector lever in position 'D', apply full throttle until 50 mph (80 km/h) is reached.
2. At 50 mph (80 km/h) move the selector lever across the gate to the Sport position; the instrument pack LCD should display 'D Sport'.
3. When selector lever is moved to the Sport position, the engine speed should increase to 5500 rev/min within 1 to 2 seconds. If this response is achieved gearbox shift operation is satisfactory.

TEST 5: Manual mode response

A stop watch and the vehicle tachometer is required for this test.

1. With the selector lever in position 'D Sport', drive the vehicle at a steady 50 mph (80 km/h).
2. Release the throttle pedal and move the selector lever to the minus (-) position (manual mode). The instrument pack should display the gear ratio number and the engine speed should rise within 1 to 2 seconds. If this response is achieved, manual mode operation is satisfactory.

AUTOMATIC GEARBOX - 'EM-CVT'

DRAIN AND REFILL

Service repair no - 44.24.02

 NOTE: The fluid should be drained with the gearbox at normal operating temperature.

 WARNING: Observe due care when draining gearbox fluid, as the fluid will be very hot.

1. Remove dipstick.
2. Raise rear of vehicle.

 WARNING: Support on safety stands.

3. Position container to collect fluid from gearbox.

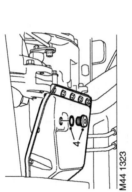

M44 1323

4. Remove drain plug using an 5 mm Allen key and discard sealing washer.
5. Allow fluid to drain into container.

NOTE: Approximately 1 litre of fluid is retained in the primary and secondary cylinders of the gearbox.

Refill

1. Clean drain plug and sealing face of gearbox.
2. Fit new sealing washer to drain plug, fit drain plug and tighten to 30 Nm.
3. Remove stand(s) and lower vehicle.
4. Remove dipstick and, using a funnel on the end of the dipstick tube, carefully fill gearbox to the minimum mark with new CVT fluid. *See INFORMATION, Capacities, fluids and lubricants.*
5. Replace dipstick.
6. Start engine and run until normal operating temperature is achieved.
7. Operate gearbox through full range of selector positions 3 times to ensure fluid is in all parts of the system.
8. With the vehicle on horizontal ground, the selector lever in the 'N' position and the engine running at idle speed, check the oil level and add oil until the level lies between the minimum and maximum marks on the dipstick.

This page is intentionally left blank

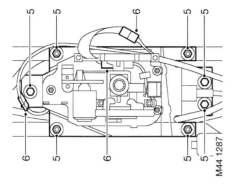

M44 1287

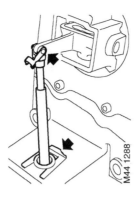

M44 1288

LEVER - GEAR CHANGE

Service repair no - 44.15.04

Remove

1. Disconnect battery earth lead.
2. Make the SRS system safe. *See* **RESTRAINT SYSTEMS, Precautions.**
3. Remove centre console. *See* **BODY, Interior trim components.**

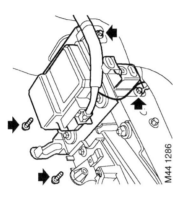

M44 1286

4. Remove 4 Torx bolts securing SRS DCU support bracket and release earth lead. Position support bracket aside.

5. Remove 3 bolts and 4 nuts securing gear lever assembly.
6. Disconnect 3 multiplugs from gear lever assembly.
7. Release gear lever from floor tunnel to access gear change cable.

8. Remove clevis pin and 'C' washer securing cable to gear lever and remove gear lever assembly.

This page is intentionally left blank

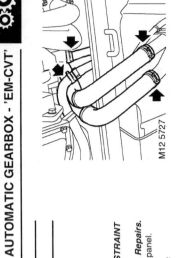

M12 5727

8. Release clips securing coolant hoses and heater hoses and disconnect hoses.
9. Tie coolant and heater hoses aside to access closing plate.
10. Place support jack underneath engine sump and support engine weight.

⚠ **CAUTION: To prevent damage to sump place a piece of wood between jack and sump.**

CABLE - GEAR CHANGE

Service repair no - 44.15.08

Remove

1. Position vehicle on a 2 post ramp.
2. Make the SRS system safe. **See RESTRAINT SYSTEMS, Precautions.**
3. Remove engine cover. **See ENGINE, Repairs.**
4. Remove engine compartment access panel. **See BODY, Exterior fittings.**
5. Drain engine coolant. **See COOLING SYSTEM, Adjustments.**

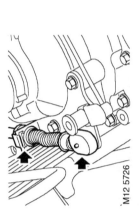

M12 5726

6. Disconnect cable from ball joint on gear change quadrant and release cable from support bracket on gearbox.
7. Remove gear change lever. **See this section.**

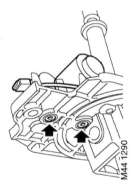

M44 1290

14. Remove 2 bolts securing park solenoid to gear lever.
15. Release park solenoid from gear lever and remove park solenoid.

Refit

1. Fit sequential gear change microswitch. Fit bolts and tighten to 12 Nm.
2. Fit microswitch spacer, position microswitch and secure with clip.
3. Secure microswitch harness clip.
4. Position park solenoid, fit bolts and tighten to 15 Nm.
5. Position selector slide and secure with screws.
6. Position lever to support bracket. Fit bolts and tighten to 10 Nm.
7. Position lever assembly to cable and secure with 'C' washer and clevis pin.
8. Position lever assembly to tunnel and connect gear lever multiplugs.
9. Fit nuts and bolts securing lever assembly to floor and tighten to 10 Nm.
10. Position SRS DCU and align earth lead. Fit Torx bolts and tighten to 10 Nm.
11. Fit centre console. **See BODY, Interior trim components.**
12. Connect battery earth lead.

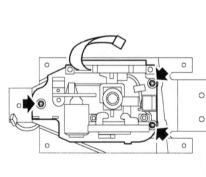

M44 1289

9. Remove 3 nuts and bolts securing gear lever to support bracket and remove lever.

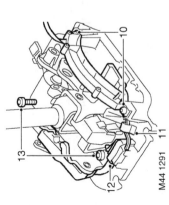

M44 1291

10. Remove 2 screws securing selector slide mechanism and remove selector slide.
11. Remove microswitch harness clip from gear lever housing.
12. Remove clip securing microswitch and collect microswitch spacer.
13. Remove 2 bolts securing sequential gear change microswitch and remove microswitch assembly.

AUTOMATIC GEARBOX - 'EM-CVT'

LED MODULE - GEAR SELECTION

Service repair no - 44.15.10

Remove

1. Remove gearchange selector knob.
2. Release gaiter from centre console.

M44 1310

3. Disconnect LED module multiplug and remove gaiter.
4. Remove 2 screws securing LED module and remove module.

Refit

1. Position LED module to gaiter and secure with screws.
2. Position gaiter to centre console, connect multiplug and secure gaiter to centre console.
3. Fit gear selection knob.

Refit

1. Position gear change cable to tunnel and feed through rear bulkhead.
2. Feed gear change cable into position in engine compartment.
3. Lubricate all cables with soft soap to ease grommet movement on cables.
4. Position gear change cable into closing plate slots and secure with grommets.
5. Align closing plate to bulkhead and secure with bolts.
6. Raise subframe on jack, fit subframe front mounting bolts and tighten to 30 Nm.
7. Connect coolant and heater hoses and secure with clips.
8. Fit gear change lever. *See this section.*
9. Connect cable to support bracket on gear box and gear change quadrant.
10. Check cable adjustment. *See Adjustments.*
11. Refill engine coolant. *See COOLING SYSTEM, Adjustments.*
12. Fit engine compartment access panel. *See BODY, Exterior fittings.*
13. Fit engine cover. *See ENGINE, Repairs.*
14. Connect battery earth lead.

AUTOMATIC GEARBOX - 'EM-CVT'

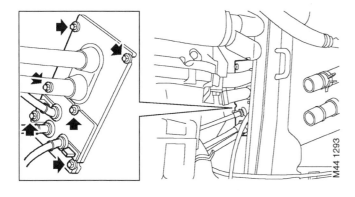

M44 1292

11. Remove 2 bolts securing both front subframe mountings to body brackets.
12. Lower jack carefully, to allow access to closing plate bolts.

⚠ **CAUTION: Care must be taken when lowering front of subframe, that no cables or pipes are stretched.**

M44 1293

13. Release 2 lower and remove 4 remaining bolts securing closing plate to bulkhead.
14. Apply soft soap to all closing plate cables, to ease movement of closing plate.
15. Release closing plate from bulkhead and slide along cables, release gear change cable from grommet.
16. Remove gear change cable from tunnel and engine compartment.

SWITCH - PRND

Service repair no - 44.15.13

Remove

1. Remove centre console. *See BODY, Interior trim components.*

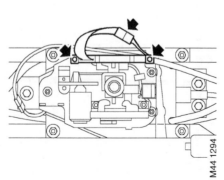

M44 1294

2. Disconnect PRND switch multiplug.
3. Remove 2 screws securing PRND switch and remove switch.

Refit

1. Position PRND switch, engage pin to gear lever and secure switch with screws.
2. Connect PRND switch multiplug.
3. Fit centre console. *See BODY, Interior trim components.*

PARK/NEUTRAL AND REVERSE LIGHT SWITCH

Service repair no - 44.15.15

Remove

1. Disconnect battery earth lead.
2. Raise rear of vehicle.

⚠ **WARNING: Support on safety stands.**

3. Position container to collect fluid loss from gearbox.

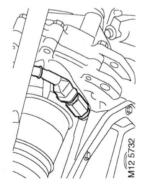

M12 5732

4. Disconnect multiplug from switch.
5. Loosen and remove switch from gearbox.
6. Remove and discard 'O' ring from switch.

Refit

1. Clean switch and mating face of gearbox.
2. Lubricate new 'O' ring with gearbox fluid and fit to switch.
3. Fit switch to gearbox and tighten to 12 Nm.
4. Connect multiplug to switch.
5. Remove stand(s) and lower vehicle.
6. Top-up gearbox fluid level. *See MAINTENANCE.*
7. Connect battery earth lead.

DIFFERENTIAL SPEED SENSOR

Service repair no - 44.15.47

Remove

1. Disconnect battery earth lead.
2. Raise rear of vehicle.

⚠ **WARNING: Support on safety stands.**

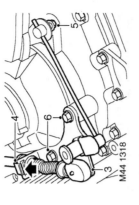

M44 1318

3. Release gear selector cable from selector linkage.
4. Release selector cable from abutment bracket by pressing tab upwards as shown.
5. Loosen nut securing connecting rod to selector bracket.
6. Remove 2 bolts securing abutment bracket to gearbox, release connecting rod from selector bracket and remove abutment bracket.

SOLENOID - SHIFT LOCK

Service repair no - 44.15.36

Remove

1. Remove gear lever assembly. *See this section.*

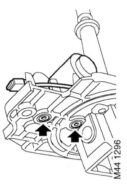

M44 1296

2. Remove 2 Allen bolts securing shift lock solenoid.
3. Release shift lock solenoid from gear lever housing and remove solenoid.

Refit

1. Position shift lock solenoid and engage to gear lever housing.
2. Fit Allen bolts securing shift lock solenoid and tighten to 15 Nm.
3. Fit gear lever assembly. *See this section.*

SWITCH - STEERING WHEEL REMOTE

Service repair no - 44.15.70

Remove

1. Disconnect battery earth lead.

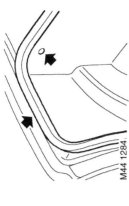

M44 1309

2. Release horn switch from steering wheel and position aside.
3. Release clip securing remote switch and release switch from steering wheel.
4. Disconnect remote switch multiplug and remove switch from steering wheel.

Refit

1. Position remote switch, connect multiplug and secure switch to steering wheel.
2. Position horn switch and secure in steering wheel.
3. Connect battery earth lead.

MICROSWITCH - MANUAL/SPORT AND +/- SWITCH

Service repair no - 44.15.72

Remove

1. Remove gear lever assembly. *See this section.*

M44 1295

2. Release clip securing harness to gear lever housing.
3. Remove clip securing manual/sport microswitch and collect microswitch spacer.
4. Remove 2 Allen bolts securing +/- switch to gear lever housing and remove switch assembly.

Refit

1. Position +/- switch to gear lever housing. Fit Allen bolts and tighten to 12 Nm.
2. Fit microswitch spacer, position manual/sport microswitch and secure with clip.
3. Secure harness clip to gear lever housing.
4. Fit gear lever assembly. *See this section.*

GEARBOX INTERFACE UNIT (GIU)

Service repair no - 44.15.81

Remove

1. Disconnect battery earth lead.

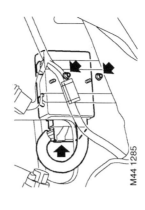

M44 1284

2. Release boot lid aperture seal from LH side of aperture flange.
3. Remove clip securing LH side of luggage compartment trim and release trim for access to GIU.

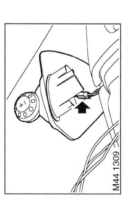

M44 1285

4. Remove 2 nuts securing GIU to body.
5. Release GIU, disconnect multiplug and remove GIU.

AUTOMATIC GEARBOX - 'EM-CVT'

M44 1319

7. Disconnect multiplug from speed sensor.
8. Remove bolt securing sensor to gearbox.
9. Remove sensor and discard 'O' ring.

Refit

1. Clean sealing faces of sensor and gearbox.
2. Lubricate new 'O' ring with gearbox fluid and fit to sensor.
3. Fit sensor to gearbox and tighten bolt to 9 Nm.
4. Connect multiplug to harness.
5. Fit abutment bracket to gearbox ensuring connecting rod is located into selector bracket. Tighten bolts to 25 Nm.
6. Tighten nut securing connecting rod to selector bracket to 6 Nm.

⚠ **CAUTION: Do not exceed the specified torque.**

7. Connect gear selector cable to selector linkage.
8. Remove stand(s) and lower vehicle.
9. Connect battery earth lead.

Refit

1. Position new GIU and connect multiplug.
2. Fit GIU to body and secure with nuts.
3. Refit trim and secure with clip.
4. Fit boot lid aperture seal to flange.
5. Connect battery earth lead.

STEPTRONIC (EM-CVT) GEARBOX

Service repair no - 44.20.02/99

Remove

1. Remove engine and gearbox assembly. *See **ENGINE, Repairs.***

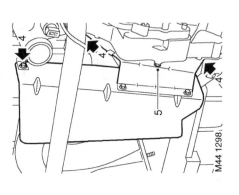

M44 1297

2. Release Lucar from starter solenoid.
3. Disconnect multiplug from actuator control motor and release lead from clip.

M44 1298

4. Remove 3 bolts securing exhaust heat shield and remove shield.
5. Remove bolt securing flywheel cover to gearbox and remove cover.

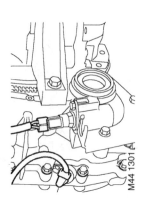

M44 1299

6. Remove 2 bolts securing starter motor to gearbox and remove starter motor.

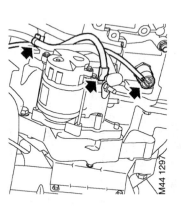

M44 1300

7. Remove 2 bolts securing rear flywheel cover to gearbox and remove cover.

M44 1301

8. Disconnect multiplugs from speed sensor and speedometer transducer.

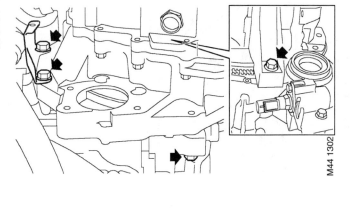

M44 1302

9. Remove 4 bolts securing gearbox to engine, and collect mounting plate.
10. With assistance remove gearbox from engine.

AUTOMATIC GEARBOX - 'EM-CVT'

Refit

1. Clean mating faces of engine and gearbox.
2. With assistance, fit gearbox and locate onto dowels.
3. Position mounting plate and fit 4 bolts securing gearbox to engine. Tighten bolts to 80 Nm.
4. Connect speed sensor and speedometer transducer multiplugs.
5. Fit flywheel rear cover and secure with bolts.
6. Fit starter motor and tighten bolts to 80 Nm.
7. Fit flywheel cover to gearbox and secure with bolt.
8. Fit exhaust heat shield and secure with bolts.
9. Connect multiplug to actuator control motor and secure lead to clip.
10. Connect Lucar to starter solenoid.
11. Fit engine and gearbox assembly. See **ENGINE, Repairs.**

SEAL - INPUT SHAFT

Service repair no - 44.20.17

Remove

1. Remove gearbox assembly. **See this section.**

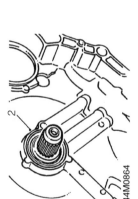

44M0864

2. Remove and discard input shaft seal using suitable lever.

Refit

1. Clean seal housing and input shaft.
2. Lubricate new seal with gearbox fluid and fit onto input shaft.

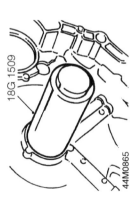

18G 1509

44M0865

3. Push seal into place using tool 18G 1509 .
4. Refit gearbox assembly. **See this section.**

AUTOMATIC GEARBOX - 'EM-CVT'

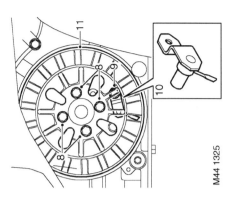

SEAL - PRIMARY COVER

Service repair no - 44.20.29

Remove

1. Raise rear of vehicle.

⚠ **WARNING: Support on safety stands.**

2. Remove air cleaner. **See ENGINE MANAGEMENT SYSTEM - MEMS, Repairs.**
3. Remove LH rear road wheel.
4. Clean area around primary cover.
5. Position container to collect fluid loss.

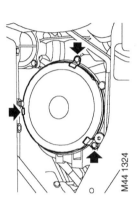

M44 1324

6. Remove 3 bolts and brackets securing primary cover to gearbox.
7. Remove primary cover from gearbox.

M44 1325

8. Remove and discard 4 bolts securing engine pitot chamber to fluid pump drive.
9. Rotate pitot chamber sufficient to remove lower RH fluid pump bolt which secures the engine pitot tube.
10. Rotate pitot tube 180°anti-clockwise and remove pitot chamber. Collect pitot tube.
11. Remove and discard primary cover 'O' ring from gearbox housing.

Refit

1. Clean primary cover and mating face of gearbox housing.
2. Lubricate new primary cover 'O' ring and fit to gearbox housing.
3. Position pitot tube in fluid pump. Fit pitot chamber ensuring pitot tube is located in fluid pick-up channel in pitot chamber.
4. Rotate pitot chamber sufficient to align pitot tube. Fit pitot tube bolt and tighten to 10 Nm.

AUTOMATIC GEARBOX - 'EM-CVT'

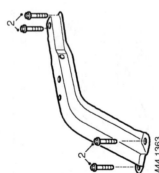

M44 1362

5. Remove and discard 2 'O' rings from cover.
6. Remove and discard split ring.

Refit

1. Clean secondary cover and mating faces of cover and gearbox.
2. Lubricate new 'O' rings with clean gearbox fluid and fit to secondary cover.
3. Fit new split ring to secondary cover.
4. Fit and align secondary cover to gearbox.
5. Fit bolts securing secondary cover to gearbox and tighten to 10 Nm.
6. Align LH buttress to subframe, fit bolts and tighten to 45 Nm.
7. Fit LH engine mounting. *See ENGINE, Repairs.*

GASKET - FLUID PAN

Service repair no - 44.24.05

Remove

1. Raise rear of vehicle.

⚠ **WARNING: Support on safety stands.**

2. Drain gearbox fluid. *See Adjustments.*

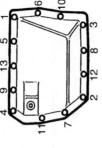

44M0880

3. Working in the sequence illustrated, loosen then remove 13 bolts securing fluid pan to gearbox.
4. Release fluid pan from gearbox and filter, remove fluid pan.
5. Remove and discard gasket.

AUTOMATIC GEARBOX - 'EM-CVT'

SECONDARY COVER SEALS

Service repair no - 44.20.33

Remove

1. Remove LH engine mounting *See ENGINE, Repairs.*

M44 1363

2. Remove 4 bolts securing LH buttress and manoeuvre buttress to access secondary cover.

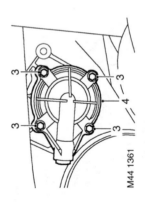

M44 1361

3. Remove 4 bolts securing secondary cover to gearbox.
4. Remove secondary cover.

5. Align pitot chamber to fluid pump drive, fit new bolts and tighten to 10 Nm.
6. Fit primary cover to gearbox.
7. Fit primary cover bolts and brackets and tighten to 10 Nm.
8. Fit road wheel(s) and tighten nuts to correct torque. *See INFORMATION, General data.*
9. Fit air cleaner. *See ENGINE MANAGEMENT SYSTEM - MEMS, Repairs.*
10. Remove stand(s) and lower vehicle.
11. Top-up gearbox fluid level. *See MAINTENANCE.*

AUTOMATIC GEARBOX - 'EM-CVT'

Refit

1. Clean mating faces of fluid pan and gearbox. Clean fluid pan.
2. Lubricate new gasket with gearbox fluid and fit to fluid pan.

⚠ **CAUTION: Do not apply adhesive to gasket.**

3. Position fluid pan to filter and gearbox.

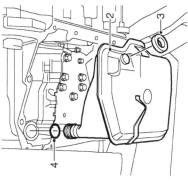

44M0881

4. Fit bolts securing fluid pan to gearbox and working in the sequence illustrated, tighten to 10 Nm.
5. Refill gearbox with fluid. **See Adjustments.**
6. Remove stand(s) and lower vehicle.

FILTER - GEARBOX FLUID

Service repair no - 44.24.07

Remove

1. Remove fluid pan. **See this section.**

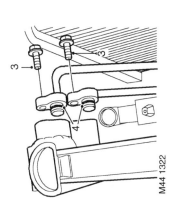

M44 1334

2. Release filter from valve block and remove filter.
3. Remove filter magnet.
4. Remove and discard 'O' ring.

Refit

1. Clean magnet and fit to filter.
2. Lubricate new 'O' ring with clean gearbox fluid and fit to filter.
3. Position filter to valve block and engage 'O' ring in valve block.
4. Fit fluid pan. **See this section.**

COOLER - GEARBOX FLUID

Service repair no - 44.24.10

Remove

1. Remove bonnet locking platform. **See BODY, Exterior fittings.**
2. Position container underneath gearbox fluid cooler connections to collect any spillage.

M44 1322

3. Remove 2 bolts securing cooler pipe connections to fluid cooler.
4. Release connections from cooler and discard 'O' rings.

⚠ **CAUTION: Plug the connections.**

M44 1321

5. Remove 2 bolts securing cooler to body and remove cooler.

Refit

1. Clean fluid cooler and pipe connections.
2. Fit fluid cooler and secure with bolts.
3. Using new 'O' rings connect pipes to cooler and tighten bolts to 14 Nm.
4. Fit bonnet locking platform. **See BODY, Exterior fittings.**
5. Top-up gearbox fluid level. **See MAINTENANCE.**

AUTOMATIC GEARBOX - 'EM-CVT'

HOSE/PIPE - FEED - INTERMEDIATE TO FLUID COOLER

Service repair no - 44.24.26

Remove

1. Raise front of vehicle.

⚠ **WARNING: Support on safety stands.**

2. Remove bonnet locking platform. *See BODY, Exterior fittings.*
3. Position container underneath gearbox fluid cooler connections to collect any spillage.

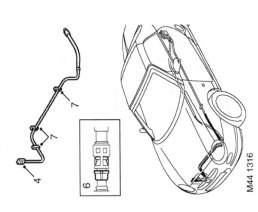

M44 1313

4. Remove bolt securing cooler pipe connection to fluid cooler.
5. Release connection from cooler and discard 'O' ring.
6. Remove release catch, refit in reverse position and release hose from intermediate pipe.
7. Refit release catch in safe position.
8. Remove pipe clamp clip, release pipe from clamp and remove pipe.

⚠ **CAUTION: Plug the connections.**

Refit

1. Clean pipe end and mating faces.
2. Connect hose to intermediate pipe.
3. Using new 'O' ring, align pipe to fluid cooler, fit bolt and tighten to 10 Nm.
4. Position pipe in clamp and secure clamp clip.
5. Fit bonnet locking platform. *See BODY, Exterior fittings.*
6. Top-up gearbox fluid level. *See MAINTENANCE.*
7. Remove stand(s) and lower vehicle.

AUTOMATIC GEARBOX - 'EM-CVT'

HOSE/PIPE - RETURN - INTERMEDIATE TO FLUID COOLER

Service repair no - 44.24.27

Remove

1. Raise front of vehicle.

⚠ **WARNING: Support on safety stands.**

2. Remove bonnet locking platform. *See BODY, Exterior fittings.*
3. Position container underneath gearbox fluid cooler connection to collect any spillage.

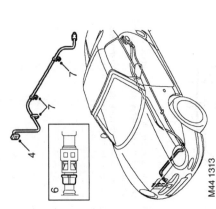

M44 1316

4. Remove bolt securing cooler pipe connections to fluid cooler.
5. Release connection from cooler and discard 'O' ring.
6. Remove release catch, refit in reverse position and release hose from intermediate pipe.
7. Refit release catch in safe position.
8. Remove pipe clamp clip, release pipe from clamp and remove pipe.

⚠ **CAUTION: Plug the connections.**

Refit

1. Clean pipe end and mating faces.
2. Connect hose to intermediate pipe.
3. Using new 'O' ring, align pipe to fluid cooler. Fit bolt and tighten to 10 Nm.
4. Position pipe in clamp and secure clamp clip.
5. Fit bonnet locking platform. *See BODY, Exterior fittings.*
6. Top-up gearbox fluid level. *See MAINTENANCE.*
7. Remove stand(s) and lower vehicle.

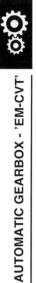

HOSE/PIPE - INTERMEDIATE - FEED

Service repair no - 44.24.28

Remove

1. Remove front underbelly panel. *See BODY, Exterior fittings.*

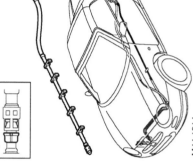

M44 1311

2. Release pipe from 5 clips.
3. Position container to catch spillage.
4. Remove pipe release catches and refit in reverse position.
5. Release hoses from intermediate pipe and remove intermediate pipe.
6. Refit release catches in safe position.

⚠ **CAUTION: Plug the connections.**

Refit

1. Clean pipe end and mating faces.
2. Position intermediate pipe and connect to hoses.
3. Secure intermediate pipe with new cable ties.
4. Fit front underbelly panel. *See BODY, Exterior fittings.*
5. Top-up gearbox fluid level. *See MAINTENANCE.*

HOSE/PIPE - INTERMEDIATE - RETURN

Service repair no - 44.24.29

Remove

1. Remove front underbelly panel. *See BODY, Exterior fittings.*

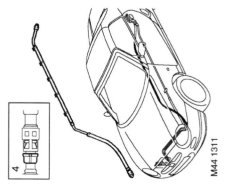

M44 1314

2. Release pipe from 5 clips.
3. Position container to catch spillage.
4. Remove pipe release catches and refit in reverse position.
5. Release hoses from intermediate pipe and remove intermediate pipe.
6. Refit release catches in safe position.

⚠ **CAUTION: Plug the connections.**

Refit

1. Clean pipe end and mating faces.
2. Position intermediate pipe and connect to hoses.
3. Secure intermediate pipe in clips.
4. Fit front underbelly panel. *See BODY, Exterior fittings.*
5. Top-up gearbox fluid level. *See MAINTENANCE.*

AUTOMATIC GEARBOX - 'EM-CVT'

HOSE/PIPE - RETURN - INTERMEDIATE TO GEARBOX

Service repair no - 44.24.31

Remove

1. Raise rear of vehicle.

⚠ **WARNING: Support on safety stands.**

2. Position container to catch spillage.

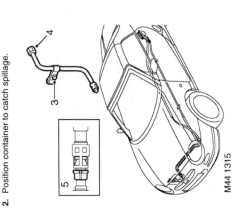

M44 1315

3. Remove bolt securing pipe clamp and remove pipe clamp.
4. Loosen union on gearbox and release pipe from gearbox. Remove and discard 'O' ring.
5. Remove release catch and refit in reverse position. Release pipe from intermediate pipe and remove pipe.
6. Refit release catch in safe position.

⚠ **CAUTION: Plug the connections.**

Refit

1. Clean pipe end and mating faces.
2. Connect pipe to intermediate pipe.
3. Using a new 'O' ring, position pipe to gearbox and tighten union to 14 Nm..
4. Position pipe clamp, fit and tighten clamp bolt to 10 Nm.
5. Remove stand(s) and lower vehicle.
6. Top-up gearbox fluid level. *See MAINTENANCE.*

AUTOMATIC GEARBOX - 'EM-CVT'

HOSE/PIPE - FEED - INTERMEDIATE TO GEARBOX

Service repair no - 44.24.30

Remove

1. Raise rear of vehicle.

⚠ **WARNING: Support on safety stands.**

2. Position container to catch spillage.

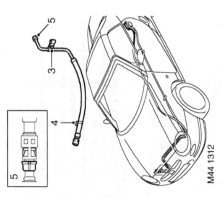

M44 1312

3. Remove bolt securing pipe clamp and remove pipe clamp.
4. Loosen union on gearbox and release pipe from gearbox, remove and discard 'O' ring.
5. Remove release catch and refit in reverse position. Release pipe from intermediate pipe and remove pipe.
6. Refit release catch in safe position.

⚠ **CAUTION: Plug the connections.**

Refit

1. Clean pipe end and mating faces.
2. Connect pipe to intermediate pipe.
3. Using a new 'O' ring, position pipe to gearbox and tighten union to 14 Nm..
4. Position pipe clamp, fit and tighten clamp bolt to 10 Nm.
5. Remove stand(s) and lower vehicle.
6. Top-up gearbox fluid level. *See MAINTENANCE.*

PRIMARY BEARING

Service repair no - 44.36.14

Remove

1. Raise rear of vehicle.
2. Remove LH rear road wheel.
3. Remove air cleaner. **See ENGINE MANAGEMENT SYSTEM - MEMS, Repairs.**

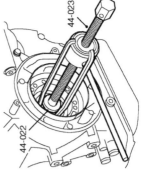

M44 1326B

4. Remove 2 bolts securing resonator to body.

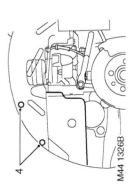

M12 5768

5. Release 2 hand brake cables and gear selector cable from clips on air cleaner mounting bracket.

6. Remove 2 nuts securing fuel filter to air cleaner mounting bracket and release filter from bracket.
7. Remove 3 bolts securing air cleaner mounting bracket to body and remove bracket.
8. Release resonator to increase access for bearing removal.
9. Remove gearbox primary cover seal.5 **See this section.**

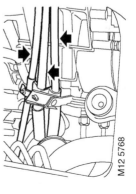

M44 1328

10. Remove 5 remaining bolts securing fluid pump.
11. With care, position 2 levers 180 ° apart and remove fluid pump.

▷ NOTE: To prevent damage to primary housing, place 2 pieces of wood between levers and primary housing when removing oil pump.

M44 1333

12. Remove and discard 2 'O' rings from oil pump.

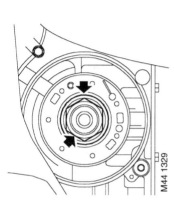

M44 1329

13. Remove and discard belleville washer.
14. Using an air impact wrench with a torque capacity of ± 300 Nm, remove primary bearing nut.

▷ NOTE: Initially start to undo nut with the impact wrench in the minimum position. Increase torque until nut is released.

15. Using a small screwdriver, lever out seal from primary bearing.

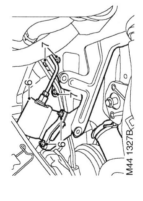

M44 1330

16. Position thrust button **44-022** into primary shaft.
17. Assemble tool **44-023** underneath the exterior ring of primary bearing.
18. Tighten centre bolt of tool **44-023** and remove primary bearing.

AUTOMATIC GEARBOX - 'EM-CVT'

DIFFERENTIAL OIL SEAL

Service repair no - 51.20.37

Remove

1. Raise rear of vehicle.

⚠ **WARNING: Support on safety stands.**

2. Remove road wheel(s).

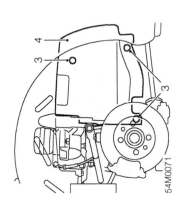

54M0071

3. Remove 2 scrivets and Torx screw securing closing panel.
4. Remove closing panel.
5. Place a jack under vehicle and raise hub.

54M0072

6. Fit a wedge between suspension upper arm and subframe. Lower suspension onto wedge and remove jack.

⚠ **CAUTION: Ensure that an appropriate wedge is used to prevent any damage occurring to the suspension components.**

7. Position drain tray to collect oil spillage from gearbox.

AUTOMATIC GEARBOX - 'EM-CVT'

Refit

1. Clean primary bearing bore and shaft.
2. Clean sealant from threads in fluid pump drive shaft and clean fluid pump housing.
3. Position primary bearing with numbers on bearing facing outwards.

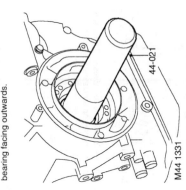

M44 1331

4. Drift in primary bearing using tool **44-021**.
5. Fit and tighten nut using an air impact wrench for sufficient duration until a minimum torque of 180 Nm is achieved.
6. Fit new belleville washer.
7. Lubricate and fit new 'O' rings to fluid pump.
8. Position fluid pump into gearbox, aligning feeder and pitot tube channels.
9. Fit 5 bolts and tighten in a diagonal sequence to 10 Nm.
10. Fit gearbox primary cover seal. *See this section.*
11. Position resonator and secure with bolts.
12. Fit air cleaner mounting bracket to body, fit and tighten 3 bolts.
13. Fit fuel filter to air cleaner mounting bracket and secure with nuts.
14. Secure hand brake cables and gear selector cable to clips.
15. Fit air cleaner. *See ENGINE MANAGEMENT SYSTEM - MEMS, Repairs.*
16. Fit road wheel and tighten to correct torque. *See INFORMATION, Torque wrench settings.*
17. Lower vehicle.
18. Top-up gearbox fluid. *See MAINTENANCE.*

ROAD SPEED TRANSDUCER

Service repair no - 44.38.08

Remove

1. Disconnect battery earth lead.
2. Remove engine compartment access panel. *See BODY, Exterior fittings.*

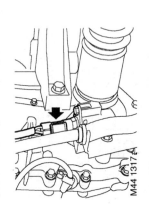

M44 1317

3. Disconnect multiplug from transducer.
4. Remove bolt securing transducer to gearbox.
5. Remove transducer and discard 'O' ring.

Refit

1. Clean sealing faces of transducer and gearbox.
2. Lubricate new 'O' ring with gearbox fluid and fit to transducer.
3. Fit transducer to gearbox and tighten to 9 Nm.
4. Connect multiplug to transducer.
5. Fit engine compartment access panel. *See BODY, Exterior fittings.*
6. Connect battery earth lead.

8. Remove bolt securing lower arm to hub.
9. Remove nut securing track control arm to hub.
10. Break taper joint using tool **18G 1584** and release track control arm.

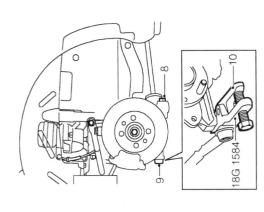

54M0073

11. Release drive shaft from differential using tool **18G 1761.**
12. Remove and discard circlip from drive shaft.
13. Secure drive shaft clear of gearbox for access.
14. Carefully prise oil seal out of differential housing.

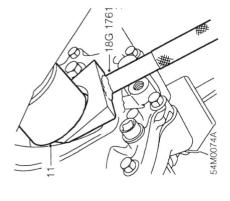

54M0074A

⚠ **CAUTION: Pull on drive shaft to ensure that circlip has engaged correctly.**

9. Locate rear link ball joint to hub and tighten nut to 30 Nm.
10. Fit bolt securing lower arm to hub and tighten to 100 Nm.
11. Raise hub on jack and remove wedge. Lower jack and remove.
12. Remove spillage tray.
13. Fit closing panel and secure with scrivets and Torx screw.
14. Fit road wheel(s) and tighten nuts to correct torque. **See INFORMATION, Torque wrench settings.**
15. Remove stand(s) and lower vehicle.
16. Check and top up gearbox oil. **See MAINTENANCE.**

Refit

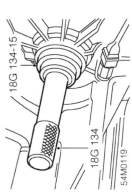

54M0119

1. Thoroughly clean oil seal recess and splines of drive shaft.
2. Lubricate NEW oil seal with clean unused gearbox oil. **See INFORMATION, Capacities, fluids and lubricants.**

3. Locate new seal on tools **18G 134** and **18G 134-15** with sealing lip facing towards differential housing.
4. Carefully drift oil seal into differential housing until it is fully seated in recess.
5. Remove tools **18G 134** and **18G 134-15.**
6. Fit NEW circlip to drive shaft.
7. Ensuring drive shaft is kept horizontal, insert drive shaft and engage with the differential splines in the housing.
8. Fully engage driveshaft into differential.

DRIVE SHAFTS

CONTENTS

Page

DRIVE SHAFT COMPONENTS

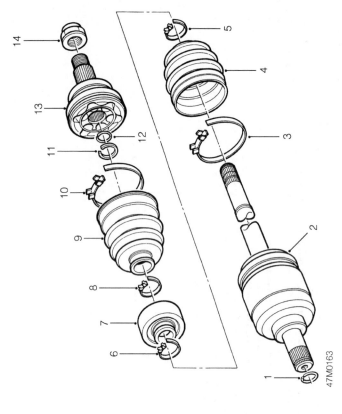

47M0163

1. Circlip
2. Inner joint and shaft
3. Large clip - inner joint gaiter
4. Gaiter
5. Small clip - inner joint gaiter
6. Damper clip - RH shaft only
7. Dynamic damper - RH shaft only

8. Small clip - outer joint gaiter
9. Gaiter
10. Large clip - outer joint gaiter
11. Stopper ring
12. Circlip
13. Outer joint
14. Drive shaft nut

OPERATION

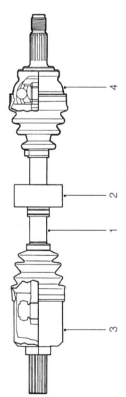

47M0164

1. Drive shaft
2. Dynamic damper
3. Inner joint
4. Outer joint

Drive from the power unit is transmitted to the rear wheels by the drive shafts. Due to the RH drive shaft being longer than the LH drive shaft, a dynamic damper is fitted to reduce harmonic vibration.

The inner joint is of the tripode type with spherical bushing to reduce sliding resistance; it cannot be serviced separate from the shaft. The outer joint is of the ball and socket type. The joints are sealed and pre-packed with grease.

DRIVE SHAFT

Service repair no - 47.10.01

⚠️ **CAUTION: The vehicle is fitted with either an early type or modified type driveshaft inner joint. The type of joint fitted will depend on the type of differential oil seal that is fitted to the gearbox. For information on types of differential oil seals. See MANUAL GEARBOX, Repairs.**

Remove

1. Raise rear of vehicle.

⚠️ WARNING: Support on safety stands.

2. Remove road wheel(s).
3. Remove 2 scrivets and Torx screw securing closing panel.
4. Remove closing panel.
5. Place a jack under lower suspension arm and raise hub.

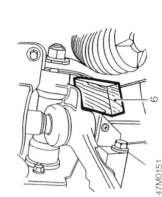

47M0151

6. Fit a wedge between suspension upper arm and subframe. Lower suspension onto wedge and remove jack.

⚠️ **CAUTION: Ensure that an appropriate wedge is used to prevent any damage occurring to the suspension components.**

7. Position container to collect oil spillage from gearbox.

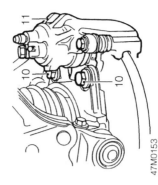

47M0152

8. With an assistant pressing the brake pedal, remove and discard drive shaft nut.
9. Remove bolt securing ABS sensor to hub and collect spacer.

47M0153

10. Remove 2 bolts securing brake caliper to hub. Release caliper and tie aside.
11. Release caliper and tie aside.
12. Remove bolt securing lower arm to hub.
13. Remove nut securing rear link to hub.
14. Break taper joint using tool **18G 1584** and release rear link.
15. Remove bolt securing anti-roll bar link to hub.

DRIVE SHAFTS

16. Bend back tab washer on upper ball joint nut.
17. Remove nut and tab washer securing upper ball joint to hub. Discard tab washer.
18. Break upper ball joint taper using tool **18G 1584.**
19. Release hub from upper arm and drive shaft.

18G 1584

47M0154

20. Use special tool **18G 1761** to release drive shaft from differential.

18G 1761

47M0155A

Refit

1. Clean drive shaft ends, hub, and differential oil seal.
2. Lubricate oil seal running surfaces with clean unused gearbox oil.
3. Fit drive shaft to differential.
4. Connect drive shaft to hub.
5. Locate upper ball joint with upper arm and fit a new tab washer. Fit a new ball joint nut and tighten to 54 Nm.
6. Bend tab washer to secure nut.
7. Locate rear link ball joint to hub and tighten nut to 30 Nm.
8. Fit bolt securing lower arm to hub and tighten to 100 Nm.
9. Fit bolt securing anti-roll bar link to hub and tighten to 35 Nm.
10. Raise hub on jack and remove wedge. lower jack and remove.
11. Untie brake caliper and align to hub. fit bolts and tighten to 85 Nm.
12. With an assistant pressing the brake pedal, fit a NEW drive shaft nut and tighten to 210 Nm. Stake the nut.
13. Fit ABS sensor to hub and tighten bolt to 10 Nm.
14. Remove container.
15. Fit closing panel and secure with scrivets and Torx screw.
16. Fit road wheel(s) and tighten nuts to correct torque. See *INFORMATION, Torque wrench settings.*
17. Remove stand(s) and lower vehicle.
18. Check and top up gearbox oil. See *MAINTENANCE.*

DRIVE SHAFTS

DRIVE SHAFT OUTER GAITER

Service repair no - 47.10.03

Remove

1. Remove drive shaft outer joint. *See this section.*

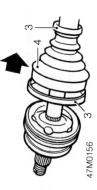

47M0159

2. Slide gaiter from shaft.
3. Inspect gaiter for signs of damage and renew if necessary.

Refit

1. Fit gaiter to shaft.
2. Fit drive shaft outer joint. *See this section.*

DRIVE SHAFT OUTER JOINT

Service repair no - 47.10.04

Remove

1. Remove drive shaft. *See this section.*
2. Place drive shaft in a vice.

47M0156

3. Release both gaiter clips and discard.
4. Slide gaiter along shaft to gain access to outer joint.

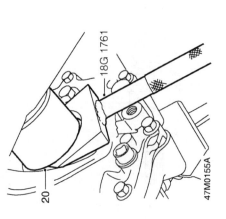

47M0157

5. Bend the joint, and using a suitable drift against the inner part of the joint, remove from shaft.

DRIVE SHAFT INNER GAITER

Service repair no - 47.10.16

Remove

1. Remove drive shaft outer joint. *See this section.*
2. Slide outer gaiter off shaft.

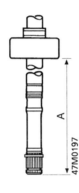

47M0160

3. Release both inner gaiter clips and discard.
4. Slide inner gaiter off shaft.
5. Inspect gaiter for signs of damage and renew if necessary.
6. Clean shaft and joint.

Refit

1. Smear grease around joint.
2. Position gaiter to inner joint and use a band-it thriftool to secure 2 NEW clips.
3. Fit outer gaiter to shaft.
4. Fit outer joint. *See this section.*

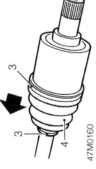

47M0158

6. Remove circlip from shaft and discard.

Refit

1. Fit NEW circlip to shaft.
2. Position outer joint to shaft, use a screwdriver to press circlip into its groove and push joint fully onto shaft.
3. Smear grease around joint.
4. Position gaiter to joint and use a band-it thriftool to secure the 2 NEW clips.
5. Fit drive shaft. *See this section.*

DYNAMIC DAMPER - DRIVE SHAFT - RH

Service repair no - 47.10.33

Remove

1. Remove drive shaft outer gaiter. *See this section.*
2. Clean shaft with emery cloth to remove rust.
3. Lubricate shaft with liquid soap to aid damper removal.
4. Slide damper from shaft.

Refit

47M0197

1. Measure along shaft for fitted position of damper.
2. Mark shaft for fitting position.
   Dimension 'A' = 398.5 mm. ± 3 mm.
3. Lubricate shaft for fitting of damper.
4. Position damper to mark.
5. Clean lubricant from shaft.
6. Fit drive shaft outer gaiter. *See this section.*

CONTENTS

Page

EPAS SYSTEM COMPONENT LOCATION

M57 0938

(RHD shown, LHD similar)

1. Steering rack
2. EPAS motor
3. Steering column
4. Steering wheel

5. Road speed transducer
6. EPAS ECU
7. EPAS System remote fuse (40A)

STEERING WHEEL

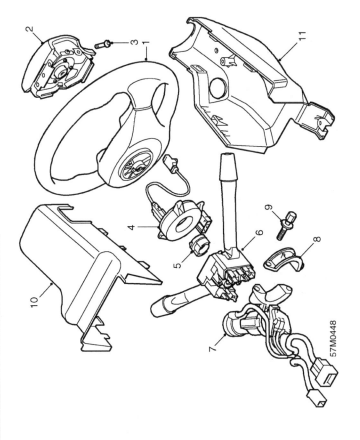

57M0448

1. Steering wheel
2. Driver's airbag module
3. Torx bolt, 2 off
4. Rotary coupler
5. Cancel cam - indicator switch
6. Lighting, indicator and wiper switch assembly
7. Steering lock assembly
8. Bracket - steering lock
9. Shear bolt - steering lock, 2 off
10. Nacelle upper
11. Nacelle lower

STEERING RACK

57M0445

1. Steering rack
2. Track-rod end
3. Locknut - track-rod end
4. Self locking nut - track-rod end to steering arm
5. Gaiter - steering rack
6. Clip inner
7. Clip outer
8. Clamp - steering rack
9. Spacer - steering rack
10. Bolt - steering rack to subframe
11. 'U' bolt - steering rack to subframe
12. Nut - steering rack to subframe

STEERING

STEERING COLUMN - WITHOUT EPAS

⚠️ **WARNING:** The steering column is not serviceable. A damaged column must be renewed otherwise crash performance may be affected.

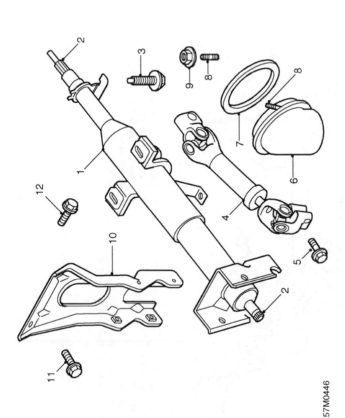

57M0446

1. Steering column assembly
2. Steering shaft
3. Bolt - steering column to body, 2 off
4. Intermediate shaft
5. Bolt - intermediate shaft, 2 off
6. Pinion cover
7. Pinion cover seal
8. Stud - pinion cover, 3 off
9. Nut - pinion cover, 3 off
10. Bracket - steering column to body
11. Bolt - bracket to body, 2 off
12. Bolt - bracket to steering column, 4 off

STEERING

⚠️ **WARNING:** The steering column is not serviceable. A damaged column must be renewed otherwise crash performance may be affected.

STEERING COLUMN - WITH EPAS1 SYSTEM (UP TO 2000MY)

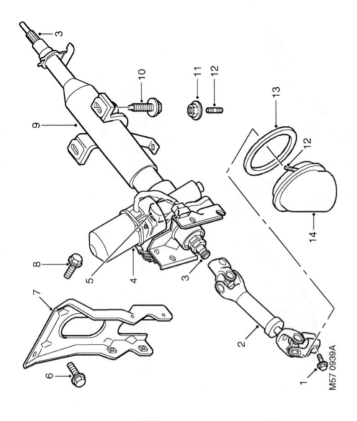

M57 0939A

1. Bolt - intermediate shaft, 2 off
2. Intermediate shaft
3. Steering shaft
4. EPAS steering motor
5. Torque sensor
6. Bolt - bracket to body, 2 off
7. Bracket - steering column to body
8. Bolt - bracket to steering column, 4 off
9. Steering column
10. Bolt - steering column to body
11. Nut - pinion cover, 3 off
12. Stud - pinion cover, 3 off
13. Pinion cover seal
14. Pinion cover

STEERING COLUMN - WITH EPAS2 SYSTEM (FROM 2000MY)

⚠ WARNING: The steering column is not serviceable. A damaged column must be renewed otherwise crash performance may be affected.

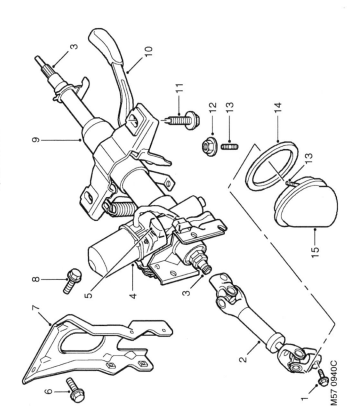

M57 0940C

1. Bolt - intermediate shaft, 2 off
2. Intermediate shaft
3. Steering shaft
4. EPAS steering motor
5. Torque sensor
6. Bolt - bracket to body, 2 off
7. Bracket - steering column to body
8. Bolt - bracket to steering column, 4 off

9. Steering column
10. Column tilt adjustment lever
11. Bolt - steering column to body
12. Nut - pinion cover, 3 off
13. Stud - pinion cover, 3 off
14. Pinion cover seal
15. Pinion cover

STEERING

EPAS SYSTEM CONTROL DIAGRAM

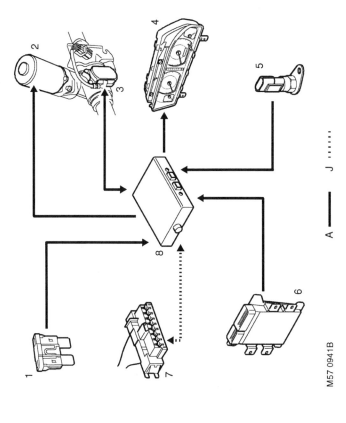

M57 0941B

A = Hardwired; J = Diagnostic ISO 9141 K Line

1. EPAS fuse 40A
2. Steering motor and clutch
3. Torque sensor
4. Instrument pack

5. Road speed transducer
6. Engine Control Module (ECM)
7. Diagnostic socket
8. EPAS ECU

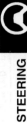

DESCRIPTION

Steering column

The steering column is secured to the body by two brackets. The column consists of two sections that telescopically collapse in the event of a frontal impact. The steering shaft also consists of two telescopic collapsible sections secured by two shear pins. The steering shaft rotates in the steering column via a ball-bearing at its upper end and two ball bearings at its base.

When the steering wheel is rotated, the turning effort of the shaft is transmitted to the pinion shaft of the the steering rack via the intermediate shaft. The intermediate shaft comprises two universal joints which counter the varying angle between steering shaft and rack; and a telescopic internal shaft which acts as a damper. This construction limits intrusion of the column in the event of a crash and also prevents suspension movement and vibration being transmitted through the steering column.

Steering column - With EPAS

The Electronic Power Assisted Steering (EPAS) system uses the same basic steering column design as the non-EPAS system but with electrical components added. The EPAS system steering column has a torque sensor, an electric motor and gearbox positioned at the lower part of the column.

No parts of the steering column are serviceable and failure of any electrical or mechanical component will require column replacement.

EPAS System

The EPAS system is based on the conventional rack and pinion steering system. The EPAS2 system introduced from 2000MY includes updated EPAS ECU software to improve steering response and characteristics and a column tilt adjustment feature.

EPAS provides variable power assistance depending on vehicle speed and driver's steering effort. Power assistance will be most evident to the driver when maneuvering the vehicle at low speeds, this assistance reduces progressively as vehicle speed increases.

Steering motor

Steering assistance is provided by a motor mounted on the steering column. The motor is attached to a cast housing which forms part of the column and is secured with two Torx screws. A single connector connects the motor to the main harness.

The motor drives a wormwheel attached to the steering shaft to provide the power steering assistance. The level of assistance provided by the motor varies according to torque sensor output and road speed.

The EPAS ECU calculates the required torque using inputs from the torque sensor and road speed transducer, and supplies a current to the motor of the appropriate amperage to provide the necessary steering assistance.

An electrically operated clutch connects the motor drive to the column when assistance is required. If a system failure occurs, the EPAS ECU will not engage the clutch, disconnecting motor assistance to the column.

Torque sensor

Driver steering effort is measured by a torque sensor mounted on the steering column. This information is sent to the EPAS ECU, which also monitors engine and vehicle speed.

The torque sensor comprises a rotary potentiometer with two tracks. The potentiometer is connected, via a pin and bearing, to a track on a slider. The slider moves axially depending on steering torque input from the steering wheel. This axial movement is converted, via the track, into rotary movement of the potentiometer in proportion to the torque input. The potentiometer passes information to the EPAS ECU for torque input and direction.

Instrument pack

The EPAS ECU uses this information to calculate the ideal level of power assistance required for the driving conditions and applies a current of the applicable amperage to the electric motor mounted on the steering column. The electric motor applies the required torque to the steering shaft via a worm gear.

EPAS ECU

The EPAS ECU is located above the glove box, behind the fascia. The ECU is rubber mounted to a bracket on the front bulkhead and is secured by a bracket with two bolts to the body cross tube.

The EPAS system incorporates fail-safe devices which cause it to revert to conventional manual steering in the event of a system failure. The EPAS ECU integral fault monitor sends a signal to the electromagnetic clutch which disconnects the motor mechanical drive to the column. Fault codes are stored in the EPAS ECU memory, for identification by TestBook.

If a fault occurs, the EPAS ECU illuminates the EPAS warning lamp in the instrument pack. If, when the ignition is switched off and back on again, the fault is no longer present, the ECU will not illuminate the fault lamp after the engine is started. The ECU stores a fault code for the fault. If the fault does not re-occur in the next twenty ignition cycles, the ECU will erase the fault code.

Field Effect Transistors (FET's) in the ECU protect the system from overload. If excessive use or component failure causes the motor to overheat, the FET's will become hot. As the temperature increases, the FET's and the EPAS ECU gradually decrease the level of steering assistance provided. As the system cools the level of steering assistance is progressively reinstated.

Permanent battery voltage is supplied to the EPAS ECU via a dedicated EPAS 40A fuse which is located remotely adjacent to the underbonnet fusebox.

Two multiplugs provide input and output connections to and from the ECU. The following tables show the harness connector pin numbers and input/output information.

Instrument pack

The EPAS ECU informs the driver of any malfunctions via a warning lamp on the instrument pack. The warning lamp receives a 12V supply from fuse 1 in the passenger compartment fusebox when the ignition is in position II. The EPAS ECU connects the warning lamp to earth when fault warning lamp illumination is required.

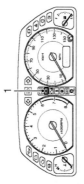

M57 0943

1. EPAS warning lamp

Diagnostics

A diagnostic socket allows the exchange of information between the EPAS ECU and TestBook. The diagnostic socket is located in the passenger compartment fusebox which is below the fascia on the driver's side.

The EPAS ECU monitors inputs and outputs relating to the EPAS system. If a fault is detected, a code applicable to that fault is stored in a fault log in the ECU.

EPAS ECU connector C0316 pin details

Pin No.	Description	Input/Output
1	Clutch earth	Input
2	EPAS instrument pack warning lamp	Output
3	Not used	-
4	Torque sensor earth	Input
5	Torque sensor	Input
6	Torque sensor 5V supply	Output
7	Road speed signal	Input
8	Ignition ON signal	Input
9	Clutch 12V supply	Output
10	Not used	-
11	Not used	-
12	EPAS1 - Potentiometer earth EPAS2 - Not used	EPAS1 Input
13	Torque sensor	Input
14	EPAS1 - 12V supply for potentiometer EPAS2 - Not used	EPAS1 Output
15	Engine speed	Input
16	Diagnostic socket	Input/Output

 CAUTION: On EPAS2 vehicles, the potentiometers are connected in series, therefore, pins 12 and 14 are not used. Wires are still present in harness connector but are unterminated in the torque sensor. DO NOT short circuit either of these pins.

EPAS ECU connector C0317 pin details

Pin No.	Description	Input/Output
1	Battery +12V permanent supply	Input
2	Motor +ve PWM signal (right turn)	Input
3	Earth	Input
4	Motor -ve PWM signal (left turn)	Input

OPERATION

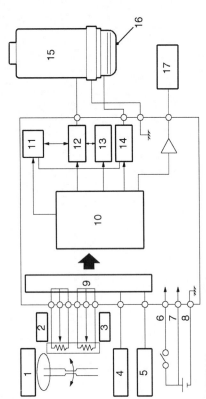

M57 0942A

1. Spring
2. Worm gear
3. Worm wheel
4. Output shaft
5. Ball bearing
6. Pin
7. Lever pin
8. Rotary potentiometer
9. Ball
10. Slider
11. Torsion bar
12. Input shaft

EPAS Mechanical operation

The motor, clutch and motor worm gear are mounted on the cast gear housing on the column. The worm wheel is attached to the output shaft. The input shaft and the output shaft are joined by a torsion bar.

When the steering wheel is rotated, torque is applied to the torsion bar which twists causing an angular deflection between the input and output shafts.

The deflection causes the slider to rotate via the balls in the ball groove which causes linear movement of the slider along the axis of the output shaft.

The rotary potentiometer in the torque sensor has pin, which is fitted with a ball bearing. The bearing locates in a groove in the slider. The linear movement of the slider is converted back to rotational movement of the potentiometer, via the bearing and pin. The torque sensor converts the torque applied into an electrical signal which is proportional to the steering torque.

EPAS electrical operation

M57 0944

EPAS ECU (EPAS1 ECU shown)

1. Torque sensor
2. Main
3. Sub
4. Speed sensor
5. Engine revolution sensor
6. Ignition switch supply
7. Battery supply
8. Earth
9. Interface
10. Main control computer
11. Fail safe relay
12. Motor drive circuit
13. Current control circuit
14. Clutch drive circuit
15. Motor
16. Clutch
17. Warning lamp

On EPAS1 vehicles (up to 2000MY), the torque sensor has two potentiometers. Each potentiometer has its own power supply and earth connection and operate in opposing directions. The ECU monitors the output from each potentiometer and can suspend power assistance and illuminate the EPAS warning lamp if a fault is detected.

On EPAS2 vehicles (from 2000MY), the torque sensor has two potentiometers. The potentiometers share a power supply and earth connection from the ECU and operate the same direction. One potentiometer provides the torque data and the other potentiometer acts as a fault monitor. The ECU checks the output from each potentiometer and will illuminate the EPAS warning lamp and suspend power assistance whilst the fault is present.

STEERING

When the ignition is switched on, the EPAS ECU performs a start-up (diagnostic) check procedure. The ECU illuminates the EPAS fault warning lamp in the instrument pack. The lamp will remain illuminated until the engine is started and the ECU receives an engine running signal from the crankshaft position (CKP) sensor.

The inputs from the torque sensor, CKP sensor (engine running signal) and road speed transducer are passed to the ECU and, via the interface, to the main control computer.

The computer processes the data and calculates the required steering assistance and outputs the required current to the motor. The motor then operates to apply torque via the worm gear in the required direction to the worm wheel.

STEERING

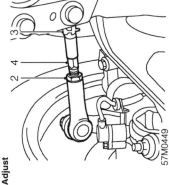

57M0449

FRONT WHEEL ALIGNMENT

Service repair no - 57.65.01

Check

1. Ensure suspension trim height is correct before checking wheel alignment. **See INFORMATION, General data.**
2. Ensure tyre pressures are correct.
3. Ensure that equipment is properly calibrated.

⚠ NOTE: Only use equipment recommended in the STEP (Service Tools and Equipment Programme) Manual.

4. Check front wheel alignment is within tolerance.

⚠ NOTE: The following steering geometry settings are given in A - degrees and minutes, B - decimal parts of a degree and C - millimetres. Steering and Suspension geometry settings are for a vehicle at unladen weight.

DATA
Front wheel alignment - toe-out - per side:
A - 0 °10' ± 0° 6'
B - 0.21° ± 0.1°
C - 1.105 mm ± 0.651 mm.

Adjust

1. Mark track-rods for reference.
2. Slacken track-rod lock nut.
3. Release clip securing gaiter.
4. Adjust track-rod to obtain correct alignment.

⚠ **CAUTION: Both track-rods must be rotated an equal amount.**

5. Tighten track-rod lock nut to 50 Nm and secure gaiter clip.

REAR WHEEL ALIGNMENT

Service repair no - 57.65.06

Check

1. Ensure suspension trim height is correct before checking wheel alignment. **See INFORMATION, General data.**
2. Ensure tyre pressures are correct.
3. Ensure that equipment is properly calibrated.

⚠ NOTE: When adjusting rear wheel alignment 4 turntables must be used, one for each wheel. Only use equipment recommended in the STEP (Service Tools and Equipment Programme) Manual.

4. Ensure front wheel alignment is correct. **See this section.**
5. Check rear wheel alignment is within tolerance.

⚠ NOTE: The following settings are given in A - degrees and minutes, B - decimal parts of a degree and C - millimetres. Settings are for a vehicle at unladen weight.

DATA

Rear wheel alignment = toe-in - per side:

A - 0° 10' ± 0° 7'
B - 0.21° ± 0.12°
C - 1.105 mm ± 0.76 mm

Adjust

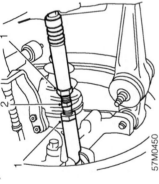

57M0450

1. Loosen 2 lock nuts securing track control arm adjuster.
2. Turn adjuster to obtain correct alignment.
3. Tighten lock nuts.
4. Settle suspension.
5. Recheck alignment, when correct tighten lock nuts to 50 Nm.
6. Repeat check and adjust operation on other side of vehicle.

⚠ CAUTION: After adjusting the rear wheel alignment, ensure that the track control arm has rotational movement. This can be checked by grasping the track control arm and rotating it backwards and forwards on the ball joints.

STEERING

STEERING RACK

Service repair no - 57.25.01

Remove

1. Raise front of vehicle.

⚠ WARNING: Support on safety stands.

2. Remove road wheel(s).

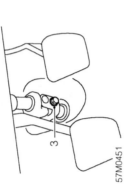

57M0451

3. Remove bolt securing intermediate shaft to steering rack.
4. Remove 3 nuts securing pinion cover.

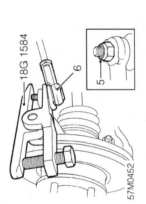

18G 1584

57M0452

5. Remove nuts securing track-rod ends to steering arms.
6. Using tool **18G 1584** break both track-rod end taper joints.

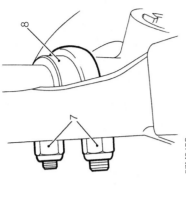

57M0453

7. Remove nuts securing steering rack 'U' bolt to subframe.
8. Remove 'U' bolt.

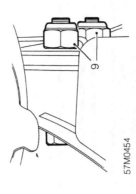

57M0454

9. Remove bolts securing steering rack clamp to subframe.
10. Remove clamp.
11. Support front subframe with trolley jack.

⚠ CAUTION: Place a piece of wood between the jack and the subframe to avoid damage.

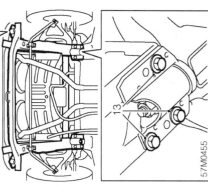

57M0455

12. Slacken 4 bolts securing front of subframe to body.
13. Remove 6 bolts securing rear of subframe to body.
14. Lower rear of subframe.
15. Release steering rack from steering column gaiter.
16. Withdraw steering rack out through drivers side wheel arch.

⚠ **CAUTION: Be careful not to damage steering rack gaiters when removing steering rack.**

17. Remove and discard pinion cover.

Refit

1. Fit NEW pinion cover and tighten bolts to 8 Nm.
2. Position rack to subframe.
3. Fit 'U' bolt to steering rack and subframe. Fit nuts but do not tighten at this stage.
4. Fit steering rack clamp. Fit nuts and tighten to 22 Nm.
5. Tighten 'U' bolt nuts to 22 Nm, ensure that thread protrusion behind each nut is equal.
6. Raise subframe into position.
7. Fit bolts securing subframe to body and tighten to:
   Front bolts = 30 Nm.
   Rear bolts = 45 Nm.
8. Connect track-rod ends to steering arms and tighten nuts to 30 Nm.
9. Connect steering column, intermediate shaft to rack and tighten bolt to 22 Nm.
10. Fit road wheel(s) and tighten nuts to correct torque. *See **INFORMATION, Torque wrench settings.***
11. Remove stand(s) and lower vehicle.
12. Check and adjust wheel alignment. *See **Adjustments.***

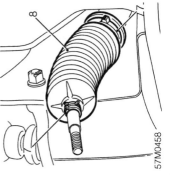

57M0458

STEERING RACK GAITER

Service repair no - 57.25.03

Remove

1. Raise front of vehicle.

⚠ WARNING: Support on safety stands.

2. Remove road wheel(s).

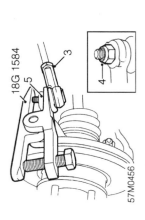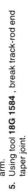

18G 1584

57M0456

3. Loosen track-rod end lock nut.
4. Remove nut securing track-rod end to steering arm.
5. Using tool **18G 1584**, break track-rod end taper joint.

57M0457

6. Noting the number of complete turns remove track-rod end, and lock nut.

7. Remove 2 gaiter clips.
8. Remove gaiter from rack.

Refit

1. Apply grease to gaiter. *See **INFORMATION, Capacities, fluids and lubricants.***
2. Position inner gaiter clip to gaiter.
3. Fit gaiter and secure with clips.
4. Fit lock nut and track-rod end to rack.

⚠ NOTE: Rotate the track-rod end the same amount of turns noted on the removal.

5. Clean taper and position track-rod end to steering arm.
6. Fit nut and tighten to 30 Nm.
7. Tighten track-rod end lock nut to 50 Nm.
8. Fit road wheel(s) and tighten nuts to correct torque. *See **INFORMATION, Torque wrench settings.***
9. Remove stand(s) and lower vehicle.
10. Check and adjust wheel alignment. *See **Adjustments.***

STEERING

STEERING COLUMN

Service repair no - 57.40.01

⚠️ **WARNING:** See *RESTRAINT SYSTEMS, Precautions.*

Remove

1. Make the SRS system safe *See RESTRAINT SYSTEMS, Precautions.*

⚠️ **CAUTION: The steering column upper mountings have breakout capsules which are critical to crash performance. Do not clamp the capsules in a vice or otherwise mishandle them.**

⚠️ **WARNING: If the breakout capsules on the upper mountings are damaged the steering column must be replaced.**

2. Remove steering column switch pack. *See ELECTRICAL, Repairs.*

57M0428

3. Loosen 2 screws securing fuse box cover to fascia and remove fuse box cover.

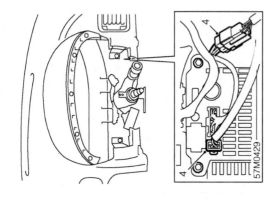

57M0429

4. Disconnect 2 ignition switch multiplugs from fusebox and harness.

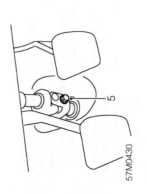

57M0430

5. Remove bolt securing intermediate shaft to steering rack pinion.

6. Remove 2 nuts securing passenger fusebox to body and position fusebox aside.

⚠️ **CAUTION: The steering column, upper mounting bolts must be removed before the lower mounting bolts. This is to prevent the weight of the steering column damaging the upper mounting breakout capsules.**

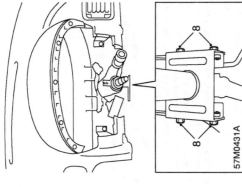

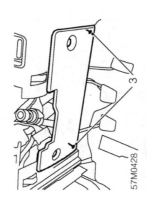

57M0432A

7. Remove 2 bolts securing upper steering column to fascia rail.

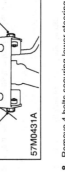

57M0431A

8. Remove 4 bolts securing lower steering column to bracket.

9. Release column assembly and remove from steering rack pinion, remove steering column from vehicle.

STEERING COLUMN NACELLE

Service repair no - 57.40.29

Remove

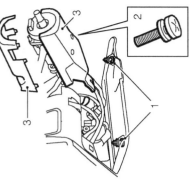

57M0362

1. Release 2 clips securing fascia fusebox cover.
2. Remove 3 screws securing nacelle to column.
3. Release upper nacelle from lower nacelle and remove from column.
4. Remove ignition switch grommet from lower nacelle.

Refit

1. Fit ignition switch grommet to lower nacelle.
2. Fit lower and upper steering column nacelle and clip together.
3. Align nacelle to fixings and tighten screws.
4. Position fascia fusebox cover and secure fasteners.

Refit

1. Remove key from ignition barrel to ensure steering lock pin is protruding.
2. Fit ignition switch to column, locating steering lock pin in groove on inner column.
3. Fit lock saddle.
4. Fit and nip up shear bolts.
5. Test operation of lock and switch prior to tightening shear bolts.
6. Tighten both shear bolts progressively to ensure lock and saddle sit level on column.
7. Tighten bolts until heads shear.
8. Remove column assembly from vice.
9. Fit intermediate shaft to steering column and tighten clamping bolt to 22 Nm.

⚠ **WARNING: Intermediate shafts are supplied in LH and RH drive variants. The two shafts have different phase angles, and cars fitted with the incorrect shafts will have defective steering.**
It is essential that all RH drive cars are fitted with shafts with blue marks, and all LH drive cars are fitted with unmarked shafts.

10. Fit column assembly to steering rack pinion.
11. Align column to lower mounting and loosely fit bolts.
12. Align column to upper mounting and loosely fit bolts.
13. Tighten lower mounting bolts to 22 Nm.
14. Tighten upper mounting bolts to 22 Nm.
15. Fit and tighten clamping bolt securing intermediate shaft to steering rack pinion to 22 Nm.
16. Fit fuse box to body and tighten nuts to 10 Nm.
17. Connect ignition switch multiplugs to fusebox and harness.
18. Fit fuse box cover and secure with screws.
19. Fit steering column switch pack. *See ELECTRICAL, Repairs.*
20. Connect battery earth lead.

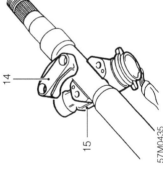
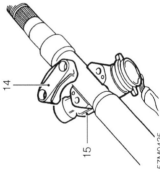

57M0435

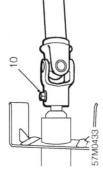

57M0433

10. Remove clamping bolt securing steering column to intermediate shaft. Remove intermediate shaft.
11. Position steering column assembly in vice.

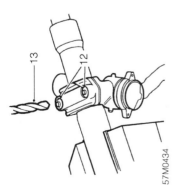

57M0434

12. Mark ignition lock shear bolt heads with centre punch.
13. Drill out shear bolt heads.

14. Remove lock 'saddle' from column.
15. Remove lock assembly from column.
16. Remove shear bolts from lock assembly.

IGNITION SWITCH AND STEERING LOCK

Service repair no - 57.40.31

⚠ **WARNING:** *See RESTRAINT SYSTEMS, Precautions.*

Remove

⚠ **CAUTION: The steering column upper mountings have breakout capsules which are critical to crash performance. Do not clamp the capsules in a vice or otherwise mishandle them.**

⚠ **WARNING: If the breakout capsules on the upper mountings are damaged the steering column must be replaced.**

1. Remove steering column assembly. *See this section.*
2. Position steering column assembly in vice.

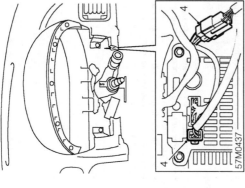

57M0416

3. Mark ignition switch shear bolt heads with centre punch.
4. Drill out shear bolt heads.

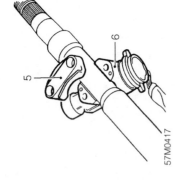

57M0417

5. Remove lock 'saddle' from column.
6. Remove lock assembly from column.

Refit

1. Remove key from ignition barrel to ensure steering lock pin is protruding.
2. Fit ignition switch to column, locating steering lock pin in groove on inner column.
3. Fit lock saddle.
4. Fit and nip up shear bolts.
5. Test operation of lock and switch prior to tightening shear bolts.
6. Tighten both shear bolts progressively to ensure lock and saddle sit level on column.
7. Tighten bolts until heads shear.
8. Remove column assembly from vice.
9. Fit column assembly to vehicle. *See this section.*

STEERING COLUMN - WITH EPAS - UP TO 2000MY

Service repair no - 57.43.01

⚠ **WARNING:** *See RESTRAINT SYSTEMS, Precautions.*

Remove

1. Make the SRS system safe. *See RESTRAINT SYSTEMS, Precautions.*

⚠ **CAUTION: The steering column upper mountings have breakout capsules which are critical to crash performance. Do not clamp the capsules in a vice or otherwise mishandle them.**

⚠ **WARNING: If the breakout capsules on the upper mountings are damaged the steering column must be replaced.**

2. Remove steering column switch pack. *See ELECTRICAL, Repairs.*

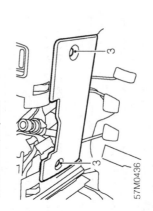

57M0436

3. Loosen 2 screws securing fuse box cover to fascia and remove fuse box cover.

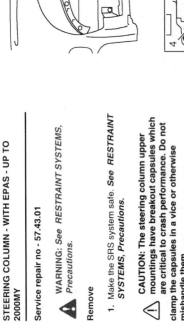

57M0437

4. Disconnect 2 ignition switch multiplugs from fusebox and harness.

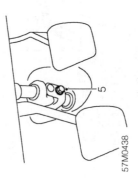

57M0438

5. Remove bolt securing intermediate shaft to steering rack pinion.
6. Remove 2 bolts securing passenger fusebox to body and position fusebox aside.

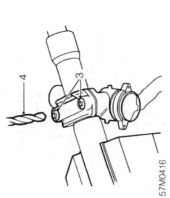

STEERING

> ⚠️ **CAUTION: The steering column upper mounting bolts must be removed before the lower mounting bolts. This is to prevent the weight of the steering column damaging the upper mounting breakout capsules.**

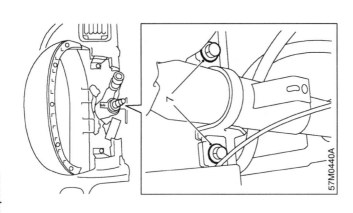

57M0440A

7. Remove 2 bolts securing upper steering column to fascia rail.

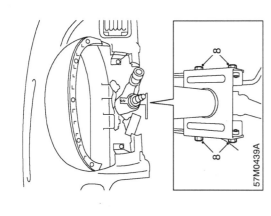

57M0439A

8. Remove 4 bolts securing lower steering column to bracket.
9. Release column assembly from steering rack pinion.
10. Remove column from vehicle.

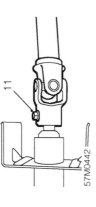

57M0442

11. Remove clamping bolt securing steering column to intermediate shaft. Remove intermediate shaft.
12. Position steering column assembly in vice.

STEERING

57M0443

13. Mark ignition switch shear bolt heads with centre punch.
14. Drill out shear bolt heads.

57M0444

15. Remove lock 'saddle' from column.
16. Remove lock assembly from column.
17. Remove shear bolts from lock assembly.

Refit

1. Remove key from ignition barrel to ensure steering lock pin is protruding.
2. Fit ignition switch to column, locating steering lock pin in groove on inner column.
3. Fit lock saddle and loosely fit shear bolts.
4. Test operation of lock and switch prior to tightening shear bolts.
5. Tighten both shear bolts progressively to ensure lock and saddle sit level on column.
6. Tighten bolts until heads shear.
7. Fit intermediate shaft to steering column and tighten clamping bolt to 22 Nm.

> ⚠️ **WARNING: Intermediate shafts are supplied in LH and RH drive variants. The two shafts have different phase angles, and cars fitted with the incorrect shafts will have defective steering.**

It is essential that all RH drive cars are fitted with shafts with blue marks, and all LH drive cars are fitted with unmarked shafts.

8. Fit column assembly to steering rack pinion.
9. Connect column multiplugs.
10. Align column to lower mounting and loosely fit bolts.
11. Align column to upper mounting and loosely fit bolts.
12. Tighten lower mounting bolts to 22 Nm.
13. Tighten upper mounting bolts to 22 Nm.
14. Fit and tighten clamping bolt securing intermediate shaft to steering rack pinion to 22 Nm.
15. Fit fuse box to body and tighten bolts to 10 Nm.
16. Connect ignition switch multiplugs to fusebox and harness.
17. Fit fuse box cover and secure with screws.
18. Fit steering column switch pack. See **ELECTRICAL, Repairs.**
19. Connect battery earth lead.

STEERING

STEERING COLUMN - WITH EPAS - 2000MY ON

Service repair no - 57.43.01

Remove

1. Make the SRS system safe. *See RESTRAINT SYSTEMS, Precautions.*

⚠ **CAUTION: The steering column upper mountings have breakout capsules which are critical to crash performance. Do not clamp the capsules in a vice or otherwise mishandle them.**

⚠ WARNING: If the breakout capsules on the upper mountings are damaged the steering column must be replaced.

2. Remove steering column switch pack. *See ELECTRICAL, Repairs.*

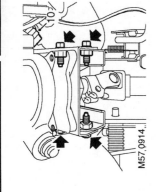

3. Release transponder coil from ignition switch, disconnect multiplug and remove transponder coil.

M57 0909

4. Loosen 2 screws and scrivets securing fuse box cover to fascia and remove fusebox cover.

M57 0910

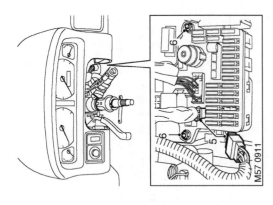

5. Disconnect ignition switch multiplugs from fusebox and main harness.

6. Remove 2 nuts securing passenger compartment fusebox to body and position aside.

M57 0911

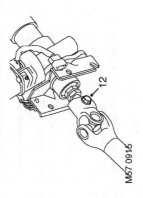

7. Remove bolt securing universal joint to steering rack pinion.

⚠ **CAUTION: The steering column upper mounting bolts must be removed before the lower mounting bolts. This is to prevent the weight of the steering column damaging the upper mounting breakout capsules.**

M57 0912

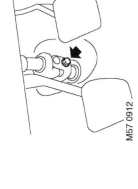

8. Remove 2 bolts securing upper steering column to fascia rail.

M57 0913

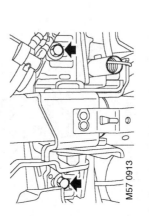

9. Remove 4 bolts securing lower steering column to bracket.

10. Lower steering column and disconnect 2 multiplugs.

11. Release column assembly from steering rack pinion and remove from vehicle.

M57 0914...10

12. Remove clamping bolt securing steering column to universal joint and remove joint.

13. Position steering column assembly in vice.

M57 0915

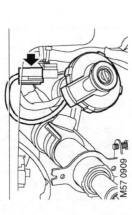

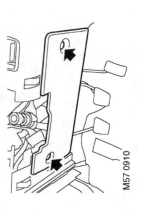

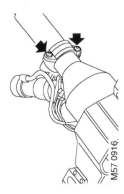

M57 0916.

14. Mark shear bolt heads with centre punch.
15. Drill out shear bolt heads.

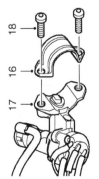

M57 0917

16. Remove lock 'saddle' from column.
17. Remove lock assembly from column.
18. Remove shear bolts from lock assembly.
19. Remove column from vice.

Refit

1. Remove key from ignition barrel to ensure steering lock pin is protruding.
2. Fit ignition switch to column, locating steering lock pin in groove on inner column.
3. Fit lock saddle and loosely fit shear bolts.
4. Test operation of lock and switch prior to tightening shear bolts.
5. Tighten both shear bolts progressively to ensure lock and saddle sit level on column.
6. Tighten bolts until heads shear.
7. Fit universal joint to steering column and tighten clamping bolt to 22 Nm.

⚠ **WARNING: Intermediate shafts are supplied in LH and RH drive variants. The two shafts have different phase angles, and cars fitted with the incorrect shafts will have defective steering.**
It is essential that all RH drive cars are fitted with shafts with blue marks, and all LH drive cars are fitted with unmarked shafts.

8. Fit column assembly to steering rack pinion.
9. Connect column multiplugs.
10. Align lower column mounting bracket and locate 2 bolts in slots.
11. Fit remaining 2 bolts into column lower mounting bracket and tighten all bolts to 22 Nm.
12. Align column to upper mounting bracket and fit bolts. Tighten bolts to 22 Nm.
13. Fit and tighten column clamping bolt securing universal joint to steering rack pinion to 20 Nm.
14. Fit passenger compartment fuse box to body and tighten nuts to 10 Nm.
15. Connect ignition switch multiplugs to passenger compartment fusebox and harness.
16. Fit passenger compartment fuse box cover and secure with screws and scrivets.
17. Position transponder coil, connect multiplug and secure transponder coil to ignition switch.
18. Fit steering column switch pack. See *ELECTRICAL, Repairs.*
19. Connect battery earth lead.

EPAS ECU

Service repair no - 57.43.05

Remove

1. Remove glovebox. *See BODY, Interior trim components.*

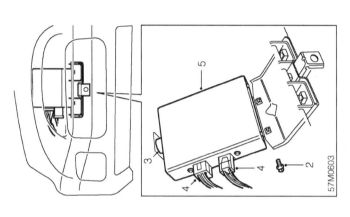

57M0603

⚠ **WARNING: Do not remove EPAS ECU bracket from fascia rail on vehicles fitted with a passenger airbag.**

2. Remove 2 bolts securing ECU to fascia rail bracket.
3. Release ECU from rubber mounting.
4. Disconnect 2 multiplugs from ECU.
5. Remove ECU.

Refit

1. Position ECU and connect multiplugs.
2. Fit ECU to mounting and tighten bolts to 10 Nm.
3. Connect multiplugs.
4. Fit glovebox. *See BODY, Interior trim components.*

TRACK-ROD END

Service repair no - 57.55.02

Remove

1. Raise front of vehicle.

 **WARNING: Support on safety stands.**

2. Remove road wheel(s).

57M0462

3. Loosen track-rod end lock nut.
4. Remove nut securing track-rod end to steering arm.
5. Using tool **18G 1584**, break taper joint.
6. Noting the number of complete turns, remove track-rod end.

Refit

1. Fit NEW track-rod end and position taper to steering arm.

   NOTE: Rotate the track-rod end the same amount of turns noted on the removal.

2. Tighten nut to 30 Nm.
3. Tighten lock nut to 50 Nm.
4. Fit road wheel(s) and tighten nuts to correct torque. **See INFORMATION, Torque wrench settings.**
5. Remove stand(s) and lower vehicle.
6. Check and adjust front wheel alignment. **See Adjustments.**

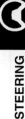

6. Attach tape across edge of rotary coupler to retain in central setting.
   Do not carry out further dismantling if component is removed for access only.
7. Release horn earth terminal from steering wheel.
8. Release 2 horn switches from steering wheel.
9. Disconnect 4 Lucars and remove switches.
10. Remove harness from steering wheel.
11. Fit harness to steering wheel.
12. Fit switches, connect Lucars and secure switches to steering wheel.
13. Connect horn earth terminal to steering wheel.

STEERING WHEEL - UP TO 2000MY

Service repair no - 57.60.01

 WARNING: See RESTRAINT SYSTEMS, Precautions.

Remove

1. Remove driver's airbag module. **See RESTRAINT SYSTEMS, Repairs.**

57M0361

2. Disconnect horn feed lead multiplug from rotary coupler.
3. Loosen steering wheel retaining nut.
4. Release steering wheel from column splines and remove nut.
5. Remove steering wheel.

Refit

1. Remove retaining tape from rotary coupler.
2. Ensure road wheels are in straight ahead position and indicator cancellation cam is aligned vertical.
3. Fit steering wheel to steering column ensuring wheel spokes are horizontal, fit NEW nut and tighten to 50 Nm.
4. Connect horn multiplug to rotary coupler.
5. Fit driver's airbag module. **See RESTRAINT SYSTEMS, Repairs.**

STEERING WHEEL - 2000MY ON

Service repair no - 57.60.01

Remove

1. Remove driver's airbag. **See RESTRAINT SYSTEMS, Repairs.**

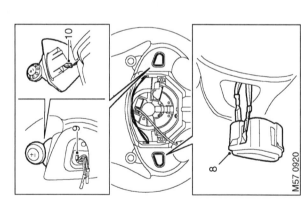

M57 0918

2. Disconnect horn/sequential gear change switch multiplug.
3. Centralise steering wheel with road wheels in straight ahead position.
4. Restrain steering wheel and loosen nut securing steering wheel to column.
5. Release steering wheel from column.
6. Remove steering wheel.

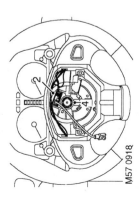

M57 0919

7. Attach tape across edge of rotary coupler to retain correct setting and to prevent rotational damage to rotary coupler.

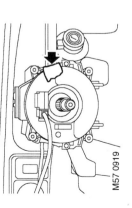

M57 0920

8. Release horn switches, disconnect Lucar connections and remove horn switches.
9. Release clips securing sequential gear change switches, release switches from steering wheel.
10. Disconnect gear change switch multiplugs and remove switches from steering wheel.
11. Remove steering wheel harness.

Refit

1. Position harness to steering wheel and locate to switch recesses.
2. Position gear change switches, connect multiplugs and secure switches to steering wheel.
3. Position horn switches, connect Lucar connections and secure horn switches to steering wheel.
4. Remove tape from rotary coupler.
5. Ensure road wheels are in straight ahead position and indicator cancelling cam is aligned horizontally.
6. Fit steering wheel to column.
7. Connect horn/sequential gear change switch multiplug.
8. Fit and tighten nut securing steering wheel to column to 63 Nm.
9. Fit driver's airbag. **See RESTRAINT SYSTEMS, Repairs.**

CONTENTS

FRONT SUSPENSION COMPONENTS

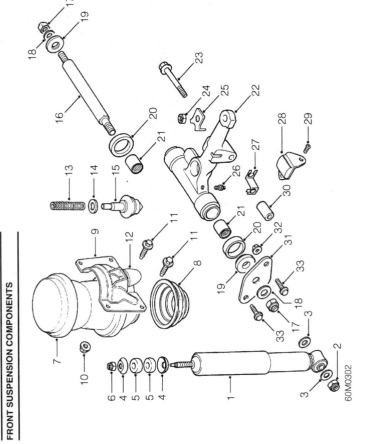

60M0302

1. Damper unit
2. Self locking nut
3. Flat washer
4. Cup washer
5. Damper, top mounting bush
6. Self locking nut
7. Hydragas unit
8. Gaiter
9. Hydragas unit retaining plate
10. Self locking nut
11. Bolts - retaining plate
12. Bump rubber
13. Return spring
14. Spacer
15. Roller foot joint
16. Upper arm pivot shaft
17. Locking nut

18. Flat washer
19. Thrust washer
20. Sealing ring
21. Needle-roller bearing
22. Suspension upper arm
23. Bolt - damper lower mounting
24. Nut - upper ball joint
25. Tab washer - upper ball joint
26. Grease nipple
27. Brake hose bracket
28. Rebound rubber
29. Screw
30. Spacer
31. Upper arm pivot shaft, retaining plate
32. Self locking nut
33. Bolt - retaining plate

REAR SUSPENSION COMPONENTS

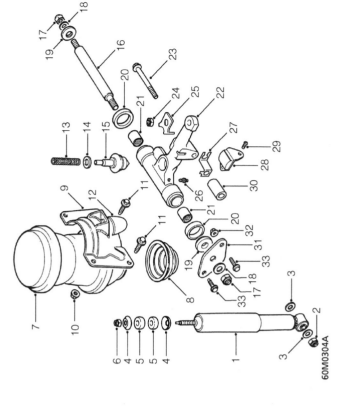

60M0304A

1. Damper unit
2. Self locking nut
3. Flat washer
4. Cup washer
5. Damper, top mounting bush
6. Self locking nut
7. Hydragas unit
8. Gaiter
9. Hydragas unit retaining plate
10. Self locking nut
11. Bolts - retaining plate
12. Bump rubber
13. Return spring
14. Spacer
15. Roller foot joint
16. Upper arm pivot shaft
17. Locking nut

18. Flat washer
19. Thrust washer
20. Sealing ring
21. Needle-roller bearing
22. Suspension upper arm
23. Bolt - damper lower mounting
24. Nut - upper ball joint
25. Tab washer - upper ball joint
26. Grease nipple
27. ABS cable bracket
28. Rebound rubber
29. Screw
30. Spacer
31. Upper arm pivot shaft, retaining plate
32. Self locking nut
33. Bolt - retaining plate

FRONT SUSPENSION COMPONENTS - continued

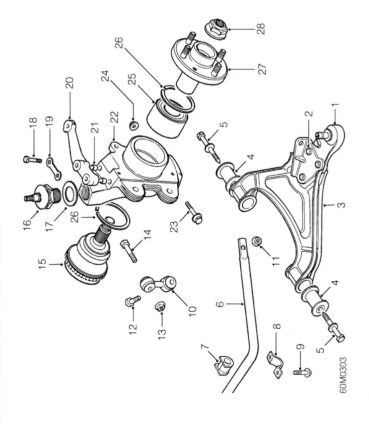

60M0303

1. Lower ball joint
2. Rivet (nut and bolt fitted when ball joint renewed)
3. Suspension lower arm
4. Lower arm bush
5. Bolt - lower arm mounting
6. Anti-roll bar
7. Anti-roll bar bush
8. Anti-roll bar, bracket
9. Bolt - anti-roll bar, bracket
10. Anti-roll bar link
11. Self locking nut
12. Bolt - anti-roll bar link
13. Self locking nut
14. Bolt - anti-roll bar link

15. Stub axle
16. Upper balljoint
17. Lock washer
18. Bolt - steering arm
19. Tab washer
20. Steering arm
21. Dowel - steering arm
22. Swivel hub
23. Bolt - lower ball joint
24. Self locking nut
25. Bearing
26. Retaining clip
27. Drive flange
28. Hub nut

REAR SUSPENSION COMPONENTS - continued

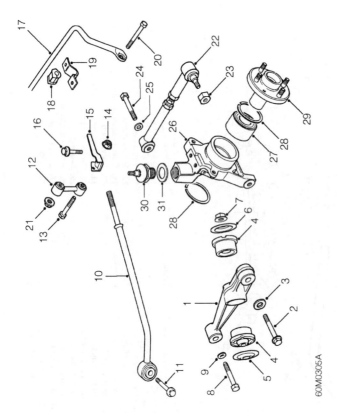

60M0305A

1. Lower suspension arm
2. Bolt - lower suspension arm
3. Flat washer
4. Bush - tie bar
5. Bevelled washer - front
6. Bevelled washer - rear
7. Self locking nut
8. Bolt - lower suspension arm
9. Flat washer
10. Tie bar
11. Bolt - tie bar
12. Anti-roll bar link
13. Bolt - anti-roll bar link
14. Self locking nut
15. Anti-roll bar link, bracket
16. Bolt - anti-roll bar link, bracket

17. Anti-roll bar
18. Bush - anti-roll bar
19. Bracket - anti-roll bar
20. Bolt - anti-roll bar link
21. Self locking nut
22. Track control arm
23. Self locking nut - track control arm
24. Bolt - track control arm
25. Flat washer
26. Hub
27. Bearing
28. Retaining clip
29. Drive flange
30. Upper ball joint
31. Lock washer

HYDRAGAS SUSPENSION

The Hydragas suspension system consists of a Hydragas unit at each wheel, mounted vertically between the vehicle's body and top suspension arm. The units are connected front to rear at each side of the vehicle via pipes, and pressurized with fluid. This method of linking the units improves the vehicle's resistance to pitch. The pitching motion occurs when the front suspension is compressed and the rear suspension is extended simultaneously.

Controlled distribution of the fluid between the two connected units combats the pitching motion. A sudden upward movement of the front wheel displaces fluid from the front hydragas unit, forcing it through the connecting pipe into the rear unit. This action raises the rear of the vehicle to the same level as the front, keeping the vehicle's body horizontal. When the front wheel descends the fluid is returned and the suspension settles to its normal position.

The hydragas system also restricts vehicle roll when cornering, this is achieved by the two outside units stiffening when under load.

Each Hydragas unit comprises of two chambers separated by a rubber membrane. The upper chamber which is sealed contains nitrogen gas, the lower chamber is filled with a water base fluid containing approximately 50% alcohol to prevent freezing, and a corrosion inhibiter.

Damping is achieved by fluid passing through a two-way valve arrangement restricting the flow of fluid in the unit. One valve provides bump control and the other restricts rebound.

FRONT SUSPENSION

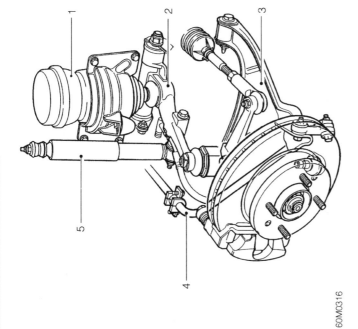

60M0316

1. Hydragas unit
2. Upper suspension arm
3. Lower suspension arm
4. Anti-roll bar
5. Damper unit

Suspension springing and damping is provided by the Hydragas unit mounted vertically above the upper suspension arm. An additional damper unit also vertically mounted to the upper suspension arm, is employed to provide a more responsive suspension. The damper unit assists in absorbing the energy stored in the Hydragas unit after passing a bump. Quickly terminating the reciprocating motion of the suspension and returning the Hydragas unit to the rest position.

The suspension lower arm is of the wishbone type and is designed to provide fore-and-aft stiffness, to restrain braking torque. Both lower suspension arms are interconnected by an anti-roll bar which provides the required stiffness to prevent body roll.

REAR SUSPENSION

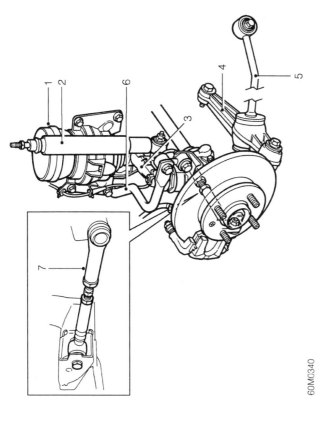

60M0340

1. Hydragas unit
2. Damper unit
3. Upper suspension arm
4. Lower suspension arm

5. Tie bar
6. Anti-roll bar
7. Adjustable track control arm

Suspension springing and damping is provided by the Hydragas unit mounted vertically above the upper suspension arm. An additional damper unit also vertically mounted to the upper suspension arm, is employed to provide a more responsive suspension. The damper unit assists in absorbing the energy stored in the Hydragas unit after passing a bump. Quickly terminating the reciprocating motion of the suspension and returning the Hydragas unit to the rest position.

The track control arm and lower arm make up the suspension wishbone to provide the necessary fore-and-aft stiffness to resist braking torque. A tie bar fitted between the lower arm and the front of the subframe, resists longitudinal dynamic loads and braking torque. Both upper suspension arms are interconnected by an anti-roll bar which provides the required stiffness to prevent body roll.

HYDRAGAS SYSTEM PROCEDURES AND TRIM HEIGHT ADJUSTMENT

Check - Trim height

1. Allow vehicle to stand in an unladen condition on a level surface.
2. Place steering in a straight ahead position.

⚠ **CAUTION: Do not check or adjust suspension trim height immediately after a road test. Allow vehicle to stand for at least two hours to allow suspension fluid temperature to equalise with air temperature.**

3. Bounce the vehicle at both ends a number of times and allow it to settle.
4. Roll vehicle forward 1 m to relieve suspension stresses.
5. Push down on front of vehicle and release, allow suspension to return unassisted. Do not apply handbrake.

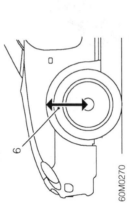

60M0270

6. Measure both front trim heights, hub centre to top centre of the front wheel arch:
   Front trim height = 368 ± 10 mm.

⚠ **CAUTION: Fluid in the suspension system is under very high pressure. Any repair or adjustment can only be carried out using specialist equipment.**

Adjust - Trim height

⚠ **CAUTION: To minimise problems caused by contamination of the hydragas system, it is important that all equipment is maintained in a clean condition. Only clean filtered fluid must be used in filling/pressurising equipment.**

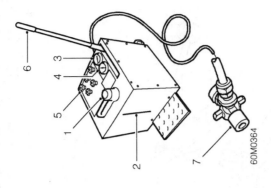

60M0364

Service tool 18G 703Q

1. Filler cap
2. Fluid level sight glass
3. Pressure gauge
4. Vacuum gauge
5. Control valves
6. Pump operating lever
7. Connector

This page is intentionally left blank

18G 703Q Hydragas Unit Valve Setting

VALVES	A	B	C	D	E
Pressure check	-	-	-	O	O
Drain	O	-	-	O	O
Evacuation	O	O	O	-	-
Fill	-	O	O	-	O
Pressurising	-	-	-	O	O

O = Valve Open
- = Valve closed

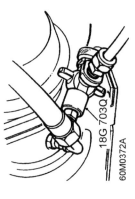

18G 703Q

60M0372A

TO ADJUST - Remove underbonnet closing panel. *See BODY, Exterior fittings.*

Fit connector of tool **18G 703Q** to displacer valve with the connector T-bar valve unscrewed. Any air which may have entered the tube during this operation should be carefully bled out by opening the bleed valve in the connector body and slowly pumping then close the bleed valve.

Ensure the service tool is ¼ full of hydralastic fluid before use.

Close valves 'A','B' and 'C'. Open valves 'D' and 'E'. Operate the pump until approx 100 psi is registered on the gauge. Screw in connector T-bar, and read pressure of displacer on gauge. Check trim height and adjust by increasing the fluid pressure to raise, or lower by slowly opening valve 'A' and reducing pressure until the correct pressure or trim height is reached.

When pressure check is completed, unscrew the connector T-bar and release pressure in unit by opening valve 'A', before removing connector from displacer.

Fit underbonnet closing panel. *See BODY, Exterior fittings.*

⚠ NOTE: Temperature will affect the suspension height. Trim height specification is correct at a nominal temperature of 17°C. Setting trim heights at temperatures above or below 17°C will cause the suspension trim height to be incorrect and should be compensated for, by the factor of 0.6 mm per 1°C, when temperatures are above or below this figure.

TO DEPRESSURISE OR DRAIN - Close valves 'A','B' and 'C'. Open valves 'D' and 'E'. Slowly open valve 'A' until pressure reads zero and movement of fluid in tube has stopped.

TO EVACUATE - Open valves 'A','B' and 'C'. Close valves 'D' and 'E'. Ensure the tubular pump is in the evacuation position, i.e. Turn pump handle anti-clockwise, lift and turn clockwise again to lock.

Operate pump slowly until 27 inches Hg is obtained and movement of fluid in the tube has stopped.

TO FILL DISPLACERS - Close valves 'A' and 'D'. Open valves 'B','C' and 'E'. Slowly open valve 'E' and wait until vacuum gauge has settled at zero.

TO PRESSURISE - Close valves 'A','B' and 'C'. Open valves 'D' and 'E'. Lower pump handle to pressurising position and pump to required pressure or trim height.

The vehicle should periodically bounced while pumping up to settle the displacer valves and avoid excessive pressure.

Drive the vehicle for a minimum of 2 miles to settle the suspension before resetting the trim height.

⚠ **CAUTION: Do not check or adjust suspension trim height immediately after a road test. Allow vehicle to stand for at least two hours to allow suspension fluid temperature to equalise with air temperature.**

HYDRAGAS UNIT TESTING

Test 18G 703Q, 18G 1743

If the trim height is low and there is no detectable fluid leak from the hydragas system, a leakage of nitrogen from one or more of the hydragas units is indicated.

1. Depressurise and evacuate the hydragas unit on the low side of the car.

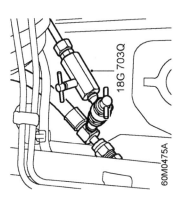

18G 703Q

60M0475A

2. Disconnect the connecting pipe from the suspect hydragas unit and fit the tool **18G 1743** to the unit. Pressurise the hydragas unit using tool **18G 703Q** and note the readings on the servicing unit pressure gauge.

3. The gauge readings should rise rapidly to 2172 kN/m² ± 3% (240 lbf/in² ± 20 lbf/in²), (this is the nominal nitrogen pressure) and then rise gradually at each operation of the servicing unit pump.

4. If the gauge reading continues to rise rapidly at each operation of the servicing unit pump after the nitrogen nominal pressure is reached, the unit is defective and must be renewed.

5. If a new Hydragas unit is fitted, or an existing Hydragas unit is refitted to the vehicle, the unit must be evacuated.

6. Adjust the pressure to give the correct trim height.

FRONT ANTI-ROLL BAR BUSHES

Service repair no - 68.10.06

Remove

1. Raise front of vehicle.

⚠️ **WARNING: Support on safety stands.**

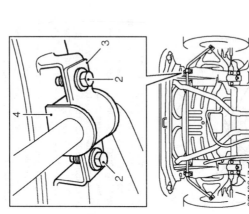

60M0317

2. Remove 2 bolts securing each anti-roll bar bush, clamp to subframe.
3. Remove 2 clamps.
4. Remove 2 bushes.

Refit

1. Clean anti-roll bar.
2. Fit bushes and align clamps to bolt holes.
3. Fit bolts to each anti-roll bar clamp and tighten to 22 Nm.
4. Remove stand(s) and lower vehicle.

REAR ANTI-ROLL BAR BUSHES

Service repair no - 68.10.07

Remove

1. Remove silencer heat shield. *See MANIFOLD & EXHAUST SYSTEMS, Repairs.*

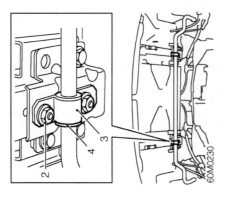

60M0230

2. Remove 2 nuts securing each anti-roll bar bush, clamp to subframe.
3. Remove 2 clamps.
4. Remove 2 bushes.

Refit

1. Clean anti-roll bar.
2. Fit bushes and align clamps to bolt holes.
3. Fit nuts to each anti-roll bar clamp and tighten to 22 Nm.
4. Fit silencer heat shield. *See MANIFOLD & EXHAUST SYSTEMS, Repairs.*

This page is intentionally left blank

FRONT ANTI-ROLL BAR

Service repair no - 68.10.09

Remove

1. Raise front of vehicle.

 WARNING: Support on safety stands.

60M0318

Anti-roll bar bushes

2. Remove 2 bolts securing each anti-roll bar bush, clamp to subframe.
3. Remove 2 clamps.
4. Remove 2 bushes.

Anti-roll bar links

5. Remove nut and bolt securing each link to anti-roll bar.
6. Remove nut securing anti-roll bar links to lower suspension arms.
7. Remove anti-roll bar links.
8. Check link bushes for wear.
9. Remove anti-roll bar.

Refit

1. Position anti-roll bar.

Anti-roll bar links

 CAUTION: The head on the bolt connecting the link to lower arm must face forward, to allow clearance between bolt and front hub.

2. Fit anti-roll bar links to lower suspension arm bolts and fit nut, do not tighten at this stage.
3. Align anti-roll bar links to anti-roll bar and fit bolt and nut, do not tighten at this stage.

Anti-roll bar bushes

4. Clean anti-roll bar.
5. Fit bushes and align clamps to bolt holes.
6. Fit bolts to each anti-roll bar clamp and tighten to 22 Nm.
7. Tighten nuts and bolts securing anti-roll bar links to 35 Nm.
8. Remove stand(s) and lower vehicle.

Refit

1. Position anti-roll bar.

Anti-roll bar links

2. Fit links to anti-roll bar, do not tighten at this stage.
3. Fit links to hub abutment brackets, do not tighten at this stage.

Anti-roll bar bushes

4. Clean anti-roll bar.
5. Fit bushes and align clamps to mounting bracket studs.
6. Fit nuts to each anti-roll bar clamp and tighten to 22 Nm.
7. Tighten nuts and bolts securing anti-roll bar links to 35 Nm.
8. Fit road wheel(s) and tighten nuts to correct torque. **See INFORMATION, Torque wrench settings.**
9. Fit silencer heat shield. **See MANIFOLD & EXHAUST SYSTEMS, Repairs.**

REAR ANTI-ROLL BAR

Service repair no - 68.10.10

Remove

1. Remove silencer heat shield. **See MANIFOLD & EXHAUST SYSTEMS, Repairs.**
2. Remove road wheel(s).

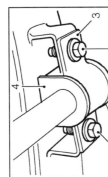
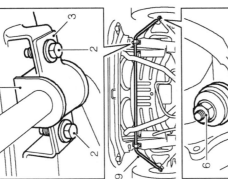

60M0231

Anti-roll bar bushes

3. Remove 2 nuts securing each anti-roll bar bush clamp.
4. Remove 2 clamps.
5. Remove 2 bushes.

Anti-roll bar links

6. Remove nut and bolt securing each link to anti-roll bar.
7. Remove nut and bolt securing each link to hub abutment brackets.
8. Remove anti-roll bar links.
9. Check link bushes for wear.
10. Remove anti-roll bar.

REAR ANTI-ROLL BAR LINK

Service repair no - 68.10.12

Remove

1. Raise rear of vehicle.

⚠ **WARNING: Support on safety stands.**

2. Remove road wheel(s).

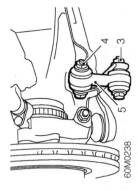

60M0232

3. Remove nut and bolt securing anti-roll bar to link.
4. Remove nut and bolt securing anti-roll bar link to hub abutment bracket.
5. Remove anti-roll bar link.

Refit

1. Fit link to anti-roll bar, fit bolt and tighten nut to 35 Nm.
2. Align link to hub abutment bracket, fit bolt and tighten nut to 35 Nm.
3. Fit road wheel(s) and tighten nuts to correct torque. **See INFORMATION, Torque wrench settings.**
4. Remove stand(s) and lower vehicle.

FRONT ANTI-ROLL BAR LINK

Service repair no - 68.10.14

Remove

1. Raise front of vehicle.

⚠ **WARNING: Support on safety stands.**

2. Remove road wheel(s).

60M0238

3. Remove nut and bolt securing anti-roll bar to link.
4. Remove nut securing anti-roll bar link to lower arm.
5. Remove anti-roll bar link.

Refit

⚠ **CAUTION: The head on the bolt connecting the link to lower arm must face forward, to allow clearance between bolt and front hub.**

1. Fit anti-roll bar link to lower arm bolt and fit nut, do not tighten at this stage.
2. Align link to anti-roll bar, fit bolt and tighten nut to 35 Nm.
3. Tighten anti-roll bar link to lower arm nut to 35 Nm.
4. Fit road wheel(s) and tighten nuts to correct torque. **See INFORMATION, Torque wrench settings.**
5. Remove stand(s) and lower vehicle.

FRONT BUMP RUBBER

Service repair no - 68.15.01

Remove

1. Raise front of vehicle.

⚠ **WARNING: Support on safety stands.**

2. Remove road wheel(s).

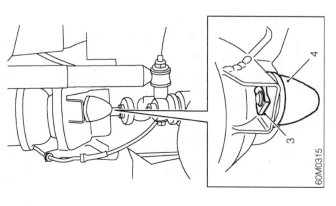

60M0315

3. Remove spring clip securing bump rubber to Hydragas unit retaining plate.
4. Collect bump rubber.

Refit

1. Fit bump rubber and secure with spring clip.
2. Fit road wheel(s) and tighten nuts to correct torque. **See INFORMATION, Torque wrench settings.**
3. Remove stand(s) and lower vehicle.

REAR BUMP RUBBER

Service repair no - 68.15.02

Remove

1. Raise rear of vehicle.

⚠ **WARNING: Support on safety stands.**

2. Remove road wheel(s).

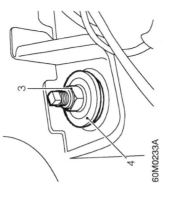

60M0315

3. Remove spring clip securing bump rubber to Hydragas unit retaining plate.
4. Collect bump rubber.

Refit

1. Fit bump rubber and secure with spring clip.
2. Fit road wheel(s) and tighten nuts to correct torque. **See INFORMATION, Torque wrench settings.**
3. Remove stand(s) and lower vehicle.

REBOUND RUBBERS

Service repair no - 68.15.08

Remove

1. Raise vehicle.

⚠ **WARNING: Support on safety stands.**

2. Remove road wheel(s).
3. Place trolley jack under hub and raise suspension.

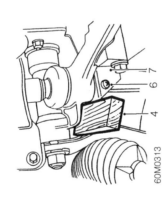

60M0313

4. Fit wedge between suspension arm and subframe. Lower suspension onto wedge and remove jack.

⚠ **CAUTION: Ensure that an appropriate wedge is used to prevent any damage occurring to the suspension components.**

5. Release ABS sensor lead from bracket.
6. Remove screw securing rebound rubber to subframe.
7. Remove rebound rubber.

Refit

1. Fit rebound rubber to subframe and tighten screw.
2. Secure ABS sensor lead in bracket.
3. Place trolley jack under hub and raise suspension.
4. Remove wedge, lower suspension, and remove trolley jack.
5. Fit road wheel(s) and tighten nuts to correct torque. **See INFORMATION, Torque wrench settings.**
6. Remove stand(s) and lower vehicle.

FRONT DAMPER

Service repair no - 68.15.16

Remove

1. Raise front of vehicle.

⚠ **WARNING: Support on safety stands.**

2. Remove road wheel(s).

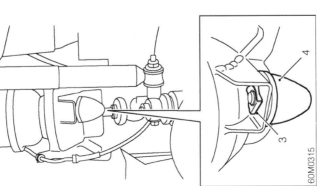

60M0233A

3. Remove nut securing damper to front wing valance.
4. Remove rubber bush and washer.

REAR DAMPER

Service repair no - 68.15.23

Remove

1. Raise rear of vehicle.

⚠ **WARNING: Support on safety stands.**

2. Remove road wheel(s).
3. Remove engine compartment access panel.
   See BODY, Exterior fittings.

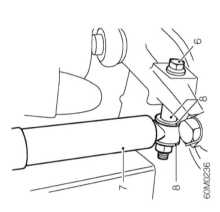

60M0235

4. Remove nut securing damper to rear wing
   valance.
5. Remove rubber bush and washer.

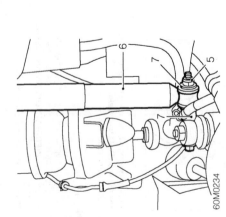

60M0234

5. Remove nut and bolt securing damper to upper
   suspension arm.
6. Remove damper.
7. Collect spacer and 2 washers.

Refit

1. Remove nut and bush from NEW damper.
2. Prime damper by operating at least 3 full
   strokes.
3. Position damper to front wing valance, fit top
   bush and tighten nut to 37 Nm.
4. Fit brake hose bracket, spacer, damper and
   washers to fixing bolt. Fit nut but do not tighten
   at this stage.
5. Fit road wheel(s) and tighten nuts to correct
   torque. **See INFORMATION, Torque wrench
   settings.**
6. Remove stand(s) and lower vehicle.
7. Tighten damper lower fixing nut to 45 Nm.

UPPER ARM - FRONT

Service repair no - 68.20.02

Remove

1. Raise front of vehicle.

⚠ **WARNING: Support on safety stands.**

2. Remove road wheel(s).
3. Remove underbonnet closing panel. **See
   BODY, Exterior fittings.**
4. Depressurise one side of Hydragas system.
   See FRONT SUSPENSION, Adjustments.
5. Remove front bumper armature. **See BODY,
   Exterior fittings.**

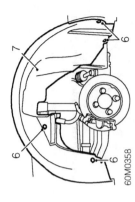

60M0358

6. Remove screw and 3 scrivets securing wheel
   arch liner.
7. Remove wheel arch liner.

60M0236

6. Remove nut and bolt securing damper to upper
   suspension arm.
7. Remove damper.
8. Collect spacer and 2 washers.

Refit

1. Remove nut and bush from NEW damper.
2. Prime damper by operating at least 3 full
   strokes.
3. Position damper to rear wing valance, fit top
   bush and tighten nut to 37 Nm.
4. Align ABS sensor bracket, fit spacer, damper
   and washers to damper lower fixing bolt, and fit
   to upper arm. Fit nut, but do not tighten at this
   stage.
5. Fit road wheel(s) and tighten nuts to correct
   torque. **See INFORMATION, Torque wrench
   settings.**
6. Remove stand(s) and lower vehicle.
7. Tighten damper lower fixing nut to 45 Nm. **See
   BODY, Exterior fittings.**
8. Fit engine compartment access panel. **See
   BODY, Exterior fittings.**

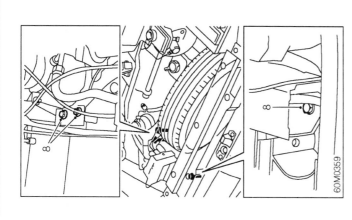

60M0359

8. Remove 3 bolts securing front subframe box section.
9. Remove box section.

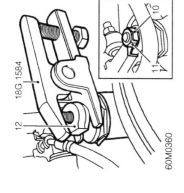

60M0360

10. Bend tab washer from ball joint nut.
11. Remove ball joint nut.
12. Break ball joint using tool **18G 1584.**

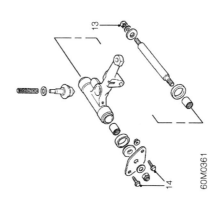

60M0361

13. Remove nut securing rear most end of upper arm pivot shaft.
14. Remove 2 bolts securing pivot shaft retaining plate.

△ NOTE: Inner bolt has captive nut.

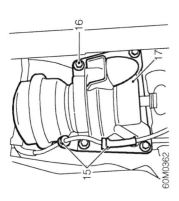

60M0362

15. Release ABS sensor lead.
16. Remove 4 bolts securing Hydragas unit retaining plate and sensor bracket.
17. Remove Hydragas unit retaining plate and collect ABS sensor bracket.

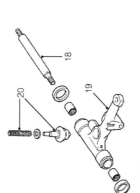

60M0363

18. Remove pivot shaft.
19. Remove upper arm from subframe and Hydragas unit.
20. Collect Hydragas roller foot joint, spacer and spring.

△ NOTE: Be aware of position of washers when removing the upper arm.

Refit

1. Fit bearings to upper arm. **See FRONT SUSPENSION, Repairs.**
2. Fit roller foot joint, spacer and spring to upper arm, secure rubber boot.
3. Position upper arm and seals.
4. Lubricate pivot shaft with Dextragrease super GP.
5. Fit pivot shaft.
6. Fit Hydragas unit retaining plate and sensor bracket, and tighten bolts to 25 Nm.
7. Tighten bolts securing pivot shaft retaining plate to 10 Nm.
8. Fit nut and washer to other end of pivot shaft, and tighten bolt to 74 Nm.
9. Fit hub to upper arm and tighten ball joint nut to 54 Nm.
10. Bend tab washer onto ball joint nut.
11. Fit subframe box section and tighten bolts to 45 Nm.
12. Fit wheel arch liner.
13. Fit scrivets and screw securing wheel arch liner.
14. Fit front bumper armature. **See BODY, Exterior fittings.**
15. Fit road wheel(s) and tighten nuts to correct torque. **See INFORMATION, Torque wrench settings.**
16. Evacuate and pressurise Hydragas system. **See FRONT SUSPENSION, Repairs.**
17. Fit underbonnet closing panel. **See BODY, Exterior fittings.**

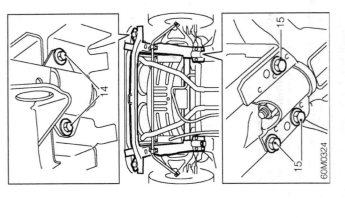

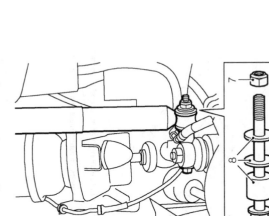

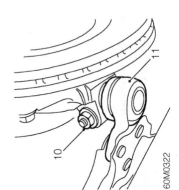

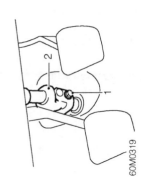

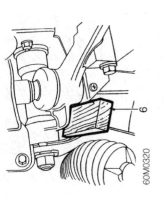

SUSPENSION

FRONT LOWER ARM

Service repair no - 68.20.10

Remove

1. Remove bolt securing steering column universal joint to rack pinion.
2. Release column universal joint from rack pinion.
3. Raise front of vehicle.

⚠ **WARNING: Support on safety stands.**

4. Remove road wheel(s).
5. Place a jack under front hub and raise suspension.

60M0319

6. Fit a wedge between suspension arm and subframe, lower suspension onto wedge and remove jack.

60M0320

⚠ **CAUTION: Ensure that an appropriate wedge is used to prevent any damage occurring to the suspension components.**

7. Remove nut and bolt, securing brake hose to upper arm.
8. Collect spacer and 2 washers.
9. Repeat steps 5 to 8 on opposite side.

60M0321

10. Remove nut and bolt securing ball joint to lower arm.
11. Release ball joint from hub.

60M0322

12. Remove nut and bolt securing anti-roll bar link to lower arm.
13. Support rear of front subframe on a jack.

60M0323

14. Slacken 4 nuts and bolts securing front subframe mountings to front panel.
15. Remove 6 bolts securing front subframe rear mountings to body.
16. Lower subframe on jack to gain access to lower suspension arm rear retaining bolt.

60M0324

Refit

1. Fit lower arm to subframe.
2. Fit bolts securing lower arm to subframe, do not tighten at this stage.
3. Raise subframe on jack.
4. Align subframe to body mountings, fit bolts and tighten to 45 Nm.
5. Tighten nuts and bolts securing front subframe mountings to front panel to 32 Nm.
6. Remove jack.
7. Align anti-roll bar link to lower arm.
8. Fit nut and bolt securing anti-roll bar link to lower arm, do not tighten at this stage.
9. Position hub to lower ball joint, fit nut and bolt and tighten to 45 Nm.
10. Fit brake hose bracket, spacer, washers and damper to upper arm bolt, tighten nut to 45 Nm.
11. Place a jack beneath hub, raise hub on jack and remove wedge. Lower jack and remove.
12. Repeat steps 10 to 11 on opposite side.
13. Fit road wheel(s) and tighten nuts to correct torque. **See INFORMATION, Torque wrench settings.**
14. Remove stand(s) and lower vehicle.
15. With vehicle at nominal trim height:
    - Tighten lower arm to subframe bolts to 85 Nm.
    - Tighten anti-roll bar link to lower arm nuts and bolts to 35 Nm.
16. Fit bolt access grommet to subframe.
17. Align and connect steering column intermediate shaft to rack pinion.
18. Fit bolt and tighten to 22 Nm.

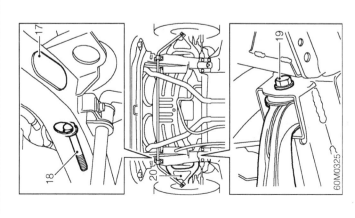

17. Remove lower arm bolt, access grommet from subframe.
18. Remove front bolt securing lower arm to subframe.
19. Remove rear bolt securing lower arm to subframe.
20. Remove lower arm.

FRONT LOWER ARM BUSHES

Service repair no - 68.20.14

Remove

1. Remove front lower arm. **See this section.**

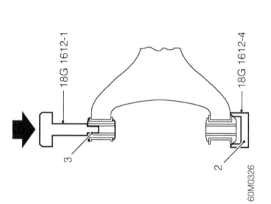

60M0326

2. Remove front bush using press, position lower arm with front bush uppermost and support with tool **18G 1612-4** under rear bush.
3. Fit tool **18G 1612-1** to front bush and press bush from lower arm.
4. Reposition arm under press with rear bush uppermost.

5. Fit tool **18G 1612-1** to rear bush and press bush from arm.

Refit

1. Clean lower arm and bush locations.
2. Position lower arm in press with rear bush located uppermost.
3. Lubricate rear bush with Marlene 148 rubber lubricant.
4. Fit tool **18G 1612-2** to rear bush location.

60M0327

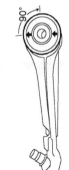

SP60 0001

5. Fit rear bush into tool **18G 1612-2** with the rounded flange uppermost with the arrows on bush pointing 90° from ball joint for MG-F Trophy and the arrows pointing towards ball joint for all other models.

18G 1612-1
18G 1612-2

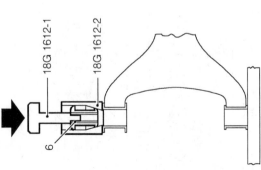

60M0329

6. Fit tool **18G 1612-1** to the rear bush and press into lower arm.

18G 1612-1
18G 1612-3
18G 1612-4

11
8
10
7

60M0330

7. Position lower arm with tool **18G 1612-4**.
8. Fit tool **18G 1612-3** to front bush location.
9. Lubricate front bush with Marlene 148 rubber lubricant.
10. Fit bush into tool **18G 1612-3** with flat flange uppermost
11. Press bush into lower arm using tool **18G 1612-1**.
12. Remove arm from press.
13. Fit front lower arm. *See this section.*

⚠ **CAUTION: Inspect and clean bearing housings prior to reassembly. If any wear or damage is present due to worn bearings, the arm must be renewed.**

UPPER ARM BEARINGS - FRONT

Service repair no - 68.20.18

Remove

1. Raise front of vehicle.

⚠ **WARNING: Support on safety stands.**

2. Remove road wheel(s).
3. Remove upper arm. *See this section.*

18G 582
18G 582/1

M60 0774

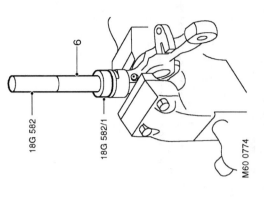

18G 581

5
4

60M0348

4. Place upper arm in vice.
5. Remove needle roller bearings using tool **18G 581**.
6. Align and press NEW needle roller bearings into upper arm using tools **18G 582** and **18G 582/1**

Refit

1. Refit upper arm. *See this section.*
2. Fit road wheel(s) and tighten nuts to correct torque. *See INFORMATION, Torque wrench settings.*
3. Remove stand(s) and lower vehicle.

UPPER BALL JOINT - FRONT HUB

Service repair no - 68.25.05

Remove

1. Raise front of vehicle.

⚠ **WARNING: Support on safety stands.**

2. Remove road wheel(s).
3. Place jack under hub and raise suspension.

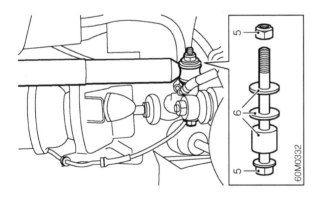

60M0331

4. Fit a wedge between suspension arm and subframe, lower suspension onto wedge and remove jack.

⚠ **CAUTION: Ensure that an appropriate wedge is used to prevent any damage occurring to the suspension components.**

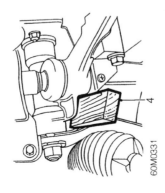

60M0332

5. Remove nut and bolt securing brake hose to upper arm.
6. Collect spacer and 2 washers.

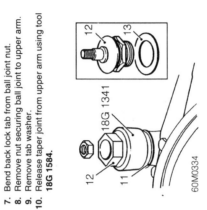

10 18G 1584

8

60M0333

7. Bend back lock tab from ball joint nut.
8. Remove nut securing ball joint to upper arm.
9. Remove tab washer.
10. Release taper joint from upper arm using tool **18G 1584.**

12   13

12   18G 1341

12   11

60M0334

11. Bend back lock washer securing ball joint to hub.
12. Remove ball joint using tool **18G 1341.**
13. Remove lock washer.

Refit

1. Fit NEW lock washer.
2. Fit ball joint to hub using tool **18G 1341** and tighten to 105 Nm.
3. Bend over lock washer to hub and ball joint nut.
4. Position hub ball joint to upper arm, fit NEW tab washer, fit nut and tighten to 54 Nm.
5. Bend over ball joint tab washer.
6. Fit brake hose bracket, spacer, washers and damper to upper arm bolt, tighten nut to 45 Nm.
7. Place a jack beneath hub, raise hub on jack and remove wedge. Lower jack and remove.
8. Fit road wheel(s) and tighten nuts to correct torque. *See INFORMATION, Torque wrench settings.*
9. Remove stand(s) and lower vehicle.

LOWER BALL JOINT - FRONT HUB

Service repair no - 68.25.06

Remove

1. Remove front lower arm. *See this section.*

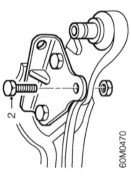

60M0339

2. Centre punch centres of rivet heads.
3. Drill pilot hole in rivet heads.
4. Enlarge pilot hole to remove rivets.

⚠ **CAUTION: Do not enlarge holes in lower arm.**

△ NOTE: Use pedestal drill for accuracy.

5. Press out rivet studs.
6. Remove ball joint assembly.

Refit

1. Fit ball joint to lower arm.

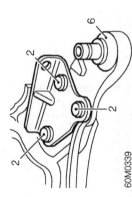

60M0470

2. Fit 3 bolts and nuts, tighten to 40 Nm.

△ NOTE: Ensure bolt heads are fitted above the arm.

3. Fit front lower arm. *See this section.*

FRONT HUB BEARINGS

Service repair no - 68.25.13

Remove

1. Raise front of vehicle.

⚠ **WARNING: Support on safety stands.**

2. Remove road wheel(s).
3. Knock back hub nut stake.
4. Remove hub nut.
5. Place jack under hub and raise hub.

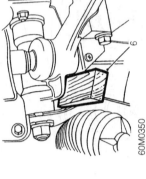

60M0350

6. Fit a wedge between suspension arm and subframe, lower suspension onto wedge and remove jack.

⚠ **CAUTION: Ensure that an appropriate wedge is used to prevent any damage occurring to the suspension components.**

7. Remove front brake disc. *See BRAKES, Repairs.*

18G 1584

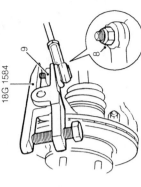

60M0351

8. Remove nut securing track-rod end to steering arm.
9. Release taper joint using tool **18G 1584**.

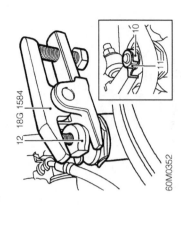

60M0352

10. Bend back tab washer from ball joint nut.
11. Remove nut and tab washer securing ball joint to upper arm.
12. Release taper joint from upper arm using tool **18G 1584**.

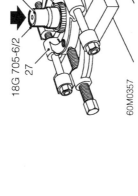

60M0353

13. Remove nut and bolt securing hub to lower arm, ball joint.
14. Release hub from lower ball joint.
15. Remove front hub assembly.

18G 1358/4

60M0354

16. Position hub to press.
17. Press out drive flange using tool 18G 1358/4.
18. Collect drive flange.
19. Remove hub from press.

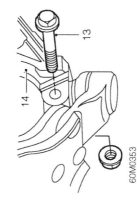

60M0355

20. Remove bearing outer circlip.
21. Remove bearing inner circlip.

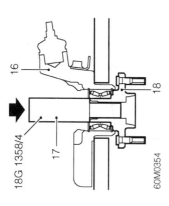

60M0356

22. Position hub to press.
23. Fit tool 18G 705-6/3 to bearing.
24. Press out bearing.
25. Remove hub from press.

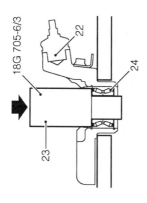

60M0357

26. Position drive flange to press.
27. Fit a universal bearing splitter to bearing. (as shown)
28. Fit thrust button, tool 18G 705-6/2 to drive flange.
29. Press out drive flange from inner track.
30. Collect drive flange.
31. Remove bearing inner track.

Refit

1. Clean hub and bearing mating faces.
2. Fit NEW bearing outer circlip to hub.
3. Position hub to press.
4. Press bearing into hub using tool 18G 705-6/3.
5. Fit NEW bearing inner circlip to hub.
6. Clean drive flange to bearing mating face.
7. Using tools 18G 134BD and 18G 705-6/3 press drive flange into hub.
8. Remove hub from press.
9. Clean drive shaft end and hub mating faces.
10. Clean lower ball joint to hub mating faces.
11. Fit hub to lower ball joint, fit bolt and tighten nut to 45 Nm.
12. Clean upper ball joint to top arm mating faces.
13. Position upper ball joint to top arm.
14. Fit tab washer and nut to upper ball joint and tighten to 54 Nm.
15. Lock over ball joint tab washer to secure nut.
16. Clean steering track-rod to hub mating faces.
17. Align steering track-rod end to steering arm, fit nut and tighten to 30 Nm.
18. Fit front brake disc. See *BRAKES, Repairs.*
19. Place jack under front hub and raise hub.
20. Remove wedge from between top arm and subframe.
21. Lower hub and remove jack.
22. Fit a NEW hub nut and tighten to 210 Nm.

▷ NOTE: Assistance will be required to depress the brake pedal to allow the tightening of the drive shaft nut.

23. Stake drive shaft nut to shaft.
24. Fit road wheel(s) and tighten nuts to correct torque. See *INFORMATION, Torque wrench settings.*
25. Remove stand(s) and lower vehicle.

UPPER BALL JOINT - REAR HUB

Service repair no - 68.25.27

Remove

1. Raise rear of vehicle.
   Remove road wheel.
   Place jack under rear hub and raise suspension.

⚠️ **WARNING: Support on safety stands.**

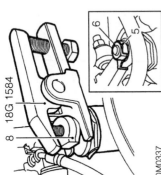

60M0335

2. Fit a wedge between suspension arm and subframe, lower suspension onto wedge and remove jack.

⚠️ **CAUTION: Ensure that an appropriate wedge is used to prevent any damage occurring to the suspension components.**

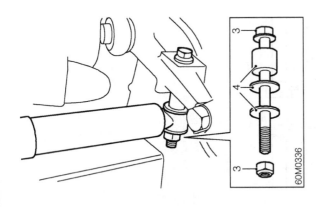

60M0336

3. Remove nut and bolt securing rear damper to upper arm.
4. Collect spacer and 2 washers.

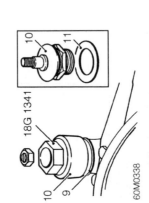

60M0337

5. Bend back lock tab from ball joint nut.
6. Remove nut securing ball joint to upper arm.
7. Remove tab washer.
8. Release taper joint from upper arm using tool **18G 1584.**

60M0338

9. Bend back lock washer securing ball joint to hub.
10. Remove ball joint using tool **18G 1341**.
11. Remove lock washer.

Refit

1. Fit NEW lock washer.
2. Fit ball joint to hub using tool **18G 1341** and tighten to 105 Nm.
3. Bend over lock washer to hub and ball joint nut.
4. Position ball joint to upper arm, fit NEW tab washer, fit nut and tighten to 54 Nm.
5. Bend over ball joint tab washer.
6. Fit ABS sensor lead bracket, spacer, washers and damper to upper arm bolt, tighten nut to 45 Nm.
7. Place a jack beneath hub, raise hub and remove wedge. Lower jack and remove.
8. Fit road wheel(s) and tighten nuts to correct torque. See *INFORMATION, Torque wrench settings.*
9. Remove stand(s) and lower vehicle.

REAR HUB BEARINGS

Service repair no - 68.25.38

Remove

1. Raise rear of vehicle.

⚠ **WARNING: Support on safety stands.**

2. Remove road wheel(s).
3. Knock back drive shaft nut stake.
4. Remove drive shaft nut.
5. Remove rear brake disc. **See BRAKES, Repairs.**

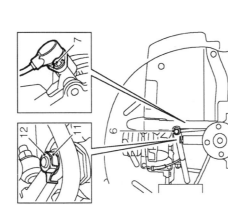

60M0281

6. Remove nut and bolt securing anti-roll bar to link.
7. Remove bolt securing ABS sensor to hub, release sensor and position aside.
8. Remove nut securing track control arm to hub.
9. Release taper joint using tool **18G 1584.**
10. Remove bolt securing lower arm to hub.

11. Bend back tab washer from upper ball joint nut.
12. Remove nut and tab washer from upper arm ball joint.
13. Release taper joint from upper arm using tool **18G 1584.**
14. Remove rear hub assembly from drive shaft.

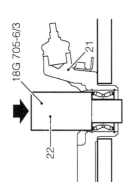

60M0282

15. Position hub to press.
16. Press out drive flange using tool **18G 1358/4.**
17. Collect drive flange.
18. Remove hub from press.

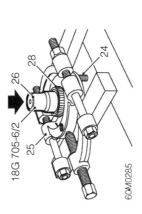

60M0283

19. Remove bearing outer circlip.
20. Remove bearing inner circlip.

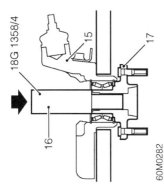

60M0284

21. Position hub to press.
22. Fit tool **18G 705-6/3** to bearing and press out bearing.
23. Remove hub from press.

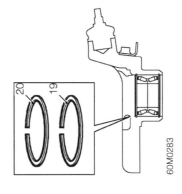

60M0285

24. Position drive flange to press.
25. Fit a universal bearing splitter to bearing. (as shown)
26. Fit thrust button, tool **18G 705-6/2** to drive flange and press out drive flange from inner track.
27. Collect drive flange.
28. Remove bearing inner track.

Refit

1. Clean hub and bearing mating faces.
2. Fit NEW bearing outer circlip to hub.
3. Position hub to press.
4. Press bearing into hub using tool **18G 705-6/3.**
5. Fit NEW bearing inner circlip to hub.
6. Clean drive flange to bearing mating face.
7. Using tools **18G 134BD** and **18G 705-6/3** press drive flange into hub.
8. Remove hub from press.
9. Clean drive shaft end and hub mating faces.
10. Fit hub to drive shaft.
11. Clean upper arm ball joint.
12. Engage ball joint pin to upper arm.
13. Fit tab washer and nut and tighten to 54 Nm.
14. Lock over ball joint tab washer to secure nut.
15. Align lower arm to hub, fit bolt and tighten to 100 Nm.

▷ NOTE: Loctite must be applied to bolt, connecting lower arm to hub.

16. Clean track control arm, ball joint.
17. Engage track control arm, ball joint to hub, fit nut and tighten to 30 Nm.
18. Align anti-roll bar to link, fit bolt and tighten nut to 35 Nm.
19. Position ABS sensor lead to hub, fit NEW bolt and tighten to 10 Nm.
20. Fit rear brake disc. **See BRAKES, Repairs.**
21. Fit NEW drive shaft nut and tighten to 210 Nm.

▷ NOTE: Assistance will be required to depress the brake pedal to allow the tightening of the drive shaft nut.

22. Stake drive shaft nut to shaft.
23. Fit road wheel(s) and tighten nuts to correct torque. **See INFORMATION, Torque wrench settings.**
24. Remove stand(s) and lower vehicle.

FRONT HYDRAGAS UNIT

Service repair no - 68.30.08

Remove

1. Raise front of vehicle.

⚠ WARNING: Support on safety stands.

2. Remove road wheel(s).
3. Remove front wheel arch liner. *See BODY, Exterior fittings.*
4. Depressurise one side of suspension. *See Adjustments.*

5. Release ABS sensor lead from 2 clips on hydragas unit retaining plate.
6. Remove 2 nuts and 4 bolts from hydragas unit retaining plate, remove retaining plate.
7. Collect ABS sensor lead bracket.
8. Loosen hydragas unit union and release pipe from unit.
9. Remove hydragas unit.

⚠ CAUTION: Plug the connections.

11. Remove retaining plate and sensor bracket.
12. Release hydragas unit from roller foot joint.
13. Remove hydragas unit.

⚠ CAUTION: Plug the connections.

Refit

1. Clean hydragas unit and roller foot joint mating faces.
2. Remove plugs and clean connections.
3. Fit hydragas unit, position pipe and tighten union to 20 Nm.
4. Align hydragas unit to subframe, fit retaining plate and ABS sensor lead bracket, tighten nuts and bolts to 25 Nm.
5. Secure sensor lead to clips.
6. Fit front wheel arch line. *See BODY, Exterior fittings.*
7. Fit road wheel(s) and tighten nuts to correct torque. *See INFORMATION, Torque wrench settings.*
8. Remove stand(s) and lower vehicle.
9. Evacuate and pressurise hydragas system. *See Adjustments.*

REAR HYDRAGAS UNIT

Service repair no - 68.30.10

Remove

1. Raise rear of vehicle.

⚠ WARNING: Support on safety stands.

2. Remove road wheel(s).
3. Depressurise one side of system. *See Adjustments.*
4. Remove engine compartment access panel. *See BODY, Exterior fittings.*
5. Remove bolts securing engine control module bracket and move aside.

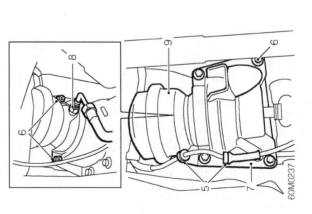

6. Loosen pipe union from hydragas unit and release pipe.
7. Remove 2 scrivets and Torx screw from closing panel.
8. Remove closing panel.
9. Release ABS sensor lead.
10. Remove 4 bolts securing hydragas unit retaining plate and sensor bracket.

Refit

1. Clean hydragas unit and roller foot joint mating faces.
2. Fit hydragas unit.
3. Align retaining plate and sensor bracket, fit bolts, and tighten to 25 Nm.
4. Secure ABS sensor lead.
5. Fit closing panel and secure scrivets.
6. Remove plugs and clean connections.
7. Reconnect pipe to hydragas unit. Tighten connection to 20 Nm.
8. Fit and tighten bolts securing engine control module bracket.
9. Fit engine compartment access panel. *See BODY, Exterior fittings.*
10. Fit road wheel(s) and tighten nuts to correct torque. *See INFORMATION, Torque wrench settings.*
11. Remove stand(s) and lower vehicle.
12. Evacuate and pressurise hydragas system. *See Adjustments.*

ROLLER FOOT JOINT - FRONT

Service repair no - 68.30.17

Remove

1. Remove front hydragas unit. *See this section.*

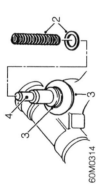

60M0314

2. Remove spring and spacer from roller foot joint.
3. Remove clips securing rubber gaiter to roller foot joint.
4. Remove roller foot joint from upper arm.

Refit

NOTE: The roller foot joint is a sealed unit and needs no lubrication. If the roller foot joint comes apart, it should be cleaned and repacked with Dextragrease Super GP.

1. Clean roller foot joint seat and strut location.
2. Fit roller foot joint to upper arm and secure gaiter with clips.

NOTE: Ensure that the lug on roller foot joint enters recess in upper arm.

3. Fit spacer and spring to roller foot joint.
4. Fit front hydragas unit. *See this section.*

ROLLER FOOT JOINT - REAR

Service repair no - 68.30.19

Remove

1. Remove rear hydragas unit. *See this section.*

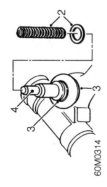

60M0314

2. Remove spring and spacer from roller foot joint.
3. Remove clips securing rubber gaiter to roller foot joint.
4. Remove roller foot joint from upper arm.

Refit

NOTE: The roller foot joint is a sealed unit and needs no lubrication. If the roller foot joint comes apart, it should be cleaned and repacked with Dextragrease Super GP.

1. Clean roller foot joint seat and location.
2. Fit roller foot joint to upper arm and secure gaiter with clips.

NOTE: Ensure that the lug on roller foot joint enters recess in upper arm.

3. Fit spacer and spring to roller foot joint.
4. Fit rear hydragas unit. *See this section.*

CAUTION: Inspect and clean bearing housings prior to reassembly. If any wear or damage is present due to worn bearings, the arm must be renewed.

Refit

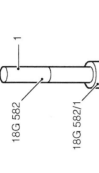
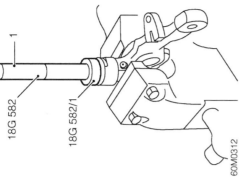

18G 582

18G 582/1

60M0312

1. Align and press NEW needle roller bearings into upper arm using tools **18G 582** and **18G 582/1**.
2. Refit upper arm. *See this section.*
3. Fit road wheel(s) and tighten nuts to correct torque. *See INFORMATION, Torque wrench settings.*
4. Remove stand(s) and lower vehicle.

UPPER ARM BEARINGS - REAR

Service repair no - 68.35.29

Remove

1. Raise rear of vehicle.

WARNING: Support on safety stands.

2. Remove road wheel(s).
3. Remove upper arm. *See this section.*

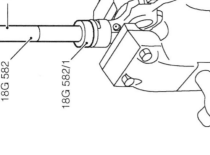

18G 581

60M0279

4. Place upper arm in vice.
5. Remove needle roller bearings using tool **18G 581**.

SUSPENSION

UPPER ARM - REAR

Service repair no - 68.35.31

Remove

1. Raise rear of vehicle.

⚠ **WARNING: Support on safety stands.**

2. Remove road wheel(s).
3. Depressurise one side of hydragas system. *See Adjustments.*

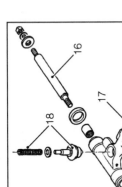

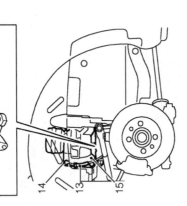

4. Remove nut and bolt securing damper to upper arm.
5. Release damper from upper arm.
6. Bend tab washer from ball joint nut.
7. Remove ball joint nut.

8. Break ball joint using tool **18G 1584.**
9. Remove 2 scrivets and Torx screw securing closing panel.
10. Remove closing panel.
11. Remove nut securing RH end of upper arm, pivot shaft.
12. Remove 2 bolts securing pivot shaft retaining plate.

⚠ NOTE: Inner bolt has captive nut.

SUSPENSION

Refit

1. Fit roller foot joint, spacer and spring to upper arm, secure rubber boot.
2. Position upper arm and seals.
3. Lubricate pivot shaft with Dextragrease super GP.
4. Fit pivot shaft.
5. Fit hydragas unit retaining plate and sensor bracket, and tighten bolts to 25 Nm.
6. Tighten bolts securing pivot shaft retaining plate to 10 Nm.
7. Fit nut and washer to other end of pivot shaft, and tighten bolt to 74 Nm.
8. Fit closing panel and secure scrivets.
9. Fit hub to upper arm and tighten ball joint nut to 54 Nm.
10. Bend new tab washer onto ball joint nut.
11. Fit damper to upper arm and tighten nut to 50 Nm.
12. Fit road wheel(s) and tighten nuts to correct torque. *See INFORMATION, Torque wrench settings.*
13. Remove stand(s) and lower vehicle.
14. Evacuate and pressurise hydragas system. *See Adjustments.*

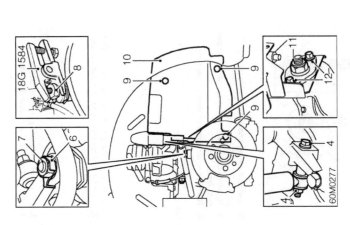

60M0278

13. Release ABS sensor lead.
14. Remove 4 bolts securing hydragas unit retaining plate and sensor bracket.
15. Remove hydragas unit retaining plate and collect ABS sensor bracket.
16. Remove pivot shaft.
17. Remove upper arm from subframe and hydragas unit.
18. Collect hydragas roller foot joint, spacer and spring.

⚠ NOTE: Be aware of position of washers when removing the upper arm.

LOWER ARM - REAR

Service repair no - 68.35.12

Remove

1. Remove tie bar *See this section.*
2. Remove grommet from aperture in subframe.

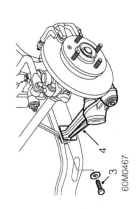

60M0467

3. Using aperture in subframe for access, remove bolt securing lower arm to subframe.
4. Collect lower arm.

Refit

1. Position lower arm to subframe and fit bolt, do not tighten at this stage.
2. Fit tie bar *See this section.*
3. With vehicle at nominal trim height, tighten bolt securing lower arm to subframe to 85 Nm
4. Fit grommet to subframe aperture.

BUSHES - LOWER ARM - REAR

Service repair no - 68.35.16

Remove

1. Remove lower arm. *See this section.*
2. Position lower arm in a press.

Inner bush

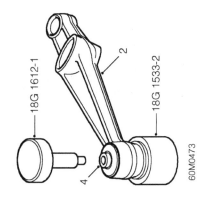

18G 1612-1
2
18G 1533-2

60M0473

> NOTE: Note the orientation of the inner bush in the lower arm.

3. Support lower arm with tool **18G 1533-2** so that smaller bevelled end of inner bush enters tool first.
4. Insert tool **18G 1612-1** into top of inner bush.
5. Press inner bush from lower arm.

Outer bush

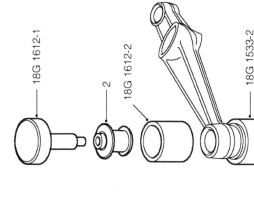

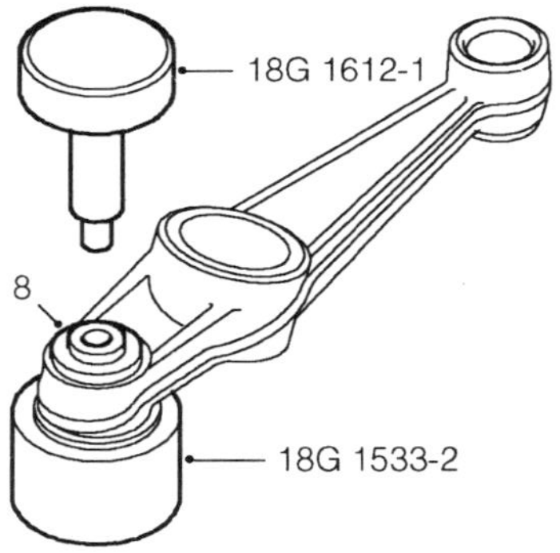

18G 1612-1
18G 1533-2

60M0471

6. Support lower arm with tool **18G 1533-2** to allow outer bush to enter tool.
7. Insert tool **18G 1612-1** into top of outer bush.
8. Press outer bush from lower arm.

Refit

1. Clean lower arm bush locations.

Inner bush

18G 1612-1
2
18G 1612-2
18G 1533-2

60M0474

2. Lubricate inner bush with Marlene 148 rubber lubricant.
3. Support lower arm on tool **18G 1533-2**.
4. Insert inner bush into guide tool **18G 1612-2** so that smaller bevelled end of bush enters lower arm first.
5. Position guide tool to top of lower arm.
6. Insert tool **18G 1612-1** into top of inner bush.
7. Press inner bush into position.

Outer bush

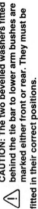

18G 1612-1

18

18G 1612-3

18G 1533-2

M60 0775

8. Lubricate outer bush with Marlene 148 rubber lubricant.
9. Support lower arm on tool **18G 1533-2.**
10. Insert outer bush into guide tool **18G 1612-3.**
11. Position guide tool to top of lower arm.
12. Insert tool **18G 1612-1** into top of outer bush.
13. Press outer bush into position.
14. Fit lower arm. *See this section.*

TIE BAR - REAR

Service repair no - 68.35.13

Remove

⚠ **CAUTION: The two bevelled washers fitted behind the tie bar to lower arm bushes are marked either front or rear. They must be fitted in their correct positions.**

1. Raise rear of vehicle.

⚠ **WARNING: Support on safety stands.**

2. Remove road wheel(s).

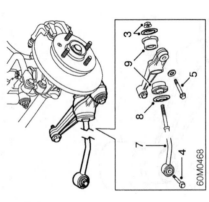

60M0468

3. Remove nut securing tie bar to lower arm, collect rear washer.
4. Remove bolt securing tie bar to subframe.
5. Remove bolt securing lower arm to hub.
6. Hinge lower arm down and remove tie bar from subframe.
7. Remove tie bar from lower arm.
8. Collect front washer.
9. Remove both tie bar bushes from lower arm.

Refit

1. Fit tie bar bushes to lower arm.
2. Position front washer and fit tie bar to lower arm.
3. Hinge lower arm down and fit tie bar to subframe.
4. Apply Loctite and fit bolt securing lower arm to hub, do not tighten bolt at this stage.
5. Fit bolt securing tie bar to subframe, do not tighten at this stage.
6. Fit rear washer and nut securing tie bar to lower arm, do not tighten at this stage.
7. Fit road wheel(s) and tighten nuts to correct torque. *See* **INFORMATION, Torque wrench settings.**
8. Remove stand(s) and lower vehicle.
9. Tighten the following fixings with the suspension at nominal trim height:
   Lower arm to hub bolt 100 Nm,
   Tie bar to subframe bolt 45 Nm,
   Tie bar to lower arm nut 80 Nm.

BUSHES - TIE BAR - REAR

Service repair no - 68.35.15

1. Refer to tie bar - rear. *See this section.*

TRACK CONTROL ARM - REAR

Service repair no - 68.35.14

Remove

1. Raise rear of vehicle.

⚠ WARNING: Support on safety stands.

2. Remove road wheel(s).

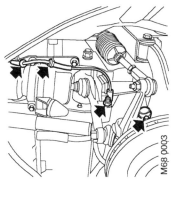

3. Remove bolt securing track control arm to subframe.
4. Remove nut securing track control arm to hub.
5. Using tool **18G 1584** release taper on track control arm, ball joint.
6. Collect track control arm.

60M0469

Refit

1. Position track control arm to subframe.
2. Connect ball joint to hub.
3. Fit bolt securing track control arm to subframe and tighten to 80 Nm.
4. Fit nut securing track control arm to hub and tighten to 30 Nm.
5. Fit road wheel(s) and tighten nuts to correct torque. **See INFORMATION, Torque wrench settings.**
6. Remove stand(s) and lower vehicle.

⚠ **CAUTION: Ensure that the track control arm has rotational movement. This can be checked by grasping the track control arm and rotating it backwards and forwards on the ball joints.**

7. Check rear wheel alignment.

---

11. Remove front road wheels.

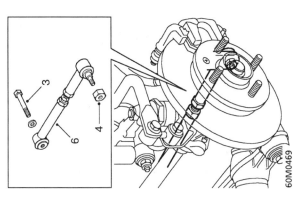

M68 0003

12. Remove nut and bolt securing LH damper to hub.
13. Remove bolt securing LH ABS sensor to caliper. Release sensor and collect spacer. Release sensor lead from grommets.
14. Release sensor lead from grommets.

SUBFRAME - FRONT

Service repair no - 68.40.01

Remove

1. Position vehicle on '2-post' ramp.
2. Disconnect battery earth lead.
3. Disconnect battery positive lead.
4. Release main fuse and fuse box connectors, and release from clips. Position lead aside.

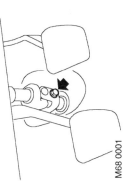

M68 0001

5. Remove bolt securing steering column universal joint to steering rack.
6. Release steering column from steering rack. **See AIR CONDITIONING, Adjustments.**
7. **Models with A/C:** Evacuate A/C system. **See AIR CONDITIONING, Adjustments.**
8. **All models:** Depressurise both sides of hydragas system. **See Adjustments.**

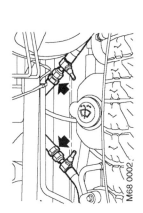

M68 0002

9. Disconnect hydragas pipe unions from valves.
10. Remove and discard 'O' rings.

⚠ **CAUTION: Plug the connections.**

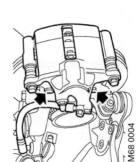

M68 0004

15. Remove 2 bolts securing LH front brake caliper to hub and release caliper from hub.
16. Tie caliper aside.
17. Repeat above operations for other side.
18. Raise vehicle on ramp.
19. Drain cooling system. See *COOLING SYSTEM, Adjustments*.
20. **Steptronic EM-CVT models:** Drain gearbox fluid. See *AUTOMATIC GEARBOX - 'EM-CVT', Adjustments*.
21. Loosen fluid cooler pipe unions and release fluid cooler pipes.

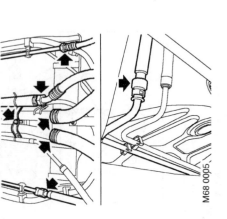

M68 0005

22. **All models:** Remove nut and bolt securing coolant pipe support bracket and remove bracket.

⚠ **CAUTION: Plug the connections.**

23. Release clips and disconnect coolant hoses under floor.
24. **Models with A/C:** Loosen A/C pipe unions under floor and release pipes, remove and discard 'O' rings.

⚠ **CAUTION: Immediately cap all air conditioning pipes to prevent ingress of dirt and moisture into the system.**

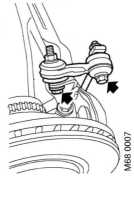

M68 0007

25. **All models:** Position suitable table beneath front subframe.
26. Lower vehicle on ramp until subframe makes contact with table.

M68 0006

27. Remove 8 bolts and 2 nuts and bolts securing subframe to body.
28. Slowly raise vehicle away from subframe.

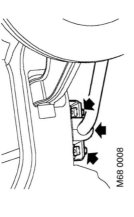

M68 0008

29. Remove nuts and bolts securing anti-roll bar links to anti-roll bar.
30. Remove 4 bolts securing anti-roll bar to subframe and remove anti-roll bar, collect anti-roll bar clamps and rubbers.

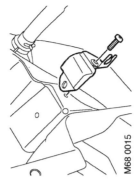

M68 0015

44. Remove screw securing bump stop to subframe and remove bump stop.

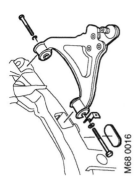

M68 0016

45. Remove front bolt securing lower arm to subframe.
46. Remove rubber grommet from subframe.
47. Remove rear bolt and spacer securing lower arm to subframe.
48. Remove lower arm.
49. Repeat above for opposite side of suspension.

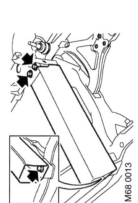

M68 0013

39. Remove 3 bolts securing LH crash can to subframe and remove crash can.

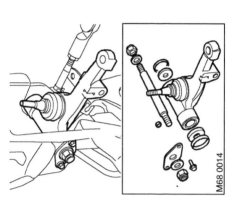

M68 0014

40. Remove large nuts either end of top arm pivot shaft.
41. Remove 2 bolts securing pivot shaft retaining plate.
42. Remove pivot shaft from subframe.
43. Remove top arm from subframe, collect thrust washers and sealing rings.

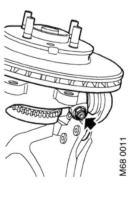

M68 0011

35. Remove nut and bolt securing bottom ball joint and release ball joint.
36. Remove hub assembly.

M68 0012

37. Remove 4 bolts securing left hand hydragas unit retaining plate.
38. Collect retaining plate, ABS sensor lead bracket, and hydragas unit.

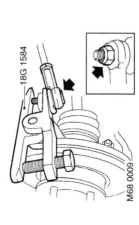

M68 0009

31. Remove nuts securing track rod ends to hubs and release tapers using 18G-1584 .

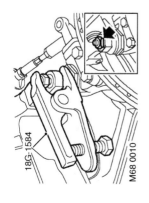

M68 0010

32. Release lock washer from top arm ball joint nut.
33. Remove nut and lock washer from top arm ball joint nut.
34. Release taper joint from top arm using 18G-1584.

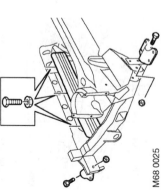

M68 0017

50. Remove 2 nuts and bolts and 'U' bolt securing steering rack to subframe.
51. Remove steering rack, collect 'U' bolt and clamp.

M68 0025

52. Remove nut and bolt securing LH front subframe mounting and collect mounting.
53. Remove nut and bolt securing LH rear subframe mounting and collect mounting.
54. Repeat process for RH subframe mountings.
55. Remove 3 nuts and bolts securing splash guard to subframe and remove splash guard.

Refit

1. Position splash guard, fit nuts and bolts and tighten to 8 Nm.
2. Position LH rear subframe mounting fit nut and bolt and tighten to 100 Nm.
3. Position LH front subframe mounting, fit nut and bolt and tighten to 100 Nm.
4. Repeat above for RH mountings.
5. Position steering rack to subframe fit 'U' bolt. Clamp and tighten nuts and bolts to 22 Nm.
6. Position lower arm in subframe, fit bolts and tighten to 85 Nm.
7. Fit grommet to subframe.
8. Fit top arm pivot shaft thrust washers and seals.
9. Position top arm and knuckle joint ball pin in subframe, and fit pivot shaft.
10. Fit retaining plate to pivot shaft and tighten bolts to 10 Nm.
11. Fit nuts securing pivot shaft and tighten to 74 Nm.
12. Position LH hydragas unit in subframe and fit retaining plate and ABS sensor lead bracket.
13. Fit retaining plate bolts and tighten to 25 Nm.
14. Repeat suspension build process for other side.
15. Fit LH crash can, fit bolts and tighten to 22 Nm.
16. Clean hub assembly and suspension arms.
17. Position hub assembly to suspension arms and engage ball joints.
18. Using a new lock washer, fit nut to top ball joint and tighten to 54 Nm and secure lock washer.
19. Ensure bottom ball joint pin is fully engaged in hub.
20. Fit nut and bolt securing bottom ball joint and tighten to 45 Nm.
21. Repeat above for other side.
22. Connect track rod ends to hubs, fit nuts and tighten to 30 Nm.
23. Position anti-roll bar, fit clamps and bolts and tighten to 22 Nm.
24. Align anti-roll bar links to anti-roll bar fit nuts and bolts and tighten to 35 Nm.

FRONT SUBFRAME - FRONT MOUNTING

Service repair no - 68.40.02

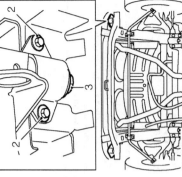

60M0344

Remove

1. Raise front of vehicle.

⚠ WARNING: Support on safety stands.

25. Slowly lower vehicle onto subframe.
26. Align subframe mountings to body.
27. Fit nuts and bolts securing subframe, tighten:
    Rear bolts to 45 Nm.
    Front bolts to 30 Nm.
28. Raise vehicle on ramp.
29. Remove table.
30. **Models with A/C:** Clean A/C pipe ends lubricate new 'O' rings with clean refrigerant oil and fit to A/C pipes.
31. Connect A/C pipes and tighten:
    18 mm dia pipe to 44 Nm,
    12 mm dia pipe to 25 Nm.
32. **All models:** Connect coolant hoses and secure with clips.
33. **Steptronic EM-CVT models:** Clean fluid cooler pipes and fit new 'O' rings.
34. Connect fluid cooler pipes and tighten unions to 14 Nm.
35. **All models:** Fit pipe support bracket, fit nut and bolt and tighten to 10 Nm.
36. Fit ABS sensors and spacers, fit bolts and tighten to 10 Nm.
37. Align front dampers to hubs, fit nuts and bolts and tighten 45 Nm.
38. Secure ABS harness in grommets.
39. Release LH and RH calipers, position to hub, fit bolts and tighten to 85Nm.
40. Fit front wheels.
41. Clean hydragas pipe ends and fit new 'O' rings.
42. Align hydragas pipe unions to hydragas units and tighten to 20 Nm.
43. Evacuate and pressurise hydragas system. *See Adjustments.*
44. Refill cooling system. *See COOLING SYSTEM, Adjustments.*
45. **Steptronic EM-CVT models:** Refill gearbox fluid. *See AUTOMATIC GEARBOX - 'EM-CVT', Adjustments.*
46. **Models with A/C:** Recharge A/C system.
47. **All models:** Position universal joint to steering column.
48. Fit universal joint clamp bolt, and tighten to 22 Nm.
49. Connect battery positive lead, fuse box and main fuse leads, secure lead in clips.
50. Connect battery earth lead.
51. Check front wheel alignment. *See STEERING, Adjustments.*

2. Remove 2 bolts securing subframe mount to body.
3. Remove bolt securing subframe mount to subframe and remove mount.

Refit

1. Fit mount to subframe and secure with bolt.
2. Fit bolts securing subframe mounting to body and tighten to 30 Nm.
3. Tighten subframe mounting bolt to 100 Nm.
4. Remove stand(s) and lower vehicle.

6. Remove pivot shaft from subframe.
7. Remove top arm and knuckle joint ball pin from subframe and collect thrust washers and sealing rings.

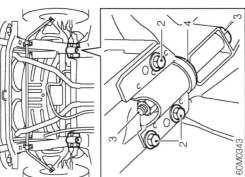

M68 0020

8. Remove bolt securing right hand track control arm to subframe.
9. Remove track control arm from subframe.

REAR SUBFRAME

Service repair no - 68.40.07

Remove

1. Remove engine and gearbox assembly. *See ENGINE, Repairs.*

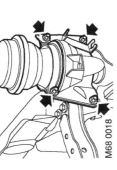

M68 0018

2. Remove 4 bolts securing right hand hydragas unit retaining plate.
3. Collect retaining plate, ABS sensor lead bracket, and hydragas unit.

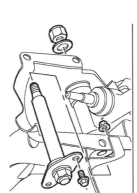

M68 0019

4. Remove large nuts either end of top arm pivot shaft.
5. Remove 2 bolts securing pivot shaft retaining plate.

FRONT SUBFRAME - REAR MOUNTING

Service repair no - 68.40.03

Remove

1. Raise front of vehicle.

⚠ **WARNING: Support on safety stands.**

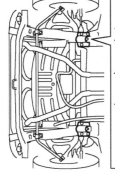

60M0343

2. Remove 3 bolts securing subframe mount to body.
3. Remove bolt securing subframe mount to subframe and remove mount.
4. Collect nylon washer.

Refit

1. Fit bolt to subframe.
2. Fit bolts securing subframe mount to body and tighten to 45 Nm.
3. Fit nylon washer and mount to bolt and tighten to 100 Nm.

⚠ **CAUTION: Ensure that the nylon washer is positioned over the mount tube, and that it does not become clamped between the mount and subframe.**

4. Remove stand(s) and lower vehicle.

12. Fit retaining plate to pivot shaft and tighten bolts to 10 Nm.
13. Fit nuts securing either end of pivot shaft and tighten to 74 Nm.
14. Position right hand hydragas unit in subframe and fit retaining plate and ABS sensor lead bracket.
15. Fit retaining plate bolts and tighten to 25 Nm.
16. Repeat suspension build process for left hand side.
17. Fit engine and gearbox assembly. **See ENGINE, Repairs.**
18. Check rear wheel alignment. **See STEERING, Adjustments.**

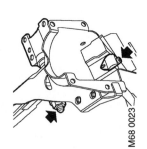

M68 0024

18. Remove bolt securing rear engine mounting tie rod to subframe and collect mounting.
19. Remove exhaust mounting rubber from subframe.

Refit

1. Fit exhaust mounting rubber to subframe.
2. Fit front mountings to subframe and tighten bolts to 100 Nm.
3. Fit rear mountings to subframe and tighten bolts to 100 Nm.
4. Fit rear engine mounting tie rod to subframe and tighten bolt to 85 Nm.
5. Position left hand buttress to subframe and fit bolts. Tighten bolts to 45 Nm.
6. Position lower arm in subframe and fit bolt. Tighten bolt to 85 Nm.
7. Fit washer and rubber on brake reaction rod, and position to lower arm.
8. Fit bolt securing brake reaction rod to subframe and tighten bolt to 45 Nm.
9. Fit rubber, washer and nut to brake reaction rod. Tighten nut to 85 Nm.
10. Fit right hand track control arm to subframe and tighten bolt to 85 Nm.
11. Position top arm and knuckle joint ball pin in subframe, and fit pivot shaft.

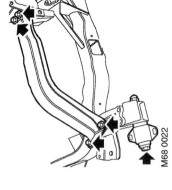

M68 0021

10. Remove nut securing right hand brake reaction rod to lower arm.
11. Remove bolt securing brake reaction rod to subframe. Remove arm and collect washers and rubbers.
12. Remove bolt securing lower arm to subframe and remove arm.
13. Repeat strip down process for left hand suspension.

M68 0022

14. Remove 4 bolts securing left hand buttress to subframe and remove buttress.
15. Remove bolt securing right hand front subframe mounting, and collect mounting.

M68 0023

16. Remove bolt securing right hand rear subframe mounting, and collect mounting.
17. Repeat process for left hand subframe mountings.

REAR SUBFRAME - FRONT MOUNTING

Service repair no - 68.40.08

Remove

1. Raise vehicle on a 2 post ramp.
2. Remove road wheel(s).
3. Support subframe with trolley jack.

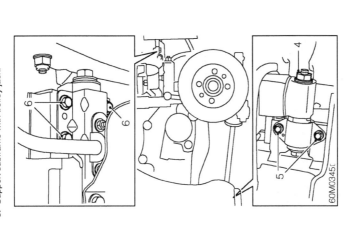

60M0345

4. Remove nut from front subframe mounting centre bolt.
5. Remove 2 bolts securing front mounting to body.
6. Remove 3 bolts securing rear subframe mounting to body.
7. Carefully lower subframe on trolley jack until sufficient room is gained to remove centre bolt and subframe mounting.

Refit

1. Fit mounting and centre bolt to subframe and loosely fit centre nut.
2. Raise subframe on trolley jack and fit 3 bolts securing rear subframe mounting to body. Tighten bolts to 45 Nm.
3. Fit bolts securing front subframe mounting to body and tighten to 30 Nm.
4. Tighten subframe mounting centre bolt to 100 Nm.
5. Fit road wheel(s) and tighten nuts to correct torque. *See INFORMATION, Torque wrench settings.*
6. Lower vehicle.

REAR SUBFRAME - REAR MOUNTING

Service repair no - 68.40.09

Remove

1. Raise vehicle on a 2 post ramp.
2. Remove silencer heat shield. *See MANIFOLD & EXHAUST SYSTEMS, Repairs.*

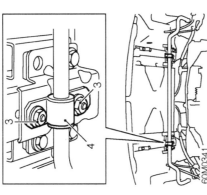
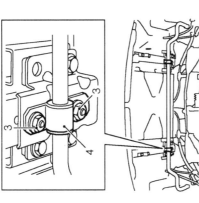

60M0341

3. Remove 2 nuts securing anti-roll bar, rubber bush to subframe.
4. Remove rubber bush and clamping bracket from anti-roll bar.
5. Support subframe with trolley jack.

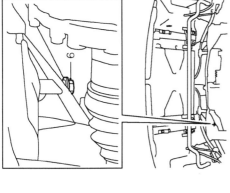

60M0342

6. Loosen rear mounting centre bolt.

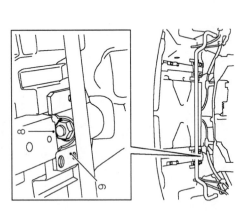

60M0346

7. Remove 3 bolts securing rear subframe mounting to body and collect anti-roll bar bracket.

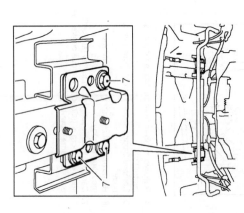

60M0347

8. Remove nut from centre bolt.
9. Carefully lower subframe on trolley jack and remove rear subframe mounting and washers.

Refit

1. Fit mounting and washers to subframe and centre bolt, and loosely fit centre nut.
2. Fit and tighten 1 bolt either side of rear subframe mounting to hold mounting in position. DO NOT fit anti-roll bar bracket.
3. Tighten centre bolt to 100 Nm.
4. Remove bolts holding rear mounting in position.
5. Fit rubber bush and bracket to anti-roll bar and tighten nuts to 22 Nm.
6. Fit silencer heat shield. **See MANIFOLD & EXHAUST SYSTEMS, Repairs.**
7. Lower vehicle.

This page is intentionally left blank

CONTENTS

Page

MASTER CYLINDER COMPONENTS

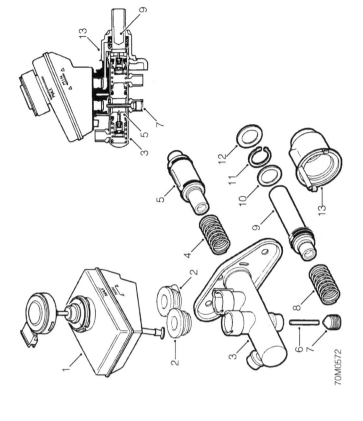

70M0572

1. Brake fluid reservoir
2. Seals
3. Cylinder body
4. Spring
5. Secondary plunger assembly
6. Stop pin secondary plunger
7. Pin securing screw
8. Spring
9. Primary plunger assembly
10. Washer
11. Circlip
12. Flat washer
13. Transfer housing

REAR BRAKE CALIPER COMPONENTS

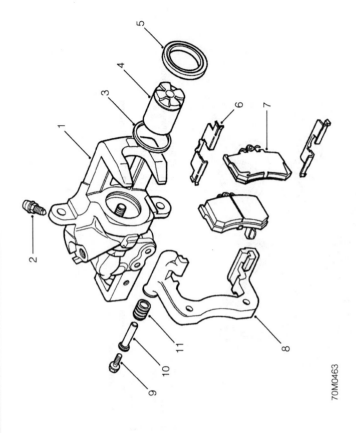

70M0463

1. Caliper body
2. Bleed screw
3. Piston seal
4. Piston
5. Dust cover
6. Shim

7. Brake pad
8. Caliper carrier
9. Guide pin bolt
10. Guide pin
11. Boot

FRONT BRAKE CALIPER COMPONENTS

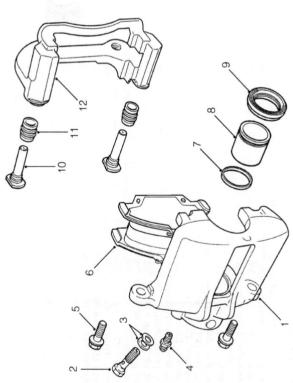

70M0462

1. Caliper body
2. Hose banjo bolt
3. Hose banjo washer
4. Bleed screw
5. Guide pin bolt
6. Brake pad

7. Piston seal
8. Piston
9. Dust cover
10. Guide pin
11. Boot
12. Caliper carrier

ABS ANTI-LOCK BRAKING SYSTEM

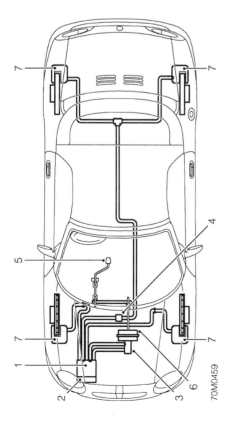

70M0459

1. ABS modulator unit
2. Electronic control unit
3. Master cylinder
4. Brake pressure proportioning valve

5. Brake pedal
6. Servo unit
7. Brake caliper

Description

The ABS system is an electronic control unit (ECU), controlled system deriving its input from four speed sensors, one mounted at each wheel, which allow the ABS to control the hydraulic modulator to prevent the wheels locking during braking.

The operation of the ABS is completely dependent upon electronic signals. To prevent the ABS responding to any inaccurate signals, a built in safety circuit monitors all electric and electronic signals, including battery voltage. If an inaccurate signal or low battery voltage is detected, the ABS is shut down immediately and the warning light on the fascia is illuminated to inform the driver that the brake system will respond to pedal pressure in the same manner as a non ABS.

Should a failure occur in one system, the remaining system will still operate effectively, although the brake pedal travel will increase.

Calipers

Pressure at the caliper forces the caliper piston against the inner brake pad and, in turn, against the disc. The caliper body reacts and slides on the guide pins to bring the outer pad into contact with the disc.

Modulator operation

Type:
ABS 5.0 up to 2000MY
ABS 5.3 from 2000MY

For information on the electrical operation of ABS 5.0 and ABS 5.3 See **ELECTRICAL REFERENCE LIBRARY, Description and Operation.**

With the vehicle in motion, the ECU receives signals from the four wheel sensors. From these signals the ECU can determine the speed of the vehicle. This is the speed which the ECU uses as a reference when evaluating the deceleration of each wheel.

This reference speed is continually calculated, even during braking. If one or more of the wheels are decelerating faster than the others, indicating a wheel is near the point of locking, the anti-lock sequence will be initiated.

The hydraulic modulator has three operation phases:

1. Increase pressure phase: The ABS system is at rest and fluid pressure from the master cylinder is allowed to pass through the solenoid valves in the hydraulic modulator to operate the caliper on each wheel.

2. Maintain pressure phase: The caliper is isolated from the master cylinder preventing any pressure increase due to increased pedal pressure.

3. Decrease pressure phase: The caliper is connected to the return pump which pumps the fluid back to the master cylinder.

Operation

Servo

Inlet manifold vacuum is transmitted through a hose and non-return valve to the servo. Inside the servo, this vacuum is felt on both sides of the diaphragm. When the brake pedal is pressed, the servo push rod opens a valve and allows atmospheric pressure to be drawn through the filter into the pedal side of the diaphragm. The pressure differential, acting on the diaphragm, increases the pressure being applied at the brake pedal and transmits it to the master cylinder through a push rod.

Master cylinder

When the foot brake is applied the primary plunger moves up the bore of the cylinder and the pressure created acts in conjunction with the primary spring to overcome the secondary spring, thus moving the secondary plunger up the bore of the cylinder simultaneously. Initial movement of both plungers causes them to be pushed off their stop pins, thus closing both primary and secondary centre valves. Further movement of the plungers pressurises the fluid which is directed into the two separate hydraulic circuits connected to the hydraulic modulator.

The primary circuit operates the front brakes and the secondary circuit operates the rear brakes.

The fluid in the chambers behind the plungers is unaffected by any movement of the plungers and can flow unrestricted between chamber and reservoir both before and during brake application.

When the brake pedal is released, the primary and secondary springs force their respective pistons back down the bore of the cylinder. As the plungers contact the stop pins the primary and secondary centre valves are opened allowing fluid to circulate unrestricted between the two hydraulic circuits and the fluid reservoir.

The movement of fluid during brake application/release is compensated for by fluid from the separate reservoirs within the supply tank moving through the feed holes in the cylinder. Conversely the final movement of the plungers causes any surplus fluid to move through the cut-off holes in the fluid reservoirs.

BRAKES

Brake pressure proportioning valve

The fluid line for the rear brake circuit is connected to the proportioning valve. The circuit for the front brakes uses a separate three way connector for distribution.

Pressure to the rear brakes passes through a piston sleeve, past a poppet valve and out to the rear brakes. The same pressure is also felt on the top of the piston, forcing the piston against spring pressure, towards the valve centre until the piston sleeve contacts the poppet valve and forms a seal. Input pressure is now balanced with output pressure. As further input pressure is applied from the master cylinder, it overcomes output pressure being felt on the piston and forces the piston outwards slightly away from the poppet valve allowing pressure past the poppet valve until output pressure is again balanced with input pressure.

HANDBRAKE OPERATION

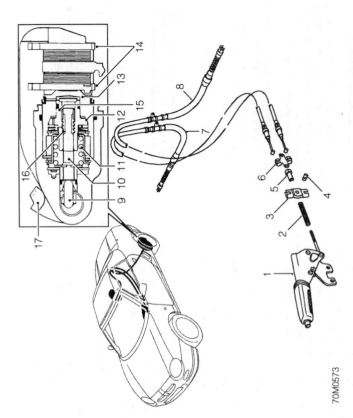

70M0573

1. Handbrake lever
2. Compensator spring
3. Compensator
4. Lever to compensator, retainer
5. Adjuster nut
6. Handbrake cable, abutment bracket
7. Handbrake cable, RH
8. Handbrake cable, LH
9. Plunger
10. Push rod
11. Spring
12. Cone seating
13. Piston
14. Brake pads
15. Adjuster nut
16. Push rod thread
17. Caliper lever

The handbrake operates on both rear discs via two rear cables, compensator and an intermediate rod which connects to the handbrake lever.

As the handbrake lever is applied, movement is transmitted through the intermediate rod to the compensator which, in turn, transmits movement to the two rear cables. Each rear cable pulls on a lever on a rear caliper.

Rotational movement of the caliper lever is changed to linear movement by a plunger which is forced out of its location by its inclined seating. The plunger contacts the push rod which, in turn, pushes the piston down its bore and forces the brake pads into contact with the disc.

Automatic adjustment of the disc brake pads is maintained by operation of the foot brake. With the brake pedal released, the piston is stationary in its bore and the adjuster nut is held against a cone seating inside the piston by the compression ring.

When the brake pedal is pressed, fluid pressure forces the piston down its bore and the compression spring causes the adjuster nut to follow. Initially the nut remains against its cone seating and just takes up the clearance between the push rod and its own thread, and if piston movement is within this tolerance no automatic adjustment takes place.

Further movement of the piston moves the cone seating away from the adjuster nut. This allows the compression spring to rotate the adjuster nut along the push rod thread until it again contacts the cone seating.

This extending action of the push rod assembly maintains adjustment of the handbrake mechanism.

When fluid pressure is released, the piston moves back and re-establishes the clearance between the push rod thread and the adjuster nut thread.

Manual adjustment of the handbrake cables is effected via the adjusting nut on the threaded intermediate rod bearing upon the compensator.
See Adjustments.

BRAKES

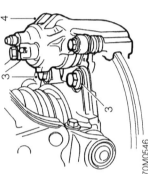

70M0547

FRONT BRAKE DISC - CHECK

Service repair no - 70.10.14

1. Raise front of vehicle.

   WARNING: Support on safety stands.

2. Remove road wheel(s).

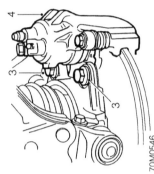

70M0546

3. Remove 2 bolts securing brake caliper to hub.
4. Release caliper from disc. Tie caliper clear of brake disc, ensuring that weight of caliper is supported.

   CAUTION: Do not allow caliper to hang on brake hose as weight of caliper may damage hose.

5. At 4 points around disc, measure disc thickness using a micrometer; renew disc if less than service limit or if maximum variation is exceeded:
   Disc thickness, NEW = 22.00 mm.
   Service limit = 20.00 mm.
   Thickness variation, maximum = 0.015 mm.

   NOTE: Maximum variation limit:
   Both brake discs must be renewed at the same time, unless one disc requires changing at 1000 mile service. Only in this situation is renewal of one disc permissible.

9. Renew disc if run-out exceeds limit even after re-positioning of disc on drive flange.

⚠ **CAUTION: Brake discs must be renewed in pairs, unless one disc requires changing before 1000 miles (1500 kilometers) from new.**

10. Untie caliper, position caliper to hub, fit and tighten bolts to 85 Nm.
11. Remove wheel nuts and spacers.
12. Apply foot brake several times to enable brake pads to position correctly.
13. Fit road wheel(s), fit wheel nuts and tighten in a diagonal sequence to 70 Nm.
14. Remove stand(s) and lower vehicle.

SP70 0003

4. At 4 points around disc, measure disc thickness using a micrometer; renew disc if less than service limit. Disc thickness, NEW = 24 mm. Service limit = 22 mm.

70M0548A

5. Position a suitable spacer to each wheel stud and secure brake disc using wheel nuts. Tighten wheel nuts in a diagonal sequence to 70 Nm.
6. Set dial test indicator 6 mm from disc outer edge.
7. Zero dial test indicator and rotate brake disc one complete turn to measure disc run-out. Disc run-out limit = 0.05 mm.
8. If run-out exceeds limit, mark disc to drive flange location; remove wheel nuts, spacers and disc retaining screws. Remove disc, rotate 180° refit disc to drive flange. Fit and tighten disc retaining screws to 7 Nm, fit spacers and wheel nuts and tighten wheel nuts in a diagonal sequence to 70 Nm.

FRONT BRAKE DISC - CHECK - MGF TROPHY

Service repair no - 70.10.14

Adjust

1. Raise front of vehicle.

⚠ **WARNING: Do not work on or under a vehicle supported only by a jack. Always support the vehicle on safety stands.**

2. Remove road wheel(s).

70M0546

⚠ **CAUTION: Do not allow caliper to hang on brake hose.**

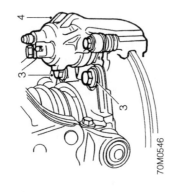

70M0548A

6. Position a suitable spacer to each wheel stud and secure brake disc using wheel nuts. Tighten wheel nuts in a diagonal sequence to 70 Nm.
7. Set dial test indicator 6 mm from disc outer edge.
8. Measure disc run-out:
   Run-out limit = 0.05 mm.
9. If run-out exceeds limit, mark disc to show position on drive flange; remove 2 screws retaining disc, remove disc and refit after rotating 180°. Tighten disc securing screws to 7 Nm and re-check disc run-out.
10. Renew disc if run-out exceeds limit even after re-positioning of disc on drive flange.
11. Untie caliper and support caliper weight.
12. Align caliper carrier to hub ensuring correct positioning of brake pads. Fit and tighten bolts to 85 Nm.
13. Apply foot brake several times to enable brake pads to position correctly.
14. Remove wheel nuts and spacers.
15. Fit road wheel(s) and tighten nuts to correct torque. *See INFORMATION, Torque wrench settings.*
16. Remove stand(s) and lower vehicle.

BRAKES

REAR BRAKE DISC - CHECK

Service repair no - 70.10.35

1. Raise rear of vehicle.

⚠ WARNING: Support on safety stands.

2. Remove road wheel(s).

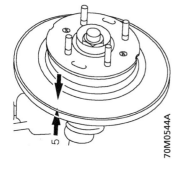

70M0543A

3. Remove 2 bolts securing brake caliper to hub.
4. Release caliper from disc. Tie caliper clear of brake disc, ensuring that weight of caliper is supported.

⚠ CAUTION: Do not allow caliper to hang on brake hose as weight of caliper may damage hose.

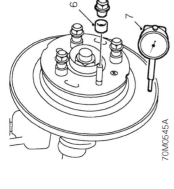

70M0544A

5. At 4 points around disc, measure disc thickness using a micrometer; renew disc if less than service limit or if maximum variation is exceeded:
   Disc thickness, NEW = 10.00 mm.
   Service limit = 8.00 mm.
   Thickness variation, maximum = 0.015 mm.

⚠ NOTE: Maximum variation limit:
Both brake discs must be renewed at the same time, unless one disc requires changing at 1000 mile service. Only in this situation is renewal of one disc permissible.

BRAKE SYSTEM - BLEED

Service repair no - 70.25.02

The following procedure covers bleeding the complete system but where only the primary or secondary circuit have been disturbed, partial bleeding is permissible if a brake pipe or hose has been disconnected with only minor loss of fluid.

⚠ CAUTION:

- Never re-use fluid that has been bled from the brake system.
- Do not allow fluid level in master cylinder to fall below 'MIN' level during bleeding.
- Do not fill reservoir above 'MAX' level.

1. Raise front and rear of vehicle.

⚠ WARNING: Support on safety stands.

2. Check all pipe and hose connections are tight and there are no signs of leakage.
3. Top-up fluid level in brake reservoir to 'MAX' mark. See INFORMATION, Capacities, fluids and lubricants.

⚠ CAUTION: Use only NEW brake fluid of the recommended grade.

70M0551

Bleed sequence - non ABS and ABS systems:
LH rear to RH rear
RH front to LH front

⚠ CAUTION: Braking efficiency may be seriously impaired if wrong bleed sequence is used.

70M0545A

6. Position suitable spacers and secure brake disc using wheel nuts. Tighten wheel nuts to 70 Nm.
7. Set dial test indicator 6 mm from disc outer edge.
8. Measure disc run-out:
   Run-out limit = 0.05 mm.
9. If run-out exceeds limit, mark disc to show position on drive flange; remove 2 screws retaining disc, remove disc and refit after rotating 180°. Tighten disc securing screws to 7 Nm and re-check disc run-out.
10. Renew disc if run-out exceeds limit even after re-positioning of disc on drive flange.
11. Untie caliper and support caliper weight.
12. Align caliper carrier to hub ensuring correct positioning of brake pads. Fit and tighten bolts to 85 Nm.
13. Apply foot brake several times to enable brake pads to position correctly.
14. Remove wheel nuts and spacers.
15. Fit road wheel(s) and tighten wheel nuts to correct torque. See INFORMATION, Torque wrench settings.
16. Remove stand(s) and lower vehicle.

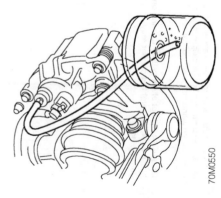

70M0550

4. Attach bleed tube to LH rear brake caliper bleed screw, submerge free end in brake fluid in a clear container.

5. Apply pressure to brake pedal several times, then apply steady pressure.

6. Loosen bleed screw to release brake fluid and air. Allow pedal to return unassisted.

7. Depress brake pedal steadily through its full stroke and allow to return unassisted. Repeat procedure until a flow of clean air-free fluid is purged into container then, whilst holding pedal at end of downward stroke, tighten bleed screw to 10 Nm.

 CAUTION: Maintain brake fluid level above 'MIN' mark during this procedure.

8. Top-up brake fluid level.

9. Repeat procedure at each wheel in the sequence shown.

CAUTION: Braking efficiency may be seriously impaired if wrong bleed sequence is used.

10. Remove bleed tube. Apply brakes and check for leakage.

11. Remove stand(s) and lower vehicle.

12. Road test vehicle. Check brake pedal for short firm travel when brakes are applied.

BRAKES SYSTEM - BLEED - MGF TROPHY

Service repair no - 70.25.02

Adjust

1. The following procedure covers bleeding the complete system but where only the primary or secondary circuit have been disturbed in isolation, it should only be necessary to bleed that system. Partial bleeding of the hydraulic system is only permissible if a brake pipe or hose has been disconnected with only minor loss of fluid.

CAUTION: Never re-use fluid that has been bled from the system.

2. Raise front and rear of vehicle.

WARNING: Do not work on or under a vehicle supported only by a jack. Always support the vehicle on safety stands.

3. Check all pipe and hose connections are tight and there are no signs of leakage.

4. Top-up brake fluid level to 'MAX' mark.

CAUTION: Use only new brake fluid of the recommended grade.

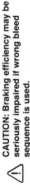

SP70 0007

5. Bleed sequence - non ABS and ABS systems: LH rear to RH rear, RH front to LH front. Note that the front calipers on MG-F Trophy incorporate 2 bleed screws on each caliper. When bleeding this system, bleed the outer bleed screw followed by the inner bleed screw in the same sequence as stated.

CAUTION: Braking efficiency may be seriously impaired if wrong bleed sequence is used.

6. Clean area around bleed screws and remove dust seals.

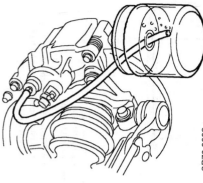
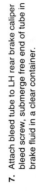

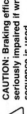

SP70 0008

7. Attach bleed tube to LH rear brake caliper bleed screw, submerge free end of tube in brake fluid in a clear container.

8. Apply pressure to brake pedal several times, then apply steady pressure.

9. Loosen bleed screw to release brake fluid and air. Allow pedal to return unassisted.

10. Depress brake pedal steadily through its full stroke and allow to return unassisted. Repeat procedure until a flow of clean air-free fluid is purged into container then, whilst holding brake pedal at end of downward stroke, tighten bleed screw to 10 Nm.

CAUTION: Maintain brake fluid level above 'MIN' mark during this procedure.

11. Top-up brake fluid level.

12. Repeat procedure at each wheel in the sequence shown.

CAUTION: Braking efficiency may be seriously impaired if wrong bleed sequence is used.

13. Remove tube from bleed screw and fit bleed screw dust cap.

14. Apply brakes and check for leakage.

15. Road test vehicle. Check brake pedal for short firm travel when brakes are applied.

BRAKES

HANDBRAKE - ADJUST

Service repair no - 70.35.10

Adjust

1. Raise rear of vehicle.

 WARNING: Support on safety stands.

2. Remove front console storage bin.

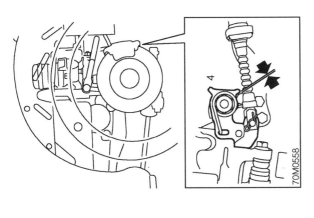

70M0557

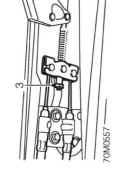 NOTE: Depress brake pedal several times to ensure that automatic adjustment clearance is taken up.

3. Tighten adjuster nut ½ turn and check caliper lever clearance.

 CAUTION: Do not depress brake pedal until caliper adjustment clearance is correct.

4. Repeat adjustment until caliper lever clearances are between 1 & 2 mm each side.
5. Fit storage bin.
6. Remove stand(s) and lower vehicle.

BRAKE LIGHT SWITCH - ADJUST

Service repair no - 70.35.41

Adjust

1. Depress and hold brake pedal.

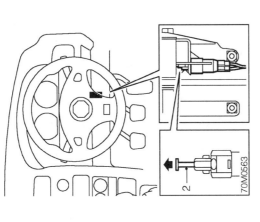

70M0563

2. Reset switch by pulling plunger.
3. Release brake pedal to set switch adjustment.

FRONT BRAKE DISC

Service repair no - 70.10.10

Remove

1. Raise front of vehicle.

 WARNING: Support on safety stands.

2. Remove road wheel(s).

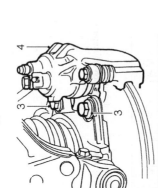

3. Remove 2 bolts securing brake caliper to hub.
4. Move caliper aside. Tie caliper clear of brake disc, ensuring that weight of caliper is supported.

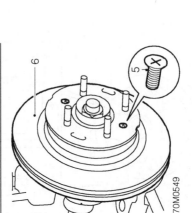

70M0549

⚠ **CAUTION: Do not allow caliper to hang on brake hose as weight of caliper may damage hose.**

5. Remove 2 screws securing brake disc to drive flange.
6. Remove brake disc.

Refit

⚠ **CAUTION: Brake discs must be replaced in pairs.**

1. Wire brush drive flange to remove all corrosion deposits. Clean new brake disc.
2. Fit brake disc to drive flange, fit screws and tighten to 7 Nm.
3. Check disc run-out. **See _Adjustments_.**
4. Examine brake pads and renew if necessary.
5. Fit brake caliper to hub, fit and tighten bolts to 85 Nm .
6. Fit road wheel(s) and tighten nuts to correct torque. **See _INFORMATION, Torque wrench settings_.**
7. Remove stand(s) and lower vehicle.

This page is intentionally left blank

FRONT BRAKE DISC - MGF TROPHY

Service repair no - 70.10.10

Remove

1. Raise front of vehicle.

⚠ **WARNING: Do not work on or under a vehicle supported only by a jack. Always support the vehicle on safety stands.**

2. Remove road wheel(s).

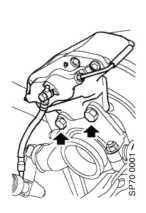

SP70 0001

3. Remove 2 bolts securing caliper assembly to hub.
4. Remove caliper assembly from hub and tie aside.

⚠ **CAUTION: Do not allow caliper to hang on brake hose.**

SP70 0002

5. Remove 2 screws securing brake disc to drive flange.

6. Remove brake disc.

⚠ **CAUTION: Brake discs must be renewed in pairs, unless one disc requires changing before 1000 miles (1500 kilometers) from new.**

Refit

1. Wire brush drive flange to remove all corrosion deposits. Clean new brake disc.
2. Fit brake disc to drive flange, fit and tighten screws to 7 Nm.
3. Examine brake pads and renew if necessary.
4. Check brake disc runout.
5. Position caliper to hub, fit and tighten bolts to 85 Nm.
6. Fit road wheel(s), fit wheel nuts and tighten in a diagonal sequence to 70 Nm.
7. Remove stand(s) and lower vehicle.

REAR BRAKE DISC

Service repair no - 70.10.33

Remove

1. Raise rear of vehicle.

⚠ **WARNING: Support on safety stands.**

2. Remove road wheel(s).

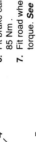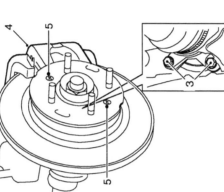

70M0460A

3. Remove 2 bolts securing brake caliper to hub.
4. Release caliper from disc. Tie caliper clear of brake disc, ensuring the weight of the caliper is supported.

⚠ **CAUTION: Do not allow caliper to hang on brake hose as weight of caliper may damage hose.**

5. Remove 2 screws securing brake disc to drive flange.
6. Remove brake disc.

Refit

1. Wire brush drive flange to remove all corrosion deposits.
2. Clean drive flange and NEW disc.

⚠ **CAUTION: Brake discs must only be replaced in pairs, unless: The vehicle has covered less than 1000 miles**

3. Fit brake disc to drive flange. Tighten screws to 7 Nm.
4. Check disc run-out. See *Adjustments.*
5. Examine brake pads and renew if necessary.
6. Fit brake caliper to hub, fit and tighten bolts to 85 Nm.
7. Fit road wheel(s) and tighten nuts to correct torque. See *INFORMATION, Torque wrench settings.*
8. Remove stand(s) and lower vehicle.

FLUID LEVEL SWITCH

Service repair no - 70.25.08

Remove

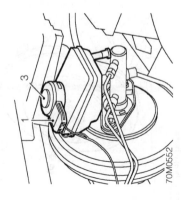

70M0552

1. Disconnect switch multiplug.
2. Clean area around reservoir cap.
3. Remove cap/switch assembly.

⚠ **CAUTION: Do not allow brake fluid to contact paint finished surfaces as paint may be damaged. If spilled, remove fluid and clean area with clean warm water.**

Refit

1. Check and top-up fluid level.
2. Fit cap/switch assembly.
3. Connect switch multiplug.

ABS HYDRAULIC MODULATOR - UP TO 2000MY

Service repair no - 70.25.12

Remove

1. Disconnect battery earth lead.
2. Position cloth under modulator to absorb brake fluid.

⚠ **CAUTION: Do not allow brake fluid to contact paint finished surfaces as paint may be damaged. If spilled, remove fluid and clean area with clean warm water.**

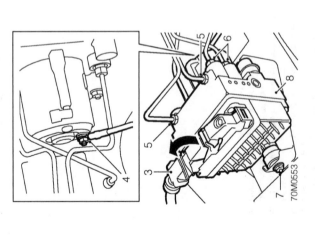

70M0553

3. Raise clip, lift rear of multiplug and disengage from modulator ECU.

---

4. Remove nut securing earth lead to motor and disconnect lead.
5. Disconnect 2 inlet brake pipe unions from top of modulator.

⚠ **CAUTION: Plug the connections.**

6. Disconnect 3 outlet brake pipe unions from modulator.

⚠ **CAUTION: Plug the connections.**

7. Loosen 3 nuts securing modulator to mounting bracket.
8. Release modulator from mounting bracket and remove.
   Do not carry out further dismantling if component is removed for access only.
9. Remove 3 mounting rubbers from modulator.
10. Fit mounting rubbers to NEW modulator.

Refit

1. Fit modulator to mounting bracket and tighten mounting nuts to 10 Nm.
2. Connect brake pipe unions to modulator, ensuring pipes are connected to their correct ports, as follows:

   MC 1 = Master cylinder primary
   MC 2 = Master cylinder secondary
   RF = Right hand front
   LF = Left hand front
   R = Rear

3. Connect earth lead to modulator, fit and tighten nut.
4. Connect multiplug to modulator and secure clip.
5. Bleed brakes. *See Adjustments.*
6. Connect battery earth lead.

ABS HYDRAULIC MODULATOR - 2000MY ON

Service repair no - 70.25.12

Remove

1. Disconnect battery earth lead.
2. Position cloth under modulator to absorb brake fluid.

⚠ **CAUTION: Do not allow brake fluid to contact paint finished surfaces as paint may be damaged. If spilled, remove fluid and clean area with clean warm water.**

M70 1003

3. Release clip securing ABS modulator multiplug and disconnect multiplug.
4. Disconnect 2 inlet brake pipe unions from top of modulator.

⚠ **CAUTION: Plug the connections.**

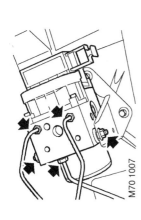

M70 1007

5. Disconnect 3 outlet brake pipe unions from modulator.

⚠️ **CAUTION: Plug the connections.**

6. Loosen 2 nuts securing modulator to mounting bracket.
7. Release modulator from mounting bracket and remove modulator.

Refit

1. Remove 2 mounting rubbers and studs from modulator.
2. Fit mounting rubbers and studs to new modulator.
3. Fit modulator to mounting bracket and tighten mounting nuts to 10 Nm.
4. Connect brake pipe unions to modulator, ensuring pipes are connected to their correct ports as follows:

   MC 1 = Master cylinder primary
   MC 2 = Master cylinder secondary
   RF = Right hand front
   LF = Left hand front
   R = Right & Left hand rear

5. Connect multiplug to modulator and secure clip.
6. Bleed brakes. *See Adjustments.*
7. Connect battery earth lead.

BRAKE PROPORTIONING VALVE

Service repair no - 70.25.15

Remove

1. Position cloth to catch spillage.

⚠️ **CAUTION: Do not allow brake fluid to contact paint finished surfaces as paint may be damaged. If spilled, remove fluid and clean area with clean warm water.**

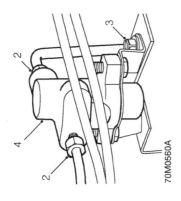

70M0560A

2. Release 2 brake pipe unions and position pipes aside.

⚠️ **CAUTION: Plug the connections.**

3. Remove 2 bolts securing valve to body.
4. Remove valve.

Refit

1. Fit valve to body and tighten bolts to 10 Nm.
2. Align unions to valve and tighten to 14 Nm.
3. Bleed rear brakes. *See Adjustments.*

ABS SENSOR - FRONT WHEEL

Service repair no - 70.25.32

Remove

1. Disconnect battery earth lead.
2. Raise front of vehicle.

⚠️ **WARNING: Support on safety stands.**

3. Remove road wheel(s).

70M0570

4. Disconnect ABS sensor lead from main harness.
5. Release ABS sensor lead from clips on Hydragas unit retaining plate.
6. Remove bolt securing ABS sensor to hub.
7. Remove ABS sensor and spacer from hub.

Refit

1. Fit ABS sensor and spacer to hub and tighten bolt to 10 Nm.
2. Fit ABS sensor lead to clips on Hydragas unit retaining plate.
3. Connect ABS sensor lead to main harness.
4. Connect battery earth lead.
5. Fit road wheel(s) and tighten nuts to correct torque. *See INFORMATION, Torque wrench settings.*
6. Remove stand(s) and lower vehicle.

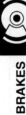

BRAKES

ABS SENSOR - REAR WHEEL

Service repair no - 70.25.33

Remove

1. Disconnect battery earth lead.
2. Remove engine compartment access panel. **See BODY, Exterior fittings.**
3. Raise rear of vehicle.

⚠ **WARNING: Support on safety stands.**

4. Remove road wheel(s).

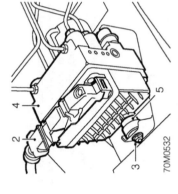

70M0534

5. Disconnect ABS sensor lead from main harness.
6. Release ABS sensor lead from clips on Hydragas unit retaining plate.
7. Remove bolt securing ABS sensor to hub.
8. Remove ABS sensor and spacer from hub.

Refit

1. Fit ABS sensor and spacer to hub and tighten bolt to 10 Nm.
2. Fit ABS sensor lead to clips on Hydragas unit retaining plate.
3. Connect ABS sensor lead to main harness.
4. Connect battery earth lead.
5. Fit road wheel(s) and tighten nuts to correct torque. **See INFORMATION, Torque wrench settings.**
6. Remove stand(s) and lower vehicle.
7. Fit engine compartment access panel. **See BODY, Exterior fittings.**

ABS ECU - UP TO 2000MY

Service repair no - 70.25.34

Remove

1. Disconnect battery earth lead.

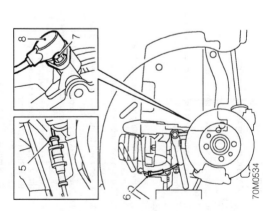

70M0532

2. Disconnect multiplug from ABS ECU.
3. Loosen 3 nuts securing ABS modulator and ECU assembly to mounting bracket.
4. Release ABS modulator and ECU from bracket.
5. Remove rubber mounting from front of ECU.

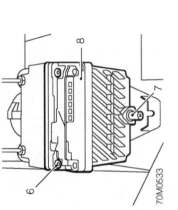

70M0533

6. Remove 4 Tx25 Torx screws securing ECU to modulator.
7. Remove mounting spigot from ECU using a Tx30 adapter.
8. Release ECU from modulator.

Refit

1. Fit ECU to modulator and tighten screws to 8 Nm.
2. Fit mounting spigot to ECU and tighten to 15 Nm.
3. Fit mounting rubber to spigot.
4. Locate ECU and modulator assembly in mounting bracket and tighten nuts to 10 Nm.
5. Connect multiplug to ECU.
6. Connect battery earth lead.

BRAKES

PEDAL BOX ASSEMBLY

Service repair no - 70.35.03

Remove

1. Remove bulkhead closing panel. *See BODY, Repairs.*

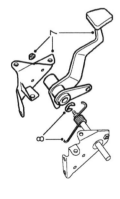

M70 1010

2. Remove 2 nuts and 1 bolt securing throttle pedal. Release pedal and position aside.
3. Release brake light switch and position aside.
4. Remove clip securing brake pedal push rod clevis pin and remove clevis pin.

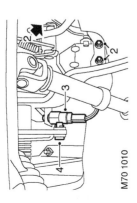

M70 1011

5. With assistance, remove 3 nuts and bolts and 4 bolts securing pedal box assembly.
6. Manoeuvre pedal box assembly over steering column and remove assembly.

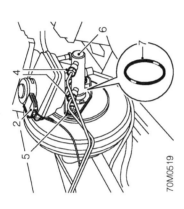

M70 1012

7. Remove nut securing end bracket and remove end bracket and pedal.
8. Remove return spring circlip and return spring from pivot shaft.

Refit

1. Position return spring on pivot shaft and secure with circlip.
2. Examine pedal bushes for wear or damage and replace as required.
3. Position pedal and end bracket, fit nut and tighten to 22 Nm.
4. Position pedal box assembly, manoeuvre over steering column and align to bulkhead.
5. Fit and tighten nuts and bolts securing pedal box assembly to 22 Nm.
6. Align brake pedal push rod, fit clevis pin and secure with clip.
7. Position brake light switch and secure in end bracket.
8. Position throttle pedal, fit nuts and tighten to 6 Nm.
9. Fit bulkhead closing panel. *See BODY, Repairs.*

BRAKE MASTER CYLINDER

Service repair no - 70.30.08

Remove

1. Remove underbonnet closing panel. *See BODY, Exterior fittings.*

70M0519

2. Disconnect fluid level switch.
3. Position cloth under master cylinder to absorb spilled fluid.

⚠ **CAUTION: Do not allow brake fluid to contact paint finished surfaces as paint may be damaged. If spilled, remove fluid and clean area with clean warm water.**

4. Disconnect pipe unions at master cylinder.

⚠ **CAUTION: Plug the connections.**

5. Remove 2 nuts and plain washers securing master cylinder to brake servo.
6. Remove master cylinder.
7. Collect and discard 'O' ring.

Refit

1. Clean master cylinder and servo mating surfaces.
2. Fit NEW 'O' ring to master cylinder.
3. Align servo push rod and fit master cylinder to servo.
4. Secure master cylinder with nuts and plain washers. Tighten to 20 Nm.
5. Connect primary and secondary brake pipes, tighten unions to 14 Nm.
6. Connect fluid level switch.
7. Bleed brake system. *See Adjustments.*
8. Fit underbonnet closing panel. *See BODY, Exterior fittings.*

HANDBRAKE LEVER

Service repair no - 70.35.08

Remove

1. Remove front console. *See BODY, Interior trim components.*

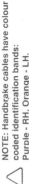

70M0556

2. Loosen cable adjuster nut and disconnect 2 cables from compensator.
3. Remove 2 bolts securing lever to body.
4. Disconnect Lucar from switch and remove handbrake lever.

Refit

1. Connect Lucar to switch.
2. Position handbrake lever to body, fit and tighten bolts to 25 Nm.
3. Connect cables to compensator.
4. Adjust handbrake cables. *See Adjustments.*
5. Fit front console. *See BODY, Interior trim components.*

HANDBRAKE CABLES

Service repair no - 70.35.28

△ NOTE: Handbrake cables have colour coded identification bands: Purple - RH, Orange - LH.

⚠ WARNING: *See RESTRAINT SYSTEMS, Precautions.*

Remove

1. Position vehicle on a 2 post ramp.
2. Make the SRS system safe. *See RESTRAINT SYSTEMS, Precautions.*
3. Remove engine cover. *See ENGINE, Repairs.*
4. Remove engine compartment access panel. *See BODY, Exterior fittings.*
5. Release handbrake to off position.

70M0565A

6. Remove and discard 2 'R' clips, and remove 2 clevis pins securing handbrake cables to rear calipers.
7. Remove and discard 2 clips securing handbrake cable abutments to caliper brackets and release cables.

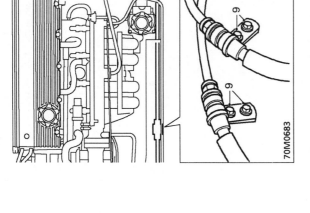

70M0683

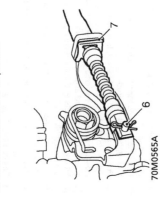

70M0566A

8. Release air intake duct from subframe clip and position duct aside.

9. Remove 2 bolts securing each handbrake cable to luggage compartment bulkhead.
10. Release handbrake cables from air cleaner mounting bracket.
11. Drain engine coolant. *See COOLING SYSTEM, Adjustments.*
12. Place support jack underneath engine sump and support engine weight.

⚠ **CAUTION: To prevent damage to sump place a piece of wood between jack and sump.**

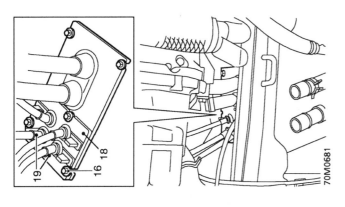

70M0681

16. Release 2 upper and remove 3 remaining bolts securing closing plate to bulkhead.
17. Apply soft soap to all four closing plate cables, to ease movement of closing plate.
18. Release closing plate from bulkhead and slide along cables.
19. Noting their fitted positions release 2 handbrake cable grommets from closing plate.
20. Remove front console. See **BODY, Interior trim components.**

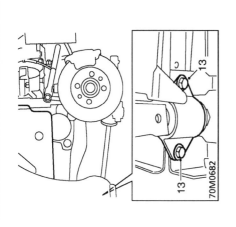

70M0682

13. Remove 2 bolts securing both front subframe mountings to body brackets.
14. Lower jack carefully, to allow access to closing plate bolts.

⚠ **CAUTION: Care must be taken that no cables or pipes are stretched when lowering front of subframe.**

15. Tie coolant pipes aside to allow access to closing plate.

Refit

1. Position handbrake cables to tunnel and feed through rear bulkhead.
2. Feed handbrake cables into position in engine compartment.
3. Lubricate all four cables with soft soap to ease grommet movement on cables.
4. Position handbrake cables into closing plate slots and secure with grommets.
5. Align closing plate to bulkhead and secure with bolts.
6. Lift subframe on jack, fit subframe front mounting bolts and tighten to 30 Nm .
7. Position handbrake cable abutments to caliper brackets and secure with NEW clips.
8. Align handbrake cables to calipers, fit clevis pins and secure with NEW 'R' clips.
9. Position handbrake cables to luggage compartment bulkhead and secure clips with bolts.
10. Position air intake duct to subframe and secure with clip.
11. Fit handbrake cables to air cleaner mounting bracket.
12. Fit cables to handbrake compensator.
13. Position cables and secure with handbrake abutment clamp.
14. Fit front console. See **BODY, Interior trim components.**
15. Untie and position coolant hoses.
16. Fill engine coolant. See **COOLING SYSTEM, Adjustments.**
17. Fit engine cover. See **ENGINE, Repairs.**
18. Fit engine compartment access panel. See **BODY, Exterior fittings.**
19. Adjust handbrake cable. See **Adjustments.**

70M0569A

21. Remove 2 bolts securing handbrake abutment clamp to tunnel and remove clamp.
22. Release handbrake cables from compensator.
23. Remove handbrake cables from tunnel and engine compartment.

HANDBRAKE WARNING SWITCH

Service repair no - 70.35.40

Remove

1. Remove handbrake lever. *See this section.*

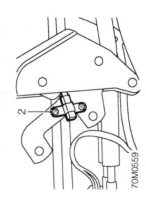

70M0559

2. Remove 2 screws securing switch to lever and collect switch.

Refit

1. Fit switch and secure with screws.
2. Fit handbrake lever. *See this section.*

BRAKE LIGHT SWITCH

Service repair no - 70.35.42

Remove

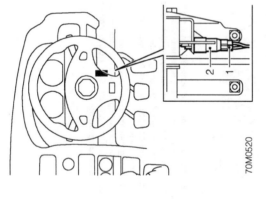

70M0520

1. Release 2 Lucar connectors from switch.
2. Release bayonet fixing and remove switch.

Refit

1. Fit switch to pedal box.
2. Connect Lucar connectors.
3. Adjust switch. *See Adjustments.*

Refit

⚠ **CAUTION: Always fit correct grade and specification of brake pads, and renew in axle set. Braking efficiency may otherwise be impaired.**

1. Clean caliper abutments and piston.
2. Clean area around fluid reservoir cap.
3. Remove cap from brake reservoir and position cloth to catch spillage.

⚠ **CAUTION: Do not allow brake fluid to contact paint finished surfaces as paint may be damaged. If spilled, remove fluid and clean area with clean warm water.**

4. Using tool **18G 590**, press piston into caliper body.
5. Remove tool.
6. Remove backings from pad shims and fit pads to carrier.
7. Position caliper body to carrier, fit and tighten guide pin bolt to 45 Nm.
8. Fit road wheel(s) and tighten nuts to correct torque. *See* **INFORMATION, Torque wrench settings.**
9. Top-up brake fluid to 'MAX' mark. *See* **MAINTENANCE.**
10. Depress brake pedal several times to seat pads.

⚠ **NOTE: Pedal travel may be longer than normal during first brake applications.**

11. Remove stand(s) and lower vehicle.

BRAKE PADS - FRONT

Service repair no - 70.40.02

Remove

1. Raise front of vehicle.

⚠ **WARNING: Support on safety stands.**

2. Remove road wheel(s).

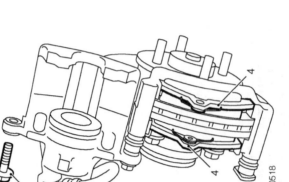

70M0518

3. Remove lower guide pin bolt from caliper and pivot caliper body upwards.
4. Remove 2 brake pads from caliper carrier.

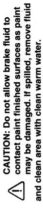

BRAKE PADS - FRONT - MGF TROPHY

Service repair no - 70.40.02

Remove

1. Raise front of vehicle.

⚠ **WARNING: Do not work on or under a vehicle supported only by a jack. Always support the vehicle on safety stands.**

2. Remove road wheel(s).

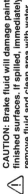

SP70 0004

3. Using a parallel punch, drift out brake pad retaining pins and collect anti-squeal plate.

SP70 0005

4. Remove brake pads from caliper housing.

Refit

1. Clean brake pad abutment area's in calipers, retaining pins and anti-squeal plates.
2. Clean area around brake fluid reservoir cap.
3. Disconnect multiplug from brake fluid level indicator, remove reservoir cap and position a piece of cloth over reservoir to collect any brake fluid spillage.

⚠ **CAUTION: Brake fluid will damage paint finished surfaces. If spilled, immediately remove fluid and clean area with water.**

4. Using a suitable flat lever, retract caliper pistons into housing.
5. Remove backings from brake pad shims.

⚠ **CAUTION: Always fit correct grade and specification of brake pads, and renew in axle set. Braking efficiency may otherwise be impaired.**

6. Fit brake pads to caliper housing.
7. Fit brake pad retaining pins and anti-squeal plate.
8. If necessary, top-up brake fluid reservoir.
9. Remove cloth, fit fluid reservoir cap and connect multiplug to fluid level indicator.
10. Fit road wheel(s), fit wheel nuts and tighten in a diagonal sequence to 70 Nm.
11. Depress brake pedal several times to seat pads.
12. Remove stand(s) and lower vehicle.

⚠ **CAUTION: Do not operate handbrake with brake pads removed.**

Refit

⚠ **WARNING: Always fit the correct grade and specification of brake pads, and renew in axle set. Braking efficiency may be impaired.**

1. Remove old shims from caliper.
2. Fit NEW shims to replacement pads.
3. Clean area around fluid reservoir cap.
4. Remove cap from brake reservoir and position cloth to catch spillage.

⚠ **CAUTION: Do not allow brake fluid to contact paint finished surfaces as paint may be damaged. If spilled, remove fluid and clean area with warm water.**

5. Screw piston into caliper using 18G 1596 ensuring piston is fully retracted.
6. Clean components using methylated spirit or denatured alcohol. Do not use any petroleum based fluids.
7. Fit NEW pads to caliper carrier.
8. Untie caliper body and position to carrier.
9. Fit guide pin bolts and tighten to 45 Nm.
10. Fit road wheel(s) and tighten nuts to correct torque. See *INFORMATION, Torque wrench settings.*
11. Top-up brake fluid to 'MAX' mark. *See MAINTENANCE.*
12. Operate brake pedal several times to adjust brake pads and the handbrake linkage.

⚠ **CAUTION: Do not apply the handbrake before the brake pads have been adjusted or incorrect brake operation will result.**

13. Remove stand(s) and lower vehicle.

BRAKE PADS - REAR

Service repair no - 70.40.03

Remove

1. Raise rear of vehicle.

⚠ **WARNING: Support on safety stands.**

2. Release handbrake lever.
3. Remove road wheel(s).

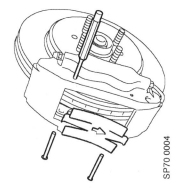 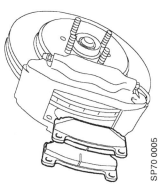 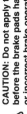

70M0554

4. Remove guide pin bolts from caliper.
5. Release caliper body from carrier.
6. Tie caliper aside.

⚠ **CAUTION: Do not allow weight of caliper to hang on hose, as damage may occur to hose.**

7. Remove brake pads from carrier.

BRAKE SERVO

Service repair no - 70.50.01

Remove

1. Remove underbonnet closing panel. *See BODY, Exterior fittings.*
2. Remove spare wheel.

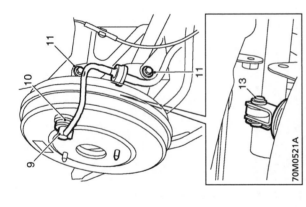

3. Disconnect fluid level switch.
4. Remove 2 nuts and washers securing master cylinder to brake servo.
5. Release brake pipes from bulk head clips.

⚠ **CAUTION: Do not bend brake pipes when removing master cylinder.**

6. Remove master cylinder from brake servo.
7. Remove 'O' ring from master cylinder and discard.
8. Tie master cylinder aside so that weight of master cylinder is supported.

70M0519A

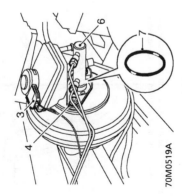

70M0521A

9. Carefully prise vacuum hose connection from brake servo.
10. Remove and discard sealing rubber.
11. Remove 2 inboard bolts and loosen 2 outboard bolts securing servo bracket.
12. Release servo from bracket for access to clevis pin.
13. Remove split pin and withdraw clevis pin securing crank to servo push rod.
14. Remove servo assembly.

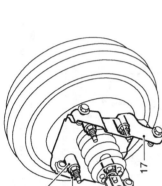

70M0522A

15. Remove 4 nuts securing bracket to servo.
16. Collect spacers.
17. Remove bracket.

Refit

1. Position bracket to servo, fit spacers and secure with nuts, tighten nuts to 20 Nm.
2. Position servo assembly and align servo push rod.
3. Fit clevis pin and secure with new split pin.
4. Align servo and engage outboard bolts to slots in bracket.
5. Fit inboard bolts. Tighten all bolts to 20 Nm.
6. Engage harness clip to bracket.
7. Fit NEW sealing rubber to vacuum hose.
8. Connect vacuum hose to servo.
9. Untie master cylinder.
10. Clean master cylinder and servo mating surfaces.
11. Fit new 'O' ring to master cylinder.
12. Align servo push rod and fit master cylinder to servo.
13. Fit nuts and washers securing master cylinder to servo, tighten nuts to 20 Nm.
14. Fit brake pipes to clips.
15. Connect fluid level switch.
16. Fit spare wheel.
17. Fit underbonnet closing panel. *See BODY, Exterior fittings.*

BRAKES

CALIPER - FRONT - MGF TROPHY

Service repair no - 70.55.02

Remove

1. Raise front of vehicle, one side.

⚠ **WARNING: Do not work on or under a vehicle supported only by a jack. Always support the vehicle on safety stands.**

2. Remove road wheel(s).

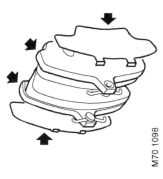

SP70 0004

3. Using a parallel punch, drift out brake pad retaining pins and collect anti-squeal plate.

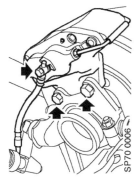

SP70 0005

4. Remove brake pads from caliper housing, mark their fitted position if they are to be refitted.
5. Use an recommended brake hose clamp to clamp brake hose.

SP70 0006

6. Remove banjo bolt securing brake hose to caliper, remove and discard sealing washers.

⚠ **CAUTION: Always fit plugs to open connections to prevent contamination.**

7. Remove 2 bolts securing caliper assembly to hub and remove caliper.

Refit

1. Rotate disc by hand and scrape all scale and rust from around edge of disc.
2. Clean mating faces of caliper and hub.
3. Position caliper to hub, fit and tighten bolts to 85 Nm.
4. Remove plug from brake hose banjo.
5. Clean brake hose banjo connection, fit NEW sealing washers and tighten banjo bolt to 35 Nm.
6. Remove clamp from brake hose.
7. Using a suitable flat lever, retract caliper pistons into housing.
8. Fit brake pads to caliper housing.
9. Fit brake pad retaining pins and anti-squeal plate.
10. Bleed brake caliper.
11. Fit road wheel(s), fit wheel nuts and tighten in a diagonal sequence to 70 Nm.
12. Depress brake pedal several times to seat pads.
13. Remove stand(s) and lower vehicle.

BRAKES

BRAKE CALIPER HOUSING -FRONT

Service repair no - 70.55.24

Remove

1. Raise front of vehicle, one side.

⚠ **WARNING: Support on safety stands.**

2. Remove road wheel(s).
3. Clamp brake hose to prevent fluid lose.

⚠ **CAUTION: An approved brake hose clamp must be used.**

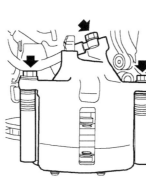

M70 1097

4. Remove brake hose banjo bolt.
5. Remove and discard 2 sealing washers

⚠ **CAUTION: Plug the connections.**

6. Remove 2 guide pin bolts.
7. Remove caliper housing from caliper bracket.

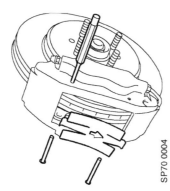

M70 1098

8. Remove 2 brake pads and discard shims.

⚠ NOTE: Note location of pads if same ones are to be replaced. Pads must be fitted in original locations.

Refit

1. Rotate disc by hand and scrape all scale and rust from around edge of disc. Scrape clean abutment surfaces on caliper carrier.
2. Clean dust from brake parts using brake cleaning fluid or industrial alcohol.
3. Using tool **18G 590** , press piston back into caliper.
4. Fit new shims to pads and fit pads to caliper carrier.
5. Position caliper housing to carrier, fit and tighten guide pin bolts to 45 Nm.
6. Clean brake hose banjo connection, fit NEW sealing washers and tighten banjo bolt to 35 Nm.
7. Remove clamp from brake hose.
8. Bleed brake caliper.
9. Fit road wheel(s) and tighten nuts to correct torque. **See INFORMATION, Torque wrench settings.**
10. Remove stand(s) and lower vehicle.

BRAKES

BRAKE CALIPER CARRIER - FRONT

Service repair no - 70.55.28

Remove

1. Raise front of vehicle, one side.

 WARNING: Support on safety stands.

2. Remove road wheel(s).

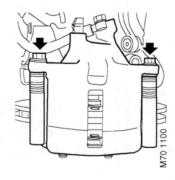

M70 1100

3. Remove 2 guide pin bolts securing caliper housing to carrier.

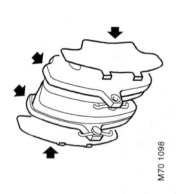

M70 1098

 NOTE: Mark location of pads if same ones are to be replaced. Pads must be refitted to original locations.

4. Position caliper housing aside and remove 2 brake pads.
5. Remove and discard 2 shims from pads.

 CAUTION: Do not allow caliper to hang from hose as damage may result.

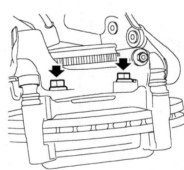

M70 1099

6. Remove 2 bolts securing caliper carrier to swivel hub and remove carrier.

Refit

1. Position caliper carrier to hub, fit and tighten bolts to 85 Nm.
2. Remove cap from brake fluid reservoir and position cloth to catch any spillage.

 CAUTION: Do not allow brake fluid to contact paint finished surfaces as paint may be damaged. If spilled, remove fluid and clean area with clean warm water.

3. Clean housing abutment and piston.
4. Using tool **18G 590**, press piston fully into caliper.
5. Fit new shims to pads and position to carrier.
6. Position caliper housing to carrier, fit and tighten guide pin bolts to 45 Nm.
7. Fit road wheel(s) and tighten nuts to correct torque. **See INFORMATION, Torque wrench settings.**
8. Remove stand(s) and lower vehicle.
9. Depress brake pedal several times to seat pads to discs. Pedal travel may be longer than normal during first brake applications.
10. Top up fluid level if required and fit cap.

RESTRAINT SYSTEMS

CONTENTS

COMPONENT LOCATION

◁ NOTE: LHD type is symmetrical to RHD type.

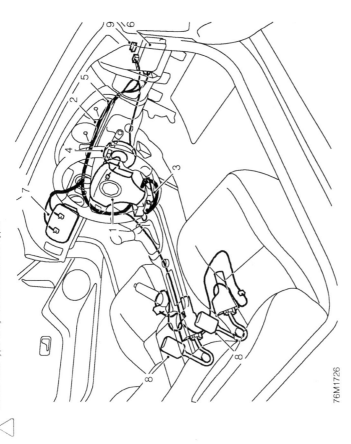

76M1726

1. Driver's airbag module *
2. SRS warning light
3. Diagnostic control unit *
4. Rotary coupler *
5. SRS harness (YELLOW) *

6. Fuse/relay box
7. Passenger's airbag module (optional) *
8. Seat belt pre-tensioners *
9. Diagnostic socket

* Components to be renewed following system deployment.

Following deployment of the Supplementary Restraint System (SRS), under any circumstances, the above components marked with an asterisk must be renewed.

Impacts which do not deploy airbags, check for structural damage in the area of impact, paying particular attention to bumper armatures, longitudinals, crash cans and bracketry.

RESTRAINT SYSTEMS

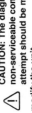

DESCRIPTION

76M1809

The airbag Supplementary Restraint System (SRS) is a safety device which, when deployed in the event of a severe frontal impact, provides additional protection to the driver's face and upper torso. The airbag is designed to inflate when the vehicle is exceeding a set speed and receives a frontal impact within the area shown.

76M1810

OPERATION

Diagnostic Control Unit

⚠ **CAUTION: The diagnostic control unit is a non-serviceable component and no attempt should be made to repair or modify the unit.**

The diagnostic control unit which is mounted within the passenger compartment performs two functions:

1. It monitors the airbag system for faults;
2. It provides a fire signal to the airbag(s) in the event of a crash.

The warning lamp illuminates to inform the driver of any airbag system faults.

The diagnostic control unit comprises of the following circuits which control the airbag system:

1. The crash sensor determines the severity of any impact and can discriminate between rough road conditions and an actual crash.
2. The safing sensor is wired in series with the crash sensor. The fire signal from the crash sensor therefore, passes through the safing sensor which confirms a crash is taking place.
3. The regulator circuit maintains stability of the system in the event of battery voltage drop.
4. The back-up power supply provides power to the system in the event of the battery being damaged or disconnected during the impact.
5. Internal diagnostics continually monitor the SRS system.

The fire signal from the diagnostic control unit passes via the airbag harness to the airbag modules and pretensioners. Grains of Nitrocellulose and Nitroglycerine inside the airbag module, ignite and combine in a chemical reaction to form a large amount of Nitrogen gas leading to inflation of the airbag in approximately 30 milli-seconds.

As the occupant moves forward into the airbag it immediately deflates to provide progressive deceleration and reduce the risk of injuries.

RESTRAINT SYSTEMS

Sequence of operation:

1. The main sensor and the safing sensor are activated.
2. Power is supplied to the airbag igniter by the battery or the back-up circuit.
3. The airbag deploys.

It takes approximately 0.1 seconds from the beginning of the airbag deployment until it is completely deflated.

System check

The warning light, located in instrument pack illuminates when the electrical circuits are switched on whilst the system performs a self diagnosis test. If the system finds no fault during self diagnosis the light will extinguish after approximately 5 seconds and remain extinguished.

In the event of a fault in the system, the warning light will illuminate continuously or fail to illuminate during the self diagnosis test.

Fault finding diagnosis

Faults in the SRS system can be identified by connecting TestBook into the diagnostic socket, located on the passenger compartment fuse box.

General

PRECAUTIONS

Making the system safe

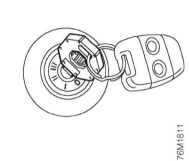

76M1811

- Remove key from starter switch, disconnect both battery leads, earth lead first, wait 10 minutes to allow the SRS back-up circuit to fully discharge.

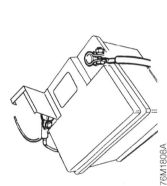

76M1808A

- Always disconnect both battery leads, earth lead first before beginning work.
- On completion of work connect battery leads, earth lead last.

76M1812

- Carefully inspect any SRS part before you install it. Do not install any part that shows signs of being dropped or improperly handled, such as dents, cracks or deformation:

  - Airbag assembly - Pretensioners
  - Rotary coupler - SRS Harness
  - Diagnostic control unit (DCU).

- The DCU is a shock sensitive device and must be handled with extreme care.
- Because the crash sensor is incorporated inside the DCU it is imperative that the bolts securing the DCU and its bracket are tightened to their correct torque.
- Never install a part that shows signs of being dropped or improperly handled.
- Do not install used SRS parts from another car. When repairing an SRS, use only new parts.
- Do not use a circuit tester to check the system.
- After completing work, check that the connectors are installed correctly.

This page is intentionally left blank

Airbag Handling and Storage

- Do not try to disassemble the airbag assembly, it has no serviceable parts. Once an airbag has been deployed, it cannot be repaired or reused.
- Be careful that the airbag assembly receives no strong shocks; it could deploy.
- Special bolts are necessary for installing the airbag assembly. Do not use other bolts.

For temporary storage of the airbag assembly during service, observe the following precautions:

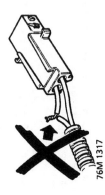

76M1813

- Always carry the airbag module with the pad surface face up.
- Store the removed airbag assembly with the pad surface face up.
- Do not allow anything to rest on the airbag module.
- Place the airbag module in a designated storage area.
- If no designated storage area is available, then the boot of the vehicle should be used. Always lock the boot when a module is stored in it and inform the workshop supervisor.

 WARNING: If the airbag is improperly stored face down, accidental deployment could propel the unit with enough force to cause serious injury.

- Store the removed airbag assembly on a secure flat surface away from any high heat source (exceeding 85°C/185°F) and free of any oil, grease, detergent or water.

⚠️ **CAUTION: Improper handling or storage can internally damage the airbag assembly, making it inoperative. If you suspect the airbag assembly has been damaged, install a new unit and refer to the Deployment/Disposal Procedures for disposing of the damaged airbag.**

Overnight storage

Airbag modules are classed as explosive articles and as such must be stored in an approved secure steel cabinet which has been registered by the local authority.

Wiring-related

76M1317

- Never attempt to modify, splice or repair SRS wiring. Never install electronic equipment such as: a mobile telephone, two way radio or in car entertainment system in such a way that it interferes electrically with the airbag harness.

◁ NOTE: SRS wiring can be identified by special yellow outer protective covering.

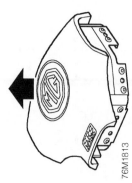

76M1318

- Always ensure SRS harnesses are routed correctly. Be careful to avoid trapping or pinching the SRS harness. Look out for possible points of chafing.
- Always use specified earth fixings tightened to the correct torque. Poor earthing can cause intermittent problems that are difficult to diagnose.
- Ensure all airbag harness connectors are mated correctly and securely fastened. Do not leave the connectors hanging loose.

WARNING LABELS

76M1670

A combination of symbols/icons are displayed (either in a suitable, prominent position or are attached to the component itself) to indicate:
(a) The need for caution when working in close proximity to SRS components;
(b) The publication where suitable reference and advice can be found (usually Workshop Manual or Owner's Handbook).

⚠ NOTE: It is imperative that before any work is undertaken on the SRS system that the appropriate publication is read thoroughly.

The following list indicates current locations for warning labels. Exact positions may vary dependent on legislation and market trends.

1. Bonnet locking platform

Refer to the Owner's Handbook for information on the airbag system.

2. Rotary coupler

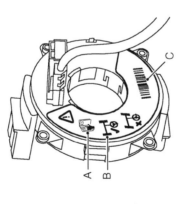

76M2319

A - SRS - Refer to the Workshop Manual for detailed instructions.
B - Ensure wheels are in the straight ahead position before removal and refitting of the rotary coupler.
C - Rover part number/Bar code: The code number must be quoted when ordering a replacement rotary coupler.

⚠ CAUTION: DO NOT ROTATE ROTARY COUPLER MECHANISM

---

3. Door glass

Refer to the Owner's Handbook for information on the airbag system.

4. Airbag module - driver

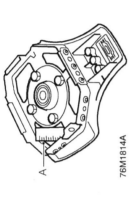

76M1814A

A - ROVER Part Number/Bar code - The code number must be quoted when ordering a replacement module.

5. Diagnostic control unit.

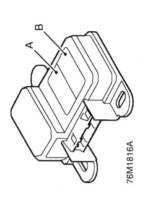

76M1816A

A - Refer to the Workshop Manual for information on the airbag system.

B - ROVER Part number/Bar Code - The code number must be recorded if the airbag control and diagnostic unit is to be replaced.

6. Airbag module - passenger

76M1815A

A - ROVER Part Number/Bar code - The code number must be quoted when ordering a replacement module.

AIRBAG AND PRE-TENSIONER, MANUAL DEPLOYMENT

 NOTE: Pre-tensioner deployment is done in car only.

If a vehicle is to be scrapped and contains an undeployed airbag module, or pre-tensioner, the components must be manually deployed. This operation should only be carried out using the following recommended manual deployment procedure.

Before deployment is started the deployment tool self test procedure should be carried out.

Deployment tool SMD 4082/1 self test procedure

1. Insert blue and yellow connectors of tool lead into corresponding sockets on face of tool.
2. Connect crocodile clips of second tool lead to battery, red to positive and black to negative.
3. Red "READY" light should illuminate.
4. Press and hold both operating buttons.
5. Green "DEFECTIVE" light should illuminate.
6. Release both operating buttons.
7. Red "READY" light should illuminate.
8. Disconnect tool from battery.
9. Disconnect blue and yellow connectors from tool face sockets.
10. Self test now complete.

Deployment of pre-tensioner

These guidelines are written to aid authorised personnel to carry out the safe disposal of the pre-tensioner.

 **WARNING:**

- **Only use the Rover approved deployment equipment.**
- **Deploy pre-tensioner in a designated area.**
- **Ensure pre-tensioner is not damaged or ruptured before deploying.**
- **Notify relevant authorities.**

1. Carry out deployment tool self test.
2. Slide seat fully forward to access pre-tensioner harness connector.
3. Disconnect pre-tensioner harness connector.

WARNING: Ensure deployment tool SMD 4082/1 is not connected to battery.

4. Connect flylead **SMD 4082/5** to pre-tensioner connector.
5. Connect flylead **SMD 4082/5** to tool **SMD 4082/1**.

WARNING: Ensure pre-tensioner is secured tightly to seat.

6. Connect tool **SMD 4082/1** to battery.

WARNING: Ensure all personnel are standing at least 15 metres away from vehicle.

7. Press both operating buttons to deploy pre-tensioner.
8. Using gloves, remove pre-tensioner from seat and place pre-tensioner in plastic bag, and seal bag.
9. Transport deployed pre-tensioner to designated area for incineration.

NOTE: DO NOT transport pre-tensioner in the vehicle passenger compartment.

Deployment of driver airbag module

These guidelines are written to aid authorised personnel to carry out the safe disposal of airbag modules when removed from the vehicle.

 **WARNING:**

- **Only use the Rover approved deployment equipment.**
- **Deploy airbag modules in a well ventilated designated area.**
- **Ensure airbag module is not damaged or ruptured before deploying.**
- **Notify relevant authorities.**

1. Carry out deployment tool self test.
2. Remove airbag module from steering wheel. **See Repairs.**
3. Position tool **SMD 4082/2** in vice, ensuring that vice jaws grip tool above bottom flange to prevent possibility of tool being forced upwards from vice. Tighten vice.

WARNING: Ensure deployment tool SMD 4082/1 is not connected to battery.

4. Secure airbag module to tool **SMD 4082/2**. Ensure module is correctly secured using both fixings.
5. Ensure airbag module mounting brackets are secure.
6. Connect flylead **SMD 4082/4** to airbag module.
7. Connect flylead **SMD 4082/4** to tool **SMD 4082/1**.

WARNING: Do not lean over airbag module whilst connecting.

8. Connect tool **SMD 4082/1** to battery.

WARNING: Ensure all personnel are standing at least 15 metres away from module.

9. Press both operating buttons to deploy airbag module.
10. **DO NOT** return to airbag module for 30 minutes.
11. Using gloves and face mask, remove airbag module from tool, place airbag module in plastic bag, and seal bag.
12. Wipe down tool with damp cloth.
13. Transport deployed airbag module to designated area for incineration.

NOTE: DO NOT transport airbag module in the vehicle passenger compartment.

14. Scrap all remaining parts of airbag system. **DO NOT** re-use or salvage any parts of the airbag system.

Deployment of passenger airbag module

These guidelines are written to aid authorised personnel to carry out the safe disposal of airbag modules when removed from the vehicle.

 WARNING:

• **Only use the Rover approved deployment equipment.**
• **Deploy airbag modules in a well ventilated designated area.**
• **Ensure airbag module is not damaged or ruptured before deploying.**
• **Notify relevant authorities.**

1. Carry out deployment tool self test.
2. Remove passenger airbag module. *See Repairs.*
3. Position tool **SMD 4082/6** in vice, ensuring that vice jaws grip tool above bottom flange to prevent possibility of tool being forced upwards from vice. Tighten vice.
4. Position brackets **SMD 4082/7** to tool, lightly tighten bolts.
5. Position airbag module to tool **SMD 4082/6**. Ensure module is correctly secured using all fixings.
6. Ensure airbag module mounting brackets are secure.

 **WARNING: Ensure tool SMD 4082/1 is not connected to battery.**

7. Connect flylead **SMD 4082/5** to airbag module.
8. Connect flylead **SMD 4082/5** to tool **SMD 4082/1**.

WARNING: Do not lean over airbag module whilst connecting.

9. Connect tool **SMD 4082/1** to battery.

WARNING: Ensure all personnel are standing at least 15 metres away from module.

10. Press both operating buttons to deploy airbag module.
11. **DO NOT** return to airbag module for 30 minutes.
12. Using gloves and face mask, remove airbag module from tool, place airbag module in plastic bag and seal bag.
13. Wipe down tool with damp cloth.
14. Transport deployed airbag module to designated area for incineration.

   NOTE: DO NOT transport airbag module in the vehicle passenger compartment.

15. Scrap all remaining parts of airbag system. **DO NOT** re-use or salvage any parts of the airbag system.

DIAGNOSTIC CONTROL UNIT (DCU)

Service repair no - 76.73.72

 **WARNING: *See Precautions.***

Remove

1. Make the SRS system safe. *See Precautions.*
2. Remove centre console panel. *See BODY, Interior trim components.*

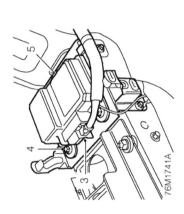

76M1741A

3. Disconnect multiplug from DCU.
4. Remove 3 Torx bolts securing DCU to bracket.
5. Remove DCU.

Refit

 WARNING: Because the crash sensor is incorporated inside the DCU, it is imperative that bolts securing the DCU are tightened to their correct torque.

1. Position DCU to support bracket, fit and tighten Torx bolts to 10 Nm.
2. Connect multiplug.

 CAUTION: Before connecting multiplug ensure that clip is in the open position, pointing away from the harness. Lock the connector into position by pushing clip towards harness.

3. Fit centre console panel. *See BODY, Interior trim components.*
4. Carry out system check using TestBook.

DRIVER AIRBAG MODULE

Service repair no - 76.74.71

 **WARNING: See Precautions.**

Remove

1. Make the SRS system safe. **See Precautions.**

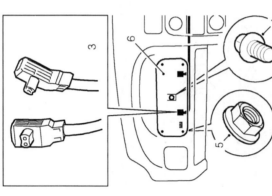

86M3733A

2. Remove 2 Tx30 Torx screws securing module to steering wheel.
3. Release air bag module from steering wheel.

 CAUTION: Do not allow the air bag module to hang by the air bag harness.

4. Disconnect multiplug from air bag module.
5. Remove air bag module.

CAUTION: Store the air bag module in accordance with the storage procedures outlined in the precautions part of this section.

NOTE: If the air bag module is to be replaced, the bar code must be recorded.

Refit

1. Position module to steering wheel and connect harness multiplug.
2. Align module to steering wheel, fit Torx screws and tighten to 8 Nm
3. Carry out system check using TestBook.

PASSENGER AIRBAG MODULE

Service repair no - 76.74.69

 WARNING: See Precautions.

Remove

1. Make the SRS system safe. **See Precautions.**
2. Remove glovebox. **See BODY, Interior trim components.**

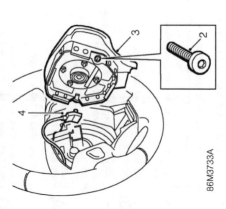

76M1795A

3. Disconnect 2 multiplugs from airbag.
4. Remove bolt securing bracket to fascia cross rail.
5. Remove 4 nuts securing airbag to bracket.
6. Remove airbag module.

CAUTION: Store the airbag module in accordance with the storage procedures outlined in the precautions part of this section.

NOTE: If the airbag module is to be replaced, the bar code must be recorded.

Refit

1. Position module to fascia bracket and tighten nuts to 8 Nm.
2. Tighten bolt securing bracket to fascia rail to 9 Nm.
3. Connect multiplugs.
4. Fit glovebox. **See BODY, Interior trim components.**
5. Carry out system check using TestBook.

SRS HARNESS

Service repair no - 76.73.73

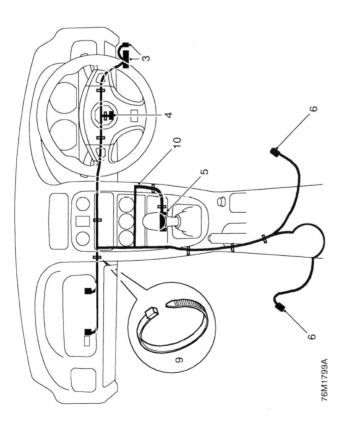

76M1799A

⚠ **WARNING: See Precautions.**

Remove

1. Make the SRS system safe. **See Precautions.**
2. Remove fascia. **See BODY, Interior trim components.**
3. Disconnect SRS multiplug and SRS fuse satellite from fusebox.
4. Disconnect multiplug from steering column.
5. Disconnect multiplug from DCU and release harness from bracket clip.
6. Disconnect 2 multiplugs from seatbelt pre-tensioners.

7. Remove 4 Torx bolts securing DCU bracket to tunnel, release harness earth and position DCU aside.
8. Remove 4 nuts and 3 bolts securing gear lever assembly to tunnel and position assembly aside.
9. Release 11 cable clips securing SRS harness to main harness.
10. Remove SRS harness.

Refit

1. Position harness to body.
2. Connect fuse satellite and multiplug to fusebox.
3. Connect multiplugs to seatbelt pre-tensioners.
4. Secure harness with clips.

⚠ **CAUTION: Ensure that pre-tensioner leads pass through grommets in centre console area.**

5. Position gear lever assembly to tunnel and tighten fixings to 9 Nm.

⚠ **WARNING: Because the crash sensor is incorporated inside the DCU, it is imperative that all bolts securing the DCU are tightened to their correct torque.**

6. Position DCU bracket to tunnel, fit harness earth lead and tighten fixings to 10 Nm.
7. Connect multiplug to steering column.

⚠ **CAUTION: Before connecting DCU multiplug ensure that clip is in the open position, pointing away from the harness. Lock the connector into position by pushing clip towards the harness.**

8. Connect multiplug to DCU and fit harness to clip.
9. Fit fascia. **See BODY, Interior trim components.**
10. Carry out system check using TestBook.

RESTRAINT SYSTEMS

SEAT BELT

Service repair no - 76.73.13

Remove

1. Remove seat. **See BODY, Interior trim components.**
2. Remove Torx bolt securing seat belt strap to seat frame.
3. Remove hoodwell trim. **See BODY, Interior trim components.**

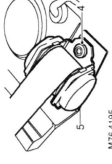

M76 4195

4. Remove Torx screw securing seat belt reel to body.
5. Remove seat belt.

Refit

1. Position seat belt reel to body, fit and tighten Torx screw to 35 Nm.
2. Fit hoodwell trim. **See BODY, Interior trim components.**
3. Position seat belt strap to seat, fit bolt and tighten to 30 Nm.
4. Fit seat. **See BODY, Interior trim components.**

SEAT BELT PRE-TENSIONER

Service repair no - 76.73.75

⚠ WARNING: *See Precautions.*

Remove

1. Make the SRS system safe. *See Precautions.*

⚠ **CAUTION: Ensure pre-tensioner multiplug is disconnected before seat is removed.**

2. Remove seat. *See BODY, Interior trim components.*

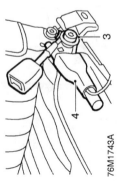

76M1743A

3. Remove bolt securing pre-tensioner to seat.
4. Remove pre-tensioner.

Refit

1. Position pre-tensioner to seat and tighten bolt to 45 Nm.

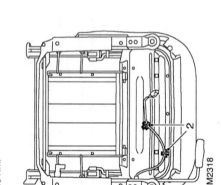

76M2318

2. Ensure that pre-tensioner lead is correctly clipped to seat base.
3. Fit seat. *See BODY, Interior trim components.*
4. Carry out system check using TestBook.

ROTARY COUPLER

Service repair no - 86.65.85

⚠ WARNING: *See Precautions.*

Remove

1. Make the SRS system safe. *See Precautions.*
2. Ensure wheels are in the straight ahead position.
3. Remove steering wheel. *See STEERING, Repairs.*
4. Remove steering column nacelle. *See STEERING, Repairs.*
5. If the rotary coupler is being re-used, place adhesive tape around moulding to prevent rotation.

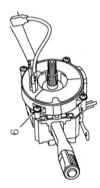

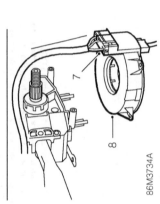

86M3734A

6. Remove 4 screws securing rotary coupler to steering column switch pack.
7. Release rotary coupler from column and disconnect 2 multiplugs.
8. Remove rotary coupler.

⚠ **CAUTION: Do not dismantle the rotary coupler. It has NO serviceable parts and must be replaced as a complete assembly.**

Refit

1. Position rotary coupler to switch pack.
2. Connect multiplugs.
3. Fit and tighten screws.
4. Remove adhesive tape.
5. Fit steering column nacelle. *See STEERING, Repairs.*
6. Fit steering wheel. *See STEERING, Repairs.*
7. Carry out system check using TestBook.

CONTENTS

CONTENTS

ELECTRIC WINDOW LIFT COMPONENTS

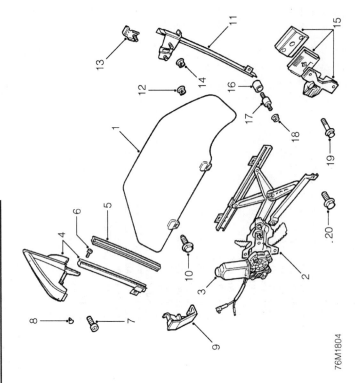

76M1804

1. Door glass
2. Regulator
3. Motor
4. Cheater assembly
5. Sash
6. Screw - sash to cheater, 2 off
7. Screw - cheater, 2 off
8. Fastener - cheater
9. Glass stop,
10. Bolt - glass to regulator, 2 off

11. Sash
12. Nut - upper rail bracket, 2 off
13. Stud bracket - glass retention
14. Nut - glass retention
15. Glass retention assembly
16. Sleeve - sash adjuster, 2 off
17. Screw - sash adjuster, 2 off
18. Nut - sash adjuster, 2 off
19. Bolt - glass retention
20. Bolt - regulator, 2 off

This page is intentionally left blank

ELECTRIC WINDOW OPERATION

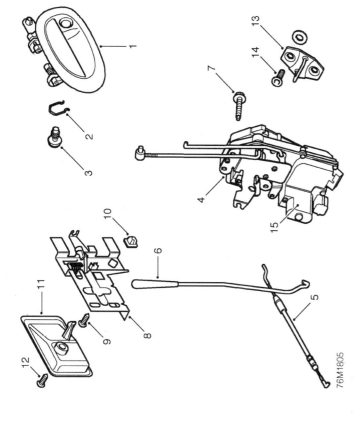

M76 3546

(RHD shown, LHD similar)

1. Window switch
2. Window lift ECU (Vehicles from 2000MY only)
3. Window relay
4. Glass
5. Regulator
6. Motor

The two window lift system is controlled by switches fitted in the centre console. When the ignition is switched on, the electric window relay located on the passenger compartment fusebox, switches power supply to the window circuit. The electric motor via an integral gearbox, operates the regulator assembly to lift and lower the window glass.

Battery supply from the electric window relay to the window switches is via two fuses, one for each door, located in the driver's compartment fusebox.

On vehicles from 2000MY, the driver's door window has a 'one-shot' down facility which allows the window to be fully lowered with a single press of the window switch. This is controlled by a window lift ECU which is located at the bottom of the 'A' post, behind the driver's window. The ECU controls all functions of the driver's window. The passenger window remains controlled by the multi function ECU and the window lift relay as on previous models.

DOOR - CENTRAL LOCKING COMPONENTS

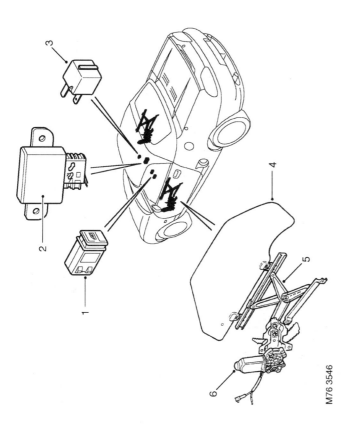

76M1805

1. External door handle assembly
2. Retaining clip - cylinder block
3. Bolt - outer door handle
4. Latch assembly
5. Cable - remote door handle
6. Sill button and rod
7. Screw - latch assembly
8. Remote door handle assembly
9. Screw - inside door handle
10. Holder - lock rod
11. Escutcheon - remote door handle
12. Screw - escutcheon
13. Striker - door lock
14. Bolt - striker
15. Lock motor

DOOR CENTRAL LOCKING - OPERATION

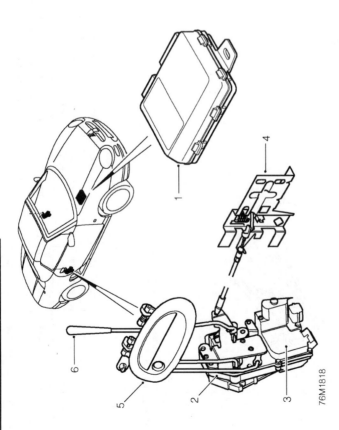

76M1818

1. Anti-theft alarm ECU
2. Latch assembly
3. Lock motor

Central door locking is operated by using any one of the following:

- Remote handset,
- Key in the driver's door lock,
- Driver's door sill button.

Both door locks are operated by separate integral lock motors which function simultaneously. They are controlled by the alarm ECU mounted behind the fascia centre console, below the heater control unit.

A signal from the remote handset is received by the alarm ECU. Depending on this signal the ECU will either lock or unlock the doors by controlling the direction of electrical current sent to the lock motors.

4. Internal door handle
5. External door handle and lock
6. Sill button

When the driver's door key is turned or the sill button is depressed, the driver's door is mechanically locked by the door latch which triggers the latch switch. The latch switch sends an earth signal to the alarm ECU, which in turn controls the electrical current sent to the passenger door motor to lock the door.

Operation of the passenger door sill button will lock or unlock the passenger door but will not operate the central door locking system.

DOOR STRIKER - ADJUST

Service repair no - 76.28.05

76M1836

1. Using a Torx bit loosen 2 striker screws and close door.
2. Check door for flush fit to adjacent panels and edges for equal gap.
3. Open door and tighten striker screws to 18 Nm.

DOOR GLASS - ADJUST

For information on adjustment of the door glass, see hood seals and door glass - adjust. *See Hood.*

DOOR - ALIGN ON HINGES

Service repair no - 76.28.07

1. Turn wheel in lock for access to wheel arch liner screws.
2. Remove 3 screws and 3 scrivets securing wheel arch liner.
3. Remove wheel arch liner to gain access to hinge bolts.
4. Open door.
5. Remove screws securing door striker to 'B' post collect striker.
6. Loosen bolts securing hinges to 'A' post.
7. Align door to meet the profile of adjacent panels, and ensure all surrounding door gaps are parallel.
8. Tighten door hinge bolts.
9. Re-check door alignment.
10. Position door striker and fit screws.
11. Adjust door striker so that the door closes without the need for slamming it.
12. Tighten door striker screws to 18 Nm.
13. Fit and wheel arch liner and secure with screws and scrivets.

DOOR MIRROR - UP TO 2000MY

Service repair no - 76.10.52

Remove

1. Remove trim casing. *See this section.*

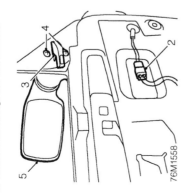

76M1558

2. Disconnect heated door mirror glass multiplug.
3. Remove door mirror adjustment lever.
4. Remove 2 screws securing door mirror to cheater panel.
5. Release mirror harness from cheater and remove mirror.

Refit

1. Feed mirror harness through cheater, align mirror and tighten screws.
2. Fit door mirror adjustment lever.
3. Connect door mirror harness multiplug to vehicle harness.
4. Fit trim casing. *See this section.*

MIRROR - EXTERIOR - ELECTRIC - 2000MY ON

Service repair no - 76.10.57

Remove

1. Remove front door casing. *See this section.*

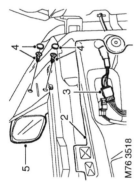

M76 3518

2. Release plastic sheet to access mirror multiplug.
3. Disconnect mirror multiplug and attach draw string to mirror harness.
4. Remove 2 screw caps and screws securing mirror.
5. Remove exterior mirror.
6. Remove draw string from mirror harness.

Refit

1. Attach draw string to mirror harness and feed harness into door. Remove draw string from mirror harness.
2. Position exterior mirror to door and secure with screws.
3. Fit screw caps.
4. Connect mirror multiplug.
5. Secure plastic sheet in correct position.
6. Fit front door casing. *See this section.*

GLASS

Service repair no - 76.31.01

Remove

1. Remove trim casing. *See this section.*

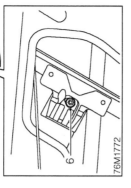

76M1771

2. Release 5 clips securing outer waist seal to door and remove seal.
3. Peel back plastic sheet to allow access to inner door.
4. Switch ignition ON and lower window to allow access to bolts.
5. Switch ignition OFF.

76M1772

6. Remove 3 bolts securing glass to regulator.
7. Remove glass.

Refit

1. Position glass to regulator and align rear guide to glass.
2. Fit bolts securing glass to regulator but do not tighten.
3. Adjust door glass. *See this section.*
4. Position plastic sheet and secure in place.
5. Fit outer waist seal and secure with clips.
6. Fit trim casing. *See this section.*

BODY

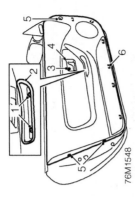

DOOR GLASS REGULATOR

Service repair no - 76.31.45

Remove

1. Remove glass. *See this section.*
2. Remove plastic sheet. *See this section.*
3. Disconnect multiplug from motor.

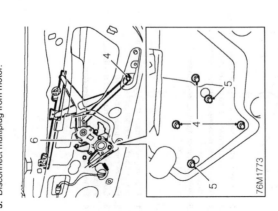

76M1773

4. Remove 4 bolts securing regulator to door.
5. Loosen 2 bolts securing regulator to door.
6. Remove regulator.

Refit

1. Position regulator to door and feed multiplug through aperture.
2. Align bolts to slotted holes and tighten to 7 Nm.
3. Fit and tighten bolts to 7 Nm.
4. Fit glass. *See this section.*
5. Fit plastic sheet. *See this section.*

OUTER WAIST SEAL

Service repair no - 76.31.53

Remove

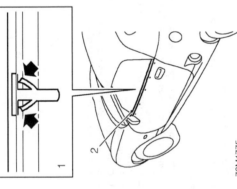

76M1775

1. Starting from the rear of the door, release 5 clips securing seal to door.
2. Remove seal.

Refit

1. Position seal to door and align clips.
2. Fit seal and engage clips.

DOOR AND HEADER SEAL

Service repair no - 76.31.85

Remove

1. Open both doors.
2. Lower both sun visors.
3. Release catches and lower hood.

76M1552

4. Remove 2 Tx30 Torx screws securing each hood striker and remove both strikers.
5. Remove 2 studs securing seal to 'A' posts.
6. Remove seal.

Refit

1. Position and centralise seal to header rail.
2. Secure seal to 'A' posts with studs.
3. Engage seal to flanges of header, 'A' posts and sills.
4. Fit hood strikers and tighten screws to 6 Nm.
5. Reposition sun visors.
6. Raise hood and secure catches.
7. Close doors.

TRIM CASING

Service repair no - 76.34.01/99

Remove

76M1548

1. Remove 2 screws securing door pull.
2. Remove door pull from trim casing.
3. Remove screw securing remote door handle escutcheon.
4. Remove remote door handle escutcheon.
5. Remove 3 screws securing trim casing.
6. Release 6 lower trim casing retaining clips, remove trim casing.

Refit

1. Fit trim casing to door and secure with clips.
2. Fit screws securing trim casing to door.
3. Fit remote door handle escutcheon and secure with screw.
4. Fit door pull to trim casing and secure with screws.

PLASTIC SHEET

Service repair no - 76.34.26

⚠ NOTE: A NEW plastic sheet must always be fitted, do not attempt to repair an existing plastic sheet.

⚠ NOTE: To obtain an effective seal when fitting a new plastic sheet, ensure that the plastic sheet and door contact surface are at room temperature: between 18°C to 30°C.

Remove

1. Remove the remote door handle. **See this section.**

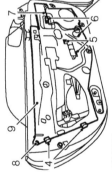

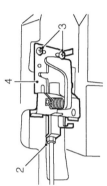

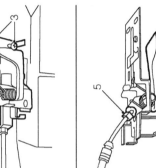

76M3612

2. Remove 3 screws securing door speaker.
3. Release speaker, disconnect 2 Lucars and remove speaker.

76M1551

4. Remove 2 trim rear fixing clips from door.
5. Remove 2 screws securing door pull fixing bracket to door, remove bracket.
6. Release 2 door harness retaining clips from door.
7. Disconnect heated door mirror multiplug.
8. Remove trim casing rear upper fixing clip from door.
9. Release plastic sheet from door. Feed harness connectors through sheet and remove plastic sheet.

Refit

1. Ensure door is clean and dry where it comes in to contact with the adhesive strip on the plastic sheet.
2. Fit plastic sheet, by fitting the adhesive strip to the bottom centre of the door first.
3. Starting from the bottom centre of the adhesive strip apply even pressure along the strip in both directions simultaneously, until the top centre of seal is reached.
4. Feed harness connectors through sheet and secure to door.
5. Fit fixing clips to door.
6. Connect heated door mirror multiplug.
7. Secure harness retaining clips to door.
8. Fit door pull fixing bracket to door and tighten screws.
9. Fit trim casing rear fixing brackets to door.
10. Position door speaker, connect Lucars and tighten screws.
11. Fit the remote door handle. **See this section.**

PRIVATE LOCK

Service repair no - 76.37.39

Remove

1. Remove trim casing. **See this section.**
2. Carefully peel back plastic sheet to allow access to inner door.

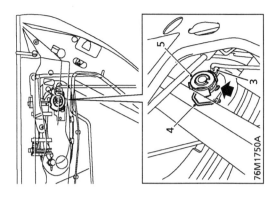

76M1750A

3. Unclip link rod from lock.
4. Release spring clip from lock.
5. Remove private lock.

Refit

1. Fit lock to handle and secure with spring clip.
2. Engage link rod to lock.
3. Position plastic sheet and press into place.
4. Fit trim casing. **See this section.**

REMOTE DOOR HANDLE

Service repair no - 76.37.31

Remove

1. Remove trim casing. **See this section.**

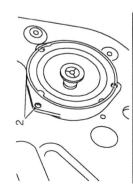

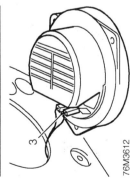

76M1549

2. Release latch operating cable from remote door handle abutment bracket.
3. Remove 2 screws securing remote door handle.
4. Release remote door handle from door by sliding in a forward direction.
5. Release clip securing latch operating cable to remote door handle, remove remote door handle.

Refit

1. Fit latch operating cable to remote door handle and secure with clip.
2. Position remote door handle to door and secure with screws.
3. Secure latch operating cable to remote door handle abutment bracket.
4. Fit trim casing. **See this section.**

BODY

OUTSIDE HANDLE

Service repair no - 76.58.07

Remove

1. Remove trim casing. *See this section.*
2. Switch the ignition ON and fully lower door glass.
3. Switch ignition OFF.
4. Carefully peel back corner of plastic sheet to allow access to door latch.

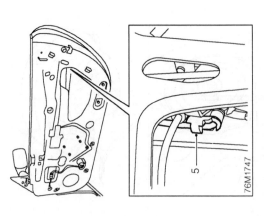

76M1747

5. Release clip securing door handle link rod to latch assembly and position aside.
6. *Driver's side:* release lock link rod from lock.

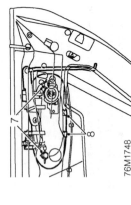

76M1748

7. Remove 2 bolts securing handle to door.
8. Release 2 clips retaining handle to door and position handle.

76M1749

9. Release clip securing lock to handle and remove lock.
10. Remove handle.
11. Remove rod from handle.

Refit

1. Fit rod to handle and position handle to door.
2. Engage handle to door and tighten bolts to 2.5 Nm.
3. Adjust rod length to align rod to latch.
4. Position rod and secure with clip.
5. *Driver's side:* engage lock connecting rod.
6. Fully raise door window.
7. Position lock to handle and secure with clip.
8. Secure plastic sheet.
9. Fit trim casing. *See this section.*

BONNET - ADJUST

Service repair no - 76.16.02/01

Adjust

1. Check alignment of bonnet.
2. Open bonnet.

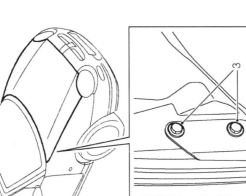

76M1777

BONNET LOCK PLATE - ADJUST

Service repair no - 76.16.20

Adjust

1. Open bonnet.

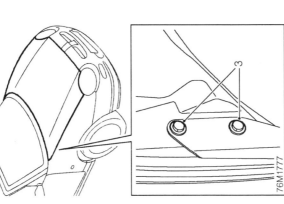

76M1778

2. Loosen 2 bolts securing lock plate to body.
3. Position lock plate fully forward.
4. Gently lower bonnet. Align striker pin with lock and ensure safety catch engages in lock plate.
5. Tighten bolts to 25 Nm.
6. Check correct operation of bonnet latch and alignment of bonnet.
7. If necessary adjust bonnet. *See this section.*

3. Loosen 4 bolts securing bonnet to hinges and adjust bonnet.
4. Lightly tighten bolts and close bonnet.
5. Check gaps are equal and bonnet is aligned with adjacent panels.
6. Open bonnet, adjust hinges if necessary and tighten bolts to 9 Nm.
7. If necessary, adjust bonnet locking plate. *See this section.*

This page is intentionally left blank

BODY

BOOT LID - ADJUST

Service repair no - 76.19.03

Adjust

1. Check for equal gaps around boot and alignment with adjacent panels.
2. Open boot lid.

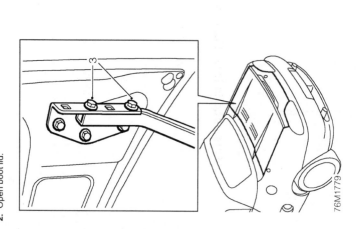

76M1779

3. Loosen 4 bolts securing boot lid to hinges and adjust boot lid.
4. Lightly tighten bolts and close boot.
5. Check alignment of boot lid.
6. Open boot lid.
7. Adjust boot lid if necessary and tighten bolts to 9 Nm.
8. If necessary, adjust boot striker. *See this section.*

BOOT LID STRIKER - ADJUST

Service repair no - 76.19.04

Adjust

1. Open boot lid.

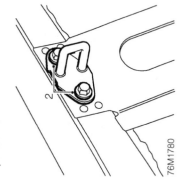

76M1780

2. Loosen 2 bolts securing striker to body and approximately position striker.
3. Lightly tighten bolts and close boot lid. Check for equal gaps and alignment with adjacent panels.
4. Open boot lid, re-position latch as necessary, tighten latch and striker bolts to 10 Nm.

FRONT WHEEL ARCH LINER

Service repair no - 76.10.48

Remove

1. Raise front of vehicle.

⚠ WARNING: Support on safety stands.

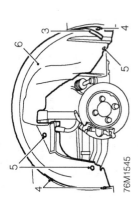

76M1545

2. Remove road wheel(s).

3. Release wheel arch flange seal from rear lower edge of wing panel.
4. Remove 3 screws securing wheel arch liner.
5. Remove 3 scrivet screws securing wheel arch liner, remove scrivets.
6. Remove wheel arch liner.

Refit

1. Fit and align wheel arch liner.
2. Fit scrivet fasteners securing wheel arch liner.
3. Fit and tighten screws securing wheel arch liner.
4. Secure wheel arch flange seal.
5. Fit road wheel(s) and tighten nuts to correct torque. **See INFORMATION, Torque wrench settings.**
6. Remove stand(s) and lower vehicle.

SPOILER - BOOT - MGF TROPHY

Service repair no - 76.10.91

Remove

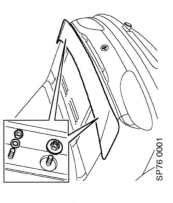

SP76 0001

1. Noting their fitted position, remove 4 nuts and washers securing rear spoiler to boot lid.
2. Release spoiler from boot lid and remove spoiler.

Refit

1. Clean spoiler and boot lid mating faces.
2. Ensure boot lid is at room temperature, fit new double sided pads.
3. Position spoiler and align to boot lid.
4. Ensuring correct orientation, fit nuts and washer and tighten to 5 Nm.

UNDERBONNET CLOSING PANEL

Service repair no - 76.10.94

Remove

1. Open bonnet.

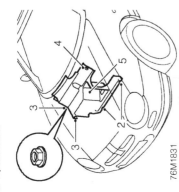

76M1831

2. Remove 2 fixings securing closing panel to spare wheel well.
3. Remove 2 fixings securing closing panel to scuttle.
4. Remove fixing securing closing panel to air intake plenum.
5. Remove closing panel.

Refit

1. Fit closing panel to body studs and secure fixings.
2. Close bonnet.

ENGINE COMPARTMENT ACCESS PANEL

Service repair no - 76.11.05/99

Remove

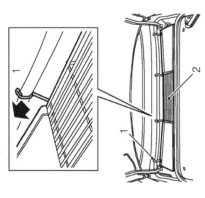

76M1745

1. Release 4 retaining clips along front edge of closing panel by pulling each clip away from the seal and lifting upwards.
2. Remove panel. *Do not carry out further dismantling if component is removed for access only.*
3. Remove 6 screws securing LH plate to panel, remove plate.
4. Remove 3 screws securing RH plate to panel, remove plate.

Rebuild

5. Fit RH plate to panel and secure with screws.
6. Fit LH plate to panel and secure with screws.

Refit

1. Fit closing panel and secure.

BONNET LOCKING PLATFORM - R/R ACCESS

Service repair no - 76.16.22/99

Remove

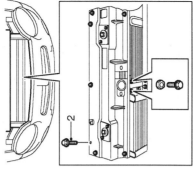

1. Remove front bumper valance. *See this section.*

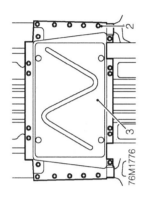

M76 3522

2. Remove 7 bolts and 2 nuts and bolts securing bonnet locking platform. Release bonnet locking platform from 4 location pegs.
3. Disconnect bonnet cable from bonnet catch and remove bonnet locking platform.

Refit

1. Position bonnet locking platform and connect bonnet cable to bonnet catch.
2. Fit bonnet locking platform and engage platform in location pegs. Fit nuts and bolts and tighten to 10 Nm.
3. Fit front bumper valance. *See this section.*

PANEL - FRONT UNDERBELLY - CENTRE

Service repair no - 76.10.50

Remove

1. Raise vehicle on a 2 post ramp.

76M1776

2. Remove 22 bolts securing underbelly panel to floorpan.
3. Remove underbelly panel.

Refit

1. Position underbelly panel to floorpan and tighten bolts to 22 Nm.
2. Lower vehicle.

BONNET RELEASE CABLE

Service repair no - 76.16.29

Remove

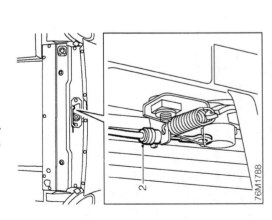

1. Remove headlamp assembly. **See** **ELECTRICAL, Repairs.**

2. Release cable from bonnet lock plate.

76M1788

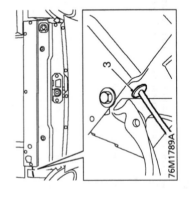

76M1789A

3. Release grommet from body
4. Feed bonnet release cable through hole.

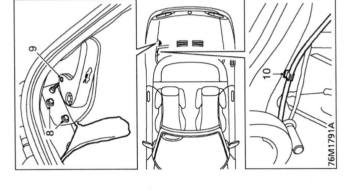

76M1790A

5. Loosen bolt securing earth header to inner wing and release cable from 2 inner wing clips.
6. Remove engine compartment access panel. **See this section.**
7. Remove hoodwell trim. **See Interior trim components.**

76M1791A

8. Position carpet aside and remove 2 bolts securing bonnet release lever to luggage compartment bulkhead.
9. Release cable abutment and cable from lever assembly.
10. Release cable from rear, inner wing clip.
11. Position felt pad aside and release grommet from hoodwell panel.
12. Feed cable through body holes and remove grommet from cable.

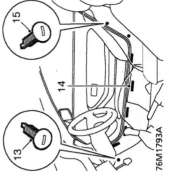

76M1793A

13. Remove stud securing carpet to inner wheel arch.
14. Release carpet from door seal and 5 velcro strips.
15. Remove 2 studs securing carpet to 'B' post, and release carpet from door seal and velcro to reveal cables.

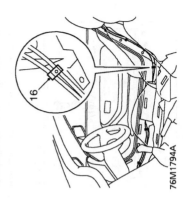

76M1794A

16. Release cable from 3 sill clips and 3 'B' post clips.
17. Release cable from floorpan crossmember.
18. Release grommet from scuttle and remove cable.

Refit

1. Feed cable through scuttle and under carpet insulation.
2. Position grommet to cable timing mark and engage grommet to scuttle.
3. Position cable to front inner wing and through hole in body.
4. Engage cable and abutment to bonnet lock plate.
5. Engage grommet to body.
6. Fit headlamp assembly. *See ELECTRICAL, Repairs.*
7. Engage cable to inner wing clip and tighten earth header bolt to 9 Nm.
8. Feed cable through floorpan crossmember and engage to clips.
9. Position carpet and secure with studs and velcro.
10. Position carpet beneath door flip seal.
11. Fit grommet to cable and position to timing mark.
12. Position cable through hole in hoodwell panel and luggage compartment bulkhead.
13. Engage cable and abutment to bonnet release lever.
14. Position lever to bulkhead and tighten bolts to 9 Nm.
15. Position carpet beneath luggage compartment flip seal.
16. Engage grommet and cable clip.
17. Fit hoodwell trim. *See Interior trim components.*
18. Fit engine compartment access panel. *See this section.*
19. Fit front bumper valance. *See this section.*

PRIVATE LOCK - BOOT LID

Service repair no - 76.19.10

Remove

1. Open boot lid.

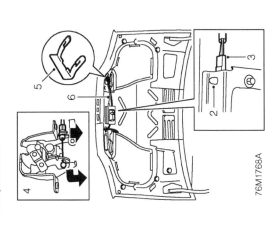

76M1768A

2. Release multiplug from boot lid latch, bracket.
3. Disconnect multiplug.
4. Disconnect release cable from boot lid latch.
5. Remove clip securing lock to boot lid.
6. Remove lock assembly from boot lid.

Refit

1. Position lock to boot lid and secure with clip.
2. Connect release cable to boot lid latch.
3. Connect multiplug.
4. Secure multiplug to boot lid latch, bracket.

BOOT LID LATCH

Service repair no - 76.19.11

Remove

1. Open boot lid.

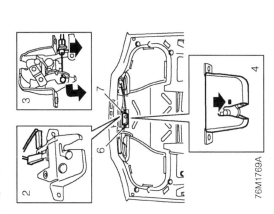

76M1769A

2. Disconnect 2 Lucars and multiplug from latch assembly.
3. Release cable from latch.
4. Release clip and remove cover from latch.
5. Mark position of latch to boot for reference.
6. Remove 2 bolts securing latch to boot lid.
7. Remove latch assembly.

Refit

1. Position latch to boot lid using reference marks and tighten bolts to 10 Nm.
2. Connect cable and secure to latch.
3. Connect Lucars and multiplug, and fit latch cover.
4. Check latch operation and if necessary, adjust boot lid striker. *See this section.*

FRONT BUMPER ARMATURE

Service repair no - 76.22.49

Remove

1. Remove front bumper valance. *See this section.*

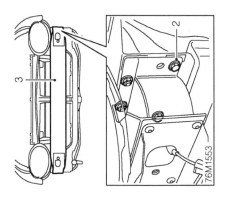

76M1553

2. Remove 2 bolts and 2 nuts securing each end of armature to front panel.
3. Remove armature.

Refit

1. Fit armature to fixing studs.
2. Fit nuts and bolts and tighten to 25 Nm.
3. Fit front bumper valance. *See this section.*

REAR BUMPER ARMATURE

Service repair no - 76.22.52

Remove

1. Remove rear bumper valance. *See this section.*

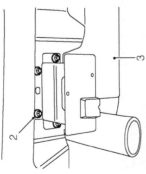

76M1798

2. Position luggage compartment carpet aside and remove 4 bolts securing bumper armature to body.
3. Remove bumper armature.

Refit

1. Align armature to body and tighten bolts to 22 Nm.
2. Fit rear bumper valance. *See this section.*

FRONT BUMPER VALANCE

Service repair no - 76.22.72

Remove

1. Raise front of vehicle.

⚠ **WARNING: Support on safety stands.**

2. Remove both direction indicators. *See ELECTRICAL, Repairs.*

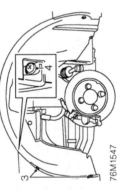

76M1547

3. Remove 2 screws securing each end of bumper valance to wheel arch liner.
4. Remove screw securing each end of bumper valance to wings.

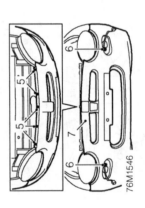

76M1546

5. Remove 5 screws securing bumper valance to bonnet lock panel.
6. Working through direction indicator housings, remove 2 bolts securing bumper valance to bumper armature.
7. Remove front bumper valance.

FRONT BUMPER VALANCE - MG F TROPHY

Service repair no - 76.22.72

Remove

1. Raise front of vehicle.

⚠ **WARNING: Do not work on or under a vehicle supported only by a jack. Always support the vehicle on safety stands.**

2. Remove front road wheels.
3. Remove both front wheel arch liners. *See this section.*
4. Remove both front direction indicator lamps. *See ELECTRICAL, Repairs.*

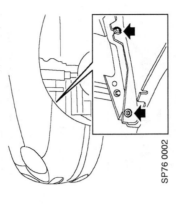

SP76 0002

5. Remove 4 screws securing each end of bumper valance to front wings.

Refit

1. Fit bumper valance.
2. Fit bolts securing bumper valance to bumper armature and tighten to 25 Nm.
3. Fit and tighten screws securing bumper valance to bonnet locking platform.
4. Fit and tighten screws securing each end of bumper valance to wheel arch liners.
5. Fit and tighten screws securing each end of bumper valance to wings.
6. Fit both direction indicators. *See ELECTRICAL, Repairs.*
7. Remove stand(s) and lower vehicle.

Refit

1. Clean mating faces of bib spoiler and bumper valance with spirit wipe or hot air gun.
2. Ensuring panels are at room temperature, fit new double sided tape to bib spoiler, ensure foam blocks are fitted to bumper valance.
3. Position bib spoiler to bumper valance and secure with scrivets.
4. Clean bumper badge and mating face, fit badge.
5. Position bumper grilles, fit and tighten screws.
6. Clean number plate and mating face.
7. Fit number plate.
8. Fit front bumper valance.
9. Fit bolts securing bumper valance to bumper armature and tighten to 25 Nm.
10. Fit and tighten screws securing bumper valance to bonnet locking panel.
11. Fit and tighten screws securing bumper valance to front wings.
12. Fit both direction indicator lamps. *See ELECTRICAL, Repairs.*
13. Fit both front wheel arch liners. *See this section.*
14. Fit road wheel(s), fit wheel nuts and tighten in a diagonal sequence to 70 Nm.
15. Remove stands and lower vehicle.

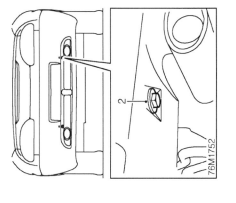

SP76 0003

6. Remove 5 screws securing bumper valance to bonnet locking panel.
7. Working through direction indicator housings, remove 2 bolts securing bumper valance to bumper armature.
8. Remove front bumper valance.

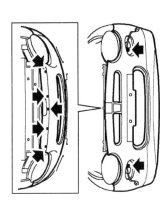

SP76 0004

9. Remove 15 screws securing bumper valance grilles and remove grilles.
10. Remove bumper valance badge.
11. Remove 4 scrivets securing bib spoiler to bumper valance.
12. Carefully Release bib spoiler from bumper valance and remove bib spoiler.
13. Remove 2 foam blocks.
14. Remove front number plate.

REAR BUMPER VALANCE

Service repair no - 76.22.74

Remove

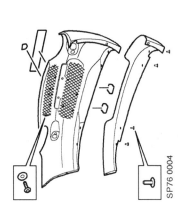

76M1751

1. Remove 4 screws securing bumper to wheel arches.

76M1752

2. Remove 2 bolts securing bumper valance to bumper armature.

Refit

1. Clean mating faces of bib spoiler and bumper valance with spirit wipe or hot air gun.
2. Ensuring panels are at room temperature, fit new double sided tape to bib spoiler, ensure foam blocks are fitted to bumper valance.
3. Position bib spoiler to bumper valance and secure with scrivets.

⚠ **CAUTION: Take care to align bib spoiler correctly before attaching to bumper.**

4. Fit scrivets securing bib spoiler to wheel arch return flanges.
5. Remove stands and lower vehicle.

EXTENSION - SPOILER - FRONT BUMPER - MGF TROPHY

Service repair no - 76.22.78

Remove

1. Raise front of vehicle.

SP76 0005

2. Remove 2 scrivets securing bib spoiler to wheel arch return flange.

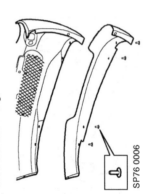

SP76 0006

3. Remove 4 scrivets securing bib spoiler to bumper valance.
4. Carefully Release bib spoiler from bumper valance and remove bib spoiler.

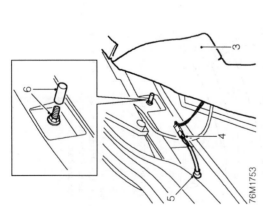

76M1753

3. Open boot lid and position luggage compartment carpet aside.
4. Disconnect 2 number plate lamp multiplugs.
5. Release 2 grommets from body.
6. Remove 3 thread covers and 3 nuts securing bumper to body.
7. Remove bumper taking care to release wires from holes.
   Do not carry out further dismantling if component is removed for access only.

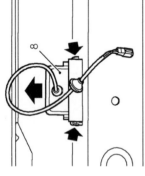

76M1754

8. Release clip securing number plate lamp assembly to bumper and remove lamp.
9. Remove other number plate lamp.

Refit

1. Fit number plate lamps to bumper and engage clips.
2. Position wires through holes and align bumper to body fixings.
3. Fit nuts and tighten to 25 Nm.
4. Fit thread covers.
5. Connect multiplugs and position carpet.
6. Fit bolts and tighten to 25 Nm.
7. Secure bumper to wheel arches with screws.

SIDE AIR VENT

Service repair no - 76.55.19

Remove

76M1651

1. Remove 2 screws securing outer grille.
2. Remove outer grille.
3. Remove 3 screws securing inner retaining plate.
4. Remove inner retaining plate.
5. Remove air intake pipe.

Refit

1. Locate air intake pipe to body.
2. Fit inner retaining plate and tighten screws.
3. Fit outer grille and tighten screws.

BODY

HOOD ASSEMBLY COMPONENTS - SOFT TOP

76M1806

1. Hood frame
2. Hood
3. Backlight
4. Backlight zip
5. Hood cover, tonneau
6. Retaining plate, 6 off
7. Tape elastic, 2 off
8. Tension cable, 2 off
9. Rear bow extrusion
10. Rear bow, canopy insert
11. Pop rivet - tonneau panel, 2 off
12. Stud - tonneau panel, 2 off
13. Link rod, 2 off
14. Front header fabric cover
15. Front header insert
16. Catch - front header, 2 off
17. Torx screw - catch, 6 off
18. Striker - front header, 2 off
19. Torx screw - striker, 4 off
20. Seal - cantrail, 2 off
21. Seal - B post, 2 off
22. Mounting plate - B post, 2 off
23. Screw - plate to body, 4 off
24. Catch - rear hoodwell, 5 off
25. Rivet - hoodwell catch, 10 off

HOOD ASSEMBLY COMPONENTS - HARD TOP

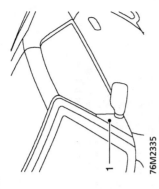

76M1807

1. Hard top assembly
2. Backlight glass
3. Weatherstrip - backlight
4. Headlining
5. Trim stud - headlining, 2 off
6. Seal
7. Finisher - lower edge
8. Block spacer, 2 off
9. Harness extension
10. Catch assembly - front header, 2 off
11. Screw - front catch assembly, 6 off
12. Catch assembly - B post, 2 off
13. Mounting plate - B post, 2 off
14. Header finisher - front
15. Clip - header seal, 6 off

HOOD SEALS AND DOOR GLASS - ADJUST

Service repair no - 76.31.04

Adjust

1. Check door alignment *See Doors.*

Cantrail seal

1. Check that cantrail seal butts up to 'A' post seal correctly, the cantrail seal must not be distorted when the hood is closed.
2. To adjust cantrail seal release hood and carefully slide seal either backwards or forwards in its channel.
3. Ensure seals are located correctly in their channels.

'A' post seal

76M2334

1. Check that 'A' post seal is positioned square at the corner of the 'A' post and header.
2. To adjust 'A' post seal remove 2 Torx screws securing header striker and remove striker.
3. Manoeuvre 'A' post seal to its correct position.
4. Close hood and secure with opposite side hood catch, apply downward pressure on hood and check that 'A' post seal is aligning correctly.
5. Release hood and fit header striker and secure with Torx screws, tighten to 6 Nm .

Cheater

76M2335

1. Check position of cheater, the cheater must be parallel with 'A' post when viewed from the side and front of vehicle.
2. If cheater is protruding out at the top when viewed from the front it will hold the door glass away from the seal.
3. To access cheater adjusters remove door speaker *See ELECTRICAL, Repairs.*

9. Close door and check cheater is positioned correctly, this can be judged by the bulge made by the glass on the 'A' post seal which should be uniform along the seal.
10. Fit speaker **See ELECTRICAL, Repairs.**
11. Fit door trim casing **See Doors.**

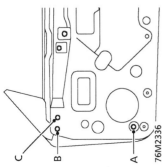

76M2336

4. Lower window and loosen screws **B** and **C**.
5. Loosen lock-nut on adjuster **A**, position adjuster screw so that it is level with the back of the nut it screws in to.
6. Push cheater down and pull inboard as far as possible.
7. Hold cheater in this position and tighten screws **B** and **C**, and the adjuster lock nut **A**.
8. Ensure window can be raised and lowered smoothly.

Door Glass

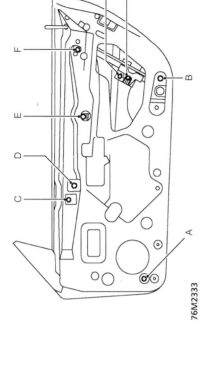

76M2333

A: This gives glass deflection adjustment (pivoting at waist rail).
B: This gives glass deflection adjustment (pivoting at waist rail).
C: This gives glass height adjustment (this is also the glass stop).
D: This gives glass lateral and vertical adjustment.
E: This gives glass lateral and vertical adjustment.

F: These give glass height adjustment (this is also the glass stop).
G: This is used at beginning of adjustment to position the door glass centrally in waist rail slot. Tighten bolt to 7 Nm.
H: This is positioned at rear glass rail at final stage of adjustment and tightened to 7 Nm.

NOTE: All glass adjustments must be done before the upstroke of the glass.

1. Remove door speaker. **See ELECTRICAL, Repairs.**
2. Peel back water shedder to access adjusters.

Height

NOTE: Glass height is correct when pressure is being applied to the soft part of the cantrail seal.

1. Lower glass slightly and loosen adjusters **C** and **F** these also act as glass stops.
2. Raise glass to height required, pull adjusters down in slots and tighten adjusters.
3. Lower glass and then raise fully to ensure required height has been obtained.

Parallelism

7mm

76M1797

NOTE: The glass is parallel when it is in the fully raised position and there is a constant clearance of 7 mm between the glass and the rear face of the 'A' post.

1. Loosen two height adjusters **C** and **F**.
2. Lower glass sufficiently to gain access to adjusters **D** and **E**, loosen adjusters.
3. Lower glass further to gain access to rear sash rail bracket.

4. Loosen adjuster bolt **H**.
5. Raise glass until adjusters **D** and **E** can be accessed, then close the door.
6. Adjust the position of the glass until it is parallel with the 'A' post, tighten adjusters **D** and **E**.

76M2332

7. Open door and lower glass then raise fully, check that front edge of glass and cheater are in line.
8. Close door by pushing on glass, check glass height.
9. If glass height is correct, pull adjusters down in slots and tighten adjusters **C** and **F**.

   NOTE: If glass height is incorrect refer to height adjustment above.

10. Lower glass to access rear sash bracket, tighten adjuster **H**.
11. Raise glass and ensure it pre-loads all surrounding seals.
12. If pre-load is not sufficient loosen lock-nut on adjuster **B**.
13. Position adjuster so that it is level with the back of nut it is screwed in to, this will tilt the top edge of the glass inwards.
14. Tighten lock-nut and check pre-load of glass on seal.
15. If pre-load is still not sufficient loosen bolt **G** and slide the bolt down one notch, tighten bolt.
16. Repeat previous instruction until pre-load is correct.
17. Secure water shedder.
18. Fit speaker **See ELECTRICAL, Repairs.**
19. Fit door trim casing **See Doors.**

CANTRAIL TENSIONING CABLES - ADJUST

Service repair no - 76.61.25

1. Partially lower hood.

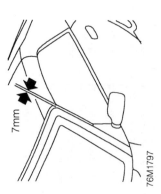

76M1612

2. Loosen cable locking screws.
3. Raise hood fully, but do not secure catches.
4. Using pliers, pull cables taught and tighten locking screws.
5. Secure hood catches and check cable tension.
6. If necessary, release hood catches, slacken cable locking screws and adjust cable tension. Tighten locking screws.
7. Secure catches.

HARDTOP - ADJUST

Service repair no -

NOTE: Check that soft top hood fit is correct before making any adjustments to the hardtop fit. *See this section.*

1. Fit hardtop. *See this section.*

Adjust

NOTE: If necessary, only make adjustments to the cantrail seal and glass height. It should not be necessary to disturb any other settings.

Cantrail seal

1. Check that cantrail seal butts up to 'A' post seal correctly, the cantrail seal must not be distorted when the hardtop is secured.
2. To adjust cantrail seal release hardtop and carefully slide seal either backwards or forwards in its channel.
3. Ensure seals are located correctly in their channels.

Glass height

NOTE: If glass height is incorrect adjust the height to the minimum requirement, to prevent too much disturbance to the soft top hood settings.

1. Adjust glass height *See this section.*

HARD TOP

Service repair no - 76.61.01

Remove

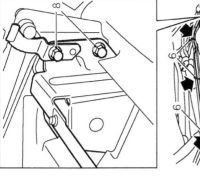
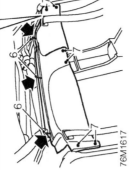

76M1783

1. Disconnect multiplug from heated rear window.
2. Release 2 catches securing hard top to header rail.
3. Release 2 catches securing hard top to hood mounting brackets.
4. With assistance, remove hard top from vehicle.

Refit

⚠ NOTE: Ensure side catches are in the raised position before fitting the hard top to the vehicle.

1. With assistance, position hard top to vehicle.
2. Secure hard top to header rail with catches.
3. If necessary, release clips and adjust catches.
4. Secure hard top to hood mounting brackets.
5. Adjust catches if required.
6. Connect screen heater multiplug.

HOOD ASSEMBLY

Service repair no - 76.61.10/99

Remove

1. Lower both windows.
2. Release both hood catches, but do not lower hood.

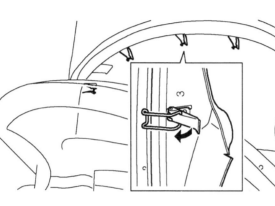

76M1608

3. Release rear edge of hoodwell carpet and release 5 clips securing hood to body.
4. Fold rear of hood, up to release from body.

⚠ CAUTION: Clips must be fully released to ensure that backlight is not damaged when hood is lowered.

5. Tilt both seat squabs forward.

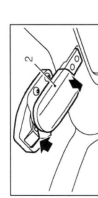
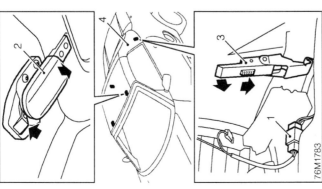

76M1617

6. Remove 3 screws securing bulkhead finisher. Collect press studs.
7. Release 6 clips and position bulkhead finisher aside.
8. Remove 4 bolts securing hood to body.
9. Collect 2 hard top strikers.
10. With assistance, remove hood assembly.

⚠ CAUTION: Support assembly beneath backlight and hinges during removal.

11. Position hood on a soft covered work surface.

Refit

1. With assistance, position hood to body.
2. Position hard top strikers.
3. With assistance, align hinge brackets to body and fit bolts but do not tighten at this stage.
4. Raise hood but do not secure catches.
5. Tighten hinge bracket bolts to 45 Nm.
6. Position bulkhead finisher and engage clips.
7. Position press studs and secure bulkhead finisher with screws.
8. Return seat squabs to original positions.
9. Engage clips to secure rear of hood to body.
10. Engage hoodwell carpet beneath flip seal.
11. Secure catches to secure front of hood.
12. Raise windows.

HOOD OUTER COVER

Service repair no - 76.61.11

Remove

The following operation involves the bonding of fabric backed vinyl to various steel components of the hood frame. If adhesive is to be applied to the fabric backing, Dunlop 758 adhesive or equivalent should be used. For direct application on vinyl surfaces, use Dunlop S1588 adhesive or equivalent.

A thin coating of adhesive should be applied to both surfaces and then allowed to cure, until just touch dry, for between 5 and 10 minutes, before the bond is made.

1. Remove both hood catches. *See this section.*
2. Remove both 'B' post seals. *See this section.*

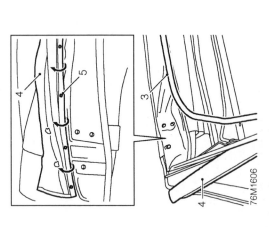

76M1606

3. With hood in the lowered position, remove edge protector from rear of header rail.
4. Release forward 150 mm of cantrail seals from retainers, release covering from rear of header rail and fold cover forward to reveal retaining strip.
5. Locally release foam from retaining strip to reveal 11 rivets, drill out rivets.
6. Collect header cover assembly.

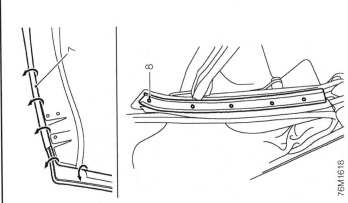

76M1618

7. Release outer cover from adhesive on underside of header rail.
8. Drill out 5 pop rivets securing each 'B' post seal retainer. Collect retainers.

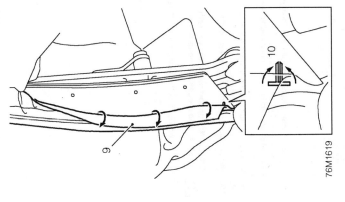

76M1619

9. Release outer cover from adhesive on 'B' post brackets.
10. Bend up tabs and release 'rivet' plates securing outer cover to base of 'B' post brackets.
11. Raise hood frame.

Refit

1. Position hood frame, fit and tighten bolts.
2. Remove any uneven deposits of adhesive from 'B' post brackets, clamp rail and header rail using a suitable solvent.
3. Position new outer cover to a soft covered work surface.
4. Fold outer cover in half and chalk centre line to aid alignment.
5. Measure and mark centre line on underside of hood header rail.
6. Apply adhesive to clamp rail and outer cover.

76M1728

7. Bond clamp rail to outer cover with larger flange towards edge of material.
8. If necessary, apply adhesive to clamp rail and felt covering. Bond covering centrally to clamp rail, ensuring that slotted ends remain free.
9. Position outer cover over raised hood frame and engage clamp rail studs to bow.
10. Secure clamp rail with nuts.
11. Apply adhesive to 3rd hood bow and mating surface of felt covering.

⚠️ **CAUTION: Ensure underside of outer cover does not become contaminated with adhesive.**

12. Bond felt covering to 3rd bow, ensuring that slots are correctly positioned around frame straps.

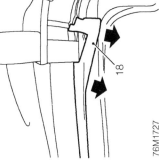

76M1727

18. Release felt covering from 3rd hood bow.

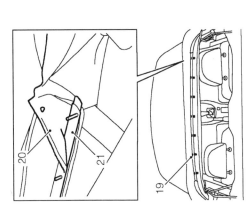

76M1623

19. Remove 7 nuts securing outer cover clamp rail to 3rd hood bow.
20. Release clamp rail studs from bow and remove outer cover assembly.
21. Remove clamp rail from outer cover.
22. Remove 4 bolts securing hood frame and with assistance remove hood frame.
23. Invert frame and shake vigorously to remove rivets and swarf from frame.

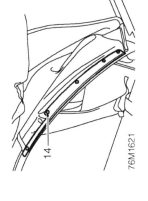

76M1621

14. Drill out 5 pop rivets securing each retaining strip and collect retaining strips.
15. Drill out any rivet heads still captive in hood frame.

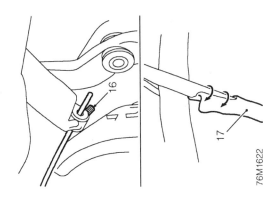

76M1622

16. Loosen cable locking screws and release cables from outer cover.

⚠️ NOTE: Leave cables attached at header rail.

17. Release outer cover flaps from adhesive on 1st and 2nd hood bows.

76M1620

12. Release rear edge of hoodwell carpet and release 5 clips.
13. Fold rear of hood, up to release from body.

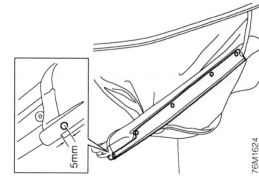

76M1624

13. Align hood rear quarters to lower rail, ensuring that:
    Lower edge of rail and cover reinforcement strip are aligned.
    Centre of rivet hole in lower rail is 5 mm from end of reinforcement strip as shown.
14. Transfer holes from lower rail into outer cover, using a bradawl or similar tool.
15. With careful use of a drill, open out holes to 3.5 mm.
16. Position retaining strips and secure hood rear quarters to lower rail with pop rivets.
17. Raise backlight into position and secure with zip.
18. Engage clips to secure rear of hood to body.
19. Engage hoodwell carpet beneath flip seal
20. Partially lower hood frame.
21. Apply adhesive to underside of header rail and mating surface of outer cover.

22. Temporarily fit hood catches.
23. Position outer cover to header, then make adhesive joint in three small areas.

⚠ **CAUTION: Do not make a permanent joint at this stage as adjustment may be necessary.**

24. Raise hood and secure catches.
25. Check outer cover tension.
26. Lower hood partially.
27. Adjust position of outer cover and recheck tension if necessary.
28. Remove hood catches.
29. Bond outer cover securely to header rail, ensuring cover does not crease.
30. Trim off excess material using a sharp knife.
31. Lower hood fully.
32. Position header cover assembly.
33. Transfer holes in header cover retainer through outer cover into header rail.
34. Secure header cover retainer with pop rivets.
35. Apply adhesive to header rail and mating surface of header cover.

⚠ **CAUTION: Ensure underside of outer cover does not become contaminated with adhesive.**

36. Bond header cover.
37. Fit edge protector to rear of header rail.
38. Secure forward ends of cantrail seals in retainers.
39. Fit hood catches. *See this section.*
40. Raise hood partially.
41. Engage outer cover rivet plates to 'B' post brackets and bend over tabs to secure.
42. Apply adhesive to 'B' post brackets and mating surfaces of outer cover.
43. Raise hood, but do not secure catches.

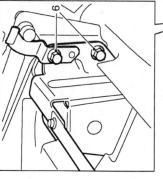 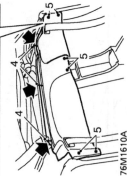

44. Thread cantrail cables through pockets in outer cover and engage in frame locations.
45. Bond outer cover to 'B' post brackets, ensuring that even tension is applied as bond is made.
46. Position 'B' post seal retainers.
47. Transfer holes in retainers through outer cover into brackets.
48. Secure retainers with pop rivets.
49. Fit 'B' post seals. *See this section.*
50. Apply adhesive to outer cover flaps and mating surfaces of 1st and 2nd hood bows.

⚠ **CAUTION: Ensure that underside of outer cover does not become contaminated with adhesive.**

51. Check cosmetic appearance of hood.
52. Adjust cantrail cables. *See this section.*
53. Remove protection.
54. Secure hood catches.
55. Close windows.

HOOD FRAME

Service repair no - 76.61.12

Remove

1. Remove outer cover. *See this section.*
2. Remove backlight. *See this section.*
3. Tilt both seat squabs forward.

76M1610A

4. Remove 3 screws securing bulkhead finisher, collect press studs.
5. Release 6 clips and position bulkhead finisher aside.
6. Remove 4 bolts securing hood frame to body.
7. Collect hard top strikers.
8. With assistance, remove hood frame.
9. Remove cantrail seals, *See this section.*
10. Bend up tabs securing cantrail tensioning cables to header rail.
11. Remove tensioning cables.

Refit

1. Position cantrail tensioning cables to header rail.
2. Secure cables top header rail by bending tabs.
3. Fit cantrail seals, leaving forward ends disengaged from retainer. **See this section.**
4. With assistance, position frame.
5. Position hard top strikers.
6. With assistance, align hinge brackets to body and secure with bolts. Tighten bolts to 45 Nm.
7. Raise hood frame.
8. Position bulkhead finisher and engage clips.
9. Position press studs and secure bulkhead finisher with screws.
10. Return seat squabs to original positions.
11. Fit outer cover. **See this section.**
12. Fit backlight. **See this section.**

BACKLIGHT

Service repair no - 76.61.15

Remove

1. Lower both windows.
2. Release hood catches, but do not lower hood.

76M1609

3. Release rear edge of hoodwell carpet and release 5 clips.
4. Fold rear of hood, up to release from body.

⚠ **CAUTION: Clips must be fully released to ensure that backlight is not damaged.**

5. Unzip backlight.
6. Lay backlight flat in hoodwell.
7. Place protective covering over backlight and boot.

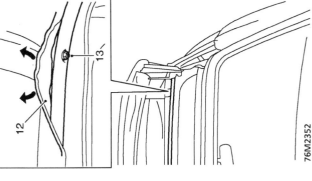

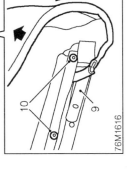

76M1616

8. Remove 2 rivets securing ends of hood rear quarter retaining strips.
9. Carefully bend back ends of strips to reveal rivets.
10. Drill out 13 pop rivets securing backlight retaining strip.
11. Collect retaining strip and remove backlight.

76M2352

12. Release felt covering from 3rd hood bow.
13. Remove 7 nuts securing outer cover clamp rail.
14. Partially lower hood frame.
15. Release clamp rail studs from hood frame.
16. Lay protective sheet over backlight, luggage compartment lid and seats.
17. Release foam from ends of zip retainer to reveal pop rivets.
18. With assistance to hold outer cover aside, drill out 9 pop rivets securing zip retainer to hood frame.
19. Remove backlight zip.

BODY

Refit

1. Drill out any rivet heads still captive in hood frame.

⚠ **CAUTION: Clear away swarf from protective covering to ensure that new backlight does not become scratched.**

2. With assistance, position backlight to frame, centralise and transfer holes into backlight.
3. Position backlight to a soft covered work surface.
4. With careful use of a drill, enlarge holes to 3.5mm
5. Position backlight to frame, align retainer and secure with pop rivets.

◁ NOTE: Start at the centre location and work outwards.

6. Secure ends of rear quarter retaining strips with rivets.
7. Position zip assembly to frame and secure with rivets.
8. Fit foam pads to both ends of hood bow.

◁ NOTE: Foam pads are designed to prevent outer cover being damaged by ends of hood bow and zip retainer.

9. Position outer cover clamp rail to frame and engage studs.
10. Raise hood, but do not secure catches.
11. Secure outer cover, clamp rail with nuts.
12. Apply adhesive to 3rd hood bow and mating surface of felt covering.

⚠ **CAUTION: Ensure underside of outer cover does not become contaminated with adhesive.**

13. Bond felt covering to 3rd bow, ensuring that slots are correctly positioned around frame straps.
14. Remove protective covering.
15. Raise backlight into position and secure with zip.
16. Engage clips to secure rear of hood to body.
17. Engage hoodwell carpet beneath flip seal
18. Secure hood catches.
19. Raise windows.

HOOD CATCH

Service repair no - 76.61.17

Remove

1. Lower hood.

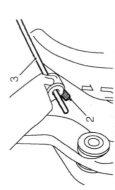

76M1611

2. Remove 3 Allen screws securing catch to hood header rail.
3. Remove hood catch.

Refit

1. Position catch and fit screws, finger tight.
2. Raise hood, but do not secure catches.
3. Align catch to striker and tighten screws to 20 Nm.
4. Check operation of hood catches. If necessary, release locking wire and turn hexagonal adjuster to give correct action.
5. Secure locking wire.
6. Secure hood catches.

6. Peel outer cover away from header in immediate area of cable location.
7. Bend location tag up by minimum amount necessary and release cantrail tensioning cable from header rail.
8. Remove cantrail tensioning cable.

Refit

1. Locate cable loop over location tag in header rail and bend tag over to retain cable.
2. Apply adhesive to outer cover and header rail.
3. Bond outer cover to header rail, ensuring that beading at side of header is correctly positioned.
4. Fit forward end of cantrail seal to retainer.
5. Partially raise hood.
6. Insert new cable into pocket of outer cover.
7. Thread cable through location in 2nd hood bow.
8. Raise hood fully, but do not secure catches.
9. Using pliers, pull cable taught and tighten locking screw.
10. Secure hood catches and check cable tension.
11. If necessary, release hood catches, slacken cable locking screw and adjust cable tension. Tighten locking screw.
12. Secure catches.

CANTRAIL TENSIONING CABLE

Service repair no - 76.61.26

The following operation involves the bonding of fabric backed vinyl to various steel components of the hood frame. If adhesive is to be applied to the fabric backing, Dunlop 758 adhesive or equivalent should be used. For direct application on vinyl surfaces, use Dunlop S1588 adhesive or equivalent.

A thin coating of adhesive should be applied to both surfaces and then allowed to cure, until just touch dry, for between 5 and 10 minutes, before the bond is made.

1. Partially lower hood.

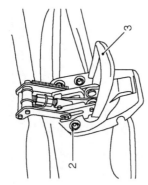
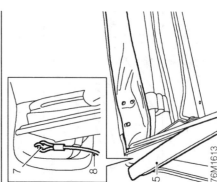

76M1613

2. Loosen cable locking screw.
3. Release cable from location.
4. Lower hood fully.
5. Release forward 100 mm of cantrail seal from retainer.

BODY

BACKLIGHT ZIP

Service repair no - 76.61.21

Remove

1. Remove backlight assembly. *See this section.*
2. Entrust replacement of zip to trim specialist.

Refit

1. Refit backlight assembly. *See this section.*

HARD TOP HEADLINING

Service repair no - 76.61.31

Remove

1. Remove front catches. *See this section.*

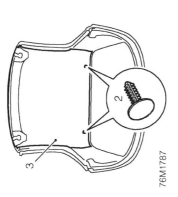

76M1787

2. Remove 2 trim studs securing rear of headlining to hard top.
3. Remove headlining.

Refit

1. Position headlining and secure with trim studs.
2. Fit front catches. *See this section.*

HARD TOP CATCH - REAR

Service repair no - 76.61.32

Remove

1. Remove hard top. *See this section.*
2. Invert hard top on a soft covered work surface.
3. Position protection over headlining and backlight.

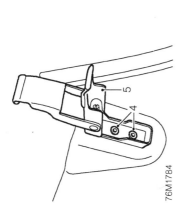

76M1784

4. Drill out 2 pop rivets securing catch to hard top.
5. Remove catch.

Refit

1. Position catch and secure with rivets.
2. Fit hard top. *See this section.*
3. Check operation of catch. If necessary, turn adjuster to give correct action.
4. Secure catch.

HARD TOP CATCH - FRONT

Service repair no - 76.61.33

Remove

1. Remove hard top. *See this section.*
2. Invert hard top on a soft covered work surface.

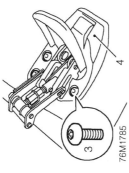

76M1785

3. Remove 3 Allen screws securing catch to hard top.
4. Remove catch.

Refit

1. Position catch and tighten screws to 10 Nm.
2. Fit hard top. *See this section.*
3. Check operation of catch. If necessary, release locking wire and turn hexagonal adjuster to give correct action.
4. Secure locking wire.
5. Secure catch.

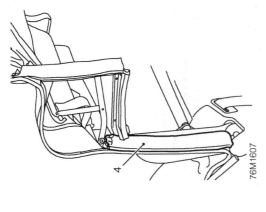

BODY

HARD TOP SEAL

Service repair no - 76.61.34

Remove

1. Remove hard top. *See this section.*
2. Invert hard top on a soft covered work surface.
3. Release seal from adhesive at header and below backlight.

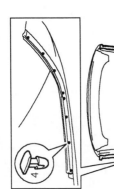
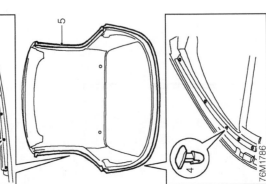

76M1786

4. Release 26 studs securing seal to hard top.
5. Remove seal.

Refit

1. Remove all traces of dirt and grease from surfaces to be bonded using a suitable mild solvent.
2. Apply Loctite 401 to hard top using old deposits as a guide.
3. Position seal, centralise and carefully bond to hard top.
4. Engage studs securing seal to hard top.
5. Fit hard top. *See this section.*

CANTRAIL SEAL

Service repair no - 76.61.35

1. Lower both windows.
2. Depress locking buttons and release both hood catches.
3. Partially lower hood.
4. Position protective covering beneath frame.

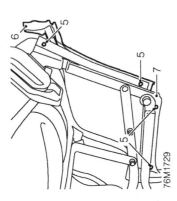

76M1729

5. Drill out pop rivets securing seal to frame channels.
6. Release seal from 2 retainers.
7. Remove seal.

Refit

1. Apply liquid soap to seal retainers.
2. Position seal and engage to retainers.
3. Raise hood and check seal fit.
4. If necessary, partially lower hood, reposition seal in retainers and recheck.
5. Carefully transfer rivet holes into seal using a 3 mm drill bit.

⚠ **CAUTION: Care must be taken not to drill through the outer surface of the seal.**

6. Secure seal with pop rivets.
7. Raise hood and secure catches.
8. Raise windows.

'B' POST SEAL

Service repair no - 76.61.38

1. Lower both windows.
2. Depress locking buttons and release both hood catches.
3. Partially lower hood.

76M1607

4. Remove seal from retainer.

Refit

1. Apply liquid soap to seal retainer.
2. Fit seal to retainer.
3. Raise hood and check seal fit.
4. If necessary, partially lower hood, reposition seal in retainer and recheck.
5. Raise hood and secure catches.
6. Raise windows.

HARD TOP - BACKLIGHT

Service repair no - 76.61.40

Remove

1. Remove hard top. *See this section.*
2. Invert hard top on a soft covered work surface.

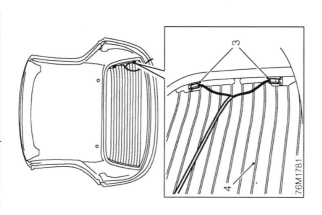

3. Disconnect 2 Lucar terminals and remove heated screen harness.

⚠ **WARNING: Gloves and suitable eye protection must be worn when removing glass.**

4. Working from inside hard top and commencing from lower LH corner, release sealing rubber. Remove glass and seal.

76M1781

⚠ **CAUTION: Use assistance to support glass as it is removed.**

5. Remove and discard rubber seal.

Refit

1. Clean hard top aperture and edge of glass.
2. Apply rubber lubricant to seal channels.
3. Fit sealing rubber to glass.

⚠ **WARNING: Gloves and suitable eye protection must be worn when fitting glass.**

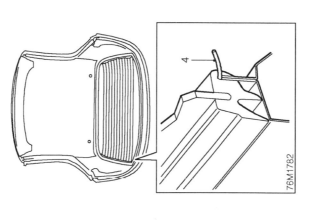

76M1782

4. Insert a suitable length of cord in hard top aperture channel of sealing rubber.

5. Using assistance, push glass against hard top aperture whilst using cord to pull lip of seal over aperture flange.
6. Clean all traces of rubber lubricant from glass and hard top using white spirit.
7. Fit heated screen harness and connect Lucar terminals.
8. Fit hard top. *See this section.*
9. Press firmly around outside edges of glass to ensure that seal is fully seated.

SUN VISOR

Service repair no - 76.10.47

Remove

1. Lower sun visor.

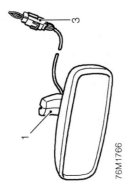

76M1556

2. Remove 2 screws securing visor to header rail.
3. Remove visor.

Refit

1. Position visor and secure with screws.

INTERIOR MIRROR

Service repair no - 76.10.51

Remove

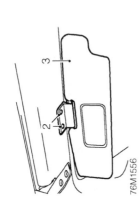

76M1766

1. Release mirror from screen mounted clip.
2. Release cable and multiplug from header finisher.
3. Disconnect multiplug and remove mirror.

Refit

1. Connect multiplug and position cable to recess in mirror mounting.
2. Fit mirror to windscreen.
3. Position excess cable and multiplug behind header finisher.

This page is intentionally left blank

HEADER TRIM

Service repair no - 76.13.69

Remove

1. Remove both sun visors. *See this section.*
2. Release catches and lower hood.

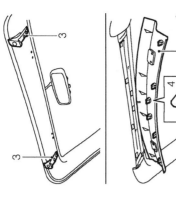

3. Remove 2 Tx30 Torx screws securing each hood striker and remove strikers.
4. Release 6 sprag clips securing trim to header rail.
5. Remove trim.

Refit

1. Position trim and engage sprag clips.
2. Fit hood strikers and tighten screws to 6 Nm.
3. Fit sun visors. *See this section.*
4. Raise hood and secure catches.

76M1555

REAR BULKHEAD FINISHER

Service repair no - 76.13.49

Remove

1. Remove front seats. *See RESTRAINT SYSTEMS, Repairs.*

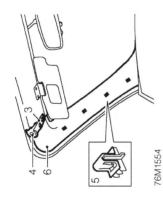

2. Remove 3 screws securing finisher and collect press studs.
3. Release finisher from fixings.
4. Remove 4 screws securing belt guides to finisher.
5. Release belt guides from finisher and remove from belt.
6. Slide seat belts through finisher and remove finisher from vehicle.

Refit

1. Position finisher and thread seat belts into position.
2. Fit seat belt guides and locate guides into position.
3. Secure guides with screws.
4. Align finisher to studs and secure into position.
5. Position press studs and secure with screws.
6. Fit front seats. *See RESTRAINT SYSTEMS, Repairs.*

M76 3528

LUGGAGE COMPARTMENT TRIM

Service repair no - 76.13.17

Remove

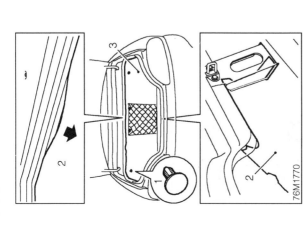

1. Remove 4 clips securing trim to engine compartment bulkhead.
2. Release trim from flip seal, bonnet release lever and boot lid striker.
3. Remove trim.

Refit

1. Fit trim and secure with clips.
2. Position trim behind flip seal.
3. Position trim to bonnet release lever and boot lid striker.

76M1770

'A' POST TRIM

Service repair no - 76.13.26

Remove

1. Lower sun visor.
2. Release catches and lower hood.

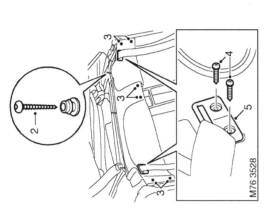

3. Remove 2 Tx30 Torx screws securing hood striker.
4. Remove striker.
5. Release 4 sprag clips securing trim to 'A' post.
6. Remove 'A' post trim.

Refit

1. Position trim and engage sprag clips.
2. Fit hood striker and tighten screws to 6 Nm.
3. Reposition sun visor.
4. Raise hood and secure catches.

76M1554

FRONT CONSOLE

Service repair no - 76.25.01

⚠️ **WARNING: See RESTRAINT SYSTEMS, Precautions.**

Remove

1. Make SRS system safe. **See RESTRAINT SYSTEMS, Precautions. See this section.**
2. Remove centre console panel. **See this section.**

⚠️ **CAUTION: Ensure pre-tensioner multiplug is disconnected before seat is removed.**

3. Remove rear console. **See this section.**
4. Remove both console closing panels. **See this section.**

76M1735B

5. Remove 6 screws securing console to tunnel.

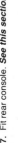

6. Loosen handbrake adjustment and position hand brake lever in ON position.
7. Release handbrake gaiter from console and remove gaiter from handbrake.
8. Release console and disconnect multiplug from cigar lighter.
9. Release volumetric sensor cable and remove console.

Refit

1. Position front console, connect cigar lighter multiplug and position volumetric sensor cable.
2. Position console and secure with screws.
3. Fit handbrake gaiter and secure with band.
4. Engage gaiter to console.
5. Adjust handbrake. **See BRAKES, Adjustments.**
6. Fit console closing panels. **See this section.**
7. Fit rear console. **See this section.**

⚠️ **CAUTION: Ensure that pre-tensioner flylead is correctly clipped to seat base before fitting seat, as shown in seat refit. See this section.**

8. Fit centre console panel. **See this section.**
9. Connect both battery terminals, earth lead last.

REAR CONSOLE

Service repair no - 76.25.04

Remove

1. Remove rear bulkhead finisher. **See this section.**

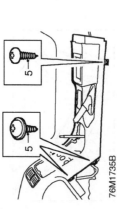

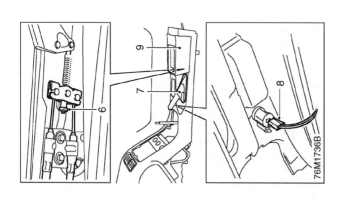

76M1734B

2. Disconnect multiplug from volumetric sensor.
3. Remove 2 screws securing rear console to rear bulkhead.
4. Open rear console lid and remove 2 screws securing console lid bracket to rear console.
5. Open front console lid and remove storage bin from front console.

GEAR LEVER GAITER - 2000MY ON

Service repair no - 76.25.06

Remove

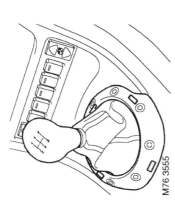

M76 3555

1. **Manual models:** Unscrew and remove gear knob.
2. **Steptronic EM-CVT models:** Select position 'D', pull gear selector lever sharply upwards and remove.
3. **All models:** Release gaiter from centre console.

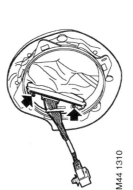

M44 1310

4. **Steptronic EM-CVT models:** Disconnect gearshift selector indicator multiplug
5. Remove 2 screws securing gearshift selector indicator and remove selector indicator.
6. **All models:** Remove gaiter.

Refit

1. Position gaiter.
2. **Steptronic EM-CVT models:** Fit gearshift selector indicator and secure with screws.
3. Connect multiplug to selector indicator.
4. **All models:** Secure gaiter to centre console.
5. Fit gear change selector knob.

GEAR LEVER GAITER - UP TO 2000MY

Service repair no - 76.25.06

Remove

1. Remove centre console panel. *See this section.*

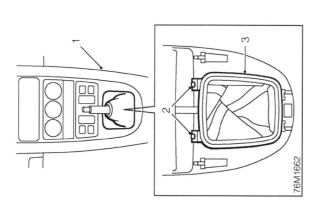

76M1662

2. Remove 2 screws securing gaiter retaining bracket to gaiter.
3. Remove bracket and gaiter.

Refit

1. Position gaiter.
2. Fit bracket and secure with screws.
3. Fit centre console panel. *See this section.*

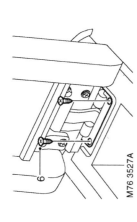

M76 3527A

6. Remove 2 screws securing console lid bracket to front console and remove console lid assembly.
7. Remove rear console.
8. Remove 2 screws securing volumetric sensor to rear console and remove sensor.

Refit

1. Fit sensor to console and secure with screws.
2. Fit rear console to bulkhead and secure with 2 upper screws. Ensure correct position of cable.
3. Fit console lid assembly and secure with screws.
4. Fit front console storage bin.
5. Connect multiplug to sensor.
6. Fit rear bulkhead finisher. *See this section.*

CENTRE CONSOLE PANEL - 2000MY ON

Service repair no - 76.25.23

Remove

1. Disconnect battery earth lead.
2. Remove radio. **See ELECTRICAL, Repairs.**
3. Remove gear lever gaiter. **See this section.**

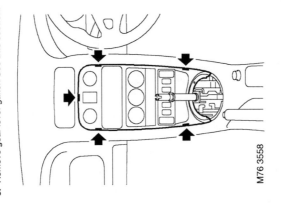

M76 3558

4. Release 5 clips securing console to fascia.

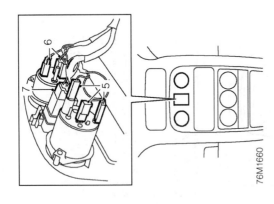

76M1661

8. Release 6 multiplugs from switches.
9. Release gaiter from gear lever and remove centre console.

Refit

1. Position console and engage gaiter to gear lever.
2. Connect multiplugs, Lucars and bulb holder.
3. Secure console clips to fascia.
4. Fit gear knob.
5. Fit radio. **See ELECTRICAL, Repairs.**
6. Connect battery earth lead.

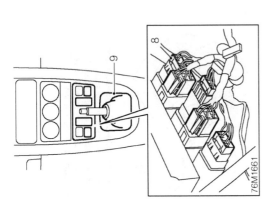

76M1660

5. Release 3 Lucars from clock.
6. Release multiplug and bulb holder from oil temperature gauge.
7. Release hazard switch multiplug.

CENTRE CONSOLE PANEL - UP TO 2000MY

Service repair no - 76.25.23

Remove

1. Disconnect battery earth lead.
2. Remove radio. **See ELECTRICAL, Repairs.**

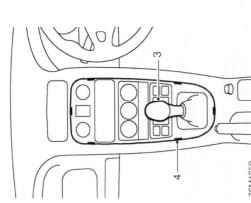

76M1659

3. Remove gear knob.
4. Release 6 clips securing console to fascia.

FASCIA PANEL

Service repair no - 76.46.23

⚠️ **WARNING:** *See RESTRAINT SYSTEMS, Precautions.*

Remove

1. Make SRS system safe. *See RESTRAINT SYSTEMS, Precautions.*
2. Remove front console. *See this section.*
3. Remove steering column switch pack. *See ELECTRICAL, Repairs.*
4. Remove instrument pack. *See INSTRUMENTS, Repairs.*
5. Remove glovebox. *See this section.*

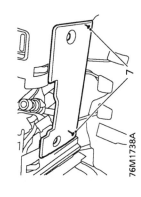

76M1737A

6. Remove 4 screws securing heater controls to fascia and position aside.

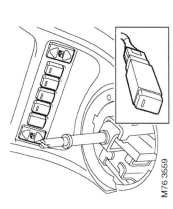

76M1738A

7. Loosen 2 screws securing fuse box cover to fascia and remove cover.
8. Release both screen heater ducts from fascia and position aside.

CONSOLE CLOSING PANEL

Service repair no - 76.25.31

Remove

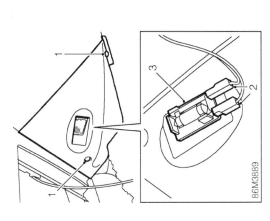

86M3889

1. Remove 2 screws securing panel to console.
2. Release panel and disconnect 2 Lucars from lamp.
3. Remove lamp from panel.

Refit

1. Fit lamp to panel and connect Lucars.
2. Position panel and secure with screws.

Refit

1. Position console and connect multiplugs, Lucars and bulb holder.
2. Secure console clips to fascia.
3. Fit gear lever gaiter. *See this section.*
4. Fit radio. *See ELECTRICAL, Repairs.*
5. Connect battery earth lead.

76M1660

5. Release 3 Lucars from clock.
6. Release multiplug and bulb holder from oil temperature gauge.
7. Release hazard switch multiplug.

M76 3559

8. Release multiplugs from switches.
9. Remove centre console panel.

HOODWELL TRIM

Service repair no - 76.67.06

Remove

1. Lower both windows.
2. Release hood catches, do not lower hood.

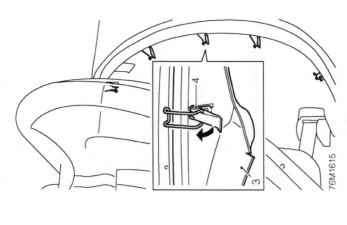

76M1615

3. Release rear edge of hoodwell trim to reveal 5 clips.
4. Release clips securing rear of hood to body.
5. Raise rear edge of hood.
6. Remove hoodwell trim.

GLOVEBOX LATCH

Service repair no - 76.52.08

Remove

1. Open glovebox lid.

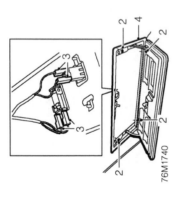

76M1767

2. Remove screw securing latch to glovebox lid.
3. Remove latch.

Refit

1. Position latch to glovebox lid and secure with screw.
2. Close glovebox lid.

GLOVEBOX

Service repair no - 76.52.03

Remove

1. Open glovebox lid.

76M1740

2. Remove 4 screws securing glovebox to fascia.
3. Release glovebox and disconnect 4 Lucars.
4. Remove glovebox.

Refit

1. Position glovebox and connect Lucars.
2. Engage glovebox to fascia and secure with screws.
3. Close glovebox lid.

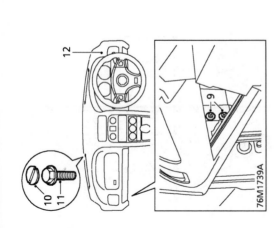

76M1739A

9. Loosen 4 nuts securing fascia to lower 'A' post.
10. Release 4 retaining bolt caps from fascia and collect caps.
11. Remove 4 bolts securing fascia to scuttle.
12. Remove fascia panel.

Refit

1. Position fascia to scuttle.
2. Align fascia and secure with nuts and bolts.
3. Fit retaining bolt caps.
4. Engage heater ducts to fascia.
5. Position fuse box cover to fascia and secure with screws.
6. Align heater controls to fascia and secure with screws.
7. Fit glovebox. *See this section.*
8. Fit instrument pack. *See INSTRUMENTS, Repairs.*
9. Fit steering column switch pack. *See ELECTRICAL, Repairs.*
10. Fit front console. *See this section.*

Refit

1. Fit trim and engage beneath lip of bulkhead finisher.
2. Reposition rear edge of hood.
3. Engage clips to secure rear of hood to body.
4. Engage hoodwell trim beneath flip seal.
5. Secure hood catches.
6. Raise windows.

HEAD RESTRAINT

Service repair no - 78.10.36/99

Remove

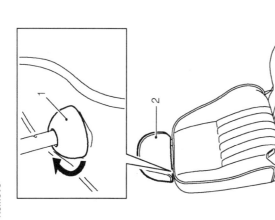

76M1707

1. Rotate inboard head restraint, guide cap 90°.
2. Remove head restraint.

Refit

1. Fit head restraint.
2. Rotate inboard head restraint, guide cap back 90° to lock head restraint.

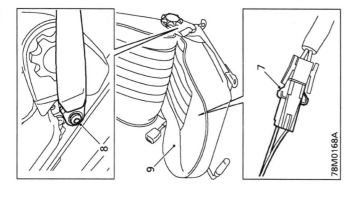

78M0168A

7. Disconnect seat belt pre-tensioner multiplug.
8. Position seat and remove Torx screw securing seat belt strap to seat frame.
9. Remove seat.

SEAT

Service repair no - 78.10.44/99

⚠ **WARNING: See *RESTRAINT SYSTEMS, Precautions.***

Remove

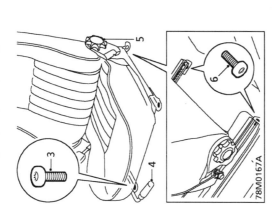

78M0167A

1. Make the SRS system safe. **See *RESTRAINT SYSTEMS, Precautions.***
2. Lift seat adjuster, move seat rearwards.
3. Remove Torx screw from front of each seat runner.
4. Lift seat adjuster, move seat forwards.
5. Rotate recline handle to tilt squab fully forward.
6. Remove Torx screw from rear of each seat runner.

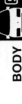

BODY

Refit

1. Ensure harness lead does not become trapped under seat runner when fitting seat.
2. Position seat belt strap to seat frame and tighten Torx screw to 30 Nm.

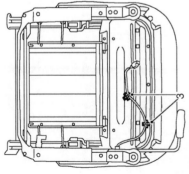

M76 4196

3. Ensure that pre-tensioner lead is correctly clipped to seat base.
4. Position seat and align runners to floor bolt holes.
5. Connect pre-tensioner multiplug.
6. Fit but do not tighten Torx screw securing rear of each seat runner.
7. Lift seat adjuster, move seat rearwards.
8. Fit Torx screw securing front of each seat runner and tighten to 45 Nm.
9. Lift seat adjuster, move seat forwards.
10. Tighten Torx screw securing rear of each seat runner to 45 Nm.
11. Connect both battery leads, earth lead last.
12. Carry out system check using TestBook.

SEAT SQUAB ASSEMBLY

Service repair no - 78.10.50/99

> **WARNING: See RESTRAINT SYSTEMS, Precautions.**

Remove

1. Make the SRS system safe. **See RESTRAINT SYSTEMS, Precautions.**

> **CAUTION: Ensure pre-tensioner multiplug is disconnected before seat is removed.**

2. Remove seat. **See this section.**

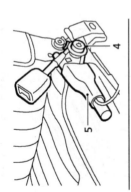

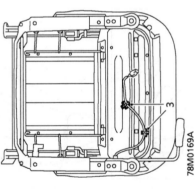

78M0169A

3. Release 2 clips securing pre-tensioner flylead to underside of seat.
4. Remove Torx bolt securing pre-tensioner to squab frame.
5. Remove pre-tensioner.

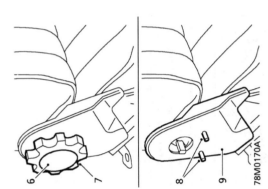

78M0170A

6. Remove outer half of squab recline handle.
7. Remove inner half of squab recline handle.
8. Using a suitable punch, drive out 2 retaining pins from the side valance.
9. Remove side valance.

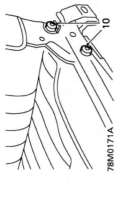

78M0171A

10. Remove 4 Torx bolts securing squab frame to cushion frame.
11. Remove squab assembly.

Refit

1. Fit squab frame to cushion frame, fit Torx bolts and tighten to 45 Nm.
2. Fit side valance and secure with pins.
3. Fit inner half of squab recline handle.
4. Fit outer half of squab recline handle.
5. Fit pre-tensioner to squab frame, fit Torx bolt and tighten to 45 Nm.
6. Secure pre-tensioner flylead clips to underside of seat.

> **CAUTION: To prevent damage to the pre-tensioner flylead ensure flylead is positioned correctly to seat, as shown in seat refit. See this section.**

7. Fit seat. **See this section.**

CUSHION COVER

Service repair no - 78.30.01

WARNING: See RESTRAINT SYSTEMS, Precautions.

Remove

1. Make the SRS system safe. *See RESTRAINT SYSTEMS, Precautions.*
2. Remove seat squab assembly. *See this section.*

76M1697A

3. Remove 2 spring clips securing front lower edge of cover to frame.
4. Release cushion cover retainers from frame.
5. Remove cover and pad assembly from frame.

Do not carry out further dismantling if component is removed for access only.

76M1699A

6. Remove 9 Hog rings securing cushion cover to pad.
7. Remove cushion cover from pad.

Rebuild

8. Fit cushion cover to pad.
9. Secure cushion cover to pad with Hog rings.

Refit

1. Position cover and pad assembly to frame.
2. Secure cushion retainers to frame.
3. Fold front lower edges of cover under frame and secure with spring clips.
4. Fit seat squab assembly. *See this section.*

PULLMAFLEX - SEAT CUSHION

Service repair no - 78.30.15

WARNING: See RESTRAINT SYSTEMS, Precautions.

Remove

1. Make the SRS system safe. *See RESTRAINT SYSTEMS, Precautions.*
2. Remove cushion cover. *See this section.*

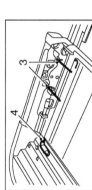

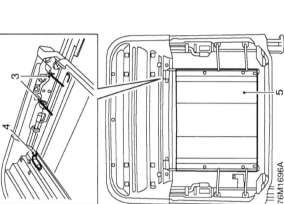

76M1696A

3. Release 4 pullmaflex straps from frame.
4. Release 2 pullmaflex frame retainers.
5. Remove pullmaflex from frame.

Refit

1. Fit pullmaflex to frame.
2. Secure pullmaflex to frame retainers.
3. Secure pullmaflex straps to frame.
4. Fit cushion cover. *See this section.*

CUSHION FRAME

Service repair no - 78.30.16

WARNING: See RESTRAINT SYSTEMS, Precautions.

Remove

1. Make the SRS system safe. *See RESTRAINT SYSTEMS, Precautions.*
2. Remove seat cushion pullmaflex. *See this section.*

Refit

1. Fit seat cushion pullmaflex. *See this section.*

CUSHION PAD

Service repair no - 78.30.30

WARNING: See RESTRAINT SYSTEMS, Precautions.

Remove

1. Make the SRS system safe. *See RESTRAINT SYSTEMS, Precautions.*
2. Remove cushion cover. *See this section.*

Refit

1. Fit cushion cover. *See this section.*

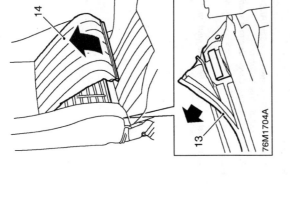

BODY

SQUAB COVER

Service repair no - 78.90.08

⚠ **WARNING: See** *RESTRAINT SYSTEMS,* ***Precautions.***

Remove

1. Make the SRS system safe. *See RESTRAINT SYSTEMS, Precautions.*

⚠ **CAUTION: Ensure pre-tensioner multiplug is disconnected before seat is removed.**

2. Remove seat. *See this section.*

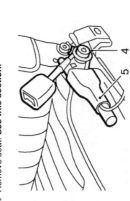

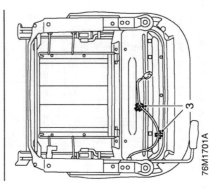

76M1701A

3. Release 2 clips securing pre-tensioner flylead to underside of seat.
4. Remove Torx bolt securing pre-tensioner to squab frame.
5. Remove pre-tensioner.

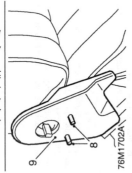

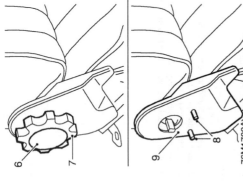

76M1702A

6. Remove outer half of squab recline handle.
7. Remove inner half of squab recline handle.
8. Using a suitable punch, drive out 2 retaining pins from the side valance.
9. Remove side valance.

76M1703A

10. Rotate inboard head restraint guide cap 90°.
11. Remove head restraint.
12. Remove head restraint, guide caps.

76M1704A

13. Release squab cover lower retainer.
14. Raise squab centre panel.

PULLMAFLEX - SEAT SQUAB

Service repair no - 78.90.21

⚠ **WARNING: See RESTRAINT SYSTEMS, Precautions.**

Remove

1. Make the SRS system safe. *See RESTRAINT SYSTEMS, Precautions. See this section.*
2. Remove squab cover. *See this section.*

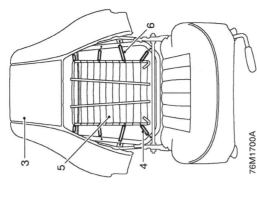

76M1700A

3. Remove squab pad from frame.
4. Release springs from pullmaflex.
5. Remove pullmaflex.
6. Noting their fitted positions collect pullmaflex springs.

Refit

1. Fit springs to squab frame.
2. Position pullmaflex to squab frame and secure with springs.
3. Fit squab pad to frame.
4. Fit squab cover. *See this section.*

Refit

1. Fit squab cover to pad.
2. Fit Hog rings securing squab cover to frame.
3. Position squab centre panel.
4. Secure squab cover, lower retainer.
5. Fit head restraint, guide caps.
6. Fit head restraint.
7. Rotate inboard head restraint, guide cap back 90° to lock head restraint.
8. Fit side valance and secure with pins.
9. Fit inner half of squab recline handle.
10. Fit outer half of squab recline handle.
11. Fit pre-tensioner to squab frame, fit Torx bolt and tighten to 45 Nm.

⚠ **CAUTION: To prevent damage to the pre-tensioner flylead ensure flylead is correctly positioned to seat, as shown in seat refit. See this section.**

12. Secure pre-tensioner flylead clips to underside of seat.
13. Fit seat. *See this section.*

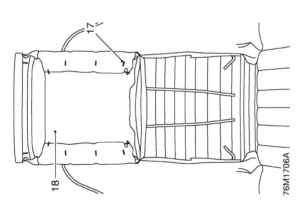

76M1705A

15. Remove 11 Hog rings securing squab cover to frame.
16. Remove squab cover from pad. *Do not carry out further dismantling if component is removed for access only.*

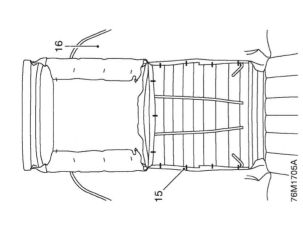

76M1706A

17. Remove 12 Hog rings securing squab cover to centre pad.
18. Remove seat squab, centre pad.

Rebuild

19. Position seat squab, centre pad.
20. Secure squab cover to centre pad with hog rings.

SQUAB FRAME

Service repair no - 78.90.22

⚠️ **WARNING: See** *RESTRAINT SYSTEMS, Precautions.*

Remove

1. Make the SRS system safe. *See RESTRAINT SYSTEMS, Precautions.*
2. Remove seat squab pullmaflex. *See this section.*

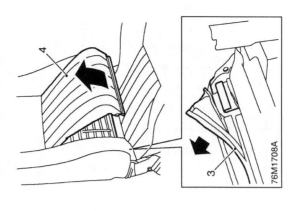

78M0172A

3. Remove 4 Tx50 Torx bolts securing squab frame to cushion frame.
4. Remove squab frame.

Refit

1. Fit squab frame to cushion frame.
2. Fit Torx bolts securing squab frame to cushion frame and tighten to 45 Nm.
3. Fit seat squab pullmaflex. *See this section.*

SQUAB PAD

Service repair no - 78.90.49

⚠️ **WARNING: See** *RESTRAINT SYSTEMS, Precautions.*

Remove

1. Make the SRS system safe. *See RESTRAINT SYSTEMS, Precautions.*
2. Remove squab cover. *See this section.*
3. Remove squab pad from frame.

Refit

1. Fit squab pad to frame.
2. Fit squab cover. *See this section.*

SQUAB PAD - CENTRE

Service repair no - 78.90.50

⚠️ **WARNING: See** *RESTRAINT SYSTEMS, Precautions.*

Remove

1. Make the SRS system safe. *See RESTRAINT SYSTEMS, Precautions.*

⚠️ **CAUTION: Ensure pre-tensioner multiplug is disconnected before seat is removed.**

2. Remove seat. *See this section.*

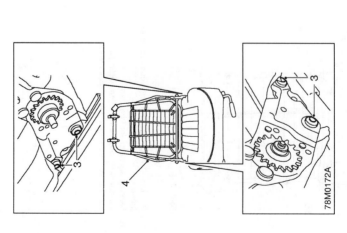

76M1708A

3. Release squab cover, lower retainer.
4. Raise squab centre panel.

WINDSCREEN

Service repair no - 76.81.01

NOTE: The following equipment is required:

**Cutting wire and handles
Windscreen repair kit
Sealer applicator gun
Suction cups**

WARNING: Wear protective gloves when handling glass, solvents and primers.

WARNING: Wear suitable eye protection when removing and refitting glass.

Remove

1. Remove air intake panel. *See HEATING & VENTILATION, Repairs.*
2. Remove header trim. *See Interior trim components.*
3. Remove 'A' post trim, *See Interior trim components.*

76M1832

4. Remove interior mirror. *See Interior trim components.*
5. Fit protection to bonnet and areas around screen.
6. Cover heater ducts with masking tape.
7. Cover interior of vehicle with protective sheet.
8. Make knife cut in sealant at bottom of 'A' post.

9. Insert cutting wire through previously made knife cut and fit handles as shown, with approximately 200 mm of wire between handles.
10. With assistance, wedge tube of handle **A** between glass and body, ahead of cutting position, and carefully cut sealer using a continuous pull on handle **B** from the outside. Ensure that glass is retained as last sealant is cut.

NOTE: If multi-strand cutting wire is used, a sawing action can be used to cut through heavy sealant deposits around corners.

CAUTION: Use of a sawing action may overheat and break single strand wire.

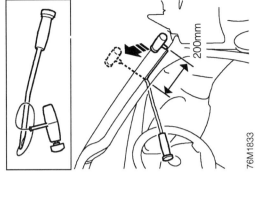

200mm

76M1833

76M1709A

5. Remove 12 Hog rings securing squab cover to centre pad.
6. Remove seat squab, centre pad.

Refit

1. Position seat squab, centre pad.
2. Secure squab cover to centre pad with hog rings.
3. Position squab centre panel.
4. Secure squab cover, lower retainer.
5. Fit seat. *See this section.*

11. Attach suction cups and use assistance to remove glass from body.

⚠ **CAUTION: Lay glass on felt covered supports. Do not stand on edge. Any chipping of glass edge may develop into cracks.**

Refit

1. Carefully remove excess sealer from body leaving a smooth surface.

2. Use a vacuum cleaner to clear away any waste.

3. Original glass: Carefully cut back old sealer to obtain a smooth surface without damaging obscuration band on glass.

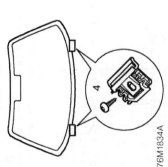

76M1834A

4. Fit 2 brackets and tighten screws.

5. With assistance, locate screen upright on brackets and then lay in position in body frame. Carefully centre screen in body frame and apply masking tape reference marks from screen to body, on each side of lower screen.

6. Carefully centre screen in body frame and apply masking tape reference marks from screen to body, on each side of lower screen.

7. Cut tape at edge of screen, and with assistance remove screen and place aside.

8. Clean frame and edge of screen with solvent.

⚠ **CAUTION: Do not touch cleaned or primed surfaces with fingers.**

9. Apply etch primer to any bare metal on frame.

10. Apply bonding agent to screen and allow to cure.

11. Apply primer over etch primer on frame.

12. Apply activator over old sealer on frame.

13. Allow activator to cure.

14. Fit pre-cut nozzle to sealer cartridge, remove lid and shake out crystals, and install in applicator gun.

△ NOTE: Nozzle will need modification to achieve required bead section.

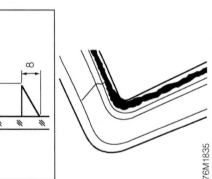
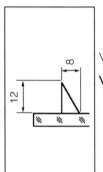

76M1835

15. Apply a continuous bead of sealer around edge of frame as shown. Make bead slightly thicker at each corner.

16. Check for breaks and air bubbles in sealer.

17. With assistance, lift screen into place and align to brackets and tape. Lightly press glass to seat sealer.

18. Remove protective covers and tape.

19. Test sealer for leaks, apply additional sealer if necessary. If water is used, allow sealer to dry before testing. Spray water around glass and check for leaks. Mark any area that leaks. Dry glass and sealer then apply additional sealer.

20. Fit 'A' post trim. *See Interior trim components.*

21. Fit header trim. *See Interior trim components.*

22. Fit interior mirror. *See Interior trim components.*

23. Fit air intake panel. *See HEATING & VENTILATION, Repairs.*

⚠ **CAUTION: A curing time of 6 hours is desirable, during this time leave a window open and do not slam the doors. If the car must be used, drive slowly.**

CONTENTS

Page

DESCRIPTION AND OPERATION

OPERATION

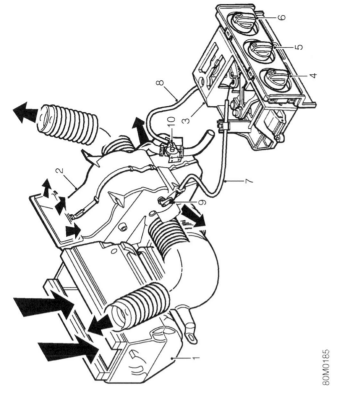

80M0185

1. Heater duct
2. Heater and blower unit
3. Heater control unit
4. Blower switch
5. Temperature control
6. Distribution control
7. Control cable - air distribution
8. Control cable - temperature control
9. Distribution control, lever
10. Heater valve

Air drawn through the intake below the windscreen, passes through a heater duct into the heater unit to enter the interior of the car through fascia vents, via a moulded heater duct in the fascia.

When the temperature control is rotated towards the heated air position it opens a heater valve in the engine cooling system allowing hot coolant from the engine to circulate through the heater matrix.

The distribution of air entering the car through the heater is dependent on the positions of distribution flaps inside the heater unit.

The distribution flaps are adjusted by rotation of the distribution control to direct the air in various proportions to the vents at face level, foot level and the windscreen.

When the blower switch is switched off, the volume of air entering the blower unit depends on the ram effect of the car's forward motion. Four fan speeds are available on the switch to supplement the ram effect.

Operation of the thumb-wheel in either, the side or centre face level vents will open or close the vents.

CONTROLS - HEATER - 2000MY ON

Service repair no - 80.10.02

Remove

1. Remove centre console. *See BODY, Interior trim components.*

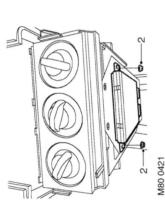

M80 0421

2. Remove 2 nuts securing alarm ECU, release ECU and position aside.

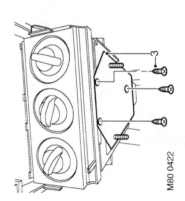

M80 0422

3. Remove 3 screws securing alarm ECU support plate and remove support plate.

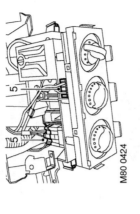

M80 0423

4. Remove 4 screws securing heater controls and release controls from support bracket.

M80 0424

5. Disconnect heater control multiplugs.

A/C

CABLE - WATER VALVE CONTROL - UP TO 2000MY

Service repair no - 80.10.07

Remove

1. Remove front console. *See BODY, Interior trim components.*

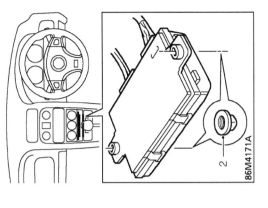

86M4171A

2. Remove 2 nuts securing anti-theft alarm ECU to heater control unit, position ECU aside.

Refit

1. Position control assembly and connect inner cables.
2. Secure outer cables in clips, do not clamp screws at this stage.
3. Connect control multiplugs.
4. Align controls to support bracket. Fit and tighten screws.
5. Turn distribution control fully anti-clockwise to face vent position.
6. Position air distribution lever fully forward.
7. Align outer cable to abutment and secure clamp screw.
8. Turn heater control to 'cold' and heater valve lever fully clockwise.
9. Secure outer cable clamp screw.
10. Position alarm ECU support plate, fit and tighten screws.
11. Position alarm ECU, fit and tighten nuts.
12. Fit centre console. *See BODY, Interior trim components.*

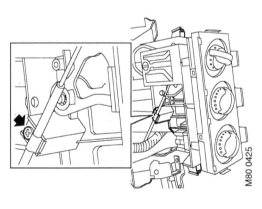

M80 0431

6. Loosen screw securing temperature control outer cable and release inner cable from control lever.

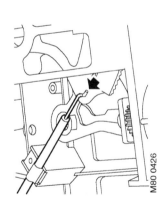

M80 0425

7. Loosen screw securing distribution cable control outer cable.

M80 0426

8. Release inner cable from control lever.
9. Remove control assembly.

A/C

CABLE - WATER VALVE CONTROL - 2000MY ON

Service repair no - 80.10.07

Remove

1. Remove front console. *See BODY, Interior trim components.*

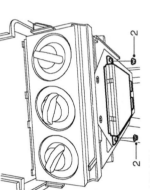

M80 0421

2. Remove 2 nuts securing alarm ECU to heater control unit and position alarm ECU aside.

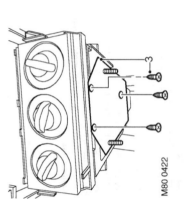

M80 0422

3. Remove 3 screws securing alarm ECU support plate and remove support plate.

M80 0423

4. Remove 4 screws securing controls to fascia.
5. Release controls from fascia.

M80 0427

6. Remove screw securing cable clamp to controls and collect clamp.
7. Release cable from controls.

80M0180A

3. Remove 4 screws securing control unit to fascia.
4. Release control unit from fascia.
5. Remove screw securing cable clamp to control unit and collect clamp.
6. Release cable from control unit.

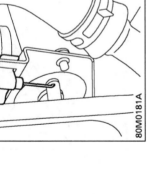

80M0181A

7. Remove clip securing cable outer to heater valve.
8. Release cable from valve and remove cable.

Refit

1. Engage cable to heater valve.
2. Engage cable to control unit and secure cable clamp.
3. Turn heater control to 'COLD' and heater valve lever fully clockwise.
4. Secure outer cable to valve with clip.
5. Position control unit to fascia and secure with screws.
6. Position alarm ECU to heater control unit, fit and tighten nuts to 4 Nm.
7. Fit front console. *See BODY, Interior trim components.*

CABLE - AIR DISTRIBUTION CONTROL - 2000MY ON

Service repair no - 80.10.12

Remove

1. Remove front console. *See BODY, Interior trim components.*

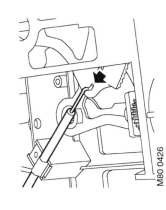

M80 0423

2. Remove 4 screws securing controls to fascia.
3. Release controls from fascia.

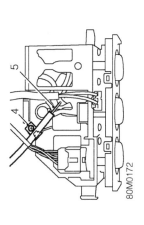

M80 0426

4. Remove screw securing cable clamp to controls and collect clamp.
5. Release cable from controls.

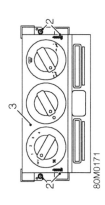

80M0173

6. Remove clip securing cable outer to heater.
7. Remove star washer securing cable to air distribution control lever.
8. Remove cable from heater.

Refit

1. Position cable to air distribution control lever and secure with star washer.
2. Engage cable to control unit.
3. Align collar of outer cable to control unit abutment and secure with clamp.
4. Turn distribution control fully anti-clockwise to face vent position.
5. Position air distribution control lever fully forward.
6. Align outer cable to abutment and secure with clip.
7. Position controls to fascia and secure with screws.
8. Fit front console. *See BODY, Interior trim components.*

CABLE - AIR DISTRIBUTION CONTROL - UP TO 2000MY

Service repair no - 80.10.12

Remove

1. Remove front console. *See BODY, Interior trim components.*

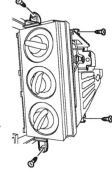

80M0171

2. Remove 4 screws securing heater control unit to fascia.
3. Release control unit from fascia.

80M0172

4. Remove screw securing cable clamp to control unit and collect clamp.
5. Release cable from control unit.

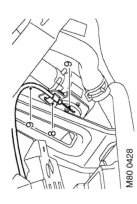

M80 0428

8. Remove clip securing cable outer to heater valve.
9. Release cable from valve and remove cable.

Refit

1. Engage cable to heater valve.
2. Engage cable to heater controls and secure cable clamp.
3. Turn heater control to 'COLD' and heater valve lever fully clockwise.
4. Secure outer cable to valve with clip.
5. Position controls to fascia and secure with screws.
6. Position alarm ECU support plate and secure with screws.
7. Position alarm ECU to heater control unit, fit and tighten nuts to 4 Nm.
8. Fit front console. *See BODY, Interior trim components.*

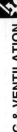

M80 0429

6. Remove clip securing cable outer to heater.
7. Remove star washer securing cable to air distribution control lever.
8. Remove cable from heater.

Refit

1. Position cable to air distribution control lever and secure with star washer.
2. Engage cable to heater controls.
3. Align collar of outer cable to heater control abutment and secure with clamp.
4. Turn distribution control fully anti-clockwise to face vent position.
5. Position air distribution lever fully forward.
6. Align outer cable to abutment and secure with clip.
7. Position controls to fascia and secure with screws.
8. Fit front console. *See BODY, Interior trim components.*

HEATER VALVE

Service repair no - 80.10.16

Remove

1. Drain coolant system. *See COOLING SYSTEM, Adjustments.*
2. Remove both console closing panels. *See BODY, Interior trim components.*

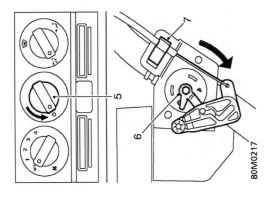

80M0169A

3. Remove 2 screws securing valve to heater assembly.

80M0179A

4. Remove clip securing cable outer to valve and release cable from valve lever.
5. Position cloth and container to catch spillage.
6. Release 2 clips securing hoses to valve.
7. Release top hose.
8. Remove valve from bottom hose.

Refit

1. Fit valve to lower hose and secure with clip.
2. Position upper hose to valve and secure with clip.
3. Engage cable to valve lever.
4. Position valve to heater assembly and secure with screws.

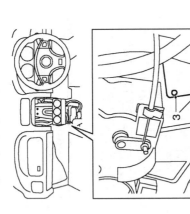

80M0217

5. Turn heater control fully to 'COLD'.
6. Turn valve lever fully clockwise.
7. Position cable outer and secure with clip.
8. Fit console closing panels. *See BODY, Interior trim components.*
9. Refill coolant system. *See COOLING SYSTEM, Adjustments.*

HEATING & VENTILATION

HEATER FAN SWITCH

Service repair no - 80.10.22

Remove

1. Remove front console. *See **BODY, Interior trim components.***

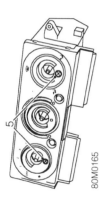

80M0163

2. Remove 4 screws securing heater control unit to fascia and position control unit aside.

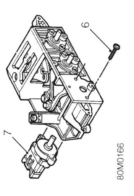

80M0164

3. Disconnect multiplug from control unit.

---

4. Remove 3 knobs from control assembly.

80M0165

5. Remove 2 screws securing illumination housing to assembly and remove housing.

80M0166

6. Remove 2 screws securing fan switch to assembly.
7. Remove switch.

Refit

1. Position switch to assembly and secure with screws.
2. Position illumination housing to assembly and secure with screws.
3. Fit control knobs.
4. Connect multiplug.
5. Position control unit to fascia and secure with screws.
6. Fit front console. *See **BODY, Interior trim components.***

HEATING & VENTILATION

FACE LEVEL VENT - RH

Service repair no - 80.15.04

Remove

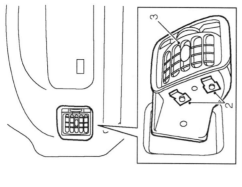

80M0175

1. Turn clips securing fuse box cover ¼ turn and open cover.

2. Release 4 clips securing vent to fascia.
3. Remove vent.

Refit

1. Fit vent to fascia and engage clips.
2. Close fuse box cover and secure with clips.

80M0176

FACE LEVEL VENT - LH

Service repair no - 80.15.05

Remove

1. Remove glovebox. *See **BODY, Interior trim components.***

80M0178

2. Release 4 clips securing vent to fascia.
3. Remove vent.

Refit

1. Fit vent to fascia and engage clips.
2. Fit glovebox. *See **BODY, Interior trim components.***

FACE LEVEL VENT - CENTRE

Service repair no - 80.15.63

Remove

1. Remove centre console panel. *See BODY, Interior trim components.*

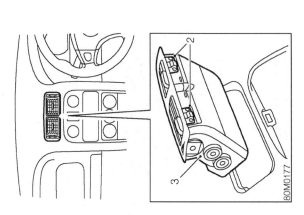

2. Release 4 clips securing vent to fascia.
3. Remove vent.

Refit

1. Fit vent to fascia and engage clips.
2. Fit centre console panel. *See BODY, Interior trim components.*

80M0177

AIR INTAKE PANEL

Service repair no - 80.15.62

Remove

1. Remove wiper arms. *See WIPERS & WASHERS, Repairs.*

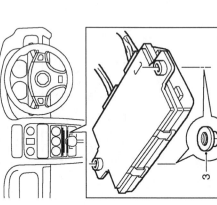

2. Remove 6 retaining screw caps from intake moulding.
3. Remove 6 screws and 6 clips securing panel to scuttle.
4. Release intake panel from clips and remove panel.

Refit

1. Position panel to scuttle and secure with clips and screws.
2. Fit screw caps.
3. Fit wiper arms. *See WIPERS & WASHERS, Repairs.*

80M0160

HEATER

Service repair no - 80.20.01

⚠ **WARNING:** *See RESTRAINT SYSTEMS, Precautions.*

Remove

1. Make the SRS system safe *See RESTRAINT SYSTEMS, Precautions.*
2. Remove fascia. *See BODY, Interior trim components.*

3. Remove 2 nuts securing anti-theft alarm ECU to heater control unit, position ECU aside. *See COOLING SYSTEM, Adjustments.*
4. Drain cooling system. *See COOLING SYSTEM, Adjustments.*

86M4178

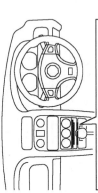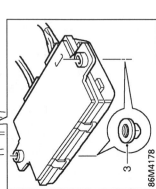

5. Remove 2 screws retaining outer cables to control unit.
6. Release cables from control unit.
7. Disconnect 2 multiplugs and remove control unit.
8. Remove 2 screen ducts from heater.

80M0146

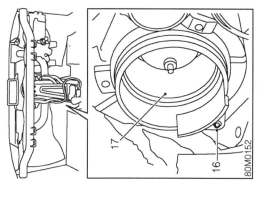

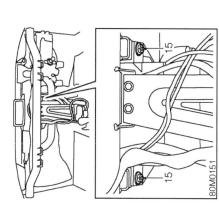

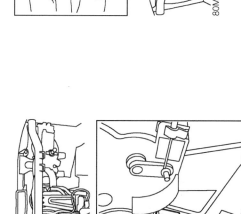

80M0150

13. Remove nut securing intake duct to body.
14. Remove intake duct.

80M0151

15. Remove 2 nuts securing heater unit to crossmember.

80M0152

16. Remove bolt securing heater unit to bulkhead.
17. Remove heater unit.

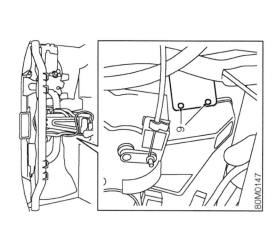

80M0147

9. Remove 2 screws securing valve to heater casing.
10. Position container beneath heater to catch spillage.

80M0149

12. Disconnect multiplug from heater blower.

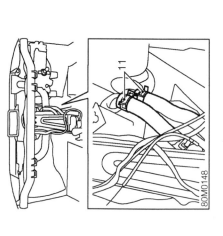

80M0148

11. Release clips and disconnect both hoses from heater matrix. Allow matrix to drain.

HEATING & VENTILATION

Refit

1. Position heater to mountings.
2. Tighten all fixings to 10 Nm.
3. Position intake duct and tighten nut to 10 Nm.
4. Connect multiplug to heater blower.
5. Connect hoses to heater matrix and secure with clips.
6. Position valve and secure with screws.
7. Fit screen ducts.
8. Connect multiplugs to control unit.
9. Position control cables and connect to control unit.
10. Align cable outers to control unit and tighten clamp screws.

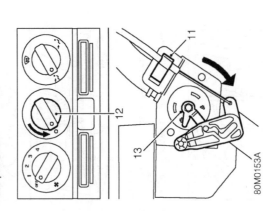

80M0153A

11. Release clip securing cable outer to heater valve.
12. Turn temperature control to COLD.
13. Push heater control valve to the cold position and secure cable clip.
14. Position alarm ECU to control unit, fit and tighten nuts to 4 Nm.
15. Refill cooling system. *See COOLING SYSTEM, Adjustments.*
16. Fit fascia. *See BODY, Interior trim components.*

HEATER - WITH AIR CONDITIONING

Service repair no - 80.20.01/20

⚠ **WARNING:** *See RESTRAINT SYSTEMS, Precautions.*

Remove

1. Make the SRS system safe *See RESTRAINT SYSTEMS, Precautions.*
2. Remove evaporator. *See AIR CONDITIONING, Repairs.*

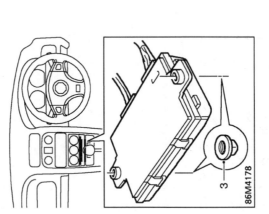

86M4178

3. Remove 2 nuts securing anti-theft alarm ECU to heater control, position ECU aside.
4. Drain cooling system. *See COOLING SYSTEM, Adjustments.*

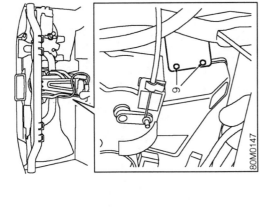

80M0146

5. Remove 2 screws retaining outer cables to control unit.
6. Release cables from control unit.
7. Disconnect 2 multiplugs and remove control unit.
8. Remove screen duct from heater.

80M0147

9. Remove 2 screws securing valve to heater casing.
10. Position container beneath heater to catch spillage.

HEATING & VENTILATION

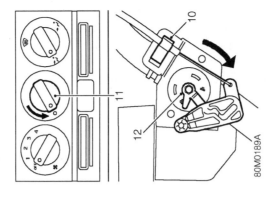

Refit

1. Position heater to mountings.
2. Tighten all fixings to 10 Nm.
3. Connect multiplug to heater blower.
4. Connect hoses to heater matrix and secure with clips.
5. Position valve and secure with screws.
6. Fit screen duct.
7. Connect multiplugs to control unit.
8. Position control cables and connect to control unit.
9. Align cable outers to control unit and tighten clamp screws.

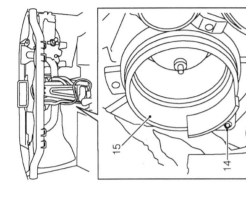

80M0188

14. Remove nut securing heater unit to bulkhead.
15. Remove heater unit.

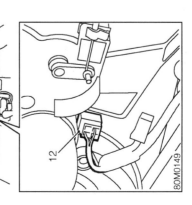

80M0189A

10. Release clip securing cable outer to heater valve.
11. Turn temperature control to COLD.
12. Push heater control valve to the COLD position and secure cable clip.
13. Refill cooling system. **See COOLING SYSTEM, Adjustments.**
14. Position alarm ECU to heater control, fit and tighten nuts to 4 Nm.
15. Fit evaporator. **See AIR CONDITIONING, Repairs.**

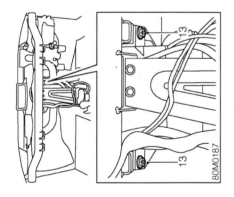

80M0187

13. Remove 2 nuts securing heater unit to crossmember.

80M0148

11. Release clips and disconnect both hoses from heater matrix. Allow matrix to drain.

80M0149

12. Disconnect multiplug from heater blower.

RECIRCULATION SERVO MOTOR

Service repair no - 80.20.10

Remove

1. Remove glovebox. *See BODY, Interior trim components.*

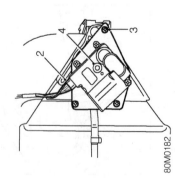

80M0182

2. Disconnect multiplug from servo motor.
3. Remove 3 screws securing servo motor to evaporator casing.
4. Remove servo motor.

Refit

1. Position servo motor and engage output crank to recirculation flap lever.
2. Secure servo motor with screws.
3. Connect multiplug.
4. Fit glovebox. *See BODY, Interior trim components.*

HEATER BLOWER

Service repair no - 80.20.12

Remove

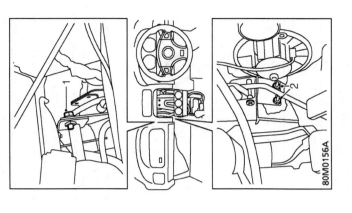

80M0154A

1. Remove bolt securing throttle pedal bracket to pedal box.
2. Remove 2 nuts securing throttle pedal bracket to bulkhead and position throttle pedal assembly aside.
3. Remove heater duct.

HEATER RESISTOR

Service repair no - 80.20.17

Remove

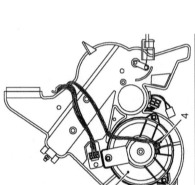

80M0156A

1. Remove bolt securing throttle pedal bracket to pedal box.
2. Remove 2 nuts securing throttle pedal bracket to bulkhead and position throttle pedal assembly aside.

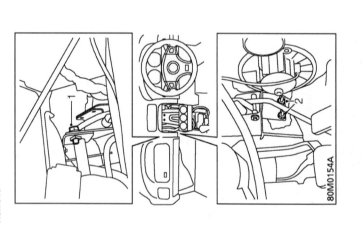

80M0155

4. Disconnect multiplug from heater blower.
5. Remove 3 screws securing blower to heater.
6. Remove heater blower.
7. Release armature cover and collect sleeve.

Refit

1. Position screw and sleeve to top location of heater blower.
2. Position blower to heater and secure with screws.

⚠ **CAUTION: Ensure screw sleeve does not fall into blower motor.**

3. Connect multiplug to blower.
4. Fit heater duct.
5. Position throttle pedal assembly, fit and tighten nuts to 6 Nm.
6. Fit and tighten bolt to 22 Nm.

HEATER MATRIX

Service repair no - 80.20.29

Remove

1. Remove heater. *See this section.*

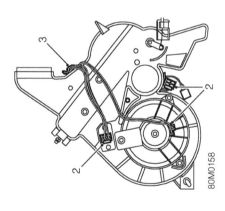

80M0158

2. Disconnect multiplugs from blower and resistor.
3. Release harness from 2 clips and position aside.

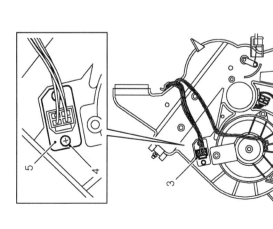

80M0157

3. Disconnect multiplug from resistor.
4. Remove 2 screws securing resistor.
5. Remove heater resistor.

Refit

1. Position resistor to heater and secure with screws.
2. Connect resistor multiplug.
3. Position throttle pedal assembly, fit and tighten nuts to 6 Nm.
4. Fit and tighten bolt to 22 Nm.

80M0159

4. Remove 15 clips and 2 screws securing two halves of casing.
5. Remove foam seal from outlet vent and matrix bleed nipple.
6. Separate two halves of casing.
7. Remove heater matrix.

Refit

1. Position matrix to heater.
2. Position two halves of casing, ensuring correct location of flow direction flap.
3. Secure casing halves with clips and screws.
4. Clean sealing faces.
5. Fit foam seals to outlet vent and bleed nipple.
6. Engage harness clips and connect multiplugs.
7. Fit heater. *See this section.*

AIR CONDITIONING COMPONENTS

82M0301

1. Condenser
2. Cooling fans
3. Evaporator
4. Compressor

5. Receiver/drier
6. Trinary pressure switch
7. Air conditioning, relay module
8. ECM

CONTENTS

AIR CONDITIONING

SCHEMATIC LAYOUT OF AIR CONDITIONING SYSTEM

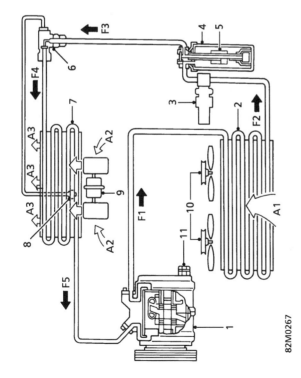

82M0267

1. Compressor
2. Condenser
3. Trinary pressure switch
4. Receiver/drier
5. Drying agent - receiver/drier
6. Thermostatic expansion valve
7. Evaporator
8. Capillary tube
9. Heater blower motor
10. Condenser cooling fans
11. Compressor high pressure relief valve

A1. Ambient air flow through condenser
A2. Ambient air flow through fan and evaporator
A3. Cooled air flow to vehicle interior
F1. High pressure, high temperature refrigerant vapour
F2. High pressure, slightly subcooled refrigerant liquid
F3. High pressure, slightly subcooled refrigerant liquid with moisture, vapour bubbles and foreign matter removed
F4. Low pressure, low temperature mixed liquid and vapour
F5. Low pressure, slightly superheated refrigerant vapour

AIR CONDITIONING SYSTEM OPERATION

The air conditioning system provides the means of supplying cooled and dehumidified, fresh or recirculated air to the interior of the vehicle. The cooling effect is obtained by blowing air through the matrix of an evaporator unit and when required, heating the air to provide the conditions required inside the vehicle. The volume of the conditioned air being supplied is controlled by a variable speed blower.

Sealed refrigerant

A sealed system, charged with Refrigerant R134a, together with a blower unit, blend unit and control system combine to achieve the cooled air condition.

The sealed system comprises of the following main components:

1. Compressor
2. Condenser
3. Receiver/drier
4. Thermostatic expansion valve
5. Evaporator

Refrigeration cycle

The compressor is driven by a belt from the crankshaft pulley. The compressor pressurises and circulates the refrigerant through the system. Mounted on the compressor, an electro-mechanical clutch maintains the correct temperature and pressure of the refrigerant by engaging or disengaging the compressor to support the systems requirements. Operation of the clutch is controlled by the engine control module (ECM), the trinary (triple) pressure switch and a thermostatic switch located on the exterior fins of the evaporator.

If the temperature at the evaporator falls low enough for ice to form on the fins, the thermostatic switch will open, breaking the circuit to the clutch and releasing the drive on the compressor. The ECM detects that the air conditioning system is not operating and switches off the condenser cooling fan. When the temperature at the evaporator rises sufficiently for the thermostatic switch to close, the air conditioning system will be restarted.

If the system pressure becomes excessive or drops sufficiently to cause damage to the compressor, a trinary pressure switch located in the high pressure line at the receiver drier will break the electrical circuit to the compressor clutch, releasing drive from the compressor. The compressor also has an internal thermal cut-out switch which disengages the compressor's clutch to prevent the compressor oil overheating. The clutch will re-engage when the oil temperature has returned to normal.

The two cooling fans are controlled by the ECM and dependent upon engine coolant temperature and air conditioning system pressure. With the air conditioning system switched off, the (radiator) cooling fans are operated with the ECM controlling the fan speed according to engine temperature. With the air conditioning system switched on, condenser (radiator) cooling fans are connected in series by the ECM and operate at low speed. As the pressure of the air conditioning refrigerant rises above the threshold of the medium pressure setting on the trinary pressure switch, the cooling fans are connected in parallel and operate at high speed.

If engine coolant temperature continues to rise with both cooling fans running at high speed, the ECM will break the circuit to the compressor clutch releasing drive to the compressor. This reduces the load on the engine whilst maintaining a high cooling fan speed to lower the engine coolant temperature. Once engine coolant temperature has dropped sufficiently the air conditioning system will be reinstated.

From the compressor, high pressure vaporised refrigerant is passed to the condenser which is mounted in front of the radiator. Ram air passing through the condenser, supplemented by the cooling fans, cools the refrigerant vapour in the condenser sufficiently to form a high pressure slightly subcooled liquid.

This subcooled liquid then passes to the receiver/drier which extracts moisture from the refrigerant as well as acting as a reservoir.

From the receiver/drier the moisture free refrigerant liquid passes through a thermostatic expansion valve to the evaporator unit. The thermostatic expansion valve incorporates a restrictor which converts the liquid refrigerant into a low temperature, low pressure liquid vapour mixture. To prevent liquid refrigerant passing into the evaporator unit, the thermostatic expansion valve senses the evaporator outlet pressure and controls the amount the valve opens and closes.

Fan blown air is passed through the evaporator where it is cooled by absorption due to the low temperature refrigerant in the evaporator. Most of the moisture being held in the air is condensed into water by the evaporator and drains away beneath the vehicle via a drain tube.

From the evaporator, low pressure slightly heated refrigerant passes to the compressor to complete the cycle. The compressor pressurises the refrigerant vapour which becomes very hot and is passed to the condenser to be converted into liquid.

AIR CONDITIONING CONTROL SYSTEM

The air conditioning control system comprises of relays, a thermostatic switch, a trinary pressure switch and a control panel. Together these controls, in conjunction with the cooling fans, compressor clutch, blower and heater distribution enable minimal input to maintain the required environment inside the vehicle.

When air conditioning is not selected, air is supplied by ram effect or blower to the areas selected by the air distribution control. The heater valve on the heater matrix controls the temperature of the air being delivered. No cooled air is available.

Selecting air conditioning provides the added facility of cooled air which can be re-heated by the heater matrix if required. When required a fully cold condition can be selected by turning the temperature control to cold, which automatically closes the heated coolant access to the heater matrix. Mixtures of cooled, fresh, and hot air can be selected to give the required interior environmental conditions by selection at the control panel.

Trinary pressure switch

The trinary (triple) pressure switch is located in the high pressure line between the condenser and the receiver drier. The trinary pressure switch detects refrigerant pressure and by means of the ECM controls the following system functions:

1. Refrigerant pressure drops below 2.0 bar (due to possible leakage), the compressors electro-mechanical clutch is disengaged. When pressure rises above 2.4 bar the compressors clutch is re-engaged.
2. Refrigerant pressure exceeds 19 bar the cooling fan speed is increased by the ECM switching the relays in the relay module to connect the cooling fans in parallel supplying a direct feed to each fan motor.
3. Refrigerant pressure rises above 27 bar even with maximum cooling fan operation (due to possible blockage), the compressor electro-mechanical clutch is disengaged. The high pressure switch resets when the pressure drops to approximately 21 bar.

ECM control

In addition to its various functions of controlling the air conditioning system, the ECM also controls the compressor's clutch for system safety.

A. To protect the discharge hose material from excessive high refrigerant temperatures produced at high speed. The ECM will disengage the compressor clutch when an engine speed of 5000 rpm is reached and re-engage when the speed drops below 4900 rpm.

B. To allow more power for vehicle acceleration the compressor's clutch is disengaged when the throttle disc angle is opened above 85°(fully open is 90°). The clutch is re-engaged when the throttle disc angle is below 80°.

C. To protect the engine's cooling system the ECM will disengage the compressor's clutch when the coolant temperature exceeds 117°C. The clutch re-engages when the coolant temperature drops below 112°C.

Condenser cooling fans

The condenser cooling fans operate automatically whenever the air conditioning system is switched on, providing the system pressure is correct.

The cooling fans are controlled by the ECM, thermostatic switch and trinary pressure switch. If engine coolant temperature and air conditioning system pressure are normal then the cooling fans operate at low speed.
If the engine coolant temperature reaches 108°C or the air conditioning refrigerant pressure exceeds 19 bar then the cooling fans will operate at high speed.

Blower control

The blower can be operated at any one of four speeds by rotating the blower switch to the required position. When the blower is switched off the air conditioning system will not operate.

The fresh air/recirculation flap has two positions and is operated by pressing the button in the centre console. In the recirculation position, air is drawn into the heater from the vehicle by closing the exterior air inlet and opening the interior inlet. In the fresh air position, air is drawn into the heater from outside the vehicle by opening the exterior air inlet and closing the interior inlet.

Heater distribution and blend unit control

Blower unit air flow, having passed through the evaporator passes into the heater unit to be heated, if required. It is then directed into the vehicle interior in accordance with the flap positions, which are designated by the air distribution control on the fascia panel.

The temperature control knob moves the heater valve, allowing engine coolant to flow through the heater matrix back to the engine when the control is moved towards the hot position. The temperature of the heated air flow into the vehicle interior is controlled by the relative movement of the heater valve.

The distribution control moves a flap which controls the direction of the air flow into the interior of the vehicle.

The face level vents have a permanent feed of heated or unheated air from the heater unit and are opened or shut by rotary thumbwheels on each face level vent.

GENERAL PRECAUTIONS

The refrigerant used in the air conditioning system is HFC (Hydrofluorocarbon) R134a.

WARNING:

- **R134a is a hazardous liquid and when handled incorrectly can cause serious injury. Suitable protective clothing must be worn when carrying out service operations on the air conditioning system.**
- **Do not allow a refrigerant container to be heated by direct flame or to be placed near any heating appliance. A refrigerant container must not be heated above 50°C.**
- **,sk.Add definate article Do not leave a container of refrigerant without its cap fitted. Do not transport a container of refrigerant that is unrestrained, especially in the boot of a car.**
- **R134a is odourless and colourless. Do not handle or discharge in an enclosed area, or any area where the vapour and liquid can come in contact with a naked flame or hot metal. R134a is not flammable but can cause a highly toxic gas.**
- **Do not smoke or weld in areas where R134a is in use. Inhalation of concentrations of vapour can cause dizziness, disorientation, narcosis, nausea or vomiting.**
- **Do not allow fluids other than R134a or compressor lubricant to enter the air conditioning system. Spontaneous combustion may occur.**
- **R134a splashed on any part of the body will cause immediate freezing of that area. Also refrigerant cylinders and replenishment trolleys when discharging will freeze skin to them if contact is made.**
- **The refrigerant used in an air conditioning system must be reclaimed in accordance with the recommendations given by a Refrigerant Recovery Recycling Recharging Station.**

 NOTE: Suitable protective clothing comprises:
Wrap round safety glasses or helmet, heat proof gloves, rubber apron, or waterproof overalls and rubber boots.

REMEDIAL ACTIONS

1. If liquid R134a strikes the eye, do not rub it. Gently run large quantities of eye wash off it to raise the temperature. If eye wash is not available, cool, clean water may be used. Cover eye with a clean pad and seek immediate medical attention.

2. If liquid R134a is splashed on the skin run large quantities of water over the area as soon as possible to raise the temperature. Carry out the same action if the skin comes in contact with discharging cylinders. Wrap effected parts in blankets or similar material and seek immediate medical attention.

3. If suspected of being overcome by inhalation of R134a vapour seek fresh air. If unconscious move to fresh air. Apply artificial respiration and/or oxygen and seek immediate medical attention.

NOTE: Due to its low evaporating temperature of -26.1°C, R134a should be handled with care.

This page is intentionally left blank

SERVICE PRECAUTIONS

Care should be taken when handling the components in the refrigeration system. Units must not be lifted by their hoses, pipes or capillary lines. Hoses and lines must not be subjected to any twist or stress. Ensure that hoses are positioned in their correct run before tightening couplings, and ensure that all clips and supports are used. Torque wrenches of the correct type must be used when tightening refrigerant connections to the stated value. An additional spanner must be used to hold the union to prevent twisting of the pipe.

Before connecting any hose or pipe ensure that refrigerant oil is applied to the seat of the new 'O' ring seals but not to the threads.

Check the oil trap for the amount of oil lost.

All protective plugs must be left in place until immediately prior to connection.

The receiver/drier contains desiccant which absorbs moisture. It must be positively sealed at all times.

⚠ **CAUTION: Whenever the refrigerant system is opened, the receiver/drier must be renewed immediately before evacuating and recharging the system.**

Refrigerant oil

Use an approved refrigerant lubricating oil:

Seiko Seiki SK-20
Unipart SK-20
Idemitsu SK-20

⚠ **CAUTION: Do not use any other type of refrigerant oil.**

Refrigerant oil easily absorbs water and must not be stored for long periods. Do not pour unused oil back into the container.

When renewing system components, add the following quantities of refrigerant oil:

Condenser 30cm^3
Evaporator 30cm^3
Pipe or hose 10cm^3
Receiver drier 30cm^3

Total amount of oil in the system: 170 cc

A new compressor is sealed and pressurised with Nitrogen gas, slowly release the sealing cap, gas pressure should be heard to release as the seal is broken.

⚠ NOTE: A new compressor should always have its sealing cap in place and must not be removed until immediately prior to fitting the compressor air conditioning pipes.

Rapid refrigerant discharge

If the air conditioning system is involved in accident damage and the circuit is punctured, the refrigerant will discharge rapidly. The rapid discharge of refrigerant will also result in the loss of most of the oil from the system. The compressor must be removed and all the remaining oil in the compressor drained and refilled as follows:

1. Remove the drain plug and gravity drain all the oil, assisted by rotating the clutch plate (not the pulley).
2. Refit the compressor with the following amount of new refrigerant oil: 170cm^3
3. Refit the drain plug and plug the inlet and outlet port.

REFRIGERANT RECOVERY, RECYCLING AND RECHARGING

⚠ NOTE: An air conditioning portable Refrigerant Recovery, Recycling and Recharging Station for use with R134a refrigerant incorporates all the features necessary to recover refrigerant R134a from the A/C system, to filter and remove moisture, to evacuate and recharge with reclaimed refrigerant. The unit can also be used for performance testing and air conditioning system analysis.

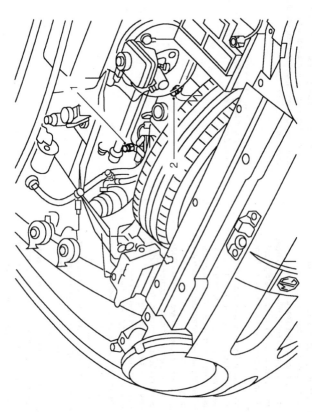

82M0302

Service connections

1. High pressure
2. Low pressure

Recovery and recycling

1. Remove underbonnet closing panel. **See BODY, Exterior fittings.**
2. Connect a refrigerant station to high and low pressure servicing connections.
3. Operate the refrigerant recovery system in accordance to the manufacturer's instructions.

 WARNING: Refrigerant must always be recycled before re-use, to ensure that the purity of the refrigerant is high enough for safe use in the air conditioning system.

Recycling should always be carried out with equipment which is design certified by Underwriter Laboratory Inc. for compliance with SAE - J1991. Other equipment may not recycle refrigerant to the required level of purity.

A R134a Refrigerant Recovery Recycling Recharging Station must not be used with any other type of refrigerant.

Refrigerant R134a from domestic and commercial sources must not be used in motor vehicle air conditioning systems.

Evacuation and recharging

1. Add calculated refrigerant oil to the compressor as necessary.
2. Renew receiver/drier. **See Repairs.**
3. Connect a Refrigerant Station to the high and low pressure servicing connections.

⚠ **CAUTION: Whenever the refrigerant system is opened, the receiver/drier must be renewed immediately before evacuating and recharging the system.**

4. Operate the refrigerant evacuation system according to the manufacturer's instructions.

△ NOTE: If the vacuum reading is below 700 mm/Hg after 15 minutes, suspect a leak in the system. Partially recharge the system and check for leaks using an electronic leak tester.

⚠ **CAUTION: The system must be evacuated immediately before recharging commences. Delay between evacuation and recharging is not permitted.**

5. Operate the refrigerant recharging system according to the manufacturer's instructions.

   Amount of refrigerant required to charge system is:
   - 620 ± 10 g for manual gearbox models
   - 720 ± 10 g for automatic gearbox models
   For each 1.2 m of hose length used to connect the charging trolley to the vehicle's air conditioning system, add 5 g of refrigerant.

6. If the full charge has not been accepted by the system, start the engine and run it at 1500 rev/min.
7. Switch on the air conditioning system, open the car windows, set the temperature control to cold and switch the blower to maximum speed.
8. Consult the Refrigerant Station Manual for the correct procedure to complete the charge.
9. Carry out the air conditioning system performance test.
10. Switch off air conditioning and wait for pressures to equalize, before disconnecting charging hoses from vehicle.

Performance Guide-lines

Carry out this test with bonnet, doors or windows open; air conditioning switched on, temperature control set to cold, face vent mode and blower at maximum speed. Set the air supply control to supply fresh air.

1. Close low pressure valve on Refrigerant Station.
2. Close high pressure valve on Refrigerant Station.
3. Connect Refrigerant Station to the high and low pressure servicing connections.
4. With a thermometer measure the air intake temperature, close to the outside air inlet at the plenum.
5. With a thermometer measure the air outlet temperature, at the centre vent outlet.
6. Run the engine at idle speed for 10 minutes or until normal operating temperature is reached.
7. Read both pressure gauges and thermometers. Check readings against the guide-lines shown in the table below.

Ambient	20°C	25°C	30°C	35°C	40°C
Outlet Temperature (°C)	5 - 10	7 - 15	8 - 20	11 - 22	14 - 25
Low Pressure (bar)	1.6 - 2.4	1.8 - 2.6	2.0 - 3.2	2.2 - 3.5	2.4 - 3.8
High Pressure (bar)	14 - 19	14 - 19	14 - 21	18 - 23	19.6 - 24.8
Notes	A + B	A + B	A + B	B	B

NOTES

- The temperatures and pressures may be slightly increased for high humidity conditions.

- The varying air conditioner pressure will dictate whether the fans operate in series or parallel, which will itself cause the temperatures and pressures to fluctuate. For example:
  A =Condenser and cooling fan both running at half speed (series)
  B =Condenser and cooling fan both running at full speed (parallel)
  A + B =Fans switching from series to parallel.

REPAIRS   1

COMPRESSOR

Service repair no - 82.10.20

Remove

1. Recover refrigerant from air conditioning system. *See **Adjustments**.*
2. Disconnect battery earth lead.
3. Raise rear of vehicle.

⚠ **WARNING: Support on safety stands.**

4. Remove alternator. *See **ELECTRICAL, Repairs**.*

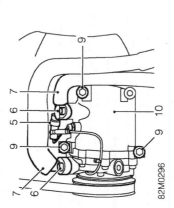

82M0296

5. Disconnect multiplug from air conditioning compressor.
6. Remove 2 Allen screws securing air conditioning pipe unions to compressor.
7. Release air conditioning pipe unions from compressor.
8. Remove and discard 2 'O' ring seals from pipe unions.

⚠ **CAUTION: Immediately cap all air conditioning pipes to prevent ingress of dirt and moisture into the system.**

9. Remove 3 bolts securing compressor to mounting bracket and collect 2 washers from each bolt.
10. Remove compressor.

Fitting a new compressor

A NEW compressor is sealed and pressurised with Nitrogen gas, slowly release the sealing cap, gas pressure should be heard to escape as the seal is broken.

⚠ NOTE: A NEW compressor should always have its sealing cap in place and must not be removed until immediately prior to fitting.

A NEW compressor is supplied with an oil fill quantity (X cm^3) of 170 cm^3. A calculated quantity of oil must be drained from a new compressor before fitting.

To calculate the quantity to be drained:

1. Remove the drain plug from the old compressor.
2. Invert compressor and gravity drain the oil into a calibrated measuring cylinder. Rotating the compressor clutch plate will assist complete draining.
3. Note the quantity of oil drained (Y cm^3).
4. Calculate the quantity of oil to be drained from the NEW compressor using the following formula:

$$X \text{ cm}^3 - (Y \text{ cm}^3 + 20 \text{ cm}^3) = Q \text{ cm}^3$$

5. Remove drain plug from NEW compressor and drain Q cm^3 of oil. Fit and tighten compressor drain plug.

This page is intentionally left blank

Fitting an existing compressor

When refitting an existing compressor a quantity of refrigerant oil equivalent to the amount obtained when the system was discharged must be added to the compressor.

Use only an approved refrigerant lubricating oil:

Seiko SK-20
Unipart SK-20
Idemitsu SK-20

 CAUTION: Do not use any other type of refrigerant oil.

Refrigerant oil easily absorbs water and must not be stored for long periods. Do not pour unused oil back into the container.

CONDENSER

Service repair no - 82.15.07

Remove

1. Recover refrigerant from air conditioning system. See *Adjustments*.
2. Remove front bumper valance. See *BODY, Exterior fittings.*

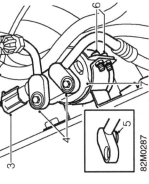

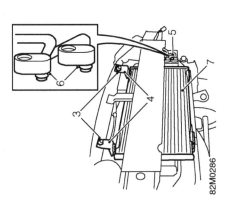

82M0286

3. Remove 2 bolts securing top condenser mounting brackets to striker plate panel.
4. Remove brackets from condenser.
5. Remove 2 bolts securing air conditioning pipe connections to condenser and release pipes.
6. Remove and discard 2 'O' rings from air conditioning pipes.

 **CAUTION: Immediately cap all air conditioning pipes to prevent ingress of dirt and moisture into the system.**

7. Release condenser from lower mountings and remove condenser.

Refit

1. Fit bolts to compressor.
2. Position compressor to engine, fit washers to bolts and tighten to 45 Nm.
3. Clean compressor and pipe connections.
4. Remove caps from compressor and pipe connections.
5. Lubricate 2 NEW 'O' rings with refrigerant oil and fit to pipes.
6. Position air conditioning pipe unions to compressor, fit securing bolts and tighten to 25 Nm.
7. Connect multiplug to compressor.
8. Fit alternator. See *ELECTRICAL, Repairs.*
9. Replace receiver drier. See *this section.*
10. Remove stand(s) and lower vehicle.
11. Connect battery earth lead.
12. Recharge air conditioning system. See *Adjustments.*

RECEIVER DRIER - UP TO 2000MY

Service repair no - 82.17.03

Remove

1. Disconnect battery earth lead.
2. Recover refrigerant from air conditioning system. See *Adjustments.*

82M0287

3. Disconnect multiplug from trinary switch.
4. Remove 2 bolts securing air conditioning pipes to receiver drier.
5. Remove and discard 2 'O' rings from pipes.

CAUTION: Immediately cap all air conditioning pipes to prevent ingress of dirt and moisture into the system.

6. Loosen 2 Allen screws clamping receiver drier bracket.
7. Position pipes aside and remove receiver drier.

Refit

1. Clean air conditioning pipe connections.
2. Lubricate NEW 'O' rings with refrigerant oil and fit to air conditioning pipes.
3. Remove caps from new condenser and fit to old condenser.
4. Position condenser to lower mountings.
5. Fit mounting brackets to condenser.
6. Align mounting brackets to striker plate panel and tighten bolts to 17 Nm.
7. Align air conditioning pipes to condenser and tighten bolts to 5 Nm.
8. Renew receiver drier. See *this section.*
9. Fit front bumper valance. See *BODY, Exterior fittings.*
10. Recharge air conditioning system. See *Adjustments.*

Refit

1. Clean air conditioning pipe connections.
2. Lubricate NEW 'O' rings with refrigerant oil and fit to air conditioning pipes.
3. Remove caps from NEW receiver drier and fit to old unit.
4. Fit receiver drier to bracket and secure bracket clamp screws.
5. Engage air conditioning pipes to receiver drier and tighten retaining bolts to 5 Nm.
6. Connect multiplug.
7. Connect battery earth lead.
8. Recharge air conditioning system. **See Adjustments.**

RECEIVER DRIER - 2000MY ON

Service repair no - 82.17.03

Remove

1. Recover refrigerant from A/C system. **See Adjustments.**

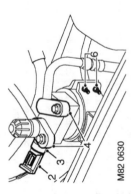

M82 0630

2. Disconnect multiplug from trinary switch.
3. Loosen and remove trinary switch, remove and discard 'O' ring.
4. Remove 2 bolts securing A/C pipes to receiver drier.
5. Remove and discard 2 'O' ring seals from pipes.

⚠ **CAUTION: Immediately cap all air conditioning pipes to prevent ingress of dirt and moisture into the system.**

6. Loosen 2 Allen screws clamping receiver drier bracket.
7. Position pipes aside and remove receiver drier.

Refit

1. Clean A/C pipe connections.
2. Lubricate new 'O' ring seals with clean refrigerant oil and fit to air conditioning pipes.
3. Remove caps from new receiver drier and fit to old unit.
4. Fit receiver drier to bracket and secure bracket clamp screws.
5. Engage A/C pipes to receiver drier and tighten retaining bolts to 5 Nm
6. Lubricate new trinary switch 'O' ring with clean refrigerant oil and fit 'O' ring to trinary switch.
7. Fit trinary switch and tighten to 10 Nm.
8. Connect multiplug.
9. Recharge A/C system. **See Adjustments.**

THERMOSTATIC EXPANSION VALVE

Service repair no - 82.25.01

Remove

1. Recover refrigerant from air conditioning system. **See Adjustments.**

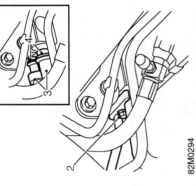

82M0294

2. Remove bolt securing pipe clamp to thermostatic expansion valve.
3. Release 2 air conditioning pipes from valve.
4. Remove and discard 2 'O' rings from air conditioning pipes.

⚠ **CAUTION: Immediately cap all air conditioning pipes to prevent ingress of dirt and moisture into the system.**

SWITCH - TRINARY

Service repair no - 82.20.86

Remove

1. Recover refrigerant from A/C system. **See Adjustments.**

M82 0631

2. Disconnect trinary switch multiplug.
3. Remove trinary switch and discard 'O' ring.

⚠ **CAUTION: Immediately cap all air conditioning pipes to prevent ingress of dirt and moisture into the system.**

Refit

1. Lubricate new 'O' ring with clean refrigerant oil and fit to trinary switch.
2. Fit trinary switch and tighten to 10 Nm.
3. Connect trinary switch multiplug.
4. Recharge A/C system. **See Adjustments.**

EVAPORATOR

Service repair no - 82.25.20

Remove

1. Raise front of vehicle.

⚠ **WARNING: Support on safety stands.**

2. Remove fascia panel. *See BODY, Interior trim components.*
3. Remove thermostatic expansion valve. *See this section.*

82M0288

4. Remove pipe clamp from evaporator pipes.
5. Remove screen vent duct from heater.

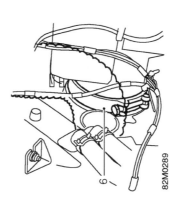

82M0289

6. Remove clamp securing evaporator to heater.

AIR CONDITIONING

CONTROL SWITCH - 2000MY ON

Service repair no - 82.20.07

Remove

1. Remove console closing panel. *See BODY, Interior trim components.*

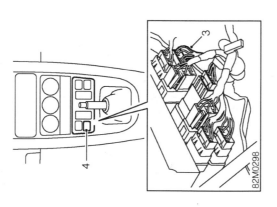

M82 0632

2. Release switch from centre console.
3. Disconnect multiplug from switch.
4. Remove switch.

Refit

1. Connect multiplug to switch and fit switch to centre console.
2. Fit console closing panel *See BODY, Interior trim components.*

AIR CONDITIONING

CONTROL SWITCH - UP TO 2000MY

Service repair no - 82.20.07

Remove

1. Remove console closing panel. *See BODY, Interior trim components.*
2. Release switch panel from centre console.

82M0298

3. Disconnect multiplug from air conditioning switch.
4. Remove switch.

Refit

1. Connect multiplug and engage switch to panel.
2. Engage panel to console and fit closing panel. *See BODY, Interior trim components.*

82M0295

5. Remove 2 Allen bolts securing evaporator pipe clamp to thermostatic expansion valve.
6. Remove thermostatic expansion valve from evaporator pipes.
7. Remove and discard 2 'O' rings from evaporator pipes.

⚠ **CAUTION: Immediately cap all air conditioning pipes to prevent ingress of dirt and moisture into the system.**

Refit

1. Clean air conditioning pipe connections.
2. Lubricate NEW 'O' rings with refrigerant oil and fit to air conditioning pipes.
3. Remove caps from NEW thermostatic expansion valve and fit to old unit.
4. Engage valve to evaporator pipes.
5. Position evaporator pipe bracket, fit and tighten Allen bolts to 7 Nm.
6. Engage pipes to valve and position pipe clamp.
7. Tighten pipe clamp bolt to 5 Nm.
8. Renew receiver drier. *See this section.*
9. Recharge air conditioning system. *See Adjustments.*

AIR CONDITIONING

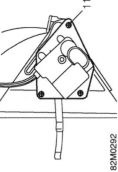

82M0290

7. Disconnect 2 multiplugs from evaporator.

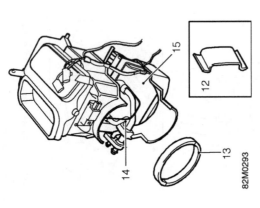

82M0291

8. Remove 2 nuts securing evaporator to lower dash panel.
9. Release evaporator drain hose from evaporator.
10. Remove evaporator assembly.

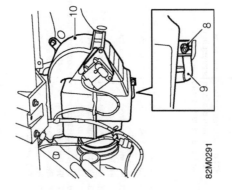

82M0292

11. Remove 3 screws securing recirculation servo to casing and position aside.

82M0293

12. Remove 7 clips securing casing halves.
13. Remove and discard foam seal from output duct.
14. Release thermocouple from evaporator matrix.
15. Separate evaporator casing and remove evaporator matrix.

Refit

1. Position matrix to casing.
2. Align casing halves and secure with clips.
3. Insert tip of thermocouple into centre of matrix fins.
4. Position servo output crank to recirculation flap lever and secure servo with screws.
5. Fit NEW foam seal to output duct.
6. Position evaporator, fit nuts but do not tighten.
7. Engage hose to drain pipe.
8. Fit clamp securing evaporator to heater and tighten nut to 3 Nm.
9. Tighten nuts securing evaporator to lower dash panel to 9 Nm.
10. Connect multiplugs.
11. Remove evaporator pipe caps and clean air conditioning pipe connections.
12. Lubricate NEW 'O' rings with refrigerant oil.
13. Fit pipe bracket to evaporator pipes.
14. Fit thermostatic expansion valve. *See this section.*
15. Fit fascia panel. *See* **BODY, Interior trim components.**
16. Remove stand(s) and lower vehicle.

WIPERS & WASHERS

CONTENTS

WINDSCREEN WIPER COMPONENTS

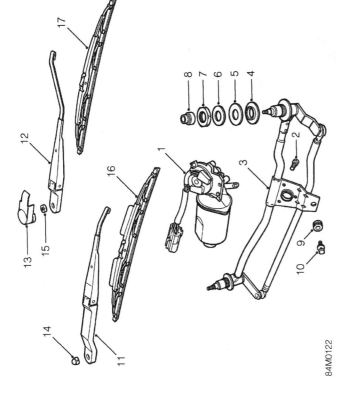

84M0122

1. Wiper motor
2. Bolt - motor to mechanism, 3 off
3. Wiper mechanism assembly
4. Sealing washer - spindle, 2 off
5. Washer - spindle, 2 off
6. Washer - spindle, 2 off
7. Nut - spindle, 2 off
8. Spindle cap, 2 off
9. Rubber grommet
10. Bolt - mechanism to body plate
11. Wiper arm - driver side
12. Wiper arm - passenger side
13. Cover
14. Bevel nut - wiper arm
15. Nut - wiper arm
16. Windscreen wiper - driver side
17. Windscreen wiper - passenger side

WASHER COMPONENTS

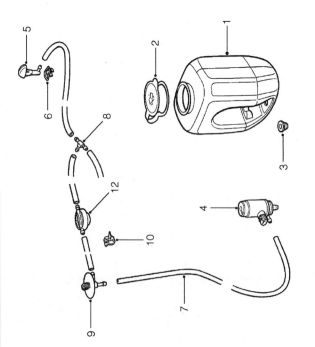

84M0123

1. Reservoir
2. Reservoir cap
3. Bush washer - reservoir
4. Pump - windscreen washer
5. Jet washer, 2 off
6. Gasket - jet washer, 2 off
7. Washer tube
8. Tee connector
9. Elbow connector
10. Clip - tube to bonnet, 4 off
11. Clip - tube to body, 2 off
12. Non-return valve

WINDSCREEN WASHER AND WIPER OPERATION

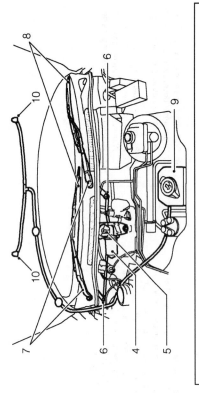
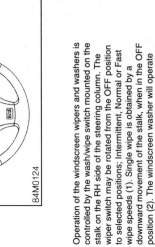

84M0124

Operation of the windscreen wipers and washers is controlled by the wash/wipe switch mounted on the stalk on the RH side of the steering column. The wiper switch may be rotated from the OFF position to selected positions; Intermittent, Normal or Fast wipe speeds (1). Single wipe is obtained by a downward movement of the stalk, when in the OFF position (2). The windscreen washer will operate when the stalk is pulled towards the steering wheel (3).

When any wiper function is selected, a 2 speed wiper motor (4) provides drive through a rotary link (5) to a wiper mechanism (6) which converts the lateral motion of the links into the sweeping motion of the wiper arms (7) and blades (8).

The fast, normal and intermittent speeds, when selected, are controlled by the multi-function unit.

When the windscreen washer is operated, washer fluid is drawn by an electric pump from the reservoir (9); located behind the spare wheel compartment. The washer fluid is sprayed onto the windscreen by washer jets (10).

WASHER RESERVOIR

Service repair no - 84.10.01

Remove

1. Remove reservoir and pump. *See this section.*

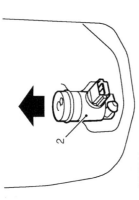

84M0114

2. Remove pump from reservoir.

Refit

1. Fit pump to reservoir.
2. Fit reservoir and pump assembly. *See this section.*

RESERVOIR AND PUMP

Service repair no - 84.10.06

Remove

1. Remove underbonnet closing panel. *See BODY, Exterior fittings.*
2. Position container to catch spillage.
3. Release reservoir from body bracket.

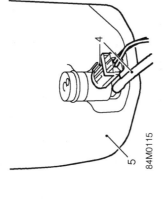

84M0115

4. Disconnect multiplug and washer hose.
5. Remove reservoir assembly.

Refit

1. Position reservoir.
2. Connect multiplug and hose.
3. Engage reservoir to body.
4. Fill reservoir with washer fluid.
5. Fit underbonnet closing panel. *See BODY, Exterior fittings.*

This page is intentionally left blank

WIPERS & WASHERS

WASHER JET

Service repair no - 84.10.08

Remove

1. Open bonnet.

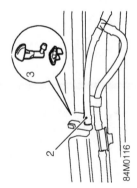

84M0116

2. Disconnect hose from washer jet.
3. Remove jet and collect seat.

Refit

1. Position seat and engage jet to bonnet.
2. Connect hose.
3. Adjust jets.

WASHER PUMP

Service repair no - 84.10.21

Remove

1. Remove reservoir and pump. *See this section.*

84M0117

2. Remove pump from reservoir.

Refit

1. Fit pump to reservoir.
2. Fit reservoir and pump assembly. *See this section.*

WIPERS & WASHERS

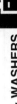

WIPER ARM

Service repair no - 84.15.02

Remove

1. Open bonnet.

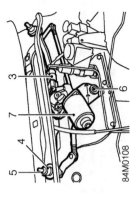

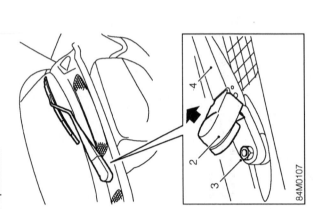

84M0107

2. Remove cover from wiper arm.
3. Remove nut securing wiper arm to spindle.
4. Remove wiper arm.

Refit

1. Fit wiper arm to spindle and align blade to screen.
2. Fit and tighten nut to 20 Nm.
3. Fit cover.

WIPER MOTOR AND LINKAGE

Service repair no - 84.15.11

Remove

1. Remove air intake panel. *See HEATING & VENTILATION, Repairs.*
2. Remove underbonnet closing panel. *See BODY, Exterior fittings.*

84M0108

3. Disconnect multiplug from motor.
4. Remove cover from spindle.
5. Remove 2 nuts securing spindles to scuttle.
6. Remove bolt securing motor to pedal box.
7. Remove motor and linkage assembly.

Refit

1. Position motor and linkage assembly to scuttle.

   ⚠ NOTE: Ensure spindle seals are correctly positioned to scuttle apertures.

2. Tighten fixings to 10 Nm.
3. Fit spindle cover.
4. Connect multiplug.
5. Fit air intake panel. *See HEATING & VENTILATION, Repairs.*
6. Fit underbonnet closing panel. *See BODY, Exterior fittings.*

WIPERS & WASHERS

WIPER MOTOR

Service repair no - 84.15.12

Remove

1. Remove wiper motor and linkage assembly. *See this section.*

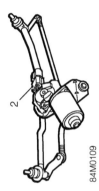

84M0109

2. Release multiplug clip from linkage.

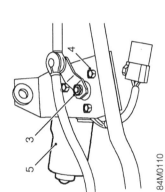

84M0110

3. Remove nut securing crank to motor spindle and release crank.
4. Remove 3 bolts securing motor.
5. Remove motor.

Refit

1. Connect multiplug to harness.
2. Operate wipers to park motor.
3. Disconnect multiplug.
4. Fit motor to linkage bracket and tighten bolts to 12 Nm.

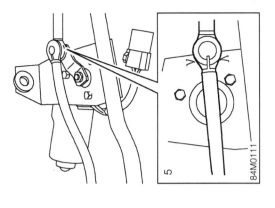

84M0111

5. Align crank between timing marks and fit to motor spindle.
6. Fit and tighten crank nut to 18 Nm.
7. Engage multiplug.
8. Fit wiper motor and linkage. *See this section.*

4   REPAIRS

This page is intentionally left blank

CONTENTS

Page

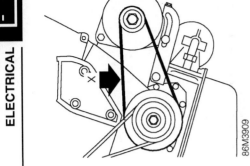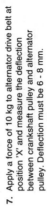

86M3909

ALTERNATOR DRIVE BELT - NON AIR CONDITIONING - ADJUST

Service repair no - 86.10.05

Check

1. Raise rear of vehicle.

⚠ **WARNING:** Support on safety stands.

2. Remove road wheel(s).

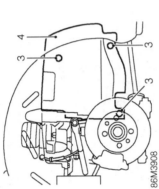

86M3908

3. Remove 2 scrivets and Torx screw securing closing panel.

4. Remove closing panel.

5. Disconnect battery earth lead.

6. Check condition of alternator drive belt. Renew a belt that shows signs of wear or splitting.

7. Apply a force of 10 kg to alternator drive belt at position 'X' and measure the deflection between crankshaft pulley and alternator pulley. Deflection must be 6 - 8 mm.

Adjust

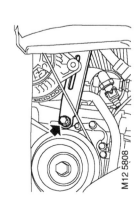

M12 5808

1. Loosen bolt securing alternator adjustment bracket.

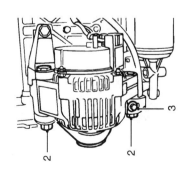

M12 5760

2. Loosen 2 alternator clamp bolts.

⚠ **CAUTION: Ensure that bolts are loosened sufficiently for alternator to move freely.**

3. Turn adjustment bolt in a clockwise direction to increase belt tension.

⚠ **CAUTION: Do not apply excessive torque to adjusting bolt or damage to bolt will result. If bolt appears to be seized or is difficult to turn, apply suitable anti-seize lubricant to bolt.**

4. Check belt tension and re-adjust if necessary.
5. Tighten clamp bolts to 45 Nm.
6. Tighten adjustment bracket bolt to 25 Nm.
7. Fit closing panel and secure scrivets.
8. Fit road wheel(s) and tighten nuts to correct torque. **See INFORMATION, Torque wrench settings.**
9. Remove stand(s) and lower vehicle.
10. Connect battery earth lead.

Adjust

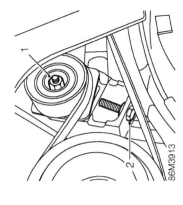

86M3913

ALTERNATOR DRIVE BELT - WITH AIR CONDITIONING - ADJUST

Service repair no - 86.10.05/20

Check

1. Disconnect battery earth lead.
2. Raise rear of vehicle.

⚠ **WARNING: Support on safety stands.**

3. Remove road wheel(s).
4. Remove 2 scrivets and Torx screw securing closing panel.
5. Remove closing panel.
6. Check condition of drive belt. Renew a drive belt that shows signs of wear and splitting.

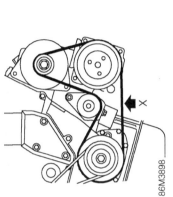

86M3898

7. Apply a force of 10 kg to the drive belt at position 'X' and measure the deflection between the crankshaft pulley and air conditioning compressor pulley. Deflection must be 9 - 10 mm.

Adjust

1. Loosen nut securing drive belt, tensioner pulley.
2. Increase drive belt tension by turning the tension adjusting bolt clockwise.
3. Tighten drive belt tensioner pulley securing nut to 25 Nm.
4. Recheck drive belt tension.
5. Fit closing panel and secure with fixings.
6. Fit road wheel(s) and tighten nuts to correct torque. **See INFORMATION, Torque wrench settings.**
7. Remove stand(s) and lower vehicle.
8. Connect battery earth lead.

ELECTRICAL

HEADLAMPS - ADJUST

Service repair no - 86.40.17

Inspect

1. Before adjustment, ensure tyre pressures and suspension trim heights are at the correct settings.
2. Line up suitable beam setting equipment to headlamp.
3. Switch on headlamps, and check alignment;
   1.4% - Vertical
   0.0% - Horizontal

Adjust

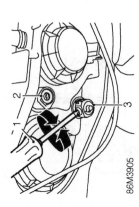

86M3905

1. Using a 6 mm hexagonal drive, adjust headlamp accordingly to achieve correct alignment.
2. Turn adjuster for vertical alignment.
3. Turn adjuster for horizontal alignment.
4. Repeat above procedure for 2nd headlamp.
5. Switch off headlamps.

ALTERNATOR - NON AIR CONDITIONING

Service repair no - 86.10.02

Remove

1. Disconnect battery earth lead.
2. Remove engine cover, See **ENGINE, Repairs.**
3. Raise rear of vehicle.

⚠ **WARNING: Support on safety stands.**

4. Remove road wheel(s).

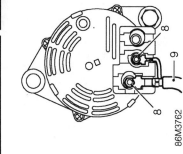

86M3761

5. Remove 2 scrivets and Torx screw securing closing panel.
6. Remove closing panel.
7. Remove alternator drive belt. **See this section.**

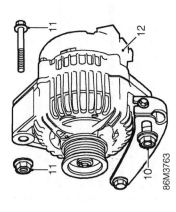

86M3762

8. Loosen 2 nuts securing cables to alternator.
9. Disconnect cables from alternator.

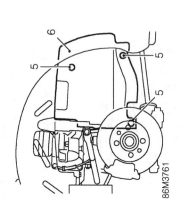

86M3763

10. Remove nut and bolt securing alternator to adjustment bracket.
11. Remove nut and bolt securing alternator to engine.
12. Remove alternator.
    Do not carry out further dismantling if component is removed for access only.
13. Restraining the alternator shaft with an 8mm Allen key, remove nut securing pulley to alternator shaft using tool **18G 1653** .
14. Remove pulley from alternator.
15. Clean pulley and alternator shaft.

ALTERNATOR - WITH AIR CONDITIONING

Service repair no - 86.10.02/20

Remove

1. Raise rear of vehicle.
2. Remove engine cover. **See ENGINE, Repairs.**
3. Remove alternator drive belt, **See this section.**

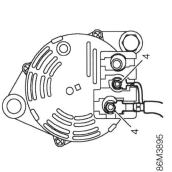

86M3895

4. Remove 2 nuts securing connections to alternator and position aside.

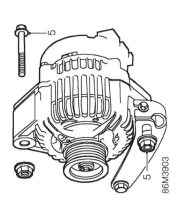

86M3903

5. Remove upper and lower bolts securing alternator to mounting bracket.

Refit

1. Fit pulley to alternator shaft.
2. Fit alternator pulley nut, hold shaft with an 8 mm Allen key and tighten nut to 25 Nm using tool **18G 1653**.
3. Position alternator to engine.
4. Fit nut and bolt securing alternator to engine, do not tighten at this stage.
5. Fit bolt securing alternator to adjustment bracket, but do not tighten.
6. Fit alternator drive belt. **See this section.**
7. Tighten bolt securing alternator to engine to 45 Nm.
8. Refit closing panel and secure with scrivets and Torx screw.
9. Fit road wheel(s) and tighten nuts to correct torque. **See INFORMATION, Torque wrench settings.**
10. Remove stand(s) and lower vehicle.
11. Connect alternator leads to terminals and tighten nuts.
12. Fit engine cover. **See ENGINE, Repairs.**
13. Connect battery earth lead.

ALTERNATOR DRIVE BELT - NON AIR CONDITIONING

Service repair no - 86.10.03

Remove

1. Disconnect battery earth lead.
2. Raise rear of vehicle.

WARNING: Support on safety stands.

3. Remove road wheel(s).

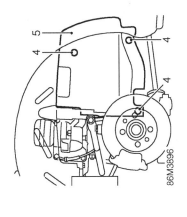

86M3896

4. Remove 2 scrivets and Torx screw securing closing panel.
5. Remove closing panel.

86M3904

6. Remove bolt and loosen nut securing alternator upper mounting bracket to cylinder head.
7. Rotate bracket aside.
8. Remove alternator.
Do not carry out further dismantling if component is removed for access only.
9. Restraining the alternator shaft with an 8mm Allen key, remove nut securing pulley to alternator shaft using tool **18G 1653** .
10. Remove pulley from alternator.
11. Clean pulley and alternator shaft.

Refit

1. Fit pulley to alternator shaft.
2. Fit alternator pulley nut, hold shaft with an 8 mm Allen key and tighten nut to 25 Nm using tool **18G 1653**.
3. Fit alternator to engine.
4. Align top bracket and tighten fixings to 25 Nm.
5. Position alternator to top bracket and tighten fixings to 45 Nm.
6. Connect cables and secure nuts.
7. Fit alternator drive belt. **See this section.**
8. Fit engine cover. **See ENGINE, Repairs.**

M12 5808

6. Loosen bolt securing alternator adjustment bracket.

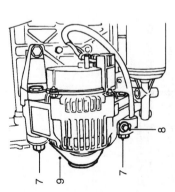

M86 5058

7. Loosen 2 alternator clamp bolts.

⚠ **CAUTION: Ensure that bolts are loosened sufficiently for alternator to move freely.**

8. Loosen adjusting bolt until there is sufficient free movement in belt to remove.

⚠ **CAUTION: Do not apply excessive torque to adjusting bolt or damage to bolt will result. If bolt appears to be seized or is difficult to turn, apply suitable anti-seize lubricant to bolt.**

9. Remove drive belt.

◁ NOTE: If belt does not show signs of wear or damage, do not renew. If belt is to be re-used, mark the direction of rotation using chalk.

Refit

1. Fit drive belt to alternator and crankshaft pulleys.
2. Adjust alternator drive belt tension. *See Adjustments.*
3. Fit closing panel and secure with fixings.
4. Fit road wheel(s) and tighten nuts to correct torque. *See INFORMATION, Torque wrench settings.*
5. Remove stand(s) and lower vehicle.
6. Connect battery earth lead.

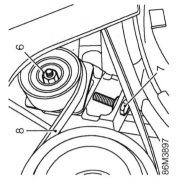

86M3897

ALTERNATOR DRIVE BELT - WITH AIR CONDITIONING

Service repair no - 86.10.03/20

Remove

1. Disconnect battery earth lead.
2. Raise rear of vehicle.

⚠ **WARNING: Support on safety stands.**

3. Remove road wheel(s).

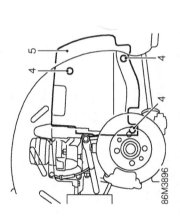

86M3896

4. Remove 2 scrivets and Torx screw securing closing panel.
5. Remove closing panel.

6. Loosen drive belt tensioner pulley securing nut.
7. Release drive belt tension by turning the tension adjusting bolt anti-clockwise.
8. Release drive belt from alternator and compressor pulleys.
9. Remove and discard drive belt.

CENTRAL DOOR LOCKING MOTOR AND LATCH

Service repair no - 86.26.08

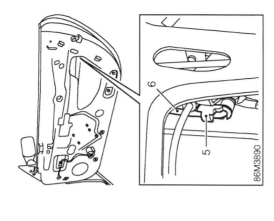

86M3890

Remove

1. Remove door trim casing. *See BODY, Doors.*
2. Switch the ignition ON and fully lower door glass.
3. Switch ignition OFF.
4. Carefully peel back corner of plastic sheet to allow access to door latch.

5. Release clip securing door handle link rod to latch assembly and position aside.
6. Release lock link rod from lock.

ELECTRIC WINDOW SWITCH - 2000MY ON

Service repair no - 86.25.19

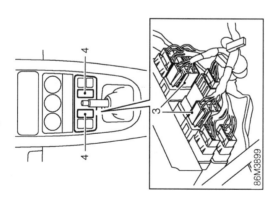

M86 5085

Remove

1. Remove console closing panel. *See BODY, Interior trim components.*
2. Release switch from centre console.
3. Disconnect multiplug from switch.
4. Remove switch.

Refit

1. Connect multiplug to switch and fit switch to centre console.
2. Fit console closing panel *See BODY, Interior trim components.*

ELECTRIC WINDOW SWITCH - UP TO 2000MY

Service repair no - 86.25.19

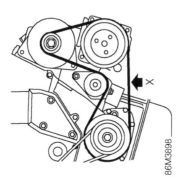

86M3899

Remove

1. Remove console closing panel. *See BODY, Interior trim components.*
2. Release switch panel from centre console.

3. Disconnect multiplug from window switch.
4. Remove switch.

Refit

1. Connect multiplug and engage switch to panel.
2. Fit console closing panel. *See BODY, Interior trim components.*

Refit

1. Clean pulley 'V's.
2. Fit NEW drive belt to crankshaft pulley and engage to alternator and compressor pulleys. Ensure grooves on drive belt and pulleys are correctly located.
3. Increase belt tension by turning the tension adjusting bolt clockwise.
4. Tighten drive belt tensioner pulley securing nut to 25 Nm.

86M3898

5. Apply a force of 10 kg to the drive belt at position 'X' and measure the deflection between the crankshaft pulley and air conditioning compressor pulley. Deflection must be 9 - 10 mm.
6. Fit closing panel and secure with fixings.
7. Fit road wheel(s) and tighten nuts to correct torque. *See INFORMATION, Torque wrench settings.*
8. Remove stand(s) and lower vehicle.
9. Connect battery earth lead.

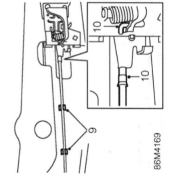

86M3891

7. Remove 3 Tx25 Torx screws securing latch assembly to door.
8. Position latch assembly and disconnect 2 multiplugs.

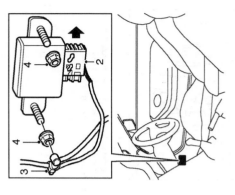

86M4169

9. Release cable from 2 inner door panel clips.
10. Disconnect cable from remote door handle.
11. Switch ignition ON and fully raise door glass.
12. Switch ignition OFF.

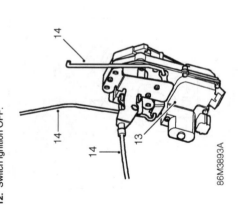

86M3893A

13. Remove latch assembly from door.
14. Remove sill button, lock link rod and cable from latch assembly.

ELECTRICAL

CONTROL UNIT - ONE TOUCH WINDOW - 2000MY ON

Service repair no - 86.25.37

Remove

M86 5055

1. Release RH lower section of door seal and carpet to access control unit.
2. Release multiplug catch and disconnect multiplug.
3. Release harness clip from control unit retaining stud.
4. Remove 2 nuts securing control unit and remove control unit.

Refit

1. Position control unit, fit and tighten nuts.
2. Connect multiplug and secure catch.
3. Connect harness clip to retaining stud.
4. Reposition carpet and door seal.

Refit

1. Fit sill button, lock link rod and cable to latch assembly.
2. Position latch assembly to door and guide sill button through door aperture.
3. Switch ignition ON and fully lower door glass.
4. Switch ignition OFF.
5. Connect multiplugs to latch assembly.
6. Connect door release cable to remote door handle and secure to inner door panel clips.
7. Align exterior handle, link rod to latch assembly and secure with clip.

▷ NOTE: A small amount of free-play should be evident between the exterior handle and latch. If necessary adjust the exterior handle, link rod trunnion.

8. Engage lock link rod to lock.
9. Fit Torx screws securing latch assembly to door and tighten to 5 Nm.
10. Secure plastic sheet to door.
11. Fit door trim casing. See BODY, Doors.

HORN

Service repair no - 86.30.10

Remove

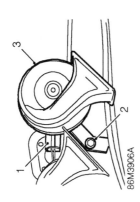

86M3906A

1. Disconnect horn multiplug.
2. Remove bolt securing horn to valance.
3. Remove horn.

Refit

1. Position horn to valance fit bolt and tighten to 8 Nm.
2. Connect multiplug.

DIRECTION INDICATOR

Service repair no - 86.40.42

Remove

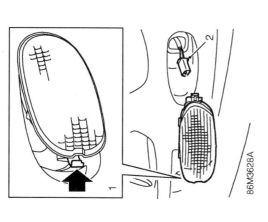

86M3628A

1. Using a slim, flat bladed screwdriver, release direction indicator retaining tab from bumper valance.

⚠ **CAUTION: Protect area of bumper valance around direction indicator.**

⚠ **CAUTION: DO NOT apply excessive force on retaining tab when levering out direction indicator.**

2. Disconnect multiplug from direction indicator, remove direction indicator.
Do not carry out further dismantling if component is removed for access only.
3. Rotate bulb holder to release from direction indicator lens, remove bulb holder.
4. Align bulb holder to direction indicator and rotate to lock.

Refit

1. Position direction indicator, connect multiplug.
2. Secure direction indicator to bumper valance.

HEADLAMP ASSEMBLY

Service repair no - 86.40.49

1. Remove front bumper valance, *See BODY, Exterior fittings.*

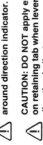

86M3613A

2. Disconnect multiplug from headlamp.
3. Remove 2 headlamp upper retaining bolts and 1 lower Torx screw.
4. Release headlamp from lower and side retaining clips.
5. Remove headlamp assembly.

Refit

1. Fit headlamp assembly.
2. Fit and finger tighten both upper bolts.
3. Fit and tighten Torx screw to 6 Nm.
4. Tighten upper bolts to 6 Nm.
5. Fit front bumper valance, *See BODY, Exterior fittings.*
6. Adjust headlamp, *See Adjustments.*

HEADLAMP LENS

Service repair no - 86.41.25

1. Remove headlamp, *See this section.*

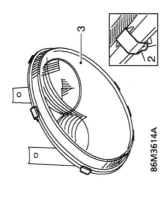

86M3614A

2. Release 5 clips securing lens to headlamp assembly.
3. Remove lens from headlamp assembly.

Refit

1. Fit headlamp lens to housing and secure with clips.
2. Fit headlamp assembly. *See this section.*

ELECTRICAL

TAIL LAMP ASSEMBLY

Service repair no - 86.40.70

Remove

1. Disconnect battery earth lead.

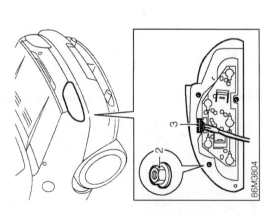

86M3804

2. Remove 3 nuts securing tail lamp.
3. Release tail lamp and disconnect multiplug.

Refit

1. Connect multiplug to tail lamp.
2. Fit tail lamp and tighten nuts to 2 Nm.
3. Connect battery earth lead.

GLOVEBOX LAMP

Service repair no - 86.45.08

Remove

1. Open glove box.

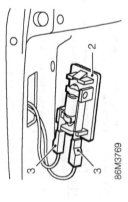

86M3769

2. Release lamp from glovebox
3. Disconnect 2 Lucars from lamp.
4. Remove lamp.

Refit

1. Position lamp and connect Lucars.
2. Secure lamp in glovebox.

BOOT LID LAMP

Service repair no - 86.45.16

Remove

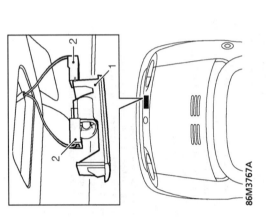

86M3767A

1. Release lamp from boot lid.
2. Disconnect 2 Lucars.
3. Remove lamp.

Refit

1. Position lamp and connect Lucars.
2. Secure lamp in boot lid.

FOOTWELL LAMP

Service repair no - 86.45.20

Remove

1. Remove console closing panel. *See BODY, Interior trim components.*

Refit

1. Fit console closing panel. *See BODY, Interior trim components.*

BONNET LAMP

Service repair no - 86.45.24

Remove

1. Open bonnet.

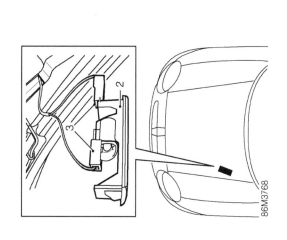

86M3768

2. Release lamp from bonnet.
3. Disconnect 2 Lucars.
4. Remove lamp.

Refit

1. Position lamp and connect Lucars.

⚠ **CAUTION: Ensure black wire is connected to terminal closest to the bulb.**

2. Secure lamp in bonnet.

RADIO

Service repair no - 86.50.03

Remove

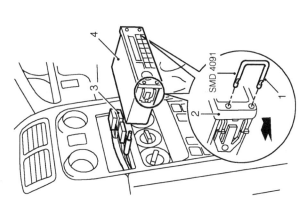

86M3907

1. Fit radio removal tools **SMD 4091.**
2. Pull tools to release radio from fascia.
3. Disconnect multiplugs and aerial lead.
4. Remove radio.
5. Remove tools from radio.

Refit

1. Position radio to aperture, connect multiplugs and aerial lead.
2. Slide radio into fascia until retaining clips engage.
3. Enter security code and check radio for correct operation.

FRONT SPEAKER

Service repair no - 86.50.15

Remove

1. Remove front door trim casing. *See BODY, Doors.*

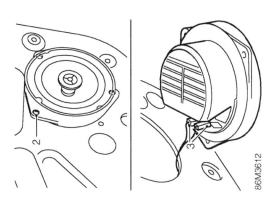

86M3612

2. Remove 3 screws securing speaker to door.
3. Release speaker from door, disconnect 2 Lucars.
4. Remove speaker.

Refit

1. Position speaker to door and connect Lucars.
2. Align speaker to door and secure with screws.
3. Fit front door trim casing. *See BODY, Doors.*

AERIAL

Service repair no - 86.50.18

Remove

1. Disconnect battery earth lead.
2. Remove engine compartment access panel. *See BODY, Exterior fittings.*

86M3803

3. Unscrew aerial from base.
4. Using a 17 mm open ended spanner, remove aerial base locking nut.
5. Collect locking nut and outer sleeve.
6. Remove aerial base from body.
7. Disconnect aerial coaxial lead from harness.

Refit

1. Position aerial base in body.
2. Fit sleeve and tighten locking nut to 3 Nm.

⚠ NOTE: If the vehicle is fitted with a rear spoiler ensure the aerial mast does not contact the rear spoiler before tightening the locking nut.

3. Connect aerial coaxial lead to harness.
4. Screw aerial into base.

SPEAKER - TWEETER - 2000MY ON

Service repair no - 86.50.34

Remove

1. Remove door casing. *See BODY, Doors.*

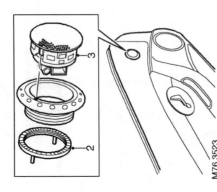

M76 3523

2. Remove backing nut from tweeter assembly and remove tweeter assembly from door casing.
3. Release tweeter from finisher.

Refit

1. Fit tweeter to finisher ensuring correct alignment of key and keyway in finisher.
2. Fit tweeter assembly to door casing and fit backing nut.
3. Fit door casing. *See BODY, Doors.*

SUBWOOFER ASSEMBLY - 2000MY ON

Service repair no - 86.50.51

Remove

1. Move both seats fully forwards.

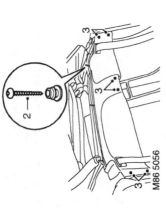

M86 5056

2. Remove 3 screws securing finisher and collect press studs.
3. Release finisher from fixings and slide downwards for access to subwoofer assembly.

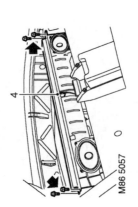

M86 5057

4. Disconnect multiplug from subwoofer.
5. Remove 4 bolts securing subwoofer to body fixings and remove subwoofer assembly.

Refit

1. Position subwoofer assembly and connect multiplug.
2. Fit and tighten 4 bolts securing subwoofer to body.
3. Align finisher to fixings and secure into position.
4. Position press studs and secure with screws.
5. Return seats to original position.

ANTI-THEFT ALARM ECU

Service repair no - 86.55.85

Remove

1. Remove 4 screws securing both closing panels to front console and position panels aside.

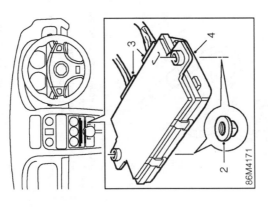

86M4171

2. Remove 2 nuts securing alarm ECU to heater control unit.
3. Disconnect 2 multiplugs from alarm ECU.
4. Remove alarm ECU.

Refit

1. Connect multiplugs to alarm ECU.
2. Position alarm ECU to heater control unit and tighten nuts to 4 Nm.
3. Fit closing panels and secure with screws.

ELECTRICAL

VOLUMETRIC SENSOR

Service repair no - 86.77.29

Remove

1. Position both seats fully forward and position seat squab forward.

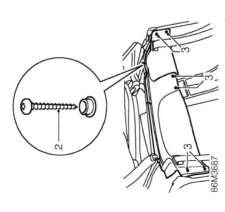

86M3887

2. Remove 3 screws securing rear bulkhead finisher to rear bulkhead and collect 3 studs.
3. Release finisher from 6 clips and position aside.

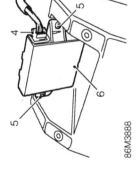

86M3888

4. Disconnect multiplug from sensor.
5. Remove 2 screws securing sensor to rear console.
6. Remove sensor.

Refit

1. Fit sensor to console and secure with screws.
2. Connect multiplug.
3. Locate bulkhead finisher and engage clips.
4. Fit studs and secure with screws.
5. Return seats to original position.

ELECTRICAL

STARTER MOTOR

Service repair no - 86.60.01

Remove

1. Disconnect battery earth lead.
2. Remove engine compartment access panel *See BODY, Exterior fittings.*
3. Raise rear of vehicle.

⚠ **WARNING: Support on safety stands.**

4. Remove LH rear wheel.
5. Release EVAP cannister from bracket and position cannister aside.

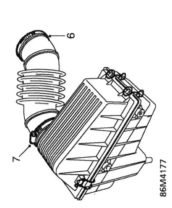

86M4177

6. Remove clip and disconnect air intake hose from throttle body.
7. Loosen clip and remove air intake hose from air filter.

86M3760A

8. Disconnect Lucar and release cable tie from starter motor solenoid.
9. Remove nut from solenoid and release 2 leads.
10. Remove 2 nuts and bolts securing starter motor.
11. Remove starter motor.
12. Remove flywheel closing plate.

Refit

1. Clean mating faces of starter motor and gearbox.
2. Fit starter motor.
3. Fit closing plate.
4. Fit bolts and tighten nuts to 80 Nm.
5. Fit leads to starter solenoid and tighten terminal nut.
6. Connect Lucar to starter solenoid.
7. Secure cables to starter solenoid with cable clip.
8. Fit air intake hose to air filter and to throttle body.
9. Tighten clip securing air intake hose to air filter, fit clip securing air intake hose to throttle body.
10. Fit EVAP cannister.
11. Fit road wheel(s) and tighten nuts to correct torque. *See INFORMATION, Torque wrench settings.*
12. Remove stand(s) and lower vehicle.
13. Fit engine compartment access panel *See BODY, Exterior fittings.*

REPAIRS 19

ELECTRICAL

STARTER MOTOR - STEPTRONIC (EM-CVT) MODELS

Service repair no - 86.60.01

Remove

1. Disconnect battery earth lead.
2. Remove engine cover. *See ENGINE, Repairs.*
3. Raise rear of vehicle.

⚠ **WARNING: Support on safety stands.**

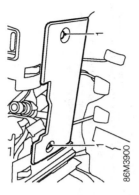

M86 5059

4. Remove bolt securing coolant hose heat shield to bracket on exhaust manifold.
5. Remove 2 bolts securing coolant hose heat shield to cylinder block and remove heat shield.
6. Disconnect Lucar from starter solenoid.
7. Remove nut from starter solenoid and release 2 leads.
8. Remove 1 bolt and remove flywheel cover.

M86 5060

9. Remove 2 bolts securing starter motor and remove starter motor.

Refit

1. Clean mating faces of starter motor and gearbox.
2. Fit starter motor and align to dowel.
3. Fit bolts and tighten to 80 Nm.
4. Fit leads to starter solenoid and tighten terminal nut.
5. Connect Lucar to starter solenoid.
6. Fit flywheel cover and tighten bolt to 9 Nm.
7. Fit exhaust manifold heat shield and tighten bolts to 9 Nm.
8. Remove stand(s) and lower vehicle.
9. Fit engine cover. *See ENGINE, Repairs.*
10. Connect battery earth lead.

STARTER SOLENOID

Service repair no - 86.60.08

Remove

1. Disconnect battery earth lead.
2. Remove starter motor. *See this section.*

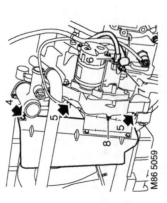

86M3914

3. Remove nut from solenoid and disconnect lead.
4. Remove 2 bolts securing solenoid to starter motor housing.
5. Remove solenoid from starter motor housing.
6. Remove plunger from starter.

Refit

1. Apply grease to lever end of plunger.
2. Fit starter solenoid to starter motor housing and tighten bolts.
3. Fit lead to rear of solenoid and tighten nut.
4. Fit starter motor. *See this section.*
5. Connect battery earth lead.

PANEL DIMMER RESISTOR

Service repair no - 86.65.37

Remove

86M3900

1. Release 2 clips and open fuse box cover.

HAZARD WARNING LAMP SWITCH

Service repair no - 86.65.50

Remove

1. Release radio from console. **See this section.**

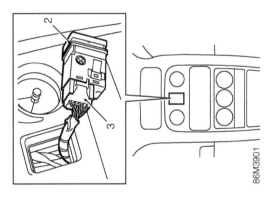

86M3901

2. Release hazard warning lamp switch from console.
3. Disconnect multiplug from switch.

Refit

1. Connect multiplug and engage switch to console.
2. Secure radio to console. **See this section.**

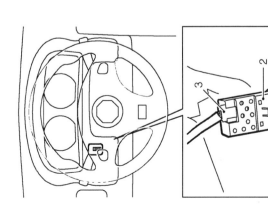

86M3902

2. Release dimmer resistor from instrument cowl.
3. Disconnect multiplug from dimmer.

Refit

1. Connect multiplug and engage dimmer to cowl.
2. Position fuse box cover and secure with clips.

STEERING COLUMN SWITCH PACK

Service repair no - 86.65.55

Remove

1. Remove rotary coupler. **See RESTRAINT SYSTEMS, Repairs.**

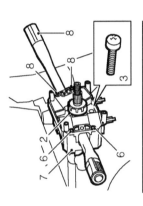

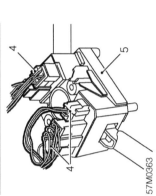

57M0363

2. Remove direction indicator cancellation cam from column.
3. Remove 2 screws securing switch pack to steering column.
4. Release switch pack from column and disconnect 3 multiplugs.
5. Remove switch pack.
6. Remove 2 screws securing direction/headlamp stalk to switch pack.
7. Remove direction/headlamp stalk from switch pack.
8. Remove 2 screws securing wash wipe stalk to switch pack.
9. Remove wash wipe stalk from switch pack.

Refit

1. Fit wash wipe stalk to switch pack and secure with screws.
2. Fit indicator/headlamp stalk to switch pack and tighten screws.
3. Position switch pack to steering column, connect 3 multiplugs and tighten screws.
4. Fit direction indicator cancellation cam to steering column.
5. Fit rotary coupler. **See RESTRAINT SYSTEMS, Repairs.**

ELECTRICAL

SWITCH - EXTERIOR MIRROR - 2000MY ON

Service repair no - 86.65.75

Remove

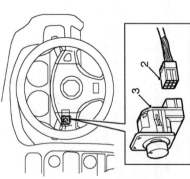

M86 5066

1. Carefully remove switch from fascia.
2. Disconnect multiplug from switch.
3. Remove switch.

Refit

1. Position switch and connect multiplug.
2. Carefully push switch back into position.

This page is intentionally left blank

CONTENTS

Page

DESCRIPTION AND OPERATION

REPAIRS

INSTRUMENT PACK COMPONENTS - REAR VIEW (UP TO 2000MY)

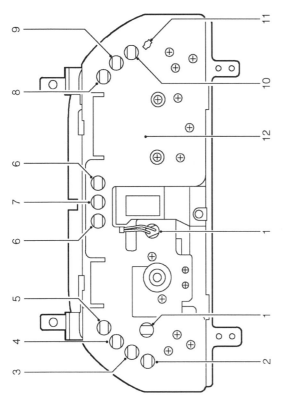

88M0113

1. Panel rear illumination bulbs
2. ABS - warning light bulb
3. Engine bay temperature - warning light bulb
4. Hazard lights - warning light bulb
5. Brake fail / handbrake - warning light bulb
6. Direction indicator - warning light bulb

7. Main beam - warning light bulb
8. Low oil pressure - warning light bulb
9. Ignition no charge - warning light bulb
10. Rear fog lights - warning light bulb
11. Catalyst over heat - warning light bulb
12. Main printed circuit

INSTRUMENT PACK COMPONENTS - EXPLODED VIEW

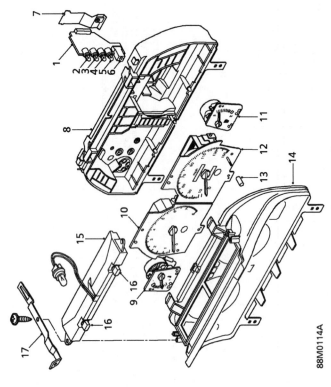

88M0114A

(Up to 2000MY instrument pack shown, From 2000MY similar)

1. Printed circuit board
2. EPAS - warning light bulb
3. Seat belt - warning light bulb
4. Oil temperature - warning light bulb (VVC only)
5. SRS - warning light bulb
6. Anti-theft warning LED
7. Circuit board cover
8. Instrument panel housing
9. Coolant temperature gauge

10. Tachometer
11. Fuel gauge
12. Speedometer
13. Control knob - trip distance
14. Instrument panel and face plate
15. Panel illumination and printed circuit
16. Panel front illumination bulbs
17. Support bracket

INSTRUMENT PACK COMPONENTS - REAR VIEW (FROM 2000MY)

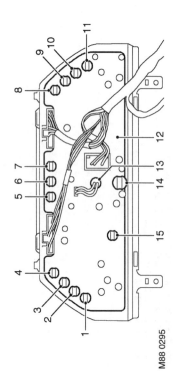

M88 0295

1. Rear fog lamps - warning light bulb
2. Gearbox fault (Steptronic gearbox only) - warning light bulb
3. Hazard warning lamps - warning light bulb
4. Brake fail / Handbrake - warning light bulb
5. RH direction indicator - warning light bulb
6. Main beam - warning light bulb
7. LH direction indicator - warning light bulb
8. Low oil pressure - warning light bulb

9. Ignition / No charge - warning light bulb
10. Malfunction Indicator Lamp (MIL) - warning light bulb
11. ABS - warning light bulb
12. Main printed circuit board
13. Panel rear illumination bulb
14. Anti-theft alarm LED
15. LCD illumination bulb

INSTRUMENT PACK

Instrument pack (Up to 2000MY)

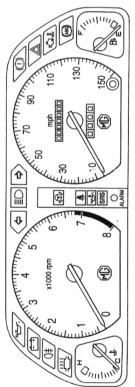

88M0115A

Instrument pack (From 2000MY)

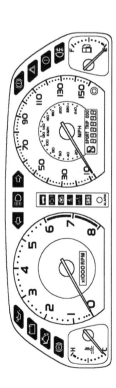

M88 0296

When the gauge unit float is at its lowest point, indicating an empty fuel tank, the resistance to earth is at its greatest. The resistance value to fuel gauge position to earth is:

Sender resistance	Fuel gauge position
105 Ω	Empty
32.5 Ω	Half full
5 Ω	Full

The fuel gauge pointer will display level of fuel in the tank when the ignition was last switched off.

Coolant temperature gauge

The coolant temperature gauge is fitted with a return magnet causing the gauge to return to zero when the ignition is switched off.

Thermistor resistance	Temperature	Gauge position
142 Ω	56°C	No movement
49 - 98 Ω	65°C - 85°C	Approx. one third
24.6 - 32.1 Ω	100°C - 110°C	Approx. halfway
16.9 Ω	125°C	Enters red sector

Instrument illumination

Four bulbs provide instrument illumination, 2 x 14V 1.4W for back illumination and 2 x 14V 1.4W for front illumination.

Operation

For operation of the instrument pack. See **ELECTRICAL REFERENCE LIBRARY, Description and Operation.**

Speedometer (Up to 2000MY)

The speedometer is driven by a worm gear system from a flexidrive input. The pointer is controlled by an eddy current movement.

A seven digit odometer and a four digit trip distance readout up to 999.9 miles or km is fitted.

Speedometer (From 2000MY)

The speedometer is operated electronically by a signal output from a speed transducer fitted to the gearbox. The transducer output is shared with the EPAS ECU.

Odometer and trip distance is displayed on an LCD located at the bottom of the speedometer. A button allows the trip and odometer to be displayed individually. The button will also reset the trip meter if pressed and held. The LCD also shows gearbox information when the vehicle is fitted with a Steptronic (EM-CVT) gearbox.

Tachometer

The tachometer signal is taken from the MEMS ECU to the control board which is secured to the rear of the tachometer sub-assembly. The instrument panel display reading is averaged over all the engine cylinders to reduce fluctuations due to individual cylinder retardation in spark timing which may occur on engines fitted with programmed ignition systems.

Fuel gauge

The fuel gauge is driven by an air cored electronic movement which is fluid damped. Fluid damping reduces the movement of the gauge pointer caused by fluid movement in the tank.

The fuel tank gauge unit comprises a float and is connected to wire-wound resistor which is connected to the fuel gauge and back through the instrument panel to earth. The resistor controls the current flow through to the fuel gauge circuit, which in turn drives the gauge movement against the resistance of the fluid damping.

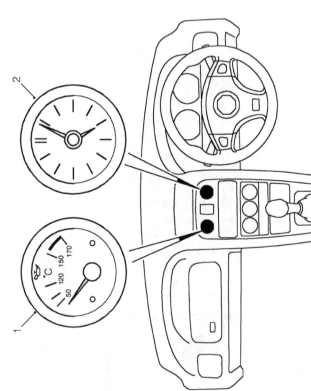

88M0116A

1. Oil temperature gauge
2. Analogue clock

Oil temperature gauge

Th oil temperature gauge (1) is fitted with a return magnet causing the gauge to return to zero when the ignition is switched off.

150°C sender (To - VIN 001017)

Sender resistance	Temperature
221 Ω ± 26 Ω	60°C
83 Ω ± 8 Ω	90°C
36 Ω ± 27 Ω	120°c

170°C sender (from - VIN 001018)

Sender resistance	Temperature
574 Ω ± 71 Ω	60°C
202 Ω ± 24 Ω	90°C
84 Ω ± 9 Ω	120°C

INSTRUMENT PACK - UP TO 2000MY

Service repair no - 88.20.01/99

⚠ **WARNING: See RESTRAINT SYSTEMS, Precautions.**

Remove

1. Make the SRS system safe. **See RESTRAINT SYSTEMS, Precautions.**
2. Remove instrument cowl. **See this section.**

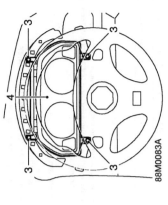

88M0083A

3. Remove 4 screws securing instrument pack to fascia.
4. Release instrument pack from fascia.

CLOCK

Service repair no - 88.15.07

Remove

1. Remove centre console panel. **See BODY, Interior trim components.**

88M0087

2. Remove 2 screws securing clock to console.
3. Remove retaining bracket, clock and 'O' ring.

Refit

1. Position 'O' ring and clock to console.
2. Fit retaining bracket and secure with screws.

⚠ NOTE: Ensure correct orientation of clock in console.

3. Fit centre console panel. **See BODY, Interior trim components.**

INSTRUMENT PACK - 2000MY ON

Service repair no - 88.20.01/99

⚠ **WARNING: See RESTRAINT SYSTEMS, Precautions.**

Remove

1. Make the system safe. See **RESTRAINT SYSTEMS, Precautions.**
2. Remove instrument cowl. **See this section.**

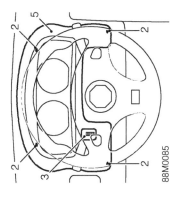

M88 0290

3. Remove 4 screws securing instrument pack to fascia.
4. Release instrument pack from fascia.

M88 0291

5. Release 3 multiplugs from pack.
6. Remove instrument pack.

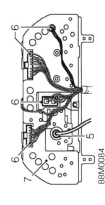

88M0084

5. Disconnect speedometer cable.
6. Release 3 multiplugs and bulb holder from pack.
7. Remove instrument pack.

Refit

1. Position instrument pack to fascia and connect multiplugs.
2. Connect bulb holder and speedometer cable.
3. Position instrument pack and secure with screws.
4. Fit instrument cowl. **See this section.**

Refit

1. Position instrument pack to fascia and connect multiplugs.
2. Position instrument pack and secure with screws.
3. Fit instrument cowl. **See this section.**

INSTRUMENT COWL - UP TO 2000MY

Service repair no - 88.20.02

Remove

1. Remove steering column nacelle. **See STEERING, Repairs.**

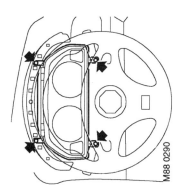
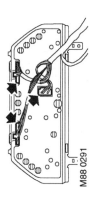

88M0085

2. Remove 4 screws securing instrument cowl to fascia.
3. Release cowl and disconnect multiplug from panel lamp dimmer.
4. Release dimmer from cowl.
5. Remove cowl.

Refit

1. Secure dimmer to cowl.
2. Position cowl and connect multiplug.
3. Position cowl to fascia and secure with screws.
4. Fit steering column nacelle. **See STEERING, Repairs.**

INSTRUMENT COWL - 2000MY ON

Service repair no - 88.20.02

Remove

1. Remove steering column nacelle. *See STEERING, Repairs.*

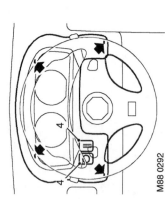

M88 0292

2. Remove 4 screws securing instrument cowl to fascia.
3. Release cowl from fascia.
4. Disconnect multiplugs from dimmer resistor and door mirror selector switch.
5. Remove cowl.
6. Remove dimmer and mirror switch from cowl.

Refit

1. Fit dimmer and mirror switch to cowl.
2. Position cowl and connect multiplugs.
3. Position cowl to fascia and secure with screws.
4. Fit steering column nacelle. *See STEERING, Repairs.*

INSTRUMENT PACK WINDOW

Service repair no - 88.20.06

Remove

1. Remove instrument illumination housing. *See this section.*

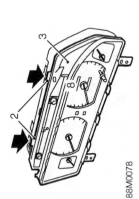

88M0078

2. Release 4 clips securing panel window to instruments.
3. Remove instrument pack window.

Refit

1. Fit pack window and secure with clips.
2. Fit instrument illumination housing. *See this section.*

INSTRUMENT ILLUMINATION HOUSING

Service repair no - 88.20.07

Remove

1. Remove instrument pack. *See this section.*

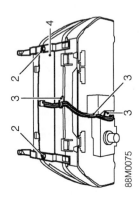

88M0075

2. Remove 2 screws securing brackets to instrument pack and collect brackets.
3. Release bulb holder from casing and cables from 2 casing clips.
4. Remove instrument illumination housing.

Refit

1. Position illumination housing to casing.
2. Fit brackets and secure with screws.
3. Secure bulb holder and secure cables to clips.
4. Fit instrument pack. *See this section.*

INSTRUMENT WARNING LIGHT PANEL

Service repair no - 88.20.18

Remove

1. Remove instrument pack. *See this section.*

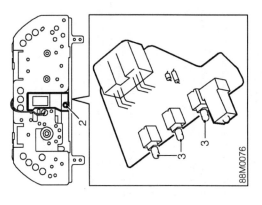

88M0076

2. Remove screw securing cover to casing and remove cover.
3. Remove warning light panel.

Refit

1. Fit panel to instrument pack.
2. Fit cover and secure with screw.
3. Fit instrument pack. *See this section.*

PRINTED CIRCUIT BOARD

Service repair no - 88.20.19

Remove

1. Remove instrument pack. *See this section.*

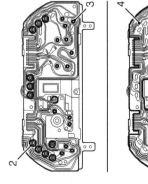
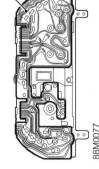

88M0077

2. Noting their fitted positions remove 12 bulbs from PCB.
3. Remove 14 screws securing PCB to casing.
4. Release PCB from 14 lugs and remove PCB.

Refit

1. Position PCB and engage lugs.
2. Secure PCB with screws.
3. Fit bulbs.
4. Fit instrument pack. *See this section.*

OIL TEMPERATURE GAUGE

Service repair no - 88.25.02

Remove

1. Remove centre console panel. *See BODY, Interior trim components.*

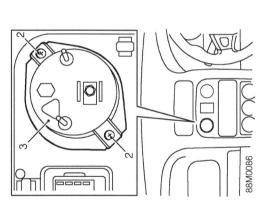

88M0086

2. Remove 2 screws securing gauge to console.
3. Remove retaining bracket, gauge and 'O' ring.

Refit

1. Position 'O' ring and gauge to console.
2. Fit retaining bracket and secure with screws.

△ NOTE: Ensure correct orientation of gauge in console.

3. Fit centre console panel. *See BODY, Interior trim components.*

COOLANT TEMPERATURE GAUGE

Service repair no - 88.25.14

Remove

1. Remove instrument pack window. *See this section.*

88M0079

2. Remove 3 screws securing temperature gauge to casing.
3. Remove gauge.

Refit

1. Fit gauge to instrument pack and secure with screws.
2. Fit instrument pack window. *See this section.*

ENGINE COOLANT TEMPERATURE GAUGE SENSOR

Service repair no - 88.25.20

Remove

1. Disconnect battery earth lead.
2. Remove engine cover. *See ENGINE, Repairs.*

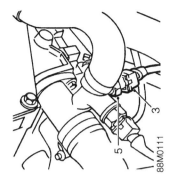

88M0111

3. Disconnect multiplug from sensor.
4. Position a container below sensor to collect coolant spillage
5. Remove sensor.

Refit

1. Clean threads of sensor.
2. Apply Loctite 577 to threads of sensor.
3. Fit sensor and tighten to 6 Nm.
4. Connect multiplug to sensor.
5. Fit engine cover. *See ENGINE, Repairs.*
6. Connect battery earth lead.
7. Top-up coolant, *See MAINTENANCE.*

ENGINE OIL TEMPERATURE GAUGE SENSOR

Service repair no - 88.25.21

Remove

1. Raise rear of vehicle.

 WARNING: Support on safety stands.

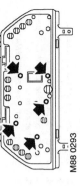

2. Disconnect multiplug from sensor.
3. Position spillage tray.
4. Remove sensor from oil filter housing.

Refit

1. Fit oil temperature sensor to oil filter housing and tighten to 15 Nm.
2. Remove spillage tray.
3. Connect multiplug to sensor.
4. Remove stand(s) and lower vehicle.
5. Check and top up engine oil level. *See MAINTENANCE.*

FUEL GAUGE

Service repair no - 88.25.26

Remove

1. Remove instrument pack window. *See this section.*

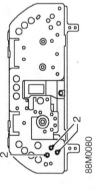

88M0080

2. Remove 3 screws securing fuel gauge to casing.
3. Remove gauge.

Refit

1. Fit gauge to instrument pack and secure with screws.
2. Fit instrument pack window. *See this section.*

SPEEDOMETER - UP TO 2000MY

Service repair no - 88.30.01

Remove

1. Remove instrument pack window. *See this section.*

88M0081

2. Remove 4 screws securing speedometer to casing.
3. Remove speedometer.

Refit

1. Fit speedometer to instrument pack and secure with screws.
2. Fit instrument pack window. *See this section.*

SPEEDOMETER - 2000MY ON

Service repair no - 88.30.01

Remove

1. Remove tachometer. *See this section.*

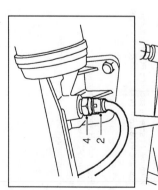

M88 0293

2. Remove 5 screws securing speedometer to casing.
3. Remove speedometer.

Refit

1. Fit speedometer to instrument pack and secure with screws.
2. Fit tachometer. *See this section.*

SPEEDOMETER CABLE - UPPER - UP TO 2000MY

Service repair no - 88.30.08

Remove

1. Remove underbonnet closing panel. **See BODY, Exterior fittings.**

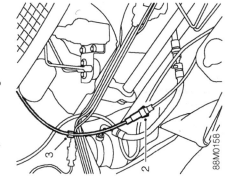

88M0158

2. Disconnect upper cable from intermediate cable.
3. Release upper cable from clip.
4. Remove instrument cowl. **See this section.**

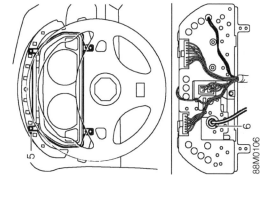

88M0106

5. Remove 4 screws securing instrument pack to fascia.
6. Release instrument pack and disconnect upper cable.
7. Release bulkhead grommet and collect upper cable.

Refit

1. Position upper cable through bulkhead and connect cable to instrument pack.
2. Fit bulkhead grommet.
3. Position instrument pack to fascia and secure with screws.
4. Fit instrument cowl. **See this section.**
5. Fit upper cable to clip.
6. Connect upper cable to intermediate cable.
7. Fit underbonnet closing panel. **See BODY, Exterior fittings.**

SPEEDOMETER CABLE - INTERMEDIATE - UP TO 2000MY

Service repair no - 88.30.13

Remove

1. Remove underbonnet closing panel. **See BODY, Exterior fittings.**

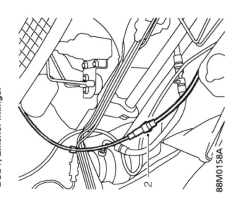

88M0158A

2. Disconnect intermediate cable from upper cable.
3. Remove underbody crossmember. **See BODY, Exterior fittings.**

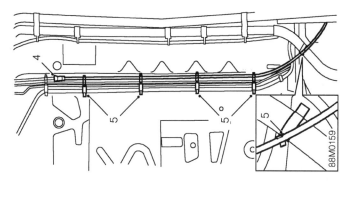

88M0159

4. Disconnect intermediate cable from lower cable.
5. Release intermediate cable from 4 underbody clips and 1 coolant hose clip.
6. Collect intermediate cable.

Refit

1. Fit intermediate cable to underbody clips and coolant hose clip.
2. Connect intermediate cable to lower cable.
3. Fit underbody crossmember. **See BODY, Exterior fittings.**
4. Connect intermediate cable to upper cable.
5. Fit underbonnet closing panel. **See BODY, Exterior fittings.**

INSTRUMENTS

TACHOMETER - 2000MY ON

Service repair no - 88.30.21

Remove

1. Remove instrument pack window. *See this section.*

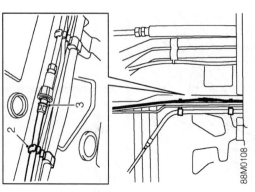

M88 0294

2. Remove 3 screws securing tachometer to casing.
3. Remove tachometer .

Refit

1. Fit tachometer to instrument pack and secure with screws.
2. Fit instrument pack window. *See this section.*

TACHOMETER - UP TO 2000MY

Service repair no - 88.30.21

Remove

1. Remove instrument pack window. *See this section.*

88M0082

2. Remmove 5 screws securing tachometer to casing.
3. Remove tachometer.

Refit

1. Fit tachometer to instrument pack and secure with screws.
2. Fit instrument pack window. *See this section.*

INSTRUMENTS

SPEEDOMETER CABLE - LOWER - UP TO 2000MY

Service repair no - 88.30.09

Remove

1. Raise rear of vehicle.

⚠️ **WARNING: Support on safety stands.**

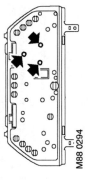

88M0108

2. Release speedometer cable from 2 underfloor clips.
3. Disconnect lower cable from intermediate cable.

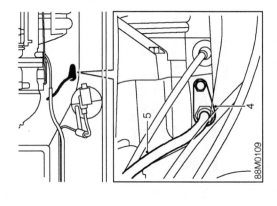

88M0109

4. Loosen cable union to gearbox and disconnect cable.
5. Remove speedometer cable.

Refit

1. Position cable to gearbox and tighten union to 19 Nm.
2. Connect lower cable to intermediate cable and secure cable to clips.
3. Remove stand(s) and lower vehicle.

Notes

....

....

....

....

....

....

....

....

....

....

....

....

....

....

....

....

Part No. RCL 0051ENG

'K' SERIES ENGINE

OVERHAUL MANUAL

This overhaul manual is applicable to 'K' Series engines fitted with either VVC or non VVC cylinder heads and 'damp' cylinder liners.

This engine is fitted to the following models:
MGF,
Rover 114 and 214/414
New Rover 214, 216, 218 and BRM
New Rover 414 and 416 Coupe,
Cabriolet, Tourer and Sports Models
Rover 25, Rover 45, and Rover 75

Publication Part No. RCL 0057ENG (6th Edition)
Published by MG Rover Group Aftersales
© MG Rover Group Limited 2000

Distributed by Brooklands Books Ltd., PO Box 146, Cobham,
Surrey KT11 1LG, England Phone: 01932 865051 Fax: 01932 868803
E-mail: sales@brooklands-books.com

Part No. RCL 0057ENG (6th Edition)

CONTENTS
Page

INTRODUCTION

How to use this manual

To assist in the use of this manual the section title is given at the top and the relevant sub-section is given at the bottom each page.

To help readers find the information they need, the first page of each section is marked with a black tab. In addition the symbol at the top of each RH page identifies each section or group of sections.

Each section starts with a contents page, listing the information contained within. Some sections are divided into sub- sections such as Description and Operation, Adjustments, Repairs and Data, Torque and Tools. To assist filing of revised information each of the sub-sections is numbered from page 1.

Each Adjustment and Repair procedure is fully illustrated showing a number against each text item. Service tools are shown in use where usage is not obvious. Each illustration appears before the text which refers to it. Adjustment and Repair operations also include relevant data, torque figures and useful assembly details.

WARNINGS, CAUTIONS and Notes have the following meanings:

 WARNING: Procedures which must be followed precisely to avoid the possibility of injury.

 CAUTION: Calls attention to procedures which must be followed to avoid damage to components.

NOTE: Gives helpful information.

References

References to the LH or RH side given in this manual are made when viewing the vehicle from the rear. With the engine and gearbox assembly removed, the crankshaft pulley end of the engine is referred to as the front.

Operations covered in this manual do not include reference to testing the vehicle after repair. It is essential that work is inspected and tested after completion and if necessary a road test of the vehicle is carried out particularly where safety related items are concerned.

Dimensions

The dimensions quoted are to design engineering specification with Service limits where applicable.

During the period of running-in from new, certain adjustments may vary from the specification figures given in this manual. These will be reset by the Dealer at the First Service, and thereafter should be maintained at the figures specified in this manual.

REPAIRS AND REPLACEMENTS

When replacement parts are required it is essential that only Rover recommended parts are used.

Attention is particularly drawn to the following points concerning repairs and the fitting of replacement parts and accessories.

Safety features and corrosion prevention treatments embodied in the car may be impaired if other than Rover recommended parts are fitted. In certain territories, legislation prohibits the fitting of parts not to the manufacturer's specification. Torque wrench setting figures given in this Manual must be used. Locking devices, where specified, must be fitted. If the efficiency of a locking device is impaired during removal it **must be renewed.**

Owners purchasing accessories while travelling abroad should ensure that the accessory and its fitted location on the car conform to legal requirements.

The Terms of the vehicle Warranty may be invalidated by the fitting of other than Rover recommended parts.

All Rover recommended parts have the full backing of the vehicle Warranty.

Rover Dealers are obliged to supply only Rover recommended parts.

This page is intentionally left blank

SPECIFICATION

Rover are constantly seeking to improve the specification, design and production of their vehicles and alterations take place accordingly. While every effort has been made to ensure the accuracy of this Manual, it should not be regarded as an infallible guide to current specifications of any particular vehicle.

This Manual does not constitute an offer for sale of any particular vehicle. Rover Dealers are not agents of Rover and have no authority to bind the manufacturer by any expressed or implied undertaking or representation.

ENGINE NUMBER LOCATION

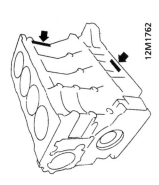

12M1762

The engine number will be found stamped either on the LH side of the bearing ladder or cast on the rear LH side of the cylinder block.

ENGINE SERIAL NUMBER PREFIXES

Engines covered by this overhaul manual have the following prefixes in the engine serial number:

H63, H64, H67, H71, H72, H75, H76, H77, H78
J31, J32, J78, J79, J89, J90
K38, K39, K40, K41, K43, K44, K45, K51, K53, K61, K63, K67, K68, K74, K76, K77, K78, K79, K80, K88, K89

L06, L07, L08, L09, L10, L24, L25, L28, L30, L31, L32, L33, L34, L35, L36, L37, L44, L45, L46, L47, L48, L49, L50, L51, L64, L67, L68, L69, L82, L97, L98, L99 K79, K80, K88, K89

M01, M21, M22, M23, M26, M27, M28, M29, M30, M31, M36, M37, M38, M39, M41, M42, M47, M48, M49, M50, M51, M52, M53, M54, M55, M56, M62, M64, M65, M67, M68, M70, M71, M72, M73, M75, M76, M79, M80, M81, M82, M83, M84, M85, M86, M87, M88, M89, M90, M91, M92, M93, M94, M95, M96, M97, M98, M99
N01

COMMENCING ENGINE NUMBERS

> NOTE: The following modifications have been introduced at the following engine numbers. Engines fitted to Rover 25, 45 and 75 models incorporate these modifications from commencement of production.

K16 Non VVC engines fitted with automatic timing belt tensioner

14K4FK76 646038, 14K4FK76 885300
14K4FK77 655218, 14K4FK77 885300

14K4FL30 153524, 14K4FL30 885300
14K4FL31 154156, 14K4FL31 885300

16K4FK79 654924, 16K4FK79 885300
16K4FK80 655078, 16K4FK80 885300

16K4FL32 153217, 16K4FL33 152709
16K4FL34 149204, 16K4FL35 145785

18K4FJ31 153993, 18K4FJ32 147263
18K4FJ78 151555, 18K4FJ79 153785
18K4FJ89 146503, 18K4FJ90 141815
18K4FL66 148135, 18K4FL67 665464
18K4KL36 118709, 18K4KL37 102149

K16 Non VVC engines fitted with modified camshafts and cylinder heads

14K4FK76 872191, 14K4FK77 872382
14K4FL30 114520, 14K4FL30 872041
14K4FL31 104073

16K4FK79 872751, 16K4FK80 872285
16K4FL32 114135, 16K4FL33 112837
16K4FL34 110965, 16K4FL35 110541

18K4FJ31 112397, 18K4FJ32 111281
18K4FJ78 115630, 18K4FJ79 112575
18K4FL66 674985, 18K4FL67 110704
18K4KJ89 110206, 18K4KJ90 683004
18K4KL36 703592, 18K4KL37 703768

Cylinder heads fitted with triple angle valve seats

14K4FK76 853697, 14K4FK77 853547
14K4FL30 684272, 14K4FL31 682772

16K4FK79 853606, 16K4FK80 853676
16K4FL32 684705, 16K4FL33 684141
16K4FL34 674898, 16K4FL35 675041

18K4FJ31 685002, 18K4FJ32 678009
18K4FJ78 679210, 18K4FJ79 682294
18K4FL66 658261, 18K4FL67 615758
18K4KL36 667388, 18K4KL37 657611
18K4KJ89 673981, 18K4KJ90 637368

Modified - type B crankshafts

11K2FK42 602582

14K2FH67 601998
14K2FK43 604022, 14K2FK44 585572
14K2FL64 589869
14K4FH71 589479, 14K4FH72 603771
14K4FK76 580134, 14K4FK77 602717

16K4FH75 597254, 16K4FH76 597902
16K4FK79 581514, 16K4FK80 583009
16K4FK88 605066, 16K4FK89 600785

18K4FJ31 599800, 18K4FJ32 577734
18K4FJ79 581514, 18K4FJ89 597466
18K4FK61 547750, 18K4FK67 526547
18K4FK68 323456, 18K4FL50 527882
18F4FL51 551737, 18K4FL82 589737
18K4KH77 585941, 18K4KH78 588402
18K4KJ90 568275

CYLINDER BLOCK COMPONENTS

1. Oil pump assembly
2. Gasket - oil pump
3. Screw - M6 x 30 - oil pump
4. Screw M6 x 20 - oil pump
5. Crankshaft front oil seal
6. Dipstick
7. Dipstick tube
8. Screw - dipstick tube and thermostat housing
9. Screw - dipstick tube
10. Gasket
11. Coolant pump
12. 'O' ring - coolant pump
13. Pillar bolt - if fitted
14. Bolt - coolant pump
15. Locating dowel
16. Thermostat housing - plastic
17. 'O' ring
18. Seal thermostat
19. Thermostat
20. Cover - plastic
21. Screw
22. 'O' ring
23. Coolant rail
24. Screw - coolant rail
25. Vent screw - if fitted
26. Sealing washer
27. Cylinder block
28. Cylinder liner
29. Ring dowel
30. Piston and connecting rod assembly
31. Big-end bearing cap
32. Connecting rod bolt
33. Big-end bearing shells
34. Top compression ring
35. 2nd compression ring
36. Oil control ring
37. Crankshaft
38. Ring dowel
39. Main bearing shells
    Plain in block Nos.1 and 5
    Grooved in block Nos. 2, 3 and 4
    Plain in bearing ladder
40. Thrust washers
41. Crankshaft rear oil seal
42. Flywheel assembly
43. Flywheel bolt - Patchlok
44. Bearing ladder
45. Bolt - bearing ladder
46. Bolt - bearing ladder
47. Ring dowel
48. Oil rail
49. Stud - oil rail
50. Nut - oil rail
51. Oil filter adapter
52. Gasket
53. Bolt
54. Oil pressure switch
55. Sealing washer
56. Oil temperature sensor - if fitted
57. Sealing washer
58. Oil filter element
59. Pressed steel sump
60. Gasket
61. Sump bolt - M6 - Patchlok
62. Drain plug
63. Sealing washer
64. Alloy sump
65. Sump bolt - M8 x 25
66. Sump bolt - M8 x 60
67. Drain plug
68. Sealing washer
69. Oil suction pipe
70. Screw - oil suction pipe
71. 'O' ring
72. Blanking plate
73. Screw - blanking plate

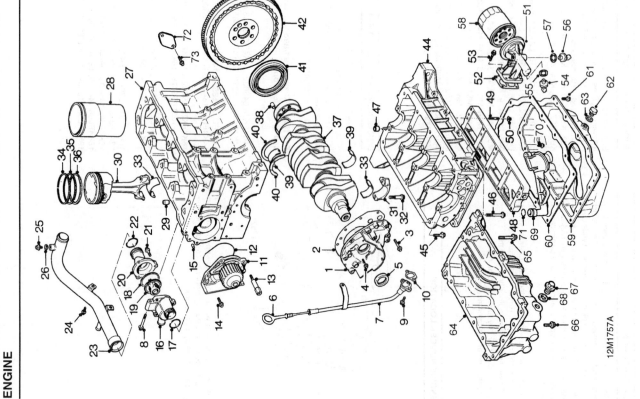

12M1757A

CYLINDER HEAD COMPONENTS - K8 ENGINES

1. Engine oil filler cap
2. Filler cap seal
3. ht clip mounting bracket
4. Clip - 2 ht leads
5. Bolt, bracket
6. Camshaft cover
7. Gasket
8. Bolt - camshaft cover
9. Cylinder head bolt
10. ht clip mounting bracket
11. Clip - 4 ht leads
12. Bolt, bracket
13. Mounting bracket - duct
14. Camshaft carrier
15. Bolt - camshaft carrier - long
16. Bolt - camshaft carrier - short
17. Locating dowel - camshaft carrier
18. Camshaft
19. Drive pin - camshaft gear
20. Camshaft oil seal
21. Hydraulic tappet
22. Collets - valve
23. Valve spring cap
24. Valve spring
25. Valve stem oil seal
26. Valve guide
27. Exhaust valve
28. Valve seat insert - exhaust
29. Inlet valve
30. Valve seat insert - inlet
31. Cylinder head
32. Coolant temperature sensor
33. Coolant outlet elbow
34. Bolt - coolant outlet elbow
35. Gasket - coolant outlet elbow
36. Spark plug
37. Cylinder head gasket
38. Fuel pump blanking plate - if fitted
39. Gasket
40. Nuts - blanking plate

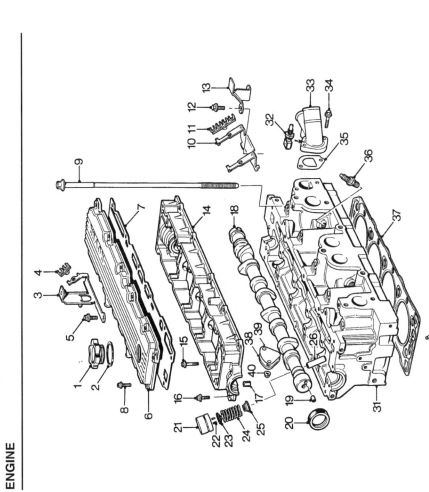

12M1760

CYLINDER HEAD COMPONENTS - K16 NON VVC ENGINES FITTED WITH DISTRIBUTOR

1. Spark plug cover
2. Screw M4 - cover
3. Screw retaining washer
4. Engine oil filler cap
5. Filler cap seal
6. Spark plug
7. Clip - ht leads
8. Bolt M6 - camshaft cover
9. Camshaft cover
10. Camshaft cover gasket
11. Camshaft carrier
12. Bolt M6 - camshaft carrier
13. Cylinder head bolt
14. Camshaft - inlet
15. Camshaft - exhaust
16. Drive pin - camshaft gear
17. Drive spindle - rotor arm
18. Camshaft oil seal
19. Hydraulic tappet

20. Collets - cap
21. Valve spring cap
22. Valve spring
23. Valve stem oil seal
24. Cylinder head
25. Ring dowel - cylinder head to camshaft carrier
26. Cylinder head gasket
27. Valve guide
28. Inlet valve
29. Valve seat insert - inlet
30. Exhaust valve
31. Valve seat insert - exhaust
32. Blanking plate
33. Screw M6
34. Gasket - coolant outlet elbow
35. Coolant outlet elbow
36. Screw M6 - coolant outlet elbow
37. Coolant temperature sensors
38. Sealing washer

12M1761A

CYLINDER HEAD COMPONENTS - K16 NON VVC ENGINES FITTED WITH PLUG TOP COIL IGNITION SYSTEM

1. Spark plug cover
2. Screw - spark plug cover
3. ht lead and plug tube
4. Oil filler cap
5. Seal - oil filler cap
6. Screws - coils to camshaft cover
7. Coil
8. Spark plug
9. Bolt - camshaft cover
10. Camshaft sensor
11. 'O' ring
12. Bolt - camshaft sensor
13. Camshaft cover
14. Gasket - camshaft cover
15. Camshaft carrier
16. Camshaft oil seal
17. Inlet camshaft
18. Exhaust camshaft
19. Bracket - multiplug
20. Bolt - multiplug bracket
21. Blanking plate - 2 off
22. Bolt - blanking plate
23. Gasket - coolant outlet elbow
24. Coolant outlet elbow
25. Sealing washer
26. Gasket
27. Coolant temperature sensor
28. Bolt - coolant outlet elbow
29. Hydraulic tappet
30. Valve spring cap
31. Valve spring
32. Valve stem oil seal
33. Collets
34. Locating dowel
35. Cylinder head
36. Gasket - cylinder head
37. Exhaust valve guide
38. Valve seat insert - exhaust
39. Exhaust valve
40. Valve seat insert - inlet
41. Inlet valve
42. Inlet valve guide
43. Bolt - cylinder head
44. Bolt - camshaft carrier

M124971

CYLINDER HEAD COMPONENTS - K16 VVC ENGINES

1. Bolts - hydraulic control unit
2. Hydraulic control unit body and spool valve
3. Solenoids
4. 'O' rings
5. Spool valve nut
6. Oil temperature transmitter
7. Piston screw, piston and seal assembly
8. Rack
9. Seal plate
10. Labyrinth seals
11. Spark plug
12. Spark plug cover
13. Oil filler cap
14. Filler cap seal
15. Screw - spark plug cover
16. Washer
17. Bolt - camshaft cover *
18. Camshaft cover *
19. Gasket - camshaft cover
20. Bolt - camshaft carrier
21. Camshaft carrier
22. Control shaft
23. Rear VVC housing and mechanism
24. Gasket - VVC housing
25. Bolt - VVC housing
26. Rear inlet camshaft
27. Front inlet camshaft

28. Front VVC housing and mechanism
29. Exhaust camshaft oil seals
30. Exhaust camshaft
31. Gasket - coolant outlet elbow
32. Coolant outlet elbow
33. Sealing washer
34. Gasket
35. Coolant temperature sensors
36. Bolt - coolant outlet elbow
37. Exhaust valve guide
38. Exhaust valve
39. Valve seat insert - exhaust
40. Valve seat insert - inlet
41. Inlet valve
42. Inlet valve guide
43. Cylinder head gasket
44. Valve stem oil seal
45. Valve spring
46. Valve spring cap
47. Collets
48. Hydraulic tappet
49. Bolt - cylinder head
50. Camshaft cover **
51. Bolt - camshaft cover **
52. 'O' ring - camshaft sensor **
53. Camshaft sensor **
54. Bolt - camshaft sensor **

*   Early engines
** Later engines

TIMING BELT COMPONENTS - K8 ENGINES

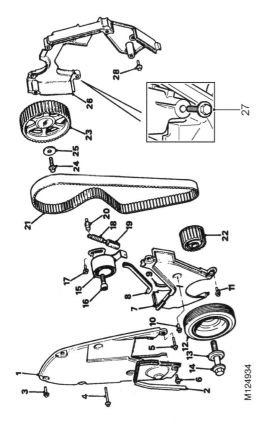

M124934

1. Upper front cover - timing belt
2. Seal - upper cover
3. Screw M6 x 16 - upper cover
4. Bolt M6 x 40 - upper cover
5. Bolt M6 x 20 - upper cover
6. Flange shoulder screw - upper cover
7. Lower cover - timing belt
8. Seal - lower cover to mounting
9. Seal - lower cover to cylinder block
10. Screw - lower cover
11. Screw M6 x 16 - lower cover
12. Crankshaft pulley
13. Special washer - pulley bolt
14. Crankshaft pulley bolt
15. Tensioner pulley and backplate
16. Allen screw - tensioner to cylinder head
17. Flange head screw - tensioner backplate
18. Tensioner spring
19. Sleeve - spring
20. Pillar bolt
21. Camshaft timing belt
22. Crankshaft timing gear
23. Camshaft timing gear
24. Camshaft gear bolt
25. Plain washer
26. Upper rear cover - timing belt
27. Screw - rear cover to coolant pump
28. Screw - rear cover

TIMING BELT COMPONENTS - K16 NON VVC ENGINES FITTED WITH MANUAL TIMING BELT TENSIONER

M124933

1. Upper front cover - timing belt
2. Screw M6 - upper cover
3. Seal - upper cover
4. Bolt M6 x 90 - upper and lower cover
5. Lower cover - timing belt
6. Seal - lower cover
7. Screw M6 - lower cover
8. Screw M6 x 16 - lower cover
9. Crankshaft pulley
10. Special washer - pulley bolt
11. Crankshaft pulley bolt
12. Camshaft timing belt
13. Camshaft timing gears
14. Camshaft gear bolt
15. Plain washer
16. Tensioner pulley and backplate
17. Allen screw - pulley
18. Tensioner spring
19. Sleeve - spring
20. Pillar bolt
21. Flange head screw - tensioner backplate
22. Crankshaft timing gear
23. Rear cover - timing belt
24. Screw - rear cover to coolant pump
25. Screw - rear cover

TIMING BELT COMPONENTS - K16 NON VVC ENGINES FITTED WITH AUTOMATIC TIMING BELT TENSIONER

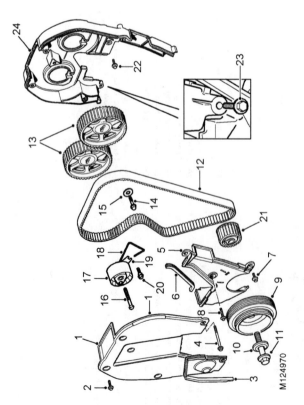

M124970

1. Upper front cover - timing belt
2. Screw M6 - upper cover
3. Seal - upper cover
4. Bolt M6 x 90 - upper and lower covers
5. Lower cover - timing belt
6. Seal - lower cover
7. Screw M6 - lower cover
8. Screw M6 x 16 - lower cover
9. Crankshaft pulley
10. Special washer - pulley bolt
11. Crankshaft pulley bolt
12. Camshaft timing belt

13. Camshaft timing gears
14. Camshaft gear bolt
15. Plain washer
16. Bolt - tensioner *
17. Tensioner
18. Index wire
19. Pointer
20. Pillar bolt
21. Crankshaft timing gear
22. Screw - rear cover
23. Screw - rear cover to coolant pump
24. Rear cover

* New Patchlok bolt must be used when tensioner is refitted

FRONT TIMING BELT COMPONENTS - K16 VVC ENGINES

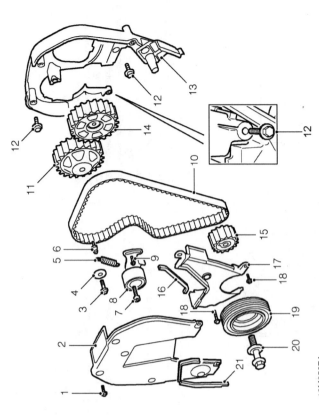

12M3527A

1. Screw - upper front cover
2. Upper front cover - timing belt
3. Camshaft gear bolt
4. Washer
5. Tensioner spring *
6. Pillar bolt *
7. Allen screw - tensioner pulley
8. Tensioner pulley and backplate
9. Flanged head screw - tensioner backplate
10. Camshaft timing belt
11. Front inlet camshaft timing gear

12. Screw - timing belt rear cover
13. Timing belt rear cover
14. Exhaust camshaft front timing gear
15. Crankshaft timing gear
16. Seal - lower front cover
17. Lower front cover
18. Screw - lower front cover
19. Crankshaft pulley
20. Crankshaft pulley bolt and washer
21. Seal - upper front cover

*These items are not fitted on production but are supplied with replacement timing belts. They must be removed and discarded on completion of belt tensioning.

REAR TIMING BELT COMPONENTS - K16 VVC ENGINES

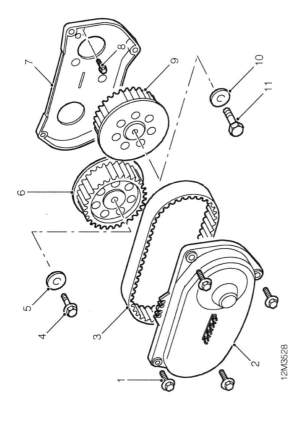

12M3528

1. Screw - rear timing belt cover
2. Rear timing belt cover
3. Rear timing belt
4. Bolt - M8 - rear timing gear
5. Washer - rear timing gear bolt
6. Exhaust camshaft rear timing gear

7. Rear timing belt backplate
8. Bolt - rear timing belt backplate
9. Rear inlet camshaft timing gear
10. Washer - rear timing gear bolt
11. Bolt - M10 - rear timing gear

Later engines are fitted with a plug top coil ignition system in which the conventional distributor is replaced by a camshaft sensor located in the camshaft carrier adjacent to the exhaust camshaft. Camshafts fitted to some early engines and all engines with plug top coil ignition have an integral reluctor ring which provides an input to the camshaft sensor. Twin coils are fitted on top of the camshaft cover, each coil supplying ht voltage to one pair of spark plugs.

Variable valve control (VVC): This system is fitted to some K16 engines. VVC is designed to provide variation in the valve open and close periods by independent positioning of the two inlet camshaft assemblies thereby giving optimum low speed driveability with no detriment to high speed performance.

OPERATION

The K Series engine is built up from aluminium castings bolted together. These consist of three major castings; the cylinder head, cylinder block and a bearing ladder which is line bored to provide the main bearing bores. Attached to these are three minor castings; above the cylinder head, the camshaft carrier and the camshaft cover. Below the bearing ladder is an oil rail.

Each of the ten cylinder head bolts passes through the cylinder head, cylinder block and bearing ladder to screw into the oil rail. This puts the cylinder head, cylinder block and bearing ladder into compression with all the tensile loads being carried by the cylinder head bolts.

When the cylinder head bolts are removed; additional fixings are used to retain the bearing ladder to the cylinder block and the oil rail to the bearing ladder.

K8 engine: The cross flow cylinder head has two valves for each cylinder and the spark plugs set at an angle. The inlet ports are of equal tract, designed to ensure a balanced mixture throughout the speed range to improve combustion and reduce exhaust emissions. The single, overhead camshaft operates both inlet and exhaust valves via hydraulic tappets and is driven from the crankshaft by a timing belt. Belt tension is maintained by a spring loaded tensioner. The camshaft is retained by a one-piece camshaft carrier sealed and bolted to the cylinder head. Positive location is by means of a flange which also controls camshaft end-float.

K16 engine: The cross flow cylinder head is based on a four valve, central spark plug, combustion chamber with the inlet ports designed to induce swirl and control the speed of the induction charge. This serves to improve combustion and hence fuel economy, performance and exhaust emissions. The twin overhead camshafts operate the valves via hydraulic tappets, one camshaft operates the exhaust valves whilst the other operates the inlet valves. The camshafts are driven from the crankshaft by a timing belt, belt tension being maintained by either a spring loaded, manually adjusted tensioner or, on later engines by an automatic tensioner. The camshafts are retained by the camshaft carrier, which is line bored with the cylinder head.

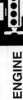

Whilst the exhaust camshaft is similar to camshafts fitted to non VVC K16 engines, there are four inlet camshafts, assembled in pairs, each individual camshaft operating the inlet valves on one cylinder. The front pair of camshafts are driven, via the front VVC mechanism, by the camshaft timing belt; the rear pair of camshafts being driven via the rear VVC mechanism by the rear timing belt which is itself, driven by the exhaust camshaft. Independent positioning of each inlet camshaft is controlled by its respective VVC mechanism. The front and rear VVC mechanisms are connected to each other by the control shaft. Movement of the control shaft is controlled by the piston and rack assembly located within the hydraulic control unit. The piston and rack assembly moves in response to engine speed and load signals received from the MEMS ECM via two solenoids mounted on the hydraulic control unit housing. As the piston and rack moves up or down in response to the signals received, the control shaft rotates and alters the position of the valve timing mechanisms.

All engines: Self adjusting hydraulic tappets are fitted on top of each valve and are operated directly by the camshaft(s). The valve stem oil seals are moulded onto a metal base which also act as the valve spring seat on the cylinder head.

Exhaust valves fitted to later engines are of the carbon break type. A machined profile on the valve stem removes any build up of carbon in the combustion chamber end of the valve guide thereby preventing valves from sticking. These valves may be fitted to all early engines.

The stainless steel cylinder head gasket has moulded seals around all coolant, breather and oil apertures and has steel cylinder bore eyelets. Compression of the gasket is controlled by limiters at each end of the gasket.

The cylinder block is fitted with 'damp' cylinder liners, the bottom, stepped half of the damp liner, being a sliding fit into the lower part of the cylinder block. The liners are sealed in the block with a bead of Hylomar applied around the stepped portion of the liner. The seal at the cylinder head is effected by the cylinder head gasket with the liner top acting as a break between the combustion chamber and gasket.

The aluminium alloy, thermal expansion pistons have a semi- floating gudgeon pin which is offset towards the thrust side and has an interference fit in the small end of the connecting rod. Pistons and cylinder liners are supplied in two grades. Big-end bearing diametric clearance is controlled by three grades of selective shell bearing.

The five bearing, eight balance weight crankshaft has its end-float controlled by thrust washer halves at the top of the central main bearing. Bearing diametric clearance is controlled by three grades of selective shell bearing. Oil grooves are provided in the upper halves of main bearings No. 2, 3 and 4 to supply oil, via drillings in the crankshaft, to the connecting rod big-end bearings.

K8 engine lubrication system

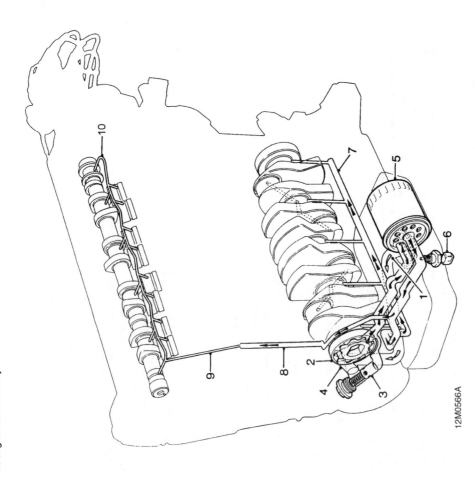

12M0566A

K16 engine lubrication system

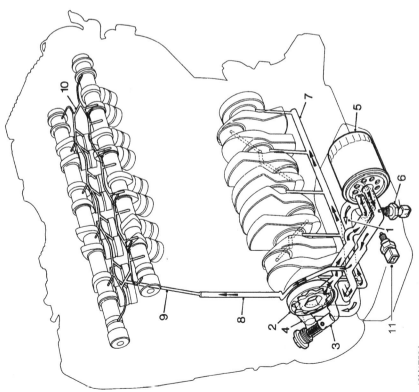

12M1758A

Non VVC camshafts illustrated

Crankcase ventilation

A positive crankcase ventilation system is used to vent blow-by gas from the crankcase to the air intake system.

K8 engine: Crankcase gas is drawn through a gauze oil separator in the camshaft cover and passes via a hose into either the carburetter or throttle body ahead of the throttle disc.

K16 engine: Crankcase gas is drawn through a gauze oil separator in the camshaft cover and passes via hoses into the throttle housing.

Lubrication

The lubrication system is of the full-flow filtration, forced fed type. The oil sump is of either pressed steel or alloy manufacture. Pressed steel sumps are sealed to the bearing ladder using a positively located gasket incorporating compression limiters. Alloy sumps are sealed to the bearing ladder with a bead of sealant applied to the sump flange.

Oil is drawn, via a strainer and suction pipe (1) in the sump, into the crankshaft driven oil pump (2) of the trochoid type which has an integral pressure relief valve (3), excess oil is diverted into the intake (4) of the oil pump. Oil is pumped through the full-flow cartridge type oil filter (5), mounted on an adapter attached to the oil pump housing. The low oil pressure sensor (6) is also screwed into the adapter and registers the oil pressure in the main oil gallery on the outflow side of the filter.

The main oil gallery (7) is fed through the oil rail below the main bearing ladder in which drillings direct the oil to the main bearings. Cross drillings in the crankshaft from No. 2 and 4 main bearings carry the oil to the big-end bearings. A passage in the oil pump housing connects to a drilling (8) in the cylinder block to oilways (9) in the cylinder head.

K8 engine: Oil is fed through the cylinder head to a drilling (10) in the one piece camshaft carrier to supply oil to each hydraulic tappet and camshaft bearing.

k16 engine: Oil is fed through the cylinder head to twin full length oilways (10) in the camshaft carrier to supply oil to each hydraulic tappet and camshaft bearing.

VVC engines: The VVC mechanisms are lubricated by oil fed via the inlet camshafts.

An oil temperature switch (11) is fitted in the oil filter head for certain models. In the event of engine oil temperature rising above a pre-set level, a warning light will illuminate on the instrument panel.

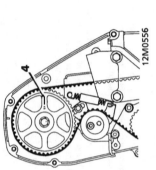

M124960

⚠ **CAUTION: Do not use camshaft gear, gear retaining bolt or timing belt to rotate crankshaft.**

5. Check that timing mark on crankshaft pulley is aligned with mark on timing belt lower cover.

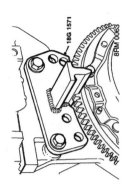

6. Position flywheel locking tool **18G 1571** to flywheel.

7. Secure with 2 bolts.

CAMSHAFT TIMING BELT - K8 ENGINES

Remove

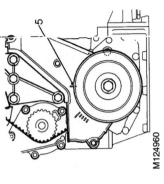

8FM 3283

1. Slacken bottom bolt securing timing belt upper front cover.

△ NOTE: Remove bottom bolt when cover is not slotted.

2. Remove 6 bolts from timing belt upper front cover.

3. Remove timing belt upper front cover and seal.

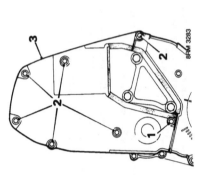

12M0556

4. Rotate crankshaft clockwise to align camshaft gear timing marks with top face of cylinder head - 90° BTDC.

This page is intentionally left blank

8RM3458A

8. Remove crankshaft pulley bolt and washer.
9. Remove crankshaft pulley.
10. Remove 3 bolts securing timing belt lower cover.
11. Remove timing belt lower cover together with seals.
12. Remove 3 bolts, mounting bracket to engine.
13. Remove mounting bracket.

M124944

14. Slacken tensioner pulley Allen screw.
15. Slacken tensioner backplate screw.
16. Push tensioner pulley down to fully OFF position.
17. Tighten backplate screw to 10 Nm.
18. Ease timing belt from gears using the fingers only.
19. Discard timing belt.

⚠ **CAUTION: Timing belt must always be replaced during engine overhaul. Do not rotate crankshaft with timing belt removed and cylinder head fitted.**

Refit

1. Clean timing gears, coolant pump drive gear and tensioner pulley .

⚠ **CAUTION: If the sintered gears have been subjected to prolonged contamination, they must be soaked in a solvent bath and then thoroughly washed in clean solvent before refitting. Because of the porous construction of sintered material, oil impregnated in the gears will emerge and contaminate the belt.**

2. Check correct alignment of timing marks for 90° BTDC:
   Crankshaft gear dots align with flange on oil pump.
   Camshaft gear mark to right aligns with top face of cylinder head.

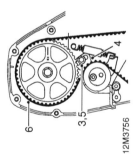

12M3756

3. Slacken tensioner backplate screw, ensure tensioner moves fully through its adjustment range and returns under spring tension.
4. Push tensioner pulley down to fully OFF position.
5. Tighten backplate screw to 10 Nm.
6. Using the fingers only, fit a new timing belt over crankshaft timing gear, camshaft gear, tensioner pulley and coolant pump drive gear, ensure belt is positioned centrally on gears and pulley and that any slack in the belt is on the tensioner pulley side of the belt.
7. Clean all traces of Loctite from engine mounting bracket securing bolts and apply Loctite 542 to threads of bolts.
8. Fit engine mounting bracket, tighten bolts to 45 Nm.

9. Ensure inserts are fitted in timing belt lower cover.
10. Fit timing belt lower cover, ensuring correct position of seals, tighten screws to 10 Nm.

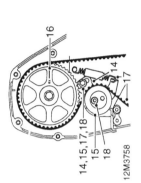

12M3757

11. Fit crankshaft pulley to crankshaft timing gear ensuring that indent on pulley locates over gear lug (arrowed).
12. Fit crankshaft pulley bolt and washer, tighten to 205 Nm.
13. Remove flywheel locking tool **18G 1571**.

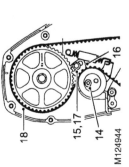

12M3758

14. Slacken tensioner backplate screw and tension timing belt by applying finger pressure to tensioner backplate.

15. With tensioner pulley against timing belt and backplate held in position, tighten backplate screw to 10 Nm.
16. Rotate crankshaft clockwise 2 complete revolutions and align camshaft gear timing mark with top face of cylinder head.

⚠ **CAUTION: Do not use camshaft gear, gear retaining bolt or timing belt to rotate crankshaft.**

17. Slacken tensioner backplate screw and check that belt is being tensioned by the tensioner spring.
18. Tighten tensioner backplate screw to 10 Nm and tensioner pulley Allen screw to 45 Nm.
19. Ensure inserts are fitted in timing belt upper front cover.
20. Fit timing belt upper front cover, ensuring correct position of seals, tighten screws and bolt to 5 Nm.

Flywheel not fitted with a reluctor ring

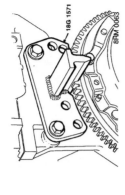

6. Fit flywheel locking tool **18G 1571**.
7. Secure with 2 bolts.

Flywheel fitted with a reluctor ring

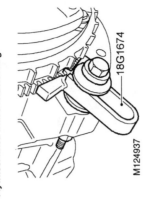

M124937

8. Fit flywheel locking tool **18G 1674**, tighten bolt.

    CAUTION: Ensure tooth on tool 18G 1674 engages with teeth on flywheel not the reluctor ring

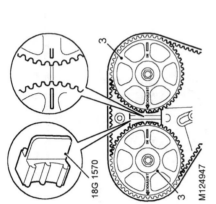

M124947

NOTE: VVC camshaft timing gear marks are shown in the inset on the illustration.

3. Rotate crankshaft clockwise to align camshaft gear timing marks - 90° BTDC.

   CAUTION: Do not use camshaft gears, gear retaining bolts or timing belt to rotate crankshaft.

4. Fit camshaft gear locking tool **18G 1570**.

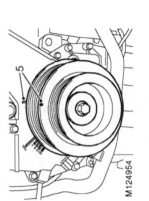

M124954

5. Check that timing mark on crankshaft pulley is aligned with mark on timing belt lower cover.

CAMSHAFT TIMING BELT - K16 ENGINES

M124974

NOTE: Two types of timing belt tensioner are fitted to K16 engines, type A is a manual tensioner fitted to some K16 non VVC and all VVC engines. Type B is an automatic tensioner fitted to some K16 non VVC engines. Commencing engine numbers for the automatic tensioner are listed in Information. The tensioners and their timing belts are not interchangeable.

The manual timing belt tensioner spring fitted to K16 non VVC engines is fitted with a sleeve, whilst on VVC engines only a spring is fitted.

Camshaft timing belt - manual tensioner - remove

CAUTION: Timing belts fitted to engines with manual timing belt tensioners are not interchangeable with belts fitted to engines with automatic tensioners.

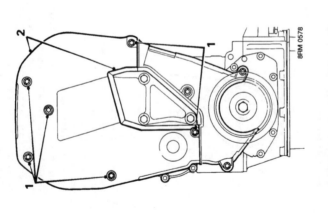

8RM 0578

1. Slacken bottom bolt and remove 5 screws securing timing belt upper front cover.

   NOTE: Remove bottom bolt when cover is not slotted.

2. Remove timing belt upper front cover and seal.

All engines

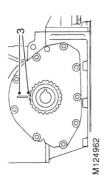

8RM3461A

9. Remove crankshaft pulley bolt and washer, remove crankshaft pulley.
10. Remove 3 bolts securing timing belt lower cover.
11. Remove timing belt lower cover together with seals.

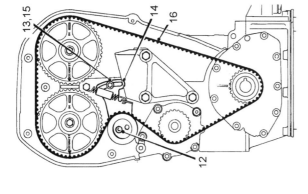

M124925

△ NOTE: Non VVC camshaft timing gears and tensioner spring illustrated.

12. Slacken tensioner pulley Allen screw.
13. Slacken tensioner backplate screw.
14. Push tensioner pulley down to fully OFF position.

△ NOTE: VVC engines:- Tensioner spring and pillar bolt are only fitted for tensioning replacement timing belts.

15. Tighten backplate screw to 10 Nm.
16. Ease timing belt from gears using the fingers only.
17. Discard timing belt.

⚠ **CAUTION: Timing belt must always be replaced during engine overhaul. Do not rotate crankshaft with timing belt removed and cylinder head fitted.**

Camshaft timing belt - manual tensioner - refit

⚠ **CAUTION: VVC engines:- When a replacement timing belt is to be fitted, it will be necessary to fit the tensioner spring and pillar bolt supplied with the replacement belt to adjust belt tension.**

1. Clean timing gears, coolant pump drive gear and tensioner pulley.

⚠ **CAUTION: If the sintered gears have been subjected to prolonged oil contamination, they must be soaked in a solvent bath and then thoroughly washed in clean solvent before refitting. Because of the porous construction of sintered material, oil impregnated in the gears will emerge and contaminate the belt.**

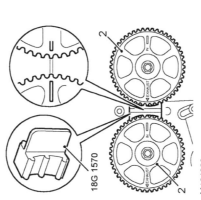

Flywheel not fitted with a reluctor ring

3. Check that crankshaft gear timing marks are aligned with flange on oil pump - 90° BTDC.

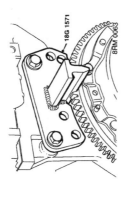

M124929

△ NOTE: VVC camshaft gear timing marks are shown in the inset on the illustration.

2. Check correct alignment of camshaft gear timing marks, fit camshaft gear locking tool **18G 1570.**

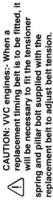

M124962

4. Fit flywheel locking tool **18G 1571**, secure with 2 bolts.

Flywheel fitted with a reluctor ring

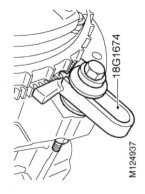

M124937

5. Fit flywheel locking tool **18G 1674**, tighten bolt.

⚠ **CAUTION: Ensure tooth on tool 18G 1674 engages with teeth on flywheel not the reluctor ring.**

6. *VVC engines:* Fit tensioner spring and pillar bolt supplied with replacement timing belt, connect spring to tensioner backplate and pillar bolt.

⚠ **CAUTION: Ensure spring is the correct type for the engine being worked on:-**

Non VVC engines:- Spring is fitted with a sleeve.
VVC engines:- Spring is not fitted with a sleeve.

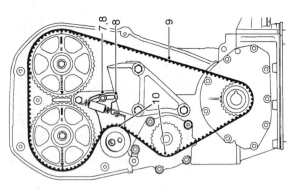

M124926

◁ NOTE: Non VVC camshaft timing gears and tensioner spring illustrated.

7. Slacken tensioner backplate screw, ensure tensioner moves fully through its adjustment range and returns under spring tension.

8. Push tensioner down to fully OFF position, tighten tensioner backplate screw to 10 Nm.

9. Using the fingers only, fit a new timing belt over crankshaft timing gear and then over camshaft gears keeping belt taut between crankshaft timing gear and exhaust camshaft gear.

10. Ease timing belt over tensioner pulley and coolant pump drive gear ensuring belt is positioned centrally on gears and pulley.

11. Ensure inserts are fitted in timing belt lower cover.

12. Fit timing belt lower cover, ensuring correct position of seals, tighten screws to 9 Nm.

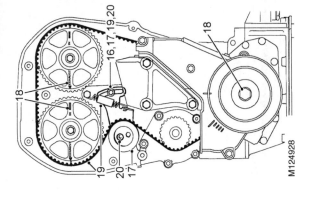

M124928

M124927

◁ NOTE: Non VVC camshaft timing gears and tensioner spring illustrated.

16. Slacken tensioner backplate screw and tension timing belt by applying finger pressure to tensioner backplate.

17. With tensioner pulley against timing belt and backplate held in position, tighten backplate screw to 10 Nm.

18. Rotate crankshaft clockwise 2 complete revolutions and align camshaft gear timing marks.

⚠ **CAUTION: Do not use camshaft gears, gear retaining bolts or timing belt to rotate crankshaft.**

19. Slacken tensioner backplate screw and check that belt is being tensioned by the tensioner spring.

20. Tighten tensioner backplate screw to 10 Nm and tensioner pulley Allen screw to 45 Nm.

13. Fit crankshaft pulley to crankshaft timing gear ensuring that indent on pulley locates over lug on gear.

14. Secure with crankshaft pulley bolt and washer, tighten to 205 Nm.

15. Remove camshaft and flywheel locking tools.

VVC engines

21. Disconnect tensioner spring from pillar bolt, release spring from tensioner: remove and discard spring.
22. Remove and discard pillar bolt.

All engines

23. Ensure inserts are fitted in timing belt front upper cover.
24. Fit timing belt upper front cover, ensuring correct position of seals, tighten screws and bottom bolt to 5 Nm.

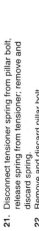

Camshaft timing belt - automatic tensioner - remove

 **CAUTION: Timing belts fitted to engines with automatic timing belt tensioners are not interchangeable with those fitted to engines with manual tensioners.**

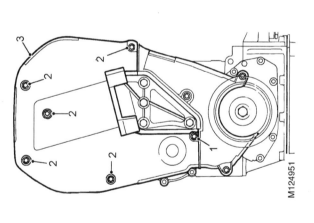

M124951

1. Slacken but do not remove bolt securing bottom of timing belt upper front cover.

 NOTE: Remove bolt when cover is not slotted.

2. Noting fitted position of longest screw, remove 5 screws securing timing belt upper front cover.
3. Remove timing belt upper front cover together with seal.

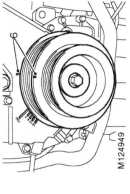
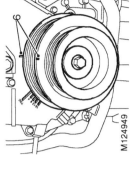

M124949

6. Check that timing mark on crankshaft pulley is aligned with mark on timing belt lower cover.

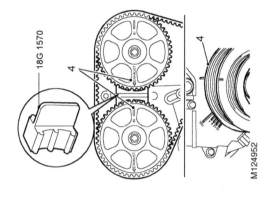

18G 1570

M124952

4. Rotate crankshaft clockwise to align camshaft gear timing marks - 90° BTDC.

 CAUTION: Do not use camshaft gears, gear retaining bolts or timing belt to rotate crankshaft.

5. Fit camshaft gear locking tool **18G 1570**.

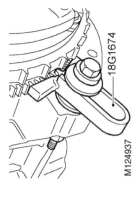

18G1674

M124937

7. Fit flywheel locking tool **18G 1674**, tighten bolt.

CAUTION: Ensure tooth on tool 18G 1674 engages with teeth on flywheel not the reluctor ring.

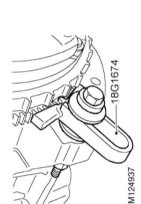

M124945

8. Remove crankshaft pulley bolt and washer.
9. Remove crankshaft pulley.
10. Remove 3 bolts securing timing belt lower cover.
11. Remove timing belt lower cover together with seals.

M124955

12. Remove and discard timing belt tensioner bolt.
13. Disengage index wire from its fitted position whilst at the same time removing the timing belt tensioner.
14. Ease timing belt from gears using the fingers only.
15. Discard timing belt.

⚠ **CAUTION: Timing belt must always be replaced during engine overhaul. Do not rotate crankshaft with timing belt removed and cylinder head fitted.**

Camshaft timing belt - automatic tensioner - refit

⚠ **CAUTION: If the sintered gears have been subjected to prolonged oil contamination, they must be soaked in a solvent bath and then thoroughly washed in clean solvent before refitting. Because of the porous construction of sintered material, oil impregnated in the gears will emerge and contaminate the belt.**

1. Clean timing gears, coolant pump drive gear and tensioner pulley.

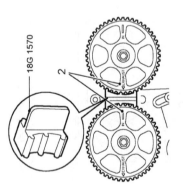

18G 1570

M124961

2. Check correct alignment of camshaft gear timing marks, fit camshaft gear locking tool **18G 1570.**

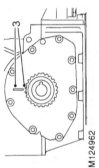

M124962

3. Check that crankshaft gear timing marks are aligned with flange on oil pump - 90° BTDC.

 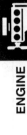

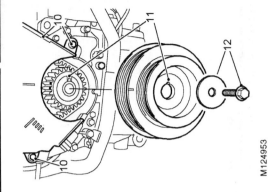

M124953

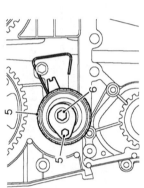

18G1674

M124937

4. Fit flywheel locking tool **18G 1674.**

M124956

5. Fit timing belt tensioner ensuring that index wire is positioned over pillar bolt and that tensioner lever is at 9 o'clock position.
6. Fit a new tensioner securing bolt and tighten bolt until it is just possible to move tensioner lever.
7. Using the fingers only, fit a new timing belt over crankshaft gear, then camshaft gears, tensioner pulley and coolant pump drive gear ensuring that the belt run between the crankshaft gear and the exhaust camshaft gear is kept taut.
8. Check that timing belt is positioned centrally around gears and tensioner pulley.
9. Ensure inserts are fitted in timing belt lower cover.
10. Fit timing belt lower cover ensuring correct position of seals, fit screws and tighten to 9 Nm.
11. Fit crankshaft pulley to crankshaft gear ensuring that indent on pulley locates over lug on gear.
12. Fit crankshaft pulley bolt and washer, tighten to 205 Nm.
13. Remove camshaft gear and flywheel locking tools **18G 1570** and **18G 1674.**

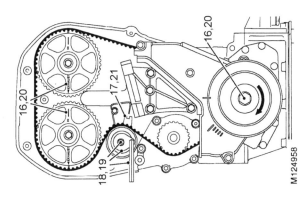

M124957

14. Using a 6 mm Allen key, rotate tensioner anti-clockwise and align the centre of the indent on the tensioner pointer to the index wire.

⚠ **CAUTION: Ensure that pointer approaches index wire from above. Should pointer go past index wire, release tension completely and repeat tensioning procedure.**

15. Ensuring that pointer maintains correct position, tighten tensioner bolt to 25 Nm.

M124958

16. Using crankshaft pulley bolt, rotate crankshaft 2 turns clockwise and align camshaft gear timing marks.

⚠ **CAUTION: Do not use camshaft gears, gear retaining bolts or timing belt to rotate crankshaft.**

17. Check that pointer is still correctly aligned with index wire.

⚠ **CAUTION: If pointer is not correctly aligned, carry out the following procedure.**

18. Slacken tensioner bolt until it is just possible to move the tensioner lever. Using a 6 mm Allen key, rotate tensioner lever clockwise until pointer is just above the index wire then rotate tensioner lever anti-clockwise until pointer is correctly aligned with index wire.

19. Ensuring that pointer maintains correct position tighten tensioner bolt to 25 Nm.

20. Using crankshaft pulley bolt, rotate crankshaft 2 turns clockwise and align camshaft gear timing marks.

21. Check that pointer is still correctly aligned with index wire.

22. Ensure inserts are fitted in timing belt upper front cover.

23. Fit timing belt upper front cover ensuring correct position of seal, fit screws, tighten screws and bottom bolt to 5 Nm.

OIL PUMP

Remove

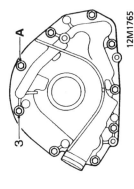

12M1765

1. Remove and discard camshaft timing belt.
2. Remove crankshaft timing gear.

3. Noting fitted position of M6 x 20 bolt 'A', remove and discard 9 bolts securing oil pump to cylinder block.

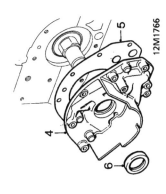

12M1766

4. Remove oil pump assembly.

NOTE: Dowel located.

5. Remove and discard oil pump gasket.
6. Remove and discard crankshaft front oil seal.

Oil pump assembling

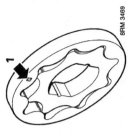

8RM 3469

1. Ensure outer rotor identification marking faces outward.
2. Lubricate pump rotors with engine oil.
3. Lubricate a new cover plate seal with engine oil.
4. Fit cover plate seal and cover plate.
5. Apply Loctite 222 to cover plate securing screws, fit and tighten screws.
6. Check that pump rotates freely.

Oil pressure relief valve

12M3531

1. Unscrew plug, discard sealing washer.
2. Remove spring and relief valve sleeve assembly.
3. Check that valve sleeve slides freely in bore and that bore and sleeve are free from scoring and corrosion.

⚠ NOTE: Light corrosion may be removed using grade 600 emery cloth soaked in engine oil.

4. Check free length of spring:
   Spring free length = 38.9 mm

   Replace relief valve as an assembly if scoring of plunger is evident or free length of spring is less than specified. Replace oil pump if relief valve bore is scored.

5. Remove all traces of Loctite from plug and threads in relief valve bore.

⚠ **CAUTION: Do not use a tap.**

6. Apply Loctite 577 to threads of plug.
7. Fit plug, use a new sealing washer.

ENGINE

Inspection

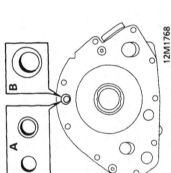
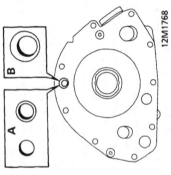

12M1767

1. Remove 2 screws and cover plate.
2. Remove and discard cover plate seal.

12M1768

⚠ **CAUTION: Two types of oil pump have been fitted. The early type oil pumps, fitted up to Engine No. 820000, can be identified by having either a plain 6 mm diameter oil feed hole or an 8 mm diameter oil feed hole with a 6 mm counterbore - A in illustration. Later type oil pumps, fitted from Engine No. 820000 all have a 12 mm diameter oil feed hole with an 8 mm diameter offset counterbore - B in illustration. Later type oil pumps may be fitted as replacements to all engines but early type pumps may not be fitted to engines from Engine No. 820000.**

4. Remove all traces of Loctite from cover plate securing screws and tapped holes in oil pump body; ensure screw holes are clean and dry.

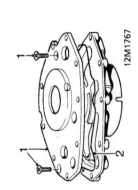
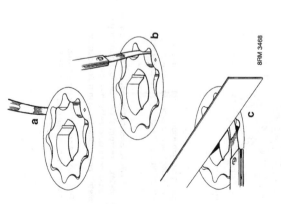

8RM 3468

3. Check rotor clearances:
   a. Outer rotor to housing = 0.28 - 0.36 mm
   b. Inner rotor tip = 0.05 - 0.13 mm
   c. Rotor end float = 0.02 - 0.06 mm
   Renew pump assembly if housing is scored or clearances are excessive.

Oil pump - refit

1. Clean oil pump.
2. Using gasket removal spray and a plastic scraper, remove all traces of gasket from oil pump.
3. Clean oil seal running surface on crankshaft.
4. Fit a new, dry, oil pump gasket.
5. Turn oil pump rotor to align drive with crankshaft.
6. Fit oil seal protector sleeve, from seal kit, over crankshaft end.

△ NOTE: This will assist in locating oil pump inner rotor.

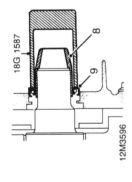

18G 1587

12M3596

8. Ensure oil seal protector sleeve is located over end of crankshaft.
9. Position new crankshaft front oil seal on crankshaft against oil pump housing. Drift seal into position using tool **18G 1587**.

⚠ **CAUTION: Oil seal must be fitted dry.**

10. Remove tool **18G 1587** and oil seal protector sleeve.
11. Clean crankshaft timing gear.
12. Fit crankshaft timing gear.
13. Fit and adjust a new camshaft timing belt.

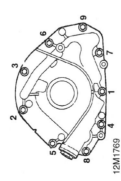

12M1769

7. Fit oil pump, fit new Patchlok bolts, M6 x 20 bolt at position 3. Tighten in sequence shown to 10 Nm.

ENGINE

Inspection

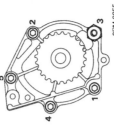

8RM 3473

1. Check for movement of pump spindle in bearing and for coolant leakage from seal.

COOLANT PUMP

Remove

1. Remove and discard camshaft timing belt.
2. Remove thermostat and housing.

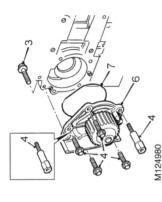

M124980

3. *Rear cover fitted:* Remove screw securing timing belt rear cover to coolant pump.
4. Noting their fitted position, remove bolts and pillar bolt securing coolant pump.

   ◁ NOTE: 2 pillar bolts are fitted to some engines.

5. Release coolant pump from 2 dowels and rear cover.
6. Remove coolant pump.
7. Remove and discard 'O' ring from pump.

Refit

1. Clean pump, mating face and dowels.
2. Fit new 'O' ring to coolant pump, use RTV sealant to retain 'O' ring.

8RM 0055

3. Fit coolant pump to cylinder block, fit bolts and pillar bolt(s) and tighten in sequence shown to 10 Nm.
4. *Rear cover fitted:* Fit timing belt rear cover securing screw, tighten to 9 Nm.
5. Fit thermostat and housing.
6. Fit and adjust a new camshaft timing belt.

THERMOSTAT

Remove

12M0558

1. Remove 2 bolts securing coolant rail to cylinder block, release rail from thermostat cover.
2. Remove bolt securing thermostat housing and dipstick tube to cylinder block.
3. Withdraw thermostat housing from coolant pump.

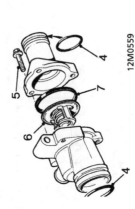

12M0559

4. Remove and discard 'O' rings from thermostat housing and cover.
5. Remove 3 bolts and remove cover from thermostat housing.
6. Withdraw thermostat from housing.
7. Remove and discard seal from thermostat.

Inspection

1. Test thermostat using thermostat test equipment, renew thermostat if necessary.
2. Thermostat open = 88° C
   Starts to open = 85° to 91° C
   Fully open = 100° C

Refit

1. Clean thermostat housing, cover and sealing faces.
2. Lubricate new 'O' rings with silicone grease and fit to thermostat housing and cover.
3. Fit a new seal to thermostat.
4. Align and fit thermostat to shoulder in thermostat housing.
5. Fit cover to thermostat housing, fit and tighten bolts to 8 Nm.

⚠ **CAUTION: Torque figure must not be exceeded.**

6. Fit thermostat housing to coolant pump, align dipstick tube bracket, fit and tighten bolt to 10 Nm.
7. Connect coolant rail to thermostat cover.
8. Align coolant rail to cylinder block, fit and tighten bolts to 25 Nm.

FLYWHEEL AND STARTER RING GEAR

Flywheel - remove

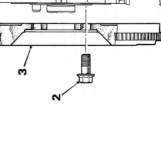

18G 1571

8RM 0063

18G1674

M124937

1. Fit flywheel locking tool:
   Flywheel without reluctor ring use **18G 1571**.
   Flywheel with reluctor ring use **18G 1674**.

⚠ **CAUTION: Ensure tool engages teeth on flywheel not the reluctor ring.**

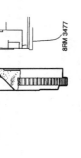

8RM 3477

▽ NOTE: Flywheel without reluctor ring illustrated.

2. Remove and discard 6 bolts securing flywheel.
3. Using assistance, remove flywheel from crankshaft.

▽ NOTE: Dowel located.

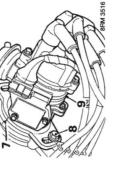

12M0549

5. Using sequence shown, progressively slacken and remove 12 bolts securing camshaft cover. Remove camshaft cover, discard gasket.

6. Remove camshaft cover, discard gasket.

8RM 3516

7. Mark distributor flange for refitting reference.
8. Remove 2 screws securing distributor.
9. Remove distributor, discard 'O' ring.
10. Remove any debris from spark plug recesses, remove and discard 4 spark plugs.

CYLINDER HEAD

Cylinder head - K8 engines - remove

⚠️ **CAUTION: If crankshaft is to be removed during overhaul, it will be necessary to check and record crankshaft end-float prior to removing cylinder head.**

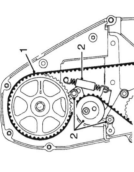

12M0553A

1. Remove and discard camshaft timing belt.

⚠️ **CAUTION: Do not rotate crankshaft whilst timing belt is removed and cylinder head is fitted, pistons will contact the valves.**

2. Disconnect tensioner spring, remove pillar bolt, screw, tensioner and spring.
3. Disconnect ht leads from spark plugs.

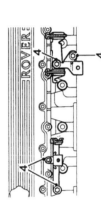

12M 0552 A

4. Remove 4 screws securing ht lead brackets, remove brackets.

Starter ring gear - remove

12M 1936A

1. Remove flywheel.
2. Drill a 3 mm diameter hole at root of 2 teeth.
3. Apply a cold chisel to root of teeth, break ring gear and remove from flywheel.

⚠️ **WARNING: Suitable eye protection must be worn.**

Starter ring gear - refit

1. Heat ring gear evenly to 350°C, indicated by light BLUE colour. Locate ring gear on flywheel and press hard against flange.

⚠️ **WARNING: Handle hot ring gear with care.**

2. Allow ring gear to air cool.
3. Fit flywheel.

Flywheel - refit

⚠️ **CAUTION: Flywheels fitted to VVC engines have a reluctor ring with 4 teeth at unequally spaced intervals missing whilst flywheels fitted to engines with plug top coil ignition have reluctor rings with equally spaced teeth . If the flywheel is to be replaced, it is essential that the replacement is of the correct type.**

1. Clean flywheel and crankshaft faces. Use a clean bolt with two saw cuts along threads and clean adhesive from threaded holes in crankshaft.
2. Using assistance, fit flywheel to crankshaft, fit and tighten new Patchlok bolts to 80 Nm.

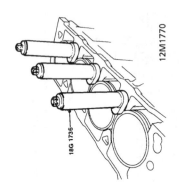

12M 0548A

11. Use tool 12-182 to hold camshaft gear against rotation.

12. Remove bolt and plain washer securing camshaft gear.

13. Remove camshaft gear.

14. Remove screws securing upper part of timing belt rear cover to cylinder head and screw securing rear of cover to coolant pump, remove cover.

⚠ NOTE: This is the longest of the rear cover securing screws.

15. Check and record crankshaft end-float.

12M 0561

16. Using sequence shown, progressively slacken 10 cylinder head to oil rail bolts. Remove bolts and store in fitted order.

⚠ CAUTION: Removal of cylinder head bolts will result in a 'tightening-up' of the crankshaft, rotation of crankshaft must, therefore, be kept to a minimum. Do not rotate crankshaft until cylinder liner retainer clamps 18G 1736 are fitted.

17. Using assistance, remove cylinder head assembly.

⚠ CAUTION: Cylinder head is dowel located, do not tap it sideways to free it from cylinder block. Place cylinder head on wooden blocks to prevent damaging valves.

18. Remove and discard cylinder head gasket.

Cylinder head - K16 Non VVC engines fitted with distributor - remove

⚠ CAUTION: If crankshaft is to be removed during overhaul it will be necessary to check and record crankshaft end-float prior to removing cylinder head.

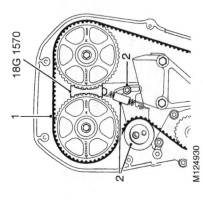

18G 1570

M124930

1. Remove and discard camshaft timing belt.

⚠ CAUTION: Do not rotate crankshaft whilst timing belt is removed and cylinder head is fitted, pistons will contact the valves.

2. Engines fitted with manual timing belt tensioner:- Disconnect tensioner spring, remove bolt, screw, tensioner and spring.

12M1770

18G 1736

19. Assemble cylinder liner retainer clamps 18G 1736 to cylinder head bolts. Position retainer clamps on cylinder liners ensuring clamps do not protrude over liner bores. Screw cylinder head bolts into oil rail and tighten sufficiently to retain clamps.

⚠ CAUTION: Ensure that bolts used are those originally fitted in that location.

ENGINE

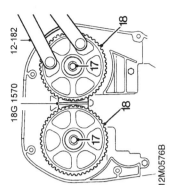

M124931

3. Release 2 screws and remove spark plug cover.

4. Disconnect 4 plug tubes from spark plugs. Remove any debris from spark plug recesses, remove and discard 4 spark plugs.

5. Lift clip plate and grommet and position plug leads aside.

6. Remove 2 bolts and air cleaner support bracket.

7. Progressively slacken then remove bolts and on early engines, 2 pillar bolts securing camshaft cover.

   ◁ NOTE: On later engines, pillar bolts have been replaced by 'cast-in' supports which are an integral part of the camshaft cover.

8. Remove camshaft cover assembly, remove and discard gasket.

9. Check and record crankshaft end-float.

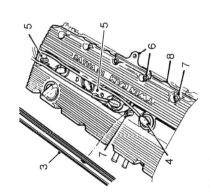

8RM 3521A

10. Release 2 screws and remove distributor cap.

11. Remove and discard screw securing rotor arm.

12. Remove rotor arm.

13. Remove anti-flash shield.

M124973

◁ NOTE: Later engines are fitted with modified camshafts which incorporate a reluctor ring and the procedure for removing cylinder head bolts differs from early engines. Commencing engine numbers for the modified camshafts are listed in information.

ENGINE

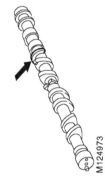

12M0576B

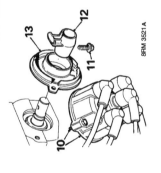

8RM 0740

14. Using sequence shown, progressively slacken cylinder head bolts:
    Early engines:- bolts 1 to 8, remove bolts 1 to 8 and store in fitted order.
    Later engines fitted with modified camshafts:- bolts 1 to 6, remove bolts 1 to 6 and store in fitted order.

   ◁ NOTE: It will be necessary to carry out the following operations in order to remove the remaining bolts.

15. Remove locking tool **18G 1570** from camshaft gears.

16. Using tool **12-182**, turn both camshafts clockwise to gain access to bolts:
    Early engines:- bolts 9 and 10.
    Later engines fitted with modified camshafts:- bolts 7 and 8.
    Progressively slacken then remove the remaining bolts and store in fitted order.

   ⚠ **CAUTION: Removal of cylinder head bolts results in a 'tightening-up' of crankshaft; rotation of crankshaft must, therefore, be kept to a minimum. Do not rotate crankshaft until cylinder liner retainer clamps 18G 1736 are fitted.**

17. Suitably identify each camshaft gear to its respective camshaft and using tool **12-182** to hold camshaft gear against rotation, remove bolt and plain washer from each camshaft gear.

18. Remove camshaft gears.

12M1770

23. Assemble cylinder liner retainer clamps **18G 1736** to cylinder head bolts. Position retainer clamps on cylinder liners ensuring clamps do not protrude over liner bores. Screw cylinder head bolts into oil rail and tighten sufficiently to retain clamps.

CAUTION: Ensure that bolts used are those originally fitted in that location.

18G 1736

12M0577A

19. Remove screws securing upper part of timing belt rear cover to cylinder head and screw securing rear of cover to coolant pump.

NOTE: This is the longest of the rear cover securing screws.

20. Remove timing belt tensioner pillar bolt.
21. Using assistance, remove cylinder head assembly from cylinder block.

CAUTION: Cylinder head is dowel located, do not tap it sideways to free it from cylinder block. Place cylinder head assembly on blocks of wood to prevent damaging valves.

22. Remove and discard cylinder head gasket.

M124950

Cylinder head - K16 non VVC engines fitted with plug top coil ignition system - remove

NOTE: Commencing engine numbers for these engines are listed in Information

CAUTION: If crankshaft is to be removed during overhaul it will be necessary to check and record crankshaft end-float prior to removing cylinder head.

1. Remove and discard camshaft timing belt.

CAUTION: Do not rotate crankshaft whilst timing belt is removed and cylinder head is fitted, pistons will contact the valves.

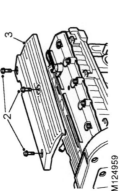

M124959

2. Noting that shortest screw is fitted in centre of spark plug cover, remove 3 screws securing cover to camshaft cover.
3. Remove spark plug cover.

If fitted

4. Disconnect ht lead and plug tube from No. 4 spark plug.
5. Remove 2 bolts securing front coil to camshaft cover.
6. Carefully raise coil until plug tube is disconnected from No. 1 spark plug. Disconnect multiplug from coil.
7. Disconnect ht lead and plug tube from No. 2 spark plug.
8. Remove 2 bolts securing rear coil to camshaft cover.
9. Carefully raise coil until plug tube is disconnected from No. 3 spark plug.
10. Disconnect multiplug from coil.
11. Release harness from clips.

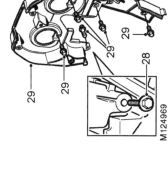

M124969

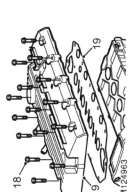

27   18G 1570   12-182

27   26

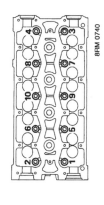

M12 4964A   24   24

◁ NOTE: Timing belt rear cover fitted to engine with 5 bolt front engine mounting illustrated.

28. Remove screw securing rear of timing belt rear cover to coolant pump.

◁ NOTE: This is the longest of the rear cover securing screws.

29. Remove screws securing timing belt rear cover, remove cover.

30. Remove timing belt tensioner pillar bolt.

31. Using assistance, remove cylinder head assembly from cylinder block.

⚠ **CAUTION: Cylinder head is dowel located, do not tap it sideways to free it from cylinder block. Place cylinder head assembly on blocks of wood to prevent damaging valves.**

32. Remove and discard cylinder head gasket.

22. Remove camshaft locking tool **18G 1570**.

23. Using tool **12-182**, rotate inlet and exhaust camshafts clockwise until reluctor rings clear bolt heads 7 and 8.

24. Progressively slacken cylinder head bolts 7 to 10.

25. Remove 10 cylinder head bolts and store in fitted order.

⚠ **CAUTION: Removal of cylinder head bolts results in a 'tightening-up' of crankshaft; rotation of crankshaft must, therefore, be kept to a minimum. Do not rotate crankshaft until cylinder liner retainer clamps 18G 1736 are fitted.**

26. Suitably identify each camshaft gear to its respective camshaft and using tool **12-182** to hold camshaft gear against rotation, remove bolt and plain washer from each camshaft gear.

27. Remove camshaft gears.

8RM 0740

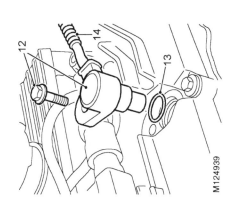

18   M124963   19   19

16   M12 4978

12. Remove bolt securing camshaft sensor to camshaft cover, withdraw sensor.

13. Remove and discard 'O' ring.

14. Release harness from clip.

15. Position harness aside.

M124939

All cylinder heads

17. Remove any debris from spark plug recesses, remove 4 spark plugs.

18. Progressively slacken then remove 15 bolts securing camshaft cover.

19. Remove camshaft cover, remove and discard gasket.

20. Check and record crankshaft end-float.

21. Using sequence shown, progressively slacken cylinder head bolts 1 to 6.

◁ NOTE: It will be necessary to carry out the following operations in order to remove the remaining bolts.

16. Remove 2 bolts securing multiplug bracket to camshaft carrier, remove bracket.

33. Assemble cylinder liner retainer clamps **18G 1736** to cylinder head bolts. Position retainer clamps on cylinder liners ensuring clamps do not protrude over liner bores. Screw cylinder head bolts into oil rail and tighten sufficiently to retain clamps.

⚠ **CAUTION: Ensure that bolts used are those originally fitted in that location.**

12M1770

Cylinder head - K16 VVC engines - remove

⚠ **CAUTION: If crankshaft is to be removed during overhaul it will be necessary to check and record crankshaft end-float prior to removing cylinder head.**

1. Remove and discard camshaft timing belt.

⚠ **CAUTION: Do not rotate crankshaft whilst timing belt is removed and cylinder head is fitted, pistons will contact the valves.**

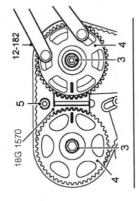

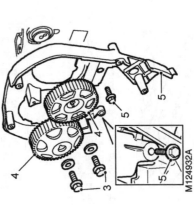

M124932A

2. Ensure that tool **18G 1570** is fitted to camshaft gears.

3. Suitably identify each camshaft gear to its respective camshaft and using tool **12-182** to restrain camshaft gears against rotation, remove bolt and plain washer securing each camshaft gear.

4. Remove tool **18G 1570**, remove camshaft gears.

5. Remove screws securing timing belt upper rear cover to cylinder head and rear of cover to coolant pump, remove cover.

▷ NOTE: This is the longest of the rear cover securing screws.

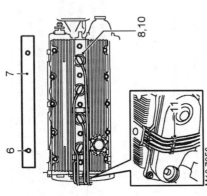

M12 7256

▷ NOTE: Camshaft cover fitted to early engines illustrated.

6. Remove 2 screws securing spark plug cover.

7. Remove spark plug cover.

8. Disconnect 4 plug tubes from spark plugs.

9. Remove any debris from spark plug recesses.

10. Remove and discard 4 spark plugs.

11. Release HT leads from camshaft rear belt cover.

Later engines

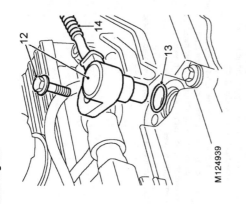

M124939

12. Remove bolt securing camshaft sensor, remove sensor.

13. Remove and discard 'O' ring.

14. Release harness from clip.

All engines

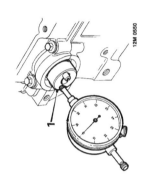

M12 6331

NOTE: Camshaft cover fitted to early engines illustrated.

15. Progressively slacken, then remove 15 bolts securing camshaft cover.

16. Remove camshaft cover, remove and discard gasket.

17. Check and record crankshaft end-float.

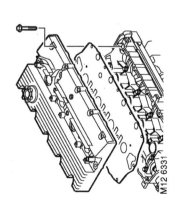

12M2034

18. Using sequence shown, progressively slacken then remove 10 cylinder head to oil rail bolts.

19. Remove bolts and store in fitted order.

⚠ **CAUTION: Removal of cylinder head bolts results in a 'tightening-up' of crankshaft; rotation of crankshaft must, therefore, be kept to a minimum. Do not rotate crankshaft until cylinder liner retainer clamps 18G 1736 are fitted.**

20. Using assistance, remove cylinder head assembly.

⚠ **CAUTION: Cylinder head is dowel located do not tap it sideways to free it from cylinder block. Place cylinder head on blocks of wood to prevent damaging valves.**

21. Remove and discard cylinder head gasket.

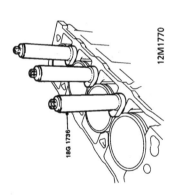

18G 1736

12M1770

22. Assemble cylinder retainer clamps **18G 1736** to cylinder head bolts. Position retainer clamps on cylinder liners ensuring that clamps do not protrude over liner bores. Screw cylinder head bolts into oil rail and tighten sufficiently to retain clamps.

⚠ **CAUTION: Ensure that bolts used are those originally fitted in that location.**

Camshafts - K8 and all K16 Non VVC engines - check end-float

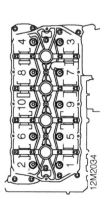

12M 0550

1. Check end-float of each camshaft using a DTI.
   Camshaft end-float = 0.06 to 0.19 mm
   Service limit = 0.3 mm

2. Renew components as necessary to achieve correct end-float.

Camshafts - K16 VVC engines - check end-float

Inlet camshafts

12M3493

1. Assemble a suitable DTI to camshaft carrier with stylus of gauge contacting face of front camshaft number 4 cam.

2. Move camshaft fully rearwards and zero gauge.

3. Move camshaft fully forwards and note end-float reading on gauge:
   Inlet camshaft end-float = 0.03 to 0.15 mm
   Service limit = 0.25 mm

4. Repeat above procedure for rear camshaft with stylus of gauge contacting face of number 5 cam.

5. Renew camshaft/VVC assemblies as necessary to achieve correct end-float.

ENGINE

Exhaust camshaft

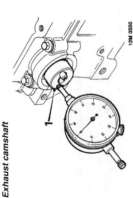

12M 0550

6. Check camshaft end-float using a DTI.
Exhaust camshaft end-float = 0.06 to 0.19 mm
Service limit = 0.3 mm

7. Renew components as necessary to achieve correct end-float.

Camshaft carrier and camshafts - K8 and all K16 Non VVC engines - remove

K8

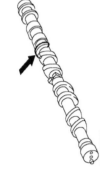

12M0578

1. Using sequence shown, progressively slacken 22 bolts securing camshaft carrier to cylinder head until valve spring pressure is released; remove bolts.

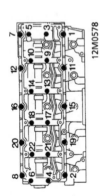

12M1994

2. Remove camshaft carrier.

▽ NOTE: Dowel located.

3. Remove camshaft.

4. Remove and discard camshaft oil seals.

5. Using a stick magnet, remove 8 tappets from cylinder head. Retain tappets in their fitted order and invert to prevent oil loss.

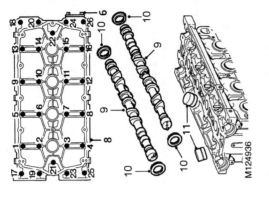

M124936

K16

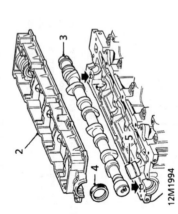

M124973

⚠ CAUTION: Camshafts fitted to later engines incorporate a reluctor ring, these camshafts are not interchangeable with those fitted to early engines. Commencing engine numbers for the modified camshafts are listed in Information.

▽ NOTE: Camshafts incorporating a reluctor ring illustrated.

6. Remove 2 bolts securing blanking plate to rear of camshaft carrier, remove plate.

▽ NOTE: On engines fitted with plug coil ignition, blanking plates are fitted for both inlet and exhaust camshafts.

7. Using sequence shown, progressively slacken 26 bolts until valve spring pressure is released. Remove bolts.

8. Remove camshaft carrier.

▽ NOTE: Dowel located.

9. Suitably identify each camshaft to its fitted position, remove camshafts.

10. Remove and discard oil seals from camshafts.

11. Using a stick magnet, remove 16 tappets from cylinder head. Retain tappets in fitted order and invert to prevent oil loss.

Camshaft carrier and camshafts - K16 VVC engines - remove

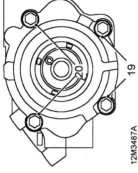

12M3481

1. Remove 4 bolts securing camshaft rear belt cover, remove cover.

 NOTE: With timing marks in this position, the lobes of numbers 3, 4, 5 and 6 cams on the inlet camshafts should be facing upwards.

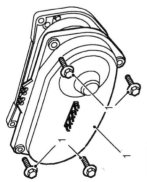

12M3482A

2. Using tool **12-182**, rotate inlet camshaft rear timing gear until timing marks on both rear gears are facing outwards.

3. Suitably identify each rear camshaft gear to its respective camshaft.

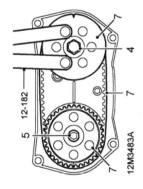

12M3483A

4. Using tool **12-182**, restrain rear inlet camshaft timing gear and remove bolt and washer retaining gear.

5. Repeat above procedure for exhaust camshaft rear timing gear.

6. Remove tool **12-182** from gear.

7. Remove both rear timing gears from camshafts, remove and discard rear timing belt.

 CAUTION: Rear timing belt must always be replaced during engine overhaul. Do not rotate crankshaft with front timing belt removed and cylinder head fitted.

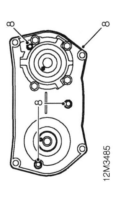

12M3485

8. Remove bolts securing camshaft rear timing belt backplate.

9. Remove rear timing belt backplate.

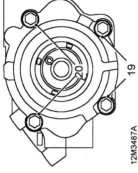

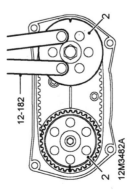

12M3487A

19. Remove and discard 2 bolts securing each VVC housing to cylinder head.

20. Slacken 2 bolts securing each VVC housing to camshaft carrier by 1 turn.

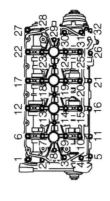 CAUTION: Do not exceed 1 turn.

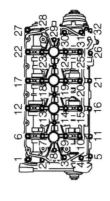

12M3488

21. Using sequence shown, progressively slacken and noting the position of 4 longest bolts, remove 32 bolts securing camshaft carrier to cylinder head.

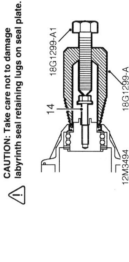

12M3486A

10. Remove oil temperature transmitter, from hydraulic control unit, remove and discard sealing washer.

11. Remove 3 bolts securing hydraulic control unit to camshaft carrier.

12. Withdraw hydraulic control unit, remove seal plate.

13. Remove and discard 2 labyrinth seals and rack seal from seal plate.

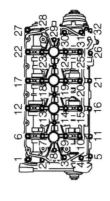 CAUTION: Take care not to damage labyrinth seal retaining lugs on seal plate.

12M3494

18G1299-A1

18G1299-A

14. Fit camshaft gear bolt to front VVC mechanism.

15. Screw tool **18G 1299A** and **18G 1299A-1** into oil seal.

16. Remove VVC housing oil seal by tightening centre bolt of tool, discard oil seal.

17. Remove camshaft gear bolt.

18. Repeat above procedures for rear VVC housing oil seal.

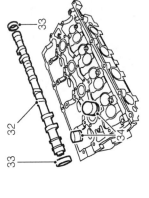

12M3489

CAUTION: During the following operations, it is essential to ensure that front and rear inlet camshafts are retained in their respective VVC assemblies. If camshafts are removed from their VVC assemblies, then complete assembly must be replaced; it is not permissible to refit camshafts to VVC assemblies.

22. Ensuring that front and rear inlet camshafts are retained in camshaft carrier and VVC assemblies, carefully release camshaft carrier from cylinder head.

◁ NOTE: Dowel located.

23. Lift camshaft carrier together with front and rear inlet camshafts off cylinder head.

CAUTION: Ensure that exhaust camshaft is retained in cylinder head as camshaft carrier is removed.

24. Ensuring that front and rear inlet camshafts are retained in camshaft carrier, invert carrier.

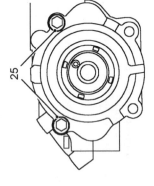

12M3526A

25. Slacken but do not remove 2 bolts securing each VVC housing to camshaft carrier.

◁ NOTE: Bolts should only be slackened sufficiently to enable timing plates 18G 1770/1 and 18G 1770/2 to be fitted.

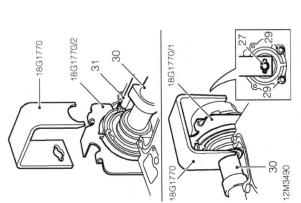

12M3490

26. Fit timing plates **18G 1770/1** to front and **18G 1770/2** to rear VVC assemblies.

27. Assemble clamps **18G 1770** to front and rear inlet camshafts and VVC assemblies, fit camshaft gear bolts and washers to retain clamps.

28. Suitably identify each VVC assembly to its fitted position. Do not attempt to interchange front and rear assemblies.

29. Remove and discard 2 bolts securing each VVC housing to camshaft carrier.

30. Remove front and rear camshafts together with VVC assemblies.

CAUTION: Do not remove clamps 18G 1770.

31. Remove control shaft from camshaft carrier.

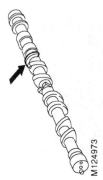

12M3521

32. Remove exhaust camshaft from cylinder head.

M124973

CAUTION: In order to commonise exhaust camshafts between VVC and non VVC engines, modified exhaust camshafts incorporating a reluctor ring are fitted to later engines, these camshafts are not interchangeable with those fitted to early engines. Commencing engine numbers for the modified camshafts are listed in Information.

33. Remove and discard exhaust camshaft oil seals.

34. Using a stick magnet, remove 16 tappets from cylinder head. Retain tappets in their fitted order and invert to prevent oil loss.

Tappets - inspection

1. Check tappets for signs of wear, scoring and overheating.
2. Measure outside diameter of tappet, measurement must be taken half-way along tappet body.
   Tappet outside dia. = 32.959 to 32.975 mm.
3. Ensure oil hole in each tappet is clear.

NOTE: Retain tappets in their fitted order and keep them inverted to prevent oil loss.

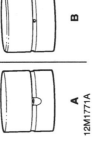

A

B

12M1771A

Non VVC engines

CAUTION: A modified tappet has been introduced and will be supplied as a replacement for all non VVC engines. The above illustration show the early tappet A and modified tappet B. When the modified tappets are already fitted to an engine, they may be replaced on an individual basis but may only be fitted as replacements for early tappets in cylinder sets.

VVC engines

CAUTION: Tappets fitted to VVC engines are lighter than those fitted to non VVC engines and whilst similar in appearance to the early tappets A illustrated above, it is essential that early tappets are not fitted to VVC engines. To ensure that correct replacement tappet is fitted, measure overall length of tappet:

Early tappet - Non VVC engines = 26.0 mm
Later tappet - VVC engines = 24.5 mm

Camshafts and timing gears - K8 and all K16 Non VVC engines - inspection

Camshafts

NOTE: Carry out camshaft inspection after removal of valves.

1. Clean camshaft(s), camshaft carrier and cylinder head bearing surfaces, use suitable solvent to remove sealant.
2. Inspect cams and bearing journals for wear, pitting and scoring; replace components as necessary.

12M0547

Checking camshaft bearing clearance - Non VVC engines

K8

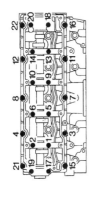

12M0563

K16

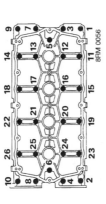

8RM 0056

3. Position camshaft(s) in cylinder head and place Plastigage across each journal.
4. Fit camshaft carrier and tighten bolts in sequence shown to 10 Nm. Do not rotate camshaft(s).
5. Progressively slacken bolts and then remove camshaft carrier.

6. Measure widest portion of Plastigage on each journal:
   Camshaft bearing clearance = 0.060 to 0.094 mm
   Service limit = 0.15 mm
   If clearance is excessive, fit new camshaft(s) and repeat check. If clearances are still excessive, replace cylinder head and camshaft carrier assembly.

CAUTION: If replacement camshafts are to be fitted, ensure they are correct for engine being worked on.

7

8RM 3526

7. Remove drive pin from old camshaft and fit to new with its split towards centre of camshaft.
8. Remove all traces of Plastigage using an oily rag.

ENGINE

Timing gears - Non VVC engines

1. Clean timing gears, check gear teeth for damage and drive pin slot for wear, replace gears as necessary.

⚠ **CAUTION: If gears have been subjected to prolonged exposure to oil contamination, they must be soaked in a solvent bath and then thoroughly washed in clean solvent.**

Camshafts and timing gears - K16 VVC engines - inspection

Camshafts

⚠ NOTE: Carry out camshaft inspection after removal of valves.

1. Clean camshaft carrier and cylinder head bearing surfaces, use suitable solvent to remove sealant.

⚠ **CAUTION: Do not remove clamps 18G 1770 whilst cleaning or inspecting inlet camshafts.**

2. Inspect cams and bearing journals for wear, pitting and scoring, replace components as necessary.

⚠ NOTE: Inlet camshafts and VVC mechanisms will only be supplied as an assembly.

Checking camshaft bearing clearance - VVC engines

1. Position exhaust camshaft in cylinder head and place a strip of Plastigage across each camshaft journal.

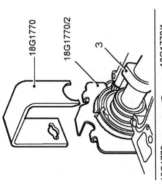

18G1770

18G1770/2

3

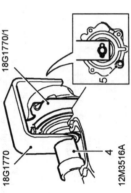

18G1770

18G1770/1

4

5

12M3516A

2. Rotate front and rear VVC control sleeves until timing plates **18G 1770/1** - front and **18G 1770/2** - rear can be inserted through the housing and into the control sleeve slot.

⚠ **CAUTION: Do not remove clamps at this stage, reposition clamps as necessary to enable timing plates to be fitted.**

3. Place a strip of Plastigage across each inlet camshaft journal on camshaft carrier and position front inlet camshaft and VVC housing in camshaft carrier.

4. Position rear inlet camshaft and VVC housing in camshaft carrier.

5. Fit and lightly tighten a slave M6 bolt to retain front and rear VVC housings to camshaft carrier.

6. Remove clamps **18G 1770**.

⚠ **CAUTION: During the following operations it is essential to ensure that front and rear inlet camshafts are retained in their respective VVC assemblies and the camshaft carrier.**

7. Invert camshaft carrier and fit to cylinder head.

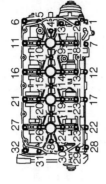

12M3503

8. Fit 32 bolts noting that 4 longest bolts are fitted at each end of camshaft carrier.

9. Using sequence shown, progressively tighten bolts 10 Nm.

⚠ **CAUTION: Do not rotate camshafts.**

10. Progressively slacken then remove 32 bolts securing camshaft carrier to cylinder head.

11. Carefully release camshaft carrier from cylinder head.

12. Lift camshaft carrier together with front and rear inlet camshafts off cylinder head.

⚠ **CAUTION: Ensure that exhaust camshaft is retained in cylinder head.**

13. Invert camshaft carrier.

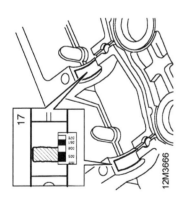

18G1770

18G1770/2

16

18G1770

18G1770/1

14

15

16

12M3518A

14. Assemble clamps **18G 1770** to front and rear inlet camshafts and VVC assemblies, fit camshaft gear bolts and washers to retain clamps.

15. Remove slave bolts securing VVC housings to camshaft carrier.

16. Remove front and rear inlet camshafts and VVC housings from camshaft carrier.

CAUTION: If new VVC housing gaskets have been fitted do not remove timing plates 18G 1770/1 and 18G 1770/2.

17

12M3666

17. Measure widest portion of Plastigage on each inlet camshaft journal on camshaft carrier:
Inlet camshaft bearing journal clearances:
25 mm diameter journals = 0.025 to 0.060 mm
Service limit = 0.1 mm
40 mm diameter journals = 0.030 to 0.070 mm
Service limit = 0.1 mm

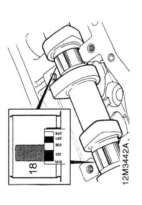

18

12M3442A.

18. Measure widest portion of Plastigage on each exhaust camshaft journal:
Exhaust camshaft bearing clearance = 0.060 to 0.094 mm
Service limit = 0.15 mm

19. If bearing clearances on any camshaft are excessive, fit new exhaust camshaft or inlet camshafts and VVC assemblies and repeat check. If clearances are still excessive, replace cylinder head and camshaft carrier assembly.

CAUTION: If replacement exhaust camshaft is to be fitted, ensure it is correct for engine being worked on.

NOTE: Inlet camshafts are only supplied with VVC mechanisms as an assembly.

20. Remove exhaust camshaft from cylinder head.

21. Remove all traces of Plastigage using an oily rag.

Timing gears - VVC engines

CAUTION: If gears have been subjected to prolonged exposure to oil contamination, they must be soaked in a solvent bath and then thoroughly washed in clean solvent.

Ensure reference marks are not erased.

1. Clean timing gears, check gear teeth for damage and drive pin slot for wear, replace gears as necessary.

Valves and springs - remove

1. Support cylinder head clear of valves; use hollow drift and tap each spring cap to free collets.
2. Position cylinder head on its exhaust manifold face.

◁ NOTE: K16 engine: Remove inlet valves with cylinder head in this position.

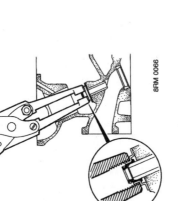

18G 1519/1 18G 1519 8RM 0075

◁ NOTE: K16 Non VVC cylinder head illustrated.

3. Using tool 18G 1519 and adapter 18G 1519/1, compress valve spring.
4. Remove 2 collets from valve stem using a magnet.
5. Remove tool 18G 1519.

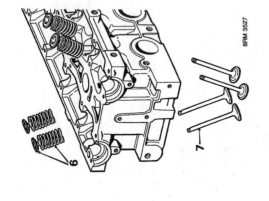

8RM 3527

◁ NOTE: K16 Non VVC cylinder head illustrated.

6. Remove spring cap and valve spring.
7. Remove valve.

Cylinder head - cleaning

1. Clean sealing surfaces on cylinder head and camshaft carrier.
   Use foam action gasket remover and a plastic scraper - DO NOT USE A METAL SCRAPER ON SEALING SURFACES.
   Clean inlet and exhaust manifold joint faces.
2. De-carbonise combustion areas of cylinder head and valves as necessary.
3. Blow out oilways and waterways, ensure oil feed to camshaft carrier is clear.

◁ NOTE: Cylinder heads fitted to later engines have a 4.5 mm diameter oil drain hole drilled through the head from the camshaft oil seal recess; ensure drilling is clear.

4. K8 engine: Check fuel pump blanking plate - if fitted for signs of oil leakage. Replace gasket if necessary, tighten blanking plate nuts to 25 Nm.

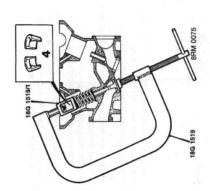

18G 1577 8RM 0066

8. Using 18G 1577, remove and discard valve stem seal.
9. K8: Repeat above operations to remove all remaining valves.
   K16: Repeat above operations to remove remaining inlet valves.

⚠ CAUTION: Retain valves and springs in fitted order.

K16

10. Position cylinder head on its inlet manifold face.
11. Repeat above operations to remove exhaust valves and valve stem seals.

⚠ CAUTION: Retain valves and springs in fitted order.

Cylinder head - inspection

1. Check cylinder head for damage, pay particular attention to gasket face of cylinder head.

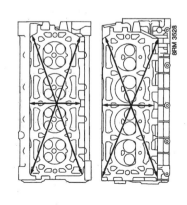

8RM 3528

2. Check cylinder head face for warping, across centre and from corner to corner:
Cylinder head:
Maximum warp = 0.05 mm
3. Check cylinder head height:
New = 118.95 to 119.05 mm.

Cylinder heads may be refaced:
Reface limit = 0.20 mm

⚠ CAUTION: Cylinder heads fitted to K16 engines with automatic timing belt tensioners are not interchangeable with those fitted to engines with manual tensioners.

Valve springs - inspection

1. Check condition of valve springs:

⚠ NOTE: Valve springs are either colour coded or plain:

K8 - Yellow/red
K16 - Non VVC engines - Plain
K16 - VVC engines - Blue

K8

Free length = 46.2 mm
Fitted length = 37.0 mm
Load - valve closed = 255 ± 12 N
Load - valve open = 535 ± 20 N

K16 - Non VVC engines

Free length = 50.0 mm
Fitted length = 37.0 mm
Load - valve closed = 250 ± 12 N
Load - valve open = 450 ± 18 N

K16 - VVC engines

Free length = 47.6 mm
Fitted length = 37.0 mm
Load - valve closed = 210 ± 13 N
Load - valve open = 440 ± 22 N

Valves and guides - inspection

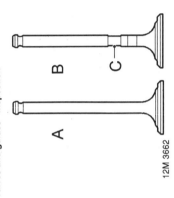

A B C

12M 3662

⚠ NOTE: Two types of exhaust valve may be fitted, standard valves, A in illustration or carbon break valves, B in illustration.
Carbon break valves may be identified by the machined profile C on the valve stem. To prevent exhaust valves from sticking, standard valves should be replaced with carbon break valves during engine overhaul.

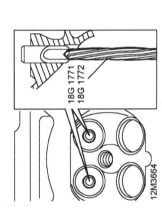

12M3663

3. Check existing valve stem diameters A, replace any valve if stem diameter is less than specified.
4. Check inlet and exhaust valve to guide clearances C using the following procedures:
5. Insert valve into its respective guide.
6. Extend valve head 10 mm out of valve guide and position suitable DTI gauge to rear of valve head.
7. Move valve towards front of cylinder head, pre-load gauge to valve head then zero gauge.
8. Move valve towards rear of cylinder head, record reading obtained to give valve stem to guide clearance B.
9. Repeat above procedures for each valve in turn.

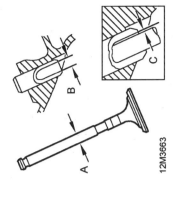

18G 1771
18G 1772

12M3664

1. Remove carbon deposits from exhaust valve guides using tool:
K8 - 18G 1772
K16 - 18G 1771

⚠ CAUTION: Tool must be inserted into valve guide from combustion face side of cylinder head.

2. Remove carbon from inlet valve guides, inlet and exhaust valves and valve seat inserts. Remove all loose particles of carbon on completion.

K8

Valve stem diameter **A:**
Inlet = 6.960 to 6.975 mm
Exhaust = 6.952 to 6.967 mm
Valve guides:
Inside diameter **B:**= 7.000 to 7.025 mm
Valve stem to guide clearance **C:**
Inlet = 0.025 to 0.065 mm
Exhaust = 0.033 to 0.073 mm
Service limit = 0.07 mm
Service limit = 0.11 mm

K16

Valve stem diameter **A:**
Inlet = 5.952 to 5.967 mm
Exhaust = 5.947 to 5.962 mm
Valve guides:
Inside diameter **B:**= 6.000 to 6.025 mm
Valve stem to guide clearance **C:**
Inlet = 0.033 to 0.063 mm
Service limit = 0.07 mm
Exhaust = 0.038 to 0.078 mm
Service limit = 0.11 mm

10. Renew valves and guides as necessary.

Valve guides - renew

1. Support cylinder head face down on wooden blocks.

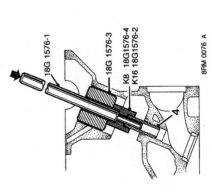

8RM 0077 A

2. Position tool guide **18G 1576-3** in tappet bore and drift out valve guide using tool drift **18G 1576-1**.

   NOTE: Retain valve guides in their fitted order.

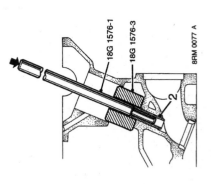

12M0007

3. Identify type of valve guide fitted:-
   A - Standard production
   C - Production oversize

   NOTE: Two replacement sizes of valve guide are available, sizes B and D. replace original guide A with B and original guide C with D.

Valve seat inserts - renew

CAUTION: Triple angle valve seat inserts have been introduced on later K16 engines; these inserts are not interchangeable with those fitted to early engines. Commencing engine numbers for engines fitted with the new inserts are listed in Information.

1. Renew valve seat inserts as necessary.

CAUTION: Do not damage counterbore when removing insert.

2. Cool replacement valve seat inserts using liquid nitrogen and press into cylinder head in one continuous operation.

CAUTION: Do not heat cylinder head.

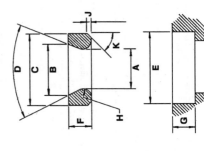

8RM 1102A

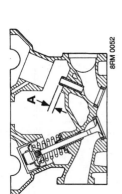

8RM 0076 A

NOTE: Cylinder head and valve guides must be at room temperature when fitting guides.

4. Locate valve guide in valve guide bore with identification groove(s) towards valve seat; position depth gauge:-
   K8 - Use depth gauge **18G 1576-4**.
   K16 - Use depth gauge **18G 1576-2**.

5. Position nylon guide **18G 1576-3** in cylinder head, press guide into bore using driver **18G 1576-1** until depth gauge contacts top of valve guide bore.

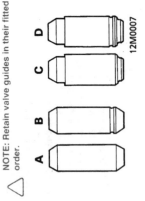

8RM 0052

6. Check fitted height **A** of valve guide:-
   K8 = 10.3 mm
   K16 = 6.0 mm

K8 - See illustration 8RM 1102A

Inlet
A:= 29.42 to 29.57 mm
B:= 31.61 to 31.91 mm
C:= 35.594 to 35.614 mm
D:= 35°
E:= 35.500 to 35.525 mm
F:= 5.45 to 5.50 mm
G:= 5.95 to 6.05 mm
H:= 2.0 mm radius
J:= 0.75 to 1.25 mm
K:= 45° **Exhaust**
A:= 26.92 to 27.07 mm
B:= 28.73 to 29.03 mm
C:= 33.06 to 33.08 mm
D:= 26°
E:= 33.000 to 33.025 mm
F:= 5.45 to 5.50 mm
G:= 5.95 to 6.05 mm
H:= 2.0 mm radius
J:= 0.75 to 1.25 mm
K:= 45°

K16 - Non VVC engines - not triple angle valve seats - See illustration 8RM 1102A

Inlet
A:= 22.98 to 23.13 mm
B:= 25.73 to 25.98 mm
C:= 29.560 to 29.573 mm
D:= 38°
E:= 29.475 to 29.500 mm
F:= 5.95 to 6.00 mm
G:= 6.53 to 6.69 mm
H:= 2.0 mm radius
J:= 0.75 to 1.25 mm
K:= 45°

Exhaust
A:= 19.58 to 19.73 mm
B:= 21.60 to 21.90 mm
C:= 25.960 to 25.973 mm
D:= 30°
E:= 25.888 to 25.913 mm
F:= 5.45 to 5.50 mm
G:= 5.75 to 6.41 mm
H:= 2.0 mm radius
J:= 0.75 to 1.25 mm
K:= 45°

K16 - VVC engines - not triple angle valve seats - See illustration 8RM 1102A

Inlet
A:= 27.38 to 27.62 mm
B:= 29.40 to 29.80 mm
C:= 32.56 to 32.57 mm
D:= 18 to 20°
E:= 32.475 to 32.500 mm
F:= 5.95 to 6.00 mm
G:= 6.46 to 6.62 mm
H:= 7.00 mm radius
J:= 0.74 to 1.25 mm
K:= 44 to 46°

Exhaust
A:= 23.68 to 23.93 mm
B:= 24.80 to 25.20 mm
C:= 28.99 to 29.00 mm
D:= 11 to 13°
E:= 28.88 to 28.91 mm
F:= 5.45 to 5.50 mm
G:= 6.00 to 6.16 mm
H:= 6.0 mm radius
J:= 0.75 to 1.25 mm
K:= 44 to 46°

K16 - Non VVC engines fitted with triple angle valve seats - See illustration M12 5536

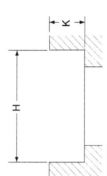

M12 5536

Inlet
A:= 15°
B:= 45°
C:= 60°
D:= 0.4 mm radius
E:= 29.560 to 29.573 mm
F:= 1.0 to 1.4 mm
G:= 26.43 mm
H:= 29.475 to 29.500 mm
J:= 5.95 to 6.00 mm
K:= 6.16 to 6.32 mm

Exhaust
A:= 15°
B:= 45°
C:= 60°
D:= 0.4 mm radius
E:= 25.960 to 25.973 mm
F:= 1.4 to 1.8 mm
G:= 22.83 mm
H:= 25.913 to 25.888 mm
J:= 5.45 to 5.80 mm
K:= 5.7 to 5.86 mm

K16 - VVC engines fitted with triple angle valve seats - See illustration M12 5536

Inlet
A:= 15°
B:= 45°
C:= 60°
D:= 0.4 mm radius
E:= 32.560 to 32.573 mm
F:= 1.0 to 1.4 mm
G:= 30.2 mm
H:= 32.475 to 32.500 mm
J:= 5.95 to 6.00 mm
K:= 6.1 mm

Exhaust
A:= 15°
B:= 45°
C:= 60°
D:= 0.4 mm radius
E:= 28.993 to 29.006 mm
F:= 1.4 to 1.8 mm
G:= 26.23 mm
H:= 28.888 to 28.913 mm
J:= 5.45 to 5.50 mm
K:= 6.54 mm

All engines

1. Cut valve seat to correct angle and width.
2. Lap valve to seat.

Valve seats - refacing

> CAUTION: Renew worn valve guides before refacing valves and seats.

1. Check condition of valve seats and existing valves that are to be re-used.

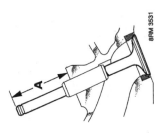

8RM 3530B

> NOTE: Triple angle valve seat illustrated

2. Recut valve seats and use pilot **MS120-6** and the following cutters:-
MS76-120 - 15° - Triple angle valve seats only.
MS76-111 60° - To narrow valve seats and obtain seat widths.
MS76-122 45° - Make final cut and remove any burrs.

Valve seat:
Angle = 45°
Width A =
Except triple angle valve seats:
Inlet - 1.5 mm
Exhaust - 1.5 mm
Triple angle valve seats:-
Inlet - 1.0 to 1.4 mm
Exhaust 1.4 to 1.8 mm

Valve face angle B:
Inlet = 45°
Exhaust = 45°

> CAUTION: Inserts must not stand proud of combustion face of head on completion of recutting operation.

3. Lap each valve to seat using fine grinding paste.
4. Apply Prussian Blue to valve seat, insert valve and press it into position several times without rotating. Remove and check valve for even and central seating:
Seating position shown by blue should be in centre of valve face.

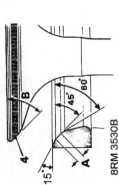

8RM 3531

5. Check valve stem fitted height A:

K8:

New = 38.95 to 40.81 mm
Service limit = 41.06 mm

K16:

New = 38.93 to 39.84 mm
Service limit = 40.10 mm

If valve stem fitted height is above service limit, fit new valve and re-check, if still over limit, renew valve seat insert.

All engines

6. Remove all traces of grinding paste on completion.

K16 VVC housing gaskets - remove

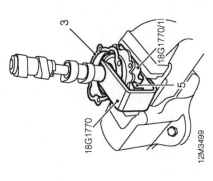

18G1770/1

12M3498

1. Secure VVC housing and camshaft in a soft-jawed vice with camshaft positioned upwards.

> CAUTION: Only tighten vice sufficiently to retain housing, damage to mechanism will result if vice is overtightened.

2. Taking care not to allow camshaft to become separated from VVC mechanism, remove clamp **18G 1770** and timing plate **18G 1770/1** - front or **18G 1770/2** - rear.

3. Remove and discard VVC housing gasket.

4. Repeat above procedures for remaining VVC housing gasket.

K16 VVC housing gaskets - refit

> NOTE: To assist correct location of VVC housing gasket in its fitted position, apply a light film of grease to gasket face of VVC housing.

1. Lubricate sealing ring of new gasket with engine oil.

18G1770/1

18G1770

12M3499

2. Fit timing plate **18G 1770/1** - front or **18G 1770/2** - rear.
3. Fit gasket, align bolt holes.
4. Assemble clamp **18G 1770** to camshaft and VVC assembly, fit camshaft gear bolt and washer to retain clamp.
5. Remove VVC housing and camshaft from vice.
6. Repeat above procedures for remaining VVC housing gasket.

Hydraulic control unit - K16 VVC engines - dismantling

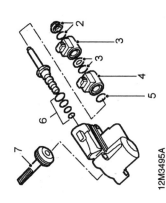

12M3495A

1. Suitably identify each solenoid to its fitted position and note the angle at which it is positioned relative to the hydraulic control unit.
2. Remove nut from sleeve bolt, remove and discard 'O' ring.
3. Remove outer solenoid, washer and 'O' rings; discard 'O' rings.
4. Remove inner solenoid.
5. Remove spool valve, remove and discard 'O' ring from spool valve nut.
6. Remove and discard 4 'O' rings from spool valve.
7. Withdraw piston and rack assembly.

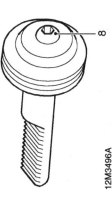

12M3496A

8. Remove and discard screw securing piston to rack, remove and discard piston and seal assembly.

Hydraulic control unit - K16 VVC engines - Inspection

1. Check piston and spool valve bores in hydraulic control unit for scoring and corrosion, replace control unit if scoring is evident.
2. Check piston for scoring.

> NOTE: Light scoring and corrosion may be removed using grade 600 grade wet or dry paper which has been soaked in engine oil for 30 minutes.

3. Check rack teeth for signs of wear or damage, replace hydraulic control unit if either are evident.
4. Check control shaft teeth for signs of wear or damage, replace control shaft if either are evident.
5. Check that oil passages in spool valve are clear.

Hydraulic control unit - K16 VVC engines - assembling

> CAUTION: It is essential to ensure that absolute cleanliness is maintained during the following operations.

1. Thoroughly clean all components, dry with compressed air.
2. Lubricate new labyrinth seals and rack seal with engine oil.

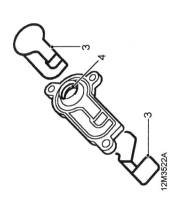

12M3522A

3. Using the fingers only, fit labyrinth seals each side of hydraulic control unit seal plate.

> CAUTION: Ensure seals are located beneath retaining lugs.

4. Fit new rack seal to plate.

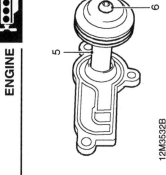

12M3532B

5. Slide piston end of rack through seal.

> CAUTION: Only insert rack through seal for a sufficient distance to enable piston to be fitted and take great care that teeth of rack do not contact seal.

6. Secure rack in a soft-jawed vice, fit new piston and seal assembly to rack, fit and tighten new screw supplied with seal kit to 9 Nm.
7. Lubricate piston bore with engine oil.
8. Position seal plate, piston and rack assembly to hydraulic control unit with rack teeth facing towards fixing hole adjacent to solenoid side of unit.

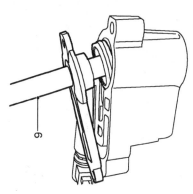

12M3658A

9. Insert piston and rack assembly into bore of housing at an angle as shown, taking care not to damage piston seal on machined edge of oil feed channel. Push piston to top of bore.

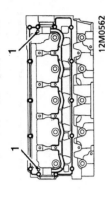

M12 7254

10. Lubricate 3 new 'O' rings with engine oil and fit to spool valve.
11. Lubricate new 'O' rings with engine oil and fit to each side of spool valve, nut, washer, inner solenoid and sleeve bolt side of outer solenoid.
12. Lubricate spool valve and bore in control unit with engine oil.
13. Position spool valve to control unit, fit valve, twisting it slightly as it is inserted to avoid damaging 'O' rings.
14. Tighten spool valve nut to 26 Nm.
15. Position inner solenoid on spool valve ensuring that lettering on end of solenoid is facing away from control unit.
16. Fit washer and 'O' ring.
17. Position outer solenoid on spool valve ensuring that lettering on end of solenoid is facing away from control unit.
18. Position inner and outer solenoids as shown, fit nut to sleeve bolt and tighten to 12 Nm.

⚠ CAUTION: Do not exceed specified torque figure.

19. Retain oil temperature transmitter with control unit, plug oil temperature transmitter port to prevent ingress of dirt.

Valves - assembling

1. Using 18G 1577, fit new valve stem oil seals.
2. Lubricate valve stems and assemble valves, using tool 18G 1519 and adapter 18G 1519/1, to compress valve spring.

⚠ CAUTION: Valve springs are either colour coded or plain, ensure correct springs are fitted:

K8 - Yellow/red
K16 - Non VVC engines - Plain
K16 - VVC engines - Blue

3. Use a wooden dowel and mallet, lightly tap top of each valve assembly two or three times to seat valves and collets.
4. Lubricate outside of tappets and fit tappets in original bores.

Camshafts - K8 and all K16 Non VVC engines - refit

K8

K16

8RM 3532

1. Lubricate bearings and fit camshaft(s) and position drive pin for 90° BTDC as follows:
   K8: Pin at 4 o'clock.
   K16: Inlet pin at 4 o'clock.
   Exhaust pin at 8 o'clock.

Camshaft carrier and oil seal - K8 engines - refit

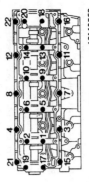

12M0562

1. Ensure 2 locating dowels are fitted in camshaft carrier.
2. Apply continuous, thin beads of sealant, Part Number GUG 705963GM to paths on camshaft carrier as shown and spread to an even film using a roller.

⚠ CAUTION: Ensure sealant does not enter lubrication grooves on camshaft carrier and that assembly is completed within 20 minutes.

3. Lubricate camshaft cams and journals with engine oil.

12M0563

4. Fit camshaft carrier, fit and lightly tighten bolts using sequence shown.
5. Tighten all bolts in sequence shown to 10 Nm.

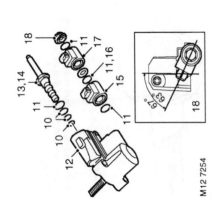

Camshaft carrier and camshafts - K16 VVC engines - refit

1. Ensure 2 locating dowels are fitted in camshaft carrier.
2. Fit new VVC housing gaskets.

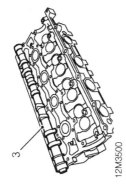

12M3500

3. Lubricate exhaust camshaft cams and journals with engine oil, position camshaft in cylinder head.
4. Lubricate cams and journal of front and rear inlet camshafts with engine oil.
5. Lubricate control shaft with engine oil.

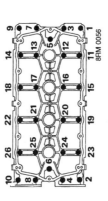

18G 1749
18G 1769A
18G 1769A
18G 1749

M12 6145

◁ NOTE: Camshaft front oil seal illustrated.

5. Position oil seal protector **18G 1749** over end of camshaft
6. Fit new camshaft oil seals using tool **18G 1769A**.

◁ NOTE: Front oil seals are coloured BLACK, rear oil seals are coloured RED.

⚠ CAUTION: Oil seals must be fitted dry. Do not use tool 18G 1769 for fitting seals as they will not be positioned correctly within recess.

7. Fit blanking plate(s), fit and tighten bolts to:
   Inlet camshaft plate - Plug top coil ignition engines only - 6 Nm.
   Exhaust camshaft plate - All engines - 25 Nm.

Camshaft carrier and oil seals - All K16 Non VVC engines - refit

1. Ensure 2 locating dowels are fitted in camshaft carrier.

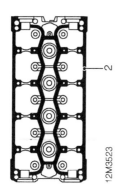

2

12M3523

2. Apply continuous, thin beads of sealant, Part Number GUG 705963GM to paths on cylinder head as shown then spread to an even film using a roller.

⚠ CAUTION: Ensure sealant is kept clear of tappet oil feed holes and lubrication grooves in carrier and that assembly is completed within 20 minutes.

3. Lubricate camshaft cams and journals with engine oil.

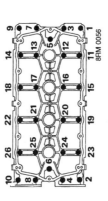

9	7	3	1
14	13	5	12	11
18	17		16	15
22	21		20	19
26	25	6	24	23
10	8		4	2

8RM 0056

4. Fit camshaft carrier, fit and progressively tighten bolts, in sequence shown, to 10 Nm.

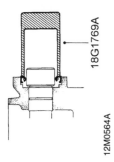

18G1769A

12M0564A

◁ NOTE: Camshaft front oil seal illustrated.

6. Fit oil seal protector **18G 1749** over end of camshaft.
7. Fit new camshaft oil seals using tool **18G 1769A**.

◁ NOTE: Front oil seals are coloured BLACK, rear oil seals are coloured RED.

⚠ CAUTION: Oil seals must be fitted dry. Do not use tool 18G 1769 for fitting seals as they will not be positioned correctly within recess.

18G1770 18G1770/1

18G1770/2 18G1770

12M3501

6. Position control shaft in camshaft carrier ensuring that shaft is fully seated journals and and centre of slot in shaft is aligned with cylinder head mating surface of carrier.

7. Position front and rear inlet camshafts and VVC assemblies in camshaft carrier at the same time engaging teeth of control shaft in VVC assemblies.

8. Check that bolt holes in VVC housings are aligned with bolt holes in camshaft carrier, that centre of slot in control shaft is still aligned with cylinder head mating surface of carrier and timing plates **18G 1770/1** - front and **18G 1770/2** - rear are correctly located in the control sleeves and control shaft is still seated in journals.

⚠ **CAUTION: If bolt holes are not correctly aligned or slot in control shaft has moved, re-position VVC assemblies and shaft as necessary until alignment is correct.**

9. Fit and finger tighten slave bolts - front and rear VVC assemblies to camshaft carrier.

▷ NOTE: Slave bolts must be replaced with new Patchlok bolts when camshaft carrier is fitted.

10. Remove clamps **18G 1770**.

⚠ **CAUTION: Do not remove timing plates at this stage or damage to VVC housing seals will result.**

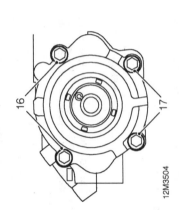

M124948

11. Apply continuous, thin beads of sealant, Part Number GUG 705963GM to paths on cylinder head as shown then spread to an even film using a roller.

⚠ **CAUTION: Ensure that sealant is kept clear of oil feed holes, oil grooves and control shaft journals and that assembly is completed within 20 minutes.**
During the following operations it is essential to ensure that front and rear inlet camshafts are retained in the camshaft carrier and their respective VVC assemblies. Take great care not to rotate camshafts or control shaft.

12. Invert camshaft carrier and fit to cylinder head.

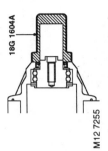

18G 1769A
18G 1749
M12 6145

▷ NOTE: Camshaft front oil seal illustrated.

18. Position oil seal protector **18G 1749** over end of camshaft and fit new exhaust camshaft front and rear oil seals using tool **18G 1769A**.

▷ NOTE: Front oil seals are coloured BLACK, rear oil seals are coloured RED.

⚠ **CAUTION: Oil seals must be fitted dry. Do not use tool 18G 1769 for fitting seals as they will not be positioned correctly within recess.**

18G 1604A

M12 7255

12M3503

13. Fit 32 bolts noting that 4 longest bolts are fitted at each end of camshaft carrier.

14. Using sequence shown, progressively tighten bolts to 10 Nm.

15. Remove timing plates **18G 1770/1** - front and **18G 1770/2** - rear.

12M3504

16. Fit and tighten new bolts - front and rear VVC housings to camshaft carrier to 10 Nm.

17. Fit and tighten new bolts - VVC housings to cylinder head to 10 Nm.

19. Fit new front and rear VVC housing oil seals using tool **18G 1604A**.

▷ NOTE: Front oil seals are coloured BLACK, rear oil seals are coloured RED.

⚠ **CAUTION: Oil seals must be fitted dry. Do not use tool 18G 1604 for fitting seals as they will not be positioned correctly within recess.**

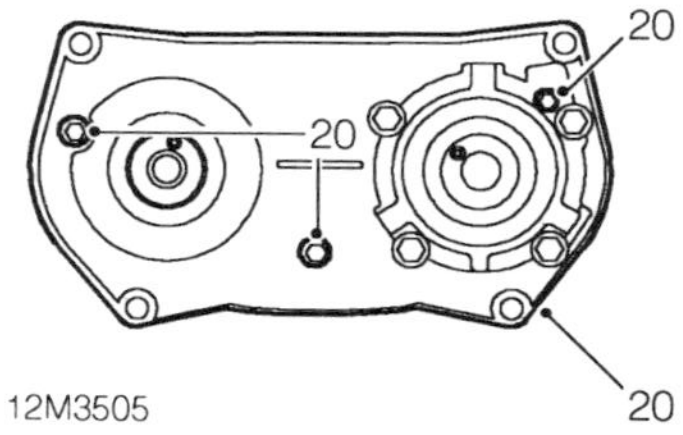

12M3505

20. Fit rear timing belt backplate, fit and tighten bolts to:
M5 bolts - 6 Nm
M6 bolts - 10 Nm.

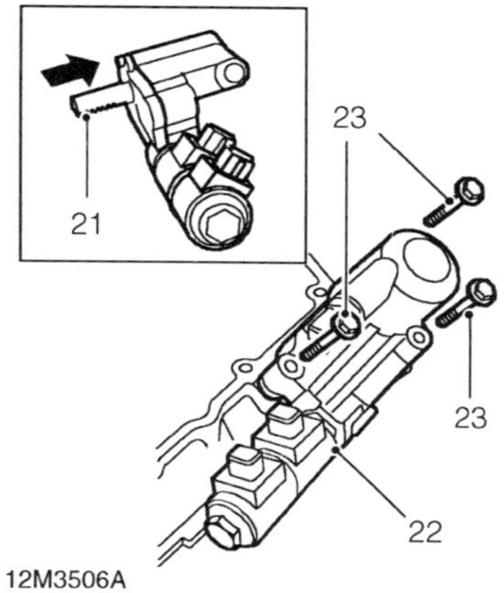

12M3506A

21. Ensure that hydraulic control piston is pushed fully to top of bore and that rack teeth will be aligned to control shaft when control unit is fitted.
22. Position hydraulic control unit and seal plate to camshaft carrier, engage teeth of rack with those of control shaft.
23. Fit and lightly tighten 3 bolts.

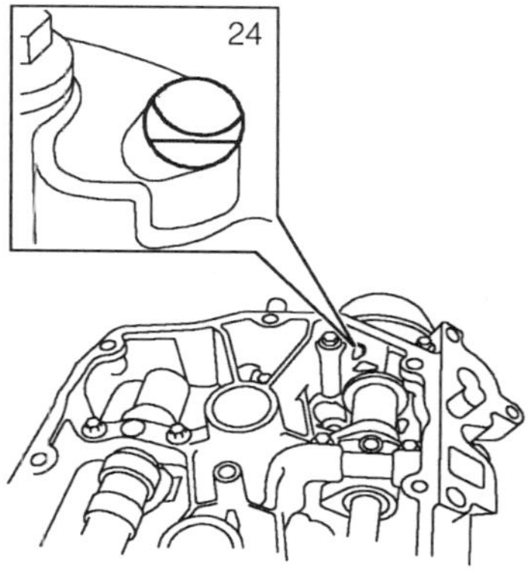

12M3507

24. Check that timing slots in front and rear VVC control sleeves are visible through holes in camshaft carrier.

CAUTION: If timing slots are not visible, carry out following procedure.

25. Remove hydraulic control unit.

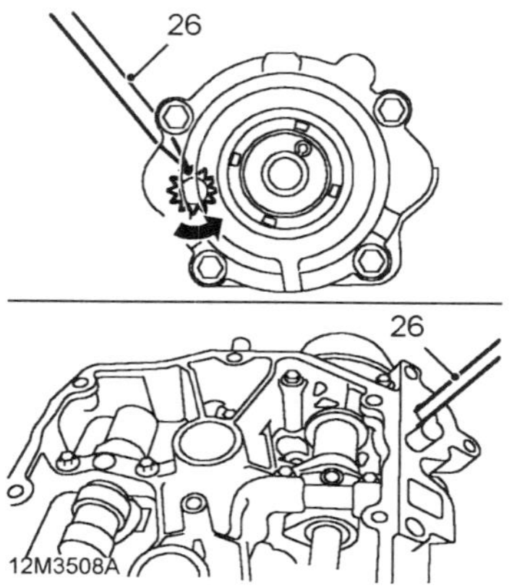

12M3508A

26. Using a screwdriver, rotate control shaft as far as possible in an anti-clockwise direction, viewed from front of camshaft carrier.

NOTE: Timing slots in both VVC control sleeves should now be visible.

27. Push hydraulic control unit piston to top of bore.
28. Fit hydraulic control unit, fit and lightly tighten 3 bolts.

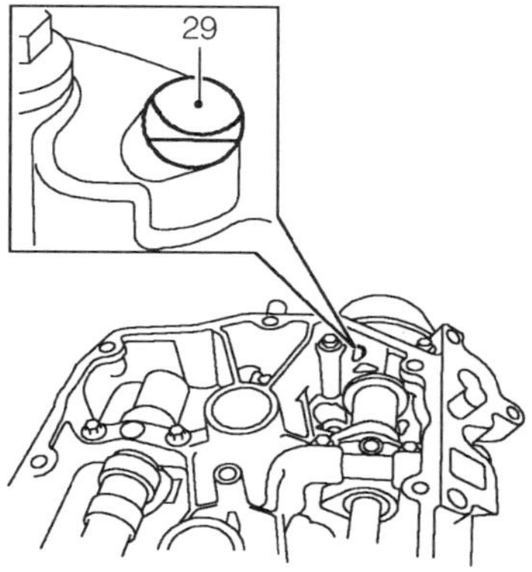

12M3524

29. Check that timing slots on both front and rear VVC control sleeves are visible. If slots are still not visible, repeat the foregoing procedure as necessary.

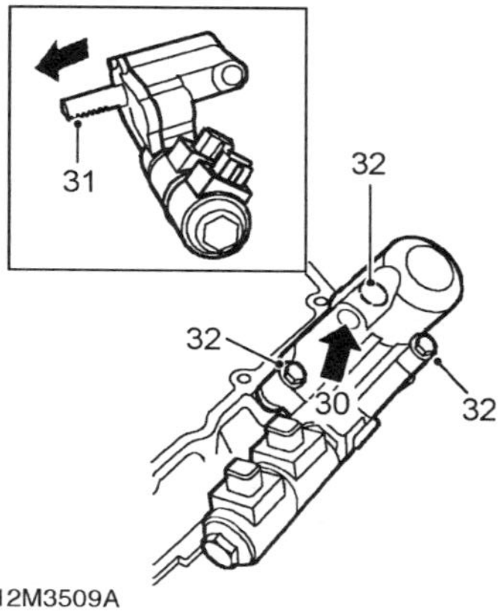

12M3509A

30. Apply low pressure air to oil temperature transmitter port in hydraulic control unit to extend rack.
31. Check that rack is fully extended i.e. rack teeth are at limit of travel and timing slots are no longer visible through holes in camshaft carrier.
32. Tighten hydraulic control unit bolts to 25 Nm.

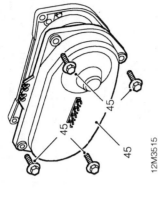

12M3510

33. Fit a new sealing washer to oil temperature transmitter,

34. Fit oil temperature transmitter and tighten to 15 Nm.

35. Thoroughly clean rear timing gears.

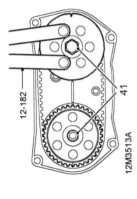

M12 3512A

36. Fit rear inlet camshaft timing gear, fit but do not tighten bolt.

37. Fit exhaust camshaft rear timing gear, fit but do not tighten bolt.

38. Using tool 12-182, rotate both timing gears until timing marks on gears are facing outwards.

39. Check alignment of timing marks using a straight edge.

NOTE: With timing marks in this position, the lobes of numbers 3, 4, 5 and 6 inlet cams will be facing upwards.

40. Remove bolt and withdraw rear inlet camshaft gear sufficiently to enable a new rear timing belt to be fitted; fit rear timing belt; refit bolt and washer.

⚠ CAUTION: Ensure that camshafts do not rotate.

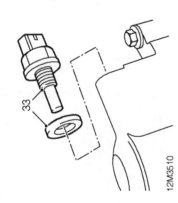

12M3515

45. Fit rear timing belt cover, fit and tighten screws to 10 Nm.

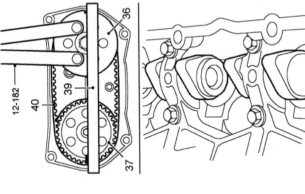

12M3513A

41. Restrain each timing gear in turn using tool 12-182 and tighten bolts to 65 Nm.

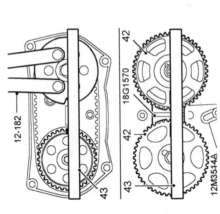

12M3514A

42. Temporarily fit front timing gears to their respective camshafts, rotate gears until timing marks on all 4 gears are aligned, facing inwards; fit tool 18G 1570.

43. Check alignment of each pair of timing marks in turn using a straight edge.

44. Remove tool 18G 1570 and front timing gears.

Cylinder head - K8 and K16 Non VVC engines fitted with a distributor - refit

⚠ **CAUTION: If crankshaft has been rotated, check that timing marks on crankshaft timing gear are aligned with flange on oil pump and that tool 18G 1571 is locking flywheel.**

1. Check cylinder head bolts in oil rail. *See Cylinder head bolt inspection.* - Renew bolts as necessary.
2. Check that 2 locating ring dowels are fitted in cylinder block.

⚠ **CAUTION: The type of ring dowel fitted must be maintained. A nylon ring dowel must not be used in place of a steel ring dowel.**

3. Oil cylinder head bolts, under head and threads.
4. Remove cylinder liner retainer clamps 18G 1736.

⚠ **CAUTION: Do not rotate crankshaft until cylinder head bolts are fitted.**

5. Fit new cylinder head gasket DRY, with identification markings facing upwards, on to cylinder block.

⚠ **CAUTION: Take care not to damage sealing faces of gasket.**

6. Using assistance, fit cylinder head on to cylinder block carefully locating ring dowels.
7. Carefully enter cylinder head bolts in their original fitted locations; DO NOT DROP. Lightly tighten bolts.

K8

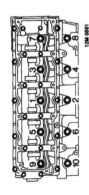

12M 0591

8. Tighten cylinder head bolts progressively in sequence shown to 20 Nm.
   Use a felt tip pen and mark position of radial mark on each bolt head.
   Tighten all bolts in sequence shown through 180°
   Tighten all bolts in sequence shown through another 180° and align mark.

⚠ **CAUTION: If any bolt is overtightened, back off 90° and re-align.**

K16

9. Temporarily fit timing gears to camshafts, fit but do not fully tighten bolts.

   ◁ NOTE: This will enable camshafts to be rotated in order to enable remaining bolts to be tightened:
   Early engines:- bolts 1 and 2
   Later engines fitted with modified camshafts:- bolts 3 and 4

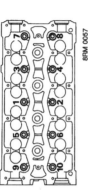

8RM 0057

10. Tighten cylinder head bolts progressively in sequence shown to 20 Nm.
    Use a felt tip pen and mark position of radial mark on each bolt head.
    Tighten all 10 bolts in sequence shown through 180°
    Tighten all bolts in sequence shown through another 180° and align mark.

⚠ **CAUTION: If any bolt is overtightened, back off 90° and re-align.**

11. Upon completion of tightening sequence, position camshafts with inlet pin at 4 o'clock and exhaust pin at 8 o'clock; remove timing gears.

⚠ **CAUTION: Ensure camshafts do not rotate when gears are removed.**

12. *Automatic timing belt tensioner:* Fit tensioner pillar bolt and tighten to 25 Nm.

K8 and K16

13. Fit new spark plugs, tighten to 25 Nm.
14. Fit camshaft cover and timing gears.
15. *K8 engines:* - Fit HT lead brackets, fit and tighten bolts to 10 Nm.

Cylinder head - K16 Non VVC engines fitted with plug top coil ignition system - refit

⚠ **CAUTION: If crankshaft has been rotated, check that timing marks on crankshaft timing gear are aligned with flange on oil pump and that tool 18G 1674 is locking flywheel.**

1. Check cylinder head bolts in oil rail. *See Cylinder head bolt inspection.* - Renew bolts as necessary.
2. Check that 2 locating ring dowels are fitted in cylinder block.

⚠ **CAUTION: The type of ring dowel fitted must be maintained. A nylon ring dowel must not be used in place of a steel ring dowel.**

3. Oil cylinder head bolts, under head and threads.
4. Remove cylinder liner retainer clamps 18G 1736.

⚠ **CAUTION: Do not rotate crankshaft until cylinder head bolts are fitted.**

5. Fit new cylinder head gasket DRY, with identification markings facing upwards, on to cylinder block.

⚠ **CAUTION: Take care not to damage sealing faces of gasket.**

6. Using assistance, fit cylinder head on to cylinder block carefully locating ring dowels.
7. Carefully enter cylinder head bolts in their original fitted locations; DO NOT DROP. Lightly tighten bolts.
8. Temporarily fit timing gears to camshafts, fit but do not fully tighten bolts.

   ◁ NOTE: This will enable camshafts to be rotated in order to enable bolts 3 and 4 to be tightened.

8RM 0057

9. Tighten all 10 cylinder head bolts progressively in sequence shown to 20 Nm.
Use a felt tip pen and mark position of radial mark on each bolt head.
Tighten all bolts in sequence shown through 180°
Tighten all bolts in sequence shown through another 180° and align mark.

⚠ CAUTION: If any bolt is overtightened, back off 90° and re-align.

10. Upon completion of tightening sequence, position camshafts with inlet pin at 4 o'clock and exhaust pin at 8 o'clock; remove timing gears.

⚠ CAUTION: Ensure camshafts do not rotate when gears are removed.

11. Fit camshaft cover and timing gears.
12. Fit new spark plugs, tighten to 25 Nm.

If fitted

13. Connect multiplugs to coils, position coils to numbers 1 and 3 spark plugs, fit bolts and tighten to 8 Nm.
14. Secure multiplug harness in clips.
15. Connect HT leads to numbers 2 and 4 spark plugs, secure leads in clips.
16. Position multiplug bracket to camshaft carrier, fit bolts and tighten to 15 Nm.

All engines

17. Lubricate new 'O' ring with engine oil and fit to camshaft sensor.
18. Fit camshaft sensor, fit bolt and tighten to 5 Nm, secure harness in clip.
19. Fit timing belt tensioner pillar bolt and tighten to 25 Nm.

⚠ NOTE: Do not fit timing belt tensioner until camshaft timing belt is fitted.

Cylinder head - K16 VVC engines - refit

⚠ CAUTION: If crankshaft has been rotated, check that timing mark on crankshaft timing gear is aligned with flange on oil pump and that tool 18G 1571 is locking flywheel.

1. Check cylinder head bolts in oil rail. *See Cylinder head bolt inspection* - Renew bolts as necessary.
2. Check that 2 locating dowels are fitted in cylinder block.
3. Oil cylinder head bolts, under heads and threads of bolts.
4. Remove cylinder liner retainer clamps **18G 1736.**

⚠ CAUTION: Do not rotate crankshaft until cylinder head bolts are fitted.

5. Fit new cylinder head gasket DRY, with identification marks facing upwards on to cylinder block.

⚠ CAUTION: Take care not to damage sealing faces of gasket.

6. Using assistance, fit cylinder head on to cylinder block carefully locating ring dowels.
7. Carefully enter cylinder head bolts in their original fitted locations; DO NOT DROP. Lightly tighten bolts.

Camshaft cover and timing gear - K8 engines - refit

1. Position a new gasket, dry, to camshaft cover.

⚠ NOTE: Ensure spigots on camshaft cover locate in holes in gasket.

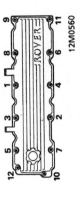

12M0560

8. Tighten cylinder head bolts progressively in sequence shown to 20 Nm.
Use a felt tip pen and mark position of radial mark on each bolt head.
Tighten bolts in sequence shown through 180°
Tighten all bolts in sequence shown a further 180° and align marks.

⚠ CAUTION: If any bolt is overtightened, back off 90° and re-align.

9. Fit camshaft cover and timing gears.
10. Fit new spark plugs, tighten to 25 Nm.

12M2037

2. Position camshaft cover on cylinder head.
3. Fit bolts and tighten progressively in sequence shown to 10 Nm.
4. Position timing belt upper rear cover to cylinder head, fit screws and tighten to 9 Nm.

⚠ NOTE: Longest screw secures cover to coolant pump.

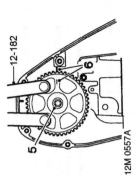

12-182

12M 0557A

5. Fit camshaft gear to camshaft, hold gear using tool **12-182** and tighten bolt to:
M8 bolt - 35 Nm
M10 bolt - 65 Nm
6. Align camshaft gear timing mark to cylinder head top face using tool **12-182.**
7. Fit camshaft timing belt tensioner.

Camshaft cover and timing gears - K16 engines not fitted with plug top coil ignition system - refit

1. Clean mating surfaces and inside of camshaft cover.
   If necessary, wash oil separator elements in suitable solvent and blow dry.
2. Fit new camshaft cover gasket dry, to camshaft carrier, with either 'TOP' mark towards the inlet manifold or 'EXHAUST MAN SIDE' towards exhaust manifold.

Camshaft cover with pillar bolts

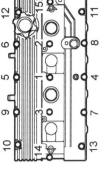

8RM 0060

3. Fit camshaft cover on to camshaft carrier, fit 13 bolts at positions 1 and 4 to 15. Fit pillar bolts at positions 2 and 3. Tighten all bolts, in sequence shown, to 10 Nm.

Camshaft cover with 'cast-in' supports

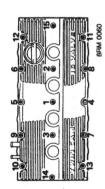

12M1772

4. Fit camshaft cover on to camshaft carrier, fit bolts and tighten in sequence shown to 10 Nm.

All camshaft covers

5. *Non VVC engines:* Fit air cleaner support bracket, tighten bolts to 10 Nm.
6. Locate HT leads in clips and press plug tubes on to spark plugs.
7. Fit spark plug cover to camshaft cover, tighten screws to 10 Nm.
8. Position timing belt upper rear cover to cylinder head, fit screws and tighten to 9 Nm.

   NOTE: Longest screw secures cover to coolant pump.

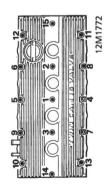

12M 3520B

NOTE: Non VVC timing gears illustrated.

9. Fit camshaft gears to their respective camshafts ensuring that, on non VVC engines, drive gear pins are located in correct slot in drive gears, hold gears using tool 12-182 and tighten bolts to:
   M8 bolts - 35 Nm
   M10 bolts - 65 Nm

Camshaft cover and timing gears - K16 engines fitted with plug top coil ignition system - refit

1. Clean mating surfaces and inside of camshaft cover.
   If necessary, wash oil separator element in suitable solvent and blow dry.
2. Fit new camshaft cover gasket dry, to camshaft carrier, with either 'TOP' mark towards the inlet manifold or 'EXHAUST MAN SIDE' towards exhaust manifold.

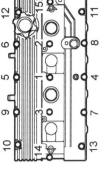

M124976

3. Fit camshaft cover on to camshaft carrier, fit bolts and tighten in sequence shown to 10 Nm.
4. Lubricate a new 'O' ring with engine oil and fit to camshaft sensor.
5. Fit camshaft sensor, fit bolt and tighten to 5 Nm.
6. Secure harness to clips on camshaft cover.
7. Fit spark plug cover, fit screws and tighten to 10 Nm.

   NOTE: Short screw is fitted in centre of cover.

8. Position timing belt upper rear cover to cylinder head, fit screws and tighten to 9 Nm.

   NOTE: Longest screw secures cover to coolant pump.

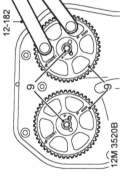
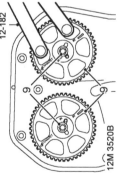

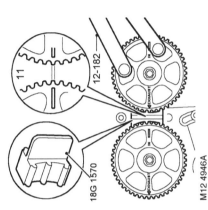

18G 1570

12-182

M12 4946A

NOTE: VVC camshaft timing marks are shown in the inset on the illustration.

10. *Non VVC engines:* Using tool 12-182, align camshaft gear timing marks.
11. *VVC engines:* Check that camshaft gear timing marks are still aligned, reposition gears if necessary using tool 12-182.
12. Fit camshaft gear locking tool 18G 1570.

Later VVC engines

13. Lubricate a new 'O' ring with engine oil and fit to camshaft sensor.
14. Fit camshaft sensor, fit bolt and tighten to 5 Nm.
15. *VVC and K16 engines fitted with manual timing belt tensioner:* Fit camshaft timing belt tensioner.
16. *K16 engines fitted with automatic timing belt tensioner:* Fit new camshaft timing belt.

12-182

M12 4977A

9. Fit camshaft gears to their respective camshafts ensuring that drive gear pins are located in correct slot in drive gears, hold gears using tool **12-182**, fit and tighten bolts to 65 Nm.

12-182

18G 1570

M12 4975A

10. Using tool **12-182**, align camshaft gear timing marks.
11. Fit camshaft gear locking tool **18G 1570**.
12. Fit new camshaft timing belt.

◁ NOTE: Timing belt tensioner is fitted when timing belt is fitted.

Camshaft timing belt manual tensioner - refit

◁ NOTE: On engines fitted with an automatic tensioner, tensioner is fitted when timing belt is fitted.

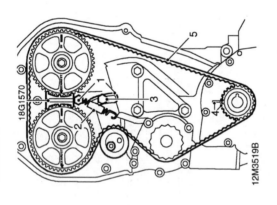

18G1570

12M3519B

◁ NOTE: K16 non VVC engine illustrated. On VVC engines, tensioner spring and pillar bolt are supplied with replacement timing belt.

1. Fit timing belt tensioner and pillar bolt, tighten bolt to 25 Nm.
2. Connect tensioner spring to tensioner and pillar bolt.

⚠ **CAUTION: Ensure correct spring is fitted:**
K8 and K16 non VVC engines - spring is fitted with a sleeve.
K16 VVC engines - spring is not fitted with a sleeve.

3. Tighten tensioner backplate screw to 10 Nm to retain tensioner in released position.

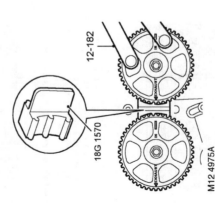

---

4. Check correct alignment of timing marks on crankshaft gear to mark on oil pump.
5. Fit and adjust a new camshaft timing belt.

⚠ **CAUTION: K16 VVC engines:- Remove and discard tensioner spring and pillar bolt on completion of camshaft timing belt adjustment.**

Distributor - K8 and K16 non VVC engines - if fitted - refit

K8

1. Fit new 'O' ring to distributor.
2. Position distributor and turn rotor to engage offset drive, align reference mark or centralise distributor and lightly tighten screws.
3. Fit distributor cap and connect plug leads.

K16

4. Fit anti-flash shield and rotor arm. Use new rotor arm screw and tighten to 10 Nm.
5. Fit distributor cap assembly.
6. Place HT lead retaining plate and grommet in position, connect plug leads.
7. Fit HT lead cover, tighten screws to 5 Nm.

CYLINDER HEAD BOLTS INSPECTION

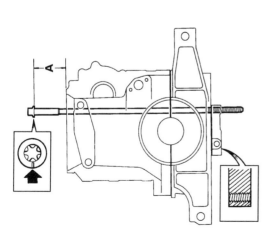

1. Retain bolts in fitted order.
2. Wash all bolts, wipe dry and lightly oil threads.

Cylinder head bolts may be re-used provided they pass one of the following tests.

Test with cylinder head removed

1. Carefully enter cylinder head bolts in their original fitted location, DO NOT DROP. Screw each bolt by hand into oil rail.

⚠️ **CAUTION: It will be necessary to temporarily remove cylinder liner retainer clamps 18G 1736 in order to test the bolt used with the retainer clamp. Retainer clamps should only be removed one at a time and replaced immediately bolt test is completed. Take great care not to rotate crankshaft or disturb cylinder liners whilst clamps are removed.**

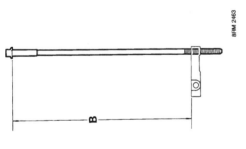

8RM 2463

2. Measure distance from cylinder block face to under bolt head 'A' in illustration:
   97 mm or less, bolt may be re-used.
   Over 97 mm, new bolt must be used.

Test with oil rail removed

1. Ensuring cylinder head bolts are in their original fitted location, screw each bolt by hand into oil rail.
2. If full length of thread is engaged, bolt may be re-used.
3. If full length of thread is not engaged, measure distance from top face of oil rail to under bolt head 'B' in illustration:
   378 mm or less, bolt may be re-used.
   Over 378 mm, new bolt must be used.

⚠️ **CAUTION: A new oil rail must be fitted if a thread is damaged. Thread inserts (Helicoil) are not acceptable.**

Crankshaft, main and big-end bearings - remove

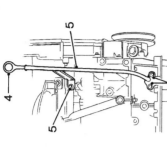

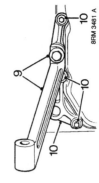

8RM 3480B

1. Remove flywheel.
2. Remove tool 18G 1571.
3. Remove and discard camshaft timing belt.
4. Withdraw dipstick.
5. Remove 3 screws and dipstick tube, discard gasket.
6. Remove cylinder head assembly.

⚠️ **CAUTION: Ensure cylinder liner retainer clamps 18G 1736 are fitted.**

7. Remove oil pump.
8. Using assistance, position cylinder block, cylinder head face down, on 2 wooden blocks.

⚠️ **CAUTION: Ensure that wooden blocks are of sufficient thickness to prevent cylinder liner clamps contacting workbench.**

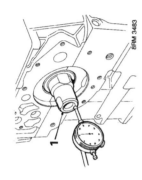

8RM 3481 A

9. Remove bolt and anti-beaming bracket - where fitted.
10. Remove 3 M6 x 35 bolts and anti-beaming bracket support; discard bolts.

CRANKSHAFT, MAIN & BIG-END BEARINGS

Crankshaft end-float - checking

⚠️ **CAUTION: Crankshaft end-float must be checked and recorded prior to removing cylinder head.**

8RM 3483

1. Check crankshaft end-float, using a DTI. Carefully lever against flywheel and press crankshaft away from DTI, zero DTI and push crankshaft towards DTI:
   Crankshaft end-float = 0.10 to 0.25 mm
   Service limit = 0.34 mm
2. Record end-float figure obtained.

Pressed steel sump

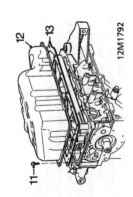

12M1792

11. Remove and discard 14 bolts securing sump to bearing ladder, (11 bolts if anti-beaming bracket support is removed).
12. Remove sump.
13. Release gasket from sump.

NOTE: Gasket may be re-used if in good condition.

Alloy sump

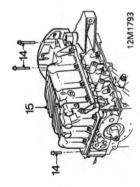

12M1793

14. Progressively slacken then remove 14 bolts securing sump to bearing ladder noting the fitted position of 2 M8 x 60 bolts.
15. Using a mallet, gently tap sump sideways to release sealant bond; remove sump.

CAUTION: Do not lever between sump flange and bearing ladder.

16. Temporarily remove cylinder retainer liner clamps 18G 1736.

CAUTION: Do not rotate crankshaft until retainer clamps are refitted.

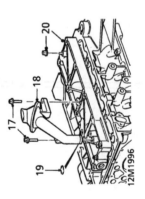

12M1996

17. Remove 2 screws, suction pipe to oil rail.
18. Remove suction pipe.
19. Discard 'O' ring.
20. Remove 2 nuts securing oil rail, remove rail.

Big-end bearings - remove

1. Refit crankshaft timing gear and pulley.
2. Fit pulley bolt and washer, lightly tighten bolt.
3. Ensure that cylinder liner retainer clamps 18G 1736 and nylon nuts are fitted and that feet of clamps do not protrude over cylinder liner bores.

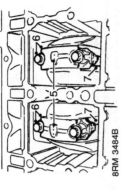

8RM 3484B

4. Rotate crankshaft to bring Numbers 2 and 3 pistons to BDC.

CAUTION: Crankshaft will be tight, do not rotate crankshaft more than absolutely necessary.

5. Make cylinder number reference mark on big-end bearing caps.

NOTE: Number stamped below cap joint is bearing bore size code. Number stamped on connecting rod is cylinder number and letter is weight code.

6. Remove 4 dowel bolts and 2 big-end bearing caps from Numbers 2 and 3 connecting rods, keep dowel bolts and caps in their fitted order. Remove and discard big-end bearing shells.
7. Release connecting rods from the crankshaft, carefully push pistons to top of their bores.
8. Rotate crankshaft 180°.
9. Remove Numbers 1 and 4 big-end caps, remove and discard bearing shells. Push pistons to top of their bores.
10. Remove and discard 4 big-end bearing shells from connecting rods.

18G 1736

12M1774A

21. Fit cylinder liner retainer clamps 18G 1736 using nylon nuts supplied to retain the clamps. Ensure that feet of clamps do not protrude over cylinder bores. Tighten bolts sufficiently to retain clamps.

Crankshaft - remove

1. Remove big-end bearings, caps and bearing shells.
2. Remove pistons and cylinder liners.
3. Using assistance, position cylinder block, cylinder head face downwards on a smooth, clean wooden surface.

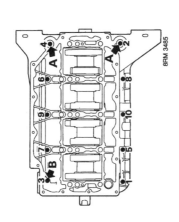

8RM 3485

4. Working in sequence shown, slacken then remove 10 bolts securing bearing ladder.

⚠ NOTE: 2 bolts 'A' are under the flanges of the rear mounting brackets. Also note position of flanged head longer bolt 'B' at front end of ladder.

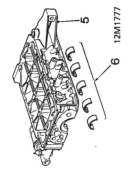

12M1777

5. Remove bearing ladder.
6. Remove and discard main bearing shells from bearing ladder.

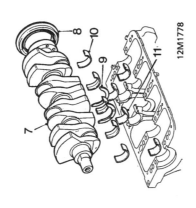

12M1778

7. Using assistance, lift crankshaft from cylinder block.
8. Remove and discard crankshaft rear oil seal.
9. Remove 2 thrust washer halves from Number 3 bearing position.

⚠ CAUTION: Do not discard thrust washers at this stage.

10. Remove and discard main bearing shells from cylinder block.

Crankshaft - inspection

1. Clean joint surfaces on bearing ladder and cylinder block using suitable solvent. DO NOT USE A METAL SCRAPER ON SEALING SURFACES. Blow out crankshaft and bearing ladder oilways.
2. Measure total thickness of thrust washers removed and compare with new. Total thickness of new thrust washer halves = 5.22 to 5.30 mm.
3. Subtract total thickness of original thrust washers from total thickness of new thrust washers.
4. Add figure obtained to crankshaft end-float figure obtained.
5. If resultant figure is within limits specified, fit new thrust washers. If fitting new thrust washers will not bring end-float within limits, crankshaft must be replaced.
   Crankshaft end-float = 0.10 to 0.25 mm
   Service limit = 0.34 mm
6. Record main bearing code letters from bearing ladder.
   Record main bearing code numbers from crankshaft front web. First letter and number is Number 1 main bearing.

⚠ **CAUTION: Crankshafts fitted to later engines have increased main journal diameters. Commencing engine numbers for the modified crankshafts are listed in Information. The modified crankshafts may be fitted as replacements to engines prior to these engine numbers. For inspection purposes, journal sizes on crankshafts fitted to early engines are listed as Type A whilst those fitted to later engines are listed as Type B. Main bearing shell sizes and colour codes for both types of crankshaft remain unchanged.**

7. Check crankshaft main journal diameters:

Type A crankshafts
Crankshaft journal tolerance:
Grade 1 = 47.993 to 48.000 mm
Grade 2 = 47.986 to 47.993 mm
Grade 3 = 47.979 to 47.986 mm
Clearance in bearings = 0.02 to 0.05 mm
Maximum out of round = 0.010 mm

Type B crankshafts
Crankshaft journal tolerance:
Grade 1 = 48.000 to 48.007 mm
Grade 2 = 47.993 to 48.000 mm
Grade 3 = 47.986 to 47.993 mm
Clearance in bearings = 0.013 to 0.043 mm
Maximum out of round = 0.010 mm

8. Replace crankshaft if outside tolerance.
9. Determine the appropriate bearing shells to be fitted from the main bearing size selection and type tables.

8RM 3489

31231

Main bearings selection

Main bearings size selection table

Bearing ladder	Crankshaft main journals		
	Grade 1	Grade 2	Grade 3
Grade A	BLUE - BLUE	RED - BLUE	RED - RED
Grade B	BLUE - GREEN	BLUE - BLUE	RED - BLUE
Grade C	GREEN - GREEN	BLUE - GREEN	BLUE - BLUE

Colour code on edge of bearing
Thickness progression:
GREEN - Thin
BLUE - Intermediate
RED - Thick

⚠ **CAUTION: If two bearing colours are to be used, thicker bearing must be fitted to bearing ladder. When original crankshaft is to be refitted, bearing shells must be as selected from table, DO NOT FIT UNDERSIZE BEARINGS.**

Main bearings type table

	1	2	3	4	5
Block	Plain	Grooved	Grooved	Grooved	Plain
Ladder	Plain	Plain	Plain	Plain	Plain

Big-end bearings selection

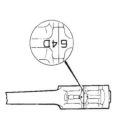

8RM 3490

1. Record big-end journal code letters from crankshaft rear web.
First letter is Number 1 big-end bearing.
Record big-end bearing bore code numbers - this will be 5, 6 or 7 located on the connecting rod bearing cap.

2. Check crankshaft big-end journal diameters:

- 1.1, 1.4 and 1.6 litre
Big-end journal tolerance :
Grade A = 43.000 to 43.007 mm
Grade B = 42.993 to 43.000 mm
Grade C = 42.986 to 42.993 mm
Clearance in bearings = 0.021 to 0.049 mm
Maximum out of round = 0.010 mm
Big-end/connecting rod end-float = 0.10 to 0.25 mm

1.8 litre
Big-end journal tolerance:
Grade A = 48.000 to 48.007 mm
Grade B = 47.993 to 48.000 mm
Grade C = 47.986 to 47.993 mm
Clearance in bearings = 0.021 to 0.049 mm
Maximum out of round = 0.010 mm
Big-end/connecting rod end-float = 0.10 to 0.25 mm

3. Select the appropriate big-end bearing shells from the table.

4. Replace crankshaft if outside tolerance.

Big-end bearings size selection table

Big-end bore	Crankshaft big-end journals		
	Grade A	Grade B	Grade C
Grade 5	BLUE - BLUE	RED - BLUE	RED - RED
Grade 6	BLUE - YELLOW	BLUE - BLUE	RED - BLUE
Grade 7	YELLOW - YELLOW	BLUE - YELLOW	BLUE - BLUE

Colour code on edge of bearing
Thickness progression:
YELLOW - Thin
BLUE   - Intermediate
RED   - Thick
If two bearing colours are to be used, thicker bearing must be fitted to big-end bearing cap.

---

5. Clean sealing surfaces on cylinder block and bearing ladder using suitable solvent.

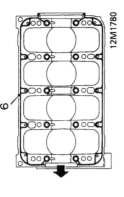

12M1780

6. Apply a continuous bead of sealant, Part Number GUG 705963GM to paths shown on cylinder block then spread to an even film using a roller.

⚠ **CAUTION: To avoid contamination, assembly should be completed immediately after application of sealant.**

Crankshaft, main and big-end bearings - refit

1. Clean all sealant surfaces on block, bearing ladder and oil rail.
Use foam action gasket remover and a plastic scraper - DO NOT USE A METAL SCRAPER ON SEALING SURFACES.
Ensure all oilways are clear.
Examine shoulder location on each big end bolt, renew if damaged.
Check that core plug at each end of oil rail is in good condition, renew as necessary.

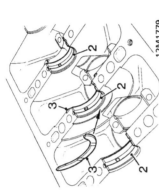

12M1779

2. Fit selected main bearing shells into cylinder block and bearing ladder as indicated in the table.

3. Fit thrust washers into block, each side of Number 3 main bearing with oil grooves facing outwards.

4. Lubricate crankshaft main journals with engine oil. Hold crankshaft with big-end journals horizontal and using assistance, lower crankshaft on to main bearings.

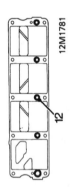

8RM 3492

7. Lubricate main journals with engine oil. Fit bearing ladder to block, fit bolts ensuring that flanged head bolt is fitted at position 10. Tighten bolts in sequence shown to 5 Nm then in same sequence to 30 Nm.

⚠ **CAUTION: With bearing ladder fitted, crankshaft will be tight; do not rotate crankshaft more than absolutely necessary until cylinder head bolts are tightened to the correct torque.**

8. Fit cylinder liners and pistons.

⚠ **CAUTION: Ensure that cylinder liner retainer clamps 18G 1736 and nylon nuts are fitted immediately cylinder liners are inserted into cylinder block.**

9. Lubricate crankshaft big-end journals and bearing shells with engine oil. Carefully pull each connecting rod into place, fit big-end caps noting that featherways abut, fit and finger tighten dowel bolts in their original fitted order.

10. Tighten big-end dowel bolts in pairs to 20 Nm+ 45°.

◁ NOTE: Until the cylinder head is fitted, crankshaft will prove difficult to rotate once big-end bolts are tightened.

---

11. Using feeler gauges, check that end-float of each big-end bearing/connecting rod is between 0.10 to 0.25 mm.

12M1781

12. Apply continuous beads of sealant, Part Number GUG 705963GM to paths on oil rail as shown, then spread to an even film using a roller.

⚠ **CAUTION: To avoid contamination, assembly should be completed immediately after application of sealant.**

13. Using assistance, position cylinder block on its side and temporarily remove cylinder liner retainer clamps 18G 1736.

⚠ **CAUTION: Take care not to disturb cylinder liners with retainer clamps removed**

14. Fit oil rail to bearing ladder, tighten nuts to 9 Nm.

⚠ **CAUTION: A new oil rail together with a plastic suction pipe must be fitted if a thread for cylinder head bolts is damaged. Thread inserts (Helicoil) are not acceptable.**

15. Fit cylinder head retainer clamps 18G 1736, screw bolts into oil rail and tighten sufficiently to retain clamps.

16. Lubricate a new 'O' ring with engine oil and fit to oil suction pipe.

17. Fit oil suction pipe, fit screws and tighten to 12 Nm.

⚠ **CAUTION: Screws used must be M6 x 20.**

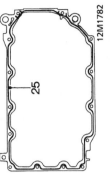

12M1782

Pressed steel sump

18. Clean inside and joint face of sump. Check condition of gasket, renew if damaged or showing signs of deterioration.

19. Fit gasket to sump, ensure its 7 pegs are fully located.

8RM 0054

20. Fit sump to bearing ladder, fit 11 new Patchlok bolts and using sequence shown, tighten to 5 Nm.

⚠ **CAUTION: Early engines: M6 bolts**
Later engines: M8 bolts

21. Fit anti-beaming bracket support, where fitted; fit and tighten 3 new M6 or M8 x 35 Patchlok bolts at positions 4, 8 and 12 to 5 Nm.

22. Progressively tighten sump bolts in sequence shown to:
    M6/M8 bolts: 10 Nm

23. Fit anti-beaming bracket where fitted, tighten bolt to 45 Nm.

Alloy sump

24. Clean sealing surface on sump flange using suitable solvent.

25. Apply a 2 mm wide x 0.25 mm thick continuous bead of sealant, Part Number GUG 705963GM to sump flange as shown then spread to an even film using a roller.

⚠ **CAUTION: To avoid contamination, assembly should be completed immediately after application of sealant. Do not use RTV or any sealant other than specified.**

37. Remove tool 18G 1574.

△ **CAUTION: Allow sealant to cure for a minimum of 30 minutes before rotating crankshaft.**

38. Fit flywheel.
39. Fit oil pump and front oil seal.
40. Fit crankshaft timing gear.
41. Fit cylinder head assembly, do not fit spark plugs at this stage.
42. Fit a new camshaft timing belt.
43. Clean joint surfaces. Use new gasket, dry and fit dipstick tube, tighten bolts to 10 Nm.

▽ NOTE: Ensure bolts securing dipstick tube to bearing ladder are flanged head and do not exceed 12 mm in length.

44. Support engine and using a socket and suitable torque gauge on crankshaft pulley bolt, check that crankshaft can be rotated in a clockwise direction without undue binding, rotational torque should not exceed 31 Nm.
45. Fit spark plugs and tighten to 25 Nm.
46. After installation in vehicle, run engine at idle speed for 15 minutes before road testing.

All engines

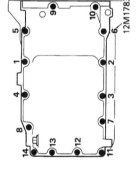

M12 5358

33. Apply a 1.5 mm continuous bead of sealant, Part No. GAC 8000 to replacement oil seal as shown.

△ **CAUTION: Do not apply oil or grease to any part of oil seal or running surface of crankshaft. Seal must be fitted immediately after applying sealant.**

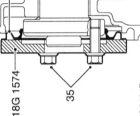

18G 1574

34

35

8RM 3494B

34. Position oil seal to cylinder block.
35. Fit oil seal replacer tool **18G 1574** to crankshaft, retain tool using 3 slave bolts.
36. Tighten bolts to press oil seal squarely into cylinder block.

▽ NOTE: Do not remove replacer for one minute to allow seal to relax.

12M1784

29
31
28
28
31
27
26
26
27

18G 1744

26. Screw alignment pins **18G 1744** into holes shown.
27. Carefully lower sump over pins and on to bearing ladder.
28. Fit 2 bolts into holes shown, tighten to 4 Nm.
29. Fit 10 bolts into remaining holes, lightly tighten all bolts.

△ **CAUTION: Ensure 2 M8 x 60 bolts are in original fitted positions.**

30. Remove alignment pins **18G 1744**, fit and lightly tighten remaining 2 bolts.
31. Using a straight edge, check that machined face of sump flange is level with rear face of cylinder block. Check in 3 positions and if necessary, tap sump gently to re-position it.

9
5
10
1
6
4
2
8
3
13
7
12
14
11

12M1783

32. Using sequence shown, tighten 14 bolts to:
    M8 x 25 - 25 Nm.
    M8 x 60 - 30 Nm

PISTONS, RINGS & CYLINDER LINERS

Pistons and connecting rods - remove

1. Suitably identify each piston assembly with its respective cylinder liner.
2. Remove big-end bearings.
3. Using assistance, position cylinder block on its side.

⚠ **CAUTION: Ensure that feet of cylinder liner retainer clamps 18G 1736 do not protrude over cylinder bores.**

4. Remove ridge of carbon from top of each cylinder liner bore.
5. Push pistons to top of their bores.
6. Carefully push out each piston assembly taking care that big-ends do not contact surface of cylinder liners.
7. Refit caps on to connecting rods, lightly tighten dowel bolts.

⚠ **CAUTION: Removal of pistons will necessitate removal and re-sealing of cylinder liners.**

Piston rings - checking

1. Using an expander, remove and discard old piston rings.
2. Use squared off end of broken piston ring and clean ring grooves.
3. Check new ring to groove clearance:

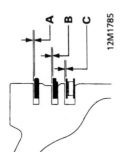

12M1785

K8 and K16 - 1.1 and 1.4
Top compression ring - **A** = 0.04 to 0.08 mm
2nd compression ring - **B** = 0.03 to 0.062 mm
Oil control rails - **C** = 0.044 to 0.55 mm

K16 - 1.6 and 1.8
Top compression ring - **A** = 0.040 to 0.072 mm
2nd compression ring - **B** = 0.030 to 0.062 mm
Oil control rails -**C** = 0.010 to 0.180 mm

Pistons - inspection

1. Check pistons for distortion and cracks.
2. Measure and record piston diameter at right angle to gudgeon pin and 8 mm from bottom of skirt.
3. Check piston diameter with figures given.
4. Measure and record piston diameter in line with gudgeon pin hole and 8 mm from bottom of skirt.
5. Check piston ovality with figures given.
6. Repeat above procedures for remaining pistons.

K8 and K16 - 1.1 and 1.4:
Grade A = 74.940 to 74.955 mm
Grade B = 74.956 to 74.970 mm
Maximum ovality = 0.3 mm

K16 - 1.6 and 1.8:
Grade A = 79.975 to 79.990 mm
Grade B = 79.991 to 80.005 mm
Maximum ovality = 0.3 mm
Service pistons are grade A and B

⚠ NOTE: Piston grades A or B are stamped on crown of piston.

8RM 3496

4. Check new ring fitted gap 20 mm from top of cylinder liner bore:

⚠ **CAUTION: Ensure rings are kept square to liner bore and that they are suitably identified to the bore in which they are checked and fitted to the piston for that bore.**

K8 and K16 - 1.1 and 1.4:
Top compression ring - = 0.17 to 0.37 mm
2nd compression ring - = 0.37 to 0.57 mm
Oil control rails = 0.15 to 0.40 mm

K16 - 1.6 and 1.8:
Top compression ring - = 0.20 to 0.35 mm
2nd compression ring - = 0.28 to 0.48 mm
Oil control rails = 0.15 to 0.40 mm

Piston to cylinder liner bore clearance - checking

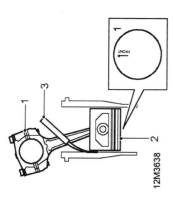

12M3638

1. Starting with number 1 piston, invert piston and connecting rod and with word FRONT or arrow on piston crown facing towards REAR of cylinder block, insert piston in cylinder liner.
2. Position piston with bottom of skirt 30 mm from top of cylinder block.
3. Using feeler gauges, measure and record clearance between piston and left hand side of cylinder liner - viewed from front of cylinder block.
4. Repeat above procedure for remaining pistons.

Clearance in cylinder liner bore: K8 and K16 - 1.1 and 1.4
0.015 to 0.045 mm

K16 - 1.6 and 1.8
0.01 to 0.04 mm

⚠ NOTE: Pistons and connecting rods are only supplied as an assembly.

Piston rings - refit

⚠ **CAUTION: Ensure that piston rings are fitted to piston for the cylinder bore in which they were checked.**

1. Fit oil control spring.
2. With 'TOP' or identification markings to top of piston, use an expander to fit piston rings in sequence; oil control, 2nd and top compression.

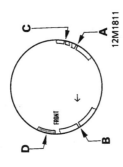

12M1811

3. Ensure rings are free to rotate, position compression ring gaps **A** and **B** at 120° to each other and away from thrust side - left hand side of piston when viewed from front. Position oil control ring gap **C** and spring gap **D** at 30° on opposite side of gudgeon pin axis.

Cylinder liners - inspection

Later 1.8 engines only

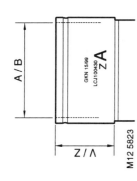

12M1786

1. Measure wear and taper in two axes 65 mm from top of cylinder liner bore.

1.1 and 1.4:
RED grade A = 74.970 to 74.985 mm
BLUE grade B = 74.986 to 75.000 mm

1.6 and 1.8:
RED grade A = 80.000 to 80.015 mm
BLUE grade B = 80.016 to 80.030 mm
Service liners are grade A and B.

Cylinder liner grade A or B together with the appropriate colour code will be found marked on outside diameter of liner.

⚠ **CAUTION: Cylinder liners with excessively glazed, worn, scratched or scored bores must be replaced, do not attempt to hone or remove glazing from bore.**

GKN 15/99
LCJ100430
M12 5823

- **A/B - Cylinder liner bore/grade**
- **V/Z - Cylinder liner step height**

⚠ NOTE: Cylinder liners fitted to later 1.8 engines have their step heights graded on production. The step heights, V or Z together with the liner part number and colour code are marked on the outside diameter of the liner. If cylinder liner(s) are to be replaced, the replacement liner(s) must have the same step height as the original liner(s). Both step heights are available in red and blue grades of liner.

ENGINE

Cylinder liners - remove

1. Remove pistons.
2. Remove cylinder liner clamps **18G 1736.**
3. Using assistance, position cylinder block on its side.

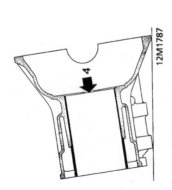

12M1787

⚠ **CAUTION: If original cylinder liners are to be refitted, use a felt tipped pen to make suitable alignment marks between liner and cylinder block. Do not etch or stamp liners.**

4. Using hand pressure, push cylinder liners out towards cylinder head face of cylinder block; remove liners.

⚠ **CAUTION: Keep cylinder liners in their fitted order.**

Cylinder liners - refit

⚠ NOTE: To enable cylinder liner retainer clamps to be fitted when liners are inserted in cylinder block, crankshaft and bearing ladder must be fitted.

1. Fit crankshaft and bearing ladder.
2. Using assistance, support cylinder block on 2 wooden blocks.
3. Remove sealant from cylinder block and if original cylinder liners are to be refitted, from shoulder of liners.
4. Clean cylinder liners and wipe dry.

⚠ **CAUTION: Ensure that if original cylinder liners are to be refitted, reference marks made during dismantling are not erased.**

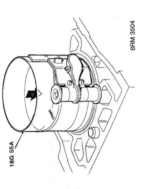

12M1788

5. Apply a 2.0 mm thick continuous bead of sealant from kit, Part Number GGC 102 around shoulder of cylinder liner.

⚠ **CAUTION: Do not use any other type of sealant.**

6. Keeping cylinder liner 'square' to cylinder block, push liner fully down until shoulder of liner seats against cylinder block. Do not drop liners into position.

⚠ **CAUTION: If original cylinder liners are to be refitted, align reference marks made during dismantling before liner is pushed fully down.**

7. Fit cylinder liner retainer clamps **18G 1736.**
8. Fit pistons.

Pistons and connecting rods - refit

1. Using assistance, support base of cylinder block on 2 wooden blocks.
2. Ensure that cylinder liner retainer clamps **18G 1736** are fitted and that feet of clamps do not protrude over cylinder liner bores.
3. Lubricate cylinder bores, pistons and rings with engine oil, ensure ring gaps are correctly spaced.
4. Fit selected bearing shells into big-end bearing caps and connecting rods.

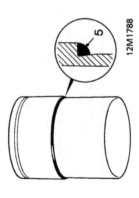

8RM 3504

18G 55A

5. Fit ring clamp **18G 55A** to each piston in turn and with 'FRONT' mark on piston to engine front, push piston into bore until flush with top face of cylinder liner.
   Remove ring clamp.

⚠ **CAUTION: If original pistons are to be fitted, ensure that each piston is inserted in its correct cylinder liner. Do not push pistons below top face of cylinder liner until big-end bearings and caps are to be fitted.**

6. Fit big-end bearings.

DATA

Oil pump

Outer rotor to housing clearance	0.28 to 0.36 mm
Inner rotor tip clearance	0.05 to 0.13 mm
Rotor end float	0.02 to 0.06 mm
Relief valve spring free length	38.9 mm

Cooling system

Thermostat starts to open	88° C
Nominal setting	85 to 91° C
Thermostat fully open	100° C

Camshafts

Camshaft end-float - K8 and K16 Non VVC engines:	0.06 to 0.19 mm
- Service limit	0.3 mm
Camshaft end-float - K16 VVC engines:	
Inlet	0.03 to 0.15
- Service limit	0.25 mm
Exhaust	0.06 to 0.19 mm
- Service limit	0.3 mm
Camshaft bearing clearance - K8 and K16 Non VVC engines:	0.060 to 0.094 mm
- Service limit	0.15 mm
Camshaft bearing clearance - K16 VVC engines:	
Inlet - 25 mm diameter journals	0.025 to 0.060
- Service limit	0.1 mm
Inlet - 40 mm diameter journals	0.03 to 0.07 mm
- Service limit	0.1 mm
Exhaust	0.060 to 0.094 mm
- Service limit	0.15 mm

Tappets

Tappet outside diameter	32.959 to 32.975 mm.

Cylinder head

Cylinder head maximum warp	0.05 mm
Cylinder head height:	
New	118.95 to 119.05 mm.
Reface limit	0.20 mm

This page is intentionally left blank

Valve springs

K8 engines
Free length	46.2 mm
Fitted length	37.0 mm
Load - valve closed	255 ± 12 N
Load - valve open	535 ± 20 N

K16 Non VVC engines
Free length	50.0 mm
Fitted length	37.0 mm
Load - valve closed	250 ± 12 N
Load - valve open	450 ± 18 N at 28.8 mm

K16 VVC engines
Free length	47.6 mm
Fitted length	37.0 mm
Load - valve closed	210 ± 13 N
Load - valve open	440 ± 22 N

Valves

K8 engines
Valve stem diameter:	
Inlet	6.960 to 6.975 mm
Exhaust	6.952 to 6.967 mm
Valve guides:	
Inside diameter	7.000 to 7.025 mm
Valve stem to guide clearance:	
Inlet	0.025 to 0.065 mm
- Service limit	0.07 mm
Exhaust	0.033 to 0.073 mm
- Service limit	0.11 mm
Valve stem fitted height:	
New	38.95 to 40.81 mm
- Service limit	41.06 mm

K16 engines
Valve stem diameter:	
Inlet	5.952 to 5.967 mm
Exhaust	5.947 to 5.962 mm
Valve guides:	
Inside diameter	6.000 to 6.025 mm
Valve stem to guide clearance:	
Inlet	0.033 to 0.063 mm
- Service limit	0.07 mm
Exhaust	0.038 to 0.078 mm
- Service limit	0.11 mm
Valve stem fitted height:	
New	38.93 to 39.84 mm
- Service limit	40.10 mm

Valve guides
Fitted height:	
K8 engines	10.3 mm
K16 engines	6.0 mm

Valve seats
Angle	45°
Width	
Not triple angle valve seats :-	
Inlet and exhaust	1.5 mm
Triple angle valve seats :-	
Inlet	1.0 to 1.4 mm
Exhaust	1.4 to 1.8 mm
Valve face angle:	
Inlet	45°
Exhaust	45°

Crankshaft
Crankshaft end-float	0.10 to 0.25 mm
Service limit	0.34 mm
Thrust washer halves thickness	2.61 to 2.65 mm
Main journal tolerance - Type A crankshaft*	
Grade 1	47.993 to 48.000 mm
Grade 2	47.986 to 47.993 mm
Grade 3	47.979 to 47.986 mm
Clearance in bearings	0.02 to 0.05 mm
Maximum out of round	0.010 mm
Main journal tolerance - Type B crankshaft*	
Grade 1	48.000 to 48.007 mm
Grade 2	47.993 to 48.000 mm
Grade 3	47.986 to 47.993 mm
Clearance in bearings	0.013 to 0.043 mm
Maximum out of round	0.010 mm
Big-end journal tolerance - 1.1, 1.4 and 1.6 litre:	
Grade A	43.000 to 43.007 mm
Grade B	42.993 to 43.000 mm
Grade C	42.986 to 42.993 mm
Clearance in bearings	0.021 to 0.049 mm
Maximum out of round	0.010 mm
Big-end/connecting rod end-float	0.10 to 0.25 mm
Big end journal tolerance - 1.8 litre:	
Grade A	48.000 to 48.007 mm
Grade B	47.993 to 48.000 mm
Grade C	47.986 to 47.993 mm
Clearance in bearings	0.021 to 0.049 mm
Maximum out of round	0.010 mm
Big-end/connecting rod end-float	0.10 to 0.25 mm

* For commencing engine numbers for Types A and B crankshafts, see Information.

Piston rings

New ring to groove clearance:

K8 and K16 - 1.1 and 1.4

Top compression ring	0.04 to 0.08 mm
2nd compression ring	0.03 to 0.062 mm
Oil control rails	0.044 to 0.055 mm

K16 - 1.6 and 1.8

Top compression ring	0.040 to 0.072 mm
2nd compression ring	0.030 to 0.062 mm
Oil control rails	0.010 to 0.180 mm

Ring fitted gap 20 mm from top of bore:

K8 and K16 - 1.1 and 1.4

Top compression ring	0.17 to 0.37 mm
2nd compression ring	0.37 to 0.57 mm
Oil control rails	0.15 to 0.40 mm

K16 - 1.6 and 1.8

Top compression ring	0.20 to 0.35 mm
2nd compression ring	0.28 to 0.48 mm
Oil control rails	0.15 to 0.40 mm

Piston diameter

K8 and K16 - 1.1 and 1.4

Grade A	74.940 to 74.955 mm
Grade B	74.956 to 74.970 mm
Clearance in bore	0.015 to 0.045 mm
Maximum ovality	0.3 mm

K16 - 1.6 and 1.8

Grade A	79.975 to 79.990 mm
Grade B	79.991 to 80.005 mm
Clearance in bore	0.01 to 0.04 mm
Maximum ovality	0.3 mm

Cylinder block

Cylinder liner bore:

K8 and K16 - 1.1 and 1.4

RED grade A	74.970 to 74.985 mm
BLUE grade B	74.986 to 75.000 mm

K16 - 1.6 and 1.8

RED grade A	80.000 to 80.015 mm
BLUE grade B	80.016 to 80.030 mm

TORQUE WRENCH SETTINGS

Air cleaner support bracket bolts	10 Nm
Alloy sump bolts*	
M8 x 25	25 Nm
M8 x 60	30 Nm
Bearing ladder to block bolts*	30 Nm
Big-end bolts	20 Nm + 45°
Blanking plate to camshaft carrier bolts:	
Not plug top coil ignition system:	25 Nm
Plug top coil ignition system:	
- Inlet camshaft	6 Nm
- Exhaust camshaft	25 Nm
Camshaft carrier bolts*	10 Nm
Camshaft cover to carrier bolts*	10 Nm
Camshaft gear bolts:	
M8	35 Nm
M10	65 Nm
Camshaft sensor bolts - K16 engines	5 Nm
Coolant pump bolts*	10 Nm
Coolant rail to cylinder block bolts	25 Nm
Crankshaft pulley bolt	205 Nm
Cylinder head bolts:*	
All bolts	20 Nm
- Mark position of radial marks	
- Turn all bolts + 180°	
- Turn all bolts another + 180° align marks	
Dipstick tube bolts	10 Nm
Flywheel+	80 Nm
Fuel pump blanking plate nuts - K8	25 Nm
ht lead brackets - not plug top coil ignition	10 Nm
ht lead cover screws	5 Nm
Hydraulic control unit bolts - K16 VVC engines	25 Nm
Hydraulic control unit piston to rack screw++	9 Nm
Hydraulic control unit oil temperature transmitter	15 Nm
Hydraulic control unit spool valve	
nut - K16 VVC engines	26 Nm
Hydraulic control unit spool valve sleeve	
bolt - K16 VVC engines	12 Nm
Ignition coils to cylinder head - plug top	
coil ignition only	8 Nm
K16 VVC housing bolts	10 Nm
Multiplug bracket to camshaft carrier	
bolts - if fitted	10 Nm
Oil filter adapter bolts	12 Nm
Oil pump bolts* +	10 Nm
Oil rail nuts	9 Nm
Oil suction pipe to bearing ladder bolts	12 Nm
Oil temperature sensor to oil filter	
adapter - if fitted	17 Nm
Pressed steel sump bolts - M6/M8* +	10 Nm

* Tighten in sequence
+ New Patchlok bolt(s) must be fitted
++ Use new screw supplied with seal kit

Rear timing belt backplate screws - K16 VVC engines:

M5	6 Nm
M6	10 Nm
Rear timing belt cover screws - K16 VVC engines	10 Nm
Rear timing belt gear bolts - K16 VVC engines Torque value changed CJ	65 Nm
RH engine mounting bracket bolts	45 Nm
Rotor arm screw	10 Nm
Spark plugs	25 Nm
Spark plug cover screws	10 Nm
Thermostat housing bolts - Alloy housing	10 Nm
Thermostat housing bolts - Plastic housing	8 Nm
Thermostat housing to cylinder block bolt	10 Nm
Timing belt tensioner bolt - Automatic tensioner+	25 Nm
Timing belt tensioner pulley Allen screw - Manual tensioner	45 Nm
Timing belt tensioner pulley backplate screw - Manual tensioner	10 Nm
Timing belt tensioner pillar bolt	25 Nm
Timing belt lower cover screws	9 Nm
Timing belt rear cover screws	9 Nm
Timing belt upper front cover screws	5 Nm

* Tighten in sequence
+ New Patchlok bolt(s) must be fitted
++ Use new screw supplied with seal kit

SERVICE TOOLS

18G 55A	Piston Ring Clamp
18G 1299A	K16 VVC Housing Oil Seal Remover
18G 1299A-1	Centre Bolt
18G 1519	Valve Lifter Basic Tool
18G 1519/1	Valve Lifter Adaptor
18G 1570	Camshaft Locking Tool
18G 1571	Flywheel Locking Tool - Flywheel Not Fitted With Reluctor Ring
18G 1574	Crankshaft Rear Oil Seal Replacer Tool
18G 1576/1	Valve Guide Remover/Replacer
18G 1576-2	Depth Gauge - All K16 Engines
18G 1576-3	Nylon Guide
18G 1576-4	Depth Gauge - K8 Engines
18G 1577	Valve Stem Oil Seal Remover/Replacer
18G 1587	Crankshaft Front Oil Seal Replacer
18G 1604A	K16 VVC Housing Oil Seal Replacer
18G 1674	Flywheel Locking Tool - Flywheel Fitted With Reluctor Ring
18G 1736	Cylinder Liner Retainer Clamps
18G 1744	Sump Alignment Pins - 2 off
18G 1769A	Camshaft Front And Rear Oil Seal Replacer
18G 1770	Camshaft Clamp - K16 VVC Engines
18G 1770/1	Timing Plate - Front Inlet Camshaft - K16 VVC Engines
18G 1770/2	Timing Plate - Rear Inlet Camshaft - K16 VVC Engines
18G 1749	Camshaft Oil Seal Protection Sleeve
18G 1771	Valve Guide Reamer - All K16 Engines
18G 1772	Valve Guide Reamer - K8 Engines
MS 120-6	Valve Seat Cutter Pilot
MS 76-111	60° Valve Seat Cutter
MS 76-120	15° Valve Seat Cutter
MS 76-122	45° Valve Seat Cutter
12-182	Camshaft Holding Tool

PG1 MANUAL GEARBOX

OVERHAUL MANUAL

This gearbox is fitted to the following models:-

Rover 218/418 Diesel
New Rover 200 Diesel
New Rover 218
New Rover 400 Diesel
Rover 220
Rover 420
Rover 600 Diesel
Rover 600 Ti
Rover 820
Rover 800 KV6
MG-F

Publication Part No. RCL 0124 ENG (2nd edition)
Published by Rover Technical Communication
© **1997 ROVER GROUP LIMITED**

Distributed by Brooklands Books Ltd., PO Box 146, Cobham,
Surrey KT11 1LG, England Phone: 01932 865051 Fax: 01932 868803
E-mail: sales@brooklands-books.com

Part No. RCL 0124ENG (2nd Edition)

INTRODUCTION

How to use this manual

To assist in the use of this manual the section title is given at the top and the relevant sub-section is given at the bottom of each page.

This manual contains procedures for the overhaul of the gearbox on the bench with the engine removed. For all other information regarding General Information, Adjustments, Removal of oil seals, gearbox unit, consult the Repair Manual for the model concerned.

This manual is divided into 3 sections, Description and Operation, Overhaul and Data, Torque & Tools. To assist filing of revised information each sub-section is numbered from page 1.

The individual overhaul items are to be followed in the sequence in which they appear. Items numbered in the illustrations are referred to in the text.

Overhaul operations include reference to Service Tool numbers and the associated illustration depicts the tool. Where usage is not obvious the tool is shown in use. Operations also include reference to wear limits, relevant data, torque figures, and specialist information and useful assembly details.

WARNINGS, CAUTIONS and Notes have the following meanings:

 WARNING: Procedures which must be followed precisely to avoid the possibility of injury.

 CAUTION: Calls attention to procedures which must be followed to avoid damage to components.

 NOTE: Gives helpful information.

References

With the engine and gearbox assembly removed, the crankshaft pulley end of the engine is referred to as the front.

Operations covered in this manual do not include reference to testing the vehicle after repair. It is essential that work is inspected and tested after completion and if necessary a road test of the vehicle is carried out particularly where safety related items are concerned.

Dimensions

The dimensions quoted are to design engineering specification with Service limits where applicable.

REPAIRS AND REPLACEMENTS

When replacement parts are required it is essential that only Rover recommended parts are used.

Attention is particularly drawn to the following points concerning repairs and the fitting of replacement parts and accessories.

Safety features and corrosion prevention treatments embodied in the car may be impaired if other than Rover recommended parts are fitted. In certain territories, legislation prohibits the fitting of parts not to the manufacturer's specification.

Torque wrench setting figures given in this Manual must be used. Locking devices, where specified, must be fitted. If the efficiency of a locking device is impaired during removal it must be renewed.

The Terms of the vehicle Warranty may be invalidated by the fitting of other than Rover recommended parts. All Rover recommended parts have the full backing of the vehicle Warranty.

Rover Dealers are obliged to supply only Rover recommended parts.

SPECIFICATION

Rover are constantly seeking to improve the specification, design and production of their vehicles and alterations take place accordingly. While every effort has been made to ensure the accuracy of this Manual, it should not be regarded as an infallible guide to current specifications of any particular component or vehicle.

This Manual does not constitute an offer for sale of any particular component or vehicle. Rover Dealers are not agents of Rover and have no authority to bind the manufacturer by any expressed or implied undertaking or representation.

Gearbox identification

This overhaul manual is applicable to PG1 gearboxes having the following Serial No. prefixes:

C4BP	R4A0
C4BS	R4DT
C6BN	S4DTU
C6BP	S4EM
C6BS	S4FTU
S6BSU	S6AO
C6DTUT	S6BN
C6DTUTH	S6BNU
C6DUTH	S6BS
C6FTUT	S7EMU
K4BS	V4DT
K4BX	V6BS
K6AO	W4DT
K6BN	W4DTUT
K6BS	Y4AO
K7BSUT	
K7BX	
M5BS	

GEARBOX COMPONENTS

1. Oil seal - differential
2. Differential housing
3. Speedometer drive pinion and housing
4. Dowel
5. Oil seal - selector shaft
6. Boot
7. Selector shaft
8. Thrust washer - sun gear
9. Sun gear
10. Thrust washer - planet gear
11. Planet gear
12. Pinion shaft
13. Ball bearing - differential
14. Final drive gear
15. Roll pin - differential pinion shaft
16. Speedometer drive gear
17. Differential casing
18. Ball bearing - differential
19. Selective shim
20. Clutch release shaft
21. Oil seal - clutch release shaft
22. Selector shaft guide
23. Dowel bolt and washer
24. Magnet
25. Detent cap bolt, ball and spring - selector shaft
26. Oil guide plate
27. Parallel roller bearing - output shaft
28. Output shaft
29. Selective thrust washer - 1st gear end float
30. Needle roller bearing - 1st gear
31. 1st gear
32. Synchro ring - 1st gear
33. Synchro spring
34. Synchro hub - 1st/2nd gear
35. Synchro sleeve - 1st/2nd gear
36. Synchro spring
37. Synchro ring - 2nd gear
38. Selective collar - 2nd gear end float

39. Needle roller bearing - 2nd gear
40. 2nd gear
41. 3rd gear
42. 4th gear
43. 5th gear
44. Ball bearing - output shaft
45. Ball bearing - output shaft
46. Tongued washer
47. Output shaft nut - L.H. thread
48. Circlip
49. Reverse idler gear
50. Thrust washer - reverse idler gear
51. Roll pin - reverse idler shaft
52. Reverse idler gear
53. Reverse selector fork
54. Oil seal - input shaft
55. Ball bearing - input shaft
56. Input shaft
57. Needle roller bearing - 3rd gear
58. 3rd gear
59. Synchro ring - 3rd gear
60. Synchro spring
61. Synchro hub - 3rd/4th gears
62. Synchro sleeve - 3rd/4th gears
63. Synchro ring - 4th gear
64. Synchro spring
65. Synchro ring - 4th gear
66. Needle roller bearing - 4th gear
67. Distance collar - 4th/5th gear
68. Needle bearing - 5th gear
69. 5th gear
70. Synchro ring - 5th gear
71. Synchro spring - 5th gear
72. Synchro hub - 5th gear
73. Synchro sleeve - 5th gear
74. Ball bearing - input shaft
75. Selective snap rings - input shaft end thrust
76. Belleville washer - input shaft end thrust

77. Oil guide plate
78. Gearbox casing
79. Reverse idler shaft bolt and washer
80. Breather pipe
81. Breather pipe bracket
82. Oil seal - differential
83. Filler/level plug
84. Drain plug
85. Access plug - output shaft bearing circlip
86. Reverse light switch
87. Interlock assembly - early gearboxes
88. Gearshift holder
89. Gearshift arm guide
90. Shift shaft
91. Roll pin - 5th/reverse gear selector
92. Gear selector - 5th/reverse gears
93. Selector fork - 3rd/4th gears
94. Selector fork - 5th gear
95. Selector shaft - 5th/reverse gears
96. Selector fork - 1st/2nd gears
97. Selector shaft - 1st/2nd gears
98. Bearing - roller **
99. Bearing - ball **
100. Retainer plate - output shaft bearing **
101. Retainer plate bolts - Patchlok **
102. Clutch release shaft bush - inner
103. Clutch release shaft bush - outer
104. Interlock assembly - later gearboxes
105. Gear selector - 5th/reverse gears/with reverse brake*
106. Spring - reverse brake*
107. Lock plate - reverse brake*
108. Taptite screws - reverse brake*

* Gearboxes with reverse brake fitted

** Fitted to gearboxes having the letter U in the gearbox serial number prefix

37M1297

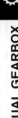
MANUAL GEARBOX

SECTIONED VIEW OF GEARBOX

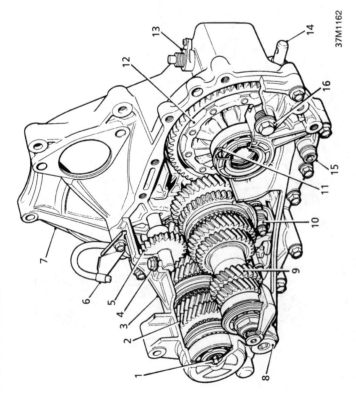

37M1162

1. Oil guide plate
2. Input shaft assembly
3. Gear case
4. Reverse idler shaft bolt
5. Reverse idler gear
6. Breather pipe and bracket
7. Differential housing
8. Access plug - output shaft bearing circlip

9. Output shaft assembly
10. Shift arm assembly and interlock
11. Selective shim
12. Final drive assembly
13. Speedometer drive pinion housing
14. Selector shaft
15. Oil drain plug
16. Oil filler/level plug

mesh with the helical gears and the spur gears mesh with those of the adjoining element gear assembly. Axial thrust of the helical gears is controlled by a combination of thrust washers and needle roller bearings located at each end of and between the two gears.

Type B

The assembly comprises a final drive gear bolted to the differential casing two helical side gears splined to the drive shafts and four pairs of element gear assemblies arranged at ninety degree intervals within the differential casing and running parallel to the side gears. Each of the element gear assemblies comprises two helical gears of unequal length, the long gears are in constant mesh with the helical side gears splined to the drive shafts and also with the short gears of the adjoining element. Axial thrust of the helical side gears is controlled by thrust washers located between the end of each gear and the differential casing and by a thrust washer and friction washer located between the two gears.

OPERATION

With the exception of reverse all gears are in constant mesh. Forward ratios are obtained by locking a gear to its shaft using its individual synchronizer hub and sleeve. Reverse gear is obtained by engaging reverse idler gear with the reverse gears changing the direction of rotation of the output shaft. When a forward gear is selected the synchronizer sleeve presses the synchromesh female cone into contact with a corresponding male cone in the gear chosen. This synchronizes the speeds of the synchronizer hub and gear. The synchronizer sleeve then engages the gear and by means of a spring ring, teeth extensions on the synchronizer sleeve and detents in the selector shaft holds the selected gear in engagement. Torque is transmitted from the input shaft through the selected gear to the output shaft pinion and final drive gear to the drive shafts.

DESCRIPTION - TORSEN DIFFERENTIAL

Gearboxes fitted to certain models incorporate a 'Torsen' limited slip differential. The word 'Torsen' is derived from torque sensing which describes the principle of operation.

Two types of differential are fitted, type A is fitted to gearboxes having serial number prefixes K4BX and K7BSUT. Type B is fitted to gearboxes having serial number prefixes C6FTUT; W4DTUT; C6DTUT; and C6DTUTH.

Type A

The assembly comprises a final drive gear bolted to the differential casing; two helical gears splined to the drive shafts and three pairs of element gear assemblies arranged at 120°intervals within the differential casing and running at right angles to the helical gears. Each of the element gear assemblies comprises a worm gear and two spur gears running on a journal pin. The worm gears are in constant

DESCRIPTION

The 5 speed constant mesh gearbox employs single helical gears for speed transmission and final drive. The input shaft carries the primary input gear, reverse pinion, 2nd gear and 3rd, 4th and 5th gear synchromesh hubs and idler gears. It is supported by two ballraces. End float is controlled by selective circlips and a Belleville washer. Its short input end eliminates the need for support in the engine crankshaft. The output shaft carries the final drive pinion, 1st idler gear, 1st and 2nd synchromesh hubs, 2nd speed idler gears and 3rd, 4th and 5th gears. The shaft is supported in the differential housing by a parallel roller bearing and depending on application, is supported in the gearcase by either a double ballrace or a single ballrace and roller bearing. Pinion location is controlled by a selective washer. The rear end of the shaft is secured by a circlip which retains the bearings in the gear case. Synchromesh is by spring rings and spline extensions in the inner faces of the synchromesh sleeves. Gear selection is via an interlock and gearshift holder assembly which transmits movement of the main selector shaft to the selector forks. Later specification gearboxes employ a reverse brake mechanism. Lubrication is by splash. An oil gutter located on the upper side of the gear case collects splashed oil and directs it to oil guide plates which distribute it to the hollow input and output shafts.

OPERATION - TORSEN DIFFERENTIAL

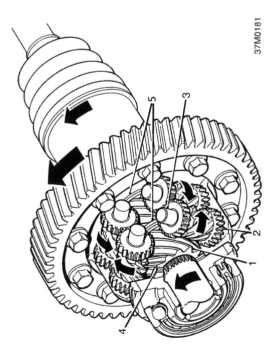

37M0181

Torsen differential - Type A - Serial number prefixes K4BX and K7BSUT

1. Helical side gear
2. Element gear assembly - worm and spur gears
3. Journal pin
4. Thrust washer and spacing washer
5. Two thrust washers and needle roller bearing

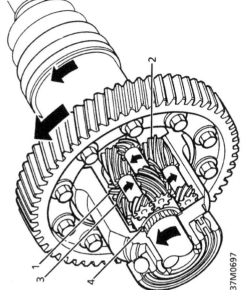

37M0697

Torsen differential - Type B - Serial number prefixes C6FTUT; W4DTUT; C6DTUT and C6DTUTH

1. Helical side gear
2. Element gear assembly - helical gears
3. Friction washers
4. Thrust washers

Unlike a conventional limited slip differential, the torque sensing differential does not rely on the locking value of friction discs but by the friction produced by the teeth of the two helical side gears splined to the drive shafts meshing with the gears of the element gear assemblies. On Type A differentials, additional locking values are generated by the thrust washers and needle roller bearings located at each end of and between the side gears; whilst on Type B differentials, a combination of thrust washers and friction washers is used.

When both front wheel speeds are equal, then the frictional loads imposed by the element gears on the side gears are also equal. However, when the drive resistance on a road wheel is reduced through loss of traction then a torque imbalance is created; less torque being required to turn the wheel with the highest speed. This torque imbalance is sensed by the differential and results in a lowering of the friction imposed by the element gears on the side gear

driving that particular wheel. This causes a reduction in wheel speed until a point is reached where traction is restored, the torque required to turn both wheels is equal and both wheels are rotating at the same speed.

DESCRIPTION - REVERSE BRAKE

A reverse brake mechanism has been introduced to the PG-1 gearbox, and is operated by the selector fork mechanism, which stops the input shaft from rotating prior to the engagement of reverse gear and provides a quiet and smooth engagement of reverse gear, providing the vehicle is stationary.

The reverse brake utilizes the 3rd/4th synchro hub for its operation. The 5th/reverse shift piece, which is secured to the selector shaft by a roll pin, and incorporates two guide lugs with two machined grooves that form a platform for a lock plate. The inner face of the lock plate is angled approximately at 45°, with two machined flanges either side of the lock plate which are positioned in machined grooves in the guide lugs. A return spring, which biases the lock plate against the stop surface, extends along the step at the front of the lock plate, with the two free ends of the spring held in position by two 'Taptite' screws either side of the shift piece. A lug on the 3rd/4th selector fork has a machined face at an angle of 45°which acts as a ramp when in contact with the angled face of the lock plate. 1st/2nd selector shaft has a machined abutment surface located below the detent grooves, the abutment surface being the area of contact for the lock plate.

OPERATION - REVERSE BRAKE

When selecting reverse gear, the 5th/reverse shift piece (1) moves upwards, and the angled face of the lock plate (3) contacts the ramp of 3rd/4th selector fork (2). The upward movement carries the lock plate (3) outwards until it contacts the abutment (4) on 1st/2nd selector shaft. From this point, continued upward movement of the 5th /reverse shift piece (1) causes the lock plate (3) to move the 3rd/4th selector and synchro sleeve (5) towards 4th gear. The movement of the 3rd/4th synchro sleeve (5) is sufficient to restrain the input shaft (6), thus permitting smooth engagement of reverse gear.

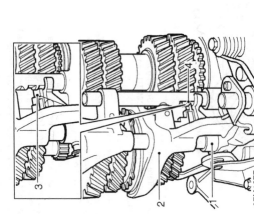

37M1277

To prevent any further movement of the 3rd/4th synchro sleeve (5) and engagement of 4th gear, the spring on the lock plate (3) moves the lock plate into the machined groove (7) above the abutment (4).

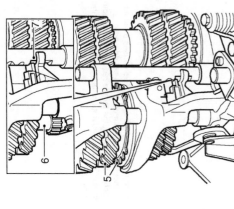

37M1278

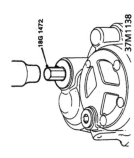

18G 1472

37M1138

5. Remove access plug using tool **18G 1472**.

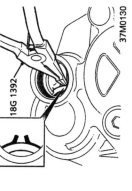

18G 1392

37M0130

6. Using tool **18G 1392**, release circlip retaining output shaft bearing.

GEARBOX DISMANTLING

1. Thoroughly clean exterior of gearbox.

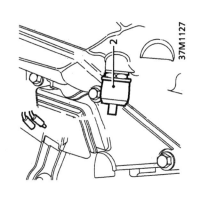

2

37M1127

2. Remove reverse light switch; discard sealing washer.

3

4

37M1163

3. Remove bolt and locating plate securing speedometer drive pinion and housing.

4. Remove speedometer drive pinion and housing, discard 'O' ring.

This page is intentionally left blank

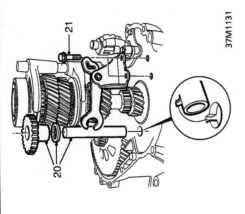

37M1131

20. Remove reverse idler gear, thrust washer and idler shaft.

21. Remove 2 bolts securing reverse selector fork bracket; remove bracket and fork.

37M1130

16. Using feeler gauges, measure clearance between reverse idler gear and selector fork.
Clearance = 0.5 to 1.1 mm

17. If clearance obtained exceeds above figure, measure width across prongs of selector fork.
Prong width = 13.0 to 13.3 mm

18. Using feeler gauges, measure clearance between pin and selector fork groove.
Standard = 0.05 to 0.35 mm
Service limit = 0.5 mm

19. If clearance obtained exceeds service limit, measure width of selector fork groove.
Groove width = 7.05 to 7.25 mm

⚠ CAUTION: If dimensions obtained exceed figures given, selector fork must be replaced.

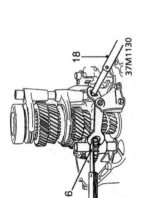

37M1154

10. Remove and discard output shaft bearing circlip from gear case.

11. Remove selective circlip from differential bearing recess in gear case; retain circlip.

12. Remove differential oil seal.

⚠ CAUTION: Two types of oil seal have been fitted, retain oil seal for reference to ensure that replacement is of correct type.

13. Remove selective circlip(s).

14. Remove and discard Belleville washer.

15. Remove input shaft oil guide plate.

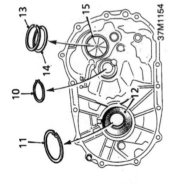

37M1128

7. Remove bolt retaining reverse idler shaft, discard washer.

8. Noting their fitted position, remove 14 bolts securing gear case to differential housing; release breather pipe bracket.

9. Using a soft-faced mallet, release gear case from differential housing; remove gear case.

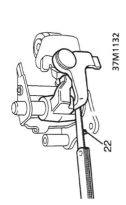

37M1132

22. Using feeler gauges, measure clearance between gearshift arm and guide.
Standard = 0.2 to 0.3 mm
Service limit = 0.55 mm

23. If clearance obtained exceeds service limit, measure width of groove in guide.
Groove width = 8.1 to 8.2 mm

⚠ CAUTION: If dimensions obtained exceed figures given, interlock assembly must be replaced.

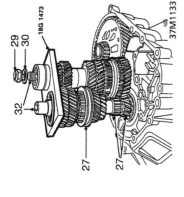

37M1164

◁ NOTE: Latest type interlock assembly illustrated

24. Noting their fitted position, remove 3 bolts and retaining interlock assembly; remove assembly.

25. Raise both input and output shafts slightly, remove selector forks and rails.

26. Using 2 suitable levers, remove input shaft bearing.

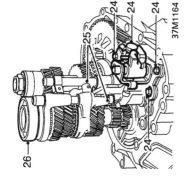

18G 1473

37M1133

27. Move synchro sleeve to engage 1st and 4th gears.

⚠ CAUTION: Damage to components will result if gears other than 1st and 4th are engaged.

28. Position tool 18G 1473 on input shaft and around output shaft bearing.

29. Release staking, remove and discard nut from output shaft.

◁ NOTE: Nut has a LH thread.

30. Remove and discard tongued washer.
31. Remove tool 18G 1473.
32. Remove input and output shafts from differential housing.

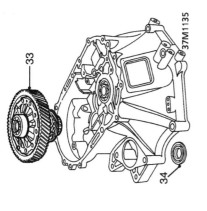

37M1135

33. Lift differential assembly out of housing.

◁ NOTE: Standard differential illustrated.

34. Remove differential oil seal.

⚠ CAUTION: Two types of oil seal have been fitted, retain oil seal for reference to ensure that replacement is of the correct type.

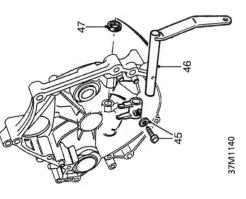

35. Using a soft metal drift, remove input shaft bearing from differential housing; discard bearing.

36. Remove and discard input shaft oil seal.

37M1136

37M1137

37. Remove and discard 2 Patchlok bolts securing output shaft bearing retaining plate - if fitted; remove plate.

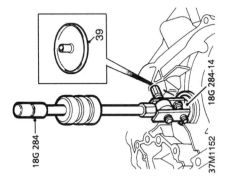

18G 284

18G 284-14

39

37M1152

38. Remove output shaft bearing using tools **18G 284** and **18G 284-14**, discard bearing.

39. Remove output shaft oil guide plate.

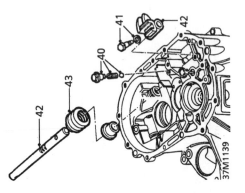

37M1139

40. Remove detent cap bolt and washer, recover detent spring and ball.

△ NOTE: Use a stick magnet to recover ball.

41. Remove bolt and washer securing selector shaft guide to shaft.

42. Withdraw selector shaft; remove selector shaft guide.

43. Remove gaiter from shaft.

44. Remove and discard oil seal.

37M1140

45. Remove bolt and washer securing clutch release fork to release shaft.

46. Withdraw release shaft.

47. Remove and discard release shaft oil seal.

Synchro assemblies

37M0148

Synchro Assembly Components

1. Synchro ring
2. Spring spring ring
3. Synchro sleeve
4. Synchro hub

▷ NOTE: Only one synchro ring and spring ring are fitted to 5th speed synchro.

37M1150

2. Remove 5th, 4th and 3rd gears.
3. Remove 2nd gear, needle bearing and collar.
4. Remove 1st/2nd synchro assembly.

⚠ **CAUTION: Keep component parts of synchro assembly together.**

5. Remove 1st gear and needle bearing.
6. Remove and retain selective thrust washer.

MANUAL GEARBOX

COMPONENT DISMANTLING

Input Shaft

⚠ **CAUTION: Keep component parts of each synchro assembly together.**

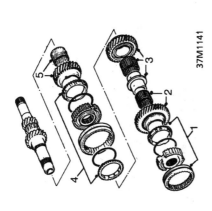

37M1141

1. Remove 5th gear synchro assembly.
2. Remove 5th gear and needle bearing.
3. Remove 4th gear together with collar and needle bearing.
4. Remove 3rd/4th synchro assembly.
5. Remove 3rd gear and needle bearing.

Output Shaft

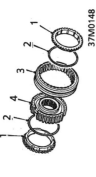

18G 2

37M0146A

1. Remove bearings using tool **18G 2**, note type of bearing fitted; discard bearings.

▷ NOTE: Depending on the application, either a double ballrace or single ballrace and roller bearing is fitted.
Gearboxes having the letter U in the serial number prefix are all fitted with a single ballrace and roller bearing.

MANUAL GEARBOX

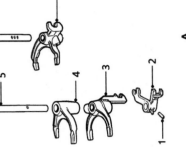

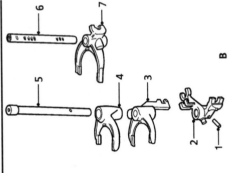

37M0149

Synchro Assembly Identification

1. 1st/2nd synchro
2. 3rd/4th synchro
3. 5th synchro

⚠ **CAUTION: Keep component parts of each synchro assembly together.**

1. Suitably mark relative position of each synchro hub to its respective sleeve.

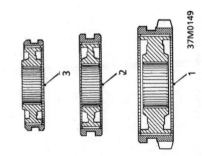

37M0150

2. Remove 2 synchro rings.
3. Remove 2 spring rings.

◁ NOTE: Only one synchro ring and spring ring are fitted to 5th synchro.

4. Remove synchro hub from sleeve.

MANUAL GEARBOX

Selector shafts

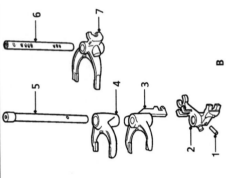

37M1147

Selector Shaft Components

1. Roll pin
2. 5th/reverse gear selector
3. 3rd/4th gear selector fork
4. 5th gear selector fork
5. 5th/reverse selector shaft
6. 1st/2nd gear selector fork
7. 1st/2nd selector shaft

⚠ **CAUTION: Two types of selector shaft assemblies have been fitted. Type A selectors are manufactured from cast steel whilst type B are manufactured from aluminium bronze and are gold in colour. Do not interchange selector forks or shafts between type A and B assemblies.**

1. Identify each selector fork and its fitted position to the relevant selector shaft. Slide 1st/2nd gear selector fork off 1st/2nd selector shaft.
2. Slide 1st/2nd selector shaft out of 5th gear selector fork and 5th/reverse gear selector.
3. Using a suitable punch, remove roll pin securing 5th/reverse gear selector; discard roll pin.
4. Slide 5th/reverse gear selector off 5th/reverse selector shaft.
5. Slide 3rd/4th and 5th selector forks off 5th/reverse selector shaft.

5th/Reverse Selector - with reverse brake

The 5th/reverse selector (1) is secured to the selector shaft by a roll pin (2). The selector incorporates the components for the reverse brake operation. This comprises of a lock plate (3) a retaining spring (4). The spring retains the lock plate in position, with The two ends of the spring located under two 'Taptite' screws (5) which are positioned either side of the 5th/reverse selector.

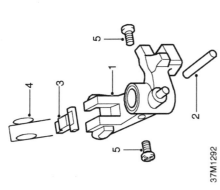

37M1292

Interlock Assembly

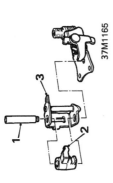

37M1165

◁ NOTE: A modified interlock assembly having 2 springs has been introduced; this assembly may be fitted as a replacement to early gearboxes.

1. Withdraw shift shaft from gearshift holder and arm guide.
2. Release lug on arm guide from slot in interlock.
3. Slide gearshift holder off arm guide.

Differential Assembly

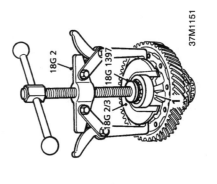

37M1151

1. Remove bearings using tools 18G 2, 18G 2/3 and 18G 1397; discard bearings.

INSPECTING COMPONENTS

1. Clean all components ensuring all traces of RTV sealant are removed from gear case, differential housing and access plug. Ensure oil drillings in input and output shafts and oil guide plates are clear. Ensure gearbox breather is unobstructed.

⚠ CAUTION: Do not clean plastic components with chlorinated solvent e.g. tricloroethane.

2. Check speedometer pinion for wear and pinion housing threads for damage.

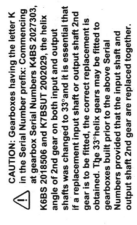

37M1155

2. Remove speedometer drive gear from carrier.
3. Suitably mark fitted position of final drive gear to carrier.
4. Progressively slacken, then remove 10 bolts securing final drive gear to carrier; remove gear.

⚠ CAUTION: With the exception of the speedometer drive gear, Torsen differentials are supplied as a complete assembly; do not dismantle.

5. Using a suitable punch, remove roll pin securing pinion shaft; discard pin.
6. Remove pinion shaft, sun gears, planet gears and thrust washers; retain thrust washers - if fitted.

 NOTE: Selective thrust washers are fitted to planet gears, non-selective washers are fitted to sun gears.

Input and Output Shaft Assemblies

1. Check gears for worn or chipped teeth, cracks or uneven wear.
2. Check coning surfaces of gears for wear.

⚠ CAUTION: Gearboxes having the letter K in the Serial Number prefix: Commencing at gearbox Serial Numbers K4BS 2027303, K6BS 2018506 and K7BSUT 2002029, the helix angle of 2nd gear on both input and output shafts was changed to 33°and it is essential that if a replacement input shaft or output shaft 2nd gear is to be fitted, the correct replacement is obtained. Tçe 33°helix gears may be fitted to gearboxes built prior to the above Serial Numbers provided that the input shaft and output shaft 2nd gear are replaced together.

3. Check needle bearings for wear and overheating (blueing).

⚠ CAUTION: Where any of the above are evident, all bearings on the shaft must be replaced.

4. Check shaft splines for wear and threads of output shaft for damage.

5. Check bearing collars for wear and damage.

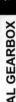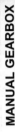

NOTE: Gearboxes having the letter U in the gearbox serial number prefix are fitted with a modified output shaft assembly having an increased diameter and shot peened gears. Due to the increased diameter of the output shaft, differential housing bearing and the method of retaining the bearing, this assembly must not be fitted to any other type of gearbox.

Reverse Idler Shaft and Gear

1. Check idler shaft for wear.

2. Check gear for wear, chipping or cracking of teeth.

3. Check needle bearings for wear, replace gear and bearings as an assembly if wear is evident.

Synchro Assemblies

1. Check component parts of each synchro assembly for wear or damage, ensure teeth on hubs and sleeves are not chipped or rounded off.

2. Ensure teeth on synchro rings are not chipped or damaged, check inner surfaces of rings for wear.

3. Ensure each hub moves freely in its respective sleeve.

4. Place a synchro ring on its respective gear cone and rotate it until it stops (approximately 10 to 20°).

37M0155

5. Measure clearance between synchro ring and gear.
Ring to gear clearance:
Standard = 0.85 to 1.1 mm
Service limit = 0.4 mm (minimum clearance)

6. Repeat for remaining rings and gears.

CAUTION: If any ring to gear clearance is less than above service limit, synchro assembly must be replaced.

Selector Shafts and Forks

CAUTION: Type B selector shaft assembly: The selector forks fitted to the 5th/reverse selector shaft are matched to the shaft and in the event of any wear or damage, shaft and forks must be replaced as an assembly.
Do not interchange selector forks or shafts between type A and B assemblies.

1. Check shafts for wear and alignment.

2. Check selector forks for wear, cracks or damage.

3. Check the retained detent balls and springs, there must be no visible 'flats' on the balls and springs must keep balls in contact with the staked portion of the selector fork.

CAUTION: It is not possible to replace balls or springs, selector fork must be replaced.

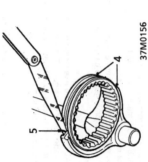

37M0156

4. Assemble each selector fork to its respective synchro sleeve.

5. Check clearance of selector fork in synchro sleeve groove.
Selector fork to groove clearance:
Standard = 0.45 to 0.65 mm
Service limit = 1.0 mm

CAUTION: If clearance is found to exceed service limit, selector fork must be replaced.

37M1156

6. Assemble gearshift arm guide to 3rd/4th selector fork.

7. Using feeler gauges, measure clearance between gearshift arm guide and fork.
Standard = 0.2 to 0.5 mm
Service limit = 0.8 mm

8. If clearance obtained exceeds service limit, measure width of tongue on gearshift arm guide.
Standard = 11.9 to 12.0 mm

CAUTION: If width of tongue is within limits, 3rd/4th selector fork must be replaced, if width of tongue is less than quoted, gearshift arm guide must be replaced.

9. Repeat above procedures for 1st/2nd selector fork.

Interlock Assembly

1. Check components for wear or damage, replace assembly if necessary.

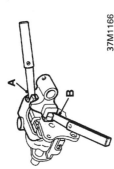

37M1166

△ NOTE: Modified interlock assembly illustrated. This assembly may be fitted as a replacement to early gearboxes but modified interlock assemblies fitted to gearboxes having Serial Number prefixes C4BP and C6BP have uprated springs and must not be interchanged with modified interlock assemblies fitted to other gearboxes.

2. Assemble gearshift arm guide to interlock assembly.

3. Using feeler gauges, measure clearance **A**.
   Clearance **A:**
   Standard = 0.02 to 0.3 mm
   Service limit = 0.55 mm

4. If clearance exceeds service limit, check width of groove in gearshift arm guide.
   Groove width = 13.05 to 13.25 mm

⚠ **CAUTION: If width of groove exceeds above dimension, gearshift arm guide must be replaced. If width of groove is within service limit, replace interlock assembly.**

5. Using feeler gauges, measure clearance **B** between interlock ball and gearshift arm guide.
   Clearance **B:**
   Standard = 0.05 to 0.25 mm
   Service limit = 0.5 mm

6. If clearance exceeds service limit, measure outside diameter of interlock ball.
   Interlock ball outside diameter = 12.05 to 12.15 mm

⚠ **CAUTION: If diameter of ball is within limits, replace gearshift arm guide, if diameter of ball is less than 12.05 mm, replace interlock assembly.**

Differential Housing

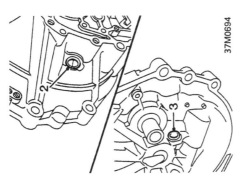

1. Check housing for damage, check that locating dowels are fitted; check clutch release shaft bushes for damage or wear and that shaft is free to turn, replace if necessary using the following procedure.

Remove

37M0694

2. *Outer bush:* Using a hacksaw blade, carefully cut a longitudinal slot opposite the split in the bush; prise bush out of differential housing.

3. *Inner bush:* Carefully prise inner bush out of differential housing.

Differential Assembly

1. Check gear teeth for wear, chipping and signs of overheating.

⚠ **CAUTION: It is not possible to overhaul Torsen differentials. Replace complete assembly if any of the above are apparent.**

Torsen differential

2. Check speedometer drive gear for damage, replace if necessary.

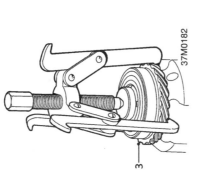

37M0182

3. Remove speedometer drive gear using a suitable three legged puller and thrust button.

Standard differential

4. Check pinion shaft for wear.

5. Check speedometer drive gear teeth for wear or damage, replace as necessary.

MANUAL GEARBOX

Refit

18G 1723-1

37M0695

4. *Inner bush:* Using tool **18G 1723-1**, drift inner bush into differential housing.

⚠ **CAUTION: Ensure end of tool 18G 1723-1 is located in inner bush.**

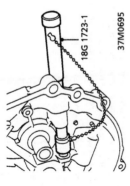

18G 1723-2

37M0696

5. *Outer bush:* Using tool **18G 1723-2**, drift outer bush into differential housing.

⚠ **CAUTION: Ensure end of tool 18G 1723-2 is located in inner bush.**

6. *Gearboxes fitted with output shaft bearing retainer plate:* Remove all traces of Patchlok compound from output shaft bearing retainer plate bolt holes using an M6 tap.

⚠ **CAUTION: Ensure bolt holes are thoroughly cleaned.**

COMPONENT ASSEMBLING

Differential

1. Assemble planet gears and original thrust washers.
2. Fit sun gears and original thrust washers - if fitted.
3. Rotate gears and thrust washers to align drillings in carrier.

⚠ **CAUTION: Do not fit roll pin or final drive gear at this stage.**

Torsen differential

4. Position speedometer drive gear on carrier.
5. Using a suitable length of tubing, drift gear fully on to carrier.

Standard differential

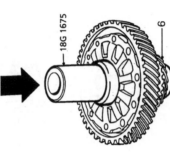

18G 1675

6

37M1143

6. Position speedometer drive gear on carrier.
7. Fit new ball bearings to carrier using tool **18G 1675.**

◁ NOTE: Larger of the two bearings is fitted on speedometer drive gear side.

Synchro Assemblies

1. Assemble each synchro sleeve to its respective hub ensuring that raised teeth on the sleeve are aligned with the deeper grooves in hub.
2. Fit spring rings to retain hub.

◁ NOTE: Only one spring ring is fitted on 5th speed synchro.

3. Assemble synchro rings to their respective sleeves.

⚠ **CAUTION: When assembling the 5th gear synchro sleeve to hub, it is possible to position the raised teeth on the synchro sleeve in the machined cut-aways for the synchro ring. Although the gearbox can be assembled, it will not be possible to select 5th gear.**

Selector Shafts

1. Slide 5th and 3rd/4th selector forks on to 5th/reverse selector shaft.

⚠️ **CAUTION: Ensure that longest portion of selector fork lugs face away from shoulder of shaft.**

2. Slide 5th/reverse selector on to 5th/reverse selector shaft; secure selector with a new roll pin.

▷ NOTE: Make sure the lock plate and retaining spring are correctly located on 5th/reverse selector fitted with reverse brake.

3. Slide 1st/2nd gear selector fork on to 1st/2nd selector shaft.
4. Locate 1st/2nd selector shaft in 5th/reverse gear selector and 5th gear selector fork.
5. Locate lug on shift arm guide in gearshift holder.
6. Position gearshift holder to interlock; fit shaft.

Reverse Idler Gear and Shaft

1. Fit a new thrust washer.
2. Smear needle bearing rollers with petroleum jelly and fit in idler gear.
3. Fit reverse idler gear to shaft.

▷ NOTE: Boss on gear must face towards thrust washer.

Input Shaft

▷ NOTE: Smear needle bearing rollers with petroleum jelly prior to assembly.

1. Fit needle bearing rollers in third gear.
2. Fit 3rd gear on shaft.
3. Fit 3rd/4th synchro assembly.
4. Fit needle bearing rollers in 4th gear, position gear on collar and fit assembly on shaft.
5. Fit needle bearing rollers in 5th gear, position gear on collar.

▷ NOTE: Boss on 5th gear must face away from 4th gear.

6. Fit 5th synchro assembly.

▷ NOTE: Machined groove in synchro hub must face towards 5th gear and large chamfer on synchro sleeve must face away from 5th gear.

7. Fit a new input shaft bearing.

---

4. If clearance exceeds service limit, measure thickness of 3rd gear.
   3rd gear thickness:
   Standard = 35.42 to 35.47 mm
   Service limit = 35.30 mm

5. If 3rd gear thickness is greater than service limit, replace 3rd gear synchro assembly; if thickness is less than service limit, replace 3rd gear.

6. Using feeler gauges, measure clearance between the spacer collar and 4th gear and spacer collar and 5th gear.
   4th and 5th gear clearance:
   Standard = 0.06 to 0.21 mm
   Service limit = 0.3 mm

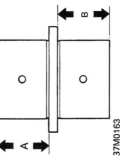

37M0163

Input Shaft Gear End-float - Check

1. Position input shaft on bed of a hand press with bearing located on a suitable socket.
2. Apply downward pressure to input shaft.

▷ NOTE: Maintain pressure whilst checks are carried out.

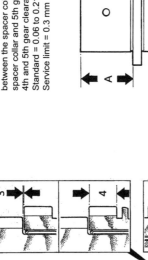

37M0162

3. Using feeler gauges, measure clearance between 2nd and 3rd gears.
   3rd gear clearance:
   Standard = 0.06 to 0.21 mm
   Service limit = 0.3 mm

7. If clearance of either gear exceeds service limit measure length of appropriate side of spacer collar **A** or **B**.
   Length A = 4th gear side
   Length B = 5th gear side
   Spacer collar length **A** or **B**:
   Standard = 26.03 to 26.08 mm
   Service limit = 26.01 mm

8. If length **A** exceeds service limit, measure thickness of 4th gear.
   4th gear thickness:
   Standard = 30.92 to 30.97 mm
   Service limit = 30.80 mm

9. If thickness of 4th gear exceeds service limit, replace 3rd/4th synchro assembly; if thickness of gear is less than service limit, replace gear.

10. If length **B** exceeds service limit, measure thickness of 5th gear.
 5th gear thickness:
 Standard = 30.42 to 30.47 mm
 Service limit = 30.30 mm

11. If thickness of 5th gear exceeds service limit, replace 5th synchro assembly; if thickness of gear is less than service limit, replace gear.

Output Shaft

⚠ NOTE: Smear needle bearing rollers with petroleum jelly prior to assembly.

1. Measure and record thickness of original thrust washer.
2. Fit original thrust washer on shaft.
3. Fit needle bearing rollers in 1st gear.
4. Fit 1st gear on shaft.
5. Fit 1st/2nd synchro assembly.

⚠ CAUTION: Ensure reverse gear on synchro sleeve is adjacent to 1st gear.

6. Measure and record length of 2nd gear collar.
7. Fit 2nd gear collar on shaft ensuring lubrication groove is towards 1st/2nd synchro assembly.
8. Fit needle bearing rollers in 2nd gear.
9. Fit 2nd gear on shaft.
10. Fit 3rd and 4th gears ensuring that bosses on gears are adjacent to each other.
11. Fit 5th gear ensuring that large boss on gear is towards threaded portion of shaft.
12. Fit new output shaft bearings ensuring that snap ring groove in ball race is towards threaded portion of shaft.

⚠ **CAUTION: Ensure that replacement bearings are the same as originally fitted. Where a roller bearing and single ballrace is to be fitted, the single ballrace must be adjacent to threaded portion of shaft.**

13. Fit a new tongued washer with dished side of washer towards bearing.
14. Secure final drive pinion of shaft in a soft-jawed vice.
15. Fit a new nut and tighten to 110 Nm.

⚠ NOTE: Nut has a LH thread; do not stake nut at this stage.

Output Shaft Gear End-float - Check

37M0164

1. Using feeler gauges measure clearance between 1st gear and thrust washer.
 Standard = 0.03 to 0.08 mm
 Service limit = 0.18 mm

2. From clearance obtained, calculate thickness of thrust washer required to give correct clearance. If clearance obtained exceeds service limit, fit a thicker thrust washer; if it is less than 0.03 mm, fit a thinner thrust washer.

⚠ NOTE: Thrust washers are available as follows:
1.96 to 2.08 mm thick in increments of 0.03 mm.

3. Select a thrust washer of the required thickness to bring end-float within limits.

4. Using feeler gauges measure clearance between 2nd and 3rd gears.
 2nd/3rd gear clearance = 0.03 to 0.10 mm

5. If clearance exceeds figure given, it will be necessary to fit a shorter 2nd gear collar; if clearance is less than figure given, it will be necessary to fit a longer collar.

6. Compare length of original collar and select a collar which will provide specified clearance. Collars are available in the following lengths: 28.99 mm and 29.04 mm

7. Having determined thickness of selective thrust washer and length of 2nd gear collar required, fit thrust washer and collar.

8. Secure output shaft nut by staking.

Input Shaft End thrust - Check and Adjust

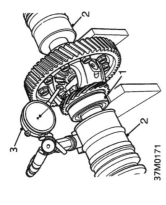

18G 1354

(18G 1354-6)

1

37M0165A

1. Fit a new input shaft bearing in differential housing using tools **18G 1354** and **18G 1354-6.**

⚠ **CAUTION: Do not fit oil seal at this stage.**

2. Position input shaft assembly in differential housing ensuring it is fully inserted in bearing.

⚠ NOTE: Position housing so that end of shaft is clear of bench.

3. Fit gear case, fit and tighten bolts to 45 Nm.

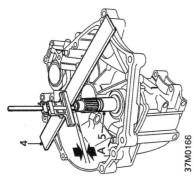

4

A 5

37M0166

4. Position a straight edge and depth gauge across face of differential housing.
5. Pull input shaft into differential housing and position end of depth gauge on end of shaft; record measurement shown on gauge.
6. Push input shaft towards gearcase, record measurement shown on gauge.
7. Subtract thickness of straight edge from above readings.
8. Subtract first measurement from second measurement; record figure obtained. Call resultant measurement **A.**
9. Calculate thickness of circlip(s) required by subtracting 0.97 mm from dimension **A.** Input shaft end thrust = 0.14 to 0.21 mm

---

10. Select circlip(s) from sizes available which equal thickness required. Fourteen circlips are available ranging from 0.5 mm to 1.15 mm thick in increments of 0.05 mm.

⚠ **CAUTION: No more than two circlips may be fitted. It is not always possible to select the exact thickness of circlips required; where this occurs, always fit a slightly thinner pack to avoid pre-loading bearings.**

11. Remove bolts securing gear case; remove gear case.
12. Remove input shaft assembly.
13. Remove input shaft bearing from differential housing using a soft metal drift.

Differential Pinion Gear Backlash - Check and Adjust

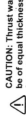

2

3

1

2

37M0171

1. Position differential assembly with bearings located in V blocks.
2. Fit both inboard drive shaft joints to align gears.
3. Assemble a DTI gauge with stylus of gauge contacting one of the planet gears; zero the gauge.
4. Measure and record planet gear backlash.
5. Repeat procedure for other planet gear.
6. Compare backlash figures obtained with the following:

   Planet gear backlash = 0.05 to 0.15 mm
7. If backlash is not as specified, remove planet gears, measure thickness of original thrust washers and from figures obtained, calculate thickness of thrust washers required to give correct backlash.

⚠ **CAUTION: Thrust washers selected must be of equal thickness, and are available from 0.70 to 0.90 mm thick in increments of 0.20 mm.**

8. Fit selected thrust washers, secure pinion shaft with a new pin.

Standard and Torsen differentials:

9. Fit final drive gear to carrier ensuring reference marks are aligned.
10. Fit 10 bolts and tighten progressively to 110 Nm.

Differential Bearing Pre-load - Check and Adjust

1. Position original selective circlip in gear case.
2. Position differential assembly in differential housing.
3. Fit gear case, fit and tighten bolts to 45 Nm.
4. Lightly drive differential assembly into gear case to seat circlip.
5. Lightly drive differential into differential housing to settle bearing.

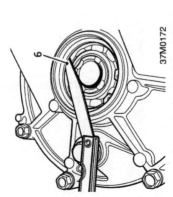

37M0172

6. Using feeler gauges measure and record clearance between circlip and bearing outer face.
   Correct clearance = 0.15 mm maximum

7. If clearance is not as specified, select the appropriate circlip from the range available.

   NOTE: Circlips are available from 2.50 to 3.00 mm thick in increments of 0.10 mm.

8. Remove original circlip through oil seal aperture using tool **18G 1392.**
9. Fit selected circlip using tool **18G 1392.**
10. Re-check bearing pre-load using above procedure.
11. Remove differential assembly, retain selected circlip.

GEARBOX ASSEMBLING

1. Lightly lubricate all components with gearbox oil.

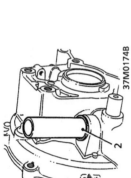

37M0174B

2. Using a suitable piece of tubing, fit a new selector shaft oil seal.
3. Fit output shaft oil guide plate in differential housing.

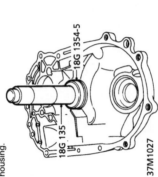

18G 135
18G 1354-5

37M1027

4. Fit a new output shaft bearing in differential housing using tools **18G 1354** and **18G 1354-5.**

   ▷ NOTE: Depending on application, output shaft bearing may have oil holes drilled in bearing cage; these holes must face towards output shaft when fitting bearing. Bearings without the oil hole may be fitted either way round.

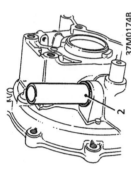

18G 1354
18G 1354-4

37M1028

5. Fit a new input shaft oil seal in differential housing using tools **18G 1354** and **18G 1354-4.**

18G 1354
18G 1354-6

37M1294

6. Fit input shaft bearing into differential housing using tools **18G 1354** and **18G 1354-6.**

REVISED: 12/97

MANUAL GEARBOX (left page)

18G 1354-16

18G 1354

A

B

37M1145

37M0178

18G 1269A

⚠ **CAUTION: Differential oil seals: Type A are fitted with early drive shafts. Type B oil seals are fitted to later drive shafts. The later oil seals are waxed and must be fitted dry. Ensure that replacement seals are the same type as those removed.**

7. Fit a new differential oil seal in differential housing using tools **18G 1354** and **18G 1354-16**.

8. Fit output shaft bearing retaining plate - if fitted.

⚠ **CAUTION: Ensure side marked TOP is facing towards output shaft.**

9. Fit 2 new Patchlok bolts to secure bearing retaining plate; tighten bolts to 8 Nm.
10. Fit selector shaft and selector shaft guide.
11. Fit and tighten dowel bolt to 28 Nm.
12. Fit detent ball, spring and cap bolt, tighten bolt to 22 Nm.
13. Position differential assembly into housing.

14. Fit seal protector, tool **18G 1269A** to input shaft, or apply masking tape to splines to protect oil seal.
15. Place input and output shafts together and fit assembly in differential housing.

▷ NOTE: Position housing so that when fitted, end of input shaft is clear of bench.

16. Remove tool **18G 1269A**.
17. Ensure output shaft nut is staked.
18. Position gears in neutral.
19. Raise both shafts slightly and fit selector forks assembly ensuring forks are located in grooves in synchro sleeves.
20. Fit reverse idler gear, thrust washer and shaft.

▷ NOTE: Large boss on idler gear must be towards differential housing.

21. Fit reverse selector fork and bracket.
22. Fit and tighten retaining bolts.
23. Fit interlock assembly ensuring base of interlock locates in slot at lower end of 1st/2nd selector shaft.
24. Fit and tighten interlock retaining bolts.

MANUAL GEARBOX (right page)

32. Position gear case over differential housing keeping gear case square to housing.
33. Lower gear case into position and at the same time, expand output shaft bearing circlip using tool **18G 1392**.
34. Push gear case fully down on to differential housing.
35. Ensure circlip is fully seated in groove in output shaft bearing, raise output shaft and a click will be heard as circlip enters groove.
36. Fit and progressively tighten gear case bolts to 45 Nm.
37. Fit reverse idler shaft bolt and tighten to 67 Nm. Use a new washer.
38. Apply thread sealant to access plug, fit and tighten plug using tool **18G 1472**.
39. Fit reverse light switch and new washer, tighten to 25 Nm.
40. Fit speedometer drive pinion and housing, use a new 'O' ring; fit retaining plate, fit and tighten bolt to 5 Nm.
41. Fit new clutch release shaft oil seal.
42. Fit clutch release shaft and fork.
43. Fit and tighten bolt to 29 Nm.

18G 1354

18G 1354 -16

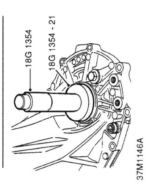

18G 1354

18G 1354 - 21

37M1146A

25. Fit new differential oil seals in gear case.

▷ NOTE: Type A oil seal - use 18G1354 and 18G 1354-16
Type B oil seal - use 18G 1354 and 18G 1354-21

26. Fit input shaft oil guide plate in gear case.
27. Fit a new Belleville washer and selected circlip(s).
28. Fit selected circlip(s).
29. Fit new output shaft circlip in gear case.
30. Fit selected circlip in differential bearing recess in gear case.
31. Apply a bead of RTV silicone sealant to mating face of gear case.

DATA

Reverse idler gear to selector fork clearance ... 0.5 to 1.1 mm
Selector fork prong width ... 13.0 to 13.3 mm
Selector fork groove to pin clearance:
  Standard ... 0.05 to 0.35 mm
  Service limit ... 0.5 mm
Selector fork groove width ... 7.05 to 7.25 mm
Gearshift arm to guide clearance:
  Standard ... 0.2 to 0.3 mm
  Service limit ... 0.55 mm
Interlock shift guide groove width ... 8.1 to 8.2 mm
Synchro ring to gear clearance:
  Standard ... 0.85 to 1.1 mm
  Service limit (minimum clearance) ... 0.4 mm
Selector shaft forks in synchro sleeve grooves clearance:
  Standard ... 0.45 to 0.65 mm
  Service limit ... 1.0 mm
Gearshift arm guide to selector fork clearance:
  Standard ... 0.2 to 0.5 mm
  Service limit ... 0.8 mm
Gearshift arm guide tongue width ... 11.9 to 12.0 mm
Gearshift arm guide to interlock assembly clearance:
  Standard ... 0.05 to 0.35 mm
  Service limit ... 0.6 mm
Gearshift arm guide groove width ... 13.05 to 13.25 mm
Interlock ball to gearshift arm guide clearance:
  Standard ... 0.05 to 0.25 mm
  Service limit ... 0.5 mm
Interlock ball outside diameter ... 12.05 to 12.15 mm
2nd to 3rd gear clearance:
  Standard ... 0.06 to 0.21 mm
  Service limit ... 0.3 mm
3rd gear thickness:
  Standard ... 35.42 to 35.47 mm
  Service limit ... 35.30 mm
4th to 5th gear clearance:
  Standard ... 0.06 to 0.21 mm
  Service limit ... 0.3 mm
Spacer collar length:
  Standard ... 26.03 to 26.08 mm
  Service limit ... 26.01 mm
4th gear thickness:
  Standard ... 30.92 to 30.97 mm
  Service limit ... 30.80 mm
5th gear thickness
  Standard ... 30.42 to 30.47 mm
  Service limit ... 30.30 mm

1st gear to thrust washer clearance:
  Standard ... 0.03 to 0.08 mm
  Service limit ... 0.18 mm
2nd to 3rd gear clearance ... 0.03 to 0.10 mm
Input shaft end thrust ... 0.14 to 0.21 mm
Planet gear backlash ... 0.05 to 0.15 mm
Differential bearing to circlip clearance ... 0.15 mm maximum

TORQUE SETTINGS

Final drive pinion nut ... 110 Nm
Differential housing to gearcase bolts ... 45 Nm
Selector shaft guide to selector shaft bolt ... 28 Nm
Cap bolts - detent balls and springs ... 22 Nm
Reverse idler shaft bolt ... 67 Nm
Speedometer drive pinion retaining plate bolt ... 5 Nm
Reverse light switch ... 25 Nm
Clutch release shaft pivot bolt ... 29 Nm
Final drive gear to carrier bolts ... 110 Nm
Output shaft bearing retainer bolts - if fitted ... 8 Nm

TOOL NUMBERS

18G 2 ... General purpose puller
18G 2/3 ... Adapter - Differential bearing remover
18G 134 ... Driver handle - main tool
18G 134-12 ... Adapter - Type B differential oil seal replacer
18G 284 ... Slide hammer
18G 284-14 ... Adapter - Slide hammer
18G 1269A ... Oil seal protector sleeve
18G 1354 ... Driver handle (main tool)
18G 1354-4 ... Input shaft oil seal replacer
18G 1354-5 ... Bearing replacer
18G 1354-6 ... Adapter - Input shaft differential bearing
18G 1354-16 ... Adapter - Type A differential oil seal replacer
18G 1392 ... Circlip pliers
18G 1397 ... Bearing puller thrust pad
18G 1472 ... 14 mm Hex key access plug
18G 1473 ... Anti-spread plate
18G 1675 ... Differential bearing replacer
18G 1723-1 ... Clutch release shaft inner bush replacer
18G 1723-2 ... Clutch release shaft outer bush replacer

Brooklands MG 'Road Test' & Restoration Titles

 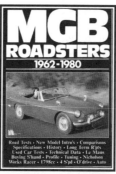  

 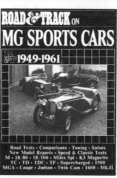 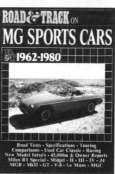 

 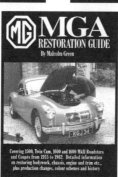 

OFFICIAL TECHNICAL BOOKS

Brooklands Technical Books has been formed to supply owners, restorers and professional repairers with official factory literature.

Workshop Manuals

Model	Original Part No.
Midget TC (instruction manual)	
Midget TD / TF	AKD580A
MG M to TF 1500 (Blower)	XO17
MGA 1500, 1600 & Mk. 2 (SC)	AKD600D
MGA Twin Cam	AKD926B
Midget Mk. 1, 2 & 3 & A-H Sprite	AKD4021
Midget 1500	AKM4071B
MGB & MGB GT	AKD3259 &
	AKD4957
MGB GT V8 Supp.	AKD8468
MGC	AKD7133/2
MGF 1995-2001	RCL0051ENG
MG TF 2002-2005	RCL0493(2)ENG BB

Parts Catalogues

Model	Original Part No.
MGA 1500 (HC)	AKD1055
MGA 1500 (SC)	AKD1055
MGB Tourer & GT (Sept. '76 on)	AKM0037

Service Book

Model	Original Part No.
Midget TF & TF 1500	AKD210A

Owners Handbooks

Model	Original Part No.
Midget TD	
MG Midget TF & TF 1500	AKD658A
MGA 1500	AKD598G
MGA 1600	AKD1172C
MGA 1600 Mk. 2	AKD1958A
MGA Twin Cam	AKD879
MGA Twin Cam (3rd edn.)	AKD879B
Midget Mk. 3 (pub. '73)	AKD7596
Midget Mk. 3 (pub. '78)	AKM3229
Midget Mk. 3 (US) (pub. '71)	AKD7883
Midget Mk. 3 (US) (pub. '76)	AKM3436
Midget Mk. 3 (US) (pub. '79)	AKM4386
MGB Tourer (pub. '65)	AKD3900C
MGB Tourer & GT (pub. '69)	AKD3900J
MGB Tourer & GT (pub. '74)	AKD7598
MGB Tourer & GT (pub. '76)	AKM3661
MGB GT V8	AKD8423
MGB Tourer & GT (US) (pub. '68)	AKD7059B
MGB Tourer & GT (US) (pub. '71)	AKD7881
MGB Tourer & GT (US) (pub. '73)	AKD8155
MGB Tourer (US) (pub. '75)	AKM3286
MGB (US) (pub. '79)	AKM8098
MGB Tourer & GT Tuning	CAKD4034L
MGB Tuning (1800cc)	AKD4034
MGC	AKD4887B

ALSO AVAILABLE: 192 page 'Glovebox' size owners' workshop manuals:

MGA & MGB & GT 1955-68
MG Sprite & Midget 1, 2, 3, 1500 1958-80
MGB & GT 1968-81

Note: SC - Soft Cover   HC - Hard Cover

Distributed by Brooklands Books Ltd., PO Box 146, Cobham,
Surrey, KT11 1LG, England Phone: 01932 865051 Fax: 01932 868803
E-mail: sales@brooklands-books.com

ISBN 9781855207165   Part No. RCL 0051ENG BB   20/12T0/2099
Printed in China   Ref: MGFWH